A TIME
FOR BUILDING

The author when he was Minister for Territories,
photograph taken in 1955

A TIME FOR BUILDING

AUSTRALIAN ADMINISTRATION
IN PAPUA AND NEW GUINEA
1951–1963

PAUL HASLUCK

MELBOURNE UNIVERSITY PRESS
1976

DU
740.75
H37

First published 1976

Printed in Australia by
Wilke & Co. Ltd, Clayton, Victoria 3168, for
Melbourne University Press, Carlton, Victoria 3053
U.S.A. and Canada: International Scholarly Book Services, Inc.,
Box 555, Forest Grove, Oregon 97116
Great Britain, Europe, the Middle East, Africa and the Caribbean:
International Book Distributors Ltd (Prentice-Hall International),
66 Wood Lane End, Hemel Hempstead, Hertfordshire HP2 4RG, England

National Library of Australia Cataloguing in Publication data

Hasluck, Sir Paul Meernaa Caedwalla, 1905–
A time for building.

Index.
ISBN 0 522 84091 4.

1. Papua New Guinea (Ter.)—Politics and
government—1951–1963. 2. Papua New Guinea (Ter.)—
Relations (general) with Australia. 3. Australia—
Relations (general) with Papua New Guinea (Ter.)
I. Title.

353.33940995

CONTENTS

v 268402

III   THE SECOND FIVE YEARS 1956–1960

IV   THE END OF TERM 1961–1963

ILLUSTRATIONS

Plates

Maps

PREFACE

This book is presented as a contemporary account of Australian administration in Papua and New Guinea between 1951 and 1963. In keeping with this purpose the names and designations of countries, government departments, public offices and institutions are given in the style of the period. Phrases such as 'before the war' and 'after the war' refer to World War II, the only conflict with direct relevance to the story. Money, weights and measures are in the old style but a conversion table is provided to help the reader to calculate today's equivalent.

One set of values for which no conversion table can be furnished concerns the social and political attitudes of the 1950s. Change in the past twenty years has been so rapid, especially in the field covered by this book, that some readers may have to make a conscious effort to appreciate the difference between 1950 and 1970. For example, Australian politics in 1950 was still dominated by the memory of the major electoral swing in December 1949 on the issue of socialism. Patriotism was still centred on the memory of World War II. The major element in public administration was the return under Menzies to orthodoxy and traditionally correct practice and procedures in the public service and scrupulous regard for the established parliamentary conventions. In economic policy, while the new government was seeking production, trade and development of resources through private enterprise, it was careful about doing everything in a regular way and with solicitude for a national reputation for dependability. It was ambitious in purpose but not adventurous in method. The advice of the central bank and Treasury economists on liquidity, the state of the overseas balances and the problem of 'walking the knife-edge of inflation' was always pondered respectfully. The balance between over-full employment and a programme of assisted migration was calculated with care. What the Opposition sometimes called a 'Stop-Go' fiscal policy was seen by the Government itself as wise and responsible budgeting to meet changes in a fickle climate. Watchfulness for danger, responsibility and making certain about the consequences of action were more highly esteemed than bold adventures or novel expedients. In world affairs, following disillusionment with the ability of the United Nations to keep the peace or to guarantee the security of any nation, and no détente between East and West having been yet achieved, events seemed to move from crisis to crisis in a way that made it easier to see the need for supporting one's own side than to discover any newly emerging pattern in international affairs. Until 1960 the preponderant membership of the United Nations was composed of long-established nations, mostly European in origin. The only African members, other than South Africa, Ethiopia and some Mediterranean Arab states, were Ghana (1957) and Guinea (1958). The rapid increase in the admission of former colonial territories and the full pressure of the 'anti-colonial', coloured and African influences on voting patterns and hence on politics within the United Nations was not seen until the 1960s.

The main influence on what happened in Papua and New Guinea was what happened in Australia during the period covered by this book, and, in many phases of administration, policy on Papua and New Guinea was decided as a subsidiary part of Australian policy. The setting in which we worked in the 1950s was different from the setting in which our successors worked in the 1970s and, as I have indicated, one does not offer a conversion table but seeks understanding.

In writing a contemporary account, I have tried to keep strictly within the period and to avoid interpreting or refurbishing what was said or done between 1951 and 1963 so that it might accord more closely with the present-day scene or present-day values. Any commentary I might make in the light of later experience is carefully separated from the narrative.

As the main documentary sources are personal papers, which have not yet been transferred to the National Archives or catalogued, it has not been possible for me to identify them by any archival reference numbers that can be used by students, and I have had to limit myself to describing and dating each document in the text.

The absence of a bibliography or references to other sources does not mean that I ignore or am unaware of other work in this field but only that I wish to avoid any false impression that, in writing my own account, I have drawn on the testimony of other witnesses or have set out to confirm or contradict what other writers have recounted.

I make grateful acknowledgement to Sir John Bunting, Mr J. L. Menadue and officers of the Prime Minister's Department, to Mr David Hay and officers of the former Department of External Territories and to Mr A. P. Renouf and officers of the Department of Foreign Affairs for the help they gave in answering the enquiries I made from time to time to check the accuracy of my own papers or my own recollection and to confirm dates and the sequence of events.

P. H.

Perth, W. A.
31 October 1975

CONVERSION FACTORS

(to two decimal places)

1 foot	0·30 metre
1 yard	0·91 metre
1 mile	1·60 kilometres
1 square mile	2·58 square kilometres
1 acre	0·40 hectare
1 pound	0·45 kilogram
1 ton	1·01 tonnes
£1	$2
1s	10c
1d	0·83c

'For everything its season, and for every activity under heaven its time: . . . a time to build up . . .'

'So I saw that there is nothing better than that a man should enjoy his work, since that is his lot. For who can bring him through to see what will happen next?'

'For who can know what is good for man in this life, this brief span of empty existence through which he passes like a shadow? Who can tell a man what is to happen next here under the sun?'

'In the morning sow your seed betimes, and do not stop work until the evening, for you do not know whether this or that sowing will be successful, or whether both alike will do well.'

Ecclesiastes (The New English Bible)

PART I

THE BEGINNING OF THE TASK

[1]

GENESIS

I will try to write only of what I know at first hand and what I did myself, offering my evidence but not completing the story. This book will thus be an account given by one witness, not the study undertaken by the historian. The chief merit of a witness is to say clearly, exactly and truthfully what he knows from his own observation and to tell his own experience. Naturally he knows more of his own thoughts, words and actions than anyone else does and of these things he can tell more than any other can tell.

Memory gives shape to my story. Whatever is most vivid in the memory is likely to have been what was thought to be most important when it happened. In details however my memory has been supported or corrected by reference to notes, letters or minutes of my own, written at the time, and in some cases these have also been checked against official records. I have not sought to do basic research in departmental archives. Except in a few places where elaboration was necessary I have not attempted to reproduce statements readily available in other forms, such as my parliamentary statements, white papers or published reports.

Others will have to write the history of Papua and New Guinea in the twelve years under my administration. It will help them to have my description of the situation I faced and my account of what I was trying to do and how I saw a number of the major tasks.

The story begins with my appointment to Cabinet in May 1951 for until then I knew little about Papua and New Guinea and had taken little interest in it and if that appointment had not been made I probably would never have had any part in its history.

I had not striven for office and certainly had not sought or even thought about the portfolio of Minister for Territories. When the electoral swing of December 1949 brought R. G. Menzies back as Prime Minister there was some expectation that in forming his first Cabinet he would pick at least one Western Australian member and there was an opinion that it might be me. The only person without parliamentary experience who was put into the Cabinet in 1949 however was Senator Spooner from New South Wales.

After the Cabinet had been chosen in 1949 the prospect I saw was that three

3

years would pass before there would be any change and so I applied my spare time to the revision of the manuscript of my two volumes of the *Official War History*.

The double dissolution in early 1951 changed that outlook. When the Government was returned I naturally wondered whether I might now be made a Minister but I was still unfamiliar with how these things were done and my year in Parliament had not brought me close to Menzies. After polling day, 28 April, I waited in Perth, did nothing to promote my own interests and, when more than a week passed without any suggestion about a place, assumed that I had been passed over again and so in the second week of May went off to Augusta with wife and two small sons for a holiday. It was the last organized holiday I attempted to have for the next eighteen years. It lasted two days.

On the evening of 9 May, when we returned all wet and sandy with a sugar bag of fish, Mrs Styles, the landlady at the little pub at Augusta, told me, 'Someone has been trying to get you urgently on the telephone and the post-mistress knows all about it.' My first thought was of family illness or fatality. The elderly postmistress, who lived and worked in a little cottage down the road, could only say that it was 'someone from Brisbane' who wanted me urgently. In those days telephone communication with Augusta closed at 5 p.m. but arrangements had been made to reopen the line at 8 o'clock. When the call came through to the hotel about 8.30 p.m. it turned out to be the private secretary of Menzies calling from a Brisbane hotel. I took the call at a telephone hanging on the wall of a passage-way in the Augusta hotel. It was one of those old-fashioned instruments with a handle to whirl when you took a call and when you ended it. Presently Menzies came on the line. He asked me where I was. He asked me if I could get to Canberra. He wanted me to do a job for him but he could not say anything over the telephone. Then, apologizing because he had to return to dinner guests, he handed the telephone back to his private secretary and we worked out some travel plans.

So the next morning two reluctant boys, a speculating wife and all our hastily packed luggage were crammed into the car with regrets at a lost holiday and I drove 220 miles back home over roads much less perfect than they are now and caught the 9.30 p.m. plane, a DC4, from Perth. I washed and shaved and put on a clean shirt while waiting for the change of aircraft at Parafield and was set down at Canberra some time after 10 o'clock. A car was waiting with a message to me to go straight to the Prime Minister's office at Parliament House and not even wait for my suitcase.

I entered the office. In a few sentences Menzies said he wanted me in the Cabinet. He had a job for me that he thought I would like. All the other Ministers had already gone out to Government House for the swearing in and he had waited behind to take me out with him. I asked what the job was and he said he was making a new portfolio of Territories out of bits of Interior and bits of External Territories. I had a feeling of dismay.

Menzies was already rising and his secretary was at the door saying that it was time to go. I had to do some quick thinking. This was all very different from how I had imagined these things were done. I was rather annoyed by the way in which it had been taken for granted that I would leap at the chance of being a Minister regardless of what portfolio it was and without even stopping to think. I would have liked to know what other newcomers were going into Cabinet. I certainly was not attracted to Territories and indeed was doubtful whether I could do any good with something of which I had no knowledge.

Resistance stirred in me. I was on the point of saying that I would have to consider the invitation. Then I had the mental picture of the waiting team at Government House and the pressmen looking on and the fuss and bother if I did not go quietly to the starting post. I followed Menzies out of the room and downstairs and into his car. He sat in front with the driver, possibly because of the leg room, and I sat alone in the back and in the presence of the driver there was no more conversation on anything except my journey from Augusta to Canberra. I thought of the sea and the rocks and the fish and the family so far away.

I was tired from sitting up all night in the aircraft and somewhat irritable. In a suit crumpled with travel I took the oaths and became a Cabinet Minister. There was no thrill about it. I felt rather cross.

I knew nothing of any difficulties that may have caused the delay of nearly two weeks between polling day and the announcement of the new Cabinet and I knew nothing of why the invitation to come to Canberra was delayed so long or why there had been no discussion with me. Instead of feeling that my merit had been recognized or that I had received the confidence of the Prime Minister I had the feeling that I had been brought in reluctantly at the last moment as a tail-ender. In the succeeding days I also began to have a feeling that the creation of the new Department of Territories had not been an imaginative stroke with a clear purpose behind it but a matter of convenience to find some rail to which another untried pony could be hitched.

I was slow to recover from my first feeling of dismay. Why use me here when there were other things I could do better? I had never been interested in or knowledgeable about the colonial question. In my undergraduate days I had done a course called History B that had a fair content of British colonial history and I had written tutorial essays on Lugard in West Africa, the Ormsby-Gore commission in East Africa, the Mandates System and Murray in Papua and I had read the relevant textbooks. As a senior officer of the Department of External Affairs, in my work on post-hostilities planning and in international discussions at the San Francisco Conference, I had necessarily given some attention to questions of colonial trusteeship but had been very happy to leave most of the work in this field to others. At the United Nations I had considerable scepticism about the outcome of the trusteeship provisions of the Charter. My dominant interest there had been in power politics and security and, linked with that, international economic relationships. Rightly or wrongly I would have claimed to know more about these fields than most people in the Australian Parliament or public service. I certainly would not have claimed to know anything more than the average graduate about New Guinea or dependent peoples. My only compensatory thought about my portfolio was that in the Northern Territory I would have some chance to renew the work which I had shared in the past for the welfare of Australian aborigines.

A day or two after the swearing in I had a talk with Menzies to find out what I was supposed to do. He said to me in effect that I would find my own way as I went along but the first thing to be done was to get a permanent head for the new department. It might take some time to get the department together.

I went away with the promise of a further conversation and on 17 May, a week after being sworn in, I addressed a letter to the Prime Minister bringing under his notice a number of questions 'of prime urgency' which I hoped might be covered in our prospective conversation. Some of these questions concerned the Northern Territory and other territories but the principal ones concerning Papua and New Guinea will be dealt with in sequence in succeeding chapters.

I had little zeal for my new job and it was not a post to my liking but I was stuck with it for the next twelve years. Why did I stay in it so long? Possibly some stubbornness, possibly some lack of political ambition. More probably the reasons were some lack of confidence on the part of others that I was capable of doing anything else and very largely the fact that no other Minister would touch the job with a barge-pole.

Territories killed me politically and I knew all the time that it was killing me, but what else could one do but stick at a job that no one else wanted. During most of my term as Minister for Territories that portfolio was not highly esteemed and it was of scant political significance. Whatever standing I gained in Cabinet was due to the strength and force with which I contributed to Cabinet decisions on other questions and not to the fact that I was doing anything in Territories that was considered to be of moment. It was an obscure and a lonely portfolio in those days. Twelve years as Minister for Territories killed in me all personal political ambition and deadened my political interest. Yet it gave me a range of administrative experience that exceeded by far that of any Federal ministerial colleague, for in a country of two million people I was virtually the Premier and the whole of a state Cabinet.

I can look back on some of the things I did for the Australian aborigines with pride and I believe that in the Northern Territory I made the first major post-war steps for northern development. The smaller island territories I handled with some skill and gained affection from their peoples. Papua and New Guinea was a task for Sisyphus. I think I did just as well as Sisyphus did and certainly got just as tired.

In the present book I do not attempt a history of what was done, but some understanding of what I was trying to do and the circumstances in which I made the attempt. Out of that may come perhaps a clearer appreciation of the situation of Papua New Guinea today and a fairer assessment of Australian administration between 1951 and 1963.

One point to keep in mind is that my work for Papua and New Guinea for twelve years only occupied about a third of my waking hours. I had responsibilities both for other territories and for my Cabinet and parliamentary duties. At a rough guess the Northern Territory took about a third of my time and effort, the smaller Territories and my work in Cabinet, Parliament and my electorate a second third, and Papua and New Guinea the remainder. Hence I am not writing here the full story of my ministerial days but only a segment of it.

[2]

FORMING A DEPARTMENT

The decision to have a Department of Territories by bringing together the Department of External Territories and the Northern Division of the Department of the Interior was presented to me as my starting point. I had no share in making that decision and knew nothing of the circumstances in which it had been made by others.

When I began to give effect to the decision, I thought I might have some advantage because of my knowledge of the public service, both of its senior membership and of its procedures. I saw at once three steps: pick a permanent head, with his help prepare proposals for a total administrative structure covering all the territories and the central office, put a submission to Cabinet so as to obtain foundational decisions both on policy and the organization to give effect to policy.

First, I had to recommend the appointment of a permanent head. I understood that Menzies conceded that I could look outside as well as inside the Commonwealth Public Service for candidates. For a few days I had the illusion that it was intended to get a big new man for a big new job but I soon found that nothing so remarkable was intended and that, in salary, the Secretary of the Department of Territories was to be among the most junior group of departmental heads.

First of all I put down three or four names. The chairman of the Public Service Board, W. E. Dunk, gave to the Prime Minister from within the service the names of J. R. Halligan, Secretary of External Territories, and C. R. Lambert, head of the Northern Territory Division of the Department of the Interior. When I mentioned the names of other senior public servants whom I fancied, I was told that these officers would not be interested. The eminence to which they all rose later both confirms my high opinion of them and helps me to understand that in 1951 they had better hopes in prospect than going into the backwater of Territories. I found that those whom I fancied from outside the service were also not interested. So our 'long list' consisted of Halligan, Lambert and one other. Our 'short list' gave a choice between Halligan and Lambert.

Halligan[1] had grown up with New Guinea, first as a pre-war clerk in the

7

Prime Minister's Department. He was a devoted, likable and thoroughly good man, helpful, warm-hearted and kindly. I had seen him at work in my own days in the public service. He seemed to me to be limited in two ways. He was a dutiful man for pushing files around but, so long as the top paper on a file had some suitable minute on it, initialled and dated, he felt that the immediate needs of administration had been achieved. In my talks with him he seemed to recognize no great problem in Papua and New Guinea and he looked at the future task as a restoration of the good things in the past. I knew and respected Halligan and was sure he could be depended on for devoted and correct service to the Government, but he would not help me to break new ground.

Lambert[2] was unknown to me. At first sight he was a less engaging man than Halligan and a much stronger character. He had come from the Rural Reconstruction Division of the Rural Bank of New South Wales into the Rural Commission set up by the Commonwealth Government in war time as part of its post-war reconstruction planning and had then passed into the Department of Interior. He had the reputation of being able to tackle a tough problem and straighten it out in an intensely practical way. He was forceful, perpetually industrious and widely experienced in public service practice. Less complaisant than Halligan, he might be more difficult to manage but he would be more likely to get work done.

Halligan knew about Papua and New Guinea but not the Northern Territory. Lambert knew about the Northern Territory but not Papua and New Guinea. The Department would be concerned with both. In a final comparison, I thought that Halligan had no capacity or quality that I could not contribute myself but Lambert could contribute qualities and in some matters show a capacity additional to anything I could myself give and thus we would make a stronger team. I recommended Lambert and on 28 May his appointment was approved by Cabinet.

Halligan became a Special Adviser and thereafter was engaged mainly on the work of the South Pacific Commission and the Phosphate Commissions.

My next hopeful venture was to try to create a territorial service to do the whole of the work of the Commonwealth Territories. I listed the topic in a letter of 24 May for discussion with Menzies. The furthest I got was a decision by Cabinet on 28 May that the practicability of establishing a territorial service be considered and that the United Kingdom Government be asked to lend the services of an officer as a consultant on the organizational problems. This request to the United Kingdom Government was made, in conformity with Cabinet instructions, but Britain was unable to respond to it at the time. There would have been early value to us in administrative efficiency, and some subsequent problems might not have arisen, if I had been able to form an Australian territorial service in 1951 but, as it was clear at the time that any decision from Cabinet was likely to be less than useful to me, I let the idea lapse. I had no faith in the results of a prolonged consultation with someone from the British colonial service and I was firmly of the opinion that waiting for a Cabinet decision on a territorial service would mean delay in getting on with the job. So I took another path.

This idea of a territorial service was linked in my mind with the planning of the structure of the Department of Territories in Canberra and with the devolution of more administrative responsibility to the local administrations in all the territories. It seemed to me that a decision should be made about the broad lines of the administrative machine to be created in the territories before we could make a sound decision on what kind of department and how big a department was to be organized in Canberra.

Some notes which I jotted down myself for use in discussion with the Prime Minister and with Cabinet show that what I had in mind was to 'end the cramping effect of remote control of the territories from Canberra and to encourage the local administrations in the territories to make and to carry out administrative decisions'; to strengthen the top level of the territorial administration by raising the status of Administrator and reinforcing him with experienced Deputy Administrators 'to direct the working of the administrative machine'; and to create a territorial public service to do the whole work of the Commonwealth territories, my belief at the time being that this larger service, allied with a new system of recruitment, would give better career opportunities for promotion, for variety in postings and for some specialization in tasks of territorial administration. This might give us a stable service with high standards. One thought in my mind was that, by reason of the distribution of powers in the Australian federation, the Commonwealth had little or no administrative experience in the sort of matters that had to be dealt with in the territories. Such matters as lands, agriculture, mining, forestry, health, education, welfare of indigenous peoples, and many aspects of works programmes (especially roads, bridges, wharves and residences) were being attended to in Australia by state governments with little Commonwealth participation at that time, so there was little experience or expertness among Commonwealth public servants in these fields. I wanted to build up expertness and experience in these practical tasks in a territorial service.

From this I also wanted to argue that, at the outset, some clear decision should be made by Cabinet on what Commonwealth departments and agencies should operate in the territories and what should be left wholly to the proposed territorial service. For example it might be readily agreed that the Australian Department of Defence should have sole responsibility for defence in the territories and that possibly the Australian Department of Civil Aviation might control civil aviation and the Department of Shipping continue to provide lighthouses and navigation aids. More complex questions might arise over the allocation of functions in such fields as post office, customs and public works.

It seemed very clear to my innocent gaze that the functions comparable to those which were performed by state public services in the Australian Commonwealth needed specialization and we should try to build a first-class service to do them. I found however that the Commonwealth Public Service and particularly Dunk, who was the chief obstacle outside Cabinet, were less modest about their native genius to do anything for which they had no training.

Some of the ideas which I put forward were of course derived from earlier public discussion of territorial questions and I claim no originality. They also were the result of my recognition of the problems already arising in other colonies in the phasing out of expatriate officers in favour of indigenous officers. I was a deluded young Minister in hoping to get either the Prime Minister or Cabinet to consider such speculative matters at that stage.

Looking back, however, I recognize that while the creation of a territorial service in 1951 would probably have given us more efficient Australian administration of a dependent territory and would have lessened the complexity of the eventual problem of phasing out expatriate officers, it would have left us with a separate problem of evolving an efficient administration to remain in Papua and New Guinea after self-government and independence. The discussion is hypothetical, for my proposals lapsed for want of a seconder.

Having failed to get a basic decision or even any guidance from the Prime Minister or Cabinet about the shape of the administrative structure I was required to create, I got to work to form the Department of Territories. We took over seventy-nine permanent officers, fifty-five temporary employees and about a dozen vacancies from the Department of External Territories. The number of officers inherited from the Northern Territory Division of the Department of the Interior was much smaller and less definite, since not all officers were willing to be transferred and we inherited none at a senior level. I knew clearly the need for an efficient department and had some experience in the Australian public service. My hope was for a strong department that would have its own expertness and independence, playing its own classical role in helping the Minister to shape policy and perfecting its own capacity to give effect to the Government's decisions promptly and successfully. I had enough experience of inter-departmental rivalries and struggles for money to know that I had to have a department strong enough to match other departments at Canberra in any case it prepared and particularly any case that required funds.

I talked over all this with Lambert. We had hopes of building such a department. One necessity would be to plan the organization of the department and then proceed to have the establishment approved by the Public Service Board, and the required positions created with classifications that would set the standard. A second necessity would be to recruit competent people into the key positions.

At any time, recruitment into vacancies in higher positions in the public service naturally is affected by the level at which the position is classified in relation to other positions in other departments and by the prospects an appointment gives of further advancement. The best men in the public service are all on the way up; some worthy ones are stationary and have reached their limit; many others, having fluked a promotion above their merits, are on the way down. If a department has the reputation of being a dead-end or too small or one that offers limited prospects of further advancement, or if the vacancies advertised are not at a classification that compares well with what is offering in other departments, the only applications the department will get will be from those officers who are on the way down. In time a department will find itself with a large proportion of its higher positions occupied by men on the way down and feel itself lucky if it has a few of the worthy and stationary ones. I knew this. Lambert knew it. Together we struggled to try to build a better department.

We failed in our hopes and we got scant understanding mainly because we could get no help in what we were trying to do from Dunk, on whose recommendations Cabinet relied. If I had not been the most junior Minister in Cabinet and if I had not had a growing feeling that there was no serious intention behind the creation of the Department of Territories, I might have tried to fight the case harder with the Prime Minister, under whose ministerial responsibility the Public Service Board worked. As it was, I accepted the reality that any real strengthening of the new department would be a slow process and in the meantime we had to do the best we could with the tools we had at hand. In my own case this meant that, not from nature or from theory but out of necessity, I turned from depending on the department to driving it hard, squeezing every bit of effort and thought that it contained. I possibly hurt some people who could not move fast enough. In the urgency of the time, we could not wait patiently for the slow coach to arrive but went ahead. It also meant that, contrary to my earlier practice and experience as a public servant, more of the new ideas had to be given as instructions from above than came up through the roots from below. Using what we had got, Lambert and I struggled to convert a mixed collection of officers into a hard-working and purposeful department. Those early days were strenuous.

As for the territories themselves, the Northern Territory was the chief sufferer, limping along as best it could with a neglected branch of the Commonwealth Public Service, in respect of which Dunk was just as unhelpful as he was over the Department of Territories. That is another story.

In Papua and New Guinea at least I had a public service of my own under the authority of the Papua and New Guinea Act and I could hope for some freedom of movement in trying to make it better. At that time, however, the staff of the Territory public service numbered only 1300, about 900 of whom were recently recruited and a large proportion poorly qualified.

I had another failure in an attempt to have a Territories Development Fund established. Although this came some months later than the other plans it sticks in my memory as being part of the initial setback.

For the financial year commencing on 1 July 1951 I inherited the preliminary estimates and had not gained enough knowledge or experience to seek to vary them to any great extent before the Budget was brought down. After six months, however, I had jotted down, both for the Northern Territory and for Papua and New Guinea, a formidable list of undertakings urgently needed to give each Territory the basic services and utilities required before any progress could be made. I also saw that, to make it possible for the Administration to undertake long-term projects, an assurance was needed that developmental measures could continue steadily over a period of years.

My jottings for Papua and New Guinea referred to wharves and jetties, roads, electricity supplies, housing, malaria control, preparation of land for settlement and provision of public services to facilitate new industries. In a second stage I noted the need for soil surveys, experimental projects, control of pests and plant and animal diseases, introduction of stock, and water supplies. The provision in 1951-2 from Commonwealth revenue was £3.6 million for the Northern Territory and £5.37 million for Papua and New Guinea. I thought I had to make a bid for higher expenditures and realized too that I had to break through the strong tradition of annual budgeting.

Early in December 1951 I prepared a proposal to create a Territories Development Fund of £100 million to be made available at the rate of £20 million a year for five years. This would be in addition to normal administrative expenditure and an expanding programme of social welfare measures in the two Territories. Claims on the fund would be made by the Territory Administration and claims would be examined by a ministerial committee of four and approved 'up to the limit of the total amount available to the fund in any one year or accumulated from the unexpended quota for previous years'. In submitting claims, the Territory would have to make proposals in concrete terms (for example a Territory could not ask for money for water supplies but would have to specify the works proposed to be done), and would have to demonstrate the practicability and the soundness of the project. In cases where difficulty arose through lack of works potential in the Territory, the ministerial committee could consult with other ministers or the Cabinet to find ways of adding to the works potential. Developmental proposals should pass the practical test of having a direct effect on production. I suggested that possibly money provided from the fund might be regarded as a long-term, low-interest advance to the territory and I envisaged as a possible eventual outcome that the revenues raised locally—in 1951–2 it was £1.7 million in Papua and New Guinea—might be drawn upon to meet the charges on much larger sums advanced from the Commonwealth for developmental purposes. The whole scheme would be covered by a Territories Development Act of the Commonwealth Parliament. I also foresaw already that when eventual self-government came to the Territory, with a great accumulation of capital works and installations, the autonomous country would have transferred to it all the assets and, if my scheme were adopted, a relatively simple piece of book-keeping could be done in settlement of whatever obligation remained in respect of the expenditures that had created those assets.

I referred my notes to Lambert for further inter-departmental study. Our target date was the next Budget. I was very hopeful. The last words of my minute to Lambert were, 'Don't be nervous about making a bold request.' On 11 January 1952 I found a chance of placing them before the Prime Minister for a preliminary discussion of the idea. We got nowhere.

It is possible that the ideas I had about a Territorial Service and a Territories Development Fund were unsound and that it would have been unwise to accept them. Any further discussion of them will not change the fact that they never became more than an idea. The historical interest is not in what might have happened but in what did happen as the result of the rejection, namely the effect on me. I was left with the impression that the Government was not really interested in the Territories and did not rate my task or my capacity very highly. I was unlikely to get any general direction or guidance on what to do in the Territories. I was unlikely to get any support for grand ideas. I had better go ahead on my own and get away with whatever I could. I started to concentrate on those matters that I could decide ministerially without bothering Cabinet. So the second chapter closed.

[3]

FIRST IMPRESSIONS OF THE TERRITORY

In July 1951 I paid my first visit to Papua and New Guinea accompanied by Lambert who was also seeing the country for the first time. Knowing nothing of the place, I left myself entirely in the hands of the Administrator who organized a grand tour and joined in with a personal staff of six of his own officers of various ranks and an enormous train of luggage.

It was much more ceremonious than I had imagined. One very vivid first impression that accounted for some of my subsequent actions was that the habits and outlook of colonialism permeated the place. I had read about colonialism of a comic kind in other lands and had seen a little of it before the war but had not expected to meet it in an Australian territory. The Administrator acted like a colonial governor and was accorded the deference due to a vice-regal rank which in fact he did not have. At his own residence, which to my surprise I found was called Government House, an aide-de-camp in uniform stood at attention when he moved from his chair. He was saluted as his car went down the street, native passers-by 'standing fast' at attention by the roadside until he had passed. At public assemblies he was greeted on entrance with 'God Save the King'. He flew the Union Jack on the flagstaff at his residence and on his car and when I asked why he did so he said that was always the custom at Government Houses and the Australian flag would not be appropriate. In and around civilian circles in Port Moresby close to the senior administrative staff, there were some of the oddities of an officers' mess full of temporary gentlemen in white ducks giving a repertory club performance of a pukka sahib who had just come in from a damned awful day of taking up the white man's burden. Several of the women talked as though they had once read a Somerset Maugham novel about planters' wives in Malaya and had sincerely admired all the things that made the author smile. The white community was stuffily rank-conscious.

When we went on our tour away from Port Moresby, the local people all travelled in 'spotless whites' with a native 'boy' carrying a big bundle the size of a bishop's swag. It was still a period of 'spotless whites' and everyone of high rank seemed to have a personal 'wash boy'. When one came in from a day's work or a day's travelling, one just kicked off the soiled whites and sweaty

13

underclothing and left them lying on the floor. A barefoot boy came in silently and picked them up, went straight to the wash tub and by some magic the clothes were clean and the suits were starched and ironed by next morning. At each senior residence or district office there were native messengers standing at the doors and doing nothing much except standing and coming to attention when a white person passed in or out. Most people seemed to have the same incapacity as newly appointed dignitaries in Australia to open a car door or carry a parcel for themselves. Everything seemed to be fetched and carried for the white man. The house boys were eager, docile and mostly sleek. They lived down the garden slope in 'boy houses' that seemed no better than huts. They were cheerful in the way in which pets are cheerful. On the New Guinea side, the younger boys were called 'monkeys'. 'Master' was the common term for a white man. The native men of status were the constabulary and, in the villages, the 'cap men' (luluais and tul-tuls), who were commended in conversation for being 'loyal' and 'having a good influence' or talked about guardedly as 'someone we will have to watch'. During the whole of this visit I never saw any indigenous person at a meal or at a social occasion with those of European race, but the Europeans would indulgently visit the natives in their villages to look at some dancing or a 'sing-sing' and the natives seemed suitably gratified at their patronage.

There is a lot more to the situation than is conveyed by the quick first impression I have recorded. I have shown the highlights only so as to illustrate the fact that, although I trotted around the Territory on my best behaviour and trying to smile like an innocent friend, I came away from that first trip revolted at the imitation of British colonial modes and manners by some of the Australians who were there to serve the Australian Government. I also had an impression that a good deal of it was a misguided or mistaken idea that such was the way in which one ruled dependent peoples. Unfortunately persons who did not have either the background or the training of the pre-war British colonial officer were imitating the outward signs and missing the inward grace. The best of the officers whom I met—and they too impressed me deeply— showed none of these oddities but went on with their job in a practical and unpretentious way.

There is a great tendency for persons in an unusual or difficult task which they have not yet mastered to romanticize themselves. It is the young and untried stockman and not the seasoned old drover who wears the fancy cowboy rig at the outback show and it is the fledgling cadet or the subordinate clerk and not the ambassador who gives the public performance of being 'in the diplomatic'. Similarly some of the colonial box of tricks I have mentioned were peculiar to the few.

The effect seemed to me however to have been heightened by other influences. There was an underlying spirit of separatism and perhaps in some cases, of resentment against Australia. This may have been the result of a feeling that they had been neglected or that they were imperfectly understood. In a few cases it may have been the result of self-importance. The man who was a diligent base-grade clerk in Australia with a state school education could be 'an officer of the colonial service' with faint but bogus suggestions of 'preparatory school, public school and the Varsity' among like-minded persons in Papua and New Guinea. I kept on hearing echoes of far-flung Empire, and 'spots of home leave' and 'going off to my cousin's place to get a bit of shooting' and never before in my life had I come across so many Australians who had lost so quickly any capacity to clean their own shoes or pour themselves another drink without the attention of a 'boy'.

This colonialism and this feeling of separateness from Australia and resentment against what was regarded as interference—mostly it was thought of as 'ignorant interference'—by Australia in Papua and New Guinea affairs were also apparent in the Administrator, Colonel J. K. Murray.[3] I shall write something later in admiration of this good and devoted man, but for the moment mention only one phase of my first meeting with him as an illustration of the matter now under notice and as an explanation of some of the factors that influenced some of my early decisions as Minister.

I think that in 1951 Murray was already a tired and disappointed man. He had been appointed from the heart of a circle of confident people at the Australian School of Pacific Administration who were glowing with ideas about the proper way to administer the Territory and how to shape the new world. He had been appointed by E. J. Ward, Minister for External Territories in the Chifley Ministry, and probably had good reason to think that he had been chosen to inaugurate and carry out vigorously an enlightened policy. His experience had been otherwise. Ward, whose major portfolio was that of Minister for Transport, contributed little to the Territory except a scandal over timber, which was the result, so I believe, not of any malfeasance on the part of Ward, whom I believe to have been a strictly honest man, but of inattention to his minor portfolio and absence of close ministerial interest in and oversight of what was going on in the Territory. Then had come a change of Government, and those sections of journalism that had any interest in the Territory, and notably the *Pacific Islands Monthly*, were predicting the end of the 'Ward-Murray policy' and the coming of a new policy less sympathetic to the native people and more favourable to European private enterprise. From what I heard after the event, I gathered that a single visit to the Territory by Ward as Minister and a bustling tour by my immediate predecessor, P. C. (later Sir Percy) Spender, had heightened Murray's misgivings about anything that came from Canberra and dampened his hopes. Spender had given me a poor account of him. Murray was most revealingly discreet whenever Spender's name was mentioned.

On arrival at Port Moresby on this first visit I found Murray correct but reticent. He gave me the impression at first that he did not think it worthwhile talking to the Minister for Territories about any major problems because anyone from Canberra would not understand them. The second and stronger impression was that he regarded the rule of the Territory as a matter for him and not for the Minister to handle. Even after I got to know him better, there was this same unwillingness to let Canberra have a part in Territory affairs. In my notes I find several instances in which I complained of his 'reticence'. In a note on a file dealing with a delicate question of policy I wrote on 19 October 1951,

This subject was one brought before me in the Territory in August last. I am amazed and annoyed that in the discussions on the spot, including a discussion resulting from some public criticism of Government policy, the Administrator never informed me of the matters of which he now complains and never disclosed anything of the background revealed in the present submissions.

It took me by surprise too to find that a man with his background and sympathies had developed an obsession about his own rank and status. It was only amusing to find that he had designed for himself and had made in London a uniform to be worn on formal occasions. The uniform was similar to that of a British Colonial Governor, with oak leaves on the collar and a white helmet with the Royal Coat of Arms in front and a silver thing on top. He said that a uniform was needed to impress the native people and they would understand a uniform of the British style better than an Australian one because it was closer to Royalty. But I was more disturbed when, sitting down by ourselves on his verandah for the first time, I asked him to tell me what he thought were the most urgent problems for me to examine and he at once started to tell me of a dispute between himself and the Naval Officer-in-Charge (NOIC) about the number of guns he was entitled to receive as a salute from a visiting French warship. The NOIC had advised the French captain to give nineteen guns and Murray thought he was entitled to twenty-one. Would I get the Governor-General as Commander-in-Chief to give a ruling?

This led at once to another topic. When, he asked, was the Governor-General going to give him his 'Instructions'? He had raised this with my predecessor but Spender had not seemed to appreciate the point. I asked him to explain and he quoted verbatim from memory Section 15 of the Papua and New Guinea Act 1949. He clearly understood this to mean that the Governor-General was to give him a formal set of 'Instructions' on taking up office and he said that since no such 'Instructions' had been given he found difficulty in carrying out his duties. I tried to discuss the constitutional relationship between the Territory Administrators and the Australian Government and between the Governor-General and his advisers in the Ministry but Murray was sure I was wrong. Although he was a little hazy about the responsibilities of a Minister, he was quite definite that 'the only way to govern Papua and New Guinea is to place it under the Administrator'. He developed an argument for self-government which meant government by himself and his staff, who were to be left free by Australia to do good as they saw it.*

In a second conversation which we had in similar circumstances, Murray returned to the topic and suggested that the title of Administrator be changed to that of Governor, which would better describe his position than the title of

---

* Subsequently, when I checked the text of Section 15, I found that it differed significantly from a similar section in the Papua and New Guinea Provisional Administration Act and I formed the opinion, from what Murray himself said, that he had something to do with the redrafting, and the change had stuck in his mind as an achievement that would free him to a large extent from political direction. After I returned to Canberra I obtained a constitutional memorandum from T. P. Fry, officer-in-charge of the Legal Research Section of the Department of Territories, on the status and powers of the Administrator in order to ensure that my own relationship with the Administrator should be constitutionally correct.

Administrator 'which was one used for places like the Northern Territory and was not suitable for colonies'. The title of Governor would show his link with the Throne.

When we passed at my initiative to talk of other topics, Murray did give to me in the course of several days some very useful information about conditions in the Territory and described well some of its immediate needs. Although he seemed to have lost confidence that the Australian Government would do much, he did have some ideas about what was needed to be done.

For the present I have recounted only lesser matters as a partial explanation of my own ministerial actions. I went back to Canberra seeing a clear need to bring about a better understanding of the constitutional relationship between the Australian Government and the Territory Administration and to develop better working arrangements for the practical and effective functioning of government in the Territory. I saw vividly too the need to combat a tendency both in the Territory Administration and in the European residents in the Territory to go 'colonial'. The need to overcome if I could the resentments in the Territory against any 'interference' from Canberra existed side by side with a need to provide much more assistance to the Administration in carrying out its job. It seemed to me that practices and procedures that had grown up in colonies remote from the homeland in an age of slow transport and poor communications were not necessarily the best model to follow in Papua and New Guinea. I was also awakened to the immediate question of fuller participation by the native people in the life of the community and in the public affairs of their land.

At the same time as I was receiving these impressions of the oddities of 'colonialism', I received a much ruder shock about the condition of the Territory public service.

After the war there was understandable difficulty in reconstructing a civil administration. During the war the Australian New Guinea Administrative Unit (Angau) had carried out many of the functions of government and the Australian New Guinea Production Control Board had managed plantations and related economic services. After the cessation of hostilities in August 1945 civil control was restored in successive stages, the last area being handed over by the Army in June 1946. The Production Control Board had become a fully civil organization in May. The Trusteeship Agreement between Australia and the United Nations General Assembly was concluded in December 1946. The Papua and New Guinea Provisional Administration Act had been assented to in August 1945 and proclaimed in October. Murray had taken up duty as Provisional Administrator in the same month.

Allowing a liberal period for the transfer, it may fairly be said that a civil administration had already been functioning for five years when I first saw it in the second half of 1951.

The Provisional Administration Act had provided for the appointment of officers 'necessary for the administration of this Act and for the proper government of the Territory' but had made no provision for the establishment of a public service. The Ordinance of the Territory for the establishment and regulation of a public service was not made until June 1949.

The fact that confronted me in August 1951, six years after the end of the war, was that the public service necessary to put into effect any decisions of policy was still in disorder. The officers from the separate pre-war administrations of Papua and the Mandated Territory of New Guinea who had been re-employed in the Provisional Administration after the war, the officers who had been transferred from Angau into the Provisional Administration, and the new recruits and officers on loan from the Commonwealth Public Service were still in many cases without confirmation of their appointments. The tedious but necessary business of the classification of positions in the service still had a long way to go. A public service inspector from the Commonwealth Public Service had been lent to the Territory as Acting Public Service Commissioner.

This temporary post was held by E. A. Head,[4] a practical, experienced and hard-working man. He was a good technician of public service administration but was working with very few members of staff who had any knowledge of the techniques. Seeing at once the deficiency in our administrative services, I drew him aside for a long talk. After some discussion, and after excluding the young officers who were out in the field as patrol officers or on similar field duties close to the indigenous people and who were doing incomparable work, we focused attention on the functioning of the main departments of the Administration in Port Moresby and Lae. He told me frankly and in confidence a disheartening story about the state of the service, the lack of public service training and the personal incompetence or unsuitability of some of the key men. He summed up, 'If you assume that the Commonwealth Public Service, which you know well, is one hundred per cent efficient, then you will be taking an optimistic view if you think of the Papua and New Guinea Public Service as being twenty-five per cent efficient.'

A good deal of the difficulty disclosed was that very few of the officers were trained public servants. Some of the pre-war officers, for example in the Customs Department, were well trained in the usages of the Territory and some of the heads of professional and technical departments, for example in the Departments of Health and Forests, knew their own professional field well. Some of the other heads of departments and senior officers either had no experience of administration at all, having been officers in the field before the war, or had previously been engaged only in minor or limited tasks and had been brought in simply because they had some knowledge of the Territory or some claim to reinstatement. The incompetence of some senior men was frightening.

The combined strengths of the public service of Papua and the public service of New Guinea before the war was only about 450 administering budgets of which the combined total was less than £670000, so pre-war experience was not much of a training in public administration. Some good material had been gained in the transfers from Angau but for the time being these young and active men were chiefly of value out in the field. At a lower level there was a distressing lack of capable clerks. In some cases clerkships had been given to men who had become unfit to continue in jobs requiring physical labour. The stores and transport position was lamentable. I soon became aware too that it was an unhappy service and indeed almost a hopeless one. Several of the senior vacancies had not yet been filled permanently.

So my first visit to the Territory brought me back to Canberra with a strong view that something had to be done to straighten out the misunderstanding about constitutional relationships, to combat the strong tendency to a 'colonial' outlook and method of administration and to get a better public service. High-minded decisions on policy would come to nothing if they could not be put into effect practically in the Territory. Policy would not be well founded unless the Territory Administration and its senior officers were helping to form it, drawing on experience in the Territory itself. Until they recognized that the path towards policy decisions led finally to Cabinet in Canberra and that the finances to support policy would have to come mostly from the Commonwealth Parliament, they would not know the effective way in which their ideas could be advanced and their experience applied.

In the course of this first visit and subsequent early visits I also became aware of the serious deficiency in buildings, public utilities and public works. The capital, Port Moresby, was still without a modern wharf; the airport was still a war-time landing strip with most of the runway made of Marsden matting and crushed coral; there was an acute shortage of housing, the most substantial structures being pre-war buildings while a large number of public servants lived in 'paper houses' erected in war time with walls of tarred paper or in 'dongas' that were little better than floored huts; hostels were badly built and badly run; the town water supply was deficient and the town electricity supply erratic. A considerable number of the 'town natives' lived in squalid humpies and the mixed-race community suffered appalling disadvantages. The offices in which the majority of the public service worked were little better than un-ventilated sheds. There was a European hospital in a pre-war building in the centre of town. The native hospital was a series of huts built out over the water at Ela Beach, the huts being connected to each other by wooden gangways, and the floors had frequent holes in them. The place was kept sweet and sanitary mainly by grace of the sea breezes and the washing in and out of the tides beneath the buildings. Roads were in bad order. Recreational facilities were scant, although an energetic Public Service Association under the leader-ship of a remarkable public-spirited officer, Ru Brennan, had constructed some amenities and a canteen for its members below the offices at Konedobu.

Rabaul was a shambles with the main port facility the upturned hull of a ship sunk in war time. Most buildings were temporary makeshifts. Chinatown was a higgledy-piggledy warren built of old iron. Everywhere was the evidence of the bombings by Allied planes when it was in Japanese occupation six and seven years earlier. The chief reason why there had been scarcely any post-war rebuilding was the lack of a final decision whether, by reason of the volcanic eruptions in 1939 and 1941, the town site should be moved. Rabaul Harbour still had scores of war-time wrecks around its shores and the war-time tunnel-ling of the Japanese was visible everywhere.

Lae was in a similar state of indecision. The town, if a straggling line of buildings can be called that, was still on the flat around the airstrip with a few war-time and pre-war buildings 'on top'. Although a decision had been made to develop the town on the plateau higher than the airstrip, an energetic and far-sighted District Commissioner, H. L. R. (later Sir Horace) Niall,[5] was unable to go ahead for lack of other decisions which would have made leases in the new town open to application. There was no proper wharf. The town hospital, in some war-time black-iron buildings, was in a deplorable condition, lacking in facilities and without the means even to repair the frequent holes in the concrete floors or to replace the leaking roofs. Out at Malahang there was a native hopsital, the wards of which were virtually no more than a series of iron roofs over damp earth floors and with no walls. It was crowded. The best shopping was at a huddle of Chinese trade stores at the edge of the jungle across the Butibum River.

Behind the town, in a group of store sheds, was a heterogeneous collection of the debris of war, on which the District Commissioner cast envious eyes if only he could have picked and chosen from it what would be useful. He had no authority to touch it.

In Madang there was a similar situation, the most substantial structures being those of the pre-war period—indeed the best of them belonged to the German period—and little post-war progress had been made in providing basic services. On a knoll near the wharf there was a decrepit wooden hospital for the Europeans, and for the natives some sheds on the outskirts. Because of the state of the hospitals, most Europeans and natives preferred to go to a mission hospital several miles inland.

Wewak was still much as the war had left it, except that the Roman Catholic mission had started building, including a cathedral. When I met the Bishop and asked him if I could do anything to help him, he said, 'A few pounds of nails would be useful.' Wewak was at the end of the line and orders for hardware often did not arrive. In building the cathedral, the mission workers were straightening out the nails recovered from old packing cases. The Administration had only constructed two small buildings since the war, and staff still lived in some hardship in substandard black-iron military sheds which had been converted into dwellings. Along the Wewak coast the rubbish of war and the bomb craters were still to be seen.

I came away with a keen sense of the inadequacy of the basic services and facilities to do what needed to be done. The little that had been done seemed only to have been done in the last twelve months under the energetic rule of Spender. I had expected to see a bigger and more useful inheritance of assets from the war-time period of construction but most of what had been there at the end of the war had been sold, dismantled, removed or broken up. I heard strange tales of the operations of the War Disposals Commission. I saw yards belonging to private interests full of material prepared for shipping to Australia or elsewhere for speculative sale although a good deal of it would have been useful in the Territory. I tried to get some account from Murray of what might still be done but in this field more than any other his hopelessness became apparent. I guessed that he must have had some discouraging experiences and had given up the struggle.

I tried to talk about houses. Murray and others in the Administration said Australia would have to be prepared to spend money, but when I agreed with that and asked for a plan for housing with estimates of costs per house, I found that they were not agreed yet on what sort of house to build. Under Spender some 'pre-fabs' had been ordered. They were still divided in opinion about whether they should import houses or build them. There was doubt about materials and when I drew attention to the possible use of pre-cut timber houses from Bulolo they condemned the idea on the ground that the houses would deteriorate quickly on the coast. When I talked of making concrete and sand building blocks they enlarged on all the difficulties of doing that. When I attempted to turn their thoughts towards a cost study of the comparative advantages of a quick supply of houses that would last for twenty years and a slow supply of houses that would last for fifty years, I seemed to have raised something beyond their competence. I could not discover any clear plan for rebuilding the administrative centre at Konedobu but only general ideas that work needed to be done.

With exceptions, here and there, I found a large part of the Administration in a mood where they automatically raised difficulties whenever a proposal was put to them and said that nothing could be done about 'this' unless something was first done about 'that'. Behind it all, the Administrator seemed to think that it was fundamental to progress that he should first get his 'Instructions' from the Governor-General as provided in Section 15 of the Papua and New Guinea Act. He seemed to be obsessed with this and referred to the absence of his 'Instructions' as a lack of policy.

On return to Australia I decided that I must try to get a lot done in housing, water and electricity supply, other utilities and services, and better office accommodation or I would not be able to recruit and hold better public servants.

This discouragement and difficulty were uppermost when I was thinking of what a Minister for Territories had to do. At the same time, as I moved from place to place, I was caught up in a proud story of adventure and saw sights that moved me deeply and made me feel that whatever little things I might share in doing would be part of a greater history.

I saw where the Kokoda Trail began. We flew across the Owen Stanley Range and landed at Dobodura. On a later visit I was to retrace the fighting at Buna and Gona. I had known men who had died there and many who had served there. On this first visit we went from Dobodura to Saiho, where an emergency camp had been set up after the Mt Lamington eruption five months earlier. Four thousand people had been killed in the eruption. We walked through some of the devastated area up to the site of Higatura, a district post which had been wiped out in a flash, killing the whole Australian staff. In a Dragon-Rapide biplane, with the vulcanologist Tony Taylor, we flew around the crater. A huge cloud of steam hung above it. A great rock the size of a house was slowly dislodged from the rim and tumbled and rolled in a ponderous way down into the mass of detritus on the hillside. Now and again the volcano gave a modest belch. 'She's quite healthy-looking this morning', said Taylor, whose job it was to make these inspection flights regularly. On the ground he showed me the instruments that took the monster's pulse, from a dozen miles away. To insert the lines he had crawled up the side of the mountain within a day or two of a lateral blast which had blown out one face of the volcano. For that and other daring he was later awarded the George Cross. He seemed to have developed a sort of affection for Mt Lamington. 'She was a bit uneasy last night.' 'She seems to be settling down.' 'She's still got one or two bad symptoms.'

In the devastated area one saw miles of country in which great tree trunks snapped off at a uniform height as the blast of heat had swept across them, and riverbeds seared by the hot ash and stones, borne on a cushion of steam, that had poured down them. Nothing had lived where that blast of heat had swept. But even now, only five months later, the sprouts of jungle growth, especially the first foot or so of banana palms, were beginning to show in the browned and blackened floor of the foothills.

At Saiho the Orokaiva people had come together in thousands. I was told that in the early post-war period they had been resistant to the restored Administration. It was feared that the losses they had suffered would have increased their enmity. But now they came to express thanks to the Administration and to Australia for the help they had given in a time of disaster. In the emergency Murray had shown up well. He had organized and directed the work of rescue and rehabilitation and had put in promptly all the required resources needed for the task.

In the Lamington area I met for the first time S. Elliott-Smith,[6] the District Commissioner. He had been a patrol officer in Papua in the time of Hubert Murray. He had also served in the region during the war. He was one of the old-time officers who had 'a way with the people'. They loved him, trusted him, and mostly did whatever he asked them to do. He could chatter endlessly with them in Motu. They enjoyed his rollicking laugh. Those who have not seen it for themselves may find it hard to appreciate the close friendship and mutual confidence that developed between such early-day officers and the people with whom they worked.

On this and on later visits I had the advantage of yarning, on many an evening, with Elliott-Smith, hearing him tell of his work with Hubert Murray and of the various 'big men' with whom he had worked in the villages. I began to feel part of a great endeavour.

One story of the Orokaiva concerned some killings just before war came to Papua and New Guinea. One of the 'big men' had been convicted of repeated murders and was in the calaboose awaiting execution. There was an urgent need for an airstrip where none had previous existed. Elliott-Smith knew there was only one man who could rally the people and he went to the condemned man to ask his help. He let him out of gaol for the purpose. Under his inspiration the people came in thousands. They cut down the kunai, carted away the stones in baskets, levelled the ground with mattocks and hoes and finally compacted the earth by dancing day and night in their thousands, stamping rhythmically up and down the hundreds of feet of strip. It was ready. The aircraft flew in. Another step had been gained in the war. The leader went back to the calaboose and in due course was hanged.

Many of the great men of pre-war Papua and New Guinea were still at work. Keith McCarthy was District Commissioner at Rabaul, Horrie Niall at Lae, George Greathead at Goroka, Charles Bates at Madang, R. I. Skinner in the highlands, and 'Bert' Jones, Alan Roberts and Ivan Champion at headquarters. On this and other visits I talked with them all. I felt that I was forming links with the pre-war romance of exploration and penetration into the unknown and sharing in a small way in an adventure and a great enterprise. I returned to Australia with my interest in the Territory awakened.

[4]

CLEARING THE DECK FOR ACTION

At the commencement of my work I found no need to restate policy. My reading of departmental papers and public pronouncements did not arouse any immediate doubts about the objectives and principles that had been declared. In any case I could not draw on any knowledge or experience at that stage which would enable me to re-examine policy intelligently. Moreover the cast of my mind and the nature of my training had given me a strong opinion that good policy and good administration are inseparably intertwined and cannot grow in a healthy way apart from each other. I have never seen much value come out of back-room planning by persons who are not engaged in any way in the administrative task and I have seen much misplaced effort when the persons who did the thinking had no part in the doing and when those who had the task of doing were not encouraged to think. I left declarations of policy to wait until I had more experience and I started to attend to administration.

I looked critically at the Papua and New Guinea Act 1949.* I thought at once that it was a poor Act. My experience in subsequent years made me think it was even worse than my first view of it and if I were not giving evidence but writing a history of Australian administration in Papua and New Guinea, I might well start by condemning the Act as one of the earliest postwar mistakes, not in purpose but in design.

Coming to office in the middle of 1951 however I saw no prospect of returning to any other starting point. The Act had been commenced by proclamation on 1 July 1949. Parts of it had not yet been put into effect. It would have been futile for me to propose an amending Bill at that stage. There would have been fierce arguments before even an amending draft could have been produced and difficulty in getting any Bill into Parliament. We had no time for those arguments. Anything that was attempted would have to be done in accordance with the existing legislation and I accepted the Act as one of the facts of the situation.

* Papua and New Guinea Act 1949 (No. 9 of 1949). Assented to 25 March 1949. Part V, Division 3 (interim legislative powers) proclaimed on the same day. The remainder proclaimed on 1 July 1949.

As I have already recounted, one of my earliest resolutions was to strengthen the Territory Administration. From the start, even before I went to the Territory on my first visit, I saw a need for strength at the top.

At first I thought the easiest way would be to raise the status of Administrator, perhaps making him a Lieutenant-Governor with something resembling a vice-regal status and relieving him of the tasks of daily administration. These tasks could be left to active men with proved administrative capacity and good public service experience who might be appointed as his deputies.

The Act, particularly Section 17, was an impediment to any clear-cut action of that kind. The section provided that the Administrator might appoint a deputy or deputies to exercise during his pleasure such powers and functions as he assigned to them. Under that section, Spender, who diagnosed the weakness of the senior level of administration much more severely than I had done, had accepted a scheme to appoint two deputies, one on the New Guinea side and one on the Papuan side, and in October 1950 applications had been called by public advertisement from persons inside and outside the public service of Papua and New Guinea for two positions of Deputy Administrator. My first view of his scheme was that it was a foredoomed attempt to change the nature of the office of Administrator. Spender had made enough progress with it however to present me with another fixed starting point.

The position I inherited was that a committee consisting of Head and Halligan had examined the sixteen applications received and interviewed eleven of them. They had recommended that only one Deputy Administrator be appointed and that he be stationed at Port Moresby; that this Deputy Administrator be given powers equivalent to those of the Administrator, except those related to the powers of the Administrator in Executive Council; that he have some of the functions and responsibility at present exercised by the Administrator and some of those of Government Secretary; and that D. M. (later Sir Donald) Cleland[7] be appointed. Spender approved these recommendations on 23 January 1951. Then it would appear—and on this I am speculating and not using any record—that Spender encountered for the first time the snag set by Section 17, which said that it was the Administrator and not the Minister who appointed deputies. There was no outcome from an attempt by Spender to clear the way by interesting Murray in taking an appointment outside the Territory. His final minute on 27 March 1951 left the question for his successor. In conversation with me after I took the portfolio he said that I would be unable to get anything done in Papua and New Guinea until I 'got rid of Murray'.

The early departmental re-examination of the question after I became Minister produced the view that we should not proceed with the appointment of a Deputy Administrator or try to make any use of Section 17 but that we should strengthen the position of Government Secretary as a senior departmental head in the Territory public service. One additional objection stated to the appointment of two deputies under Section 17 was that such action would seem to create a regional administrative structure, which might have results conflicting with the objectives sought when Australia gained authority to join the Trust Territory of New Guinea and the Australian Territory of Papua in an administrative union.

The departmental views were modified by me and on 9 July I informed the Secretary of the Department of my decision to appoint Cleland as an officer of the public service of the Territory with the title of Assistant Administrator. In taking this course I was using the powers that Division 4 of the Papua and New Guinea Act gave to the Governor-General, and by delegation to the Minister, in respect of the public service.

A minute I addressed to the Department on that date expressed my own thinking at that time. In a covering note I had said that the second of the recommendations made by Head and Halligan to Spender, in defining the powers of the Deputy Administrator, had virtually proposed a change in the office of Administrator. In my opinion the time was not opportune to make such a change nor was I prepared to recommend it without much fuller consideration of the whole structure of the Administration. In the formal minute I said that I wanted the Assistant Administrator to act as 'chief executive officer' to free the Administrator to give attention chiefly to general policy and major executive acts and to carry out his duties as chief representative of the Commonwealth Government in the Territory and as President of the Legislative Council when it was inaugurated; the Assistant Administrator should also help ensure the smooth running and efficiency of the various departments of the Administration at the departmental level. I continued,

It is my wish that the Administrator should delegate to the Assistant Administrator such powers as will be necessary to fulfil the intention in his appointment. The question of delegation of powers by the Administrator does not arise for the present appointment in any different form than in regard to other officers of the service. The Administrator should be encouraged to delegate his powers to both the higher and lower levels of the service in order that administration may be prompt and effective, but this delegation is an act to be performed by the Administrator and, unless and until there is any evidence that administration is being impeded by failure to make such delegation, I will rely on his judgement. If concrete instances can be shown that a power of delegation does not exist in cases where delegation is desirable, proposals for the introduction of amending ordinances can be considered on their merits.

In this I was relying on the interim legislative powers of the Governor-General under Section 54 to make ordinances until such time as a Legislative Council was inaugurated in accordance with Section 35, and although, as will appear later, I had already decided to inaugurate the Council, I believed this should be a good enough hint to Murray that if he did not make the necessary delegation, I would advise the Governor-General to make an ordinance or ordinances to do it in his stead. My minute continued,

Behind this appointment is the desire to encourage the Administration in New Guinea to accept increasing responsibility for making local decisions on matters not involving policy and to prepare their own submissions for transmission through the Department of Territories to the Minister. The officers of the Administration should not wait on requests from Canberra but should initiate action themselves. They should not seek instructions on matters of detail in the execution of policy when policy is clear. They should develop the habit of either acting when the course of action is plain or of presenting promptly their own recommendations for action when higher approval is necessary. The smooth working of such a system will depend to a considerable extent on close understanding and confidence between officers of the Administration in the Territory and officers of the Department of Territories in Canberra. Having regard to modern facilities for travel and communication, it should be possible for consultation at the early and formative stages to be much more common than it has been in the past and, to this end, while the Assistant Administrator will be responsible to the Administrator in the same way as other officers in the Territory and will necessarily refer to him all major questions affecting policy, I would hope to see working arrangements which would allow the Assistant Administrator direct communication with the Department of Territories on appropriate matters.

This appointment and these arrangements will be without prejudice to any subsequent and more fundamental examination of the structure of the Administration in the Territories, and it is my hope that experience gained under the change now proposed may be useful in shaping decisions or any further adjustments.

This minute was followed by further discussion of detail between Lambert, Murray and Head, and eventually with Cleland, and the actual appointment was made by me on 9 August. I quote a minute I wrote on that date, since it is a basic document in the post-war Territorial Administration:

Consequent on public advertisement for applications for two positions of Deputy Administrator . . . Mr D. M. Cleland is to be appointed to the post of Assistant Administrator.

The title of Assistant Administrator is being used to avoid confusion with the provisions for appointment of a Deputy Administrator contained in Section 17 of the Papua and New Guinea Act. The appointment it is now intended to make is of a different kind to that contemplated in Section 17 . . .

On the recommendations of the Public Service Commissioner I have decided to create within the Public Service of the Territory of Papua and New Guinea a new department, to be designated The Department of the Administrator and to create within that department the new office of Assistant Administrator . . .

The intention in the appointment of an Assistant Administrator is to create a permanent senior position at a level higher than any of the departmental heads in the Territory. The occupant of this office will

(i) assist the Administrator in the carrying out of his functions and for that purpose exercise such delegations as may be given to him by the Administrator;

(ii) be responsible to the Administrator for the co-ordination and efficient functioning of the departments of the Administration and for the promotion of development policies;

(iii) advise the Administrator generally.

Consequent on decisions made by my predecessor, it is apparent that District Commissioners in the Territory must be relied upon to a considerable extent for the general oversight and direction of administration within their respective districts. This means that District Commissioners have departmental responsibility as regards those phases of administration which come under the Department of District Services and Native Affairs and a general responsibility to the Administrator for the efficiency of their districts. Insofar as this general responsibility is concerned, it is desirable that there should be direct communication between them and the Assistant Administrator.

This appointment does not alter in any way the character of the office of Administrator.

Some points need to be made clear as a number of false statements about this appointment have gained currency. Cleland was selected from among several applicants and recommended for appointment by an interviewing committee, and the recommendation was supported by Spender before I came to office. In this matter no representations were made to me except on the single point of the need to make an early decision in fairness to all applicants. The only discussion I had with Cleland before the final decision to appoint him concerned solely my intention to create a position of Assistant Administrator inside the Territory public service. This discussion was necessary because he had made his application for a position of Deputy Administrator. No question arose then or later about any claim by Cleland to succession to the Administratorship.

One early consequence of this decision was that it was possible to proceed with the filling of other positions as heads of departments in the Territories and to get on with my plans for improving the public service. As announced when we discarded the idea of appointing Deputy Administrators, we placed higher responsibility on District Commissioners to ensure the efficiency of administration in outlying regions. In those districts where we had men of quality as District Commissioners this system worked reasonably well in practice. As we found at the outset and at every subsequent reshuffling of appointments, however, we did not have enough men of superior capacity to do the job well in all of the fifteen districts.

Another question I inherited concerned the harvesting of the Bulolo pine forest. At Bulolo there was a good forest of Klinkii pine. It was coveted by many timber millers. Certain dealings in the time when Ward was Minister had led to a public inquiry and subsequently to the trial and conviction of Ward's private secretary 'Jock' Garden on charges of conspiracy and forgery.

Following this scandal, Ward announced on 7 November 1949 a proposal for an agreement with the Bulolo Gold Dredging Company, which already had plant and installations at Bulolo, to form a joint company to work the pines. Before the change of government in December 1949, heads of agreement had been drawn up but not signed.

After the change of government Spender recommended that the new Government should proceed with the Chifley Government's plan and this proposal had been before Cabinet on four occasions during 1950. It became my responsibility to continue the negotiations with the company and to work out a good deal of detail that was still controversial.

In doing this I ran into my first political tangle. Certain timber interests in Queensland saw the Bulolo stand as a natural source of supply of logs for Queensland plymills and they lobbied hard and influentially to try to bring about that result. The contrary view which I pressed was that any timber industry should be primarily for the benefit of the Territory and not for the benefit of Queensland and that the Territory should not export logs but manufacture finished plywood and veneers. That fight was a hard one, but I won it.

A strong section of Government supporters condemned Commonwealth Government participation in ownership and control of an industrial operation, saying that it was a disguised form of socialism. The contrary view which I urged was that, with the background of scandal, it was inopportune to call public tenders and give the timber to the highest bidder, that Bulolo Gold Dredging already had the water power, the local establishment and the experience to bring a timber industry into production faster than any other potential operator, and that some Commonwealth participation was necessary in order to ensure control of policy, the fulfilment of our obligations under the Trusteeship Agreement and to counter the criticism that would arise at giving the whole of a benefit to one company.

Two other arguments which appealed to me strongly but seemed to cut less ice with others were that in any major industrial enterprise—and this was the first big one the Territory had known—it was desirable for the Government to retain some share for the sake of future native participation in the ownership of industry, and that if we regarded the forest as a continuing asset to be farmed in perpetuity, we had to treat it as a trust for the future generations, and Government participation in investment and control would help to maintain the trust. I had tough negotiations with the company, much opposition in the Government party room, strong lobbying against the proposal by the Queensland timber interests and eventually a good deal of hard talking in Cabinet. By the end of February 1952 the Prime Minister was able to announce the plan, and in June the legislation approving the agreement between the Commonwealth and Bulolo Gold Dredging to form Commonwealth New Guinea Timbers Ltd with a capital of £2 million was passed.*

These negotiations brought me in close touch for the first time with the Director of Forests, Jim McAdam.[8] He was a dedicated lover both of the Territory and of forests. As a forester he was a purist and idealist, so pure and so idealistic that he seemed to me at first to be living in perpetual fear of the rape of his beloved trees while doubtless to him I appeared possibly as a brutal assailant. As we worked together however both on this matter and later on questions of land settlement we came close to each other in sympathy, action and friendship. He was one of the finer persons with whom I had the good fortune to work.

Another acquaintanceship that developed over this transaction was with Mick Leahy.[9] I had met him and his family at their farm at Zenag on my first visit to the Territory. He said some hard things about the Administration. He also gave me more than one glimpse into the past adventurous history of Australians in Papua and New Guinea in the early days. I had an instant liking for this forthright, hot-headed, Irish Australian. I respected the way in which he had put back into the Territory everything that he had got out of it. He was a known opponent of the Government, of the Administration and of the 'big men' and so when it was heard that he was in Australia at the time when the

* New Guinea Timber Agreement Act 1952 (No. 40 of 1952) and New Guinea Timber Agreement Act 1953 (No. 73 of 1953).

party-room opposition to the Bulolo timber deal was strongest, some of the group of young and impetuous Liberal members who were strongest in attacking me arranged for him to come to Canberra and organized a private meeting so that he could address them. Mick Leahy came readily and gave his gospel. It was not what they had expected. In effect he told them that the Government proposal was a good one, that Bulolo, which he hated, was the only show that would ever be likely to do an efficient job in present circumstances, and that the Minister was on the right lines and knew what he was about. It was quite different from what the organizers of the meeting had expected and hoped he would say. It turned the tide in the party room.

As I have already indicated, another clearing-up job that called for attention was the work of the War Disposals Commission. I started to dig into its operations but quickly realized that it would be a profitless diversion of effort and possibly a harm to the Territory to scratch over that ground again. I did not think that I could regain anything of much value to the Territory and was sure that the delay, distraction and contention that would be bound to arise in any investigation would cause harm. So I left the mess to take care of itself.

Another piece of unfinished business I inherited was the proposed transfer of the town of Rabaul to another site on Blanche Bay. I could not get a firm and clear recommendation from the Territory. There had been a public announcement in 1947 that the new administrative headquarters would be 'in the Kokopo area' but I could not get a clear statement of the facts. Information about any plans for the new site was vague. At Rabaul during my first visit and later at Port Moresby I was mostly given conflicting opinions but the citizens of Rabaul were pressing for a decision so that they could get on with the business of living. In September 1951, following abortive discussions, I gave the Administration three months to examine the problems of transfer and to furnish a report. In particular I asked for detailed facts about the alternative site for the town, the new works that would be required, the stages in which any transfer could take place and the total cost at each stage.

The inadequacy of the attempts of the Administration to supply the required report was only repaired in January 1952 when Cleland, visiting Rabaul for the first time as Assistant Administrator, re-examined the whole position and produced the sort of document for which I had been asking for nearly six months and backed his own judgement by making recommendations. The Administrator disagreed with his report. Murray took the matter to the Territory Executive Council, which supported him against Cleland and favoured transferring the town to the Rapopo-Kokopo area. The papers came to me in Canberra and were the subject of further checking and inquiry by the Department of Territories. I made an early decision to support Cleland and started the Department in preparing a submission for Cabinet. My main difficulty was to get money in advance of the following year's Budget. The additional material I had obtained from the vulcanologists of the Bureau of Mineral Resources gave sufficient support to uphold my proposal against any transfer to a new site and to argue that a warning system and escape routes were practicable. On 13 June 1952 I was able to announce publicly a decision to rebuild the town and port of Rabaul on the old site in Simpson Harbour, the maintenance of an observation and warning system, the preparation of escape routes and evacuation centres in case of any further eruption and, what gave greatest joy to the townsfolk, the commencement at once of work on a new wharf at Rabaul.

Ministerially I made some other decisions, also contrary to Administration advice, concerning the town plan for Rabaul—one against designating any part of the town as Chinatown and another against forming a new residential area for Europeans only. I ruled that there were to be no limitations on the freedom of anyone to be granted blocks, either for residence or business, anywhere in the town. In 1951 Rabaul was a strongly racialist town with clear divisions between Europeans, Chinese, mixed race and indigenous people both socially and in administrative practice.

I had similar but less difficult decisions to make in the case of Lae. The granting of leases in a new townsite was held up by lack of decision on whether applications for business leases in the new town should be restricted. I gave a direction that ended uncertainty.

While the work on the spot was done by others—and done very well—I had some feeling of personal satisfaction in later years, as both Rabaul and Lae developed into thriving urban communities, that I had at least fired the starting pistol that set them on their way and that I had established the principle of no racial discrimination in town leases.

In the neighbourhood of Lae there was indecision too about the Markham River crossing for the road leading to Bulolo and Wau. It had been decided in principle to bridge the river but there was argument about the site, no final design had been made and hence no money obtained. The crossing was still by a vehicular ferry of truly remarkable oddity. I heard both arguments, had some difficulty with my colleague the Minister for Works, but got a decision on the site and cleared the way for a bid for funds. The site of the Markham River Bridge may be the wrong one. For all I know there may be a better one. But I got a decision and the Territory got a necessary bridge simply because I cut through the argument and made a decision.

Some uncertainty about Port Moresby was also cleared up in the first few months. Murray had some rather vague ideas that the capital of the combined territories should be in the congenial climate of Wau and not on the coast. He talked of building a new Government House as his own official residence at Wau. He had a plan for a centre of higher education there and saw Wau as the site of a future university. I confess I never really examined the proposal in the way it may have deserved. Murray's account gave it a dream-like quality but, for all I know, there may have been a well-conceived and practicable plan. I made no judgement on that, for no firm case had been presented. What I did was recognize the fact that Port Moresby existed, that the Administration could be made to get results there more quickly than if we waited to transfer it to some yet unbuilt 'Canberra' in the highlands, and that Port Moresby was functioning as a port and as a centre of industry. Communication with Wau was still difficult and uncertain. To start building an administrative capital there would be a diversion of scant resources and an interruption of more urgent tasks. I told Murray to forget about Wau for the time being and get on with the improvement of facilities at Port Moresby—the harbour, housing, office buildings, power station and town water supply. As far as I can remember or have noted on paper, I did not consider such broader questions as whether the capital of the administrative union should be in New Guinea or in Papua, on the coast or on the higher land, in a totally new development with modern planning or in an old European port. It was a pragmatic decision. It may have been the wrong one. But it helped us to get on with the jobs that were waiting to be done instead of putting them aside to undertake a new job.

Another of these clearing-up jobs concerned the racial situation. Being clearly of the mind that the future of the country was self-government by the indigenous people, I was equally clear that the future problems would be less complicated if we did not have a multi-racial population but one immigrant group alongside one indigenous group. This initial view on policy governed my decisions on several particular issues.

The actual situation in 1951 was that the 'immigrant group' consisted of about 11 000 persons of European race, about 2000 persons of Chinese origin, about 1300 persons of mixed race of various origins, and a very small number of others—Indians and Samoans principally—who had come in as missionary staff. I soon discovered that there was very strong pressure to bring in Asian labour 'to help develop the country' and some pressure too from the Christian missions to bring in other Asians as mission workers. I resolved to resist the introduction of Asian labour because I thought it would impede immediate progress in the advancement of the indigenous people, lessen their chances of employment in the future and unnecessarily complicate the social problems and the possible political conflicts at the time of self-government. Fiji and East Africa seemed to me to signal the need for caution in introducing immigrant labour. In order to strengthen my own position in resisting the pressure for introducing Asian labour, I decided that I also had to resist the requests from the missions. My uppermost concern was to keep the population as uncompli-cated as possible against the day when the indigenous people would make their own decisions on the composition of their country's population. This seemed to me to be as necessary as the parallel policy of checking the alienation of land from indigenous possession and occupation.

As a consequence of these views, I was also resolved to reduce the non-indigenous population to one integrated immigrant group. This meant that the mixed-race people should be given the chance to identify themselves either with the Europeans or with the indigenes and to be received into whichever group they chose. Since the rejection of the mixed-race by the indigenous people was more marked than their rejection by the Europeans, this really meant that most of the mixed-race people would have to be accorded the same position in law and in social relationship as the Europeans.

As for the Chinese, I saw at once that the only way open was to give them full Australian citizenship, with the right of permanent residence in Australia and to give every possible encouragement to all of them to identify themselves with Australians as part of a single immigrant community.

These ideas were quite contrary to prevailing opinion in the Territory and in Australia at that time. The mixed-race people were outcasts living at a depressed standard. The Chinese were considered dangerous rivals and they had been made subject to all sorts of handicaps (for example in land-holding) in order to lessen the danger that they would swamp white enterprise.

Using my powers as Minister I was able to administer the immigration laws of the Territory to protect the indigenous majority. I did so and clamped down very severely on the further immigration of any persons likely to add to a third or fourth racial group in the Territory. For the rest, I had to persuade Cabinet to a more liberal view on Australian citizenship for the Chinese and mixed-race people. I had to go through a long period of resistance, contention and delay before I succeeded but I did get my way in the end. That story belongs to a later period.

In the meantime, in the domestic affairs of the Territory, I went ahead to remove any discriminatory treatment of the Chinese and mixed-race people, to break down the social barriers between them and the Europeans, to give better opportunities to them, and to prevent the introduction of new and separate immigrant groups. I met a good deal of criticism, misunderstanding and mis-representation. Some of my own officers could not discover the consistency of a Minister who, inside the Territory, showed he was 'fond of the Chinks' and yet kept on rejecting recommendations for the entry of new Chinese 'helpers' or 'assistants' or of Asian brothers and sisters to staff the missions. Some sections of private enterprise thought I was as bad a socialist as Ward because I refused to let them have Asian labour.

I also had to face some criticism from some of those who sympathized with my views against racial discrimination. They expected me to be more peremp-tory in dealing with some incidents that arose in the Territory. My own view is that when racial differences emerge as a social crisis, wisdom lies in trying to avoid any clash. A clash, or even the making of a challenge, tends to harden prejudice. The improvement of race relations calls for a softening of attitudes, the easing of tension and a moving away from established positions. I have seen too many cases in which the zeal of reformers has increased racial antipathy and increased tension. I tried to move easily, avoiding confrontations and had the eventual happiness of seeing a much more general acceptance of the Chinese and mixed-race people as fellow-citizens than had at first been thought possible.

The problem of the mixed-race people was more acute in Port Moresby than elsewhere. Although in Rabaul there was the 'Kombiu' community of long standing which suffered some discrimination and lack of privilege, it was not so utterly rejected and in such a distressing condition as the mixed-race people on the outskirts of Port Moresby. The younger section of mixed-race people in Port Moresby included a fair number of children from casual war-time mating of soldiers with Papuan women. I gathered that before the war some half-caste children had been acknowledged and supported by their white fathers but, with the death of parents and with the consequences of war-time evacuation of civilians, many such links had been broken, so a large section of the mixed-race people under twenty-one years were 'orphans'. Catholic sisters at Bomana and Koki were giving devoted care to some of them.

The adults and family groups lived in wretched conditions in a gully behind Koki to which they had virtually been banished. I could not accept the official claim that this allotment of an area in which some temporary buildings could be built was a measure for their betterment.

When I first encountered them and sat down for talks with them in a recreation hall they had built near Koki, their chief requests were that they should be recognized as a mixed-race community—'mixed-race' was the term they themselves chose in preference to any other term—and that their claims to rights and privileges as a separate community should be recognized. They wanted such things as a mixed-race school, some better land for a mixed-race village or villages, and financial assistance to obtain materials for building better houses for themselves. It was largely a self help and regenerative movement, but a movement that I feared would end in separate development. The Catholic sisters pleaded mostly for some help in overcoming the hopelessness of the future for the children in their care. When they could no longer keep the boys and girls at their orphanage, there was nothing for them to do and nowhere to go. Low-wage labouring and cadging for the boys and prostitution for the girls were the chief prospects. The sisters were thinking of a mixed-race vocational training school.

My first suggestions that the future might be sought not in forming and solidifying a separate mixed-race community with immediate but minor benefits for itself, but in helping them to join either the indigenous or the immigrant community were not readily understood. When it became clearer that I was serious in giving them full status and opportunity in the white community if they wished it, including especially employment opportunity in the public service, and that I was also serious about a fuller opportunity for the indigenous people, they moved to an acceptance of my ideas. Luckily their leader at that time was one of the most articulate and quick-minded men in Port Moresby, John (later Sir John) Guise,[10] then a Warrant Officer in the Royal Papuan and New Guinea Constabulary. He was at first an earnest and eloquent spokesman for a separate mixed-race community with its own privileges. He saw the trend of my thinking more quickly than most and, after it had become clear that a path should be chosen either to the indigenes or to the Europeans and that there was no future in trying to be leader of a separate mixed-race community, Guise chose to identify himself through his wife's family with the indigenous people, although he continued to help the mixed-race community at Port Moresby to overcome their disadvantages. Since then he has given notable service and risen to an eminent position as a Papuan. If he had chosen to take the other path and joined the Europeans, I am sure that he would also have found opportunity to advance, but I think myself that he made the better and more enlightened choice in becoming a spokesman for Papua and New Guinea rather than a senior Australian official of an Australian Administration. He probably had good personal reason too, at that time, for doubting how far he could go and what acceptance he would enjoy in the Australian Administration, for he had had some discouraging experiences.

It took a good while to do all that I wanted to do in respect of the mixed-race people both in Port Moresby and Rabaul but the course I set was the result of one of my 'clearing-up' decisions made soon after taking office.

Yet another clearing-up job concerned the Customs administration. The Territory had its own tariff and a Customs administration separate from that of Australia. There were differences of opinion both in Australia and in the

Territory about whether this separateness should continue. I received representations both in the Territory and in Australia urging me to bring the Territory within the Australian tariff system.

In the post-war years the trade of the Territory had not revived to any great extent. A good deal of its export trade was still in shipping out stuff salvaged under war disposals or in sending 'returned empties' (oil drums, cans, bottles and other containers) to Australia. Territory exports were liable to duty on entering Australia; the Territory did not get the advantage of the Australian protective tariffs; some necessities imported from Australia paid duties on entering the Territory. The arguments for or against separate systems were closely related to the line of business conducted by the debater.

My own immediate view, having in mind the goal of ultimate self-government, was in favour of a separate Customs system. There was however less certainty that the short-term advantage of the Territory would be served by remaining separate and, as I saw it, a good deal of the hesitation both in the public sector and in the private sector in making decisions affecting the economy of the Territory was linked with this uncertainty. A clear and early decision had to be made but it would only be accepted as final and convincing if it were based on some re-examination of the facts of trade and industry.

In February 1952, after preparing the ground as best I could and overcoming a few obstacles both in the Territory and in Canberra, I was able to obtain a Cabinet decision for the appointment of a committee of three to inquire into and report upon future Customs policy for the Territory. Professor S. J. Butlin of the University of Sydney was chairman, and the members were drawn from the Commonwealth Treasury (H. J. Goodes) and the Commonwealth Department of Trade and Customs (V. A. Clark). The committee did a thorough job, taking evidence from interested parties as well as collecting and studying relevant statistics and documents.

On 21 November 1952 in Port Moresby I was able to announce that the Territory would continue to administer its own Customs system.

We reaped some incidental advantages from this inquiry. It was the first expert description of the economy of the Territory that had been made. It gave the Government a review of many of the factors that had to be taken into account in making decisions on the economic affairs of the Territory and in Goodes and Clark we had in the Commonwealth Treasury and Trade and Customs Department, perhaps for the first time in history, two senior officers who knew something about the distinctive elements in the Territory economy. Although the committee suggested that the whole issue of Customs policy be re-examined in three to five years' time I felt able to regard the decision as a lasting one. It was the decision I had wanted on other than economic grounds and I intended to see that it stuck.

During the same period I was able to make another decision which had been hanging in doubt since the end of the war by reaffirming the separateness of the Papua and New Guinea Post Office. The first step was to prepare for the first issue of postage stamps for the administrative union of Papua and New Guinea and to discontinue the use of Australian postage stamps which had been current since the war. This move was ready for announcement by July

1952. Then in October 1952, after with some difficulty disposing of doubts about the technical capacity of a Territory service, I made the definite announcement that the Territory Post Office was to remain separate from the Australian Post Office.

In coveting a wider dominion the Australian Post Office undoubtedly had strong arguments about superior efficiency and the earlier provision of wider services if it took over but, although services in the Territory, especially telephone and telegraph, were the subject of many complaints, on this issue local patriotism was strongly on my side.

Another bit of 'cleaning up' concerned internal airlines. Qantas, with commendable enterprise, very skilful flying and good organization, had established regular air services to and from Australia and over an internal network. What they were doing was of immense value to the Administration and by friendly co-operation their services had become a necessary adjunct of administration in outlying centres. Qantas was well managed, well staffed and dependable. At the same time other private operators were flying commercially in the Territory —Mandated Airlines, Gibbes-Sepik, which at that stage of its history was in some difficulty, and several small services operated chiefly as charter flights by young pilots with one or two small aircraft apiece. (At that stage the flying of light aircraft by or in the interests of the Christian missions or by other private owners was not yet significant.) The Department of Civil Aviation under a very resourceful and energetic regional director, John Arthur, was still in an embryonic stage of development. Most of the landing strips had been developed by the patrol officers of the Administration or by missions and had no equipment except a wind-sock and perhaps a line of white stones to mark the borders of the strip. Even the best of the landing fields in the main towns could only be described as re-established war-time airfields. At Lae the only navigational aid was the upturned bow of a war-time wreck in the bay, the assertion being that an approach directly over this iron tooth at a certain altitude gave the assurance of touching the strip at the right place even in a fog or rainstorm.

Some of the private operators were at a hazardous stage both financially and mechanically. Qantas, the Department of Civil Aviation and the Administration favoured a move to make Qantas the sole civil air operator in the whole Territory. Murray was strongly in favour of this, his arguments being that Qantas was Government-owned and should be protected from competition, that the airlines in the Territory should be used as an instrument of administration, and that Qantas should be made subject to direction and subsidized to serve that purpose as the sole operator. At present the chance of reaching this objective was being spoilt by small private operators who would fly a charter the day before a scheduled Qantas service and poach some of the traffic.

The handling of this question was complicated slightly because some of the small operators had been war-time mates in the RAAF with some of the younger members in the Government party room at Canberra and had complained to them that the Administration had issued an order that all Administration business must be given to Qantas. There was no real difficulty in the party room discussion however, for, before it began, the Minister for Civil Aviation, H. L. Anthony, and I had already started to attend to the problem and were already shaping the details of measures to rationalize and improve services, and we had already decided against the attempt to have Qantas designated the sole operator.

While all this was going on I was also trying to expedite the classification of the public service and the re-examination of the departmental structure of the service. In this field more than any other I felt that the lack of achievement during the six post-war years under Murray had given me a deadening handicap. I found it impossible to get quick results after making a decision or, in some branches, even the smallest improvement. Only those who tried to work in those times could really appreciate the difficulties set by such defects as poor accounting, an ill-equipped and incompetent stores system, and the lack of vehicles and of office equipment including desks, chairs and typewriters, the lack of trained clerks, the use of strange and unsuitable procedures, imperfect financial control, bad offices and faulty communications, whether by post, telegraph or telephone. For various reasons some of which will appear later, it took at least another five years before we began to have the physical equipment, the organization and the staff that would justify me in expecting something like efficient administration. For the time being I had to drive people relentlessly and learn to be very patient when all that could be raised was a stumbling trot.

[5]

THE LEGISLATIVE COUNCIL INAUGURATED

Among the matters of 'prime urgency' which I listed in my letter of 17 May 1951 for discussion with the Prime Minister was 'The early inauguration of the Legislative Council in Papua and New Guinea and the attendant problems of (i) franchise for the Asiatic population, and (ii) the urgent need to clear away an accumulation of pending legislation before the Council is inaugurated.'

On 18 June 1951, in a minute to the Secretary of the Department of Territories, I set the target for the first meeting of the Legislative Council in November 1951 and instructed that drafts be prepared of the necessary Territory ordinances.

The Papua and New Guinea Act 1949 provided that there should be a Legislative Council for the Territory, that it should commence to perform its powers and functions on a date to be fixed by proclamation and that the date should be 'as soon as practicable after the expiration of one year after the commencement of this Act'. That date had been reached on 1 July 1950.

There was considerable hesitation both in the Territory and in the Department over the inauguration of the Council. After examining the files, the only two practical difficulties I would admit were those I mentioned in my letter to the Prime Minister.

The first had been raised in the Territory. The Act provided (Section 36(c)) that three of the twenty-nine members of the Council were to be elected 'by electors of the Territory'. There was no proposal at that stage that indigenous persons should have the vote, since separate provision was made in the Act for the appointment of 'three non-official native members' (Section 36(e)). Difficulty was seen however in admitting to the vote persons who had only recently come to the Territory, temporary residents and persons of Asian or mixed race. Some of these persons were aliens, some were British subjects and some had undetermined status.

The second problem was of concern both to the Administration and to the Department. They both found it convenient to have ordinances made, as required, by the Governor-General-in-Council instead of by a deliberative legislature but their hopes and intentions in that regard had been checked by delay in drafting ordinances.

The decision that the Council be inaugurated in November 1951 was an arbitrary decision on my part. It was made before I had been to the Territory. So far as I can recall, I made the decision without any deep consideration of the long-term constitutional development of the Territory. The decision flowed rather from my early conclusion that the Papua and New Guinea Act could not be amended at that stage and it was my job to give effect to its provisions. The Act provided for a Legislative Council and, unless there were strong reasons against it, the Council should be inaugurated in the way Parliament intended. I did not take the matter to Cabinet but, after discussion with the Prime Minister, used my own authority.

Both the Department and the Administration continued to express their doubts as to whether 'the time was ripe'. Was there a building big enough for a Council meeting? What would be the qualifications of voters to take part in the poll for three elected members? Who could be nominated to represent the native peoples? How could services be provided for the legislature? Most important of all in the minds of both Department and Administration was the twofold problem of losing some measure of control over the making of ordinances and the need to clear away a backlog of drafting and enactment of ordinances already approved in principle. The procedures of enactment of laws by a Legislative Council would be slower, more complicated and more public than preparing ordinances for enactment by the Governor-General-in-Council.

Here I will make a digression to consider the state of the laws of the Territory. Before the war, there had been two sets of statute law—one consisting of ordinances made for the Territory of New Guinea and another of those made for the Territory of Papua. When, in the later stages of the war, planning began for the eventual restoration of civil administration, attention naturally turned to the body of law. All reserve stocks of laws in the Territory had been lost and only a few official copies could be found in Australia, so Cabinet decided in 1945 to print a new consolidated edition. For this purpose a Legal Research Section was set up in the Army Directorate of Research* under Dr T. P. Fry,[11] who was put into uniform and made a Lieutenant-Colonel for the purpose. Never was there any scholar who looked less like a soldier.

In early 1947 Fry and his small staff were transferred to the Department of External Territories to become the Law Revision Section. The publication of the consolidation in ten volumes (five for each of the two Territories), covering laws in force up to 1945, was not completed until after I had become Minister. In the meantime the decision to administer the two Territories in an

---

* The Army Directorate of Research originated in April 1942 as a research branch attached to the Adjutant-General but from October 1943 was made directly responsible to General Blamey. Its functions were subsequently defined as to keep the Commander-in-Chief and certain other officers informed on current events affecting their work, to undertake specific inquiries requested by principal staff officers, and to assist other government departments in work concerning the Army. Its claim to have a function in respect of Papua and New Guinea was based on the interest of the Commander-in-Chief in all matters relating to the administration in occupied or reoccupied territories. (See Gavin Long, *The Final Campaigns* (Australia in the War of 1939-1945, ser. 1, vol. 7), pp. 377-405.

administrative union had been made and the enactment of new post-war legislation had begun.

The position I found in May 1951 was that very little had been done on the second task of amalgamation and revision of existing laws to bring them up to date and there was considerable delay in the preparation and enactment of new ordinances. Fry, whose approach was that of a painstaking scholar, was of the opinion that any revision and amalgamation of laws had to be based on intensive research requiring a larger professional staff than he had. Although he was able to list a number of ordinances that might involve few major problems, he also pointed out that some of the subjects in which revision was most urgently needed would require both substantial legal work and some policy decisions.

The enactment of new legislation had gathered pace under Spender. Out of a total of 121 ordinances made since 1945, 61 were made in the twelve months immediately before I took office. Yet the Department reported to me that 42 other ordinances, which were immediately required, were waiting to be drafted. The list was being added to continuously.

A minute I wrote on 4 June 1951, after a visit to the Law Revision Section, which worked in Sydney in isolation from other instrumentalities, expressed my concern at the lag in the work of amalgamation and revision, the lag in preparing current legislation, the fact that some new ordinances were being drafted in the Department by clerical officers and made without legal advice, and the 'apparent friction between Canberra and the Law Revision Section'. I expressed the tentative view that law officers stationed in the Territory should draft current legislation in consultation with the officers of the Territory Administration who initiated the request for legislation; the work of any legal section in the Department of Territories or of the Attorney-General's Department in Canberra should be limited to advising the Minister on his function of recommending assent to ordinances; the work of amalgamation and revision should be more closely associated with current administration. All this I linked directly with the inauguration of the Legislative Council. 'The main point of interest', I wrote, 'is that the early inauguration of the Legislative Council for Papua and New Guinea is desirable but, before that can be done, the accumulation of current legislation has to be cleared out of the way.'

Tom Fry was a singular man with exceptional gifts and, as far as I could judge, a lawyer-scholar of distinction, but he lacked the worldly practicality to advance his own interests or to meet any unscholarly demands made on him. He could not compromise on a comma or forfeit one footnote to suit administrative convenience. We had a mutual regard for each other and I like to think that one of the happier periods of his working life, before his untimely death in September 1952, was when he worked with my support, encouragement and friendship. He was one of the few I pushed hard without bruising and yet he was possibly one of the most sensitive of the lot.

The unintelligent and ill-qualified officer in the Department, who, under pressure from his superiors, had been trying to take over the direction of Fry's work without having the professional competence to do it, was less fortunate. He became frantic and less dependable under my demands and directions.

My attempts to have more drafting done in the Territory led to even slower progress, for the Administration lacked skilled officers. We had not cleared the backlog of legislation before the Council was inaugurated. After it started work we were continually running into difficulties over the drafting of the Bills. Affairs might have been tidier if we had delayed the inauguration of the Council for another one or two years, but I believe I was right in forcing my decision against the advice of the Department and the Administration in 1951.

The practical difficulties in the way of deciding on the membership of the Council were wider than the single policy question of whether Asians could go on the electoral roll. The majority of the members were to be nominated. Choosing the sixteen official members was fairly straightforward. We fixed on the Assistant Administrator, the heads of the major departments of the Administration and four senior district commissioners. The departmental heads would be required to act in the role of ministers in presenting business to the Council.

The non-official nominated members were harder to choose. I relied wholly on Murray and he pondered long and deeply on the problems, hesitating over various patterns of representation and trying to find acceptable persons to fit the patterns. I gathered from him that, when the Act was being drafted, the number three in each of the three categories of nominated non-official members had been chosen in order to give representation to Papua, the New Guinea mainland and the New Guinea islands. That accurately reflected the current state of affairs, for at that time the highlands districts, with their massive population, had not been developed and much of the area was still not under administrative control.

For the three mission representatives Murray superimposed on the regional pattern the further pattern of two Protestant and one Roman Catholic and for the three 'other members' he superimposed representation of commerce, mining and plantation interests. The greatest difficulty was over the three 'native members'. Here he looked for personal qualifications, among which he placed very high a capacity to use the English language so as to understand what was going on in the Council and to express views fluently. His choice for Papua was easy and instant. Merari Dickson, of Kwato, conversed easily and correctly in English. The Kwato mission, near Samarai, was highly regarded by Murray as a hopeful example of the way in which the Papuan people could be advanced, and Dickson seemed to him to be the ideal person for nomination as a native member. In the New Guinea islands, he eventually fixed his choice on Aisoli Salin, a young school-teacher, who also had fluency in English. On the New Guinea mainland however he could not find anyone who measured up to the test of being able to follow the proceedings in English, of knowing even a little of the parliamentary process and of being able to express himself in English. It is a basic fact of the 1951 situation that there was only a skimpy handful of indigenous people in the whole Territory who could converse confidently in English. Most communication was still in Police Motu in Papua and Melanesian Pidgin in New Guinea. Finally Murray picked rather hesitatingly Simogun Peta, of the Sepik district, partly on his war-time record and partly on the energy he had shown in growing cash crops since the war for local food supply.

On one of my visits to the Territory Murray asked me to look over his three candidates. He was quite confident about Merari and Aisoli, but hesitant about Simogun. I reassured him by expressing an opinion that Simogun would be the best politician of the lot. Simogun, I said, also appealed to me because he had a base among his own people and a standing among them, whereas the other two seemed to me to be less representative of their own people. They were shining examples of the few who had made a quick acceptance of European ways.

The three native members were regarded in a kindly way as an acceptable novelty by most Europeans in the Territory but it was assumed at the start that the chief practical source of information about native needs and interests would be those official members who had some direct administrative responsibility for native welfare, especially district commissioners. There would also be the mission representatives to advocate their cause.

Simogun developed into an independent and forceful spokesman of his people. He was a man of strong character and had a penetrating and practical understanding of any situation within his own experience. I came to regard him as one of the really big men of his country.

Aisoli Salin did not last long but, before he left, he figured in an incident which, since it occurred while I was on a visit to the Territory, sticks in my mind as an illustration of other ways in other days. There was a storm at sea when he was due to come in from an outlying island by canoe to attend one of the Legislative Council sessions and he did not arrive. The alarm was raised. Someone suggested rather timidly that perhaps the Air Force might be able to help in the search. The RAAF Squadron of Lincolns at Townsville swept into full-scale action. They had received a signal to search for a missing member of parliament. They had scarcely begun their operations over New Guinea waters when Aisoli, who had taken shelter behind an island until the storm had passed, paddled in to the coast of New Ireland. The squadron leader was thanked and told the story. His dismay overcame his discretion: 'What! Have I been out searching for a bloody boong! I thought it was a member of parliament. There are no gongs in this. I won't even get my name in the paper.' And he laughed bitterly.

Regarding the three elected members, Murray's clear view was that the intention of the Act was that they should be elected by the European community to represent the Europeans. The first difficulties he saw were that many of the missionaries of long standing and good repute were not British subjects. The second was that many of the Australian population were recent arrivals who knew little of the Territory and who might turn out to be only temporary residents. A third difficulty that emerged in discussion was that the number of adult Asian permanent residents on the New Guinea islands was possibly large enough to outvote the 'white' residents and large enough on the New Guinea mainland to influence the result. Another problem was that of a small mixed-race minority. In the Territory there was a strong opinion that the electoral roll should be narrowly limited and that aliens, Asians, mixed-race and short-term residents should be excluded.

As early as 18 June 1951, in instructing the Department to expedite the inauguration of the Council in November, I directed that immediate consultation take place with the Administrator to prepare firm recommendations on the provisions of an ordinance for the holding of elections and I made two comments of my own. One was that a way of overcoming one of the difficulties caused by the presence of short-term residents in the population of the Territory might be to stipulate different qualifications for a member than for an elector. Let the customary Australian period of residence qualify a citizen for voting but ask for a longer period of residence as a qualification for nomination as a candidate. My other comment was that, in any proposals about qualifications of electors, care should be taken 'to avoid setting up in perpetuity a separate class of non-native residents'. I was very much in favour of a certain looseness and even inefficiency in building up an electoral roll at that stage. I did not mind much who went into it so long as it did not become an exclusive roll.

In the event, an ordinance providing for the holding of elections within the narrow purpose of the Papua and New Guinea Act 1949 had to make rather more precise and some more exclusive provisions than I wished to see. The ordinance provided that adults, other than natives or aliens, who had resided in the Territory for the last twelve months were entitled to enrolment as electors, and if they had three years' continuous residence, they were eligible to stand as candidates. Most of the Asians were thus eligible both as electors and candidates. The total enrolment in the three electorates was only 1700 although possibly twice that number were eligible to enrol.

My views persisted in another form when in January 1952 the Administration proposed to make enrolment compulsory, thus solidifying the restrictive nature of the electoral roll. I directed that compulsory enrolment was not to be introduced, although every reasonable effort should be made to encourage enrolment. In a confidential memorandum the Administrator was told that all questions of racial discrimination on this or any other question of citizenship rights were to be avoided. Issues were not to be forced.

Already, in my private mind, I was aware of the dangers of dual citizenship in the Territory and I foresaw that eventually we would face the question of a common electoral roll. In the Territory, however, such ideas would have been alarming both to many of our own officers and to the non-native community, for the three elected places on the Council were generally regarded as being the only means by which the non-native community could protect its interests both against officialdom and against the preponderant native interest. This was also the way in which the three elected members appeared to interpret their duties. I tried however to keep the position fluid.

I find a slightly apologetic note in some of the statements I made at that time. For example a press statement of 2 October 1951 announcing the names of official and nominated members and the date of the elections contained this passage: 'Mr Hasluck concluded that, in deciding to inaugurate the Legislative Council immediately, he had been bound to accept the provisions of the Act as it stood at present. Until the Act was amended, the Council could not be inaugurated in any other form.'

During this period I was fortunate to have occasional conversations with the Governor-General, Sir William McKell, who took a very keen interest in the Territory. He helped to educate me and had a quick understanding of my own ideas. It was a disappointment to both of us that he was on leave at the time of the inauguration of the Council, and so the ceremony in Port Moresby was performed by Sir John Northcott, who was Administrator of the Commonwealth Government in the absence of the Governor-General. Sir John himself, after resuming duty as Governor of New South Wales, proved a very firm friend and helper to the Territory.

The speech which I wrote for Sir John Northcott to deliver at the inaugura-tion ceremony reveals clearly the way in which I then viewed the outlook, after having had only six months' experience as Minister. Reading the speech again after a lapse of years, the point that strikes me most vividly about the political situation in 1951 was that I felt strongly a need to reassure the white minority in Papua and New Guinea and to bring them to a clearer understand-ing of the future of the land in which they lived and worked and a fuller acceptance of the policies of the Australian Government. At that time the people of European race were the only articulate group in the Territory. In my few but broadly representative conversations with planters, businessmen, missionaries and those engaged in transport I had found that they were not the unpleasant people that sections of politicians and the press made them out to be. There was much about them that was kindly, unselfish and, in Territory terms, patriotic.

They were attached to the Territory as to their home and they had a good intention towards its people. But even the kindliest had a limited view. They saw the good of the Territory as a good that would be given to it by them-selves. Their criticism of Ward as a Minister was not so much that he wanted to help the natives but that he did not know what was the best way of helping them and that he would in fact do harm or had already done so. There were some Europeans who were more selfish than this, and such persons were even more highly suspicious of any change in their relationship with the native people.

Both in peace and in war, or so I understood the attitude of the majority, the indigenous and the expatriate people had worked together satisfactorily inasmuch as it was in a way that was understood and was acceptable to both. Security, good order, a better way of living, an end to savagery and some gradual improvement in the standard of living of all would continue to grow out of the old relationship. Such growth would be menaced by those, either native or European, who broke away from the old relationship. They might break away dangerously at either end of the scale. The over-indulgent employer and the harsh employer were both dangerous, and so were the over-familiar or 'sophisticated' natives as well as the rebellious ones. To keep both white and black in their 'proper place' was not an unkind or intentionally repressive code. It was the maintenance of a relationship that had been found to work well in the past.

In 1951, as I read this situation, this code of conduct was largely accepted in both native and non-native communities, and by a great number of officers in the Administration. It was equally plain to me that such a relationship would not last and that such a code would block change.

In my judgement, what was best in the code had some temporary and transitional value. My own preference in administrative method is not to force a crisis unless the issue and the situation demand it. We had to soften any opposition and especially reduce the dismay and resistance that had been generated by the way in which the so-called 'Ward-Murray' policy had been presented to the planters and traders by the *Pacific Islands Monthly*. I felt a need to persuade the influential people in the Territory—and these were mostly in planting, in trade or on the long-established missions—to think about change and not simply to be alarmed by the rising murmur of change.

Looking at the situation for something good on which to build, I saw clearly then, as I continued to see for many years, that perhaps the most valuable product of the old system and of the existing code was the trust and confidence that had grown up between native persons and those most closely in touch with them. The native people believed what the 'master' said and the whites respected the native people.

The attitudes I have attempted to describe were derived from the pre-war situation in both New Guinea and Papua. In spite of the differences in theory in the administration of pre-war Papua and pre-war New Guinea, and in spite of the strong claims made by those who favoured the Papuan style of benevolent gradualism, I could not myself see that the end result in the relationship between the Europeans and indigenous people was basically different in the two Territories.

Now, however, the wish to rebuild the pre-war understanding was further affected by some post-war developments. One element in the new situation was the expectation of further European settlement. The prospects on the price of copra were reasonable, interest in cocoa and coffee was just awakening, and although rubber faced some marketing difficulties, there was an ambition to grow more. In some quarters there was a strong sentiment that because Australian troops had defended the country—other phrases were 'kept it free' or 'driven out the enemy'—Australians were entitled to draw benefit from Papua and New Guinea. Enterprising individuals thought mostly of plantation industries. In the time of the Labor Government, there had been considerable fear inside the Territory of a planned and controlled economy in which the planter would have no safe place, and this had given way, under the encouragement of some statements by my predecessor and the interpretation of them by the *Pacific Islands Monthly*, to a somewhat exaggerated hope that the 'menace of socialism' had vanished and that better times were coming. I had been made aware of a rising pressure for more land and more native labour under terms favourable to the Europeans.

Another new element was the presence of a number of people, particularly among the government employees, the wage-earners of private industry and the missionaries, whose knowledge and interest in the Territory were recent. Some of those who professed an enlightened view of the future of dependent peoples and some of those who thought they were walking into an old-style romantic colonial situation where there was cheap native labour seemed to me to present a more difficult problem than the old hands. The new dreamers and the new greedy were both a risk.

Although the non-native population in 1951 was less than 20 000 as against the hundreds of thousands of indigenous people, they were, at that stage in the Territory's history, a more significant element in the political scene than the native people, who were still largely an inarticulate and wholly dependent mass. This was all going to change very quickly. Perhaps invisible changes were already beginning, but I deal solely with the scene that I saw in November 1951.

One of the tendencies I detected was for the government of the Territory to become a sort of match between 'The Administration' and 'The Rest', with the native population looking on at the contest. I found no expectation of early participation of the natives in the game either as voters or as public servants. The information given to me on all sides was that the native people would not know how to vote. Both Territories had been accustomed in the pre-war period to a wholly white legislature and a wholly white administration. Only a few people had thought ahead to any other prospect and there was still a firmly held belief among many people of good intention that a native was happiest when he had someone to tell him what to do. The great majority of the native people most closely in touch with the Europeans looked for that guidance. The district officer, the missionary and the employer of good repute were the ones who knew best and, being educated, were the ones who had a 'magic' to be relied upon.

When I sat down to write the speech for Sir John Northcott, I had this situation in mind and was also aware that, in the circumstances of the day, the speech would reach mostly a white audience. This is the background to such passages as the following:

It is pleasing on this occasion to notice the presence in the Legislative Council of some of those who, as settlers, officials and servicemen, have served this Territory notably in the past, and who now join with the men and women of a younger generation in meeting the problems and the opportunities of today.

It is also a pleasing and memorable feature of this Council that its membership includes, for the first time in the history of any Australian legislature, the representatives of the native peoples. They, too, have a very special contribution to make to the progress of the Territory and the advancement of the interests of their people . . . For the first time in the history of the Territory there are elected members.

We do not, however, regard this Council as being divided into two groups of official and non-official members but look on the Council as one body, each and every member of which is imbued with an equal resolve to advance the interests of the Territory and to bring his own individual store of experience to the discussion of the problems.

The functioning of the Council will be watched closely and with sympathy by my advisers and if and when it should be discovered that the interests of the Territory can be served by altering the composition of the Council, the necessary changes will be sought in the Commonwealth Parliament. Any change to increase the number of elected representatives will necessarily be related to the size of the electorate and to evidence that all those entitled to play their part in the political life of the Territory are prepared to do so.

It would be contrary to the whole history of our country if the Australian-born residents of this Territory did not show independence of spirit and a democratic aspiration towards self-government. The more numerous indigenous population are also encouraged by the terms and the Trusteeship

Agreement in respect of New Guinea and by our commitments in the United Nations Charter in respect of all territories to look for a progressively increasing share in the conduct of the affairs of the Territory. The eventual attainment of this goal will depend, to a large degree, on the way in which the indigenous population and the immigrant population can find a balance between their interests and work out the way in which they can live and work side by side with mutual respect for each other's rights . . .

The speech discussed the responsibilities of the Commonwealth Parliament and Government, constitutionally, politically and internationally, in respect of the Territory and referred to the intention to strengthen the structure of administration both in the Territory and in Canberra. It then passed to economic development. The significant passages, drafted to carry a message to the Territory audience, were:

While determined that the rights of the natives shall be respected, we believe nevertheless that the long-term interests of the native peoples are directly dependent on a sound and extensive economic activity in the country from which, ultimately, all government and social services must derive . . . We look to private enterprise to take an active part in this development and in providing ancillary services . . . For some years to come, private enterprise will largely mean the enterprise of Australians. That will not be absolute for all time. Although experience up to date has not been wide enough to allow a clear forecast of the exact nature of the part which the native people will play in this development, the use of the term 'private enterprise' does not exclude enterprises initiated by them on their own part.

My Government recognizes that land is the key to development. An established policy is that land can be acquired from native owners only by the Administration and that, before acquisition, the Administration must be satisfied that the sale is voluntary and that the land is not essential to the native's own needs. Subject to that policy, the Government wishes to see more land made available for settlement, and the processes of acquisition and leasing made more expeditious. We are taking measures to that end and to promote settlement.

Problems of land use extend to the use of it made by the natives. More extensive measures should be taken for the improvement of village agriculture to ensure more stable and more varied food supplies and for the production of additional cash crops from which the newly acquired needs of the villagers can be satisfied. The work in village agriculture and husbandry must keep pace with any measures for the acquisition of land. In other words, the use of land must be considered by the Territorial Administration as a problem covering the total lands and the total population of the Territory.

For some time to come, the employment of native labour is likely to be a customary feature of industry in the Territory and, believing that carefully supervised native labour can be both a major factor in promoting the material welfare of all inhabitants of the Territory and one of the most useful agents in the education of the native, the Administration will facilitate its use. At the same time, native labour cannot be regarded as an unlimited and perpetual supply. Already changes in the personal inclination of the natives, who are free agents in this matter, are discernible, and already native labour is ceasing to be cheap labour. Looking to the future, we believe that the Territory will have to think more purposively in terms of greater mechanization and the raising of the skill of the individual workman.

After referring to the need for the provision of basic services and for social measures, especially in health and education, the speech came to the climax:

> Behind all questions affecting this Territory lies the necessity of ensuring that the indigenous people and the immigrant peoples can find a way of living side by side to mutual advantage and with mutual respect for each other's rights and personal dignity. In all measures, care should be taken to preserve the balance between the interests of the natives and the development of the country's resources, and to assist the advancement of the welfare of the native peoples.

Part of my endeavour in the early stages of the Legislative Council was to build up its status and its independence and to accustom the Administration to the fact that it was not another instrument of the executive to be used to put the views of the Administrator into effect. In a speech of my own at the opening session of the Council, after I had been invited to take a seat on the floor of the Chamber, I stressed the fact that, once the Council had been constituted, the Minister for Territories could not intervene in its proceedings and that, subject to the terms of the Act under which it was created, the Council henceforth managed its own affairs. My duties in advising the Governor-General in the exercise of his powers to disallow or to assent to ordinances would be discharged after giving full weight to the views expressed in the debates of the Council as well as to the text of its legislation. I hoped the debates would flow freely and reasonably. I also welcomed the prospect that the Council would express responsibly but without qualification or reticence the views held in the Territory and by frequent and searching questions keep the government alert and introduce the first measure of accountability by the Territory Administration to the people of the Territory.

In subsequent years there was always some difficulty in getting public servants, both in the Territory and in Canberra, to think of the Legislative Council as other than an obstacle. They wanted to make laws in the way that suited them and were also inclined to regard the passage of a bill through the Legislative Council as a procedure that they were obliged to follow rather than as the essential and constructive work of law-making. I had moments of near despair at the signs I saw that officers could see no difference between the work of the Legislative Council and the drafting of new regulations except that the Legislative Council procedure was slower and less predictable.

In giving directions that the drafting of ordinances should be done in the Territory, not in Canberra, I relied on the Administrator to clear with his Minister any points of policy or public controversy in the same way as a Minister in the Commonwealth clears such matters with Cabinet. This hope was not always realized. At an early stage I was obliged to give a specific direction that any bill for an ordinance that had to be reserved for the Governor-General's assent should be cleared with the Minister before its introduction. I did not want a position in which the Governor-General could only exercise the responsibility that the Act placed on him for the approval of laws on certain specified matters by exercising a veto and taking a public stand against the Council. It would be better not to introduce a bill if the policy it applied or the principles it followed were so clearly unacceptable to the Governor-General-in-Council that assent was bound to be refused. This direction was not always observed. The worst embarrassments came however from the drafting defects in legislation prepared in the Territory, sometimes ending in a submission to me by my departmental officers that a bill that had been passed contained grave defects but that disallowance should not be recommended because of an expectation that at a later session a new amending bill would be introduced to rectify the defects.

My exasperation rose to a peak in June 1953. I had expressed concern to the Administrator about the position after I had in fact signed a recommendation to the Governor-General not to disallow a bill containing numerous defects, and added, 'While we want to place full responsibility on the Crown Law Office, Port Moresby, for drafting the legislation, we also want to maintain proper standards and we look both for greater care in the Crown Law Office and a more meticulous regard to any attempts made by the Government's advisers in Canberra to help maintain better standards.'

My patience finally snapped. Two more cases came up, both on matters on which legislation had to be reserved for assent. I wrote, 'I have become finally fed up with being asked to recommend assent to defective legislation and will not do it on this occasion. The responsibility rests squarely on the Crown Law Office to prepare its bills properly. Prepare new minute papers for disallowance.' This was soon magnified into a popular report that I was a very unreasonable Minister and that Canberra was trying to dominate Port Moresby.

My hopes that the Legislative Council might serve to keep the Administration up to the mark were also doomed to some disappointment. The basic loyalty of its non-official members was to the existing establishment in the Territory. A member might speak strongly when some matter touched his particular field of interest, but was otherwise seldom critical. The official members had had limited political experience. They belonged to the community as well as to the public service and understandably did not like to be either unpopular or even different from the community. With exceptions, they seldom expounded any doctrine or advocated any measure that was out of keeping with the prevailing ideas of the Territory 'whites'.

In other smaller ways I tried to build up the status of the Legislative Council. Immediately after its inauguration I took steps to have it recognized by the Commonwealth Parliamentary Association. My colleague, Harold Holt, who was chairman of the General Council of the Commonwealth Parliamentary Association at that time, gained a decision in February 1952 that both the Northern Territory and Papua and New Guinea Legislative Councils could become subsidiary members of the Commonwealth of Australia branch of the association. Through the presiding officers of the Commonwealth Parliament, I gained for the Legislative Councillors the privileges of Australian parliament houses.

In the Territory itself one visible recognition of their status was in the precedence accorded at official functions. The Territory had previously applied some rather odd notions about who was important and who was not, and we had some amusing incidents in the shuffling of presentation lines at airports or formal receptions during VIP visits after I had given a direction that the Territory members of parliament were to rank next after the Administrator and Chief Justice. One very worthy gentleman who, as president of a private voluntary organization, had been accustomed to take the front row on all public occasions, retired in indignation when he found that legislators, black as well as white, were to stand above him and, as he departed, was understood to be calling on God Almighty, in language not canonical, to tell him what would happen to a country where 'pooh-bahs and boongs' were preferred to 'decent citizens'.

Another minor step I took with the same purpose caused some misunderstanding. To overcome the inconvenience of the absence of an official member on leave, the Administrator used to propose that another official become a member for one or two meetings. I refused to recommend such appointments to the Governor-General-in-Council. One minute I wrote concluded, 'This is a parliamentary body, not a cricket team.' About the same time, facing a similar tendency in the Northern Territory, I wrote this minute:

These councils are parliamentary institutions. Membership of them carries a responsibility and a status quite different from and higher than the occupation of an office in the public service or any other kind of official appointment and it also endows the member with privileges that are not to be granted lightly. Furthermore the councils themselves cannot be used simply for the convenience of an Administration but are part of the whole structure of Government in the Territories. [Minute of 18 May 1953.]

[6]

THE OFFICE OF ADMINISTRATOR

The retirement of Colonel Murray in the middle of 1952 has been much misrepresented in popular accounts. According to some stories the retirement took place immediately after a change of government or was due to some difference over policy. If it were not for this misrepresentation, the incident could be allowed to pass with a due recognition of Murray's services.

Murray was a man of dedication and had deep sympathy for the country and the people. Because he was that sort of man, it was very unpleasant to do anything to hurt him. Furthermore, in the course of his six years in the Territory, he had gained a knowledge and understanding that could have been valuable to the Australian Government in the years to come and there were several other fields in which his abilities could have been used.

His retirement as Administrator came two-and-a-half years after the change of government in December 1949 and over twelve months after the change of Ministers in May 1951. My predecessor, Spender, after twelve months with the portfolio, had reached an opinion that, in the interests of the Territory, there should be a change and he handed this opinion on to me. I took another twelve months before on my own experience I reached the same opinion as Spender.

Looking back on the situation, my view today is that the original appointment was the wrong one. Murray had only a few of the many and varied qualifications needed for the post of Administrator. He had an enlightened and sympathetic approach to the problems of dependent peoples. He had been a professor of agriculture in the University of Queensland and, before the war, a citizen soldier. During the war he had been in command of training depots and later was chief instructor at the School of Civil Affairs at Duntroon. He had good knowledge of some of the subject matter of his field of duty but scant knowledge of public administration and no experience in running a large organization. It surprised me to find in 1951 that, after some years as Provisional Administrator and Administrator, he still had somewhat sketchy views on how the machinery of government worked, how funds were obtained, how estimates were prepared and what procedures would produce results. His views about politics and constitutional relationships were quite unreal. To put it bluntly,

50

he not only was unskilled in the use of the tools of public administration and politics but did not know what some of the tools were.

One has to recognize the enormous difficulties in the immediate post-war period but, after making generous allowances for that, little was accomplished in the first five years. Murray had been unable to put in much of the essential groundwork of government or to make much progress with the practical tasks of providing services and utilities. This was not because of lack of ideas or lack of intention but because of lack of experience in the routine of administration.

I would suggest too that during this period he had suffered a good deal of discouragement and disappointment and had felt considerable physical strain. His age of sixty-two years when I became Minister was perhaps not too advanced for active service, although sixty was generally considered the retiring age in tropical countries, but he was a very tired man. He was lacking in energy. He talked more of what needed to be done than of what was being done or planned. He was nervous about making decisions lest something should go wrong. Under pressure of demand for a firm proposal or recommendation, he retreated into the need for further investigation. When decisions were made or works inaugurated in spite of his hesitations, he became resigned and aloof.

There was probably failure on my side to handle him properly, but the plain fact is that I could not get him to work with me or with the Department in a practical way. He became less willing to communicate. He became more markedly sad. He gave me the impression that he wanted to govern the Territory by himself and not with the rest of us. He found Lambert too energetic and Lambert found him too remote from daily affairs. Lambert was the better-trained and more capable man and the stronger driving force, but I wanted him to work alongside the Administrator and not over him. There was little prospect of reaching that sort of co-operation.

An observation I recorded at the time was that Murray's appointment to the Territory had been to him the beginning of his great moment in history and now he saw his role slipping away from him under the greater energy and the stronger direction of others. I felt more and more that he was becoming resentful of what both Lambert and I were doing as part of our job to push ahead in the Territory. I record this observation as a reflection of my own state of mind at the time.

After the appointment of Cleland as Assistant Administrator, Murray seemed to show an increasing disposition to retreat 'up the hill' to Government House. Once it had become plain that I had no hope of getting a Lieutenant-Governor to sit on the hill doing only the 'honorific stuff', I wanted a hard-working Administrator as well as a hard-working Assistant Administrator. The drive and direction of the Territory Administration had to come from the Administrator and great forcefulness was needed.

I took the problem to Cabinet. It was decided that Murray should go. The only point at issue was his administrative efficiency. It was also agreed on my recommendation that he should be treated generously. I had personal talks with Murray. The terms, which included a financial provision, seemed to be acceptable to him and I had the impression that he was somewhat relieved, after all, to be going with the prospect of honourable reinstatement in Australian life. On 10 May 1952 I issued a statement the terms of which had been agreed to in consultations with Murray. The statement read as follows:

> After six years' service in the Territory of Papua and New Guinea, first as Provisional Administrator and later as Administrator, Colonel J. K. Murray will relinquish his position as from 30 June next. Mr D. M. Cleland, who was appointed Acting Administrator when Colonel Murray went on leave last March, will continue as Acting Administrator.

Then followed about two hundred words of tribute to Murray's work in the Territory.

Three weeks passed before there was any controversy. On 10 June a protest against Murray's retirement was made by the Bishop of New Guinea, who had apparently been given the impression that the retirement expressed a change of policy. In a public statement on 11 June I said that the policy of the Government towards the native peoples of Papua and New Guinea was unchanged. The decision had been made so that

> the efficiency of the Territorial administration would thereby be improved and the welfare of the natives and of the Territory in general would thus be better served . . . The termination of Colonel Murray's appointment does not express the slightest change in the Government's firm intention to protect and advance the welfare of the natives and to co-operate with the Christian missions in so doing.

I also wrote personally to the Bishop and other churchmen, but nevertheless the controversy in public continued, with the usual imputations of improper motives to the Government and myself. It was clear that from some quarter the churchmen were being told the story that we were removing Murray so that we would be able to carry on an unimpeded policy hostile to the Christian missions and against the interests of the native peoples. The allegations against the Government continued and in the course of a further public statement on 2 July I felt obliged to be more explicit about the reasons for the retirement:

> I am forced to say in public what I would rather leave unsaid. The Government does not regard the administrative capacity of Colonel Murray at the present day as adequate for the duties of his office. In saying that, I have a full appreciation of the heavy demands made on him during the past six years, of the toll which life in the tropics takes and of the fact that he is well past the age at which every other official in the Territory Administration retires. Surely the official who occupies the most onerous post of all in the Territory Administration can be regarded as being affected by the same circumstances which have led to the fixing of a comparatively early retiring age for all other officials in the Territory. My appreciation of what Colonel Murray has done in the past and my respect for the loftiness of his purpose do not absolve me from my responsibility to the Government and to the Parliament for the prompt and effective carrying out in Papua and New Guinea of the routine tasks of administration and the measures on which the Government may decide from time to time. Only after twelve months' careful observation did I recommend to Cabinet that a change be made.

Ward, the former Minister, also came into the argument, asking for a public inquiry, and muddied the pool. In a statement of 4 July I replied to the imputations he had made:

There has never been the slightest imputation against the personal character of the former Administrator or against his probity as an official. He is rightly respected as an honourable man. There is no mystery about the termination of his appointment and no doubt about the competence of the Government to make arrangements to improve the energy and efficiency of public administration in the Territory. There has been no change of policy. The retiring Administrator had no fixed term of office but was appointed during the Governor-General's pleasure. The Government, as an act of grace, has given him a very generous retiring allowance. The above statement leaves nothing undisclosed about this administrative act. We would have wished that the Administrator's service could have concluded with fitting tributes to his work during six arduous years in the Territory, two and a half years of which were served under the Menzies Government. It is not the doing either of the Government or of Colonel Murray that the dignity of his retirement has been marred.

A little over a week later, to my surprise, Murray made a statement containing recriminations. My own belief is that he was misled by the then editor of the *South Pacific Post* (Port Moresby). Murray took his final leave and embarked for Australia without saying anything, but after his departure the *Post* came out with a statement which was also telegraphed to newspapers all over Australia. It did Murray more harm than good.

As already stated, it was arranged that Cleland should continue as Acting Administrator. At that stage Cabinet was unwilling to make a decision on the Administratorship. We wanted to look around for the best man for the job. Part of the discussion regarding Murray's retirement concerned the need for a man of greater vigour, greater administrative capacity, and greater strength to stand up against the Department of Territories—a view which I myself introduced. We widened the search and I showed to Menzies an impressive list of names and we started to make soundings. Some of the most highly fancied candidates proved to be either not available or unwilling to act. In the long run, after a period of probation as Acting Administrator during which he did well, Cleland was appointed Administrator early in 1953.

It is untrue to say that Murray was retired to make way for Cleland. The decision to retire Murray and the decision to appoint Cleland were separated from one another both by a period of time and by reason of a distinct and wholly separate examination by Cabinet of the possible appointments to the vacancy.

The office of Administrator in Papua and New Guinea in the early 1950s was extremely difficult to fill. The post called for a wide range of qualifications. To direct the Territory Administration, the Administrator needed professional qualifications in public administration equal to those of the permanent head of one of the larger Commonwealth Departments. Indeed the diversity of subject matter coming under his notice was greater than the business attended to by any single head of a department in Australia, for his duties extended over the full range of government and he had the oversight of many departments of the

Territory Administration. Secondly he was the representative in the Territory of the Australian Government and was responsible on the one hand for ensuring that the policy and decisions of the Government were put into effect and on the other hand for ensuring that those decisions and policy were shaped with a full awareness of conditions in the Territory at any given time and with a full appreciation of the needs, interests, shortcomings and opportunities in the Territory. Thirdly, under delegations and under direct statutory authority, the Administrator was vested with specific functions and powers. He had a responsibility of his own to discharge and was expected to discharge it in a way that would not set up conflict between him and the Australian Government on whose behalf he acted. This called for political appreciation, political judgement and some political courage. He would fail in his duties if he became subservient to the Government and yet he should not defy the Government he served. Fourthly, the Administrator became locally the 'head man'. Many of the local population expected him to stand up for their interests against the distant authorities in Australia. He was flattered by them by being accorded at times a position of honour that did not belong to his office. He was called upon frequently to perform ceremonial and other public duties closer to those of a head of state than those of a functionary of government. He was at the apex of whatever social structure existed among the expatriate population and was undoubtedly regarded as 'Number One' by the mass of the indigenous population. He needed the social graces, the personal dignity and graciousness and the standards of personal rectitude necessary to maintain respect for one who was above the crowd. Lastly, in much the same way as a good general, he needed to have the qualities to inspire to greater effort all of those under him both in the public service and in the general community. The tone of the service and of the community was set by him. A great Administrator would have a comprehensive grasp and a tremendous drive.

This is a picture of a superman. My own view, indicated at the commencement of my term and renewed from time to time without result, was that it would have been better to have distinguished between those activities of an Administrator resembling the duties of vice-regal office and those activities concerned with putting policy into effect promptly and practically. There was personal resistance to all my suggestions along these lines, and this resistance was fortified by constitutional arguments. I still think a practicable solution would have been, while maintaining the position of the Governor-General as vice-regal head of the Territory, to create a deputy of the Governor-General to reside in the Territory, perhaps with the title of Lieutenant-Governor and to exercise under delegation from the Governor-General or by statutory authority such functions of a vice-regal kind as were limited in their application to the Territory. He would act under ministerial advice and there would be a close resemblance between his duties and those of the Governor of one of the Australian States. A separate office of Administrator could have been created to do the rest of the job without distraction. This was not provided in the Act of 1949 and was not favoured when I suggested it, so any discussion of the idea now is theoretical.

In practice the office of Administrator was bound to work imperfectly. It would not have worked as well as it did if it had not been that Cleland had a level head, kept his feet on the ground, and had a clear view of his loyalties, both where and how far his loyalty to the Territory and to his own officers carried him and where and how far his loyalty to the Australian Government carried him. Very seldom, if ever, did he become confused over the boundary lines either of functions or of powers. He knew when the decision had to be made elsewhere. He knew those things on which he was answerable to the Government and those on which an Administrator could seek to serve the community. Both in the sense of Kipling and in the sense of the Tudor Age he kept his head.

The Australian system of government of dependent territories unavoidably set up some stress between the Administrator in the Territory and the Department of Territories in Canberra. The Minister, being responsible for several territories, required the services of an efficient department close to him. Personally, taking what some have called a classical view of the public service in the British tradition, during my score of years as a Minister I never built up a separate ministerial staff around myself (other than one private secretary and stenographers kept chiefly for my parliamentary and constituency work and for Cabinet duties outside my own department) and I never made any personal attachments between departmental officers and myself. I made the department work for the Government and I insisted that it work independently of me under its own permanent head, preserving its independence and its separate and distinctive responsibility in the structure of government. I leaned over backwards to respect the independent and separate strength and a distinctive function for the public service because, as a public servant in the time of H. V. Evatt, I had seen what an unholy mess a Minister can create when he tries to make a department his personal possession.

Similarly, as Minister for Territories, I insisted on the separate and independent status and function of the Territory Administration. In copies of minutes addressed either to the Department or to the Administration I find repeated reminders to them that this or that function belonged to one or other of them, and I would not allow one to trespass on the other's ground, nor would I allow either of them to pass the buck by not making the required decision or recommendation. I was perpetually urging both to do their job and not expect me to run either the Department or the Administration. Perhaps I was too classical in my approach to the structure of government.

In a talk I gave to a public service gathering early in my term as Minister I compared the job of Minister for Territories to that of a circus rider with a foot on the back of each of two horses (the Administration and the Department). They had to gallop side by side, neither getting in front of the other and both keeping close to each other. A Minister is foolish if he thinks he can do that sort of balancing act while driving them tandem. My problem as Minister was that the animals were not uniform in strength and eagerness. I would not make unfriendly comparisons between them. If I said that the Administration was sometimes wilful, I would match it by saying the Department was sometimes possessive. The Administration might wish to bolt ahead blindly on one subject but the Department might sometimes prance around ignorantly on another. The Department might lag cautiously over a proposal on which it was suspicious but then we might find the Administration was going very slowly on some other subject that it disliked. The circus rider on top had to try to keep them both moving together.

In this situation my experience was that the Department of Territories was the stronger horse and needed firmer handling. In a wider number of customary practices in public administration it had greater knowledge and skill than the Territory public service. Being in Canberra, it was closer to other Commonwealth Government departments and instrumentalities and could consult more readily with them. It was more familiar with the requirements of other branches of government and with policies on the whole range of governmental activity. While theoretically its function was to help the Territory Administration to do the jobs that belonged to the Administration, the fact that it knew how to get results often led it to try to do the job itself. I had many occasions to pull the Department up sharply for taking too much on itself.

The major advantage of the Department of Territories however derived from the fact that it was necessarily the channel of communications between the Territory Administration and the Minister (either for his own decision or for a recommendation to Cabinet) on which the main lines of policy were laid down and the higher direction given to the Administration, and that it necessarily was closely involved in the annual bid for funds.

The Administration was never as strong as I wanted it to be. In succeeding chapters will be found many instances in which I was critical and sometimes exasperated by the inefficiency of the Administration. My final judgement on that fact however is not to place blame on the Administrator but to criticize the system that had been devised and to say also that the Australian Government failed to provide Papua and New Guinea with an Administration fully equipped to do promptly and effectively all it was asked to do.

In this uneven situation, the only way in which the Department could be checked in its attempts to run the Territory from Canberra was for the Minister to be stronger than the Secretary of the Department and for the Administrator to have a clear and calm view of his own duties and powers. I think we had this situation during my term.

I maintained my own position in various ways. I refused to make a decision on a departmental submission unless the Administrator's own submission on the subject, either made before or after the departmental recommendation, was attached to it. Having obtained the concurrence of the Prime Minister, I arranged that departmental officers could travel between Canberra and Port Moresby and Administration officials down to Canberra for discussion as required. I inaugurated a system under which the Department lent officers to the Administration to help in preparing special projects. I also inaugurated Territory participation in inter-departmental discussions in Canberra. I avoided rigidly anything that might give an impression that one or another of the team was my right-hand man whose word would be bound to prevail.

In all this I was greatly helped by both Lambert and Cleland. Lambert was eager to get things done—he was a strong character—but he knew I was just as eager, he found I was a bit stronger, and we grew in respect for each other as we worked together. It is remarkable that for nearly twelve years Papua and New Guinea was served by the same Administrator, the same Secretary of the Department of Territories and the same Minister and, very diverse in character and talent as we were, that we managed to pull in harness together and at the end each of us could look back with some satisfaction on our joint achievement. By a strange trick of fate, each of us was in the right place and none of us would have been well suited to do the job of the other two. Cleland was a far better Administrator than either Lambert or I could have been but he would have been poorly fitted to be either Secretary or Minister for Territories.

During this continuing tussle, some senior officers of the Department found reinforcement for their views in an opinion held in some authoritative circles around Canberra that the best way of governing Papua and New Guinea was to govern it from Canberra. I have a personal letter from one highly placed Commonwealth servant saying that the Colonial Office tradition was no longer applicable in times when modern transport was available, and urging me to 'integrate' the Territory Administration and the Department in Canberra. 'When you can get from Moresby to Canberra in a day', this public servant wrote, 'I see no reason why you need to have an Administration which is separate from the Department any more than you need to have a separate organization in the Supply Department which is located in Melbourne.'

Personally I saw lots of reasons against this view and quote it merely to indicate that the claim for departmental authority sprang from theory as well as ambition. Perhaps in subsequent years the theory gained in acceptance. The way I saw it, as I have already recounted, there was a need for the Territory Administration and the Administrator personally to recognize the constitutional supremacy of the Australian Parliament and hence of the Australian Government and to accept policy direction and there was also a need for the Territory Administration to be built up in strength and capacity so as to carry out more promptly and more efficiently its functions and exercise its powers. I did not see this however as a question that required the supremacy of the Department of Territories over the Territory Administration and thought the supremacy had to be exerted by the Minister over both. I refused to identify the Secretary of the Department of Territories with the Minister and, while accepting the necessity of the channel of communication, did not make a devolution of authority from Minister to Secretary and from Secretary to Administrator.

Perhaps I have laboured this point too much but, whether I was right or whether I was wrong, some misunderstanding appeared among a few officers of the Department and among journalists who picked up gossip from them about my relationships with the Department. Some of the departmental officers got some pretty hard slaps for trying to run New Guinea on their own and they did not like it. They readily gave me a reputation for 'interfering', and journalists, who had run stories about wicked bureaucrats who tried to run the country, found a new angle in stories about a wicked Minister who kept public servants in check.

Naturally I have sometimes reflected on whether the retirement of Murray in 1952 was necessary and whether I was too rough on him. Given the constitutional and administrative structure of the day, my considered judgement is that the action was necessary. I am sure that I could never have been able to achieve a balanced relationship between Department and Administration if Murray had remained Administrator. Canberra would have overrun him after Murray had lost time defending the wrong positions. Furthermore I could not have gone ahead purposefully in giving the Administration any of the improved capacity it needed in order to maintain its position and to do its job.

As will appear in subsequent chapters, there were other much weaker reeds than Murray. One of my faults as a Minister was in not being ruthless enough in disposing of them. I had not intended to 'dispose of' Murray but hoped to use him in other ways for the good of the Territory and indeed, after the bitterness of retirement had passed, he did resume service to the Territory in a helpful role.

[7]

THE BID FOR FUNDS AND STAFF

In our effort to strengthen the Territory Administration we met two related difficulties—obtaining funds and recruiting staff.

There was a tendency in the Territory to ascribe every disability to the unwillingness of the Commonwealth to make larger grants of money. The fact was that in 1951 and 1952 the Territory was unable to make effective use of the money it already had. There was under-expenditure, a lack of practical and detailed planning either to produce a good case for more money or to ensure effective use of the money granted, and a good deal of waste. I formed an early opinion that we were not getting good value for the money we did spend. I kept that personal opinion private but, in making a bid for funds, had to face the Commonwealth Treasury's argument that some of our proposals to embark on new expenditures were badly prepared and that our control over spending was incomplete.

Initially I had to improve our methods, increase our efficiency and stabilize expenditure before I had any hope of succeeding in a bid for more funds. I saw the immediate problem as being primarily one of staff. Before I discuss that aspect, however, I should say something about the way in which claims on the Budget were made.

When A. W. (later Sir Arthur) Fadden was Treasurer, under Menzies, the pattern was regular. Each year a date was set, usually in February, for the lodging of departmental claims for funds. These claims were discussed, usually at the level of assistant secretary, between the Treasury and the claimant department and by the end of April or thereabouts the first draft of the estimates of expenditure would take shape. Eventually when Ministers met, usually in early July, for a week-long series of Cabinet meetings on the Budget, the Treasurer had final figures for the past financial year and a preliminary list of expenditure in the coming year. He would also have his figures on any exceptional calls that might have to be met, such as loans falling due, and figures of anticipated revenue. The Treasurer always prepared for Ministers a number of papers on various aspects of the economy. Cabinet would discuss first the national economic situation and outlook and this would lead to a tentative view on the kind of Budget that was in prospect. Perhaps some Ministers might think chiefly of the Budget as the major instrument for the management of the national economy; perhaps some might have in mind chiefly how much extra expenditure the economy might be made to bear. Politicians are seldom purists in making economic decisions. They want to keep the pack-horse healthy enough not to break down under the load, but they want it to carry everything it can and, in choosing new items for the load, they think more of political advantage than of economic theory.

Nevertheless, after the first day's discussion of the economic situation, it was usually clear to Ministers whether there was going to be a 'tight' Budget or an 'easy' one, whether it would be intended to give a stimulus to spending or restrain spending, and whether it would be planned for a surplus or a deficit. During this period of fiscal orthodoxy Menzies often reminded us all that we were walking the 'knife-edge of inflation', and he strongly maintained the economic purpose of each Budget.

The next stage of discussion usually brought an overall look at the draft estimates of revenue and expenditure. Estimates of expenditure were always higher than those of revenue. The vital figure was the one showing the width of the gap. With the size of the gap and the tentative view on the economic situation in the minds of Ministers, discussion turned to the next stage. After hearing the Treasurer's views on how a deficit could be financed, or how a surplus would be applied, Ministers had to face critical practical questions such as whether there would have to be a cut in the expenditures already listed in the draft, or an increase in revenues by taxation changes. Any increase in revenue was only discussed in general terms, and details of any taxation measures or changes in duties were left for final and secret determinations by Treasurer and Prime Minister. At this stage attempts were made to lay down a rule such as that expenditure should be pegged at last years' level or that, across the board, there should be a fixed limit to the percentage increase. These earlier stages having been passed, Ministers started to take the draft estimates of expenditure department by department. This stage of discussion tended to become a succession of arguments between the Treasurer and the Minister primarily concerned with each item. Ministers seldom came to the aid of their distressed fellows. If one Minister got away with an extra million, someone else had a lesser chance of getting a million for his pet project. As the contest proceeded, the Treasurer kept a running score sheet by which he could know whether he was reducing or widening 'the gap'.

It seemed to me that budget-making was not a highly intelligent exercise because on the expenditure side the Government did not carefully choose its priorities or evaluate various items in comparison with one another. If and when discussion widened and Ministers started to express opinions about a claim for expenditure, it became obvious that there were very wide disparities in ministerial experience. By the nature of their portfolios, some Ministers had never been in charge of a 'spending department' and had an experience wholly different from that of other Ministers and a limited understanding of the problems of those Ministers who were making the major bids for extra funds. Personally I usually found it easier to argue with Fadden than to overcome the views of some of the senior Ministers who had never had a 'spending department', knew little about budget details and found no complications in a decision that all departments should cut their estimates by 10 per cent or some other agreed percentage.

The chief impediment to intelligent choice between items of expenditure was a certain inflexibility in the system of Australian budget-making. The decisions were made in departmental compartments and each claim for funds was tested by comparing 'this year' with 'last year'. Certain items were carried on from year to year with accretions due to such factors as rises in salary, higher costs of supplies or normal progression of services and activities. There were other items which were virtually untouchable either because they had been incurred for a period, such as bounties and subsidies, or it was politically impossible to do anything except to increase them, such as repatriation and social service benefits. There were some, such as defence expenditure, that were part of a forward programme. The departmental maintenance votes offered little scope for economy, for they could only be reduced if Cabinet would face a decision to dismiss several thousand public servants. Thus the room to practise economies or to limit increases in expenditure was very narrow. The attack could really only be made on proposals for doing something that had not been done before. The Department of Territories was probably trying to do more new things than anyone else, so we were a prime target when cuts had to be made on the claims for expenditure.

The targets for attack included the Commonwealth works programme and, in respect of that programme, in certain circumstances economic arguments could also be raised in times of 'over-full employment' and 'inflationary pressure' that Commonwealth works should be cut since they were creating demands for labour and materials and diverting to the public sector resources that might be applied more productively in the private sector. During this period the Commonwealth Government was financing some of the State as well as its own works programmes out of revenue. By the time we did our own budget-making, the commitment to a total for a States works programme had already been made and any later economic arguments about public works were applied to the Commonwealth programmes alone. Year after year I saw the cuts of a few extra millions made by deletions from the bids made on the works programme by the Post Office and by Territories. They were the easy marks, for they were making a bid for new work.

Before passing on to examine the way in which Papua and New Guinea fared in the contest for funds, let me digress to remark that in over seventeen years in Cabinet, facing this procedure in budget-making, I was continually irked by the clumsiness of the way in which the Australian Government made a choice between the various activities in which it might have engaged. I can illustrate my thought by referring to one trivial example. In one budget I was cut down heavily in an attempt to make better provisions for education of aborigines in the Northern Territory. I wanted a few thousand pounds for school-rooms. Cabinet had no opportunity during the budget discussions for saying whether it was more important to build new school-rooms on an aboriginal settlement in the Northern Territory or to spend the same sum to replace porcelain by stainless steel in all the lavatories in Parliament House,

Canberra. Yet the second work was done and the first was not done simply because the Parliament House job was fitted into a regular works vote that was no higher than the stipulated percentage above the vote for the previous year, and the Northern Territory work was not done because it could only be managed by a bid for additional funds for which no comparison with a previous year could be made. Many examples could be multiplied to show in every budget the spending of millions on one undertaking and the failure to provide money for another without any direct comparison having been made between them either of value or urgency. My opinion is that, if intelligence is revealed by comparison and choice, there was scant intelligence in the way expenditures were distributed by the Australian Government.

Another condition that irked me was that, in arguments about any larger expenditures on a works programme in the Territory, we were always confronted with statements to the effect that we did not have the works potential in the Territory to carry out the work, yet every time we proposed some measures to improve the works potential, we were resisted. At times, it seemed to me, we were resisted so that the chief argument against our bids for a bigger works programme would not vanish. That view may owe something to the irksome reiteration of the argument against us without any assistance to improve our capacity. We could gain scant attention for the argument that the raising of the works potential and the provision of a bigger works programme must go hand in hand. Instead, each year, we had a 'hen and egg' futility.

This was linked to some extent with a view that Ministers for Works and the Works Department held strongly that the Commonwealth Department of Works should be the major instrumentality for construction in the Territories. We had great difficulties with that department and I remain highly critical of its outlook and its administration in the 1950s. It was costly, unimaginative and hidebound and not closely informed in unfamiliar fields and it gave the Territories very inefficient service.

Against the background of this brief summary of the way budgets are made, I shall give some particulars of my contest for funds for Papua and New Guinea. It should be remembered that at the same time I was also fighting for additional funds for the Northern Territory and for the strengthening of the Department of Territories in Canberra. I am afraid that as a young Minister I got something of an unfavourable reputation for greed. Strangely, among all my colleagues, 'Artie' Fadden, who as Treasurer was my principal opponent, seemed to understand best what I was trying to do and there was more than one occasion when he bent the advice of his departmental officers and the opinion of Cabinet and yielded a few hundred thousand dollars more than I might otherwise have got, even if it was still a couple of million less than I wanted. I did not have much help from anyone else.

One of my difficulties in the bid for funds was that I started from a very small base. The total public expenditure in the Territory was only a little over £4 million in 1948–9. Even a 10 per cent progression on that would only yield an increase of £400 000. The works programme in that year was less than £500 000, so a 10 per cent progression would give me less than £50 000. The total number of full-time officers at the end of 1949 was 1174. To recruit anything over 200 a year was to approach a public service growth rate of 20 per cent, at a time when many ministers held the opinion that the public service should be pegged to existing levels.

During his brief term Spender had boosted the vote so that total public expenditure was given as £6.4 million in 1950–1. In my first budget, three months after taking office, it was lifted to £7.7 million. But when I got down to details, I found serious under-spending, a scramble to get rid of the vote at the end of the financial year and considerable waste. The next year I was cut back to £7.1 million and I think I was lucky to get that. At last, however, I had a firmer foundation. The real contest for funds began from the base set in the 1952–3 Budget.

Papua and New Guinea received an annual grant from the Commonwealth. To this was added the amount of revenue raised locally. After the Legislative Council was inaugurated I won a hard fight to enable the Territory Treasurer to introduce his own Budget in the Legislative Council for the Territory, making use of both sources of funds. A separate Territory Budget seemed to me basic to the future constitutional progress of the country, but this view was not readily accepted. I might have done better in the short term if, instead of taking an annual grant, I had allowed Territory revenues and expenditures to be included in detail in the Australian Budget.

Although I gained the form, the Territory was not financially autonomous in practice. The Commonwealth grant was shown in the Commonwealth Budget as a one-line entry without any details of expenditure, but in making out our case for the annual grant, we were obliged to go through items of expenditure with Treasury officials, and when the Territories were under discussion in the budget sessions of Cabinet, I was expected to give some detailed information in support of any request for more money. So, in effect, although the Territory Budget, mainly financed by a Commonwealth grant, was passed by the Legislative Council for the Territory, it had previously been approved in detail for submission by the Commonwealth Treasury and in broad outline by the Cabinet. The interest of Treasury officials even extended throughout the year to the way in which we applied our funds, and any major diversions of funds from one item of the Territory Budget to another item required their approval.

Our own departmental preparations for the Territory Budget began with a request to the Territory Administration to make its bid in the form of its own draft for the Territory estimates. At first this work was inadequately done. There have been published occasionally unjustified statements by Territory officials, especially district commissioners, about being 'starved for funds'. I encountered several cases in which, when I followed up these stories and set out to get money for a project, I found that no request for funds or any case in support of a request had ever been made by the district commissioner who was complaining. Some of the biggest blowhards had done least to help us get money. Gradually we got better preparation, especially after I arranged that the Treasurer of the Territory should come down to Canberra to take part in the arguments with Commonwealth Treasury officers. Thus he at least became aware of the sort of case demanded by them. Over the years the Territory Treasurer, Harold Reeve,[12] did a manful and difficult job well, with little thanks, in helping us to get funds. Reeve and his successor, A. P. J. Newman,[13] both deserve well of Papua and New Guinea for the efforts they made. They fought hard to straighten out procedures and prepare a stronger case for funds.

Our contests each year with Treasury officials in Canberra helped in promoting greater efficiency in our own service. I have no criticism to make of senior Treasury people. They were strict, hard-headed and reasonable and, although we fought them hard, men like Roland (later Sir Roland) Wilson, C. L. (later Sir Lenox) Hewitt and H. Goodes did a lot of solid good for us in helping officers of the Department of Territories and the Administration to do their job better. At first the Treasury officers could point to many shortcomings in the Territory in the control of expenditures and in the systems used in the Territory public service. Whenever we proposed a new activity, we had to demonstrate that staff were available and that works potential existed or could be built up readily. The Territory officers gradually learnt that they could not hope to get more money unless they could show that they could use it.

In the Cabinet argument over the 1952–3 Budget, I gained approval of the principle of 'expanding expenditures' for the Territory. It was also recognized that the annual grant by the Commonwealth and local revenues should progress together. For me this meant that the growth of internal revenues of the Territory would bring an additional argument for the growth of the Commonwealth grant, although I am afraid some Territory residents read it simply as a device to extract more money from them.

By September 1954 I was able to talk in a public statement about 'the substantial progress made in reorganizing the administration, improving its strength and efficiency, and raising the capacity of the building and construction industries'. I added, 'Until this foundation work had been done and fair progress made with reorganization it was difficult to undertake any major expansion. It is believed that the curve of accomplishment can now rise more steeply.' (Notes for the Budget Debate, 1 September 1954.)

In the next ten years, before I left the portfolio, the Commonwealth grant was lifted from £5.5 million to £25.3 million and local revenue from less than £3 million to £10.5 million. The total of the Territory Budget grew, in round figures, from £7 million to more than £37 million during my term of office. Every year throughout that period we had to fight for our money. I never came out of Cabinet in any year without disappointment and a feeling that I had failed again to persuade the Government fully of the urgent needs of the Territory. Not a penny of our money came easily. We would have got far less if it had not been for the work we did in 1951, 1952 and 1953 in establishing a sounder base for our requests.

After we had established this base and I had lost some of my nervousness lest our more grievous faults be discovered, I adopted the practice of asking the Department to prepare for circulation among members of parliament and the press each year a paper called 'Notes for the Budget Debate'. It ran from eight to twelve mimeographed pages and summarized progress in the past year and explained the main projects for the coming year. A set of these papers provides one of the best published cumulative records of what happened from 1953 to 1963. Members of parliament used it freely. The press gallery in Canberra consistently ignored it year after year.

I return now to discuss the related problem of raising the standard of staff. I fastened on to recruitment as a high priority and, at a time when reduction of Government employment in Australia was being considered, obtained Cabinet agreement to an establishment and a fixed rate of recruitment for Papua and New Guinea that freed me of any immediate numerical restriction. Recruitment alone is not enough. The officer has to have a place to live, a place to work and the tools and materials with which to do his job. A large element in our incapacity was that we did not have the staff to work out housing, building and equipment programmes in a practical way. Nor did we have the works potential to put the construction programmes into effect.

We set out to recruit at a time of growing employment opportunities in Australia and the response to our advertising of vacancies was sometimes discouraging. In such circumstances there is a temptation to take anyone with two hands, but I had set my sights on raising the quality of staff as well as getting more staff, and in some cases this search for better people checked the rate of engagement.

My notes throughout 1951 and 1952 give a record of frequent direction and exhortation on my part and much dissatisfaction with the result. Perhaps the situation in recruitment, as seen from my standpoint, is most comprehensively summed up in a long minute I addressed to the Secretary of the Department on 23 March 1953. It followed a number of less comprehensive minutes on particular aspects of the public service during the second half of 1952. I felt I had to write at length, almost like a textbook or a lecture to a class, because, as I saw it, the idea of planned recruitment had not yet been understood or, if understood, had not been accepted by officers. This minute records my own ministerial approach to this phase of my duties at this time. 'Our broad aim', I wrote,

> is (a) to construct a balanced and efficient public service and, *as part of that aim*, (b) to recruit men of a higher calibre, both in their personal character and in their professional qualifications . . . All that is done about recruitment has to be done in relationship to the total problem of constructing the Territory service, and never in isolation from it.

I continued that the need to take exceptional measures in regard to recruitment arose from past neglect and inefficient handling of the Territory public service. Too many vacancies had been left unfilled. There had been too many resignations or dismissals and too many 'duds' in the service. The age-grouping in the service and the proportion of temporary to permanent appointments were out of balance. There was a shortage of good clerical officers capable of being advanced to higher clerical positions, and the service could not provide from within itself enough officers to take higher administrative positions. There was lack of staff to carry out declared policy in respect of uncontrolled areas, health, education, agriculture, lands and forests. Difficulty was experienced in providing students for the Australian School of Pacific Administration, and other in-service training was inadequate. Many of these defects could be overcome or mitigated by better methods of recruitment.

Among the apparent faults in recruiting, I continued, were a lack of uniformity and some carelessness in selection methods. We lost potential candidates because we missed the best times for advertising and were slow in making decisions on applicants. We lost other potential candidates because we could not advise enquirers about prospective opportunities. There was no orderly and regular intake. We filled some vacancies from the tail-end of lists that had been compiled from applications received over a period of years. Our standards of admission were too low. Departments in the Territory never seemed to know what they wanted or what they were likely to receive.

After an initial period of exceptional effort to 'patch up the service', I said recruiting should settle down to an orderly system in which there would be forward estimating of needs and forward planning of recruitment with an orderly intake of new officers in order to produce a balanced service. The new system of selection, including interviews, should be fair to candidates by reason of its uniformity and should lessen the risk of failures by providing an opportunity to assess the personal qualities as well as paper qualifications of candidates.

Regarding forward planning, I said that I wanted departments, particularly those which must expand to give effect to policy, to indicate how many officers they needed and would be able to absorb year by year for at least three years ahead. Each department should have a clear plan of development of its activities, and exact estimates of wastage.

> The first step in a planned recruitment is to ensure an orderly intake. We cannot swallow a large number of officers in one lump and then go through an uncomfortable and sluggish period while the service digests them. The orderly intake has to be planned in relation to such factors as the classification of officers within each department, the rate of expansion of the work of the department concerned, the facilities available for them to work and the residential accommodation of officers.

This long minute contained a great deal of other detail. At that period it was necessary for the Minister to spell out his requirements in a precise way to overcome the haphazard practices hitherto followed. In later years I kept a close and firm grip on both recruitment and the Budget. Statutory responsibility for finance and for certain appointments was placed on the Minister for Territories. In Papua and New Guinea the Minister had the power, delegated by the Governor-General, to make public service appointments and, under ordinances of the Territory, was head of the Territory public service.

When I was first appointed a Minister in 1951, my old friend and mentor, Sir James Mitchell, then Governor of Western Australia, asked me to call on him to receive his congratulations. He also gave me some advice. He said it was easy to be a good Minister and even easier to be a bad one. The most important thing was strict care over public expenditures and public appointments. I took the advice to heart and on my own experience believe it to be sound. Perhaps a few additional qualities are needed to be a really good Minister, but lack of the two qualities I have mentioned would make failure as a Minister certain.

There is a tendency for all persons who have power to approve expenditures and make appointments to start thinking that the money and the offices belong to them. In my observation during my period in politics this tendency is more marked in public servants than in Ministers although Ministers are not immune. Time and time again one finds the official talking about 'finding some money' for this or that or, in the case of an applicant for employment, 'fitting him in' somewhere or saying, 'I think we could use him in our department.' Most of the circumvention of the precautions against venality or favouritism in a public service in my experience were not attempted by politicians—maybe because they were too shrewd—but by senior public servants whose vanity was gratified by the use of power.

I was very strict and very careful about spending and appointing. So far as appointments were concerned, I never intervened in the process of selecting candidates for appointment, but at the start of the process, when applications were called from outside of the service, I insisted on approving personally the terms in which a newly created position was established and advertised. I had seen too many cases where the description of the job is tailored to fit a person already favoured for appointment. When the recommendations for appointment were put before me I insisted that they came forward in the form of a report by the selection committee on all candidates. I had seen too many cases where the recommendation of a single name is the method of favouritism, whereas if a committee has to report at least on all candidates on the 'short list' it is obliged to make a comparison between them and justify its recommendation. On a very small number of occasions out of hundreds of appointments made, I used my authority to reject a recommended candidate and refer the applications back to the selection committee, but the value of the method was that when departmental officers or a committee knew that their work would come under final ministerial scrutiny, they took exceptional care to make sure that their recommendations were soundly based. The discipline is that the ministerial approval will not be a formality but a deliberate judgement. In the case of my officers they came to be watchful so that their recommendations would not be returned with the marginal note 'Why?' or 'I am unconvinced.'

Whatever the achievement was, the fact is that for twenty years from 1951 onwards the greater part of the work in Papua and New Guinea was done by officers who were appointed under the recruitment policy and practices I inaugurated and in the public service I had strengthened for the task ahead. That work could never have been done and many of the key men in doing it would not have been available if it had not been for my ministerial direction in the early 1950s.

In this phase of my work too I had to watch the relationships between the Department in Canberra and the Territory Administration. As an example, early in July 1954, when we were 'vetting' the Territory's draft estimates, and the Department had been rather strict in establishing sounder practices, I wrote the following minute commenting on a memorandum from Lambert:

> We need to be careful that, in exercising its proper function of ensuring that all things are done 'decently and in order' and that there is realism in our budgeting, the Department does not curb the enthusiasm and the energy which we so sadly need in the Territory. I want to see the Administration and the Administrator personally straining to do more and more at this stage rather than thinking that it is their duty to consolidate and to avoid going too far. There is a risk that the Administration efforts may get out of balance,

but for heaven's sake don't let them see this as a risk that they can do too much. Keep them highly ambitious.

In my conversation with the Prime Minister today consent was given to the submission to Cabinet of a three-year programme relating to both the Northern Territory and Papua and New Guinea, which can be adopted in principle by Cabinet and become the policy directive on which our next three Budgets will be based. The points you make in the present submission should be reconsidered in connexion with the preparation of the submission to Cabinet.

At the same time Lambert made proposals for more direct oversight by the Department of Territory finances. I gave him this minute:

I think that these proposals, if carried out, would eventually result in the Department of Territories' becoming, in effect, the Treasury of each Territory. This tendency would not be in keeping with our policy of trying to build up and strengthen Territory Administrations over the years to permit of more and more local responsibility. I would prefer appointments to be made, not in the Department, but in the Territories in order to strengthen the local management of revenues and expenditure. The Department can, of course, continue to assist as the occasion arises and as the Administrators desire. We must oblige the Territory Administrators to live up to their responsibilities.

[8]

THE OUTLOOK IN 1951 AND 1952

The first considered statement I made to an Australian audience about Papua and New Guinea was an address to the William McGregor Club in Sydney at a dinner in my honour on 20 November 1951.

At that time I had less than six months' experience of the Territory. The William McGregor Club was composed of private persons, all of European race, who had interests of one kind or another in the Territory but most of whom had been there before the war. They were proud of being 'Befores' and carried that nickname as a kind of certificate that they were better qualified than anyone else to say what was good for the country and its people. A large percentage were in private industry. Some were retired officers of the service. I felt that they were more than a little doubtful about me and that such welcome as I may have had was due less to the fact that I was myself than to the fact that I was not Eddie Ward.

In my after-dinner talk I may have squared off to them a little. I certainly did not wish to scare or estrange them. As I remember it, however, I do not think I really clicked with my audience.

One early point I made was that in Papua and New Guinea the colonizing process was taking place after the colonial age had ended. Any nation administering such a territory today must place in the forefront of its thinking the conception that the people had rights of their own. Colonial days had passed and the Territory could never be treated as a colony in the old meaning of the term.

Looking to the future, I foresaw that, as a result of health measures and better nutrition, there would be an increasing native population. 'We will see a better educated native people, a more politically conscious and politically active native population who, very gradually, over a number of generations, will take an increasing interest both in running their own enterprises and in taking a share in their own government.' Two revealing phrases are 'very gradually' and 'over a number of generations'. That is the way I saw the scene in 1951.

Then I remarked that all these changes could not come without the help of white men and women. They too would grow in numbers and become a second element in the situation. I therefore suggested that

69

the basic problem of all our work in New Guinea from this time onwards is the problem of race relations. It is a problem of finding a way in which two peoples at different but slowly converging standards of living and cultural habit can live in harmony with each other and with respect for each other's rights and each other's dignity and self-respect. A realization of that factor is basic to wise administration in New Guinea.

I criticized the old 'master' and 'boy' relationship of the colonial days because it tended to smother in both parties of the contract most of those qualities which would be needed if any other relationship were ever attempted. Both the private settler and the government servant had to realize that in the eventual outcome both indigenous inhabitants and immigrant people would be living side by side and when that time came the relationship of planter and labourer would no longer be applicable nor would the relationship of ignorant savage to civilized white man any longer exist.

Our task is to apply our minds to discover those principles of conduct in New Guinea and of relations between the two races who are destined to work together there which will be just as relevant in three or four generations as they are today. If we base our conduct on such principles we are more likely to build soundly for the future.

Later I spoke of Papua and New Guinea as 'an attempt at co-operation and mutual service between two peoples, a guardianship in which both the guardian and the guarded are to survive.' I hoped that the people of Papua and New Guinea would develop first towards greater participation in the local management of purely local affairs and eventually beyond that to some form of self-government. Yet, in the nature of things, that self-government could not come until the two races in Papua and New Guinea had solved the major problem of living and working together. It was certain that the problem could not be finally solved until the native peoples had advanced to a point where a large majority of them could in fact participate in management of the life, industry and politics of the country.

Looking back I see now that what I said was very heavily influenced by my distress at the signs of colonialism on the part of both officials and private persons on my first visit to Papua and New Guinea and by the impression I had formed, from the present backwardness of the native people and the absence of any real participation by them in daily affairs, that the progress towards self-government would be likely to take several generations. The impression was understandable at that time, for in 1951 I saw no evidence at all of significant social, economic or political progress by the people. I was also facing the fact that most of the talk about self-government at that stage was centred on representation of the white minority.

Some time later I had two reports, given gratuitously, about the impression I had made on my audience. The most favourable one was that my remarks were 'very thoughtful'. The other, by an old-timer in response to a question about what he throught of the new Minister, was, 'He's no use to us. He's just another one of these kanaka-lovers.'

I had found an unacceptable colonialism among many officials of the Administration. Now, among those Australians, both resident in Australia and in the Territory, who had the closest interest in the affairs of the Territory, I found that there was a limited conception of the best way of running the affairs of what they thought of simply as an Australian colony on the pre-war model of the more enlightened British colonies. If we did what the British had done in Africa and did it better, all would be right. As in the Cabinet itself, there was a belief that we could get very good guidance from the British colonial experts.

My views were otherwise. In August 1952, when I had a little less than fifteen months' experience, I contributed two articles to the *Sydney Morning Herald* under the general heading 'Policy in Papua and New Guinea'. They reveal the sort of questions that had mainly occupied my attention during the first year and my approach to them. One task was to clarify the constitutional relationship between Australia and the Territory and to establish a good working relationship between the Australian Government and the Territory Administration. Another task was to develop local political institutions so that the ambitions for a higher measure of local autonomy could be realized. The Territory Administration would have to be improved before heavier administrative duties were placed on it. My endeavour would be to develop the local institutions and particularly the Legislative Council and the public service. Any change to make the Legislative Council directly representative of the people could not be made without regard to the fact that the vast majority of the population were native people. Continued progress in their social advancement and education would have to be made before they could take part in political life, and the Australian Government could only withdraw from the legislative field as and when it became possible to increase the representation of the native community in the legislature. More immediate changes towards increased local authority could be brought about by encouraging a capable, well-staffed and active Territory Administration to do more and more on the spot. I concluded this part of the article with the comment, 'The immediate need is for administrative efficiency rather than constitutional dream castles.'

In arguing along these lines in 1951 and 1952 I was responding to the fact that both in Australia and in the Territory at that time any public discussion about self-government for Papua and New Guinea stemmed mainly from white objection to what was called remote control from Canberra. Much of the talk of political or constitutional change at that time and the only pressure for change favoured the giving of greater power and responsibility to the local white minority of planters, traders and those public officials who had wholly identified themselves with the local white community and wanted to run the Territory in their way.

In the second of the two articles I was again addressing the white minority and those in Australia who sympathized with their views rather than all the people of the Territory. This minority was in fact my only audience, for very few others could read what I wrote. So I set myself to argue about the fact that 'some people see a conflict between economic development in Papua and New Guinea and the advancement of the natives'. Economic development and native welfare were like the front legs and hind legs of a horse. They had to go together. After elaborating on the need to promote development of resources to meet the needs and provide the opportunities for an advancing people, I wrote of some of the new dangers that might be created by development and pointed to the need to set some limit to development 'in order that it shall not be injurious to native interests and so that, in the long term, it will not set up barriers to native participation in the enjoyment of the life and wealth of their own country'. I drew examples from the administration of land policy, the improvement of village agriculture, native enterprises either through co-opera-tive societies or by personal capitalist ventures, and measures in education and health. The articles concluded:

> In this process of change all manner of things may go wrong. The social advancement of the natives is not a subject on which dogmatic assertions can be made. We have to progress step by step, watching for facts as well as cherishing our hopes. The time will come when to an increasing extent some of the native peoples of the Territory will want to take a hand in deciding their own destiny. From time to time we may encounter one of the most serious dangers to the future of the whole of the people—the influence of the native demagogue—and we may have to walk very carefully to avoid checking a legitimate aspiration while we protect the mass of the people from inexperience or ambition. The Government is well aware that we have no easy task in Papua and New Guinea and that our short-term decisions can create long-term difficulties. The Government is also well aware that underneath all that is done in the Territory is a problem of working out our own relationship with the native people.

I quoted what I had said to the McGregor Club, about the basic problem of race relations and added, 'Insofar as we succeed in that task the history of Australia and New Guinea will be a common history in the centuries to come.'*

From these articles it is clear that at that stage I saw the future of Papua and New Guinea as being largely in our keeping; that there was virtually no expression at that time of native aspirations, and it is doubtful whether any clear ideas about the future were then held by the indigenous people; and that there was an assumption that the self-governing country of the future would be one in which the white Australian residents would be in some form of close and harmonious association with indigenous people. At that time the idea of a 'blending of cultures' was current. These articles also reflected the ideas of a 'civilizing mission' and of 'tutelage' which were then considered part of the enlightened view about the trusteeship of dependent peoples. I had derived them from my university tutorial classes before the war and from the talk at the United Nations Conferences at San Francisco in shaping the trusteeship chapters of the Charter.

Some rough notes, never published, which were pinned to my typescript of these articles are worth quoting, not because they served any purpose at the time but because they give a further revelation of my private thoughts in this period. In this patch of communing with myself, I wrote:

> Part of the difficulty of the administration of a dependent territory and part of the difficulty of working out relationships between the dependent

*Contributed articles in *Sydney Morning Herald*, 4, 5 Aug. 1952.

peoples and the immigrant peoples is that the officers on the spot and the members of the white community directly in touch with the dependent peoples are themselves imperfectly aware of the nature of the civilization to which they belong or of the difference between civilized man and un-civilized man. They reduce the contrast so often to differences in dress and diet, personal hygiene and technical skill. They are unaware of what else makes a man civilized. Small wonder that a pattern is set in which the native who has learnt to wear trousers, use a water closet, speak English and handle tools regards himself as being civilized for in fact the civilized man whom he sees daily does not often reveal that civilization consists of anything more than clothes, diet, hygiene and technical competence. We need a fuller and richer view of both personal and communal life in civilized society before we are able to communicate it. One reason why I sometimes feel doubtful about the outcome of our task is that I doubt whether in the whole of the administrative, commercial and productive community in Papua and New Guinea there are more than half a dozen individuals who could be called civilized in the full sense of the term. We are engaged on a civilizing mission using imperfect agents.

The phrases that I find revealing today, twenty years later, are 'the outcome of our task' and 'engaged on a civilizing mission'. It is also evident that, in my own mind, I saw the desirable end as being the emergence of a society that lived on the highest standards of civilized man. When I talked about social advancement, I had in mind a great many more benefits than better housing, better sanitation and a balanced diet. In a statement I made to a mission con-ference in November 1952 I spoke of the hope 'that all the people in Papua and New Guinea may live together usefully and happily and that in this land humanity can rise to the best of which it is capable'. Besides measures for raising their standard of living and adding to their skills, I spoke of 'opening their minds and raising the level of their vision'.

With longer experience I might not today be so ready to generalize about the native condition of the people, but I would still hold my faith in civiliza-tion. I would recognize today that both the colonial attitude, which I con-demned and corrected, and the missionary zeal for civilization,* which I encouraged, do promote a tendency to underestimate the objects of attention. Phrases such as 'the heathen in his blindness', 'dependent peoples', 'tutelage' and 'trusteeship' all connote much the same state of mind in persons who in their various ways are trying to do good for other people. Such an effort can only arise from a belief that the other people are in need of help because they are in some condition of sin, misfortune, wretchedness or helplessness. The exhortation to effort relies a good deal on the description of their plight, and exaggeration follows. The moral I drew from my observations was that when one gives a hand to a lame neighbour, one has to take care not to act as though he is weak in the head as well as wobbly in the legs.

---

* There were some exceptions to my generalization about 'missionary zeal for civiliza-tion'. Some Christian missionaries and some older administrative officers believed that the happiest future for the people was to retain the simplicities of their village life unaltered by anything other than the practice of the Christian religion (in the case of the mission-aries) or obedience to the laws against killing and theft, and the practice of better sanitation (in the case of the officers).

PART II

THE FIRST FIVE YEARS
1951–1955

[9]

EXTENDING LAW AND ORDER

When I became Minister, I was shown maps on which parts of the Territory were marked as 'controlled areas' or 'uncontrolled areas'. Other maps elaborated the theme by showing areas that had been explored but not brought under control and areas partly under control.

The meaning of 'control' in its barest essentials was that an area had been penetrated by Administration patrols, contact had been made with most of the people in the area, a number of patrol posts had been set up as points of continuing contact, the people had been roughly enumerated and made familiar with the basic idea of law and order, namely that they should not kill each other, that they should take their disputes to the white officer of the Administration to be settled, and that they should respect government authority. With discretion, white missionaries and traders and the occasional traveller or anthropologist were allowed to go into controlled areas. Entry into uncontrolled areas was prohibited because their safety could not be assured.

This was a wise policy insofar as it meant that, in the frontier days of the post-war years, clashes between whites and the indigenous people were prevented and there was no pattern of killing or even attacking each other. It also lessened the difficulty, time and labour of sending out patrols or search parties to recover persons who had got into dangerous situations. The Administration made its own judgement on when an area was sufficiently 'under control' for it to permit the unescorted entry of strangers.

In passing, it should be made clear that bringing an area under control was not the same thing as allowing any white settlement or any alienation of native lands. These were separate and subsequent decisions to be made in the light of other judgements on the situation.

Controlled areas included some districts where Australian administration, both before and during the war, had been closely familiar to all the people and where agricultural and commercial enterprise had been carried on for half a century or more. Yet even in some places close to these well-established districts there were small pockets of uncontrolled country, for example in the mountains behind Finschhafen, in parts of New Britain and in the country behind Wau.

77

Spender had made a decision that the whole of the Territory should be brought under control by December 1955. My reading of his decision was that, responding to what seemed a lack of effort in the Territory, he set his officers a task in order to spur them to greater effort. It was in effect a requirement that the Administration should produce a five-year plan.

Both the Administration and the former officers of the Department of External Territories were still resisting Spender's decision when I became Minister and they tried hard to get me to alter it. Part of the resistance was due to theory and part to incapacity. The theory was that it was better to do a little well than to do too much and do it all badly. It was linked with a view that the best way of building for the future of the Territory was to concentrate on getting a first-class result in part of the Territory and then use the skills and resources created by intensive effort in that part of the Territory to extend gradually into the parts that had been left backward. At least that was the way I understood the theoretical argument and that was the argument I rejected.

My rejection of it was influenced more by practical considerations than by any claim to have a better theory. I saw great urgency in the total situation. I was deeply impressed by the diversity among the peoples of the Territory. I thought that a sense of unity and some measure of homogeneity among this diverse population was an essential foundation for any viable and equitable self-government. I had a stubborn doubt about either the practical wisdom or the justice of excluding perhaps half the population of the country from the benefits of the first intensive effort, although some officers of the Administration did try to convince me that the coastal peoples were the most enterprising and intelligent part of the population and were the 'born rulers' of the land. I was also influenced by the impressions I had formed of the Administration and, like Spender, was disposed to demand more work from it for the good of its own soul.

My doubts about the capacity of the Administration held me up a little longer than my doubts about the theory. It was short-staffed. Many of the patrol officers were very junior and lacking in experience. Some of the pre-war men who had come back were past their physical prime. I had very grave doubts whether the head office of the Department of District Services at Port Moresby had any idea about how to prepare a five-year plan in a practicable way, but that was something on which Lambert might be able to help them.

I was also influenced by the fact that Spender had announced his policy in Parliament in a statement of 1 June 1950. I would have to give Parliament convincing reasons for going back. I confirmed Spender's decision. On 29 November 1951 I directed, 'The decision of my predecessor is to stand . . . No adjustment in District Services likely to affect the attainment of this aim is to be made without prior reference to me.' As I saw it, we did need a broader base than we had for the advancement of the people. The pacification of an area and the establishment of government influence were an essential starting point for all other measures to promote the welfare of the people. Looking back, I feel sure it was the right decision. Subsequent measures of economic development and political progress could not have taken place when they did and in the way they did if, under pressure in 1951, I had gone back on

Spender's decision. The participation of hundreds of thousands of highlands people in the life of their country would have been delayed.

Some of those who held the contrary theory continued to resist. Some of the hesitations and resistance were linked with separate difficulties I was having with the reorganization of the administrative structure. In October 1952 I had to assert again, 'The target set by my predecessor should be maintained.'

The doubts about the Spender policy were revived again, but on the grounds of capacity only, after Cleland became Administrator. In effect he doubted whether he could succeed in the task set. I instructed him that the target was unchanged. He was to do his best to achieve it. If he did his best, he need not worry about 'failing' in a set task. My judgement would be on the effort made and not on whether he reached a particular goal.

The task turned out to be bigger than originally estimated. In the five years up to 1956 we were able to report that 142 912 square miles were 'under Administration influence', 10 692 square miles were 'under partial influence' and 9892 square miles had been 'penetrated by patrols'. In the course of this work, contact had been made with a 'new' population numbering about 400 000 people in 'new' areas totalling about 65 000 square miles. For the sake of comparison, the area of the State of Victoria is 87 884 square miles. This work had been done in an area about three-quarters the size of that State over a terrain where the mountains are twice as high and the rainfall more than ten times as heavy and consequently where rivers and swamps present bigger obstacles and where the jungles are thick and the ravines steep. Many of the patrols had been into country where the inhabitants lived in a condition of almost constant belligerency with one another and the bow and arrow were often at the ready or the long-handled axe was always close to hand.

After the initial patrols, many new permanent patrol posts had been established. Original patrols, as part of their job, would report on possible sites for a patrol post, having regard to local population, terrain and access. In the course of the new programme, we began to use light aircraft to make reconnaissance both for planning the route of the original patrol and for locating areas in which patrol posts might best be established. The initial journeys still had to be made on foot over the mountains and along the valleys at a rate of six miles a day.

To establish a post, perhaps two young patrol officers would set out accompanied by a corporal and six constables of the Royal Papua and New Guinea Constabulary and a 'doctor boy' of the Department of Health. A line of hired labourers would carry the supplies in boxes. When they reached the chosen spot and sat down, the patrol officers had conversations with the local people. Because of earlier contacts, relations at the outset were usually good. With the friendly co-operation of the local people the construction of the post began, first the clearing for the station and the erection of the native-material houses for the patrol officers, the police, the storehouse, the doctor-boy's clinic and the office. There was always a flagstaff. Neatness and regularity in a station were the pride of those who built it. Each morning the Australian flag was raised ceremoniously with the police presenting arms and a bugle sounding. At sunset it was lowered. The people stood by in silent respect.

The next stage was the airfield. It was put to the local people that this would be to their advantage. They mobilized labour for the clearing, the levelling of the earth and the removal of all obstructions. The ends were marked with white stones. The wind sock was erected. On the transceiver, district head-quarters was told that the strip was ready. The first plane flew in.

I had the privilege on four occasions of being a passenger on the first aircraft to land on a newly constructed strip—once near Saiho in the Northern district in a Dragon Rapide biplane, once on the Sepik coast in a Norseman, and twice in the Southern Highlands in a Cessna. Pilots approached cannily and low and had a good look. Their worry seemed to be not so much whether they could land but whether they could get out again. After close inspection from the air, they landed rather gingerly. An awe-stricken multitude was always waiting at the edge of the strip as we taxied. When we stopped and doors opened, my first brief impression was of silent staring suddenly broken by the blossoming of grins on hundreds of faces and then jumping and waving of hands, and then silence again and pointing as we walked towards them leaving the aircraft on its own with a police constable standing proudly on guard. Even at places where previous flights had been made, the curiosity was enormous in the early years. People came in thousands to watch the arrival of an aircraft.

The work of establishing a post was done partly by the voluntary co-opera-tion of the people and partly by payment. The patrol post also bought a good deal of its fresh food from the local villages. At first, payment was in kind, for the use of money was unusual and sometimes unknown. At one newly established patrol post I saw an ingenious device by which a patrol officer established the idea of a fair price. He had attached a huge clock-face to a pair of hanging scales and had stuck to the outer rim the articles which would be paid for the respective weights of foodstuffs—a single razor blade at one o'clock and two razor blades at two o'clock, and so on to a flashlight at six o'clock and a hatchet at nine o'clock. Building material for the Administration houses was also paid for in kind.

Thus, from the day it opened, a patrol post commenced a course of education in economics. The clinic began to treat ailments and injuries. After the aero-planes started to arrive the people became accustomed not only to visitors and supplies coming in but to the idea that a doctor or nurse could also fly in and that the man, woman or child whom they expected to die would be taken away to a hospital and come back well.

The basic first lesson however was that of law and order. They were told they must not kill. Anyone who killed had to be punished, but he should be brought in to the patrol post, not punished by his own people. If they had disputes, they should tell the patrol officer about them.

In the very early period of first contact, one of the most difficult roles for the patrol officer was to break the chain of fighting and reprisal that had been going on for generations. The 'pay-back killing' had to be stopped before peace could come. Others who did the work have written about this and I would not attempt to tell how they did it. But they pacified a troubled country and they did it without bloodshed.

On one occasion I happened to visit a recently opened patrol post shortly after there had been a killing by natives of a native in a nearby village. The patrol officer was still engaged in arranging the settlement and had taken the alleged murderer into custody. The prisoner would be brought to trial in due course, instead of being killed and thus continuing unbroken the chain of pay-back killing. There was still the business of compensation to the family of the victim. Both family groups had come in to the post to work out the terms and I stood by while the final stages were being discussed. The argument seemed to be whether, in addition to the goods already agreed upon and visibly stacked on the ground, the family of the killer should hand over another four bags of 'kau-kau' (sweet potato). They objected that these were not due because on a previous occasion when one of their group had been killed there had been no compensation. The patrol officer fixed it up to the satisfaction of all with the handing over of only two bags of 'kau-kau', since there was a possibility that the earlier death might have been in part due to other causes.

After the 'compensation case' had been fixed up and the patrol officer was confident that they would go away without further grudge against each other, I asked him what had happened. A few days earlier he received word of trouble at a nearby village and walked out there with his corporal and two constables. He arrived to find 'a fearful row going on' and 'just walked into the middle of it and told them to stop'. I could not follow the exact proceedings masked by this laconic account, but I gathered that, at the climactic moment, the patrol officer and his three policemen were standing in the centre of the village with a raging mob with bows drawn on one side and a raging mob with bows drawn on the other side. I asked whether he felt nervous. 'It was a bit dicey for a few seconds', he said. 'I was watching their eyes and when nothing came at me in the first couple of seconds I knew I could handle it.' When the points of the arrows had been lowered and the bows slackened, he calmly and deliberately went and sat down on the step of one of the houses and asked for a coconut. They brought him one and sliced off the top for him to drink and then they started to talk.

The practice of charging a man with murder and bringing him to trial in a white man's court was sometimes ridiculed by writers who only bothered to look at an incident and not at a situation. These trials, conducted in the districts where the alleged crime took place, with the full ceremony of a Supreme Court and with great patience and due care, were the outward and visible sign of a method other than the pay-back killing for dealing with murder. They introduced the idea of justice and the idea of substituting punishment by the State for revenge in the hands of the individual.

I shall be writing in a later chapter about the administration of justice so will not digress further into the subject. In our work of establishing law and order and achieving the pacification of areas of first contact, the public arrest and public trial of offenders took an essential and useful part. Although death sentence was passed, there was only one instance in my term when it was carried out, although in another instance the condemned man avoided the gallows by taking his own life. In all other cases the sentence was reduced to a term of imprisonment, after taking into account the reports of the judges and the Administration and the compulsion of native custom that may have led to the killing. In one year I recommended to Executive Council ninety-five mitigations of the death penalty passed on natives who had been found guilty of murdering other natives. Since probably three-quarters of these came from areas of early contact, the figure gives some indication of the fierce and merciless pattern of killing that was interrupted and ended by our work of extending control.

I have another and less solemn personal memory of first-contact work. At Ialibu in the Southern Highlands, shortly after first contact, I flew in to a half-completed airstrip. A sturdy and capable young patrol officer showed me around. He had walked in across the mountains only a few months earlier with a corporal of police and half a dozen constables. He had mobilized the local people, cleared and built the strip, put up the first buildings out of local materials and then started patrolling the surrounding villages. He showed me around with justifiable pride, pointing to his hut, the office, the police barracks, the aid post, the store, the landing strip. I was aware of one omission and enquired rather casually whether he had found any need yet for a calaboose. He said, perhaps a little too off-handedly, 'Oh yes, it's a bit of a walk to get to it. It's on the other side of the strip.' I told him that I might as well look at it and, on the way over, asked him if it had been used yet. Yes, he had used it. How many prisoners were there now? He said thirty—all men, all from one village. There had been some trouble at one of the villages and he had brought them all in on the one patrol.

I remembered what a very senior district commissioner had told me about the way he kept a steady workforce, and said, 'Were you getting short of station labour?' He laughed and said, 'No. It wasn't like that.' There was silence for a time. I waited for him to go on. 'I was trying to make up my mind what I should tell you', he said at length. 'You may not approve. I went to this village and found there was a lot of trouble because the young men had been playing around with the wrong women. I knew I would have some killing on my hands. I also knew that if I stepped in after the killing to arrest the murderers, I would have to face some very angry old men and would lose their support in the village. I haven't enough police to go walking out to distant villages to arrest murderers or stop fighting, so instead I arrested all the young men and brought them back here and put them in the calaboose. It seemed to satisfy everybody.'

I asked if the prisoners had been brought before a court yet. He said, 'Oh yes. I knew the instructions and I have power to form a court, so I held a court and sentenced them all to three months. I thought that in three months tempers will cool down.'

'What was the charge?' I asked.

He said, 'That was my real trouble. I searched all through the book and couldn't find anything that seemed to fit, so I invented an offence of my own. I charged them all with illicit fornication. I wrote it all down on the sheet as required and then I found them all guilty and gave them the three months. Everyone's happy and there has not been any killing.' The prisoners, all robust, active young men, certainly all seemed happy and made no complaints.

Thus were the ends of administration served by means of the judicial process. In that situation, I did not feel that I was called upon to do anything except admire the magnificent view of the distant cloud-capped mountains and compliment the patrol officer on his work in establishing a new post. I did both and, so far as I know, the thirty convictions he recorded for 'illicit fornication' have not become an established legal precedent in the Territory.

I experienced a proud and moving moment in Perth in 1960 when I had a conversation with Sir William (later Viscount) Slim at the conclusion of his term as Governor-General of Australia. Slim had taken a great interest in all the Australian territories and had visited them and gone into some outback places on several tours. As the senior Federal Cabinet Minister from Western Australia I had to farewell him at Fremantle on his final departure from Australia. My wife and I attended a small luncheon at State Government House in his honour and, after coffee, he and I retired to the library alone for our last formal Executive Council conversation. We discussed one or two official matters and then a little gruffly, as was his habit when he came to the edge of sentiment, he asked me to accept a copy of one of his books. He had written on the fly-leaf 'To Paul Hasluck, with admiration for what he has done in the Territories, Bill Slim.' I thanked him. He looked out of the window and looked at his watch, and his mouth creased into the grim line that served him as a smile. 'In an hour or two, I'll be out to sea and I won't be Governor-General any longer', he said, 'so I'm going to say something that I suppose I shouldn't say. I don't admire everyone in your Government and I don't admire everything your Government has done. In fact I think they've done some damn silly things and some of your colleagues have said even more silly things than they have done. But there is at least one thing that your Government has done well and perhaps it is their best job. I do admire you and I do admire what you have done in New Guinea. I know something about this. It's the sort of thing I was trying to do during most of my life. Your young chaps in New Guinea have gone out where I would never have gone without a battalion and they have done on their own by sheer force of character what I could only do with troops. I don't think there's been anything like it in the modern world. And so many other things you are doing in New Guinea are good.' Then he made his remarks more personal and in some ways less complimentary to the reputation of others and concluded, 'Even if your colleagues can't understand what you are doing and the rest of Australia takes no notice of it, I just want you to know that I mean what I put in that book.'

What moved me was his particular references to our patrol officers. When every other word of criticism has been spoken and other defects in our administration have been discussed, I stand in amazement close to reverence at what was done, to my personal knowledge, in the ten years between approximately 1952 and 1962 by young Australian patrol officers and district officers in areas of first contact. There were a few mistakes and a few weak brothers, but the achievement, with the resources available, revealed a quality of character and manhood that should make our nation mightily proud that these fellows were Australians.

I was stirred by another tribute earlier than the one that Slim had paid. In the mid-fifties I visited for the first time a post in the highlands which had been open for about eighteen months. Remarkable progress had been made in that time and already the post was beginning to change from the early stage of bush huts alongside an airstrip to a station developing the facilities for the second stage of our work. As one index of that, it had a wheeled vehicle and three extra members of European staff and was just installing a lighting plant. It was in the midst of a very heavy population and about six thousand people had gathered for the first visit by a minister. They were in two different language groups, and the groups sat apart from each other down the slopes of the ridge on which the station was built. The official party stood midway between them. On this occasion we were served by two of the old-time native interpreters in their blue serge tunics with a distinctive coloured edging. The patrol officer had explained to me that both groups were very eager to make speeches to me, for this was a region of great speech-makers. Neither of the interpreters knew the local languages, but each of them knew a language also known to some of the local people. So we had the speech by the native leader, this was translated by a tribesman into a local language known by the native interpreter, and then one native interpreter turned his lot into English and the other, whose English was limited, turned his lot into pidgin.

The orators stood. Their magnificent voices rolled over the valleys and awakened the echoes from the opposing slopes. I felt a strange peacefulness as I looked from our hilltop over the grand panorama of the highlands, a light decoration of clouds on the far ridges and patches of sunlight on the nearer slopes and valleys. The oratory, first of one leader and then of the other, in organ tones, seemed to accentuate the untroubled grandeur of the scene. When they ceased, a calmness settled on the crowd and then came a gentle rumbling murmur of approval rising to a chant. We waited for the translations before the meaning came to us in two stages. Both spokesmen had said much the same thing. They had said, 'Thank you for sending the patrol officer to us. Thank you for making the patrol post. We used to be frightened people and now we are not afraid any longer. There used to be killing but killing has stopped and we can work in our gardens in safety.'

They then got down to a few more practical questions. They had heard that some other people nearer the coast had hospitals and schools and roads. It was about time that I got around to giving them hospitals and schools and roads, for they were a great and numerous people.

The leaders watched intently as the translation proceeded and when they were satisfied that it was over and we had understood, they signalled to their people and a great roar of approval came from six thousand highland voices. It was much more eloquent than words in any document about freedom from fear. We gave that freedom to half a million people who had not known it before.

[10]

NOT ENOUGH SCHOOLS

Education was one of my most difficult problems of practical administration. I wanted to give it a very high priority in funds, recruitment and works construction. I had no theories of my own and was ready to accept professional advice on the educational system for the Territory and on educational method. I took the rather simple view, possibly derived from the early history of education in the pioneering days in Australia, that education meant providing teachers and school-rooms. I also thought that the first need for an illiterate people—and it is necessary in the present day to remind readers that the indigenous people had no written language of their own—was to learn to read and write as the first step to all other learning. Moreover literacy in one language would lower the barriers to communication. We needed more native people who could understand what we were saying and who could themselves speak more freely to each other. I was distressed by the scarcity of educated native people and regarded this as a handicap to all other efforts.

At the start I expected to have a great number of proposals for educational work. I did not receive any. Then I asked for them. Then I started to demand them. But I still did not get them. If there had been someone in the Education Department who showed some drive, I would have been ready to back his judgement on what schools were needed, where they were needed, what we should do about recruiting or training teachers and what we should teach. In the early stages all I wanted was a practicable proposal for which I could obtain funds. I could not get it.

Murray used to talk to me about an 'elite' in a way that gave me an exasperated dislike for the word, but he produced no plan. He kept on using the catch phrase 'We are spreading our butter too thinly', and, as I noted at the time, the phrase seemed to have dimmed in the minds of those who used it any ideas about trying to get more butter.

The chief impediment was the Director of Education, W. C. Groves.[14] He was a man for whom I had a high personal regard. I admired greatly the voluntary work that both he and his wife did selflessly in the community. I respected his professional standing in education and was ready to accept his views on educational objectives in the Territory. But what I wanted from him more than anything else was a carefully prepared scheme for more schools and more teachers—something my officers in Canberra could use in making a case for funds to the Treasury. I wanted him to make a bigger bid for education in the estimates. Groves however wanted me to listen to his enthusiasms about visual aids in education, the merits of the series of Oxford readers prepared for African countries, and the value of some ideas he had himself formulated about educational methods in dependent territories. He had a great enthusiasm for seminars and wall charts and UNESCO pamphlets and used a vocabulary quite unfamiliar to me. When I wanted to ask him about his plans for opening more schools, he usually wished to talk about his hope that he or one of his officers might be chosen to attend some UNESCO conference in South America on overcoming problems of illiteracy. I never succeeded in any one of many attempts I made to have a down-to-earth talk with him about the administration of his department.

I made an early decision in my own private mind that I would have to ease him out into another position and, for a start at least, get a different even if less enlightened man as Director of Education. I made various suggestions of 'promotion' to him, even to his beloved United Nations, but I failed. Looking back, I am glad I did not hurt him, but I confess that one of my failures as Minister for Territories was in not dealing more ruthlessly with the administration of the Education Department in 1952. If I had done so, the story might have been different. Instead, continuing with Groves, I had to move into the educational field decisively but ignorantly myself and had difficulty both in forming education policy soundly and having it applied effectively.

One of the further problems in the educational field was set by the fact that there were far more children in schools conducted by the Christian missions than in schools conducted by the Administration. The round figures in 1951 were over 100 000 in mission schools and about 3000 in Administration schools.

These figures were not a true description of progress in education. Some mission schools were good and many of them were bad. It was the aim of nearly every newly established mission to conduct a school. Some missions had qualified teachers. Many mission schools however were conducted by persons of undoubted dedication but little schooling. I saw more than one school where a dear earnest person who had been moved to bring the 'light of the gospel to the heathen' was conducting a school in a grass shed with practically no equipment of any kind and no idea of teaching except getting the children to imitate the sound of the Bible texts she recited or the Sunday school hymns she sang in a quavering treble. I remember one school where fifteen- and sixteen-year-old youths, with beards sprouting, sat at the feet of an elderly woman teacher making sounds to the tune of 'Jesus bids us shine with a clear pure light' (Chissus pitser syne willa clee poo lye). They thought they were learning English and the dear soul thought they were learning about Christ, but I doubt whether either end was being accomplished. Very few even of the more efficient mission schools carried the pupils beyond the equivalent of the third or fourth standard of the Australian primary schools. Many of the mission schools taught in the local vernacular. A missionary would first set himself to learn the local language, then try to put the Lord's Prayer and some part of the gospels or the church service and a few hymns into a written form of that language and teach it back to the children. Others taught in pidgin and also reduced the sounds of pidgin to print. Those missionaries with a higher standard of training themselves could then proceed to introduce the idea of a written language, and this became the start of a literate schooling. Some never seemed to get beyond the point of seeking an elementary literacy in either the vernacular or pidgin so as to give further religious instruction.

The stronger and more highly organized missionary bodies, especially the Roman Catholics, Lutherans, Methodists and Anglicans, could do this with a very much higher degree of efficiency than smaller mission organizations. I could fully appreciate the educational soundness of this approach to literacy, but it seemed to me that the early outcome was to give the people some chance of being converted from paganism to Christianity but little chance of acquiring a skill that they could use for further advancement in learning or for doing good on earth.

My administrative task was secular, yet I valued what the missions were doing and valued even more highly their potential to give more and better schooling without undue delays. I set myself the aim of assisting them to turn as many mission schools as possible into efficient schools in the secular as well as the religious sense.

Groves wanted the supremacy of secular education and the building up of an Administration-controlled education system. This was understandable in a Director of Education. It derived largely from his professional views on education. It was some time before I found out from a very frank and intimate conversation with Groves himself, after he had discovered that I was neither a Freemason nor a Catholic, that his views were also affected by his own personal interpretation of the course of modern history.

I made ad hoc a decision to support mission schools financially. My view was uncomplicated. The mission schools were in existence and were being attended by tens of thousands of children. I had to help them to make their teaching efficient by providing some financial support and I could oblige them to do better by making this financial support subject to conditions about their standards of teaching. This was about ten years before Australian Governments started to finance church schools. The idea was less acceptable at that time than it became later.

Necessarily I concentrated first on getting more primary schools. Taking education to the people, this meant largely village schools. I have often been criticized for allegedly concentrating on primary schools and not doing enough to provide secondary schools so as to produce an elite. I leave on one side for the time being my views on the production of an elite and set out the facts of the situation in Papua and New Guinea as I saw them in the early 1950s. We had in fact scarcely any native children ready to go to secondary schools. I can see now that, in discussion on secondary schools, I had in mind then a picture of secondary schools similar to those with which I was familar in Australia. In our own setting, where English is the mother tongue of the children and they can all talk it before they start school, where literacy is the normal condition and where, outside school hours, most children are surrounded by influences that support or enlarge what they are being taught in the schoolroom, we have found it necessary for a child to go to a primary school for five or six years from the age of six to the age of twelve or thereabouts before he is ready to go to any secondary or post-primary school with any expectation of benefit. In Papua and New Guinea we were starting with children to whom the language of instruction was a foreign one, who could not speak it when they started school, who mostly lived in communities where literacy was scarcely understood except as 'white man's magic' and where family and social influences were mostly turning their thoughts in a different direction from what they were being taught at school. We would be lucky to get even the bright ones ready for secondary school in five or six years. If we wanted enough children to fill even the smallest secondary school, we had to get busy with primary schools first.

As I will show presently, we had problems enough in getting efficient primary schools. If that struggle for efficient primary schools had not been made, Papua and New Guinea would be even further away than it is today from having men and women able to do the work of an independent nation.

Looking back on those days, I have wondered whether there would have been value in trying to establish schools for older children on some model other than that of the secondary schools in the Australian education system. Such schools would not have attempted very much class-room work or sought a high standard of literacy. They would have kept older boys and girls at school a little longer and taught them something that might have been useful to them and to the community. We had such schools in embryo. At one end of the scale we had, in the Health Department, schools conducted in pidgin which took village youths who had virtually no education and after two years turned them out as medical orderlies able to detect common complaints and to administer simple standard treatments. Our purpose was to combat disease, not to educate an 'elite', and this was the response to an urgent medical need and not to an educational policy.

Similarly in the Royal Papua and New Guinea Constabulary we had schools, some conducted in pidgin, to produce non-commissioned police officers out of young men who had joined the force straight from a village without any prior schooling. At a slightly higher level, in the Department of District Services, we had remarkably successful schools to teach young men to become officers of native co-operative societies. On our agricultural stations we were training young men as agricultural assistants. At a somewhat later stage we started training schools in the Territory Department of Posts and Telegraphs. In the Education Department we took young men into training schools to learn to be village teachers even when they themselves had not completed a full primary school course up to Australian standards. We had also made a start with technical schools—an activity which I strongly encouraged—and in these schools, in the beginning, much of the instruction was at the level of 'see' and 'do'. We might have done more along these lines and called it 'secondary education'. Indeed it was remarkable how many of the young men who took a leading part in public affairs in the 1960s were those who had been trainees in the police, health, postal and other service training schools. Yet, useful as this groundwork was to them, they were still handicapped by not being fully literate.

If such methods were ever discussed as part of the deliberate planning of secondary education, they were never put before me. I concentrated on trying to make the primary school system more efficient so that it could start producing an annual quota of students reasonably well prepared for any academic secondary school course.

Even if my views had not been narrowed by thinking of secondary education only in the Australian context, I could not have done much about secondary schools in the Territory in the early 1950s. Our difficulties in getting money and staff were so great that we had to concentrate on the more important priorities and we had great difficulty in doing something about the poor condition of the existing primary schools. Moreover some prior decisions set the pattern of what we could do.

A decision had been made that education should be in the English language. This decision had little to do with educational theory. Indeed I conceded to mission schools, against the advice of my own experts, that they could use the vernacular as a transition to eventual teaching in English. The decision was in recognition of the facts that, in the absence of any predominant local language the only hope for an independent and united nation to gain a means of communication among its peoples was to have the common bond of English and that there was no hope for advancement to higher learning or training for trades and professions among its peoples except by becoming literate in a modern language. While each language group could retain its 'place talk', a common language was needed and English was the one that the people themselves preferred. The eagerness that many showed for schooling was an eagerness to learn to speak, read and write in English.

Another early decision had been made, not solely on educational grounds but on what might be termed social grounds, for the secondary education in Australia of white children from the Territory. With some minor exceptions among missionary staffs this was already the pattern. In keeping with the ideas I have already expressed about relationships between the indigenous and immigrant races, I was myself disposed to reject any idea of segregation in secondary schools. While in primary schools it was a necessity that there should be village schools attended by native children only, I laid it down that at the secondary school level, in those fields of study where the task of teaching and the level of student qualification were necessarily the same and the language difference had been overcome, there should be no segregation. We would not build separate secondary schools for racial groups.

Moreover it was plain that in the early days, at least, secondary schools would not be local schools but regional schools. Whereas it was practicable to have a village school at the primary level, even with only a score or so of children being taught by one teacher, the problems of staffing, organizing and accommodating a secondary school meant that there had to be some centralization in order to bring together a large enough body of pupils and to provide adequate staff and facilities for efficient instruction at the secondary level.

In the beginning I hoped—and so it turned out to be—that our early secondary schools would be built up from the children of Australian, Asian and mixed-race people living in the Territory and that native children would join them in increasing numbers as the years passed. For a brief period, for lack of qualified candidates, the indigenous people would be a minority, but they would soon become the majority and eventually there would of course be district high schools where practically all the pupils would be indigenous children.

The establishment of such secondary schools with a nucleus of white children as the beginning was delayed by the decisions that had been made before my time with the primary purpose of providing education for white children. The Education Department had already established a separate educational system to provide for the children of European race. This was designed to fit in with the Australian education system from which many of the children had come and to which most of those who sought higher education would eventually go. The Administration conducted primary schools for European children with European teachers in most of the main towns or centres of European population, and the total enrolment was in the neighbourhood of 1000. There was also a system of secondary school allowances to assist white parents to send their children to secondary schools in Australia after they had done their primary schooling in the Territory.

Murray seemed to be in favour of the early development of secondary schools in the Territory but, before my time, a proposal by him to establish a secondary boarding school at Wau had been set aside. The exact circumstances are outside my field of knowledge but they had left him hesitant about advocating Territory secondary schools. At first I was myself disposed to favour the early creation of Territory secondary schools and to save the money that was being spent on allowances for white children sent to secondary schools in Australia, but I soon accepted the political fact that most white parents wanted their children to go to Australia and would fight like hell to keep the allowance. We also faced the administrative reality that we had a slim chance of providing either accommodation or staff for secondary schools in the Territory at that stage.*

White children going to Australia for secondary education were provided with return fares and a subsidy. While this allowance could be claimed by all parents, those in public employment looked on it as part of the terms of their engagement, for, when officers were being recruited or appointed, the existence of this allowance was always mentioned to them, along with information about leave and other entitlements, as part of the benefits to be enjoyed or as one of

---

* A departmental memorandum supplied to me in March 1955 for purposes of discussion with the Administrator on a new step in secondary education reviewed past history. According to this memorandum, Murray recommended in February 1949 that a secondary school be established in the Territory 'if adequate allowance for education in Australia could not be made' and in April 1950 Spender approved Murray's recommendation for a secondary boarding school at Wau. In October 1950, however, the Australian Government, having examined the estimates, decided that the whole question be re-examined and, 'as an interim measure' an annual allowance to parents for secondary education in Australia be made. When, early in my term, I maintained the principle that a secondary school be built in the Territory, the Department of Territories found difficulty in getting practical action in the Territory and the view expressed in the departmental memorandum in March 1954 was that the approval of the subsidy 'drove a wedge into the Territory enthusiasm for the school', that from the beginning the proposals were not based on any sound appreciation of costs and proper educational development, and that the Director of Education had changed his views about the project. In any case the Wau secondary school was planned for only eighty children, mostly white.

the compensations for taking up an appointment outside Australia. The strong pressures for extending the benefit were constant. Proposals for establishing secondary schools in the Territory were resisted even inside the Administration itself as a threat to this allowance. Moreover one had to recognize the truth of the case made by the Australian parents for secondary education of their children in Australia as being preferable to anything offering in the Territory at that time, even if one did not wholly accept the common view that it was either impossible or undesirable for white children to be brought up in the Territory setting. A number of parents chose to send their children to primary school in Australia, but they did so at their own expense.

For a start I tried to deal justly with all residents of the Territory by extending the benefits of secondary education in Australia to all who were qualified for it. In the case of the mixed-race and indigenous children I did this by introducing a scholarship system. Again I was very much influenced by Australian experience. I had received my own secondary education as a child in Australia by winning a scholarship. If creating secondary school scholarships for the indigenes was a foolish move, I am wholly to blame, for I insisted on it against Territory opposition. It meant that until such time as we had the resources and the potential number of pupils to establish a secondary school system in the Territory itself, each year a quota of indigenous and mixed-race boys and girls went to secondary schools in Australia, having been selected by competitive examination.

We still had difficulty in finding enough children for the places offered. The first selection at the end of 1953 yielded only nineteen indigenous students who had reasonable prospects of entering on a secondary course in Australia. A large proportion of them came out of mission schools and the scheme was helped very much by the fact that the missions concerned often went to some trouble to find places for the children in boarding schools run by their respective denominations in Australia.

I made several tours personally around the schools in Australia to see how the children were progressing. Nearly all of them fitted well into the social life of their schools and gained a great deal of ease in the English language and in personal relationships. The scholastic results were not remarkable, those who managed to pass the Junior (or Intermediate) examination—the examination then taken by Australian children at about the age of fifteen—being counted the successes. Their teachers said they were handicapped by the lack of a good basic primary education and this confirmed my opinion that we could not hope for much from higher education until we had laid a better foundation of primary education. In the course of the years, however, many scores of bright boys and girls did have the chance of secondary education in Australia as the result of the scholarship scheme I established.

I find in my own notes that from time to time I had to keep reminding officers both in the Department and the Administration that our objective was still to have secondary schools in the Territory. For example on 1 February 1954, in connection with the preparation of the draft estimates for the coming year and the deletion of an item in the works programme, I told the Department that the proposal to build a high school at Wau still stood and the immediate question was only how to fit it into the works programme. 'I am convinced', I said, 'that there is a need for secondary schools in the Territory side by side with the schools in Australia. We should concentrate on going ahead with the project in the most practical manner possible.'

As the years passed and the primary school system began to produce more of those who could speak, read and write in English and do some arithmetic, we ran into another impediment to secondary education. The partly educated indigenous boys and girls were in instant demand both by private employers and by the Administration almost as soon as they could read, write and count. When a minimum qualification would get him a job and a better wage than those in the labour line, it was hard to keep a boy at school any longer. The inducement to get education for the sake of a better job was satisfied too early. Gradually the age of seeking employment and the level of education rose but, even after we established secondary schools, we still faced the difficulty of keeping the pupils at school long enough to proceed towards matriculation.

The schooling of girls was impeded by other causes, such as the value of a girl to her parents as a potential bride and the fear that too much schooling might either expose her to the risk of losing her value or impair her filial obedience. While experience varied from place to place in the Territory, there was often resistance to the idea that girls also needed to be educated.

In enlarging on these problems of secondary education I have run ahead of the chronological narrative on education. In the course of my attempts to improve the efficiency of the Territory Administration, I had personally asked the Public Service Commissioner, Head, who had necessarily been concentrating on some of the basic problems of classification of officers, to review broadly the state of those departments that were causing most concern. In particular I asked him to examine the Education Department. At the end of May 1952 Head reported, 'I desire to advise that I have had no confidence in the organization of the Department of Education . . . and I propose to undertake a thorough investigation into the actual work being performed in that department.' In forwarding the report to Canberra the Acting Administrator, Cleland, supported these views and expressed the opinion that 'there was a lack of direction arising primarily from no definite objective in the policy of the department.'

This report came to me during the period when I was having difficulty over Murray's retirement, to say nothing of a few problems of senior staff in Mining and Native Welfare in the Northern Territory. I was also trying to get the Education Ordinance finalized in a way that might help to bring harmonious relationships with the Christian missions after the damage done by false stories told during the Murray episode. I felt a need for the time being to continue to work with and through Groves. Better a cart with two wobbly wheels than no cart at all. Nevertheless I wonder now whether at this point of time I should have been more brutal.

Instead of disrupting the Education Department, I tried to clean up other matters. The delay only confirmed my ill opinions of the efficiency of education in the Territory. My notes during 1953 show several instances in which I found fault with Groves's administration. In April a minute placed by me on a departmental submission regarding a report on educational planning from the South Pacific Commission said that I wanted the whole question of education in Papua and New Guinea to be considered 'more broadly and more thoroughly'. In September, after discussion with Lambert, I authorized an 'investigation under Sections 10 and 12 of the Public Service Ordinance into the administration, organization and methods of the Department of Education'. Two senior officers from the Department of Territories—R. Marsh[15] and Dudley McCarthy,[16] both of whom had teaching experience before entering the Department—were appointed to assist the Public Service Commissioner, T. A. Huxley,[17] who had succeeded Head, in making the investigation. Their report did not reach me until 18 November 1954.

This investigation was purely an in-service procedure for internal administrative purposes, and the report was referred to the Director of Education for his comments before being submitted to me. In total there was an enormous volume of paper. I was somewhat disappointed both at the length of time taken to produce the report and a lack of concentration on the matters for prior decision. The document will need fair study by anyone who attempts to write a fuller history of education in the Territory. On 24 February 1955, after studying the two volumes of the report and the accompanying files, I sent a long memorandum to Lambert with an instruction that it be communicated to the Administrator, the Public Service Commissioner and the Director of Education.

Reading this memorandum again, I recall that I was still mainly concerned as Minister with trying to lay down the objectives and the purposes to be served in education rather than trying to tell the Education Department how to do its job. I saw a need to define the tasks to be done before making decisions on the organization and staffing of the Department of Education. Other notes made by me in the course of 1954 also recall to my mind that at this time I was trying hard to get the Administration, now with Cleland as Administrator, to show more initiative and to accept more responsibility. This meant some restraint by me on Lambert who, in the interests of efficiency and promptness, was showing a disposition to do in Canberra the work that the Territory Administration should be doing. Part of my own aim was to try to force the Administration and, in the case now under notice, the Department of Education in particular to do its own job and build up its own strength.

At the outset, I asked what were our overall objectives. The departmental officers had criticized Groves's use of the phrases 'mass literacy and blending of cultures' as being 'completely indefinite'. I disagreed with them and wrote,

> These two phrases carry an exact meaning to my mind and it seems to me that they call for close and careful examination at the start of any inquiry in order to determine whether these are two of the objectives which the Government should adopt. If we adopt the idea of 'mass literacy' as one of our overall objectives then we will see the way clear to working out an administrative plan to provide means by which every child will be taught to read and write. If we adopt 'blending of cultures' then we will try to work out an educational system which will draw on the best elements in the native life as well as on selected elements in Western civilization. To reach an opinion on this we have to form a judgement on whether we want to make

the Papuan* people into 'coloured Europeans' or whether we want to make them into Papuans with their own distinctive culture (including a distinctive language, laws, arts, social habit and custom, and institutions). We will probably turn away from both of those paths, if for no other reason, because the history of culture contact raises substantial doubt whether, irrespective of what we may wish or not wish to see, either of these ends can be attained. The circumstances are such that the native can never become wholly European nor remain wholly Papuan. There are bound to be enduring influences from both sides. In other words the blending of cultures is inevitable. The major task of education in Papua and New Guinea is surely to help make the eventual outcome of this blending of cultures give satisfaction to the individual native, lead to the growth of a Papuan community that has all the qualities of a sound social order, and leave goodwill and harmony between Papua and Australia.

The investigation committee had written of the phrase 'advancement of the natives' as a 'vague and general' objective. Again I took issue with them and, after recalling the reference in the United Nations Charter to the purpose of 'the political, economic, social and educational advancement' of dependent peoples, I said of the Charter phrase,

if adopted as an objective, it can at once be applied to mean that their education should be such as to enable them in time to take part in the management of their own political affairs, to engage in various sorts of economic activity and to manage their economic affairs, to change from the social habits and customs of a primitive society to those of a civilized society and to develop their primitive social organization into a social organization better suited to their changing political and economic circumstances; and to acquire knowledge and understanding of themselves and the world about them beyond what they had as primitive villagers . . . If we accept 'the advancement of the natives' we are not accepting something 'vague' and 'general' but we are deciding that the aim of education shall be to give fuller scope to the individuality of each of them and to fit all of them for shaping the political, economic and social changes in which they are bound to take part.

After clearing the ground about the overall objectives, my minute continued as follows.

10. I would not pretend to be able to speak with a full knowledge of all aspects of the educational problem, and therefore am not sure that I can state the objectives of Government policy without omissions. It is clear to me however that those objectives include the following:

    (a) the political, economic, social and educational advancement of the peoples of Papua and New Guinea;

    (b) a blending of cultures;

and, in the absence of any indigenous body of religious faith, founded on native teaching or ritual,

    (c) the voluntary acceptance of Christianity by the native peoples.

11. In consequence of the acceptance of these objectives, we move to the acceptance of the following administrative purposes:

* The word 'Papuan' in this context covered all the people of the Territory of Papua and New Guinea.

(a) To achieve mass literacy, that is to say to attempt to teach all native children to read and write in a common language.

(b) To show them the way, awaken their interest in, and assist their progress towards a higher material standard of living and towards a civilized mode of life.

(c) To teach them what is necessary to enable them, step by step as changes take place in the native communities in which they live, to manage their own political affairs, to engage in economic activities to sustain a higher material standard of living, to adopt the practices of civilization in regard to social habit and custom and their daily mode of life and to develop and express their own personalities.

(d) To retain what is best in native life and to blend it with the influences of Western Civilization so that, while gaining the advantages of Western Civilization, they will not lose their proper pride in the fact that they have an identity as Papuans [or New Guineans] and so that, when in the generations to come, they may be required to manage their own affairs to a greater degree, they may feel a common bond among themselves as a people.

(e) To replace paganism by the acceptance of the Christian faith and the ritual of primitive life by the practice of religion.

(f) As a consequence of the foregoing, to strengthen the bonds of respect, mutual interest and loyalty to one another between Papua and New Guinea on the one hand and Australia on the other.

12. It may be that I have overlooked some considerations which may make it desirable to add to or modify the statement of overall objectives and the consequential administrative purposes which I have sketched in paragraphs 10 and 11 above. Assuming that those statements are reasonably complete however we now have to consider the broad means of achieving the objectives.

13. It is obvious that the question concerns the whole of administrative activity. The Departments of Native Affairs, Health, Agriculture, Lands and many others will have to advance this policy as well as the Department of Education. Indeed educational activity, in the meaning attached to it above, is the concern of the whole Administration. Therefore, before we consider the particular phases of the task to be undertaken by the Department of Education it is necessary to consider two other points. The first is the need to ensure the closest possible relationship between the Department of Education and the other departments of the Administration both in regard to what they are trying to do and the pace at which they are doing it. This is primarily the responsibility of the Administrator and I assume that such devices as are already employed by him (such as conferences of heads of departments and of district commissioners) and his own tours of inspection are sufficient for the discharge of that duty. If they are not it is for the Administrator to develop whatever machinery he requires. He is to ensure (a) that the Director of Education administers his Department in such a way as to conform to the policies being applied in other departments and that these other departments, by their work in their own fields, reinforce the work of the Department of Education and (b) that, in various parts of the Territory, a close relationship is kept between the pace of progress in the various phases of administration. For example the point in time at which the Education Department embarks on teaching hygiene should coincide with the point of time at which the Health Department is doing parallel

work, and similarly political education goes step by step with the work being done by the Department of District Services. The second point is that there is an obvious need for a good deal of flexibility both in the curricula and teaching methods adopted by the Education Department and in their application in various parts of the Territory and they must pay regard to the fact that these changes are not occurring uniformly throughout the Territory. I don't think a school at Hanuabada has, at this moment of time, exactly the same task as a school at Telefomin would have.

14. Looking more narrowly to the means by which the Department of Education will achieve the objectives, I think that the distinctive nature of its work (as contrasted with the work of, say, the Department of Native Affairs or the Department of Lands) is the conducting of schools. There are other activities in which a Department of Education might usefully engage, but having regard both to the nature of the present situation and the limits of our capacity to do everything at once, I think that in the immediate future the main work of the Education Department should be to make it possible for more children to go to school and ensure that they do so. The first need is primary education. There can be no higher education without primary education. The first requirement for primary education and for administrative success in other fields is a means of communication. While I do not propose to issue any direction against the use of pidgin or against the use of selected native languages for teaching purposes, I propose to confirm what has been laid down before that the goal of primary education should be literacy in English. As indicated above my interpretation of the objective of 'mass literacy' means ability to read and write a common language. That common language is to be English. I set the goal and the Administrator and the Education Department, in co-operation with the missions, are to work out the best means of reaching it as early as possible. That is their first target.

15. Next to teaching reading and writing to establish a means of communication, I think the most urgent need in the primary schools in the new areas is to reinforce what other departments are doing to improve hygiene, to ensure the understanding and co-operation of the native peoples in what we are trying to do to establish law and order and to combat disease, and to teach them to grow better food and use it more wisely, to improve their houses and to overcome social customs which hold a primitive people in a primitive condition. The contribution which an Education Department makes, as distinct from other departments engaged in the same tasks, is to introduce the idea of these changes into the minds of a new generation.

16. These are the basic and immediate needs over the greater part of the Territory. Beyond them, there is also a need for instruction in the use of tools, materials and methods by which these material improvements will take place. In the immediate present at least, over a great part of the Territory, I think that this 'technical' education has to be carefully adjusted to go side by side with the changes which are being brought about in the minds of the natives. At present I would not myself place much emphasis on technical training solely for the purpose of increasing our work force or for the purpose of enabling a native to gain a higher wage for himself. It should be regarded rather as a means of enabling him, as an individual, to do those things and to make that progress which his primary education has revealed to him to be possible . . .

17. Because the Christian missions do in fact provide a large proportion of

the primary schools in operation and because the teaching of religion—and in our case this means Christianity—appears to me to be an essential in the progress of a pagan and primitive people, it is apparent that the work of mission schools is an essential and important part of the means for achieving our educational objectives. I agree, in general principles, with the recommendations of the Investigation Committee in paragraph 111 but also think that, beyond the matters there discussed, there lie deeper problems of the relationship between the Department of Education and the Missions. These will have to receive very careful attention but for the time being I do not propose to embark on them. The policy of financial aid by the Government for mission schools teaching at a required standard has already been established.

18. For the performance of these tasks I recognize the great need for teachers, both European and native. I also recognize the special value of a corps of native teachers, but, from observation, I also know that it is quite useless to send native teachers out to primary schools unless they are soundly trained and that it is also necessary to take exceptional measures to see that, over the years, they are kept up to the mark.

19. The foregoing observations, which are intended to apply to the big mass of school-age natives, must of course be modified by reason of the unevenness of the progress of education. Where, in fact, some native schools have reached a point at which my remarks become inapplicable, an exception will have to be made.

20. I am not prepared at this stage to approve formally of the recommendations by the Investigation Committee at paragraph 144, although I do not wish it to be thought that I wholly disagree with those recommendations. At this stage I prefer to set out the immediate tasks of the Education Department as follows:

(a) First attention to be given to primary schools with the goal of teaching all children in controlled areas to read and write in English.

(b) For the above purpose,

(i) efforts to be made to ensure the co-operation of the Christian missions, and,

(ii) special attention to be given to teacher training.

(c) Manual training and technical training to be developed both in conjunction with the primary schools and in special schools in response to the developing needs of the people.

The fixing of these three tasks means that they are selected as being the first in order of time and that the Department of Education is required to do them well before it shoulders other tasks. The laying down of these tasks does not exclude other phases of educational activity and does not diminish in any way the importance of the overall objectives set out in paragraphs 10 and 11 above.

21. I do not offer any observations on the precise means by which these tasks will be accomplished or on any matter relating to the organization of the Education Department. I have tried to make clear:

(a) The Government's objectives, and

(b) The particular job that the Government wants to be done immediately.

I shall be glad to receive a further submission on the way the Government's wishes are to be turned into a programme of action.

Looking at this memorandum across a gap of nearly twenty years and realizing that it had been framed as a guide to officers in both the Department of Territories and the Administration, I can see that the shape of it was influenced to some extent by such facts as that I had been distracted a little by criticisms from certain churchmen which I felt had been founded on a deliberate misrepresentation of my views, that I was still having no success in diverting Groves to some other employment, that Lambert had to be restrained in his zeal to run the Territory from Canberra, and that some officers in the Department had revealed a strong disposition to write the ticket for Territory education along lines of expert advice from the Commonwealth Office of Education while I was rather stubbornly of the view that an education system had to be worked out and developed in the Territory and not imported as a package. These were some of the reasons why my directions were spelt out in such a tedious and dogmatic way.

In the meantime we had succeeded in establishing the statutory base for the education system with an Education Ordinance. Before I became Minister, work had been commenced on the preparation of this measure and this work was continued in the Department at Canberra throughout 1951 and early 1952 with a good deal of discussion between officers below the senior level. A draft of an ordinance came before me in July 1952. In my notes in a minute of 28 July I dealt severely with the draft and gave directions for further work. Proposals for an education board and for district education committees were criticized by me, not for the idea behind them but for the vagueness of the provisions regarding their powers, functions and methods of working. Other draft clauses were taken to pieces and criticized as a 'hotch-potch'. I also insisted on consultations with the missions and co-operation between the Department of Territories and the Administration. Eventually, in October 1952, a different draft was approved by me and a Bill introduced in the Legislative Council and passed. The Ordinance came into effect at the end of March 1953. I think that it suited the times when it was made, but it took some effort on my part to get the departmental officers to shape it in the way that I thought the situation needed.

I set some hope on the provisions for district education committees and an education advisory board to overcome political opposition inside the Territory and to draw the Territory community into the tasks of education. The registration of teachers and schools was part of the attempt to raise the efficiency of mission schools and give a basis for financial support to them.

The education advisory board was constituted by the Administrator on 30 June 1953. It was composed of the Director of Education, four members appointed by the Administrator to represent the missions and voluntary education agencies of the Territory, and four others selected by the Administrator. The Administrator for a start balanced the mission representatives by selecting all the other four members from the Administration service, whereas I had rather hoped that there might have been some independent minds. A stronger disappointment came with the way the board operated. It met infrequently and its second meeting came a year after its establishment. On 7 July 1954 I received the minutes of this second meeting, but without any indication of what action, if any, had been taken on the views expressed. I wrote to the Administration saying that the education advisory board should be made an effective part of the education system and that its members should feel that their recommendations were of some account. I would be interested to hear from the Administrator what steps he took to achieve this desired result. Looking back, I think that minute was far too mild. I should have made more fuss and done more to make the education advisory board do what I had intended it to do. I had to keep on pressing the Administrator to make the Director of Education use the board.

My disappointment with the work done by the Administration continued and was often expressed. Some additional money was provided but I could have fought for funds harder and more hopefully if I had been furnished with fully developed practical proposals from the Territory. I was given lots of figures, but some of them turned out to be a false guide largely because the state of education is a qualitative as well as a quantitative measure, and partly because the collection of statistics by the department was unreliable.

One fact that helps to explain the slow achievement was the lack of teachers. We could not find enough young native men and women in the Territory with a good enough basic education for training as teachers. Attempts to recruit teachers from outside the Territory were hampered because of the shortage of trained teachers everywhere. Those trained in Australian teachers' colleges were bonded to mainland education departments and there was an understandable reluctance by Australian authorities to make teachers available for Papua and New Guinea when they did not have enough for their own needs. We recruited as best we could but with limited response.

I am not satisfied with what I did in education. We made some headway but not enough. A report distributed by me at the end of 1955 recorded a growth in a period of five years of enrolment of native children in mission schools from 105 000 to 153 000 and in Administration schools from 2690 to 6000. The vote for the Education Department rose in five years from £147 288 to £575 000. There were 326 native teachers on duty and 227 in training. Technical training had started in three centres.

The real progress in education belongs to a period after this. The sad fact is that, partly under the previous ministers and partly under my own administration, the first ten years after the cessation of hostilities in 1945 were years of poor achievement so far as education was concerned. My own error in this period was not any error of trying to establish a broad base of primary education on which the education pyramid would rest, but my lack of ruthlessness in taking measures to produce the results I wanted.

[11]

HEALTH SERVICES

The need for health services was plain and immediate. We had a duty to treat the sick, resist disease and establish the conditions for physical health. This practical approach was confirmed by another consequence of medical work. Perhaps the quickest way to find an entrance to the trust and confidence of the people was to treat their ills and ease their suffering. In areas of first contact the initial breakthrough to closer understanding often came when, as the result of our ministry someone who was expected to die did not die or someone who was in pain and distress was brought back to health.

From the start I also found myself emotionally awakened to interest in the subject. The need for health measures is seen first in human bodies. A heightened awareness of bodies came with my first close experience of life in the tropics. The arid lands of Australia are for contemplation of the whole of existence and a vision of eternity; the fecund tropics reveal the struggle of staying alive, however briefly, on the earth—in this festering eruption of animal life at the insignificant tail of galactic space. In the tropics one looks at rampant life and not at distant stars.

In the tropics teeming life abounds but droops early to decay. On the coastal plains the kunai grass, tougher, thicker and higher than maize, flourishes like a crop gone wild. In the jungle, vines writhe and twine impenetrably. Huge trees, raised by massive and distorted roots out of the dense undergrowth, lift grey columns to support a canopy of silent leaves. When they fall, the trunks start to rot almost as soon as they touch the earth, and within a few years the logs are crumbling and spongy and new monsters are rising in their place. In the deltas of southern rivers giant mangroves grow out of oozy black mud. In the Sepik swamps, the sago palms hide strange, silent and unthreaded corridors of water. In the mountains the pines crown the sides of the ravines, their dark greenness gashed here and there by a landslide. A stick thrust in the roadside soil takes root and flourishes and demonstrates its new life by violent blossom. A snapped flower withers and hangs in damp tatters. The sense of thrusting, abounding, riotous, insecure life in the humid heat—life proliferating because it is precarious—is one of the most vivid experiences of the newcomer to Papua and New Guinea. I felt the physical thrust in the same way in

100

the swarming of peoples. A stranger from a sparse and arid Australia, I had an urgent sense of our common flesh in a way I had not known before. It may have been the numbers. It may have been the nakedness. The physical presence of a multitude of human bodies worked on the mind in the same way as the luxuriance of tropical growth.

I am writing of the early 1950s and mostly of newly opened areas. In those days European dress was uncommon among the native people. Even in urban centres, such as Port Moresby and Rabaul, and on labour lines on plantations and about the house few men wore anything other than a 'lap-lap' (a cloth wound around the hips), and the women mostly wore grass skirts and nothing else. On some missions and in some houses of Europeans the women had a 'house dress' like a pinafore, with skirt and bib, but shed it when not on duty. In some of the remoter areas men walked naked except for a belt of hair or bark or, in some areas, a phallocrypt, displaying rather than concealing their possessions, and the women wore only a *cache-sexe* the size of a very small sporran. The less scantily clad men and women in other areas of first contact wore a bunch of leaves fore and aft. In the Chimbu and neighbouring areas the long tasselled apron of string gave the men distinction. Other minorities had cloaks of bark or tapa cloth, hammered out of mangrove bark and stained in varied patterns.

When, as 'No. 1 bilong Sydney', I travelled around the Territory to places where the visitor was still a great novelty, the people came down in thousands to stare, pressing around me in big-eyed, smiling curiosity. Bodies, bodies, bodies pressed as closely as the kunai on a narrow track as I walked through a gradually yielding pathway. Knowing neither them nor their language, I had no contact except the touch of our bodies. Out on the Bamu River, at the 'Mission in the Mud', near-naked women lay prostrate on the river bank for me to step over them one by one in a ritual welcome. At Menyamya sturdy warriors pressed around, touching me with their hands, feeling my muscles and more intimate parts of the anatomy. At Mendi, in the Southern Highlands, wholly naked bodies smeared with tree oil and ochre stained my shirt as they pressed closer to me to show their friendship.

One soon becomes accustomed to the breasts of nubile girls when, glistening with oil or grease or sweat, they bob around in thousands of pairs as the highland dancing goes on for hours. Like male genitalia, breasts become as unimportant, unvaried and impersonal as the nose or the chin. Seen one, seen all, and, seeing so many, one ceased to see any. But the sense of bodies remained. The large numbers of people and the customary nakedness or near-nakedness of most of them had the effect of making me more acutely aware of the bodies of humanity than of their personalities or minds.

This vivid presence of bodies influenced the starting point of my administrative concern with health. The physical welfare and the physical needs of the people impinged on my mind dramatically. It was not that all the bodies were beautiful but that they were alive and vibrant. I became aware of the fecundity of life in the thousands of naked youngsters crawling or scampering around and in the obvious pregnancy of so many of the women.

Then, by one question, I learnt, not the birth rate but the survival rate, for in some parts infant mortality (death under twelve months) was as high as one in three. I saw the unusual distension around the middle of some striplings and, asking what it was, heard of enlarged spleens, the consequence of early malaria. In hospitals and in village huts I saw wasted bodies and was told of tuberculosis. I walked through crowded wards and shook the outstretched hands and patted the shoulders of lepers when that seemed to be what they expected. I watched the dressing of tropical ulcers. I touched the dry cheeks of those with lolling heads stricken with some strange disease. I saw both sick and injured with the ghastly grey that the dark skin takes in the imminence of death, more agonizing even than the glazed ivory pallor of the dying European.

I discussed as best a layman could with medical assistants and the doctors the difficulties of this or that case, the response to this or that drug. I read lots of reports. And everything I was told and all I read was made vivid by this awareness of bodies, bodies, bodies. 'Suffering humanity' and 'relief from pain' are phrases that only take on meaning from an awareness of the physical body that is afflicted. Hitherto, in Australia, I had been too healthy and too clean. I had not been sufficiently aware of bodies as something just as real, as sensitive, as transitory as flowers that are trodden on, crushed and bruised as they lie on the earth or fade on the broken stalk.

I saw babies enfeebled with dysentery, and youngsters suspected of having intestinal parasites. I saw others suffering from malnutrition, starving to death not through lack of food but from other causes. In villages I saw bodies, otherwise healthy and shapely, whose skin was covered with a grey scurf and, asking, was told that 'grilli' was the outcome of nutritional deficiencies. I saw men and women with parts of their features eaten away or disfigured with yaws.

Incidentally, when trying once to awaken the House of Representatives to problems of health in the Territory, I said something about the campaign to overcome yaws, and one of the parliamentary buffoons, who habitually laid claim to much deeper feelings of compassion than Jesus Christ ever did, interjected with a grin, 'What's yours?' and at once he became the corner-man for his customary ape to cry, 'Make mine a schooner.' Through the sickening vulgarity of the laugh that followed, I saw vividly the disfigured faces in a welcoming line of village councillors at a recent stopping place on the Sepik, and I felt sick not for the natives, for they were men of dignity, but for the chosen and elect in Canberra—fat and pink men who stared daily into bathroom mirrors as they dabbed their smooth, self-satisfied proletarian cheeks with after-shave lotion as advertised in every women's weekly. Perhaps because of such experiences, I find in these later years that, excepting only two or three friends, I am not stirred deeply by the memory of any comradeship or esteem from my associates in parliament, but my emotions come welling from the depths at the recollection of some nameless little scared pot-bellied youngster who took my hand for comfort in New Guinea, or the clinging fingers of some newly born infant, yielded to my arms from his mother's lap, or some leper who smiled through his disfigurement. Long before I had found any way of talking to the people and entering their minds, I had awareness of them by this dumb communication of physical sympathy.

Reviewing some of my experiences of this period, I wrote at the time,

A layman travelling in tropical regions is probably impressed more dramatically by the interplay between human fecundity and human mortality than by anything else. The human body naked and vigorous in the sun or the human body crumpled and ashen as it waits for death in the shade tells as boldly as the bright tropical blossoms tell the swift chapters of being born, flourishing and dying. Disease is not screened and the physical is not obscured. Hence the immensity of the task of health is visible . . .

Although I had no medical training of any kind, I found that I could understand the immediacy and the range of the health problems in the Territory more readily and more clearly than I could understand some of the other problems.

This was also due in large part to the quality of the Director of Health, Dr John (later Sir John) Gunther.[18] I had heard about him before I met him. Some persons in the Territory went out of their way to warn me that he was a difficult man to handle and wanted everything his own way. I should be careful not to 'let him get away with too much' or I would have trouble. In fact he was not too bad at all. Although at our first meeting he may have been inclined to regard me as just another one of those politicians and hence of somewhat doubtful quality, I found he had the sort of mind and character I liked. I appreciated the blunt way in which he told me the first time I met him in Port Moresby in 1951 about all that was wrong with the Department of Health and all the things he had not done and how inadequate all the present health services were. Most of the others in the Administration had been telling me how well everything was going or about the personal hardships that they had to endure in serving the country. I also liked the fact that he knew what he wanted to do next. He had quite a number of demands ready.

After the first rather brief conversation in the somewhat decrepit war-time iron building at Konedobu occupied by the Department of Health I still thought there might be something in the warning that he was difficult and that he thought nothing else mattered so long as the Health Department got what it wanted. After I had been around the Territory however and had seen a little of the situation for myself I came back for a further and longer talk with him and this was the beginning of a real appreciation of the quality of the man. I moved from a high respect for his work to warm regard and friendship. I know of no one who, in successive capacities, did better work for Papua and New Guinea in the post-war years than John Gunther did.

When we first met, Gunther had been on the job for five years, first on a one-year appointment as Acting Director in the Provisional Administration and later as Director of Public Health, but, for reasons set out in my separate discussions of the public service, his appointment as head of the Department of Public Health was not actually gazetted until June 1951. Handicapped by lack of staff and an incomplete departmental structure, he had achieved much. He was easily the strongest single driving force in the Administration as well as being one of the very few senior men with a trained intelligence and a practical political sense.

In the Department of Health he knew his own job. If I mentioned some incident I had observed or spoke about some member of his staff or one of his aid posts, he knew the subject and could tell me what action had been taken. When I discussed tentatively some of my own impressions about the basic problems of hygiene, sanitation, nutrition, maternal and infant welfare and routine medical examinations, it was plain that he had thought about these matters and had developed ideas on how they should be tackled. When I asked about the major diseases and their treatment and control or eradication, he revealed that he saw those problems in their full depth and breadth. On questions of staff, medical stores and equipment and hospital building he was well furnished with facts and ready to make plans and he was also clearly aware of the practical problems of putting plans into effect and the political problems of obtaining approvals for forward programmes and of obtaining money.

It is a small thing but of some significance that, in all my own notes and jottings and instructions during my first five years as Minister, there is less about the Department of Health than about any other subject, although it was one of my major interests and the field in which we did most in those five years. Here I had someone who needed no pushing. It was the one field in which I inherited some good basic work and found plans for the next step already in formation. If there had been six other senior officers of the Administration as good as Gunther in 1951, the whole of the story I am telling would have been vastly different. Gunther had not yet received any major policy decisions on health and he had been given scant funds, but he had gone ahead without waiting for either. I was strongly impressed by how much he had done through improvisation and determination.

In June 1949 the total number of doctors in the Territory was 32, of whom 18 were official and 14 non-official (missions and industrial and commercial organizations). There were 131 trained nurses (91 of them non-official) and the health services of the Administration depended very heavily on 93 officers described as medical assistants. These were chiefly men who had gained experience as medical orderlies or sick-bay attendants in the armed services during war time and a few who before the war had been medical assistants on plantations. Although their paper qualifications were no higher than that of first-aid certificates or training as a male nurse, several of them had gained by experience a remarkable competence in the treatment of tropical diseases and in the handling of the more common emergencies and they were the backbone of medical services for the native people. A few were of doubtful reliability either on the medical or personal side but most were of good value. If we take for granted that 80 of these European medical assistants were worth their place, it was still not a very impressive medical coverage for two million indigenous people. They were helped by 145 native medical assistants and 895 medical orderlies. These were nearly all illiterate, but a few of the native medical assistants had a useful capacity for routine and conventional treatments and the orderlies were very helpful in fetching and carrying, cleaning up and keeping watch.

When I became Minister in 1951, Gunther, with some understandable impatience at the lack of other support from government, was going ahead vigorously with this method of taking medicine to the people. In his first five years he raised the number of posts (hospitals, clinics and aid posts) from 150 to over a thousand. The numbers of staff more than doubled, the most notable increase being in the numbers of medical assistants and native medical orderlies.

There are few more romantic stories in the early post-war history of Territory administration than this expansion of medical services for the native peoples. I was often moved to a deep admiration of the work I saw being done devotedly under almost impossible conditions. In remote parts of the Territory I met European medical assistants who had just come in from patrols on foot around a circuit of villages. In posts of first contact, recently established by young patrol officers, I saw the aid post established by a native medical assistant. In many places I visited the hospitals—huts of native materials, earth floors, rows on rows of beds made of planks supported on forked posts, hundreds of patients being nursed, hundreds of relatives camped outside or even alongside and under their rough beds, operating theatres of crude simplicity. The Health Department had not waited for fully polished and nicely streamlined plans to be approved or for someone to give them both instructions and money, but had done with energy and directness whatever tasks of healing immediately awaited them.

A hospital that was treating two or three hundred patients may have cost only a few hundred pounds to build. The native people had done the work with native materials under the guidance of the European medical assistant who had been sent out to establish it. We had some notable builders of hospitals among these men. In general the style followed the native building practice of the district concerned, that style itself being usually dictated by local conditions and availability of materials. For example in some places the wards had earth floors. In others they had raised floors made of split poles. In some places, especially where there were earth floors, there might be one enormous bed like a platform of planks. In some, the patients spread their mats on the raised floor. In others, individual bunks were made of bush timber. In a few I even saw iron bedsteads, salvaged from war-time establishments.

Yet, although the buildings and furniture were rough, a high standard was set for medical attention and hospital hygiene, and the supply of drugs, sera and other medical materials and equipment was modern and well kept.

One piece of improvisation that amazed me was the training of native medical assistants. I spent some time at a 'medical school' in some old army huts at Finschhafen. Their recruits were young men from the villages who could neither read nor write, for, by reason of conditions I have described in chapter 10, our education system had not yet started to produce any quota of young fellows with even a modest primary schooling. The medium of instruction was pidgin which, if he came from the highlands, the trainee probably had to learn as a new language before he could understand the teacher. The main course was of two years, although there were some variations on this. At the end of the course, the best of these bush boys were ready to go out as native medical assistants carrying their lecture notes with them as a sort of medical encyclopaedia and take charge of an aid post.

The lecture notes were largely pictorial, concentrating on symptoms and treatments. For example one page might show the picture of a patient with a dripping nose and a headache, followed by a picture of the thermometer and the reading of his temperature and a picture of the medicine to be given to him, the quantities to be given being pictured in spoons or numbers of tablets. Medicines were identified by distinctive shapes and labels. Each aid post was kept supplied with its readily identifiable set of standard remedies. The medical assistant was also taught to observe the results of initial treatment. He was taught to distinguish between those minor conditions which could be treated at an aid post and those which would require the services of a doctor and the sending of the patient into hospital.

These men were the advance guard on the frontiers of medicine. They could skirmish with danger and dispose of the lesser threats and give warning and call reinforcements to handle the greater threats. The job of this 'doctor boy' was to give simple aid to the people, to establish better hygiene practices and to encourage the sick and injured to seek admission to the hospitals.

On several occasions, at patrol posts, I made my own rough tests by putting myself in the position of a patient and describing a simulated pain or a sick feeling and asking the 'doctor boy' what he would do, and I always found that he had been well drilled in his job. Among other services they performed was a simple form of reporting from which the pattern of medical need was becoming factually clearer throughout the Territory.

Of course we had a few breakdowns. There was the tragedy of Faita. At Faita in the Madang district in mid-1954, when trying to do good, we killed off seventeen men, women and children, most of the population of the hamlet.

We had inaugurated a campaign for the eradication of yaws. It called for three successive injections of a drug. To cover the hundreds of thousands of people involved, a team of native medical assistants and native hygiene assistants was organized to go on foot to every village and hamlet, over the mountains, down the valleys, searching out all human beings and persuading them to have an injection. They had to do the same thing on three successive patrols. It was hard going and perhaps monotonous. Each of these native workers was equipped with his hypodermic syringe, a bottle of tablets and a gallon jar of distilled water. He had been drilled on dissolving the proper number of tablets in the proper quantity of sterile water and injecting the proper quantity in the proper rumps. Hundreds of thousands of injections were given and eventually yaws was subdued. In the course of this campaign a native hygiene assistant, growing a little weary of carrying the large jar of water on his shoulder, recalled that during his war-time association with Australian soldiers there had been an occasional practice when no sterile water was available of using the milk of a freshly opened coconut as the most nearly sterile liquid. So, on several occasions, he left his jar behind and used the fresh coconut milk to dissolve his tablets. Apparently no harm followed. At Faita, however, after opening a coconut and covering it with a clean cloth to keep contamination away, food-time distracted him. After the meal he came back, dissolved his tablets in the milk and gave his injections. Most of the people in the hamlet died in pain before nightfall. That was an exceptional incident and we took measures to lessen such risks.

Looking back, I am still moved by wonder and admiration at how much good was done and how little ill was suffered by the early reliance on the help of these uneducated, crudely trained and devoted native medical assistants to bring healing and relief to hundreds of thousands of their people in the early days of post-war health services.

The annual figures of the health services gave a heartening story of progress. Expenditure on health services rose from £605 000 in 1948–9 to £1.4 million in 1953–4, to £1.7 million in 1954–5 and to £2 million in 1955–6. The number of trained medical personnel of all kinds rose to approximately 2500. The number of Administration institutions—hospitals, clinics, aid posts and leprosaria—passed a thousand in 1954.

This period of improvisation however led to a problem of construction. The life of a native building was anything from three to five years and sometimes less. Repairs and replacement created an almost perpetual demand for the continued co-operation of the villagers and others. In some areas there was a shortage of native building materials or they had to be carried long distances on people's backs. In some cases the first hospitals had been badly located. With earth floors, poor drainage and very limited plumbing they presented sanitary problems. Yet every aid post and hospital that had been opened was in full and constant use and could not be closed or restricted without causing distress and disappointment. Most of them had created a growing need for expanding health services. The temporary stopgap was becoming the major part of our total establishment. Alongside them, the war-time sheds and huts that had been occupied were becoming more and more dilapidated. While I was at one place at Milne Bay, half of the hospital, chiefly wooden, fell over. At Daru, walking incautiously in one of the wards, I fell through the raised floor, disappearing from the incurious gaze of half a dozen women patients. They took even less notice of my strange behaviour than fellow-members used to take of a speech in the House of Representatives.

By the end of 1953, over 750 medical institutions—hospitals, clinics and aid posts—had been provided at a capital cost roughly calculated to be less than £200 000, not counting the inheritance of war-time huts and sheds and the few survivals of the pre-war years. To keep them in existence in a reasonably sound and efficient condition meant prospective works programmes of millions. I saw an enormous need to do more than we were doing, and yet I also had to face this special problem of maintaining the service provided in the makeshifts we had already got. One of my early failures was in being unable to convince my Cabinet colleagues and the senior officers of the Commonwealth Works Department and the Treasury of our special circumstances. All they seemed to be able to understand was that I was asking for more money to build hospitals and they pointed out that it was so many thousands more than I spent on hospitals in the previous year. Gunther's improvisations in providing structures at a cost of next to nothing became an argument why we could not expect more money for the permanent structures.

The special problem of hospitals was parallel to the problem of houses and offices for our staff, a large proportion of whom were dwelling and working in decrepit survivals from war time or in native structures they had built for themselves with the help of the people. At this early period I found not only a complete lack of understanding of our peculiar problems by the Commonwealth Department of Works but a positive impediment in its procedures and outlook to my attempts to get work done.

During 1950, under Spender's impetus, a hospital requirements investigation committee, composed of Drs Gunther, E. T. Brennan and W. B. Kirkland, had examined the hospital needs of the Territory and had recommended the location of base hospitals and smaller hospitals and the order of priorities in a construction programme. Spender had accepted their report as a basis for a submission to Cabinet, but no decisions had been made on a building programme. I decided that I must persist in trying to get a Cabinet decision for a major hospital building programme, but that to maintain our existing work and to meet even a few of the unsatisfied needs for medical services, I would have to continue to improvise for a number of years by using all the local resources at my command.

Early in 1952, with the help of Lambert, I drafted submissions for Cabinet on hospitals for Papua and New Guinea and for special measures on tuberculosis. In July 1952 I had to inform Lambert that we had no hope of success with our submissions and the best we could do would be to get 'a few thousand here and there' for additional appointments or essential equipment for the Health Department by making a bid to raise the grant in the Commonwealth Budget for 1952–3. Regretfully I wrote,

> Our practical task, particularly in housing and the improvement of the hospitals, is to see if we can use local resources to a far greater extent and to modify plans so as to make the money we get go further. It would be worth going through the various constructional projects to see which ones lend themselves to the use of local material and local labour. It will be better to have a reasonably useful building that will serve the purpose for the next fifteen years than to have none at all . . . I am conscious of the fact that a great proportion of the wartime heritage of buildings in New Guinea are rotting away or are just about to fall down . . . Of necessity, the Territory will have to accustom itself to the idea of replacing many of them with buildings which will be better than the wartime ones but which will still not be the perfect and final structure.

Unfortunately, in moving into this second phase of local endeavour, Gunther and I found the going less simple than the pioneering phase. It had been comparatively simple to send out a competent medical assistant to mobilize the villages with the aid of a patrol officer and build the first aid post. It had also been comparatively simple to put up a hospital in huts made of native materials or, if one were as enterprising as Gunther and his men, to move into an unused line of war-time sheds. This second phase of local building in more durable materials however required some planning and calculating and control over funds. We ran into some difficulties in the clerical weaknesses in the Territory Administration and in the small Territory Department of Works whose skill and capacity were then limited.

My special bid for a major hospital building programme was renewed in

1953. After the departmental officers had their preliminary inter-departmental discussions on the works programme for the 1953–4 Budget, I wrote:

> We have to make the most strenuous efforts possible this year to undertake a much larger proportion of the hospital plan this year, basing our case on the fact that a Cabinet decision has been made on the policy of large-scale hospital development but has not yet been carried out; that the wasting and decay of temporary and wartime hospital accommodation has reached a point where extensive replacement is necessary to maintain even existing services; and that there are extensive needs (e.g. in leprosy and tuberculosis) which are still wanting attention. The whole hospital works programme needs reconsideration and a more determined effort to remedy the appalling shortage of up-to-date buildings which exists, particularly in native hospitals. [Minute of 5 March 1953.]

On 16 April, after the Department had engaged in further talks with the Administration and the Director-General of Works and were proposing further discussions between officers, I wrote to Lambert again asking that every possible effort be made to ensure that construction of a substantial section of the total hospital plan was commenced that year.

In 1954 we started on the hospital building programme, comprising 3 base hospitals, 7 major regional hospitals, 8 minor regional hospitals, 51 subregional hospitals, 4 tuberculosis hospitals and 5 leprosy hospitals.

We increased financial aid to missions to assist them to expand their medical services. Child and maternal welfare centres and mobile infant welfare clinics were introduced. Training facilities were extended. Town sanitation was improved. Malarial control work was started. Further work in nutrition was done. Planning was started for a Central Medical School in the Territory. A tuberculosis survey, psychiatric survey and an ophthalmic investigation were conducted. Painfully and in the face of a good deal of difficulty and many disappointments, we recruited more and better staff. We introduced the practice, lacking other means, of arranging with mainland hospitals to send special surgical teams into the Territory, an experience which, later, in a different portfolio, helped me to increase the effectiveness of our Colombo Plan aid in Asia and our civil aid during the war in Vietnam. The organizing of medical teams for civil aid in Vietnam was directly due to the measures I took as the result of my Papua and New Guinea experience.

Besides the provision of buildings and facilities, we had a difficult problem in obtaining staff. While the eventual goal would be an indigenous medical service, it was plain that in the short term we would have to rely on doctors, trained nurses and medical technicians from outside the Territory. There were no native candidates for higher training who had the required basic education. It was extremely difficult to recruit doctors. Some very useful relief was given by recruiting New Australian immigrants who had practised medicine in Europe but whose qualifications were not recognized for registration in Australia. We gave them a Territory registration. We also inaugurated a scheme of medical cadetships. We got some good young doctors out of this but I must say I was rather disillusioned by the cold-blooded way in which some bright young students, having been assisted by us on their way through the university, then told us they had no intention of going to Papua and New Guinea and either forfeited the bond of £1000 by which they were obligated to give five years' service or just skipped out of any responsibility towards us.

The training of native candidates as assistant medical practitioners at the Central Medical School, Suva, had started in 1947 but, of the first six students sent there, one fell sick and the other five had to be transferred to a preparatory school because of lack of basic educational qualifications. We did not get the first qualified assistant medical practitioner from the Suva school until January 1952. The next quota of three were ready to commence work with us in 1953. At the beginning of 1954 we were able to send eight more students, bringing the total then in training to eleven. At the beginning of 1955 we sent a further sixteen. Thereafter we began to receive a small annual quota of qualified men. These arrangements eventually gave place to the establishment of our own Medical School in Port Moresby, a development that had been planned from the beginning.

In 1956 I wrote, 'The achievement of the Health Department in post-war years has been little short of amazing when one considers the difficulties. It appears pathetically inadequate when one considers the needs . . .' I wrote too of the need for 'considerably increased financial support' and the 'top priority' to be given to the medical training of the indigenous people.

In giving more attention to health, we ran into the usual contest between the claims of the European community and the indigenous community. Their respective standards of health and hygiene and the pattern of medical need were then much more widely separate from each other than they have since become. As far as I can remember there was no hospital in common use by both Europeans and natives in 1951 but only distinct and separate hospitals. This was part of the reality of life there. Nearly all native babies were still being born 'in the bush'. Very few, if any, native patients were accustomed to sleeping in a European-style hospital bed. It would have been against the prevailing habit and custom of both communities to give any order then that they had to go into the same hospitals or the same wards. The path of progress was to raise the level and extend the services of 'native hospitals' so that they and not the 'European hospitals' became the norm of hospital services in the Territory. Clearly too we had to bring a recognition that the major tasks of the Health Department were for the native people. Yet at the same time in our efforts to recruit staff and to get more vigorous administration we had to give to the Europeans working in the Territory some confidence in the availability and reliability of medical services. Most of the European hospitals were also in a bad state of repair, poorly equipped and under-staffed.

Throughout 1952, 1953 and 1955 I find several instances in which I gave directions for keeping some kind of rough balance between European and native requirements. For example in 1953 I reprimanded the Department for proposing to make some much-needed improvements at the European hospital at Port Moresby by diverting funds that had been voted for native requirements, and in November 1954 there was another direction to the effect that, since the far greater need existed among the natives than among the Europeans, we should 'ensure that a liberal provision for one does not unduly deprive the other of the bare minimum'.

Meanwhile a stronger popular pressure for medical services was growing up among the European community than among the native people. Indeed among newly arrived Australians, accustomed to the idea of having a doctor, chemist or hospital available wherever they lived, we had a more difficult job than among some of the pre-war settlers and public servants in establishing the idea that the major problems of health and the highest priorities in health were among the indigenous people and that a 'balanced' programme did not mean equal expenditures but a very heavy preponderance in favour of native health.

During 1953 it seemed to me that there was a regrettable diversion of administrative effort both in Canberra and in Port Moresby in a diligent attempt to work out a 'contributory medical benefits scheme' in the Territory. The impetus came mainly from public servants and they spent a lot of time on it. On the one hand there were public servants in Canberra who were worried over the looseness of a practice under which any white family who was sick was treated by the nearest available doctor or hospital or got a dose of medicine as a matter of course without any fee being charged. On the other hand there was the advocacy of some public servants in the Territory that there should be a medical and hospital benefits scheme available to them both in the Territory and on the Australian mainland. There was much discussion on the ins and outs of such a scheme, but no finality was reached.

Throughout this early period I was aware of some hindrances to Gunther, both in the Department at Canberra and in the Territory Administration. Sometimes his proposals for staff were whittled down, sometimes his comments were not sought on medical matters, sometimes his views on the reorganization of his department were side-tracked. This was probably nothing more than the view of the public servant that he knows best about everything and that a professional man is necessarily a poor administrator. One of my senior officers in Canberra (not Lambert) habitually seemed to regard Gunther as a dangerous man. There was a marked disposition both in Canberra and Port Moresby to keep him in check. I preferred that he should have an easier rein. I made sure he got it and he did an admirable job.

I would not wish to claim that Gunther's achievement was my achievement, but I permit myself some associated credit for having helped lay the foundations of post-war medical services, carry out some fundamental investigations, establish the first comprehensive hospitals system and start medical education in the Territory. I was happy that I remained Minister long enough to see the opening of the major hospitals at Port Moresby, Madang, Rabaul, Wewak and Daru and to see well-appointed district hospitals, and clinics staffed by native medical practitioners at many other places. At these opening ceremonies I was one of the few present who could recall mud floors, crumbling walls, a fall through the rotting floor of a ward, and also the patience and hopelessness of unrelieved suffering where no aid of any kind was at hand.

In these early years I was a bystander at several medical emergencies. I was at Daru in 1952 when, one Sunday morning on the regular two-way transceiver 'sked', a patrol officer out in the Fly Delta reported the medical emergency of a woman in difficult childbirth. 'They only brought her in after the village women had finished jumping on her belly. She's in a bad way.' The young man was on his own at the patrol post. At Daru the European medical assistant and his wife asked for fuller details. 'Roger', 'Over', 'I'm hearing you'. Backward and forward the staccato conversation went. She was in a bad way. A few temporary instructions were given for tucking certain things back inside her and for this and that. Meanwhile a canoe was got ready. It went out on a good tide, two native boys paddling, the nurse herself and her case, shrouded against sun and spray, sitting in the stern. There were scores of miles to go. We waited. On the next 'sked' the mother was still alive. Next morning we heard the canoe had got there. Treatment started. Towards evening nurse and patient were on their way in. A day later they were in hospital, put into the same ward that still had the hole in the floor where a visiting Minister had fallen through. The patient lived.

On another occasion I was on a chartered single-engine aircraft of the Missionary Aviation Fellowship flying to Kiunga on the Upper Fly. A medical emergency call came. This was the only aircraft anywhere in the vicinity. The young Australian pilot asked me what he should do. By himself there would be room in the aircraft to get the patient to hospital. I told him to put me down and go off on his job. He landed at some little strip—an isolated patch of solid green with a lot of water all around it—and unloaded both me and our overnight bags. I sat there for about three hours reading Racine and slapping insects. He came back, cheerfully. He had 'uplifted' the patient and a nurse from a mission, taken them to hospital and flown back to me—a circuit of four hundred miles or so—and, having already refuelled, was all set to go on to Kiunga.

At a small post in the highlands, returning late one afternoon from a visit to surrounding country, I was told there had been an accident with explosives in a neighbouring village. When the story was pieced together subsequently, it turned out that an unexploded hand grenade from war time must have been picked up somewhere down near the coast, passed from hand to hand and carried as a curiosity into the highlands and then discarded, or it may have been a war-time souvenir brought in by some European and then stolen from him. In the village, it being a cold day, the men were clustered after the mid-day meal in a hut, lying down with their backs to the fire. Drowsily one reached for some knobby bits of firewood and put them on the fire. Among them was the grenade. After a time there was an explosion and one man was writhing in pain. He was thought to be dying, so they carried him, wailing and despairing, over the hill tracks to the grass-walled hospital. We went rather anxiously to ask after the patient. The European medical assistant said 'she' was in a bit of a mess but he thought he could fix her up. We questioned the use of the pronoun 'she'. 'Oh, the man's backside was only peppered with ashes,' the medico said, 'but I picked out most of the bits.' The real patient was his wife. Being told that her husband had been killed, she had gone into immediate mourning, pounding her left hand with a heavy stone till it was a mashy pulp.

Casualties in the bush hospitals were of all kinds. In one I saw three youths in succession with bandages around the middle. The first one said he had been bitten by a pig. Apparently when a pig turns frantic or savage, it leaps and bites boy or man in the fleshy middle. The second one had also been bitten by a pig. The third one too. 'Was it the same pig?' I asked. 'One-fella pig, trifella belly tasol', said the grinning boy.

Falls from trees and from palms were a frequent cause of injury. In coastal towns a new cause, mostly of broken feet, was football. I seldom saw wounds inflicted with weapons. Usually if a man was hit with an axe, the job was complete.

In Telefomin I was going through a dark ward where the women patients were sitting on their plank beds. Some were nursing their young. One had to ask sometimes whether mother or child was the patient. At the dim end was a woman with twins, one on each breast. I asked the medical assistant if multiple births were frequent. He stared at me. I said that this was the first time I had seen a woman with twins in the highlands. 'Twins?' he said. 'You'd better look again.' I did. One of the twins was a little sucking pig, happily feeding at one breast while the baby fed at the other. I had seen on another occasion a woman suckling a pig in a village and apparently this woman had brought her pet in with her to hospital as well as her own child.

When I opened the hospital at Nonga, near Rabaul, the architect-engineer was very keen that I should see the morgue as well as all the other wonders. It was the best of its kind in the Territory and had refrigeration so that a corpse could be kept for several days. He was obviously waiting for the day when it could stow away its first cadaver. He touched a button and out rolled the shining tray. It was stacked with sandwiches and other goodies for the festivities that were to follow the official ceremony. The Territory is essentially a practical place and, in all matters concerned with hospitals, one of intelligent improvisation.

The extent of health services was widened by the work of the Christian missions. We introduced a scheme to subsidize the missions by issuing drugs, dressings and minor hospital appliances free to all recognized health workers in the mission field, by making a grant of £650 a year for each qualified medical practitioner and £250 a year for each trained nurse, and by capital assistance in building hospitals. The missions also had access to the services of the various departments of the Administration. I met some opposition in both the Administration and the Government when I provided capital assistance in building hospitals for missions. Perhaps I was at fault. One or two hospitals on which we placed high hope were slow in starting to function. Others were an early success. The chief argument in persuading me was that missions had staff and were already in touch with patients.

I have said little about other basic medical work that was going on—the anti-malarial work, nutritional surveys, investigation of psychiatric disorders, the mobile infant welfare clinics, dental services and so on. I claim no personal credit for inaugurating these and other similar measures, but I backed them to the hilt.

In my first five years I felt that we had done well in health and had laid the foundation for doing much more good in the future. It was an exciting period of making something shift and seeing immediate benefits follow.

[12]

LANDS POLICY

There was a saying in the Territory that the chief causes of trouble were land, pigs and women. Most disputes were about land, pigs or women. Fighting and killing were due to land, pigs or women. The things of greatest importance in the eyes of the native people were land, pigs and women—in that order.

From the beginning I recognized the importance of lands policy and administration. I was surrounded by experts. Lands administration was a field in which Lambert had wide Australian experience. Rupert Wilson,[19] who was appointed Assistant Administrator after Cleland was raised from that post to Administrator, was chosen chiefly because of his qualifications in land administration and land settlement. In the Territory itself, in the first Director of Lands in my time E. P. Holmes,[20] we had a man with a high local reputation in this field. Others appointed to perform special roles had similar high reputations. Personally I knew little or nothing about lands administration except in the setting of the early Australian colonies. I endorsed without question the long-established policy of protecting native land rights. I was slower in realizing how much was required as well as a policy.

In settling the Australian colonies the practice had been that, by the act of possession, all land was regarded as having become Crown land and the Crown proceeded to give titles in the land to the settler. Both in Papua and in New Guinea the land was regarded as still belonging to the indigenous inhabitants until the Crown (or other authority) acquired it from them, and the Crown (or other authority) only gave titles to others over portions of the land it had acquired. Land used for public purposes was also acquired by one procedure or another from the native people, and only land so acquired was used for public purposes. Broadly all other land belonged to the native people. There was a good deal of cloudiness about the nature of their ownership and about the status of wastelands which did not seem to be claimed by anybody. There were also lands in dispute among themselves. This is an over-simplification of a complicated history and of intricate and varied ideas about rights to land.

The existing situation in 1951 was broadly that a very small percentage of the total area of the Territory had been alienated in the sense in which lands officers use the term. Some of the alienated land was used for public purposes,

114

some was held by land-holders under individual titles of various kinds, and some was still 'owned' by the Administration and was either being used by the Administration for such purposes as the offices, residences, establishments of the various departments or public utilities and roads, or was 'vacant' and available for allotment to the settler or, although this idea had not been embraced by most Europeans, for allotment to native persons who had no land. All the rest of the land, except possibly some areas of 'waste land', was regarded as being in native ownership.

In the speech drafted for the Administrator of the Government of the Commonwealth to deliver at the inauguration of the Legislative Council in November 1951 I wrote,

> Our established policy is that land can be acquired from native owners only by the Administration and that, before acquisition, the Administration must be satisfied that the sale is voluntary and that the land is not essential to the native's own needs. Subject to that policy, the Government wishes to see more land available for settlement and the processes of acquisition and leasing made more expeditious. We are taking measures to that end and to promote settlement.
>
> Problems of land use extend to the use made of it by the natives. More extensive measures should be taken for the improvement of village agriculture to ensure more stable and more varied food supplies and for the production of additional cash crops from which the newly acquired needs of the villagers can be satisfied. The work in village agriculture and husbandry must keep pace with any measures for the acquisition of land. In other words, the use of land must be considered by the Territory Administration as a problem covering the total lands and the total population of the Territory.

Up to that time the lands problem had come before me in unrelated bits and pieces. In Port Moresby in 1951 it was impressed on me that the big task in hand was the 'restoration of titles'. That meant titles held by expatriates. A great part of the Lands Department records had been lost in the war and, because a large proportion of the alienated lands had been in the coastal areas overrun by the Japanese and subsequently devastated in military operations, private documents had also been lost and landmarks obliterated. It was said that for most of the information the Administration was depending on the phenomenal memory of Holmes, who had joined the old New Guinea service in 1923, been Secretary of Lands in that service from 1932 until the war and returned in 1946 to become Secretary of Lands in the Papua and New Guinea Provisional Administration. He was supplementing the lands office records from his own personal knowledge of ownership and pre-war transactions in alienated land. I can understand the circumstances which meant that in the post-war years up to this time most of the administrative efforts had been in reconstituting the departmental records and restoring lost titles. It was a work mainly benefiting the Europeans and not touching on fundamental lands policy.

About the time I became Minister, Holmes had the misfortune to be involved in a forced landing of a light aircraft in the jungle, escaping miraculously from the tree tops but seriously injured. In July 1952 he was obliged to retire. He had done good work on a narrow front and, as the outcome of this work, the New Guinea Land Titles Restoration Ordinance was made in 1951 and under it C. P. McCubbery[21] was appointed Commissioner of Titles in February 1952.

Holmes had not been able to pass on to me any understanding of the broader issues of lands policy. During his incapacity and following his retirement there was a period in which I was receiving little advice from the Administration about lands.

Lambert was seized of the problem but saw it mainly against the background of his Australian experience. Largely owing to his prompting, we obtained the appointment of a Director of Lands from outside of the Territory in the person of D. E. Macinnis,[22] a well-trained and experienced lands officer and solicitor. In the face of very great difficulties, amid a complexity that he had to discover for himself, he worked prodigiously hard. Holmes had done well in trying to complete the necessary task of rebuilding the pre-war lands administration. Macinnis was the true builder of the post-war lands administration.

Nevertheless, coming straight from a wholly different Australian setting, it took Macinnis a year or two to thread his way through some of the complexities and peculiarities of lands in the Territory and to be able to assist me to shape policy. With proper respect to both Lambert and Wilson, I doubt whether either of them ever freed himself from the habits and outlook of a very strong Australian specialization in land settlement questions and I owed more to Macinnis than to them in making decisions on land questions, and Macinnis understood more clearly and accepted more fully my ideas on policy than they did. They had a prior interest in land settlement and perhaps part of their handicap was in thinking of land settlement as the chief, if not only, entrance to the problem of lands administration. The basic problem, as I see it now, was land tenure and land use in a deeper sense than land settlement.

Meanwhile, having received my first impression from Holmes of the priority to be given to 'restoration of titles', I paid my first visit to the Northern district of Papua in 1951 and received deputations from native leaders who wanted to be given back land that they claimed had been wrongly 'sold' to the Administration in former years. The lingering resentment and sense of injury in a new generation at having lost their lands to the Administration for an inadequate 'payment' in kind in past years—a payment made in some cases to a person who may not have had the right to sell the land—became even more marked when I went to the Gazelle Peninsula. It was hard for a newcomer to distinguish the rights and wrongs of the cases which were being pressed for greater compensation in money (rather than goods) for land 'purchased' from the natives by either Germans or Australians in past years or for the return of the land to those who now claimed it. It was plain that these disputes or grievances over land already alienated had become more acute with the progress of agriculture and the movement into cash cropping. People were now coveting what they had previously disregarded. In the Gazelle Peninsula in particular, it was also evident that any claim to a right to a piece of land would raise many counter-claims, native against native, native against European (or Chinese) land-holder, both native and non-native against the Administration, and, in the case of disputes involving Chinese, some social animus of native against Asian. The Tolai, or sections of the Tolai, who urged that Europeans had 'stolen' their land, were also charged by other local peoples with having themselves 'stolen' the land from other New Guineans. These early representations and disputes over land tended to focus my attention on the need to establish and to register the ownership of land which was not the subject of recognized titles.

My next early introduction to land problems came in discussions with those whose function it was to promote agriculture and forestry or to control urban housing and industry. They were all up against difficulties in obtaining land of the kind they wanted in the places where they wanted it. There was much coveting of land to use it for better purposes. District officers and others charged with the task of obtaining land for some necessary purpose told me of the practical difficulties they encountered in identifying owners and in negotiating a purchase from them.

This administrative advice confirmed that the registration of native ownership of land was one of the major tasks. This was also urged upon me by Murray. Neither of us foresaw at the start the immensity and complexity of the work that would be involved.

As the outcome of work done before my time, the Native Land Registration Ordinance was made in 1951 and Ivan Champion, a veteran officer of the Papuan Service, was appointed by me as Chief Native Lands Commissioner. He was given the assistance of two other commissioners and they started their work of identifying owners and registering ownership with a great deal of earnest encouragement from me. It took me a few years to wake to the full scale of the difficulties to be overcome in this work and the futility of a large part of their labour. My main delusion was in placing too much hope on the outcome of this phase of lands work in helping to overcome the basic problems.

At that stage, 1951 and 1952, not much work had been done by anthropologists on land questions or, if it had been done, it was not readily available to the layman. We did not then have the benefit of the more comprehensive work done in the late fifties and sixties. Personally I can remember being made aware by conversations with our own field officers and missionaries that a native claim to rights over land might be of various kinds. One person or group of persons might have the right to make a garden on some ground and another native or group of natives might have usufructuary rights over the same ground. We knew there were different ways in which such rights might be handed on from one generation to another. This scant knowledge led us to be concerned with the problems that would arise when, under our encouragement, the native people started to establish tree crops such as cocoa and coffee, which required some harder work in preparing the ground and planting, which did not come into full fruiting for several years and which stayed in one plot instead of being shifted from patch to patch with each season. Those who did the work would want the reward and the control over the inheritance of the groves they had established.

All this confirmed our view of the need to establish and to register some native title in native lands. We were not yet familiar with the full complexity of native land-holdings.

The first definite expression of my own opinion on lands matters was made in January 1952. Some proposals had been prepared by the Administration about land settlement (by Europeans) for commercial agriculture. Lambert had taken these in hand rather energetically and improved on them. He drew up a plan for more orderly procedures in acquisition of land, the subdivision into blocks, and their allotment to applicants. I gave a slight check to him saying that I wanted him 'to give the Territory Administration some practical guidance on how to do the job and some energy in doing it' rather than to do the job himself. Instead of approving Lambert's proposals, I said that I wanted to refer them to the Administrator for action, and added,

> At the same time as we are pushing on with land settlement for commercial agriculture, it is fundamental in our policy that equal or even greater efforts are being made by us in the improvement of village agriculture. I will not favour any alienation of native land unless it goes side by side with the better use of the remaining land by the natives. Your proposals should be enlarged to include suitable provision of staff in the Departments of Agriculture and District Services for this purpose and for constant consideration of this question by your proposed Committee. [Minute of 14 January 1952.]

Other aspects of this question will be dealt with more fully in chapter 26, on agricultural development, but in July 1952 I was still expressing concern over this aspect of lands policy. In some instructions sent on 30 July 1952 to Lambert, who was then in Port Moresby, I said that in his talks with Cleland on land settlement he should emphasize the importance I placed on the improvement of village agriculture as 'an essential corollary' to European land settlement, as a means of ensuring a stable food supply and participation by the natives in the development of the Territory, and added, 'It is also directly related to the question of how much land has to be reserved for natives both for village gardens and, over the coming generations, to produce the income which they will need for the raising of their standard of living and for their social advancement.' (Letter to Lambert dated 30 July 1952.)

During the second half of 1951 and 1952, work also proceeded in the Administration and in the Department of Territories on the preparation of new ordinances dealing with lands. Procedures and forms of title rather than any basic questions of policy were foremost in the discussions. The measures were designed as a revision of the previously existing laws in order to bring them up to date with current conditions and practices rather than to change policy. Towards the end of 1952 I was giving the officers 'hurry-up' reminders, but I did not discuss anything fundamental about lands policy.

Both in my memory and in my notes, I find the first indications of a stronger and more direct and more comprehensive interest in lands policy in 1953. In connection with some reports about the use of land in the upper Bulolo valley, I asked the Department to prepare for me a summary showing the extent of the present alienation and the various uses of land, future development policy, the prospective European and native populations and the prospective activity of both. (Minute of 16 April 1953.) On 14 May, commenting on some suggestions made at the time of assent to the Lands Acquisition Ordinance 1953,

I wrote, 'It is not policy to extend the power of compulsory acquisition of native land.'

My major step and my real awakening came as a result of the rapid growth of European settlement in the highlands. To put my action in perspective and to relate it to my slow introduction to the lands question, I must say something about my first visits to the highlands.

I first saw the highlands in June 1951. We flew in to Goroka in a DC3. About two thousand people were at the airstrip, the men decked out in elaborate head-dresses and not much else. The bones through the septum of the nose and the coloured designs on their faces gave them a ceremonial air. I thought that they were a welcoming party arranged for a ministerial visit but was told that this finery and display were normal and that the crowd was just the daily assembly of strip-squatters who had come in the hope of seeing another aircraft on the ground.

George Greathead[23] was district commissioner. As we wandered through the crowd, he explained through the occasional pidgin speaker that I was 'No. 1 bilong Sydney' and Murray was 'No. 1 bilong Moresby'. When this was turned into their own talk, they looked puzzled for a time and then some confabulation among themselves was translated as a question why I had come. The answer was that I had come from the Australian Government to see how they were getting on. There was more confabulation. Then one spokesman made what sounded like a speech. Translated it said in effect, 'That's all right, but what about taking some of us down in the aeroplane to see how you are getting on. You come up here but we never go down there.' Greathead told me that this was a common sentiment. Very few of the hundreds of thousands in the highlands had even been to the coast. None had been to Australia. They were curious to know where we had come from and in addition there seemed to be a notion that if we came to look at their land, it was only polite on both sides that they should return the visit. I made a mental note to explore the value of visits by New Guineans to Australia. Local Administration was not in favour of it and, as I jotted down at the time, feared that the people would be 'spoiled' by such a visit if it were made too soon.

The township of Goroka was small—about three timber houses for Administration people, some native-material huts for the Administration offices, police quarters and calaboose on the little plateau above the town site, a hospital built of native materials a mile or so farther away and, among some other huts, a curious little timber frame house of two storeys where Jerry Pentland[24] lived. A few miles out of town, on his farm, was a somewhat similar small two-storey house where Jim Leahy lived. We had a men's dinner there on the first night —Leahy the host, Murray, Lambert and myself—the numbers being kept to four because that was all his bachelor dining-room would hold. In the evening all the Europeans came out for an evening party in the open air, just sitting around yarning and having an occasional drink and something to eat.

It was a pleasant balmy evening, the company was very friendly and relaxed. Someone remarked that it was the biggest gathering they had ever had in Goroka. They meant by that the biggest gathering of Europeans. They counted heads. There were twenty-one, nine of them being from the party travelling with Murray and myself. They said that 'everyone' was there, except a New Australian medical assistant who was on duty at the hospital in town and was acting as baby-minder for the white children, most of whom belonged to the Greatheads. The European rush into the highlands had not yet started.

Greathead was a quiet, good and resolute man. His dedication was wholly to the indigenous people. Talking of the future, he talked of the way in which they might be encouraged to improve their gardens to produce marketable vegetables for sale on the coast, to grow more passion fruit so that some pro- cessor might come in and create a bigger market for it and, with this gradual introduction to a cash economy, to pass to growing coffee. A small start had already been made in coffee growing by one enterprising native man. Great- head thought too of doing something to improve their breed of pigs and to raise the levels of nutrition by bringing in new crops.

On subsequent days I flew alongside him for hours in a light aircraft over the surrounding country, looking down from a low level on the villages, on the mountain ridges, on the wide valleys of the Wahgi. He told me quietly of one situation after another, speaking with care, exactness and moderation. Although at that time some European settlement had begun, the thought and care in his mind as he looked towards the future was for a region in which the principal change would come through the advancement of the indigenous people rather than through a major incursion of Europeans. He was familiar in general terms with the problems of land tenure and the risks of alienation of land from the native occupiers. I found him very well informed about the indigenous social structure, but both careful and modest in the expression of his views. I learnt a great deal from him, both in basic information about the highlands and regarding the broad shape of the problems of administration to be faced here. Greathead had perhaps more influence on me than anyone else in matters relating to the highlands, partly because he was the first person who revealed the situation to me with care, clarity and exactness and because he was so patently good and never pushed either a theory or an interest of his own. It was a matter of regret to me personally and a loss to the Administra- tion when he resigned from the service, following the death of one of his children in circumstances that led him to think that he had received less consideration than he might reasonably have expected from the heads of the service. He was later employed by private interests in the highlands and I continued to enjoy occasional conversations with him on visits to that part of the Territory.

After this initial visit to Goroka, I saw little of this desirable part of the highlands again until early 1953. With my preoccupation with other urgent matters, I did not give close first-hand attention to changes in the highlands. Greathead has been succeeded as District Commissioner of Goroka by a young and energetic officer, Ian Downs.[25] On all sides I heard good accounts of his work. He was much praised by Cleland. The highlands were said to be going ahead in fine style. Then my suspicions were aroused by a certain glibness in talk about 'economic development'. On the one side this seemed good. The establishment of a passion-fruit processing plant by Cottee's seemed only to have raised questions of a fair price for the fruit and those questions were settled. The native people were getting a cash crop.

The real problem came over land and then over roads. The lands branch of the Territory Administration was beset with various problems beyond the capacity of its officers to handle. A land settlement board, which had been set up in Port Moresby in 1952 to co-ordinate the work of all departments concerned in land development was being side-stepped. In the highlands, partly because of the energy and self-confidence of Downs and partly because of the inability of the Lands Department to handle the problem, a situation had grown up in which anyone wanting land just saw the district commissioner. The rush into coffee growing by Europeans began. The district commissioner was a bustling man dedicated to the 'progress' of his district and proud that it was making faster 'progress' than any other district. What was happening was that the prospective coffee grower went up to the highlands to get some land. Sometimes he spotted the bit of land he wanted and had an informal talk with the villagers, offering allurements, and then went and told the district commissioner that he had found some land and the natives were willing to sell. In other cases he went to the district commissioner first and asked if there was land to be had and was directed to various areas that might become available or that the district commissioner had already bought from the natives in anticipation of a growing demand for land. Strictly in conformity with policy, land could only be acquired from the native owners by the Administration and could only be acquired if the native owners were willing to sell. Strictly in conformity with policy, no acquisitions were to be made in disregard of the present and prospective land needs of the native people themselves, but in fact we were back to the days of 'Have a yarn with the district commissioner and he will fix you up.' In practice the district commissioner, with the best of intentions and with an undoubted idea of bringing benefits to the native population, had become a promoter of settlement. He was urging his officers to buy land, which really meant inducing natives to sell land, as one of their main duties, he was making a rule-of-thumb decision of his own on how much land the natives needed for their own use, and then he also decided which of the European land-seekers should have this or that block. This inevitably meant the encouragement of 'good types' and the discouragement of 'the sort of chap we don't want'. Downs was the 'father' of the highlands. I should like to make it plain that there was never the faintest suggestion that he had ever acted without the highest motives of public service and the highest standards of probity. Indeed I found a certain innocence in the way in which he failed to see that such a method of handling so valuable a property as coffee land exposed the Administration and individual officers to unfair risks. He also did not appreciate the points I made about lands policy being the responsibility of the Administration and of the Australian Government and not only of the district commissioner.

Downs was not one of my admirers. Although I thought him something of a prima donna, I valued very highly his services. He was one of the few senior people with energy. He had a real dedication to his work. He was closely in touch with the native people and kept their interests at heart. He was a good first-contact district commissioner.

Downs had grown up in the service when district commissioners were the local rulers of a district. Even a patrol officer was the whole of government authority in his post. Downs was unfamiliar with the rest of the administrative machine and he could not always see a relationship between his own local endeavours and a wider programme for the whole Territory. His work was self-centred and so this zealous, energetic, capable officer, acting on his own interpretation of lands policy, was actually helping to promote a land-grab that seemed to me to be very dangerous, but he was greatly admired by the people around him and highly praised by the Administrator as his best district commissioner. I was not understood at first when I took a less enthusiastic view of the 'progress'. I was quite unpopular when I checked it.

What was happening and what I was determined should not go on was that the Europeans were getting all the best coffee land; they were grouping themselves in very pleasant enclaves; the native people were being left far behind and looked like having a future only as houseboys or labourers for white settlers, or the growers of small cash crops to be sold cheaply; it was doubtful whether the needs of the heavy native population for nutrition, health and social welfare were being fully foreseen and properly protected. Perhaps mistakenly, for I then had no first-hand knowledge of Africa, I referred to it as a 'Kenya situation'.

By this time the Lands Department under Macinnis had begun to gain some competence in lands administration although it was still very much under strength; the Departments of Agriculture, Forests and Health had shown broad interest and a more comprehensive approach to problems of the use of Territory resources and the needs of the indigenous people. I decided that they all must have a say in the allocation of lands. We were also moving further into the administrative reforms under which I had made district commissioners responsible to the Department of the Administrator—the rough equivalent of a Prime Minister's Department—instead of being in their own exclusive department, and I was requiring them to accept responsibility for the overall observance of government policy. I used these structural reforms in introducing a new system of applying lands policy.

During the public controversy over the check I gave to land distribution in the highlands, there was much misrepresentation by interested parties of what we were trying to do. I need not revive the bitterness.

While I was becoming disturbed over what was happening in the central highlands, I was also becoming disturbed and uncertain over lands policy generally. On 3 August 1953 I reminded the Administrator that I wanted as early as possible his proposals on improving the work of registering native lands and added,

We must take early and effective action to give reality to our professions. It should also be clearly understood that, much as I want to see development in the Territory, I will make any further granting of land to any European contingent on (i) a decided improvement in our present measures to raise the standard of native agriculture and (ii) more rapid progress in the registration of native lands. The position in respect of both is far below the standard necessary. I am considering the need to suspend any further acquisition of native land in any circumstances unless there is an improvement. Please re-submit with a submission on that particular point on 30 September next.

On the following day I wrote a stronger note for the personal attention of Lambert and Cleland. I said that the effect of my minute was intended to be that all acquisition of native land would cease on 30 September unless in the meantime I could be convinced that effective action was being taken for agricultural extension work among the native villages and for the registration of native lands. I referred to the 'total inadequacy' of the plans for the work of the Native Lands Commission and to my opinion that there had been no more than 'a token effort' on both matters.

As I hoped, this minute scared the Administration. The Administrator replied on 18 August explaining and justifying what was being done and questioning the relationship of my two conditions to land settlement. I said I was not impressed by his reports. I spelt out the earlier expression of my views into a firm instruction:

> Any increase in non-native land settlement can only take place if at the same time we are taking steps to ensure that the natives can and will make better use of the land remaining to them.
>
> An essential element in the administration of our lands policy is the work of the Native Lands Commission. Measures for the improvement of village agriculture and the registration of native land are to proceed side by side with and at the same time as acquisition of land from natives. This means that a balance has to be kept between the progress made in each of these measures . . . In my considered opinion they are not at present in the desired relationship to one another. To adjust this relationship the acquisition of native land has to be slowed down; the measures for the improvement of native agriculture have to be increased; the work of the Native Lands Commission has to be given some chance of making reasonable progress. As regards the improvement of native agriculture, it is essential that the activity should take place not only in old-established areas but also in any new area where land is being acquired from the natives. [Minute of 8 September 1953.]

At the end of the month I received a better memorandum from the Administrator. The stirring up had done some good. I minuted the papers to the effect that it would be a matter for the Administrator's own careful judgement how the parallel lines of policy were to be kept in the proper relationship one to the other. He should report to me in three months' time on the progress made. (Minute of 1 October 1953.)

In all these matters the weight of advice both from the Department and the Administration favoured an easier policy in respect of the acquisition of native lands in order that agricultural development by Europeans might be facilitated. They gave the economic development of the Territory a higher priority than I was prepared to give it at that stage. The basic difference between the Administration and myself was probably one of judgement on method, not one of intention. My judgement was that if the amount of land left to the native people was reduced without an improvement of native farming, there would be harmful results in a fall in the native production of food both immediately and, after a growth in population, in the longer term. There could be further harmful results in limiting the opportunity of the native people to participate in the economic development and the higher standard of living resulting from it. My thinking on these matters was very much influenced by an opinion that, with the bringing of peace and better health services, the expectation of life would rise, infant mortality would fall and the numbers of indigenous population would grow. Furthermore I was very sensitive to the belief that loss of land would breed animosity among future generations. The native people should have preserved for them some capacity to make their own decisions on the use to be made of their resources. I also had a view, perhaps less persuasive, that acquisition of more land from the natives was the easy and obvious way out for the European and allowed the Administration to avoid the harder task of doing better with the land it already had.

Towards the end of the year I found occasion to scold the departmental officers again. John Willoughby,[26] one of Lambert's assistant secretaries, had approved an article on economic development and written about the availability of land for the potential settler or investor and the way in which officers would help them to get it. I wrote that the statement in the article on lands policy was 'incomplete and unacceptable' and continued,

> There are definite and early limits to the taking up of land in the Territory and consequently to the extent to which all officers 'go out of their way' to encourage settlement. It has been repeatedly made clear by me that these limits are set by the overriding considerations of native welfare. The effects of the alienation of land and the settlement of land on native welfare are the prime determinants of land policy and this must set limits to the activities of the Lands Department.

I asked that this minute be sent to the Administrator and Director of Lands, also reminding them of my requests for regular reports on acquisition and expressing appreciation of 'the very noticeable improvement in the methods and procedures of the Lands Department under Mr Macinnis'. (Minute of 5 December 1953.)

Other indications of resistance in the same quarter are given in minutes in March and April of 1954. In the March minute I asked departmental officers in Canberra to

> refrain from any action which might embarrass Mr Macinnis in the difficult task which the Government has laid upon him. Our objective regarding the methods of land grants is to establish an orderly and just system and to end the possibility of land-grabbing or undue favouritism, as well as loss of control over land policy which might be the consequence if the old methods continue to be followed . . . It is the Government and not the land-seeker which should be the master of the granting of land in Papua and New Guinea. Unless our procedures and methods make this a matter of routine we would lose control over the carrying out of established policy in regard to land. [Minute of 11 March 1954.]

In the same minute I advised the Department to get on with its work on the preparation of a new lands ordinance, the completion of which 'is at the present moment a more urgent task than any attempt to stimulate the land-seeker'.

One of the earliest fruits of the new methods of orderly land settlement was the plan for the Markham Valley. A soil survey was made, the present and prospective needs of the native population discussed with District Services and Health, the valley divided into agricultural and pastoral leases, plans made for road and bridge building and the land thrown open for application in planned stages. I have longish notes of personal discussions with Cleland and Macinnis in Port Moresby in February 1954 on this project.

The best way I can recapitulate what I did is to quote again a long letter, in clarification of policy, that I wrote to the Highland Farmers and Settlers' Association on 11 October 1954. After it had been received by the association the letter was also issued as a public statement dated 21 October. At the outset I stressed that the basic policy of respecting native ownership of land had not changed. An instruction had been given that the Territory Lands Department was to handle all lands questions and was being strengthened for that purpose. The process of lands acquisition in the past had been 'somewhat haphazard' but in future the procedure would be such that all relevant factors would be considered at a senior level by all the departments concerned. Instead of acquisitions being made at the initiative of the European land-seeker, the Lands Department was to give first attention to areas of land adjacent to exist- ing services and facilities and it was instructed to examine more closely the lands it already had before moving out to new acquisitions. Until we knew more about native claims to ownership of land, we had to proceed carefully and try to learn more about the nature of native title to land. 'It may be that, in the future,' I wrote, 'the needs of an expanding native population may not be met by inheritance in the traditional system of tenure and we may have to keep in mind the possibility that some of the natives themselves may require land under a European form of tenure.'

It was also apparent, I continued, that any question regarding the present and prospective needs of the native people for land was related to the way they used their land. The calculation of native needs had to be related to changing conditions. A clear instruction had been given that measures for the advance- ment of native agriculture had to go side by side with and keep pace with measures for European settlement. When for any reason the advancement of native agriculture was lagging, the acquisition of land should be slowed down.

I then developed my own philosophy:

> I believe that, for the sake of a successful outcome of Australian adminis- tration in Papua and New Guinea, with a free, close and permanent asso- ciation with the indigenous peoples for many generations to come, we have to be very careful in the present generation to keep a balance between the development of the country and the advancement of the natives. If we do not, we will find that in the course of time the native people will be sub- ordinated to the needs of industry, or, on the other hand, that they will develop interests and needs which there is no means of satisfying. In either case there will be discontent and unrest. Hence the pace of development is necessarily related to the pace of native progress towards civilization. The administration of lands is the chief means by which this balance can be preserved, and it will be consciously used for that purpose, either to speed up or to slow down development to keep it in close relationship with the changes taking place among the native peoples. One of the chief responsi- bilities of officers in the Administration, in all departments, is to watch that balance.

Regarding the allocation of land, I said that it was our responsibility to ensure that it was 'disposed of equitably according to well-established procedures without favour to one land-seeker above another'. Land should be advertised publicly as open for application, and applications should be dealt with impartially by a land board. It was also our responsibility to ensure the effective use of land granted. Therefore the Lands Department had been instructed to make a land-use plan before advertising blocks for application. Finally I summarized the instructions I had given:

(a) The further acquisition of land should be supervised by the Lands Department, acting in consultation with the Departments of District Services, Health, Agriculture and Forests regarding present and prospective native needs and the best economic use of any land acquired.

(b) Land held or acquired by the Administration should be examined by the Lands Department, in consultation with the other departments concerned, to determine the best use to be made of it, and a land use plan should be prepared.

(c) Land available for disposal in accordance with a land use plan should be advertised and applications for it should be considered by a Land Board.

I inherited a basic policy of preserving the land for the indigenous people and limiting the alienation of land to what was required for necessary public purposes and economic development. I was stricter on these limits to further alienation than any of my advisers or my predecessors wished. I also prevented any direct negotiation, let alone direct sale, between the native land-owner and the expatriate land-seeker. Yet at the same time as we were trying to preserve the land jealously for the original owners, we were shaping a practice that would eventually require us to obtain land to meet the needs of the landless indigenes, or those native people who, for commercial or agricultural reasons, might not want to use the land they already had but land somewhere else. We were forcing transformation without thinking enough about the ways in which a basic social and economic change, namely in land ownership, could best be made.

If all our other aims were to be achieved, there would have to be enormous changes to rights in land. There had to be an end to the almost perpetual disputation about land that went on year after year in all parts of the country and had been apparently going on long before white intrusion into land matters. There would have to be a change in the basic native concepts of rights to use, occupy or cultivate land. There would have to be changes in the methods of land use, particularly in the practice of shifting cultivation. There would have to be transfers of population more rapid than the slow pressures of population moves in ancient time and a means by which a new population got access to land by some method other than stealing it from the people whom they displaced. There would have to be a firmer delineation of boundaries. They would have to have a recognized and transferable title.

More essentially all these changes would have to be understood, recognized and accepted by the indigenous occupiers and claimants to land. In working out lands policy, far more deeply than in questions of law and order, education, health, and economic development, we were disturbing an old order and could not always show the immediate advantage of doing so, and we kept on assuring the people that in fact we were not intending to disturb it but were protecting the old order.

In our own countries, most great disturbances in land occupancy and claims have been carried out somewhat harshly. The enclosure movement, the industrial revolution and the urbanization of Britain took place with little regard for the rights or the comfort of those who were displaced or disturbed. In the Soviet Union, after the revolution, there was scant tenderness for those who owned or occupied the farm lands, and a theory took precedence over human life. In Papua and New Guinea we were starting a revolution—and before long most commentators were saying the revolution was too slow—but we were still not facing the consequences of a revolution. In the early years of my ministry my lands administration was protective but not constructive (see chapter 27).

I do permit myself some satisfaction at what I prevented, if not in what I achieved. As the time of independence approached, a senior Australian diplomat visited Papua and New Guinea and had talks with the Chief Minister, Michael Somare. It was reported to me that the Australian said to him, 'At least you can enter on self-government without any fear of having to argue with an Ian Smith in New Guinea. Do you know why? Simply because of Paul Hasluck and nothing else.' Somare told me this himself when he called on me in Canberra.

[13]

ECONOMIC DEVELOPMENT

What I shall say here about economic development may be misunderstood unless it is read against the background of the situation in the Territory between 1950 and 1956 when we were making first contact with hundreds of thousands of highlands people who had little previous knowledge of white ways and little direct experience of coastal conditions except when they went to plantations as native labour. In the early post-war years there was no single economic system for the Territory. Most of the native inhabitants lived in a subsistence economy growing what they ate and having a limited and seasonal barter trade. A cash economy was largely built around European enterprises and only a minority of the indigenous people in long-established coastal centres had any share in it. Even in the Gazelle Peninsula a 'big man's' treasure house containing great hoops of shell money threaded on fibres was a more significant element in a village fiduciary system than a bank or the Administration Treasury.

In that situation I was unable to think about economic development without thinking about the prior problems of food supply, native labour and lands policy. After early visits to the country, I found some of the papers prepared at Canberra for a planned economy and the attraction of Australian enterprise somewhat unreal. In economic matters I turned away from the lead given by Spender.

Concern about the food supply had a strong influence on me. This was due in part to my reading of the report of the New Guinea Nutrition Survey Expedition of 1947. The report convinced me that one of our earliest tasks was to introduce new food crops and to take other measures to improve the diet of the people. My concern was also due in part to the strong view I formed that a growth in population and higher standards of nutrition, as a consequence of the success of the policies we were applying, would create big additional demands for food.

A further fact that worked on my mind was that in early post-war Papua and New Guinea, with limited opportunities for export trade, the importation of food had greatly increased. We could improve the terms of trade by growing more of our own food in replacement of imports as well as by increasing our exports. In the search for gainful occupation for those people who were beginning to move from a subsistence economy to a cash economy, one of the readiest markets would be found in replacing imported foodstuffs.

Thus food took a prominent place in my thinking about economic development and influenced my policies on alienation of land and recruitment of native labour. The opinions I formed about lands policy and native labour in turn also helped to confirm my views on the promotion of agriculture.

This bias was accentuated by the strong views I held on two other subjects. One was the necessity for indigenous participation in all economic enterprise for the sake of the long-term structure of the ownership of economic activities. The other was the wisdom of avoiding harsh disruption of indigenous social organization and any sudden breakdown of social cohesion and discipline.

I saw plainly that an independent country would need an economic foundation for its independence and, as will be shown a little later, I followed various avenues in search of economic development, but I believed that economic development had to be selective and that the measurement of its success would be in the social consequences as well as in the statistics of export production.

I took it for granted that, for a generation or so, services, utilities, amenities and the whole economic infrastructure would have to be provided by Australia and not from the earnings of the Territory itself. Perhaps eventually the Territory would be able to service long-term debts for such necessities, but even that would require Australian support.

My reference to the growth of population may need some elaboration. The patrolling in uncontrolled areas had disclosed a larger population than had hitherto been enumerated. In a very short period we moved from estimates of a population of 1·3 million to a guess of 2 million. The health measures and our determination to do a great deal more than we were doing led to an assumption of rapid growth in population. One informed guess was that the average expectation of life in the Territory was about thirty-two years. If this were true, and if we raised the expectation of life by ten years, crude mental arithmetic suggested that in one generation of thirty years, hundreds of thousands who were expected to die would still be living. At the other end of the scale, if we lowered the very high rate of infant mortality—in some places 300 per thousand births—the annual increment from natural increase would be greater. The Department made various predictions of a great increase in the population of the Territory and I planned on the assumption that it would be sure to take place.

Moreover such moves towards other economic activity as were being made and the move from subsistence to a cash economy would increase the demand for food from those who did not produce food themselves. Already the minority who had been withdrawn from village life to work as native labour were compulsorily receiving their food on a ration scale (including meat and rice or wholemeal flour and other foods unknown in most villages) that raised their standard of living and was likely to create a demand for such foods in the future. Already other people who were in touch with trade stores were acquiring, either by cash or exchange, commodities of a more diverse range than their own gardens or the jungle yielded. Already some of the officers administering the recruitment of labour had warned us against the withdrawal of men from the food-producing round of daily village life lest villages should go hungry or would have to be fed from provisions supplied from public funds.

Uppermost in my mind was the belief that the major problem was to ensure a sufficient food supply for a rapidly growing population at an improved nutritional standard. Related considerations were that no major diversion of land for the production of export crops (either by indigenous land-owners or by white settlers) would be possible until some progress had been made in food production; that labour needed for other developmental projects, including development for export trade, could not be diverted from the effort of sub-sistence until the country was producing food more efficiently; and that the steps towards a viable economy included the replacement of imports, especially imports of food, by local production. Each year the Territory was bringing in larger and more expensive quantities of meat, fish, rice, sugar, milk products, vegetables and fruit, to feed both the expatriates and the indigenes. A great deal of this could and should be produced inside the Territory.

Against this background I stressed repeatedly that the improvement of agriculture meant in the immediate future a high priority for the production of food. This meant primarily better gardening by native gardeners and their use of new crops, new methods and new implements. We should be able to get quick results from a food production programme of this kind, since there would be no complications about access to land, recruitment of labour, difficulties of marketing or delays in payment for the product, and there would be no need to make transfers of population or large acquisitions of land. Many of the people were already gardening on their own land. We should increase the range of crops they grew and raise their efficiency in growing them.

I also had it in mind that in due course larger numbers of native people would be withdrawn from village life into employment on the public payroll in education, health, the public service, transport and service industries, and they would then depend on others to produce their food and would be cash customers for the product.

Taking this view and regarding the economic problem as being more compli-cated than just raising crops for export, I did not give the same urgency to development and land settlement by European immigrants as some of the officers both in the Department and in the Administration did and I saw more limits on it than they allowed.

I had some ideas, which some of my officers and critics thought perverse, about native labour. Some good and experienced people argued cogently about the educational value of native employment, the immediate raising of the standard of living of the wage-earner compared with the villager, and the essential contribution of native labour to the economic development of Papua and New Guinea and the country's eventual economic viability. They believed that if the terms and conditions of employment were properly regulated and strictly supervised and if the rate of withdrawal of the able-bodied younger persons from any district were watched, nothing but good would come. My perversity was that, as conditions were at that time, it seemed to me that much of this 'watching' was no more expert than 'backing a hunch', for we had so little information. The possible social problems of transfers of population were probably more complicated than anything described to me. I also thought that we should be cautious about building up an urban proletariat or disturbing the attachment of people to their own family groupings and the compulsions of their own social system until we had some prospect that the transition to a different condition among various urban communities of landless wage-earners could be made without harm. In this matter I thought in practical rather than theoretical terms. For example one concern was that displaced urban workers should have a form of housing suitable for urban conditions and not merely live in huts on the outskirts of towns. I thought they needed some training in how to run a household under urban conditions and do their shopping wisely. In the longer term I could not regard an increase in the number of native people living in 'boy houses' in towns or on plantations as being any sort of an advance. Even at Government House in Port Moresby and at the residences of district commissioners the customary 'boy house' seemed to me to offer no greater social advancement than a dog kennel. In urbanized villages on the edge of Port Moresby there was reported to be malnutrition mainly because in moving from subsistence to cash incomes families had not yet learnt fully how to make the wisest use of the new foods available to them for money.

Being more of a politician than an economist and being inclined to test historical events more by their social consequences and their effect on the life of the individual than by any yardstick of progress, I also foresaw as undesirable the development of rootless urban communities. I had some ideas, which some of my officers thought odd, if not foolish, about the political effects of an imperfect or deranged social adjustment. I do not think many of them shared my fears about the political difficulties that would ensue in a self-governing country if our administration produced in the coastal towns of the Territory a large, discontented, badly housed, socially maladjusted population of wage-earners who had no other hope of compensation for their efforts, or solace for their discontent, than to get more money to misuse and who had become detached in family and in sympathy from the remainder of the population. This foreshadowing of political disunity was another reason for my cautiousness in respect of large diversions of native labour.

I expressed my view most frequently by simply saying that political, economic and social change had to go hand in hand. I was inclined to slow down economic development until the indigenous people could share in it on a more equitable footing, whether working on their own account or as employees, and I hoped to lessen some of the social and political maladjustment that might complicate political advancement. I made the scale of recruitment and the terms of engagement of native labour subject to the longer-term interests of the indigenous population and not simply a response to the requirements of quick economic development. I shall deal more particularly with native labour policy in chapter 14 and mention it now only to explain my general approach to economic policy.

One of the difficulties in giving effect to views of the above kind is that in public administration if a Minister withholds approval of some proposal, there is a tendency to simplify his decision by saying that he is against the proposal, whereas the decision may have been only that he withheld approval of action of that kind, at that place, at that time or in that form, and would be in favour of action with a similar objective to the proposal but at some other time or place or by a different procedure. My view that care and wisdom were needed in proposals for economic development was read by some officers and some critics to mean that I was against such development. As a consequence of this I had to expend almost as much energy to push people into preparing developmental proposals as I had to expend in ensuring that economic development took place in the way that would create fewest complications. Among political supporters in Australia, still living in the political climate of the 1949 election, I had to face the suspicion of being a socialist because I set limits on enterprise.

In implementing a policy on the development of agriculture we had to lean heavily on the Agriculture Department of the Territory. When I became Minister no permanent head of the Department had yet been appointed to succeed a former director who had retired in 1950, and this indecision was producing further indecision. Murray, as a former professor of agriculture, took a keen personal interest in this field and probably knew more about the subject than he did of any other phase of administration. He had set out to lay a good foundation of experimentation to discover the best crops and the best methods. His own qualifications in agriculture may have made him set high standards for a director. He repeatedly stressed the need to attract some first-class man, and Lambert too had a similar view on the need to look outside the Territory for a candidate. I kept pressing for an appointment, but it was only in September 1952, after Murray had left office, that Lambert reported to me, 'We have made very exhaustive enquiries, but have been unable to interest a suitable person in this position.' He discussed the situation and ended by expressing the view that R. E. P. Dwyer,[27] who had been acting director for some time, was the 'best choice for the position among the members of the Papua and New Guinea Public Service'. On the same day that I received this report, I approved of Dwyer's appointment. (Minute of 10 September 1952.)

Dwyer had been an economic botanist in the pre-war Department of Agriculture in the Mandated Territory of New Guinea and since then had filled a number of positions as an agricultural officer in the Territory. He knew the local conditions and was a widely respected man. In the view of Lambert and myself, Dwyer had considerable technical knowledge, experience in tropical agriculture and a fairly good appreciation of what needed to be done, but he was very weak in expressing himself and in directing others. Indeed when he tried to tell anyone orally, let alone in writing, what he had in mind, he seemed to be going through a sort of obstacle race difficult both for himself and for the listener. We did not want an orator but we did want someone who could convert his ideas to plans for action and, having done so, control and direct the implementation of his plans. His appointment was made with a recognition that he would need a great deal of support from time to time in developing action plans.

In a press statement on 24 September 1952, announcing his appointment, I reviewed the activities of the Department at that time. A lowland experimental station at Keravat (28 miles from Rabaul) was working on cocoa breeding, selection and propagation, manila hemp selection and propagation, entomological research on various pests, production of seed for various crops, and

A river valley in the highlands showing the rugged terrain typical of Papua New Guinea

The Coronation contingent from the Royal Papua and New Guinea Constabulary, England, June 1953

Back row: L.-Cpl Ganki, Consts Duna, Koisen, Katka.

Third row: Consts Dau, Kemai, Kaporis, Sgt Keivi, L.-Cpl Kamai, Const. Augwi, Cpl Ehau.

Second row: Sgt-Majs Kari, William, Sgts Sorovi, Koninoro, Cpl Auwai,
L.-Cpl Wangu, Const. Peiwa, Sgt Daemen, Sgt-Majs Ligo, Saura.

Front row: Sgt-Majs 1st Cl. Merire, Guise, Insps Burns, Sinclair,
Sub-Insp. Broman, Sgt-Maj. 1st Cl. Christian, Sgt-Maj. Sairere.

demonstration and testing of various plants and crops of possible economic importance. The highland experimental station at Aiyura was working on cinchona, coffee, tea and native food crops. A subsidiary station in the Mekeo was working on rice, one at Garaina on tea and one at Bubia (near Lae) mainly on cocoa, fibres and food crops. Livestock stations were located at Baiyer River, Goroka, Erap (near Lae) and near Port Moresby, but their activities were very limited. A small beginning had been made in agricultural extension work. The recital was more impressive than the facts, for all of these stations were handicapped at that time by lack of qualified staff and facilities.

One of our first steps must be to improve the staffing and equipment. We created a number of new scientific and technical positions in the Department of Agriculture and I inaugurated a scheme of agricultural cadetships to produce more graduate officers. Nevertheless progress was slow and the response to recruiting often disappointing.

Some of the slowness in getting results may have been due to my own approach. More active promotion of land settlement by expatriates and large-scale cropping by efficient Europeans might have produced more foodstuffs more quickly than village agriculture did. Lambert and the Department of Territories favoured this and also thought that quicker results would be obtained if they took the matter in hand. I checked them. A minute of 14 January 1952 expressed my point of view. 'As I see it', I wrote after receiving some proposals from Lambert for action on land settlement, 'the problem is basically one of making the Territory Administration do what we expect it to do to carry out Government policy.' After recognizing certain weaknesses in the Territory, I added that what was needed now was to give the Administration some practical guidance on how to do the job and some energy in doing it. The responsibility however should be placed squarely and fairly on the Administration, and the Department should help but not try to take over the job. At the same time I reaffirmed that any land settlement for commercial agriculture had to be accompanied by 'equal or even greater efforts' in the improvement of village agriculture.

I crystallized my views on the second point in a letter dated 30 July 1952 to Lambert instructing him on a visit to Port Moresby to emphasize the importance of the improvement of village agriculture 'both as a means of ensuring a stable food supply and of leading the way to increased production and participation by the natives in the development of the Territory'.

There was also some pressure in the party room in Canberra and from two Cabinet colleagues in favour of soldier settlement schemes in the Territory. I agreed that we should deal fairly with ex-soldiers in the Territory but resisted proposals for encouraging ex-soldiers in Australia to settle in Papua and New Guinea in large numbers. I did not have a hard struggle on this, since the capital cost of establishing an Australian on a plantation would have been much higher than the customary advance made to soldier settlers in Australia.

On the side of food production, a large part of my original interest centred on rice. In a minute of 5 May 1952 I wrote,

> During my recent visit to the Madang and Sepik districts I was very greatly impressed by the way in which many native villages had commenced rice production under the encouragement of district officers. The possibilities

of a very rapid increase in rice production for local use are very great and I should like immediate attention to be given to them.

In view of the general importance of food production, the difficulty of obtaining rice supplies from Australia and the value of rice as a village food, I think we should make a special project of expanding village rice production to some thousands of tons in the Madang and Sepik districts (and any other district if prospects are equally favourable) within the next three or four years. I am certain that this can be achieved. The immediate need appears to me to be for:

(a) Agricultural extension officers of the right type to work in conjunction with District Service officers in encouraging, instructing and supervising village rice production.

(b) Better seed (i.e. better varieties).

(c) Light machinery and hand implements for cultivating and harvesting.

(d) Mills, including simple power-driven mills, for establishment in the larger villages and in the natural centres.

(e) Arrangements for purchase of rice surplus to village requirements for use by the Administration and by plantation and town labour throughout the north coast.

There did not seem to me to be any major transport difficulties involved in the growing of rice for local consumption, nor did there appear to me to be any great necessity for organizing village co-operatives on any elaborate scale as the natives already seem to be capable both of engaging in rice growing and rice selling as individuals and of co-operating as village communities in the purchase and operation of mills.

I instructed the Secretary to collaborate with Territory officers to prepare for my consideration a project that could be pushed ahead vigorously and urgently. I waited until December to receive a departmental submission on the subject and this ended only with a recommendation to adopt certain suggestions 'in principle'. On 19 December 1952 I wrote rather angrily, 'This is lamentable. We keep on drawing up proposals and approving them in principle. I want to approve some action. I want people to start growing rice.' Instead of approving their suggestions 'in principle', I selected a number of proposals from the report and directed that action on them start at once. More agricultural extension officers should be put into the field as soon as possible and there should be an increased use of officers of the Department of District Services. I saw the task as mainly one of agricultural extension and encouragement of native enterprise.

During this period we had also set on foot an investigation of rice production in the Territory by W. Poggendorff of the New South Wales Department of Agriculture. His full report, which I received in October 1952, has been published and is a basic document in the post-war history of agriculture in Papua and New Guinea. While he agreed that the native upland culture of rice—the village rice growing that had attracted my attention—deserved continued encouragement, he recommended that the development of flooded culture on flatlands suited to mechanization on the Australian system should be given the highest priority because of the greater potential returns from a given expenditure of capital and labour. In taking this view, he had in mind developments that would make the Territory a major exporter of rice. With this end in view he thought that 'in the absence of a huge population practising traditional Eastern rice-growing methods by hand labour, large-scale mechanization, including eventually sowing and weed-control from the air, is the only possible means of relatively rapid development.'

The fact of the situation then was that there was no visible prospect of attracting, either from public or private enterprise, the sort of capital needed for this type of development involving large-scale engineering, or of making readily available the vast areas of land needed for such a rapid development of a great rice-exporting industry. My own administrative aim continued to be the more modest one of making the Territory self-sufficient in rice, while at the same time expanding local consumption as part of the general measures to raise nutritional standards, and I saw native agriculture in villages as the quickest and most practical way of reaching this first goal. It also seemed to me to be the best step to take at that time, when one considered the social problems related to any form of agricultural development.

My early hopes in rice were not fully realized. There were various reasons. Some of them lay in the habits of villagers. After the first burst of enthusiasm, they found the year-round industry of planting rice, harvesting, threshing and milling rather more exacting than growing a vegetable crop, pulling it up and eating it. Other reasons lay on the agricultural side. We might have done better if we had been able to get more first-class extension and district officers to encourage and supervise the work. Another strong impediment was the availability of rice in the stores. It was easier both for the officers of the Administration and for the native people to get Australian rice by the ton in bags than to grow and process it. If an officer's main interest is in feeding people, tons of bagged rice in a shed are more convenient than a few hundred acres of untilled land capable of growing rice. Some rather amusing negotiations Lambert and I carried out with the Australian rice growers, and a threat we made to buy rice wherever we could get it in Asia, had resulted in a fairer price and a better delivery, and so our success in improving the terms by which the Territory purchased about 15 000 tons of rice a year from Australia lessened one of the arguments for replacing imports by home production. Incidentally, as the years went by, one of the nutritional arguments for village rice, namely that it was left brown and unpolished, lost its force when, for reasons of status, the native people who advanced to cash incomes coveted white rice as a status symbol because it was what the white people ate.

Besides rice, we did a lot of other work in improving food supply. I encouraged as strongly as I could all moves for more peanuts, grain sorghum, other food grains, improved sweet potatoes and other root crops, and the addition of other protein foods. We tried to improve the strain of pigs, although for breeding from our introduced boars we had the problem of persuading village people, accustomed to 'fencing out' the pigs to keep them from their gardens, to accept the idea that they should 'fence in' the pigs to feed and tend them better and superintend their mating. We also tried to introduce cattle into village areas (as part of larger plans of cattle introduction) and we started fish ponds in the highlands. We embarked on various schemes of trying to improve methods of village gardening. This was a phase of our work on which I was very keen and to which I gave my utmost encouragement.

The weight of departmental opinion and advice was on the side of producing crops for export and, to that end, embarking on planned development with white settlement and white ownership. I was certainly not opposed to promoting production for export and will recount some of the measures I took to that end but, looking back, I think that one of the services I gave to the Territory in the early 1950s was to emphasize the basic importance of food for the people. If it had not been for my obstinacy on this, greater difficulties would have been met in later years and greater hardship and greater inequality suffered by the native people.

My broader views on agricultural development were set out in a press statement I made in April 1952 following a visit to the Territory. After referring to village agriculture and rice-growing, I continued that, while the importance of village agriculture was great, it could not alone meet all the opportunities for agricultural development in New Guinea. I was looking both to the individual settler and to the big plantation companies for a substantial contribution of capital, enterprise and effort to promote tea, rubber, fibre crops, coffee, cocoa and rice. We were trying to build up our experimental and advisory staff to assist such enterprise. I stressed the need to develop plant and machinery for cultivation and processing suited to Territory conditions and also to the problems of access by road or sea. This phase of our work can be best illustrated by reference to particular products.

Tea experiments had started and tea seed had been produced for distribution to private growers. My impression was that, although it had been proved that the tea plant grew vigorously and many cultivation problems had been mastered, there was little knowledge of the processing. On a visit early in 1952 I drank some tea made from Territory leaf. My Parliamentary Under-Secretary, John Howse, gave it generous praise, saying that it had 'a wet taste like the smell of a dog who has been out in the rain'. A year or two later I drank some that was much more palatable.

In early 1952 we began to receive enquiries from established firms who were looking for 'fall-back positions' if conditions changed in tea-growing countries when they gained independence. None of these produced any immediate result. The enquirers sought either permission to introduce Indian or Ceylonese labour or to obtain conditions in respect of indigenous labour that I would not entertain, and they also sought exceptional privileges in respect of land. Furthermore their examination of other problems, especially transport, in the New Guinea highlands at that time left them doubtful about the economics of an investment in tea growing there. We shared expenses with one large tea company in an investigation by an expert. His report, made in mid-1953, found two major drawbacks in labour and in communications and explored the possibility of mechanization of tea growing, necessitating the use of large areas of flat land in the highlands.

Copra was a well-established industry and provided the staple export. Before I became Minister a nine-year contract had been entered into with the United Kingdom Ministry of Food for the purchase of all copra exports surplus to Australian requirements with an annual review of price. Marketing was under the control of the Australian New Guinea Production Control Board. Spender had announced in June and again in July 1950 that responsibility for marketing copra would be transferred from the Board to private enterprise and, pending that transfer, he had given representation on the Board to producers. Nevertheless there was still a strong disposition in the Territory Administration towards control. The representatives of the copra industry themselves were reported to be unwilling to assume responsibility for marketing, and the Ministry of Food contract required a single marketing authority. There was some dissatisfaction in the industry over the price—the returns from the contract being rather lower than the rising world price—but the most immediate path to benefit for the European growers was thought to be the adjustment of the contract price by negotiations conducted by the Production Control Board. Furthermore in April 1951, shortly before I took office and apparently during a period when Ministers were engrossed in elections, the Administrator placed the operations of the New Guinea Coastal and Inter-Island Shipping Service under the Production Control Board. The Territory Administration and the Department of Territories went ahead with legislation to create a Commerce Board with very extensive powers to succeed the war-time Production Control Board. My intervention is best described in a minute of 8 February 1952 telling the Secretary that I proposed to recommend the disallowance of the Commerce Board Ordinance:

I accept the responsibility for some negligence on my part in giving approval to the draft Ordinance on 30 November 1951. My error on that occasion was in accepting the departmental submission dated 29 November at its face value without examining in detail for myself the full implications of the measure.

The Ordinance goes beyond present necessity. A new Ordinance should be limited to
   (a) validating the Acts of the Production Control Board,
   (b) the control of copra as necessitated by the agreement with the UK,
   (c) the machinery clauses.
I do not approve of extending the functions of the board to cover anything except copra. The board should be called the Copra Marketing Board.

Whether or not a delegation is given to the Board in respect of shipping is subordinate to future policy regarding Territory shipping.

My minute gave directions for preparing a draft of a new ordinance and for deletion or amendment of various clauses of the ordinance to make sure that the Board had no powers or functions in respect of Territory products other than copra. In a press statement on 22 February announcing that the Governor-General-in-Council had disallowed the Commerce Board Ordinance and that a Copra Marketing Board Ordinance would be introduced, I said,

The reason why disallowance was recommended was chiefly that the Commerce Board Ordinance contained provisions by which the marketing of any Territory product could be brought under control by the direction of the Minister. I consider that controls should not be imposed unless they are necessary and, at the present time, there is no immediate necessity for control in respect of any Territory product except copra. If and when it should become necessary to consider controls in respect of any other product action can be taken by the introduction of a separate ordinance, thus giving an opportunity to the Territory residents concerned to voice their opinions through their representatives in the Territory Legislative Council.

The Copra Marketing Board was established in March, with its limited functions, and the Production Control Board went out of existence.

In February I also gave an instruction that immediate attention be given to creating a copra stabilization fund in consultation with the producers. (Minute of 22 February 1952.) A sum of £1 500 000, which had accumulated in a fund from export levies imposed by the Production Control Board, was coveted by some planters for immediate distribution. One view was that the contract with the United Kingdom gave promise of stability for the coming years, but my view was that the industry should prepare for a possible fall of prices at the end of that agreement. In May, little progress having been made, I suggested discussions in the Territory with the Copra Marketing Board, the planters' associations and independent producers of copra such as the missions and the native people. (Minute of 2 May 1952.) Lambert had discussions with the two planters' associations, one in Papua and one in New Guinea, in September 1952. Commenting on his report, I expressed the view that the Government should make a definite proposal for a stabilization fund in a form clear enough for it to be submitted to a vote of producers. I rejected a request that the money in the old fund should be handed back to contributors. In Port Moresby on 21 November I announced publicly a proposal to create a stabilization scheme to be administered by a board, the majority of members of which should be elected by producers, and I committed the Government to transfer the accumulated sum of £1 500 000 to inaugurate the scheme.

Rubber was grown only on the Papuan side. Pre-war plantings had suffered from war-time neglect and were of low-yielding strains. The owners to whom properties had been returned were trying to rehabilitate the industry and to expand. The difficulties on which they made early representations to me concerned chiefly native labour, marketing problems, including access to the Australian market, and the need for better planting material. I shall leave the problem of labour for separate discussion. We were able eventually to obtain some high-yielding rubber clones that had been developed in Malaya, thanks mainly to the fact that the Department of Agriculture had developed some high-grade cocoa strains that were coveted by Malayan planters. We bargained one against the other.

Access to the market was more difficult. One approach we made with the full co-operation of the Papuan Planters' Association was to try to improve the product and to standardize the grading of it. This was smoke-dried rubber, mainly used in automobile tyres. I accepted the advice that the best, if not only, hope of disposing of the total yield was in the Australian market and, in a minute of 13 October 1952, instructed Lambert to work towards obtaining the most suitable arrangements for ensuring purchase of the total product in Australia. We faced various difficulties. There was still a reserve of rubber in Australia left over from war-time stockpiles. The Australian tyre industry was itself passing through a difficult trading period and its demands for rubber had been reduced. Other departments of the Australian Government were considering separately the purchase of Malayan rubber for reasons of trade and foreign relations, and a delegation was in Malaya for that purpose. In a further minute of 31 December 1952 I asked my Department to continue to do 'the utmost possible' and to press a case for import restrictions on foreign rubber until Papuan rubber had been absorbed. We had numerous conferences with all the interests concerned. I publicly announced a 'clear objective' of 'an assured market in Australia for all Papuan rubber'.

We eventually succeeded and further reference to the marketing will be made in chapter 26. Except possibly on the question of labour, the rubber planters showed appreciation of what I did to re-establish rubber as a significant element in post-war economic development with an assured market in Australia.

In July 1952 we had appointed C. E. T. Mann, Director of the Rubber Research Institute of Malaya, to visit the Territory to advise on technical aspects of rubber planting and on measures that might be taken to expand the industry. His report, made public in August 1953, was informative and encouraging, and helped in the improvement of production.

While we were trying to re-establish and expand the major primary industries of copra and rubber, we were also looking hopefully towards three new crops—coffee, cocoa and fibres. I valued these because native growers were also producing them. I saw opportunities for the native grower, using his own land and the labour of himself and his family or clan, to grow the crop and deliver the produce to central 'factories' which would process and market the finished product. Such plants could be established either by native co-operative organization under Administration guidance or with native participation in private enterprise. In the early stages the European could also bring immediate benefits. We had one such example in a passion-fruit processing plant, established at Goroka by an Australian firm, which provided an immediate opportunity to the native people by providing a market for a fruit that previously had no market, and giving them their first cash crop with a regular demand.

It was a period of rising hope in money to be made from cocoa and coffee. Most of the development of these crops took place during my time. In 1950–1, only 317 tons of cocoa beans and 33 tons of coffee beans were exported and by 1961–2 the figures were 10 014 and 3444.

I thought there should be more native participation in the growing of these orchard crops as one of the few prospects by which the villager might be able to support a rise in his own standard of living. In the immediate present there was only a handful of exceptional native people who had the interest and skill to manage a new form of cultivation and to handle a crop that could not be consumed immediately but, after harvesting, had to be processed and then transported to some remote place to be sold. We had to move from a system of growing a crop and then eating it or exchanging it in barter for something else, to a more complicated economic system. In particular we had to find means, in a cash economy, of bridging the gap between harvesting and being paid for what was harvested. In some districts, such as the Gazelle Peninsula, where the people had experience of marketing cash crops, we faced the additional problem that those people who might be interested in growing cocoa might not have access to land or a right to establish a permanent tree crop on the land to which they had access. These problems became more acute at a later stage and will be dealt with in chapter 27.

For a time we placed high hopes on a fibre crop, kenaf, which showed good promise as a substitute for jute. The Australian pastoral industry used great quantities of jute for wool-packs, and there was also a big potential demand for coarse fibres for burlap, carpet backing and many similar uses. The kenaf plant grew readily. It appeared to offer great promise as a village industry inasmuch as the crops could be grown seasonally, cut, the stalks mechanically decorticated by a relatively simple process, and the fibres delivered to mills. R. A. Colyer, the head of the long-established trading firm Colyer, Watson Pty Ltd, showed great personal enthusiasm and took the initiative in many of the moves to try to establish the industry. In co-operation with him we promoted an investigation and report by an American expert. Our hopes were not realized. The major reason was that the price of jute came down, whereas much of the early economic calculation rested on the expectation that it would remain high.

During the period when I was grappling with some of these problems of economic development, I had set on foot an inquiry by three academic experts from the Australian National University—O. H. K. Spate (Professor of Geography), C. S. Belshaw (Research Fellow in Anthropology) and T. W. Swan (Professor of Economics). The Commonwealth Bank made available an officer of its Economic Department, D. H. McKenna, to assist mainly with the statistical work. The report was eventually completed in March 1953 and forwarded with a characteristic note from Spate, whom I had the happiness to call a personal friend, expressing his sorrow at the 'prolonged delay' due to circumstances, including his own illness and the perfectionism of Swan, which were beyond his control as convener of the committee.

Partly because of this delay, the Spate-Belshaw-Swan report describes a situation at about the time I took office rather than at the time the report was dated. It also drew heavily on files relating to the period 1947–9, rather than on more recent material available in the Department. Consequently it tells of what I inherited rather than what I did. This fact gave some ground for a departmental criticism, made in a minute to me of 27 April 1953, that there were errors of fact and perspective and that the report brought forth and demolished statements that had appeared more than three years ago and had since been contradicted officially. Nevertheless I found myself in accord with most of the descriptions and the conclusions in the report and it did fulfil the hope, expressed by Spate in a personal letter to me, that 'in certain directions the report might strengthen your hand, both within your own department and in relation to others'.

In the inquiry, Spate worked chiefly on 'Problems of Agricultural Development', Belshaw on 'Native Society and Economic Organizations' and Swan on 'The Market Economy and Public Finance'. There was an appendix, for which McKenna did most of the work, on 'The Social Accounts of the New Guinea Market Economy for 1949–50 and 1950–51'.

Some officers of my department were rather sensitive about the report, feeling that it did not appreciate sufficiently what they were doing, and complained that it was 'academic'. Personally I read it as an analysis of the situation with which we were attempting to deal rather than a criticism of what we were doing. It is certainly a basic document in any study of the post-war economic policy in Papua and New Guinea.

I found in the report much reinforcement of my own thinking, and confirmation of my own judgements on the existing difficulties and dangers in the Territory. The gist is in its final paragraph.

> Our inquiry, conducted along three distinct lines of approach by students of three distinct backgrounds and disciplines, has resulted in a significant convergence of opinion:
>
> (i) An economist reports that, apart from the chance of striking oil, European industry on the whole is making little if any headway, and may even be in a state of slow decline rather than of development. The running down of the staple industries of copra and gold is scarcely balanced by development in new directions, other than the search for oil.
>
> (ii) An anthropologist argues that native society offers a basis for economic organization for productive purposes, through individual enterprise, native co-operatives and looser forms of community development— given the right approach and guidance.
>
> (iii) A geographer points out that the New Guinea terrain does not lend itself to widespread European settlement, but does present many opportunities for the development of native crops (both for immediate consumption and commercial sale, including export). The scope for expansion of European enterprise seems to be mainly in extractive industries, the more highly capitalized secondary industries, and the larger operations of overseas trade.
>
> Our central thesis, then, is that a prosperous New Guinea economy can be built on the foundations of native society, and that this is not only socially the most desirable trend but economically the most feasible. Plans for a vast or rapid development of European enterprise, except in a few limited fields (such as oil and timber) can only issue in frustration and will serve neither native interests nor the commercial and political interests of Australia. In terms of immediate Government action, the Territory's major needs are more roads; a strengthening of the Administration's agricultural work and other developmental services, particularly in the direction of promoting native agriculture; and a thorough-going fiscal reform. These remain urgent needs on any view of the Territory's future.

In elaboration of the reference to fiscal reform as a major need, the report suggested some immediate steps: the abolition of export levies as a means of raising income locally; the introduction of income taxation; placing on a commercial basis some of the services operated by the Administration (harbour services such as stevedoring, postal and telecommunications, electricity and water supply), all of which contained a strong element of subsidy almost solely enjoyed by Europeans; the reconsideration of the subsidies to shipping and air; and an approach to the International Bank for Reconstruction and Development for a loan, for example for transport development projects. My own thinking had also reached out for such measures and already I had become aware of some obstacles in the way.

The report also discussed the annual Commonwealth grant, suggesting that it might be varied from year to year according to 'principles bearing some resemblance to those by which the Grants Commission relates its recommendations to the relative disabilities of particular States', rather than to finance a particular set of expenditure proposals for any one year. I was sceptical about this method. I was not clear about what set of principles would convince both Treasury officials and Cabinet and persuade them to provide more money at that stage in the neglect of the Territory. My pragmatic judgement was that, since the 'needs' were much greater than any funds we were likely to obtain or had the capacity to spend, an annual bid based on 'needs' would give a better result than making a case about our 'disabilities'.

Another suggestion was that the financing of new works projects should be considered separately from general revenue, as in the case of the Australian States, and might similarly take the form of interest-bearing loans to the Administration rather than of grants. This appealed to me but already I had found that, at that stage, any submission to Cabinet to that end would be unlikely to succeed.

The suggestions about putting services on a commercial footing ran into two difficulties. At that time the services, including electricity and water supply, were far from efficient. The first step must be to improve the service; then we could fairly review the charges to the customer. The other difficulty was that all the advantages of open and disguised subsidies were enjoyed chiefly by the European community, including our own public servants, and were regarded by them not as a concession or a privilege but as an essential condition of life in the Territory. Artie Fadden used to say, 'You can't take butter out of a dog's mouth and when your own advisers are the dog it becomes an act of indecency even to mention it.'

One early achievement in this direction however was the improvement of the postal and telecommunications services. I tackled this not as a fiscal reform but to provide an essential service for better administration and for better social and commercial facilities. The post office was in a deplorable state. As recounted in chapter 4, I had defeated the attempt of the Australian Postmaster-General's Department to take it over but, then, I faced the fact that our post office was poorly staffed and badly equipped and complaints were being made all over the Territory about mails being delayed, letters not delivered, telephones not working in the main towns, and the communication on radio schedules to outlying places constantly breaking down.

Fortunately, after one false start, I managed to appoint W. F. Carter[28] as Director of Posts and Telegraphs in 1954. It was one of the best appointments I made. Carter was virtually the creator of the post-war Papua New Guinea postal and telecommunications system. He did a stupendous job and deserves high credit for his service to Papua and New Guinea. Facing difficulties that must have seemed scarcely credible to him against the background of his experience in the Australian Postmaster-General's Department, he went to work quietly, cheerfully, methodically and with technical skill. He was also one of the first to accept fully my own ideas that the indigenous people had to be used to create and to run their own services and he started to recruit and train young officers in all branches. Carter also made a notable contribution in

various public causes to promoting the advancement of the indigenous people
and creating good relationships between them and the expatriates. For myself,
impatient and exacting as I am, the best tribute I can give is that, once Carter
had started the job, I seldom had to worry about the Postal Department again
and only needed to back him in his direction of it.

One other early success was in improving coastal shipping. During war time
most of the coastal vessels had been commandeered, and after the war the fleet
of small vessels continued to be run as a Government shipping service. The
fleet was making heavy losses, which were a charge on the scant revenues of
the Territory, and there were many complaints about the service. The simple
solution of reviving private enterprise shipping was impeded by the fact that,
before my time, the Administration had entered into a strange arrangement by
which the State-owned ships were actually operated by the bigger trading
and plantation companies under terms that gave them an income from running
the fleet, left them no risk of bearing any loss, and allowed them to arrange the
services for their own benefit in disregard of rival traders or unco-operative
planters. There were even allegations to me by individual planters that if they
did not sell their copra or buy their stores through the operating firm, they
would find that the expected coastal vessel did not turn up at their landing-
place. I had many complaints about the service. I was aware of the loss being
charged to our own revenue, and could foresee growing burdens of repair and
replacement.

Spender, highly critical of the strange arrangement made by the Administration, had taken a decision to sell the Territory shipping services to private
enterprise and, soon after taking office, I received a departmental submission
on the ways of giving effect to this decision. In a minute of 7 September 1951
however I said that the achievement of the ultimate aim of selling should be
subordinate to (a) the provision of the best possible transport service, (b) the
protection of the public investment in the existing service and (c) the protection of public revenue. While the weight of evidence under (c) would
incline us to sell as early as possible, the weight of evidence under (a) and (b)
would persuade us to be more cautious. The decision at the moment was not
between private or public ownership and operation but on the best means of
maintaining an essential service with due regard to public finances. Steps to
reduce the losses on the services and to make the ships more attractive to
private enterprise were of more immediate importance than an early sale of the
Government ships. I would not favour any arrangement that handed over
profitable services to private enterprise and left unpayable services to the
Government.

In order to serve these objectives I gave various directions in detail and also
sought the support of a Cabinet subcommittee on shipping. The real progress
towards success came a year later with the appointment of Captain J. H.
Evans[29] as shipping manager of the Papua and New Guinea Commonwealth
Shipping Service in October 1952, and the subsequent withdrawal of the
delegations in respect of shipping from the Copra Marketing Board.

Evans did a very good job of making the shipping service more efficient and,
in the course of doing that, of uncovering and discontinuing some rather odd
little practices. He took a determined but humorous view about the various

dodges and, on visits to the Territory, I shared some of the amusement and learnt a good deal about some of the less orthodox persons and practices in post-war New Guinea.

My main purpose was achieved. In November 1952 we had the first realistic offer for the purchase of some of the vessels and sold seven with satisfactory undertakings on the maintenance of the service. In December 1953 eleven more were sold and eventually we disposed of the whole fleet at prices that pleasantly surprised the Commonwealth Treasury and under conditions that ensured a competitive and improved coastal service.

We were not so readily successful in doing all we wanted to do in improving shipping to and from the Territory. Our ports had limited facilities and there was a good deal of contention about claims to priority in berthing. Other arguments concerned the right claimed by Burns, Philp & Co. to carry all the copra to Australia. This story became entangled in Australian shipping policies and it would be wearisome to tell the ins and outs of discussions that my Cabinet colleague, the Minister for Shipping and Transport, Senator George McLeay, and I had with Australian ship-owners, the Seamen's Union, and overseas ship-owners and various other interests. George McLeay was a cheerful colleague and remained untroubled in any crisis. The difficulty was that one was never quite sure which of the several positions he took up would be the one on which he intended to stand. In Cabinet once, on another matter, dear rubicund George read out some arguments and recommendations, smiled, put his elbows on the table and said in effect, 'That's the stuff my department gave me. Now what I think we should do is . . .' When Menzies said, 'But, George, your name appears on that submission and you made those recommendations', George smiled, quite unabashed, and said, 'Oh, I just signed those to keep McFadyen [his departmental permanent head] from bothering me. What we should really do is . . .' On another occasion, when we were preparing for a meeting, McFadyen, who always spoke at length, presented a case with which I disagreed. I took him to pieces bit by bit with great deliberation and sometimes perhaps rather harshly. After the meeting, when we were alone, I apologized to George for treating his permanent head in that way. George, as cheerful as ever, said, 'I'm glad you did it. You were right. It's better for you to do it than for me to do it. You don't have to work with him.'

We improved and diversified overseas shipping, our task being aided by the improvements we were making at the same time in the Territory in the port facilities and in the more efficient handling of copra by the Copra Marketing Board, but we did not reach as full a success on overseas shipping as I had hoped.

One of the other 'major needs' referred to in the Spate-Belshaw-Swan report was strengthening the Administration's agricultural work and other developmental services, particularly in the direction of promoting native agriculture. As mentioned earlier in this chapter (p. 133), this was one of the first steps I had tried to take. Again I could not get quickly all the results I wanted, almost wholly because of lack of qualified staff and the difficulty of recruiting them. Nevertheless, year by year, we improved.

The last of the 'major needs' mentioned in the report was more roads. Before I discuss this, it is necessary to digress on the problem of public works.

One of my comparative failures was in the field of public works. I saw then and I see more clearly now that it was necessary to build up a strong Territory Department of Works under the Territory Administration, to break free from the control and influence of the Commonwealth Department of Works and to attract more private contractors into the Territory to do work under competitive tendering. I did not succeed in going as far in these directions as I wanted to or as far as, in my opinion then and now, the good of the Territory required. My only excuse is that we were working in a period of unusual difficulty in the whole Australian region. Construction anywhere faced difficulties in shortage of materials, plant, labour and higher skills and in Papua and New Guinea, as in the Northern Territory, we were at the far end of the receiving line. Administratively the Australian Government had not yet broken free from habits and practices in public works that had been formed in war time. It was also a fact of those times that major overseas contractors had not become an important factor on the Australian scene—it was the Snowy Mountains Authority that started the breakthrough—and any idea of attracting them to Papua and New Guinea independently of attracting them to Australia would have been opposed. We also faced strong opposition on the lesser issue of importing materials such as cement directly from overseas instead of from Australian producers, even when Australian producers could not guarantee supplies or quote competitive prices.

The Territory Department of Works was small and weak in plant and manpower. The Commonwealth Department of Works was strong, located at the centre of power and authoritarian. I faced initially pressures to abolish the Territory Department and to leave the Commonwealth Department as the sole constructional authority for Papua and New Guinea. I resisted such a move and ensured the survival of the Territory Department although necessarily accepting an arrangement by which the Commonwealth Department would be responsible for all major works. We did not have adequate engineering and design staff in the Territory and had no prospect then of recruiting them. Local plant and equipment were narrowly limited and we had no prospect of improving them.

The major handicap we faced with the Commonwealth Department of Works was that Papua and New Guinea was regarded by them as just another 'client department', not another country. They fitted our claims for a works programme into a corner of a total Commonwealth works programme, somewhere at the bottom of the list of Commonwealth departments. If only we could have been regarded as having a loan works programme like the Australian States, it would have been better, but instead we were treated as just another departmental claimant on the Commonwealth works programme.

What the Territory needed was a strong Territory works organization, planning its works with close knowledge of local needs and opportunities. Instead it had to limp along with a weak works branch of its own and take what could be allotted to the smallest of the regional branches of the Commonwealth works organization. In our claims for funds each year we had to endure the screening of our works proposals by a committee, on which we were not represented, dominated by a Commonwealth Co-ordinator-General for Works. Our bids had to survive comparison with works to be done anywhere in the

Australian continent, and most other jobs, including the financial allocation to the States, led to greater political advantage and readier engineering recognition than a job in Papua and New Guinea. At a time when Cabinet was not persuaded of the importance of Papua and New Guinea, a Co-ordinator-General of Works (a left-over of war-time construction and the previous post-war government) could not be expected to change his outlook and he was an obstacle we had to overcome and not an agent for advancing Territory policy.

Throughout this early period we faced delays in designing our works, all design being done in Melbourne, and we were perpetually arguing against adjustments that were being made in designs by persons unfamiliar with the Territory and who planned to meet Australian mainland standards rather than Territory requirements. We were perpetually having our estimates of costs lifted to levels where high cost became an argument against doing a necessary work. On some jobs an original estimate might be trebled by the time we had to fit the project into a limited budget. In nearly all cases, after a project had been admitted to the Budget, estimates were further increased so that we had to defer other works in order to divert funds for the completion of a job in hand.

Decisions on the relative importance of works are necessarily related to cost and time of completion. Whereas one might decide to spend a quarter of a million on a project to be completed in eighteen months, one would not select that project if one could have known that in fact the work would cost three-quarters of a million and not be completed for three years. Yet this was the pattern of our experience.

In my view, which possibly few engineers would support, we would have done better at that stage in the Territory's development to design and build on standards of economy, for an initial period of twenty years or so, to meet immediate and urgent needs rather than to aim at permanent and perfect projects. The best was the enemy of the good.

There was a strong tendency at that stage for the Commonwealth Department of Works to undertake as much construction as possible itself instead of letting contracts. One consequence was that it built up in Papua and New Guinea too large a body of white Australian workers on the departmental payroll. They were expensive, not efficient in Territory conditions and in some cases a very bad social influence in the community. The use of white Australian truck drivers, plant operators and lower-skilled tradesmen and labourers was excessive and against our interests. More painstaking attention should have been given to the use of indigenous labour, but this was wholly beyond our control, for the Commonwealth Department of Works was master of its own affairs and sent up a pretty choice collection of white 'drongoes' and social misfits to add to our administrative problems. Even among the best of them the majority were birds of passage.

In our Budget discussions, we faced constantly the argument about 'lack of potential' in the Territory as a reason for not admitting a project to the works programme. At the same time we failed to receive any help in building up the 'works potential' either in the public or the private sector. My own departmental officers, understandably, accommodated themselves to a works programming procedure that they could not alter, and any proposal for a big increase in finance for works always met the arguments from my own department based on fears that too large a 'forward commitment' for works would mean that in future years all new works would be crowded out and our works programme would be 'out of balance'. They were rightly concerned about keeping a proper proportion of 'revotes' and 'new works' in each year's programme and in practice this meant that they tended to set a monetary limit each year on the new projects to be admitted.

I got no encouragement in Cabinet for suggestions that we should have our own loan works programme. My failure was in not being able to break through this situation more quickly. I should have contrived more shrewdly, been more subtly persuasive and been much more obstreperous and insistent. If I had my time over again, this is one field in which I would have forced issues and fought harder than I did. I did not do as well in this as I should have done if I had been a tougher, relentless, bull-dozing Minister and if I had been able to build up separately a better-qualified and better-equipped Territory Department of Works and to attract at an early stage more private constructional capacity in the Territory than I did. The question was of course inseparable from the annual battle for funds. Perhaps my frontal attack in order to get money, in the singleness of its purpose, lessened my chances of success on the flanks.

What I did succeed in doing was to use the Territory Department of Works to a significant extent for housing and minor buildings and gradually to interest more contractors in contracts for residences. When eventually we started on the building of central hospitals, we also took steps to try to induce the successful tenderers, if they were new to the Territory, to stay on for the variety of small works under our control.

The immediate need for roads for inland communication was clear. Everyone had ideas and plans, mostly on a big scale. Two major impediments to doing something about roads were firstly the magnitude of the claims made by advocates of roads and secondly the entrenchment of aviation. The aeroplane had played a notable, romantic and novel part in overcoming the difficulties of inland transportation in the pre-war and post-war years, and a great number of persons were dedicated to aviation to such an extent that they could scarcely contemplate any substitute for it or even any auxiliary to it. Aviation was a proud achievement as well as an established service and had a prior claim for further development.

The advocates of roads all thought on a grand scale and conjured up such pictures of mammoth engineering, with bridges and highways costing millions, that they reinforced the argument that the aeroplane was the most practical and economical form of transport.

The Administrator told me that the Government must be prepared to spend millions. I had to say plainly, 'I have not got a hope in hell of getting millions of pounds for roads at this stage. We have to make another approach.' We did obtain some funds and some engineering capacity to build a few lengths of major road and to improve the largest existing road of economic importance—

that from Lae to Bulolo. For the early years of my term, however, most of our road work was done in other ways using local labour.

There has been some fanciful writing about the origins of this scheme. In fact it began in a conversation between Cleland and myself. I told him again that, for the time being, there was no hope of mammoth expenditures on roads and hence no chance of attracting mammoth engineering capacity to build roads. I recalled an element in Australian pioneering—first a cart-track, then a cleared track, then year-by-year improvement and eventually the major road. I said that, flying over the country, one could see from the air networks of paths from village to village, mostly on the contour lines or by the easiest practicable route. I said that the one great road-building resource that the Territory had was manpower. Let us mobilize the manpower to turn tracks into better tracks and then to pave them, first in the soft places and then on longer stretches. Let us put bridges over the smaller streams by using bush material. Let us get prefabricated material, such as Bailey bridging, for erection by our own engineers at the more difficult crossings. For the time being we might have to use punts or barges at big streams. The rest of the work would be organized by our own staff—the old-time 'road-masters', of whom a handful were still left in the Territory, and the practical young patrol officers. Cleland and I discussed the ins and outs of these ideas for some time. The upshot was a ministerial direction that each district commissioner was to be instructed to encourage and direct the building of roads in his district according to the needs and opportunities of his district, gaining the co-operation of the local people to provide the labour. In the estimates for each district in the coming year a claim should be made by each district commissioner for vehicles, spades, shovels and picks for this work.

This was not novel. District officers before the war and since had customarily required village people to keep tracks open. What was novel was to introduce a Territory-wide policy of road building with native labour at their own villages and to provide funds specially for the purpose. The move forward in this post-war building of light roads was this ministerial direction.

By the end of 1955 we had built over a thousand miles of these light roads as well as done some engineering work of a higher standard on the Lae–Wau road, the Rabaul–Kokopo road and the Port Moresby–Brown River road. The results varied a good deal from district to district according to the energy of the district commissioners and the local opportunities. No single district commissioner was the originator of the scheme, nor was credit for its success due to only one. Some, however, notably the district commissioner at Goroka, had outstanding results.

As early as 30 September 1953 Cleland was able to report that the district commissioner at Goroka, Ian Downs, had crossed the Chimbu–Goroka divide on 25 September at a height of 8000 feet using a land-rover and a weapon carrier, both fully loaded. A press statement on this occasion recalled that shortly after Cleland took up his post it was agreed between him and the Minister that, instead of waiting for the construction of conventional roads by engineers at a cost that would be beyond the capacity of the Territory, the Administration itself should try to pioneer new routes.

An assembly of highlands people gathered at an airstrip

Village potter at work, Aibom, Madang district

Building the first roads: every pebble carted and laid by hand

More modern road building: Leron bridge, Markham Valley

The theory was that, if a commencement were made by constructing a suitable and trafficable jeep track, using local resources of material and labour, such a track would provide communication during a pioneering phase of development and in subsequent years, as opportunity offered and funds became available, these jeep tracks could be converted into roads.

One of the first major pioneering works of this kind was the opening of an access road into the central highlands. In July 1953 the road was traversed for the first time between Gusap (at the head of the Ramu Valley) and Kainantu. The second stage, which had now been completed, made it possible to travel by motor vehicle from Gusap to Mt Hagen, a distance of nearly 200 miles on the map. My statement continued that the measure of this achievement could only be understood by those with first-hand experience of the difficulties of the terrain. The road passed over mountainous country and made use of passes at heights of up to 8000 feet. It involved many crossings of streams and the cutting of benches around steep hillsides in order to negotiate valleys and ravines. The achievement of Downs and the other officers of the Administration showed that the epics of Australian pioneering achievement were being repeated in New Guinea by active and imaginative men.

As intended at the start, in the course of time some of these early tracks became great all-weather roadways, strongly paved and served by permanent bridges. In the early stages, however, this pioneering effort of road building brought its own peculiar problems. The village people, who had built them, rightly regarded them as their roads. The roads helped them to move more freely and more easily with the loads they carried on their backs. They made it possible for Administration officers, with jeeps or motor-cycles, to visit them more often and more readily and for mobile medical services to serve their people. When however Europeans who had done nothing to build the roads started to cut them up with vehicles carrying commercial loads, the villagers naturally began to murmur and to lose their enthusiasm for shovelling dirt and carting stones from riverbeds to keep a road in order.

A minute I wrote on 5 August 1954 records the situation. The occasion of this minute was a report from the Territory about roads in the Eastern Highlands. It included a reference to the 'increase in volume of heavy traffic created by the rapid expansion and development of this progressive district' and this seemed to me to disregard instructions on policy I had given at Goroka in January 1954 when my attention had been drawn to the use of the roads by company trucks. I recalled those instructions as follows:

At Goroka, last January . . . I expressed the view that when roads were built with the co-operation of the native villages and with voluntary village labour, we necessarily must regard the villages as having a special and prior interest in the road. The primary purpose of such roads was administrative, both for the convenience of access they afforded and for the value of the road as a civilizing agent. The co-operation in building and maintaining a road, the use of the road in bringing services to the villages, the establishing of assembly points on it, and the use of the road by natives in travelling and transporting their produce could establish it both as a symbol and as a demonstration of the benefits of Australian administration.

We could not, at the present stage, allow other users to impair the realization of this primary purpose. To take the extreme example, if heavy trucks run by Europeans in commercial ventures were to cut up the roads which we had persuaded the villagers to make for their own benefit, the natives might properly begin to distrust our good faith and also doubt the value of giving their labour free just to suit the Europeans . . . So long as the voluntary co-operation of the villages is a major component in the building and the maintenance of a road, the public use of the road has to be limited. The limits (which in the present stage of development will probably apply to the weight and types of vehicles rather than to the frequency of use) will have to be decided locally by district commissioners, who will pay due regard to those broad administrative purposes indicated in the preceding paragraph . . . These roads are being built with amazing cheapness and speed because of the help of the natives. Their purpose is chiefly administrative and they are developmental roads only in the sense that they provide access. In the course of time, according to the economic need and justification for the work, the access roads will be converted to transport routes by expenditure on metalling them, stronger bridges and so on. At that stage, when public expenditure outweighs the contribution of native labour, the whole nature of the road and consequently the use made of it will change. We have to be careful not to use them for purposes for which they were not designed.

The construction of these hundreds of miles of light roads at so small a cost was a stupendous achievement parallel to the building of hundreds of landing strips for light aircraft. As I moved around the Territory on my frequent visits, I often saw the people at work, swarming in hundreds—men, women and children—on a hillside, digging, rolling boulders aside, carrying smaller stones in baskets. They waved and cheered and called 'arpynoon' as we passed, clustered around when we stopped, and showed their work with pride. Several times, on my visits, I was asked to perform an impromptu ceremony of opening a bridge, perhaps fifteen yards long, by breaking a ribbon of flowers and vines stretched across the track, and no public gathering was ever so gleeful and so proud as those occasions. After accompanying me on one such journey, that veteran political survivor of cliff-hanger elections, Hubert Opperman, said, 'If Australians thought as much of you as these people do, you could win every seat in Australia.'

One of the most thrilling journeys I have ever made was the first journey by car, as contrasted with four-wheel-drive vehicles, from Goroka over the Chimbu–Goroka divide to Chuave. The road climbed thousands of feet on benches cut by hand out of the steep mountainsides. We climbed to the head of each valley to cross the streams where they were narrowest, and snaked along ridges, to gain access to higher valleys. Here and there along the way, where a village squatted on a platform, a jubilant people who had built the road and, in some parts, were still at work on it had gathered in thousands, waving with open hand and spread fingers, smiling and cheering. When we paused at the top of the pass, the mountains were echoing with the yodelling of the songmen who were sending news, by voice, miles ahead of us to tell that we had reached the top and would soon be on our way down. At Chuave an enormous crowd, magnificent in tall head-dresses, had gathered to sing and stamp and shout with joy as the motor-cars—the first some of them had seen—rolled down the road.

Equally thrilling was the experience, come by chance in the Southern Highlands a year or two later, to be on the spot when a bridge was being commenced. A great tree trunk weighing hundreds of tons was being hauled by ropes of jungle vine by the strength of hundreds of men and then finally slid into position by a shrewd use of gravity to become one of the main bearers of a bridge across a ravine. This was not engineering. It was a miracle wrought by men who knew their own jungle.

The construction of these pioneering tracks also tested the need for and use of a road. We found out where the permanent all-weather roads should best go and developed them accordingly. They also served a major administrative purpose of access to villages and from the villages to centres of local administration. By tradition, too, roads were places of neutrality and thus were a strong agent in the extension of control and the maintenance of order.

At the same time, work was proceeding on wharves, public buildings, water supply, electricity, landing strips and other capital works at a growing rate. In round figures expenditure on capital works progressed annually from £1·2 million in 1952–3, to £1·9 million in 1953–4; £2·3 million in 1954–5; £2·6 million in 1955–6 and £3·1 million in 1956–7. The infrastructure was being steadily strengthened.

In chapter 4 I referred to the establishment of the plymill of Commonwealth New Guinea timbers at Bulolo. We also took other measures to promote the timber industry, and Jim McAdam, a good forester, was careful about indiscriminate or unrestrained cutting of timber. I was careful of the same thing because I wanted to see the planned use of the timber resources of the Territory so as to preserve a continuing economic asset for the independent country of the future and to preserve opportunities for the indigenous people. In the early 1950s we did not have enough information to make final decisions on those areas which might well be cut out and converted to agriculture after the timber had been harvested and those which should best be kept as permanent forest, so we tended to play safe and make sure that potential permanent forests were not lost for ever in one harvest. We did get considerable development of the timber industry and kept standards which both McAdam and I, from our individual standpoints, found acceptable.

Oil search was being conducted, but in regions where present and prospective disturbance of native populations was light. We thought about the particular administrative problems of labour, resettlement, ownership and contribution to public revenues which would arise from a discovery of oil in commercial quantities and made preliminary plans for handling an oil strike but, though hopes of such discoveries were occasionally stimulated, the situation did not in fact arise.

So far as other secondary industry was concerned, I saw the most immediate practical opportunity in service industries and food processing which could find a ready local market in replacement of imports. Already the best prospects were for biscuit factories, 'lolly water' factories, tyre retreading, cement products and the servicing of vehicles.

The measures taken to improve the production and marketing of copra and rubber, the progress made with coffee and cocoa, and the commencement of the post-war timber industry brought growth of exports. Increased expenditures by the Administration, a large part on salaries, wages and materials, built up the spending power in the Territory and stimulated imports of consumer goods, plant and equipment. The Commonwealth grant rose from £4·3 million in 1950–1 to £9·6 million in 1956–7, and in the same period total Administration expenditure rose from £6·3 to £13·7 million. Exports rose from £7·3 of £13 million, in spite of a decline in gold production, and imports rose from £10·8 to £19·5 million. Our own recruitment, expansion of mission work and general development increased the non-indigenous population by some thousands although the total of both Europeans and Asians at the beginning of 1957 was still only about 21 000.

This growth stimulated trading and the setting up of service industries in the main towns and ports and increased the local market for produce. For a start the main beneficiaries of briskness in business were the Europeans, but they were also the main contributors of services. In time, the indigenous people also found opportunities of various kinds in meeting the rising demand for goods and services.

The original limits on the participation of the indigenous people in the new enterprises were set partly by their lack of experience or knowledge of business ways and partly by their lack of capital. Co-operative societies were highly favoured by the Administration as a means of overcoming these handicaps. I did a great deal to help promote co-operative societies. By the end of 1956–7 financial year there were 260 societies with an annual turnover of about £1·2 million, compared with £62 000 in 1950. A press statement I made in July 1955 referred to steps to provide additional capital; the consolidation of existing societies, placing greater responsibility on the native staff; in the case of older societies, the transfer of native staff from the Administration payroll to the payroll of the co-operative societies themselves; the increased training of native inspectors, store managers and storemen and the completion of a new co-operative school at Port Moresby.

All this was to the good but, as the years passed, I continued to doubt whether the co-operative movement was the whole answer to native participation in economic enterprises. I saw more and more instances of the way in which the exceptional native kept on emerging in business affairs. The native community produced its own tycoons, mobilizing their own families or clans, and this form of private enterprise seemed at times to be more closely in keeping with the outlook of the people and more striking in its achievements than the co-operative society.

Some of our young and zealous officers engaged in the co-operative section were inclined at times to regard any form of indigenous economic activity outside a co-operative society as being wicked, sowing the evil seeds of a capitalistic society. My influence was used to keep the field open and not to force the people into an economic mould of our choosing. I did a great deal to promote co-operative societies, but I never saw them as an end in themselves. They were a means to help the native people to mobilize capital, conduct their own trading and producing concerns and manage them in their own interests.

I expressed these views on co-operatives as early as 7 August 1952 in a minute to the Department:

> Although we accept native co-operatives as one of the instruments of native advancement and their greater participation in the economic life of the Territory we should not regard them as the only instrument and we must avoid regimentation of the natives. The co-operatives are a means of meeting the needs of the natives as and when those needs develop. The co-operative movement is not to be regarded as the only means available to us, nor is it to be developed to the exclusion of other forms of development for which the natives themselves may show a preference, and, while it can be a convenient way of assisting the education of the natives in handling their own affairs, it should not be regarded as a substitute for the traditional methods of administering native affairs. In short, we should be cautious about forcing natives into a mould which may not be the best one for all of them and we should always be on the watch against turning one of the instruments of development into an objective of its own.

The occasion for writing this minute had been the submission of a Native Economic Development Ordinance passed by the Legislative Council. The Department objected to it because of the large number of drafting defects in it. I found additional objections to it in the wide powers it would give to officers of the Administration to take charge of native activities in an extreme form of economic paternalism. I did not recommend disallowance of the ordinance by the Governor-General but instructed the Administrator not to bring it into operation and to redraft it for resubmission to the Council.

A number of our field officers seemed to me to underrate the capacity of the native people in economic affairs. I myself thought them much more quickly responsive to chances of improvement in their material lot than to any suggestions for having village councils and starting on the way to political advancement. I had noticed in some villages the readiness with which they had adapted to their own traditional uses the new hand tools and utensils and new building materials; the readiness with which they accepted electric torches first of all and then village lighting plants; the interest in our vehicles; the quickness with which they learnt routine industrial processes at a plymill or an oil rig. These were things they wanted to learn. Indeed in many cases the chief inducement to forming village councils was that forming a council was a way in which they got a village sawbench, a village rice mill or lighting plant or a village truck rather than a way in which they could govern themselves and hold elections and keep minute books.

I remember a meeting one morning at a village in the Sepik somewhere in the higher country where the people had hitherto had little contact with the outside world. All the people, perhaps fifty or sixty, squatted around me in the shade for a talk, the men in front and the women and children peeping shyly but inquisitively from behind their backs. It was my routine way of letting them say whatever they wanted to say. A patrol officer translated from pidgin. He said they wanted me to give them some money. I was puzzled because they were not a mendicant people. The patrol officer repeated that they were asking me for some money. That was all they were interested in. They were always asking for money. I said, 'Do they mean coins?' He said that was it.

They hoarded coins in old fruit tins buried under their houses. I asked him to tell them that money was not of much use. If they were sick, they needed a 'doctor boy' or a hospital, not a handful of money. If they were hungry, they needed some food out of the garden and could not get fat by eating money. They looked as puzzled as I had been. Something was missing in our talk. I called over the district commissioner and said I doubted whether the translation was correct. He tried his hand. He said that, not being coastal people, their pidgin was not very good. He tried again and said that they asked for money and probably meant material possessions. This village had a reputation for being acquisitive. I had an inspiration and asked him, 'How would you translate "economic opportunity" into pidgin?'

The district commissioner said they were a bit early for that sort of idea, but there might be something in it. He then went into a long and roundabout speech in pidgin with a lot of phrases like 'all time he come up, he come up goodfella' and 'he got and he no got' and 'kissim disfela sumting'. The men grinned and nodded assent and jabbered excitedly. The district commissioner checked in further roundabout pidgin and eventually said that what they meant was not a handful of coins but 'economic opportunity'. They had heard that people on the coast had got some new plants which they grew and then sold for money and with the money bought things like pressure lamps and spades and axes and even trucks. The coastal people had business. Up in the hills they wanted to have some business too.

In such contacts I found at many levels of material welfare a great eagerness for native economic enterprise on their own and a great deal of what a socialist would probably call individualist greed.

I have said elsewhere that I think it is folly to try to export social theories without regard to the nature of the society to which a theory is being sold. Socialist theory about a planned and controlled economy undoubtedly had some influence on some of the early post-war administration of the Territory, but it should be recognized that this tendency towards planning and control was also influenced by a view about the protection of the interests of the indigenous people. Spender bucked against the theory. If I read some of his decisions aright, they reflected a view, supported by a majority of Australian voters in the 1949 Australian elections, that private enterprise was good and socialism bad. Personally I am not doctrinaire. My rejection of a planned and controlled economy in Papua and New Guinea came from doubt whether it would suit the Territory conditions and whether it would permit the native people to participate in the economic development of the resources of their land. From the little I had seen of their economic efforts I read them as an individualistic and somewhat materialistic people who would find an incentive in doing things for themselves and for their own direct benefit. In any case they had to work it out for themselves and not have imposed on them a Western theory of the best way of running an economy in the interests of all. I had practical misgivings about the prospective efficiency of the controlling authorities. Perhaps the bent of my mind can best be summarized by saying that it seemed to me that the economic doctrinaires were always likely to act so that the means to an end became an end in itself.

In the Department of Territories in Canberra there were also tendencies at a senior level, derived mainly from experience with the Department of Post-War Reconstruction, to try to plan and control the economic development of the Territory, and I was perpetually resisting attempts to persuade me to put this or that project under the charge of one official or another or to prepare schemes of development by this or that governmental agency. The officers had a greater confidence than I had in their capacity to manage any enterprise better than anyone else. My main reason for resisting these influences however was an opinion that when a scheme for development became an end in itself, the interests of the indigenous people and their opportunity and capacity eventually to run their own affairs would not be advanced.

My contemporary fate was that I copped criticism from both sides. Private European industry in the Territory and Australia criticized me for not being as strong against the 'Ward-Murray policy'—the catch-phrase of the *Pacific Islands Monthly*—as Spender had been. A number of Canberra officials and the occasional academic criticized me for my lack of enlightenment on social and economic theory. My own chief economic theory was not to have one but to give the people a chance to shape their own future. In this situation I did not accept *laissez-faire* as a reproach but as something better than a system of economic paternalism.

[14]

A NEW LOOK AT NATIVE LABOUR

Before I became Minister, there had been some reform in native labour conditions. The principal employers were the plantations and the Administration itself. A contract system resembling indentured labour was in course of being replaced by employment under agreement for a fixed term. There was also provision for employment of casual labour under permit.

The agreements set out the terms and conditions of employment and the obligations of employer and worker to one another. The recruitment of labour and the inspection of labour, including ration scales, accommodation, issues of clothing, and the transporting of the labourer to and from his home at the beginning and end of the period of his agreement were reasonably well supervised and generally the system was regarded by the Administration as satisfactory.

The early representations I received from the Territory were mostly from employers about the problems of enforcing the agreements. There were no penal sanctions and the remedy for breach of an agreement was sought in civil proceedings. Whereas an employer who was detected in some breach of the agreement would be prosecuted promptly by a labour inspector, an employee who left his work, or stole or destroyed the issues made to him was not so readily subject to civil legal redress. 'Absconding' or 'desertion'—both terms were used—was said to be frequent. Some plantations, especially rubber plantations, also complained of difficulty in obtaining skilled labour. They wanted either a longer term of agreement than two years or a system of repeated re-engagement so that they would have labourers long enough to train them as tappers instead of having successive intakes of ignorant village boys.

Some of the workers themselves felt the lure of foreign parts and avoided the compulsion to return home at the end of the agreed term. Official policy was strict on the repatriation of workers to their own villages once an agreement had expired, and labour officers supervised the transport for that purpose. Labour travelled mostly by air and the flights of DC3 aircraft with cargo and a 'labour line' aboard were a noticeable feature of traffic between the coast and the highlands.

The size of the native labour problem is indicated by the figures in January

156

1952. Private enterprise employed 19 698 workers under agreement and 14 980 as casual workers, and the Administration and Commonwealth Departments, such as Works and Civil Aviation, employed 12 295, making a total of 46 973. By June 1955, with economic expansion and greater Administration activity, the numbers had grown to 29 390, 25 823 and 13 323 respectively, making a total of 68 536. The demand for 10 000 more workers under agreement had been met mainly by recruitment from the highlands, and the demand for 11 000 more for casual work had been met from all over the Territory, often by native workers who had completed a term of agreement labour and sought the attractions of continuing employment with free engagement.

Shortly before I became Minister, a committee in the Territory had examined the working of the new ordinance, and, on their recommendation, I approved submissions made in December 1951 for some amendments which it was thought would help the working of the existing Native Labour Ordinance. At the same time I raised questions or made comments on other suggestions.

At the end of February 1952 I found occasion to make some rather terse observations to the Department about their failure to give me fuller replies to my comments. My dissatisfaction with the way in which the Department and the Administration were handling the subject grew. In a minute of July 1952 I wrote,

> There are, to my mind, very few subjects more important in the Territory of Papua and New Guinea at the present time than the regulation of native labour and it is regrettable to see the scrambling way in which the Ordinance now under notice was handled both in Canberra and Port Moresby. As a result we have an amending Ordinance that is riddled with faults and we have left untouched several other proposed amendments.

I asked the Department to 'consider further the final objective' and to look at the possibility of having 'one sound and comprehensive piece of work' resulting in a consolidated Native Labour Ordinance to replace existing legislation and also to introduce some new ideas. We should 'sort out our ideas about native labour more clearly and state them more exactly'. I reinforced this view in a further minute of 8 July on a Mines and Works Regulations Ordinance saying that I did not like 'pecking at little bits of the problem of native labour'.

At that time the division of the Department responsible for this subject was still headed by one of the pre-war officers of the old External Territories Branch, a man of good and pleasant character who had no imagination and the very simple approach of a public servant who never does anything except what has been done before. The Administration, still under Murray, was wedded to the new legislation it had devised to deal with one immediate practical problem.

After more frustration and more complaints on my part at the attempts at the 'piecemeal improvement', I took a new step in December 1952, having waited a year for the officers to reconsider the whole of native labour policy. I directed that J. H. Jones,[30] a senior officer of the Administration with extensive experience both before and after the war, should be brought to Canberra to engage on 'a re-examination of the whole of native labour policy and of the legislation in which that policy is to be expressed'. As a first step, Jones should 'attempt to draw up for discussion with the other authorities concerned a statement of the underlying principles of native labour administration'. When these principles had been approved, they could be regarded as instructions for the preparation of draft legislation. I stressed the need for consultation and the clearing of contentious points with the Minister as they arose. I wanted to ensure that policy was shaped 'as a result of a thorough and comprehensive view of the problem and not as the result of making a series of adjustments in order to meet difficulties as they arose'.

I was in for a further disappointment. Jones had prepared a statement of sorts by June 1953, but it was not placed before me until the end of October and in the meantime Canberra and Port Moresby officers had been embellishing it on their own. When I eventually received both the Jones statement and the departmental submission and had studied them, I told them they were 'on the wrong track'. Jones had dealt mostly with the particular problems of how best to hold native labour to the job. He recommended the reintroduction of the pre-war contract system with penal sanctions against 'desertion'. He wished to restrict narrowly the engagement of casual labour. In general, he concentrated on measures to produce a well-regulated and well-protected workforce. My complaint about the way the Department and the Administration had dealt with his report was that they continued to deal with particular complaints from employers or from labour inspectors without reconsidering the aims of policy. The papers did not seem to me to be based on any thorough re-examination of the facts of the situation but to start from old pre-war suppositions.

I then sat down and, drawing on my own knowledge and on my own views about native labour—a subject on which up to that point I had been awaiting the help of more experienced and more knowledgeable people—I wrote a long minute and sent it directly to the Administrator as well as to the Secretary:

> It should be clearly understood at the outset that in shaping native labour policy we are to pay regard primarily to the welfare of the native peoples and their social and economic advancement. The social consequences of the employment of natives and the effect of employment on the individual native have to be considered before we admit any arguments relating to the economic advantage of employing them. It is only because we think that economic advantage has to be limited by consideration of the effect of employment on natives that we have any native labour policy at all. Otherwise there would only be humane laws to prevent ill-treatment and no attempt to do more.
>
> That means in practical terms that the numbers of natives employed, the terms and conditions under which they may be employed, and the obligations placed on both employer and employee have to be determined in such a way as to foster desirable social effects and to minimize any undesirable social effects of employment.
>
> When we have determined the basic requirements of our social policy these will become part of the general conditions in which economic development takes place. It is a factor in development in just the same way as climate, soil, or markets are factors of development. Such factors can be modified by a variety of devices and improvisations but they can neither be ignored nor over-ruled.

The first set of principles of native labour administration therefore have to be sought in an examination of the desirable social consequences. As an example of what I expected, there might have been set out such objectives as the following:

On the negative side—

(a) Avoidance of any abrupt changes in native social organization (e.g. disruption of village life).

(b) Avoidance of conditions likely to lead to depopulation (e.g. disruption of the pattern of marriage and the raising of families).

(c) Avoidance of conditions harmful to health.

(d) Avoidance of conditions seriously affecting the local food supply.

On the positive side—

(e) Promotion of better living standards.

(f) Promotion of the educational value of employment, using 'education' in its widest possible sense to cover technical skill, greater ease in communication between European and native and growth towards civilized ways.

Under headings such as the above—and they are put forward as illustrations and not as the result of any claim by me to have expert knowledge on the subject—there might have been developed factual statements of what has happened or is happening and an attempt might have been made to describe with some exactness the conditions which lead to the desirable result and those which bring about the undesirable result. We should then know what we are trying to promote and what we have to guard against. We should then also be able to derive from such a statement of objectives certain basic principles of native labour administration . . . [Minute of 17 November 1953.]

In the same minute I referred to the way in which conditions in the Territory were changing.

The whole structure and content of the existing legislation regarding native labour were first shaped in a period during which plantations were almost the sole employers, when labour was recruited from 'unsophisticated' natives living in the same general locality as the plantation, and when labour was regarded as being normally abundant. The legislation of today has to fit a situation in which the economy is becoming diversified, when 'town' labour is as much in demand as 'plantation' labour, when the proportion of 'unsophisticated' natives to 'sophisticated' natives has changed, when more natives are engaging in money-making activities on their own account, when natives are acquiring some skills (e.g. truck drivers, carpenters), when the opportunities in Administrative service and the requirements of Administration (police, soldiers, clerks, medical assistants, school teachers, tradesmen) are growing, when recruitment has to take place in the remoter parts of the Territory because large bodies of natives in the older areas are no longer interested in becoming employees under contract, when an early limit to the amount of labour available can be seen, when the introduction of machines, vehicles and other facilities is likely to alter the old ideas about the possibility of employing Europeans and has made possible economy in the use of labour, when possible economic changes (e.g. the discovery of oil or the planting of tea estates) may impose special requirements in regard to labour, when with rising standards food importation (especially meat and rice) has reached a level which makes it a major item of policy to improve local food production, when the number of untapped reservoirs of labour is diminishing, when the proportion of consumers (as distinct from producers) of food in the community is changing and when many other changes in social habit and custom are taking place. It is against that sort of background of social conditions and not against the background of existing legislation that I want officers in the Territory to consider the Native Labour Ordinance.

Finally I directed that before officers proceeded further with examination of particular sections of the ordinance, they should go back to the starting point. Officers should dismiss temporarily from their minds any ideas they might have about the merits or defects of the existing legislation, and looking steadily and clearly at the situation in the Territory today and the prospective situation in the future, try to find answers to such questions as the following: (a) What are the desirable social results we want to bring about? (b) What are the undesirable social results we want to avoid? (c) What factors will help the good results and what will bring about the bad results? (d) What is the present-day situation to which the labour laws will be applied? From the answers to such questions, they should draft a clear statement of objectives and the principles of labour administration derived from those objectives. Let me first clarify what we were trying to do before we got down to a detailed discussion of how we were going to do it.

This minute reveals the way in which I tried to approach any question of major policy and the motivation of many of my decisions on economic policy. In both respects I found myself at variance with some of my senior officers in both the Department and the Administration. They did not themselves approach these questions in that way nor did they share my views on the social limits on economic development.

As a digression, I might mention that in that period I found little impetus from Australian industrial and political circles towards improved labour conditions in Papua and New Guinea. Indeed the main Australian criticisms for which I had to be watchful were that the products of Australian workers should not have to compete with the products of 'cheap black labour'. Australian trade unionists' views on 'exploitation' revealed less concern about what was fair to the native than about what might be unfair to the Australian wage-earner.

Following my directions at the end of 1953, further work was done, and early in 1955 I received a long report entitled 'A Review of Native Labour Policy for the Territory of Papua and New Guinea', prepared by J. H. Jones and R. Marsh (an Assistant Secretary of the Department of Territories) following studies and consultations in the Territory. This is a basic document in any history of native labour administration in the Territory.

In one part of this lengthy review, particular questions were raised or proposals made about the regulation of the terms and conditions of labour. By answering those questions or commenting on the proposals, I helped the move towards the preparation of amending legislation. In a further long minute of 2 March 1955, however, I still found a need to discuss basic concepts. At one level, I agreed that the aim of native labour policy was to contribute to the achievement of our general policy, but I added that, at another level, the aim was fair treatment for the people both as individuals and as a group and ensuring that employment would bring them positive advantages. I still would not subordinate native labour policy to the claims of economic development. In this minute, perhaps in reaction to the pressure on me to move in other directions, I stated my views about the social consequences of employment rather more strongly than I probably intended or would express them now. In making a list of the purposes our policy was to serve, I included the purpose 'To help control and regulate the pace of the vast social change that is taking place in the Territory and to help shape the nature of that change'. At another place in my minute I spelt out my meaning:

> The established policy of preserving the natives' rights in land or, in the future, ensuring that they will be able to obtain land should their own system of tenure and inheritance not provide it for them, will only prove effective if, in practice, the natives live on their land and work it, using it to greater advantage than in the past, either for a higher level of subsistence or for the production of marketable crops. Over a great part of the Territory this means, in the present generation at least and possibly for some generations to come, a continued attachment to the villages in which they were born.
>
> The village is also regarded as the main centre of native social organization and as a point of stability in a time of social change. It affords the best setting in which social, economic and political advancement can take place. Therefore the preservation of the village and the continued attachment of natives to their villages are regarded as so important that native labour policy should serve those ends.

What I was doing, at a time when native labour meant largely unskilled, low-level, low-paid labour for a European employer on a distant plantation or in an urban industry, was to keep for the native worker of the future the chance to work for himself if he chose and to have some practical means of doing so. I was also resisting a widely held view that native labour policy should be formulated in the interests of industry. Undoubtedly native labour was one of the major elements in the economic development of the Territory and undoubtedly most industries depended very largely on native workers. Some of my officers saw this as the whole of the situation and I felt the need to stress that we did not control and regulate native labour solely to meet the needs of industry and promote economic development or produce a supply of labour for an industry but that our overall objective was to protect labour and to serve our policies for the advancement of the people, including their own economic advancement.

Elsewhere in the same minute I again stressed the purposes of native labour policy of advancing the education of the worker in the broadest sense, protecting the individual from harm, and promoting the 'development of the resources of the Territory, with native participation'. I also stressed again that the situation was perpetually changing and that changes should be closely watched.

Action consequential on the Jones–Marsh report belongs to a later period and I will resume the narrative in chapter 21. At the moment I recount only the steps taken to check what I regarded as a bad approach to native labour questions.

It was about this time that I encountered in the Territory and was influenced by two officers who later helped a great deal in the developing of new labour policies—Lalor[31] and Parrish.[32] In them I found persons who could help me develop my ideas and promote them.

The fulfilment of my ideas about native labour required some training of the workers to give them higher skills. At a time when a large proportion of recruited labour went on to the labour lines of coconut plantations to gather the nuts and to make copra, there was little opportunity of on-the-job training. Secondary industry and a number of Administration services still relied on immigrant white workers from Australia for all except low-skilled manual labour. Our own Government, in the Commonwealth Department of Works, followed the same pattern. The first time I saw recruited labour used in driving vehicles or mechanical plant was on the oil search in the Gulf of Papua. Gradually, at the plywood mill at Bulolo, the labourers were given a wider range of tasks. In the Administration and in Australian departments not under the Administration we might have done more to employ the native worker in skilled tasks at an earlier stage than we did and given them on-the-job training.

In spite of my attempts, technical education did not go as fast and as far as I would have liked. Basically I think this was because the experts who devised the system and the officers who worked zealously in this field, had too much of an Education Department view of what was good technical education. Eventually they had some encouraging results in turning out a small number of students, with a certificated skill in one trade or another, better qualified for employment. In the early years of my term I would have preferred to see more of our resources applied to giving training to people in the occupations in which they were already engaged or which lay ready to hand, building on the knowledge they already had. We did some of this low-level 'technical training' in the Department of Agriculture and the Department of Forests. I should have liked to see these efforts intensified to give to more people a greater capacity to engage in gainful occupation on their own account on their land or in their own villages, as well as some skills that might earn a higher standing for those employed on wages. We might well have done more ourselves and might well have insisted that the private employer give more training.

Native labour did a great deal in bringing about the incentive for economic change among the people. The regulated rotation of labour under the agreement system meant that large numbers of the younger men gained experience of the outside world, of the ways things were done and of the usages of a cash economy. Native labour also provided new incentives to economic effort by creating new demands—for torches, for leather belts, for blankets, for steel tools, for tinned meat, for tobacco—which the returned labourer could only satisfy by earning money or selling produce. Native labour, both under agreement and casually, was for many of the people an educational course of learning by doing and in some cases a chance to pick up some English. The pity was that for so many of them it was only a matter of fetching and carrying for a white master and being spoken to in a mixture of signs and bad pidgin.

[15]

THE BEGINNING OF POLITICAL ADVANCEMENT

Most of what is said or written about political advancement in Papua and New Guinea gives scant weight to the differences between the situation in 1951 and in 1971. I write in this chapter of the situation as I saw it in 1951.

Although under the Trusteeship Agreement with the General Assembly of the United Nations the Australian Government had the right to administer the trust territory of New Guinea and the Australian possession of Papua in an administrative union, most of the residents of the territories, both indigenous and expatriate, still thought of two territories. There were very few Papuans in the trust territory and very few New Guineans in Papua. The indigenous people knew little of each other at that time. One exception was probably in the constabulary, although there was a tendency to keep New Guinea men serving in New Guinea and Papuan men serving in Papua.

One practical reason for this separation was that on the New Guinea side pidgin was essential while on the Papuan side the lingua franca was Police Motu. For the same reason and because of personal preferences, our own Australian officers tended to have most of their service on one side of the boundary or the other. A fluent speaker of pidgin had no use for this skill in Papua and a fluent speaker of Police Motu had no use for it in New Guinea. Among Europeans in private enterprise or in mission work, the attachment to one territory or the other was similar. In my first few years as Minister, listening to much talk by the expatriates, I was often quietly amused by the calm assumptions of the people in Papua that they were more enlightened and liberal, in the Hubert Murray tradition, than the 'kanaka-bashers' on the New Guinea side while, with equal certainty, the people in New Guinea naturally assumed that they were more industrious, more productive, and generally much more progressive than the 'kanaka-lovers' on the Papuan side.

To talk of political advancement in national terms was unreal at that stage because the idea of unity of the two Territories was not yet commonly accepted either by the indigenous people or by the Europeans. Travelling around on the New Guinea side during my first few years as Minister, I found that the resentment against Port Moresby among the whites, both officially and in private enterprise, was even stronger than the resentment against

Canberra. Among our own officers complaints of neglect or misunderstanding were mostly against Port Moresby. In and around Port Moresby I found many officers who thought of New Guinea as being 'over the range', and some of them had not yet been there.

Among the indigenous people I also found many instances of division, some general and some particular. The more sophisticated people on the coast would often describe a less sophisticated person from a new district as just a 'bush kanaka' or 'rubbish man' who knew nothing. Whenever peoples from various districts were brought together, as in plantation labour lines or in the police force, old animosities often flared and it became plain that men did not think of themselves as all being Papuans or New Guineans but as being Keremas, or Sepiks, or Bukas, or Tolais, or some other language group. All except their 'one-talks' were strangers. In an unfamiliar part of the country they sought out their 'one-talks' for companionship and did not mix with the local community. The Administration had very much less trouble from public disorder directed against official authority than from public disorder arising from clashes between one native group and another.

In the early 1950s it was not just a case of doing something to soften the animosities. The basic concept of belonging to some larger community than a clan had to be introduced as a new concept. The only evidence I saw on my early trips of broader loyalties was firstly among those who professed Christianity or were members of the Boy Scouts, and secondly in the highly disciplined loyalty of the constabulary. Those exceptions covered only a minority, and even in those groups there was certainly no homogeneity in respect of anything except the central purpose of their association, and the old divisions often were perceptible.

In due course I directed that a variety of measures be taken to try to introduce and strengthen the concept of one people. We posted our own administrative officers more freely in either one of the two old territories. As indigenous school-teachers became available to teach in English, we sent Papuans into New Guinea and New Guineans into Papua. In all administrative acts we stressed the fact of the administrative union. In everything we did we tried to make one country out of the two territories under Australian rule.

This was done of course not only for the sake of promoting a sense of national unity as a prerequisite for political advancement of the indigenous people but also because it accorded with another aim of Australian national policy, to keep the territories as one so long as they were under Australian rule and if possible to have an integrated and not a fragmented country as our northern neighbour after independence. Indeed, as I remember the early policy instructions from Evatt to Australian delegations at the General Assembly of the United Nations, the idea of an administrative union of the trust territory and Papua and the negotiation of a trusteeship agreement along these lines was shaped by considerations of Australian foreign policy and defence with scant influence, if any, from those more directly concerned with the welfare of the two territories. New Guinea was tied into the administrative union because it would not suit Australia to see the trust territory go a separate way after the ending of trusteeship.

Education: the author visiting a primary school

Technical education: a well-equipped trade school

Malaria control: spraying for mosquito eradication, Northern district of Papua

The development of highly sophisticated medical care: Nonga Base Hospital, Rabaul

Even after more than twenty years of consistently promoting the unity of the two territories and of the indigenous people, we find today, at the time of independence, that unity has not been fully achieved and lack of unity is still an impediment to nationhood and a cause of doubt about the possibilities of stable government after independence. In 1951, administrative union was policy, but the concept of a political unity among the people was dim or unknown.

Another reality that many writers about political advancement do not face is that there was no political structure on which to build and no local political interest or political organization with which to co-operate.

Before I discuss this aspect, let me confess one of my own prejudices. Since undergraduate days I had been somewhat sceptical about the Lugard gospel of 'indirect rule' as expounded and applied in West Africa. It seemed to me to be a device by which colonial rule could be assisted and perpetuated rather than a path towards the development of indigenous political institutions. In Papua and New Guinea I found that British colonial practice in Africa was much quoted by those few officers who thought at all about political advancement and it seemed to me that their acceptance of the idea of 'indirect rule' had led some of them to exaggerate the relevance and the value of indigenous practice in our part of the world in promoting a policy of political advancement. I thought there was some artificiality about the attempts, influenced by pre-war practice, to adapt village custom to the post-war participation of the people in their own government, much as I valued those measures during a transitional period in assisting the Administration to carry on its colonial-type rule over wholly dependent peoples. The system of 'luluais' and 'tul-tuls' in New Guinea and 'village constables' in Papua certainly helped district officers and patrol officers to do their work better in a colonial setting, but I could not see that system as a framework on which to plan the political advancement of the people. It was a helpful method by which a tutelary power could run a dependent country but had little value for building the political structure of a nation.

As far as I could gather information about them, 'the system of government' indigenous to the country and the 'process of decision-making' were limited to small groups and local affairs. The communities themselves were small, sometimes as small as a few hundred people and never larger than a few thousand. Most decisions for common action were limited to what should be done in one village or one group of villages and hamlets and what should be done by a number of people closely linked by kinship. The topics on which decisions had to be made concerned such matters as where to make a garden, when to rebuild or repair houses in the village, what action should be taken against some offender against custom, the settling of disputes between their members and, the biggest decision of all, whether to take action against a neighbouring clan in reprisal for some earlier injury or to seize something, such as women, which they coveted. The method of reaching decision was by confabulation. A district commissioner once described it to me as 'government by jabber'. I saw something of it. The men sat around talking. They all seemed to be talking at once. Voices rose in excitement or they subsided to murmurs. The jabbering often went on for hours. Then all at once as though someone had said, 'Well, that's it. Let's go', the confabulation ceased. They were of one mind—unless someone started the jabber again.

There was no chieftainship (except in a few instances) in the clans, but there were 'men of influence' or even 'women of influence', persons who by superior possessions, or courage in fighting or strength of character had a degree of influence higher than that of others, but, as I understood it, none of these was in a position to make decisions on his own or to give orders that the others would be certain to carry out, and there was apparently no chieftainly command or clan loyalty in the Scottish pattern. There was no means of ensuring a succession of power.

In pre-war days the Australian administrations, both in Papua and in New Guinea, had devised a means of communication between the Administration and the people and an adjunct to the rule of the territories through district officers and patrol officers by picking out these 'men of influence', winning them over to the side of the Administration, giving them a local status and using them as the go-betweens. These 'cap men'—so called because a military-style cap was given to them as a badge of office in New Guinea—were relied on by the district officers and patrol officers to tell them what the people wanted and to tell the people what the Administration wanted. They were relied upon also for an assurance that when an understanding was reached, it would be put into effect. Sometimes the wrong man was picked. Sometimes a man who had been rightly chosen, subsequently lost his influence with his own people. But by and large the system seems to have worked so long as government was concerned only with local situations and local affairs and was under the direction of Australian officers and final decisions had to be made by an Australian officer. After the war the system was continued in the long-established areas and introduced in the newly opened areas. As I have said, it suited a period of first contact when rule by officials was the only rule possible.

I took over a situation in which the basis of day-by-day government of the whole Territory in most of the matters that touched the people in their daily lives was rule by the officers of the Department of District Services and Native Affairs. This system was strongly entrenched and was to be stoutly defended by the 'old hands' in the Administration. It also had to be recognized as a fact that for the vast majority of the indigenous people, indeed for all except a few thousand of them, 'government' meant an officer on the spot—a patrol officer, a district officer or a district commissioner. He was the one who appeared to them to decide what was right or wrong, what should or should not be done and what benefits could be obtained, and he was certainly the one who told them what was going to happen next, enlisted their aid in common projects, heard their complaints and exhorted them to be better citizens. For the vast majority this was still the centre if not the whole of politics in 1951, and the habit of mind of many of our best officers in the field was also in the same mould.

One of the first things I saw—and I made a few notes on it at the time— was that this simple view of government was doomed by everything else we were proposing to do in changing the lives of the people. As we expanded the scope of governmental activity—for example into health, education, agriculture and forestry—there were more and more matters on which the patrol officers and district officers no longer were making decisions. Throughout the country there were more and more Australian officials, additional to the patrol officers and district officers, who were carrying out duties for which they were responsible to their own departmental heads and about which the patrol officer or district officer might have little knowledge. The post-war commitment to the advancement of the people unavoidably brought centralization of policy-making and administrative direction. It also added to the range and complexity of subjects that came within the province of government. Political advancement really began when, as a result of a wider range of governmental effort, people in remote parts of the country, in fact all over the country, began to be familiar with the idea that decisions were being made, money provided, and requests granted by someone centrally situated and having an authority wider than that of the local patrol officer or district commissioner.

Two other aspects of this increased effort were apparent. On the one hand, our new administrative structure was not suitable for the tasks of ruling the people in the old way. On the other hand, the indigenous clan system of government—'government by jabber'—was unlikely to master the whole field of affairs. As a further complication, our plans for extension of administrative control meant that for a period of years we would have a need for operating at one and the same time the old-style rule in newly opened areas and a new-style rule in developing areas. Our aim was the unity of the country and its people, and some progress towards unity and homogeneity was essential for the creation of a nation. Our aims to promote a sense of unity were being complicated by the energy with which we were bringing hundreds of thousands of people in the remote areas into a scene previously occupied mainly by the hundreds of thousands in the coastal areas.

We were moving, by reason of our proclaimed intention to work for the political advancement of the people, into a period when rule by district officers would have to be replaced by greater participation by the people in their own affairs, when the fields covered by Administration would grow in number, range and complexity, when centralization of decision and direction in many fields would necessarily replace local decision and direction in all fields, when national unity would be promoted to lessen diversity and conflict of interest and when, as the result of other phases of our intention to advance the people, we would be accentuating the contrast between methods in newly opened areas and those in developing areas. If politics were defined narrowly as the art and science of government, the position was that we were moving out of micro-politics into macro-politics, but we could not tackle the problems of macro-politics on their own, for micro-politics would still necessarily engage the thoughts and the daily efforts of the vast majority of the people. Political advancement would mean a shift in authority, but the area of doubt was whether we could ensure that those who were in authority had the knowledge of what was needed and that those who had knowledge of what was needed would have both the opportunity and the capacity to exercise authority. Because we were taking other measures of economic, social and educational advancement of the people, we would have to change the administrative structure of government and make these administrative changes before the political changes took place. We could make the administrative changes more readily than put into effect whatever ideals we set for political change, yet, in contrast, we could possibly produce some indigenous people capable of taking part in some political activities before we could produce some indigenous people capable of the higher duties of administration. For a time the indigenous politician in a representative role and the mass of the indigenous people in an electoral role were likely to be dependent on and subordinate to the senior administrative official.

It is necessary for a full understanding of my approach to the tasks of political advancement to describe some of my own views on the study of politics, for much of the criticism of me has been a discussion by academics rather than by persons engaged in the practice of politics and I would probably be found to differ from some of my critics in basic ideas about the study of politics. In my own reading, writing and teaching of political science, I distinguish between political philosophy—a subject for the university discipline of philosophy—and politics, which I would narrowly define in terms that related to the art and science of government. In my own academic study of politics I had a strong bias towards studying the structure and functioning of political institutions, discovering the political ideas, purposes and practices by seeking both the historical and contemporary account of what those institutions were, what they did and how they did it, and the relationships between them. By the same method I would seek an understanding of the sources of political power and I would seek an appreciation of political doctrine by analysing what was done and not only what was said.

This explanation—or perhaps some university colleagues would describe it as this confession of ignorance and bias—of my own approach to political science may reveal why, in my efforts to promote the political advancement of the people of Papua and New Guinea, I was somewhat sceptical about theories that pointed to a quick transformation. I looked rather towards the practice of politics, the functioning of political institutions, and the capacity of people to use the administrative machinery of government.

For the sake of those readers who may not be familiar with the term, I might add that I regard 'political institutions' as including a great number of institutions besides the legislature, the courts and the public service. For example, in many of their activities, I regard the press, the trade unions, the party organizations, and the associations of employers or producers as being among the political institutions that function in Australia.

There was a press in the Territory but it was wholly Australian-owned and Australia-oriented. It resisted nearly everything I did for the indigenes and criticized me whenever I did not serve Australian commercial interests. There were organizations such as Chambers of Commerce and Planters' Associations to make forceful representations to and perhaps to negotiate with the government, but they had no indigenous members in 1951. It was not until about 1955, under my own encouragement, that as Minister I began to receive deputations from the native people to give me their point of view. I tried to force the growth of these other political institutions among the indigenous people by requiring them to speak for themselves.

Because I took this view of the study of politics, I was predisposed to the view that the tasks of political advancement in Papua and New Guinea required the promotion of the growth of the political institutions best suited to the country and people and the participation of the indigenous people in the working of these institutions. This would mean in practice much more than getting a few native members into a legislature. It meant getting many more native members of the public service, native representation on boards and agencies, and some association of like-minded native people to advance their common interests. At the other end of the scale it also meant having newspapers or other media of communication conducted by native people. It required party organizations composed of native people. Merely stuffing a few talkative men into one room for a few weeks each year to pass some bills would not be political advancement if a fuller range of indigenous political institutions did not exist and function. Yet so many journalists continued to utter criticisms as though, in spite of their professed contempt of all politicians, the only way to measure political advancement in Papua and New Guinea was to count the number of indigenous politicians in the legislature without regard to the way the legislature functioned as a political institution and without regard to indigenous participation in all other phases of government. My assessment of the situation in the Territory also meant that the nearest we could get to what was already familiar to the people was by promoting their more active participation in the work of village councils and of boards and committees created by us to handle matters in which they were already involved and interested.

Before I took office some decisions had been made which set the direction of political advancement. The Papua and New Guinea Act provided for nominated native members of the Legislative Council, for native village councils, for advisory councils for native matters and for the creation of lower courts and tribunals 'in which natives may sit as adjudicating officers or assessors'. These decisions left the native people in a subordinate place in government. They did point however in the direction of a representative and democratic form of government and a rule of law.

At the time I took office in May 1951 the ideas about the government of the Territory were still centred on the fact that power and responsibility were wholly in the hands of the Administration created by the Australian Parliament and placed under a Minister in the Australian Cabinet. In 1951 there were no perceptible pressures for political advancement. It was not in the forefront of any discussion I had or of any advice I received. As I have recounted in chapter 5, the decision to inaugurate the Legislative Council was made by me against the weight of current advice. This was a field (as compared with, say, questions of economic development, health and methods of establishing law and order and extending administrative control) in which I was more interested and better informed than most of those with whom I was working at that time. My opinions counted in the beginning in this field more than in other fields because few other opinions were being advanced. If there was one activity in which I was the pioneer and the chief urger, it was political advancement. Political advancement would not have been pushed until some years later if I had not personally pushed it.

One opinion I formed was that peaceful transition was preferable to a struggle for independence or a revolutionary war. I saw peaceful transition as the growth in needs, interests and experience, as a sensitive response to the new situations brought by this growth, and as change by constitutional means. On the Australian historical analogy, representative government could be succeeded by responsible government and from that the Territory would move to autonomy under constitutions granted successively by the Australian Parliament and, if independence were the eventual outcome, under terms negotiated between two nation states respecting the rights of each other. The bogies I saw were a seizure of power, a war of independence, expropriation and confiscation, the protection of rights by force of arms, and lasting resentments. My only concern about independence was that it should come peaceably and on negotiable terms, with magnanimity on the Australian side and respect for agreed obligations on the other.

My opinions on political growth were also shaped by a belief that social and political change should go side by side and that tensions and unrest arise when political relationships in a community are out of harmony with social relationships. In practice, government functions most smoothly when the pace of social change sets the pace of political change and neither races ahead of the other. I did not want to see a political advancement in which minorities suffered or used power brutally. The major argument for democracy and the ground for my faith in it is that government will respond to the social condition as it exists from time to time. Effective and peaceful democratic rule requires a high degree of homogeneity in society, otherwise the rule of the holders of power, whether benevolent or autocratic, is not government by the people but government by syndicates who do not have to answer to the people but only keep the people quiet either by persuasion or by authority. Even if we may seem to be deteriorating towards this style of democracy in Australia itself —a style of government by public relations exercises—my hopes in 1951 for the future of Papua and New Guinea were based on an older concept of good government.

In the particular situation in Papua and New Guinea I could see no political advancement in any change that meant that absolutist rule by a white minority of Australian administrative officers had given place to absolutist rule by a dark-skinned minority of indigenous potentates. Political advancement surely had to mean that government by an administering authority answerable to the Australian Parliament should give place to a government by indigenous authorities answerable to the indigenous people. If the direction of political advancement was to be towards democracy, democracy had to be deeply rooted in the community. I observed that in the villages the people already had the idea that everyone took part in public affairs, even if the very young were expected to be silent and women dutiful. Government by jabber allowed a high measure of participation in decision-making. What they needed were some new ideas about the processes of democracy. Voting, as an orderly way of reaching a decision by all, was somewhat novel. So was the idea of electing a representative to go to some other place, sit in some other assembly and join with other representatives in taking votes for making decisions which they would be bound to accept even if they did not like them. In these and other ways they had to learn the methods and procedures of politics, the practice of voting, the principle of majority rule, the representative principle, and all the other complexities that make politics the art of the possible.

The earliest directions I gave for political advancement, besides the decision to inaugurate the Legislative Council and thus start on the path of constitutional progress, were for the more rapid development of village councils, the appointment of more native members to district advisory councils and urban councils, the membership of native persons so far as possible on any boards or agencies of a semi-governmental kind, greater opportunities for experience in the running of native co-operatives, and more native members of the Territory public service. The purpose was to familiarize them more rapidly with the processes and institutions of politics.

Our most encouraging early advance was in creating local government councils, a title which replaced that of village council when in practice it was found that the best method was to group several villages into a local government district. Outlining our hopes in 1956, I wrote, 'The intention is that these local government councils, as they mature in administrative experience and demonstrate their competence in local self-government will, while remaining under the ultimate guidance of the central administration, be gradually dovetailed into the territorial political system.' By that sentence I meant that, on this base, we would expand the Legislative Council into a representative legislature.

I attended many meetings of local government councils and always made a point in my tours of the Territory of recognizing their importance. Among other good results, they familiarized numbers of people with the idea of electing representatives by a vote and of reaching decisions in an orderly way.

We also introduced native leaders to sitting alongside whites on town advisory councils and district advisory councils. Twenty years later, after I had become Governor-General, I conducted an investiture at Port Moresby, and among those honoured was a New Guinean whom I had first met at Aitape in 1952. I recalled the meeting. He was then the only native member of the district advisory council but, when I asked for comments, he was the only one who spoke. He had a serious complaint. Our patrol officers were being moved about too often and never got to know the place. In pidgin, he said that no sooner had a new patrol officer come to Aitape than he was off again. He sat down and jumped up and was off 'all same nail he shootim arse'—just like a man who had sat on a drawing pin. By the time of the investiture he was speaking a little English and we chuckled together over the memories of twenty years earlier.

His presence and the memory of our former association confirmed my belief that a very large number of those who had been drawn into some form of local government work in the early years were well prepared to take a lead when we started to spread the idea of elected and representative institutions more widely.

I suggest that commentators have also underestimated the value in political advancement of what was done by so many voluntary non-governmental bodies, the Highland Farmers and Settlers' Association and the Returned

Servicemen's League in particular, in giving experience to native representatives on how meetings were conducted and how people could best make their points of view known and get them accepted.

There was no indigenous press other than the smudgy mimeographed or typewritten sheets put out by various missionary and Administration groups and circulating within a narrowly restricted area. I felt at the time that we should have done more in this field. The experience was however that there was no one capable at that time of conducting a truly indigenous newspaper or other form of communication, so they tended to be a white-directed version of what it was thought the native people should know.

Some undated notes I jotted down in about 1956 showed some speculation about how political groupings were going to emerge, although I saw no sign of such groupings at that stage. My jottings expressed a hope that when political activity came the country might be fortunate enough to avoid divisions based on old rivalries between dominant groups such as Tolais, Sepiks, Keremas and Highlanders, or divisions between employer and wage-earner, or between land possessors and the landless people. I hoped too that the political rallying cry would not be against 'foreign exploiters', bringing racial antagonism. But I could not clearly foresee what would be the basis of future party political organization, and at that time there were few signs of political interest among the indigenous people. Even those persons referred to as leaders of the people were mostly habituated to looking to the white official or the mission for guidance on the correct way to do things.

[16]

THE ADMINISTRATION OF JUSTICE

Writing as a layman mainly for laymen, perhaps I should introduce a discussion of the administration of justice by a few remarks about the general problem as I see it.

In our own community in Australia we are accustomed to a legal code that applies to the whole population and a body of law that can be written down and studied in books. Our habit of obeying the law is linked with other ideas about sovereignty, a constitution, a continuous law-making and law-amending procedure in the legislature, and the probity and good sense of courts of justice. It may be difficult for some readers to imagine a country in which there is no written language, no legal code applying uniformly to the whole population, no formal process of law-making and law-amending, and no independent and authoritative interpretation of what the law is at any given time. Instead of all this, each of numerous language groups follows certain recognized customs and lives by rules that are verified by talking about what suits the group and accords with tradition. The rules may impose obligations or restraints, and the way in which a group makes sure that rules are observed or that some variations are allowed can be described by the rather vague term 'social pressure'. Such a system cannot work except in a community so tightly knit with ties of kinship, belief, sentiment and tradition that the 'social pressure' is the expression of a common interest and outlook. Such a system does not adjust itself readily to unfamiliar or quickly changing situations in regard to which 'social pressure' may be weak simply because a common view has not yet been formed.

In Papua and New Guinea there was not one society but hundreds of separate societies, each with its own customs and rules, each deciding for itself what was the proper thing to do. Although there were resemblances between the customs and rules of the various societies, there was nothing resembling a legal code accepted by all and applied uniformly to all by some independent interpreter of custom.

Long before I came on the scene in Papua and New Guinea, a process had started to replace the old order, in which numerous societies each followed its own customs, by a system in which a superior authority (the Administration)

173

enforced laws imported from overseas and started to make new local laws by statute. This superior authority was also insisting that most of these laws should apply uniformly throughout the country. At the same time it paid some deference to the local custom so long as this did not conflict with the broad aims of the Australian Administration.

At the heart of the administrative problem is the question whether a people can live under two wholly different systems of law and, if so, what arrangements should be made to enable them to do so. This problem became more pressing when administrative control extended over the whole country and started to affect more directly more phases of the daily life and behaviour of more people. My own experiences in this phase of my work follow.

Looking over the briefs that were prepared for me by departmental officers for my visits to Papua and New Guinea in 1951 and 1952, I find no reference to the administration of justice. This confirms my recollection that this was not a question under notice. In one brief, prepared in November 1952, there is one sentence saying that work on a native courts ordinance had been delayed by 'the pressure of work in connexion with matters requiring more urgent attention'.

I became interested in the subject as a result of chance observations in the Territory. At every centre I visited I saw a calaboose. Nearly all the inmates were native prisoners, for, with occasional exceptions, European prisoners were transferred to gaols in mainland Australia. Apart from a central prison at Bomana, near Port Moresby, most of the prisons were very primitive places consisting of a few huts inside a high netting fence. In some of the outlying districts, where short-term prisoners were retained, arrangements were somewhat casual. In the morning the prisoners went out to work, cutting grass or mending roads, with a constable standing watch over them, and in the afternoon they returned. More than one officer told me there was no need for great security because once a prisoner had been told he was in prison, he accepted the fact and did not try to get away even if the gate to the yard were still open. The physical standard of living was probably a good deal better in gaol than at home.

More than one officer frankly admitted the value of a calaboose in providing a labour line for carrying out local services. Once when I commended a district commissioner for certain improvements around the town, he made deprecatory noises and explained that there had been some 'rioting' at a nearby village and so he happened to have a rather good lot of prisoners with nothing else to do but build a new road and plant some trees along it.

The constabulary ran the prisons and a district officer was usually the gaol superintendent. While I saw nothing myself that suggested any objectionable conduct, it seemed to me that we were not doing all we ought to do either for correction or education of the prisoners. In an early minute, I wrote of our missed opportunity. In the Territory I asked that the question of setting up a separate prisons organization be examined. When Cleland became Acting Administrator, attention was given to my request, and a comprehensive report by him on control of prisons and prison reform was received in November 1952.

At the same time I noticed that boys sentenced for crimes were put in the same prisons as men. I believed that there was a need for a different system, perhaps reformatory schools, for juvenile offenders and directed that this question also be examined. Cleland's report dealt with this too. Although a period of disappointment and delay followed before I could get the results I wanted, this report was the beginning of a comprehensive prison reform.

Looking at prisoners, I began to think about the processes that led to conviction, and the fact that already the Australian Administration was making laws to take the place of custom and was enforcing them with the aid of police, magistrates and judges. The Administration had introduced new laws and punished people for breaking them, and that seemed to be all that was happening.

My second introduction to the question came in a deputation from the European community at Rabaul complaining that there was no trial by jury. The reason, I was told officially, was that there was not a large enough literate community to form a jury who were not personally acquainted with the defendant or sufficiently free from personal involvement in any case at issue. So the trial judge sat as a jury and, when he had delivered his verdict to himself, sat as a judge to determine any question of law and deliver sentence. The whites complained of the denial of trial by jury to Australians. It was all right for natives but not all right for them. When they talked of trial by jury, of course they were thinking only of white jurors.

Alongside their complaint was a further request that more justices of the peace should be appointed so that cases could be disposed of more expeditiously and heard not by Administration officers sitting as magistrates but by an 'independent bench'. The difficulty I foresaw against granting this request was that, in any case between a native and a European—say a native labour suit— the European litigant was almost bound to be a friend or associate of the justices sitting on the bench and, however noble was European probity, the native party could scarcely be expected to keep a full trust in the processes of the law. I took early steps to require the appointment of stipendiary magistrates in the main centres, both to lessen dependence on Administration officers as magistrates and to avoid using a white bench of justices of the peace.

Hearing these requests from Europeans, I faced the question whether justice meant one thing for a white man and something else for a brown man.

At this time, being rather doubtful about the capacity of anyone in my own Department or of myself to analyse these matters, I asked Professor (later Sir Kenneth) Bailey, who was keen to make a visit to New Guinea for other purposes, to investigate and report on criminal justice in the Territory. Unfortunately other demands crowded in on him and, although he made the inquiry, it was a long time before we got any result from it and then in a less comprehensive form than I had hoped.

My early interest in the work of the courts also became relevant to the effort to shape a new administrative structure. The diversification of administrative activities in the various districts by reason of an increased effort in agriculture, health, education and other functions of government, and the steps I took to give district commissioners a general responsibility for all that was done in their respective districts, answerable to a new Department of the Administrator, meant a change from a situation in which native affairs officers ran everything to a situation in which they were only one element in government. Some district commissioners could not get out of the old habits, and they and a number of native affairs officers sometimes fought stubbornly against the changes. Their proud claim was that they knew more about native custom than anyone else and were more experienced in 'handling natives' than anyone else. Against the background of their own work in areas of first contact either before the war or since, they made public order the prime consideration and thought that the making of arrests, police action, punishment of offences, custody of offenders and supervising the day-by-day life of the people were all part of the same picture of 'total government'. I could recognize the value of having close knowledge of local custom and language and the need for strength of personality, character and experience in close contact with the people in order to win their trust. But some of the native affairs officers spoke too confidently of their own wisdom and I was gradually confirmed in my own ideas about the need to ensure that the courts and the police and the prisons were not regarded simply as instruments to serve the ends of orderly administration and to carry out the decisions of native affairs officers who were sometimes rather junior and often had a narrow view of their objectives and duties.

Thus quite early in my experience, without the benefit of any advice, I became aware of two existing tendencies. One was to regard the administration of justice as a means of helping the Administration to do its job; the other was to apply the law in one way for the native people and in another way for the expatriates. My reaction against both of these tendencies coloured my directions on policy.

I may have been influenced too strongly by my studies of early contact between settlers and aborigines in Australia. In my book *Black Australians*, I give attention to the decline in the legal status of native peoples who had been declared to be British subjects equal before the law with other British subjects. The decline in their legal status had started with a practice of interpreting the law and applying it in one way for the black and in another way for the white, even though this was often done with the good intention of dealing fairly with the black.*

My memory focuses on small incidents. On my first visit to the Territory in 1951, at a subdistrict post, I was shown among other sights a court room built of native materials where the assistant district officer sat as magistrate whenever required. It was already set up for some business to be done on the next day, and at one end of the hut was a table covered by the Union Jack and behind it the chair at which the magistrate would sit. The officer, a serious young man, explained that he always liked to give a court room a special appearance of solemnity to help create a proper respect for the courts. I asked why the British and not the Australian flag. He said that was what they always did. The Acting Government Secretary, who was travelling in Murray's entourage—a pre-war officer with a British colonial style—explained patiently to me, like one talking to an idiot child, that these were the King's courts and so the Australian flag was quite unsuitable. They were administering 'British justice' and had never used the Australian flag, which was the flag of the

* See Paul Hasluck, *Black Australians: a survey of native policy in Western Australia 1829-1897*, Melbourne, 1970, ch. 5.

Australian Government, but had used the British flag, which was the King's flag. When I suggested that the courts were also applying statute law made under an Australian administration, he did not seem to understand the point, and it was plain that he himself, as a former district officer, had always relied on a code, free of 'legalism', which he called 'British justice' and that was what the courts were applying, symbolized by the British flag.

When I continued the conversation with the officer about the cases to come before the court on the morrow, I was told with some exactness the details of each case, the sentence the officer proposed to give, and the good effect the sentence would have in serving the aims of the administration of the district. He had worked it out in his own mind, without waiting to hear the case, that some of the people would expect such and such a penalty and might take revenge into their own hands if they did not get it, and others would hope for a much lesser penalty and become 'cheeky' if they managed to 'get away with' anything so light. We would fix one that would be neither too hard nor too light but would leave no lasting grievances. This attitude to 'justice' was less easy to change than the draping of the table with the wrong flag.

Even in higher circles in Port Moresby and in the Crown Law Office itself it seemed to be taken for granted that the courts, even the Supreme Court, had a prime duty to help the Administration to enforce the law and little concern to give the subject the protection of the law. My own scant reading about the administration of justice had given me some basic ideas about the role of the courts in protecting the rights of the individual and about the independence of the courts from political direction. For a variety of other reasons my Australian and international experience had given me a veneration for the law and deep respect for the loftiness of judges.

As in so many other matters in 1951, the only representations made to me in the Territory about the administration of justice were by Europeans about matters affecting only Europeans. On the official side there seemed to be satisfaction with conditions as they were. We should go on with courts in which 'British justice' was applied by persons who 'understood Territory conditions'.

Early in my ministerial experience I came to know and to form a friendship with the Chief Justice of the Territory, Mr. Justice (later Sir Beaumont) Phillips, and with Mr Justice Gore. They were men of long experience and great dedication and enjoyed wide respect. Both had pre-war experience, one on the Papuan side and one on the New Guinea side. I drew a great deal on their experience in conversations with them. No two men could have better exemplified the merits of the established ways. They were a living demonstration of the way in which the ultimate ends of justice might be reached by having a kindly interest in the native people, mingled with some shrewd but tolerant insight into some of their 'tricks', and not being too pernickety over legalisms. I formed the impression, which may not have been wholly true, that in their own minds they made a distinction between cases in which they made judgments as lawyers and those in which they made judgments on what would be best for all concerned, including the accused. At the same time they were inculcating an idea of justice and of the independence and fairness of the courts. They were carrying justice to the people. I was inspired by the story of their journeys, by land or by sea, sometimes in discomfort, going on circuit, making justice accessible to all.

So far as I was aware in 1951, the native people had adjusted themselves to the situation and valued it. Justice was certainly to most of them a 'white man's affair' to be left in the hands of the white man. The extent of the adjustment was illustrated two or three years later when official steps had to be taken to bring about a new trial. At one calaboose a prisoner presented himself to the gaoler and said it was time for him to go home. The official looked up the records and said he had two more years to serve. The prisoner said, oh, no, his time was up this month. Out of the argument it turned out eventually that, when there had been a killing in a village, the people, knowing someone would have to be punished for it, had got together, decided who could best be spared and appointed him to be the 'bunny' who would be convicted of the crime after assuring him that he would be back in two years. At the trial the confession and supporting statements were so well made that even so experienced a judge as Phillips was taken in by them. The 'bunny' was sentenced but the village plot was upset when the sentence of death was commuted to four years and not to two years' imprisonment. The 'murderer' wanted to stick by the bargain that had been made between him and his kinsmen. There was a retrial and we patched it up somehow, with some compensation to the man wrongly convicted and a mitigated penalty to the true offender who now came forward.

On my first visit to Mt Hagen, then a place with only about a dozen nonindigenous residents, I had a glimpse through the eyes of the district commissioner of justice on the frontier. One afternoon, while at his table in his office —a native-material hut on the side of the airstrip—he heard sounds of a distant commotion and went to the door, which was approached by a short flight of three or four wooden steps. From this elevation he could survey the whole station by looking up and down the airstrip. Out of the jungle at the far end of the strip rushed a desperate native, running almost at the point of exhaustion. He was a few hundred yards down the strip when behind him emerged a yelling and frantic mob. The fugitive made a last wild effort as the gap between him and the mob narrowed. He reached the office hut, crawled up the steps between the legs of the district commissioner, standing akimbo at the top, and collapsed on the floor behind him. The mob, waving axes and other weapons, swarmed around the foot of the steps. The district commissioner stood his ground and asked what was the trouble. There had been a killing. The alleged murderer had just crawled between the district commissioner's legs and was now lying mute and terror-stricken on the floor behind him. The district commissioner told the mob that the prisoner was in his custody and would be dealt with. The court would deal with him. The fury quietened. The mob told its story and eventually dispersed. The fugitive confirmed that the story against him was true. In a village more than a dozen miles away he had killed his wife and then set off to give himself up to the 'kiap'. On the discovery of the body, the avengers had set out after him. In a thirteen-mile run he had beaten them by less than a hundred yards. But instead of village justice with a slow painful death he had got white man's justice with a commutation of a death sentence to three or four years' imprisonment and, by the good offices of the district commissioner, the arrangement of some suitable compensation in kind to stop the chain of pay-back killings.

I have recounted elsewhere an incident of my first visit to Tapini.* There had been some killing and the alleged killers had been brought in the day before I arrived. A deputation of hundreds of people waited on me and with great eloquence asked that the prisoners be put to death. I explained the processes of our courts. They said they knew the judge, a nice old man and a good man, but he would just put the offenders into prison and in a few years they would be back again, fat and boastful. When I again said that we would leave them to the justice of the courts, the spokesmen said in effect, 'Very well. We know that is the way you like doing things. But when they are out of gaol, send them to some island and let them die there, and after a few years collect the whitened bones and bring the bundle of bones back here and show them to us to let us know they are dead.' When I recalled that some of their own people occasionally committed murder, and justice must be even, they replied that by all means, if they deserved it, we should kill them too. They believed strongly in capital punishment.

Out of these and other chance experiences I formed an impression that the native people, especially those in the newly opened areas, had little or no idea of justice as a concept with some merit in itself. They were more interested in fixing up the situation created by what we would call an anti-social act. I doubt whether they had clearly formulated any body of law, as Australians would understand it, but rather had ideas about rights and obligations of members of a social group and the procedures by which any disputes about them or any deliberate infraction of them should be handled. In many matters —especially where our rules (such as the rule that they must not kill each other) were easily understood—they accepted the advantages that came to them from 'white man's justice', such as the relief from fear, but in more involved matters including those that might be regarded as the commission of a sin rather than as a breach of the law they probably thought 'white man's justice' inapplicable. To some extent this was recognized by the officers of the Administration. In practice a great deal was done by a process of arbitration and negotiation by patrol officers and others in settling questions without legal process. The skill and success with which they did this varied a good deal according to the capacity and experience of the officer. Their successes tended to confirm the idea that good administration was better than good law courts and led to a situation in which crimes of the more striking kind, such as killing each other, or crimes against the white man, such as stealing, formed a much more significant part of the work of the courts than what might be termed civil disputes among themselves or minor offences against the laws of the Territory.

In my early days I assumed that, as their familiarity with white man's ways and their separation from closed indigenous societies widened, more and more of the native people would become litigious persons and the work of the courts would tend to change in character and increase in volume. Even in the

* See *Australia's Task in Papua and New Guinea* (Roy Milne Memorial Lecture, Australian Institute of International Affairs, 1956), pp. 8-9.

short term we were likely to have some difference in the relationship of people to the courts in the coastal regions and in the areas of first contact in the high-lands. Thus the difficulty of deciding what to do about the administration of justice was increased by the lack of uniformity in the need for legal remedies in different parts of the Territory.

As I tried to come face to face with the problem, I met further confusion in what might be described briefly as a tussle between the idea of applying native customary law in native courts with rules and procedures of their own and the idea of trying to establish a system of justice derived from British tradition and in so doing to familiarize the people with the concept of protection of the rights of the individual, the strict and even applications of the statute law created by ordinances of the Territory and, starting with the inheritance of the English common law, the evolving of their own common law understood and accepted by the indigenous people but based on a concept of rights different from the idea of retribution—the savage 'pay back' or the exaction of harsh forfeits or punishments for deeds that might be regarded as grave moral offences in a primitive community but might be less seriously regarded in a different social organization. There was a small body of opinion in the Administration which had made almost a religion out of their plans for native courts and, it seemed to me, had greatly over-stated their case and were arguing too fiercely against anything other than native customary courts. I myself was still some-what confused and in particular wanted to see more clearly how a native courts system applying customary practice would operate in civil cases between citizens as well as criminal charges brought by the Crown against the subject, and how, out of the wide variety of local customs, the nation of the future would be able to evolve a system of justice that would fully protect the individual and be widely understood and respected by all the people in all parts of the country. I had myself a strong doctrinaire faith that when self-government came to a country such as Papua and New Guinea, the lot of the ordinary man and woman could be precarious and sad if they did not have the benefit of independent and well-qualified judges interpreting a recognized and accepted body of law based on the principle of justice and if the govern-ment itself was not subject to the law. I would have been ready to embrace any proposal that clearly led towards that eventual outcome, but unfortunately the advocates of native courts seemed to present native courts as being good in themselves regardless of what happened to the offender, the injured party or the litigant, and they gave no clear account of how this system would evolve into an accepted and practicable system of law and justice when self-government came to the future nation.

Another particular difficulty was that, within the Administration, the Crown Law Office had not yet been fully organized and staffed. The position of the head of this office, called the Crown Law Officer, was still vacant. The staff was limited. So far as I could see, they did little at that stage to counteract the tendency of district officers to run the minor courts in their own way, and both in respect of the native people and the Europeans supported the colonialist idea of doing what was best for the Territory.

Several incidents came under my notice of misuse of legal power by Administration officers acting against Europeans and led me to speculate that

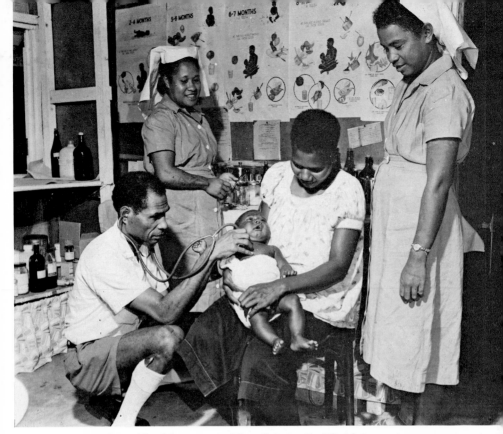

A rural health centre in New Britain: Dr W. Moi examines a small patient

In the maternity ward of Nonga Base Hospital

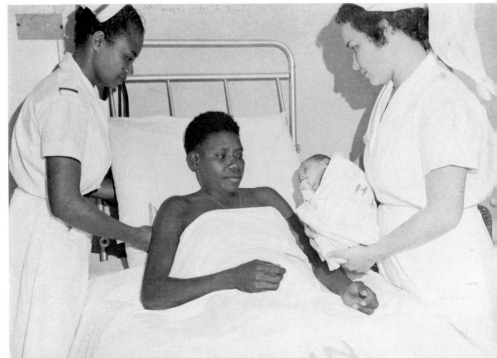

Simogun Peta, the first indigenous member of the Legislative Council, making his maiden speech

if they did such things to Europeans, what would they not do to native subjects. In 1952 I was on a visit to the district headquarters of one of the long-
established areas in Papua, mainly to look at some proposals for land settlement by Europeans and to receive some deputations from Europeans. After a
busy round of deputations, I was leaving for lunch when I noticed a slim
young European waiting rather furtively in the shade of the building. Since I
thought I had met all of the small number of Europeans in the area, I asked
the district commissioner who he was. The district commissioner, who had only
recently taken up his post, said that he was a 'bad lot' and a 'trouble-maker'.
Indeed his deportation from the Territory had been recommended. The man
had wanted to see me but, after hearing about him from his staff, the district
commissioner had crossed the name off the list of interviews, since he did not
think I would wish to be bothered by 'trouble-makers'. I said, 'Put his name
back on the list and give him an appointment immediately after lunch.' During
lunch time the official version I was given by the district officer, who had been
in charge of the district in the gap between two district commissioners, was
that the man had been ill-treating his native labour and was a type that caused
a lot of bad feeling towards the whites. The district would be better without
him. We didn't want his sort around the place.

When I saw the man, he seemed to me to be just an ordinary and not very
bright Australian. He said he had come up to the Territory to work on a
plantation with the prospect of being able to obtain a share in it. He admitted
that he did not know much about handling the labour line and had an argument with one of the 'boys' who would not do what he was told. This 'boy' had
then made up a story that some of the workers had been 'bashed'—a story
which the young man said was wholly false—and had gone off and told the
district officer. The district officer sent for him and started to condemn him
and rouse at him without listening to his side of the story, and the young man
admitted he 'lost his block' and had a row. Then the district officer 'lost his
block' and told him he was going to 'run him out of the country'. He had been
brought before the court and convicted. He was not sure what he had been
convicted for but now they told him he was to get out of the Territory. He
thought it all a bit rough, seeing that he would lose all his prospects.

I made no judgement on whether the young man had committed any
offence, but decided to look into the manner in which the proceedings had
been taken. I found that the district officer, in one capacity, had received the
original complaint by the native worker and decided without further investigation that it was well founded. He had then laid a charge, instructed his patrol
officer to bring the man in, prepared the case for the prosecution and
instructed the patrol officer how to present it, and then sat on the bench as
sole magistrate and without much difficulty found the accused guilty. He had
not taken any evidence from the accused. He had then, as acting district
commissioner, sent a rather unbalanced report of the case to Port Moresby
with a recommendation for the man's deportation from the Territory.

There were hints of earlier contention between the two men on a wholly
personal matter and there was no doubt that the district officer had already
decided to believe the native and disbelieve the white man before he took his
seat on the bench. The only evidence about the alleged incident was the

original complaint by a native who was apparently vindictive and was reporting not what had happened to himself but what was alleged to have happened
to other natives, none of whose testimony was ever taken.

What left me aghast was that the district officer could see nothing ques-
tionable about his own conduct. He was rather inclined to snub me at first. 'I
think, sir, that with more experience you will find that is the way we have to
do things here. It's our policy to get rid of troublesome elements.' The officer's
own experience, both of the English language and Australian policy, had been
very much enlarged after he heard my views. In later years the poor fellow
always seemed to look sick whenever I met him. Then when I looked further
into the papers I found that the Crown Law Office, accepting the proposal
for deportation, had regarded all this as more or less the normal routine procedure with nothing odd about it.

It was out of this confusion of impressions that I tried to find my way to
clearer directions on the administration of justice. Eventually it seemed to me
that two elements were more important than any others. One was that practices that differentiated, even with a good intention, between the position of
the European and the position of the indigenous person under the law and
before the courts of the Territory were likely to lead to a situation where there
was one law for the white man and another law for the coloured man, and one
standard of justice for the white and another standard for the coloured. Looking
to the future and having the interests of each racial group and of the total
Territory community in mind, I was sure that would be bad. We should work
towards a single body of law and a single system of justice, equally accessible
to all and even in its incidence. The other was that in the longer term, when
self-government and independence came, there should be a soundly based
and universally recognized rule of law, administered by independent courts on
high standards of probity, to ensure the protection of the individual against
the State. The courts should be freed from Administration influence so that in
future years they could not become the instrument of any government. I
decided to work towards both these ends.

Looking over my personal records, I find that on 8 January 1952, in the
course of a minute to Lambert about a case on which representations had been
made to me, I wrote,

> I am extremely unwilling to intervene politically in the processes of
> justice and in any case I have not yet had time to familiarize myself with the
> operations of the courts in the Territory but from the present case and from
> three or four other matters that have come under my notice I am beginning
> to think that the whole of the processes of justice in the Territory may need
> review . . . Will you let me know whether the Department has formulated
> any views on this matter . . . At present I have little knowledge but a very
> uncomfortable feeling on the subject.

The Bailey inquiry was part of this same attempt to get guidance and
advice. In April and June 1953 I complained that this inquiry was 'dragging
badly' and tried to get some report. I also started to press harder for attention to
other matters, especially the reorganization of the Crown Law Department as
a prelude to other measures. On various occasions during visits to the

Territory I discussed with the Administrator or his officers matters related to the work of the lower courts, the way in which native offenders were handled and the state of the prisons and expressed my dissatisfaction. No improvement seemed to be made. About the end of 1953 I began to lose my temper. In a memorandum of February 1954 I recounted step by step the delays in both the Administration and the Department in attending to a minute of 21 July 1953 about magistrates. Similarly in August 1955 I was still pressing for recommendations for the better handling of juvenile prisoners. When I received a submission at the end of October, it was so unsatisfactory that I directed that the whole question be re-examined. The information given in the submission did not seem to me to be in accord with the facts I had myself observed.

Up to this point I had placed the onus on the Administrator to repair faults or make recommendations on the matters to which I drew attention. I now saw that little would be done in this area unless I intervened. The first field I selected was the prisons system. On 18 March 1955, at Port Moresby, I gave written instructions to the Administrator about the 'custody of native prisoners' and directed that 'action be taken urgently to bring about a comprehensive reform'. I expressed my growing dissatisfaction with the lack of response to earlier requests for attention by the Administration to matters I would normally have regarded as the business of the Administrator rather than of the Minister, and also indicated what I found wrong in the prevailing practice:

The legal requirements in respect of the arrest and trial of a native, committal to prison, custody in prison and release are to be observed as strictly as in the case of any other subject of the Crown.

Immediately the new Prisons Ordinance is passed, steps are to be taken to create a Prisons Branch in the appropriate Department of the Administration, under a Controller of Prisons, with its own corps of gaol guards, warders, instructors and other officers distinct and separate from the Constabulary. I should like to see proposals for this new organization not later than 31 May 1955.

Custody of prisoners is to be regarded not only as a measure of restraint but as an opportunity for reformative and educational measures. Proposals regarding methods and establishment to serve this end should be prepared by the Controller of Prisons as soon as possible after his appointment.

For the above purposes, central gaols are to be established at suitable locations and all prisoners who have been sentenced to long terms (say, more than twelve months) are to be transferred to these central gaols. They are to have sufficient area of ground and suitable plant and facilities to ensure that there can be useful full-time work by the prisoners embracing training useful to them. Bomana is an example of the possible lines of development.

Short-term prisoners (say, those serving less than twelve months) can be kept at district gaols under the general system at present operating, except that they will also be placed under the authority of the Prisons Branch and an improvement is to be made in regard to the standard of accommodation and surveillance. Prisoners in district gaols will be available for administration labour but every opportunity has to be taken to make their work a form of training. Such training shall embrace such matters as hygiene and standard of living, and speaking either English or pidgin, as well as how to grow or make useful things.

Without exception, every prisoner should undergo a medical check and the Department of Health should undertake whatever remedial or preventive measures this examination may prove to be necessary.

After discharge, steps should be taken by the Department of Native Affairs to ensure that the discharged prisoner returns at once to his village or, if that is undesirable, that he is placed in occupation.

My deadline of 31 May was not met. I jogged the Administrator again on 6 June. At the end of June I received a recommendation that the creation of a position of Comptroller of Prisons be deferred to allow consultation with the Queensland Government about pay and conditions in a prisons branch. In approving, I wrote on 1 August, 'This must be expedited.' After some further delay, the services of W. Rutherford, Comptroller-General of Prisons in Queensland, were obtained. He made the investigation and presented a report on 28 October. A month later, when I asked what had happened, I was told that his report was still being examined. A month later still I lost my patience and, in a minute of 25 January 1956, said that Rutherford's report was so straightforward and so clearly confirmatory of the policy decisions already taken by me that it could be readily converted into proposals for immediate action. I expected to see the new system in operation without further delay.

On 3 February 1956, after receiving the Administrator's report, I confidently announced the appointment of a Comptroller of Corrective Institutions. I said that the first duty of the officer appointed would be to reorganize the prisons system in the Territory, and the custody of prisoners was to be regarded not only as a measure of restraint but as an opportunity for taking reformative and educational measures. I elaborated my ideas and recapitulated the directions I had given in March 1955 about such things as care and training while in custody, after-care on discharge, medical checks on all prisoners, and separate measures for the care of juvenile offenders. I was rather proud of that press statement. It was a long way in advance of anything else that had been done on prisons in the Commonwealth jurisdiction up to that time. Perhaps I had the vanity of thinking I had taken some place in history as a prison reformer. The statement concluded, 'It is a lost opportunity on our part if any man or woman leaves a prison with a worse understanding of our aims for advancing their welfare and with a worse spirit towards us.'

A little later I asked for the plans of the newly appointed Comptroller for setting up the new organization and learnt that, having landed the job, he had gone off to Europe to spend ten months' accumulated leave before taking up his new post. It was not until December 1957 that the first stage of the attempted reform was completed with the assent to the Corrective Institutions Ordinance. Something I had seen as urgent in 1952 had taken five years to start.

Another subject that attracted my attention in this period was the casualness about the holding of inquests on the death of any native person. Two or three rather odd cases had come under my notice during visits to outlying districts. Natives had been found dead from some undefined cause or had died apparently as the result of injuries or an unreported accident, and district officers, being busy, saw no cause for further official notice of the fatality.

When I asked about an inquest they told me in effect, without any intention of covering up the incident, that they had heard the report so long after the event, or the village where it happened was so far away, that they had simply noted the report. They had not thought that any inquest was required. This casualness, which was understandable in areas of early contact, also seemed to have continued in more stable districts, and an idea was growing up that the formality of an inquest on the unnatural death of a native could be dispensed with if the native affairs officer thought an inquest would serve no useful purpose. My initial concern, as in other matters, was that this casualness was tending to establish one law and set of practices for the Europeans and another law and set of practices for the natives. In the course of 1954 I had occasion, as the result of an incident, to give a minute about the necessity for conducting an inquest on deaths from violence. My views were expressed as follows on 28 June:

> Please watch carefully all such cases to ensure that coroners' inquests are held promptly and that, so far as local conditions permit, they fulfil the strictest requirements of inquests and do not become a mere form. I recognize that such incidents are more likely to occur in the remote areas than near the centres of population and I also recognize that it may be difficult to avoid a situation, in which the ADO [Assistant District Officer] first conducts the police inquiry and then puts on a necktie and conducts the coroner's inquest. The Administrator, being a legal man himself, will appreciate the need for overcoming such situations in the interests of the officers concerned and of the reputation of the Administration generally, as well as to ensure the requirements of the law and the theory of the law in respect of any death by violence are satisfied. Unusual difficulties can be used to explain why this standard cannot always be achieved but they do not allow us to give up trying to reach the standard. I should like these observations to be brought under the personal notice of the Administrator as apparently my two previous inquiries were handled at a lower level and in a manner which I do not think the Administrator would himself use . . .

This did not have the effect for which I hoped. Following an incident in which a number of natives had been killed by explosives, I sent a sharp minute on 20 January 1955 asking for a report on 'current practice in regard to the holding of inquests on the death of natives in Papua and New Guinea, the policy directions on which that practice is based and any other circumstances that governed the adoption of the practice' and continued,

> As a general principle, the requirements for holding an inquest in the case of the death of a native should be no less strict than in the case of the death of a European. If the Administration wish to depart from this principle they should advance a case for my consideration.

Following this, I wrote on 17 May,

> The report furnished by the Administration after a delay of five months is not as full and detailed as I require. Please obtain without delay a return showing the number of coronial inquests held on the death of natives in the past two years and a return showing the number of cases of death of a native in which formal decisions were made that an inquest was unnecessary. These returns should show details of each case.

On receiving this report, after a delay of three months, I directed that a return of the same sort should be made every six months. Each report was carefully scrutinized by me and, after making some strong comments on the continued slipshod procedures, I gradually managed to get some regularity and strictness in formal inquests into the unnatural death of natives. Arising out of this regular reporting, I was also able to introduce some stricter attention to the right of natives to compensation in cases of accidental death or injury in their employment.

It is plain to me now that I did not give a strong direction on these matters as early as I should have done, that I was too diffident about my own views on a subject on which I was unsure of my own knowledge and on which I received little advice or guidance from either Department or Administration, and that I was not firm enough in insisting that my questions or requests were answered promptly, and I relied too much on the Administrator. It was a disappointing experience.

Although the Administration and Department generally seemed to give a low priority to reforms of this kind and did not appear to see that they were part of a larger problem of establishing the legal status and the equality before the law of the native person, there was one subject on which some of the senior officers at least took a fervent interest, namely the constitution of native courts. Among them was one of the most intelligent and articulate of the pre-war officers, David Fenbury.[33] He was an experienced officer and had read much more widely than any of his colleagues as well as having had a term on exchange service in East Africa with the British colonial service. He had a tendency however to take possession of an area in a somewhat exclusive way and enjoyed being an apostle for the true faith in a world peopled by the less enlightened. He had apparently been working hard on a system of native courts, but it was a long time before the results of any of his work came up to my desk.

In January 1955 the draft of a bill for a native courts ordinance was placed before me. It had been brought down to Canberra specially by another enthusiastic and highly intelligent officer, C. J. Lynch,[34] whom I had just promoted to Deputy Crown Law Officer. Lynch, like Fenbury, was intellectually above most of his colleagues and knew it. He always gave me the impression of being impatient with persons like his Minister who did not immediately accept his views, but I valued him as a keen and constructive mind.

The submission of the draft bill led me to call for the files. A long minute dated 27 January 1955 sets out my side of a story which, in various published papers, has been slanted generally on the side of Fenbury and Lynch. The opening sentence of my minute, addressed to Lambert, reads, 'For some reason which I cannot discover none of the matters contained in this file has ever been brought under my personal notice, although as long ago as 1952 and again in 1953 there were requests from the Territory for a Ministerial decision on policy.'

After remarking that, although no policy decision by any Minister had been made, a bill had been drafted and adopted by the Executive Council of the Territory for submission to the Legislative Council, I went back over the whole of the information on the file. It seemed to me that not enough attention had been given to the basic question of whether a separate system of courts for natives was either necessary or wise. I noted that in May 1950—before my time—the Attorney-General's Department had advised that an ordinance then proposed 'involves a completely new departure in the administration of justice in the Territory', and added,

> I have so far failed to discover any close argument or presentation of fact to help us to decide whether we should make that departure. The Attorney-General sought an assurance nearly five years ago that the main principles of the legislation had ministerial approval but so far his request seems to have been ignored. Even on the submission now made to me belatedly I am asked to approve only the contents of a draft ordinance and it is still taken for granted that there is no need to examine the fundamental question of whether or not we should have a separate system of native courts at all.

The remainder of the minute records my views at that stage so precisely that I quote it in full:

> The Ordinance proposes to establish native courts to deal with both civil and criminal cases to which all parties are natives. The courts will be composed of natives. The matters with which they may deal will be limited to local matters, that is to matters which originate in the village where the court sits and to which only villagers are parties. They may impose fines and sentences of imprisonment. The jurisdiction, the membership of the courts, the judgements of the court and nearly every phase of their work would appear to be subject to control (either by direction, revision or suspension) by officers of the Administration. The courts and the district officers can also apparently have considerable liberty in the methods they use and the rules they disregard, provided that 'substantial justice' is done.
>
> In the earlier stages of drafting questions were raised by the Attorney-General's Department on various points. It seems to me that these questions, which to my mind raised valid objections to the proposals, have never been properly answered and they have been avoided in the final draft, which, on most of the contentious matters, only says that regulations shall 'prescribe' what is to be done. I should like to make it clear at once that, even if I can be eventually persuaded that a system of native courts is necessary and wise, I would not accept the present draft ordinance. If an ordinance is ever introduced that ordinance itself will have to lay down precisely the main provisions in regard to the constitution of the courts, their jurisdiction, their powers and their procedures. The draft now before me comes very close to saying only that there shall be a system of courts to do what regulations say they can do or what certain designated public servants think they would like the courts to do. Officers should be aware now that I hold very narrow views on the question of law-making by regulations.
>
> Pursuing the same line of examination, I would also raise in passing the question of whether the present proposals amount to anything more than an elaborate sham. Is this in reality a proposal to add some lower courts to the existing judicial tribunals or is it only proposing something that looks judicial but is in fact designed to meet the convenience and to serve the purposes of administration of native affairs?
>
> That question is pertinent. It also should have been posed and answered five years ago before the Department and the Administration embarked on

the labours of drafting an ordinance. The direction which was taken suggests that the answer given in the minds of officers was to the effect that a system of native courts should be devised as part of the judicial system of the Territory, but the result of their five years of drafting has been to produce a final draft which subordinates these courts to administrative convenience to such an extent as to prove that their first answer was the wrong one.

Assuming however that the draft ordinance now before me is put forward as a proposal to add to the judicial system of the Territory, it becomes my immediate concern to consider any facts or arguments that may be presented in support of the idea that special native courts should be established. Before anything further is done in preparing or submitting legislation, a ministerial decision on that fundamental question has to be made. I want to receive a reasoned submission on that point.

My own preconceived ideas are against any such move and, so that the Administration and the Department will know what prejudices they have to overcome, I shall state my views in broad outline.

It is basic to my thinking that the primitive person who comes under our protection and trusteeship by reason of our occupation of his land has the benefits of the law to no lesser extent than any other 'subject' of the Crown. It is quite true that, by reason of his ignorance, remoteness or social habits, those benefits may not be accessible to him in the same way as they are accessible to an Australian. It is also quite true that he would suffer rather than benefit if the strict letter of the law and the strict processes of the law were applied to all his actions, and compliance with the law were exacted from him without regard to the fact that he is also bound by his duties as a member of a native society and influenced by the claims of his own native law and custom. It is one thing however to pay regard to such circumstances and administer justice flexibly and quite another thing to take any action which marks out a separate province of the law and a separate group of persons, under the sign 'For Natives Only'. If, even with the best intentions, you prescribe matters and groups of persons to be dealt with by a special system, by that action you also may tend to place the benefits of the common law out of the reach of such persons.

In history, the most striking examples may be found in respect of loss of life and the loss of personal freedom. A policy which starts with a humane intention of recognizing that a killing done in obedience to a tribal law is not to be punished as murder, in our sense of the term, sometimes ends by rating the importance of the life of a native victim very much lower than that of other 'subjects' of the Crown. We can slip very easily into an almost casual attitude towards the 'value' of a native as compared with the 'value' of a white man. Similarly, there may be a need to make special regulations or adopt special conditions for the custody of native prisoners, and, doing so, we may easily slip into the habit of regarding their imprisonment as being different from the imprisonment of other persons. You may have noticed recently my request for information from the Territory regarding the present practice on the holding of inquests on the death of a native and for information about the custody of prisoners. I have not yet received replies but I shall not be surprised, assuming the replies are adequate, to find that there is some casualness in the Territory about the death or the custody of a native as compared with what would be regarded as essential in the case of a European.

It is also basic to my thinking that the processes of justice, once commenced, are free from any outside influence until they are completed, and that, in the appropriate forms, the judicial system provides its own opportunity for appeal from one tribunal to a higher tribunal and that there is the same independence from outside direction at all stages of the process of appeal. The courts not only punish a person for a breach of the laws; they also protect him.

Furthermore, I have an old-fashioned regard for the Crown as the fount of justice and an old-fashioned respect for English law. In a dependent and primitive society, such as that in New Guinea, I think the individual native would have a greater expectation of justice, in the fullest sense of the term, by arrangements which would make courts in the British tradition more easily accessible to him, with a bench appointed in the customary way, observing the customary forms, and patiently applying the laws applicable to 'subjects' of the Crown, than he would have in village courts set up by an administrative officer, with a bench composed of village natives following variable rules and applying a variable body of custom. We should not let ourselves be persuaded overmuch by bodies such as the Trusteeship Council, which expresses as much prejudice against 'colonial' powers as it expresses any knowledge of conditions in the Territories. I think the answer to them should not be lip-service to the idea of native courts or a pretence that we really have them. If we believe it, we should be prepared to say straight out that we believe the courts of the Territory will give to the native a more substantial measure of justice than native courts. I think too that we should scout the notion that a court administering justice should have a representative character. Indeed my views go so far as to say that representatives are almost certain to be bad judges in any cause. To put six villagers on a bench to try a cause between two other villagers is not, to my mind, bound to bring a greater assurance of justice to the litigants than they would have from a visiting magistrate. I am also unreceptive to the idea that the judicial system of the Territory should be tampered with for the sake of the political education of the natives.

Finally, although I notice that certain safeguards are introduced in the ordinance, I think that in Papua and New Guinea we have to be careful about what we may do to create an impression among any group of natives regarding the sources of justice. It is, in historical fact, a gift that we have brought to them. In the interests of good administration and the advancement of the natives, (quite apart from any old-fashioned prejudices I may have myself) I believe there is a great deal to be said for presenting the idea that the Queen (someone above government) is the fount of justice and that the courts are the Queen's courts. I think a good deal of mischief could be done if it could be represented that the courts belonged to the Administration, or to the district commissioner, or to the village or to anyone else. It would be particularly unfortunate if it were thought in any village or group of villages that this or that influential native on the bench was running the Court, that this was 'his' court or that he was the person to look to in order to win a case or avoid punishment. The existence of this last-mentioned danger is indicated by the fact that in the present ordinance all sorts of provisions have been made to prevent just that sort of outcome and those precautionary provisions have been carried so far that, as I suggested earlier, it may turn out that the ordinance is just a sham and a pretence.

At all events, it will be necessary to convince me on the points presented in the three preceding paragraphs before I would approve of the principle that there should be a system of native courts.

Lest my viewpoint should be misunderstood, I ought to make it plain that I appreciate the necessity for some of the practices at present followed in the Territory and raise no objection to them. First of all I understand that the existing courts, when dealing with cases involving natives, do take cognisance of the existence of tribal institutions, customs and usages of the natives when they are evaluating the evidence and particularly when they are deciding on a penalty or an award. Secondly, although I cannot claim to have a knowledge of more than a fraction of the laws of the Territory, I know that some of the ordinances of the Territory contain special provisions inserted to protect the interests of the natives and to pay regard to native usage. In my view this method of respecting native custom and usage might even be extended. Thirdly, I am aware that, in an informal way, officers of the administration, using good sense rather than a legal form, help natives to settle purely local affairs or themselves mediate to achieve rough justice on small matters of local and domestic concern. The continued use of such *administrative* methods of establishing and maintaining order in the villages and commencing the process of advancing the natives seems to me to be unobjectionable, and necessary in the early stages of contact. It is a different thing to formalize the process into a system of established judicial bodies administering their own system of law. The present ordinance obviously would apply chiefly, not in the stage of first contact, but in those villages where the natives have already advanced to the stage of having village councils. It is open to question whether they would appreciate courts which are 'run' specially for them by the district commissioner or district officer as much as they would appreciate courts which accord more closely to the normal judicial system. Do we, at this point in the growth of the natives' ideas, direct them down a branch path or towards the main course of development in civilization?

It may be that, on reflection, the Department and the Administration may come to the conclusion that what they are really seeking is not a separate system of Native courts at all but really some approval and perhaps some clearer directive on the administrative methods for handling the trouble-some individual and settling disputes in villages during the period of first contact with the natives. They would find me receptive to any ideas of this kind that they might put forward although I can see no reason or necessity to incorporate *administrative methods* in an ordinance. I would also think that such arrangements should be transitional.

At present I cannot approve the proposal to establish native courts of the kind provided in this draft ordinance as part of the system for the administration of justice. My own tentative views are that if native courts are needed, they should be established in a form in keeping with the established judicial system of the Territory. Steps can be taken—for example the strengthening of the magistracy—to make it more easily accessible. If natives are to be appointed to a bench—and I raise no objection to the appointment of natives—they are to be appointed for their competence to administer justice according to the customary standards and not in a representative or semi-representative capacity. If, in the long term, it is intended to make native customs and usages part of the general body of the laws of the Territory it can best be done by inserting suitable provisions in the relevant ordinances of the Territory. In the short term, regard can be paid to native customs and usage by the courts, according to their own wisdom, in the manner in which they already do so. During periods of establishing law and order and accustoming natives to Australian practices it is assumed that officers of the Administration will continue to conduct 'courts' in villages, but these should be clearly distinguished as serving the purposes of administration and not as part of the judicial system. If required, a directive and rules for the conduct of such 'courts' can be drawn up but the need for an ordinance for this purpose is not seen nor is it envisaged that such 'courts' could exercise the same powers of the established courts of the Territory either in civil or criminal cases.

It surprises me that, as well as not bringing this matter under ministerial notice, the persons engaged in drafting appear to have forgotten the existence of the Chief Justice of the Territory, who has had a longer experience of these matters than most others, and of the Solicitor-General, Professor Bailey, who carried out a special inquiry into the judicial system of the Territory at my request. I think they should have an opportunity to comment.

The response to this minute came twelve months later. The belated memorandum from the Administrator, dated 17 January 1956, did not satisfy me as an answer to the questions I had raised, and I decided that special native courts of the kind proposed in the draft ordinance that had been placed before me should not be established. (Minute of 27 January 1956.)

The matter was listed for discussion with the Administrator in Canberra and I directed that discussion should concentrate on what action was needed immediately 'to ensure that, within the established system of the administration of justice . . . the ends of justice and humanity will be served in all dealings with the native peoples and that, in due course, there will be fuller participation by the native peoples themselves in the administration of justice'. I regret that nothing much came of this discussion. Then, as it appears to me, the Administration lost interest. It may have been that, with the secondment of Fenbury to the United Nations Secretariat in 1956, the chief exponent of a comprehensive system of native courts was temporarily absent from the Territory. In any case I did not obtain any full discussion with the Administration of the doubts I had raised. In the light of later events, it would seem however that the resistance to my views did not cease but went underground. The outcome is recounted in chapter 29.

[17]

TASKS AND POLICIES: A SUMMING-UP IN 1956

In 1956 I received two invitations to deliver public lectures and I used the occasion both to sort out some of my own thinking and to bring some facets of Australian responsibility before a thoughtful section of the Australian public.

The first of the two addresses I called 'Australia's Task in Papua and New Guinea' and the second 'Australian Policy in Papua and New Guinea'.* Both were published and widely circulated. I cannot claim that anyone took much notice of them or that they had much effect either in communicating facts or in influencing opinion. I return to them now for their historical interest as a record of my state of mind after five years of hard work in the portfolio. It is proper to present them as my own view for, as with all my speeches and lectures, I wrote them myself, and at some points I am sure my officers would have differed from me.

It is plain to me now that I was very much influenced at that time by my awareness that few Australians were interested in or well informed about the Territory. I laboured some points that would now seem obvious. I was also influenced by the experience of five years of working with men whose boast was in being 'practical', and hence I felt a need for fuller discussion of ideas and for the clearer definition of principles. In these lectures I indulged myself in discussion about questions on which I had found no one to talk to in my daily work. I may have asserted some platitudes too strongly. I may seem to have toyed academically with too many propositions of the universal and not enough of the particular. If this is so, the fact is historical evidence of the way in which I read the situation in the Territory and my view of the gaps in the Australian approach to the tasks of Administration in 1956.

In the first lecture, given at Perth in September, I distinguished between two levels in our task—at one level the various duties in health, education, law and order, development of resources and so on; at the other level what we hoped to see as the eventual outcome of all our efforts. Discussing the 'over-all objective' I warned against positive assertions. It was beyond our power to

* The seventh Roy Milne Memorial Lecture, 10 Sept. 1956. Australian Institute of International Affairs. The George Judah Cohen Memorial Lecture, 4 Oct. 1956, University of Sydney.

predict with certainty the course of human behaviour or to prophesy the shape of historical change. Societies built themselves. Institutions grew out of the needs and the opportunities of societies. We should take care over the principles that governed our conduct before we made blueprints. If we were sure of the principles on which a good society rested and followed those principles, we could rely on society to work out its own future.

Commenting on this part of my lecture in the light of later years, I would say now that a good deal of journalistic misunderstanding of my actions as Minister would have been avoided if only one or two journalists had read and understood this description of my own approach to the task. For example, if they had understood my basic belief that a society has to 'work out its own future' they might have hesitated over their repeated assertions that I was trying to impose 'the Westminster form of government', or that I was reluctant about self-determination or that I was obstinate in not declaring 'target dates' for this or that change, or that I was 'opposed to creating an elite' or that I was trying to 'hold the people back'. When they made such assertions, they showed scant understanding of the foundation of my policy of making it possible for a new society to shape itself.

In the Perth lecture of 1956 I proceeded to ask what were the principles that should govern our conduct. I referred to the 'great moral principles on which civilized human conduct rests' and also gave some examples of other principles on which to shape our administrative actions. One example was the principle of justice. 'It means', I said, 'that without fear, favour or privilege, each person is assured that his rights will be protected, that any wrongs against him will be redressed, and that any wrong he commits against others will be corrected. Each man, woman and child can rely on being dealt with justly.' Another example was the principle of freedom. I indicated ways in which people in New Guinea were not yet free and the steps by which freedom and liberty could be gained.

> Freedom and liberty make a slippery path unless, as the primitive man advances step by step towards them, he is also advancing step by step towards civilization. Thus, in serving our principles, we not only have to make intelligent adjustments to meet prevailing conditions . . . but we also have to exercise an intelligent control over the pace of change so that each new right falls into hands which will use it and not destroy it.

A third example was the 'representative principle' based on 'the idea that a people should be able to choose those who will serve them in government and that those who are chosen should be answerable for their actions to the people.' The representative principle, I continued, led eventually to responsible government. It was a means by which a community might freely and yet in an orderly way build the institutions it wished to have, shaping them to meet its changing needs, and evolve, without undue stress and without coercion, into the sort of society it wished and needed to be, bound together by laws and customs of its own making. I discussed some of the difficulties in applying this principle and warned that there could be 'coloured privilege and coloured tyranny just as well as a white tyranny or a white privilege'. Nevertheless we should keep the principle steadily in mind. The fourth example was the 'principle of trusteeship'. We were not governing Papua and New Guinea to serve our own advantage or to place our own gain above the welfare of its people but accepted an obligation towards the people.

The discussion of these principles was undertaken in order to reveal to the audience the 'moral and intellectual responsibility placed on those who undertake the tutelage of a primitive people'. We had the task of guiding a people towards their ultimate good. We should recognize that their ultimate good would be the building of a society 'founded on such principles as those I have discussed—those and others of their kind'. We had to apply our principles with an intelligent appreciation of the changing situations with which we were dealing. One of the pitfalls of administration was set by this necessity to make adjustments, for the official might forget in his preoccupation with the day-by-day task that what he did to overcome the local conditions was only an expedient to help him reach the higher goal. One of the follies of administering powers was to mistake an expedient for a settled rule.

Rounding off this discussion of the need to be guided by principles while being 'realistic and practical about the daily tasks of administration', I added,

> We can find our surest guide if we hold to a fundamental belief that each individual has a value as an individual—a belief in the worth and dignity of the human person. If we find that we are doing or contemplating anything that devalues the individual, then let us look most carefully at the state of our administration.

In this section of my address I presented the view that, if we did our task in accordance with certain guiding principles, we could await with confidence the evolution of the future society and form of government in the Territory. Reading my argument again across the distance of many years, my memory is that, so far as my remarks were combative, I had been moved in part by tendencies still strong in a few of my departmental officers who had been influenced by the early days of the Australian School of Pacific Administration to a view that almost everything could be achieved by planning and control as laid down by them and by no one else. I was also moved in part by my resistance to some academic popularization of the idea that the Soviet authors on the rule of colonial peoples had the only true gospel. I wished to emphasize a view on the evolution and growth of society and social institutions rather than to accept that a new society in Papua and New Guinea could be constructed to order. I was not the 'paternalist'. Those who sometimes used that word in criticism of me made far more plans than I did about the sort of society they wished to impose on the New Guinea people.

In the second half of my address I turned to some particular tasks. The first was race relations. In the future all the peoples of the Territory of all colours would 'have to live alongside each other in mutual respect and trust and for a common benefit . . . Underlying all we do in Papua and New Guinea is a problem of race relations. That problem, too, is never solved by rules, but only by the practice of simple human virtues.'

Then I discussed the task of the development of the resources of the Territory as part of the process of education, as a means of maintaining a higher standard of living and as a help in providing services and facilities for the community. I also stated a view which, after my time, became a lost cause. Talking of the obligation to make untapped resources available to the world, I said, 'I would regard that however as incidental to development in the broader sense. Indeed I would go so far as to say that the too rapid development of these resources at any stage, simply to satisfy a demand from the outside world, should be avoided if in any case it would prove injurious to the welfare of the people.' I am aware that this statement shocked and annoyed some of my hearers and was always resisted by a few of my departmental officers.

Then I passed to some of the basic tasks of daily administration—establishing law and order and making friendly and helpful contacts with the people, health, education, and the improvement of agriculture. After that would come further measures for economic development to maintain a higher standard of living. The changes our administration was producing would lead to changes in social organization and would awaken eager demands by the people for further changes. Our experience was that this demand came first for social welfare, then for economic opportunity and then for political progress.

In a brief reference to political change, I spoke of the need for the people to develop a sense of community, which at present was lacking, and to overcome the barrier set by hundreds of different languages. A path could be found in our efforts to give them a common language and a common stock of ideas. Yet we should remember that they already had a culture of their own.

> Scores of different groups knowing no relationship with each other may gradually become a Papuan people joined by a common language, living at a common standard of material well-being, and with a common culture, strongly influenced by Christian teaching and by Australian social, economic and political practice, but preserving and enriching all that is best in their native cultural heritage. They will certainly not remain as they have been for centuries. They certainly will not be exactly as we are. They will be a new people living a new life in a new land.

I emphasized strongly the rapidity of the change and the strong influence Australia was having on the nature of change. The nature of what we did in the Territory and the way in which we did it were more important than the number of things we did. Our concern had to be with the quality of our actions rather than with the quantity of our effort. Yet we had to recognize too the urgency set by the pressure of world events and by the rapidity of change among the people themselves. We had to be watchful and careful in this period of rapid change and, not least, we had to watch ourselves and be careful about our own motives and purposes. 'Rule over dependent peoples calls for intelligence and high personal qualities, and not the least of these qualities is unselfishness carried to the point of self-effacement. It also calls for constant watchfulness and freshening of the mind, and not the least of the purposes of this watchfulness is to guard against the ill consequences which any form of rule has on the ruler.'

My memory is that these concluding remarks were influenced to some extent by my observations on visits to the Territory of the continuing tendency of our Administration officers to develop colonialist habits and outlook and the unavoidable elements of paternalism in a great number of the decisions and actions we were all taking to help the people of the Territory. I also wrote, 'Paternalism should not be accepted as a term of abuse or criticism. At the same time we need to be aware . . . paternalism becomes oppressive if it is carried too far and for too long, and if it is exercised not for the good of the children but for the comfort and well-being of the father.' At that time, there was a good deal of rather glib writing and talking about 'paternalism' as though it was the most serious offence that could be alleged to anyone who was governing dependent peoples. 'Tutelage' had been a rather cleaner word but was now outworn and 'trusteeship for dependent peoples' had been hallowed by the United Nations Charter so was only used with reverence. 'Paternalism' was the dirty word for the same thing.

I would admit to having been paternal if it were defined very narrowly to mean caring for, teaching and paying the expenses of a people in situations wholly unfamiliar to them and beyond their capacity to handle, the clear intention being to prepare them for full responsibility. Unfortunately many of those who used the term never distinguished between a form of paternalism that had as its purpose the preparation of men in as short a period as possible to take on the full responsibilities of adulthood and a paternalism that would have the effect of keeping them constantly in a state of infancy. The test question of course is, Who decides when the child has become an adult? Objection to paternalism properly arises if the 'father' claims that he alone can say when the 'child' can go out on his own.

I found the frequent use of the word both irritating and misleading because its use promoted too many doubtful analogies with the relationship of father and child. I think the idea that the administering country is a 'father' to the dependent country is historically untrue, factually inexact and administratively inapplicable. In the case of a community, I do not think one can fix an 'age of majority', an 'age of consent' or an age when the 'child' becomes responsible for paying his or her own bills, and in any case these are not matters in which parental authority or a superior law will prevail. I felt too that the terms expressed and helped to perpetuate too many false notions—on the one hand the native people regarding the Australian Government simply as 'papa bilong me' to give them everything for which they asked; on the other hand some Administration officers and planters justifying their attitudes by saying amiably, 'They are only children and have to be treated as such.' I myself disliked the idea of being the big white father, but every time I started to ask for more money for the Territory, some of my more foolish parliamentary colleagues would use the tag to my very great annoyance at this misunderstanding of what I was trying to do by those on whom I depended to support me in doing it. I lost my patience in more than one argument with Territory people who persisted in the 'treat them as children' argument.

In the second of the two lectures in 1956, delivered in Sydney, I devoted a good deal of my time to recounting what we had done in the Territory and describing factually the rising scale of effort. In my five years as Minister, the scale of our work had trebled. All this is part of the record and need not be repeated here. At the moment, I refer to my second lecture only for the light it may give on policy towards the end of 1956.

First I emphasized that Papua and New Guinea had its own characteristics and its own problems, indicating my view that what was done there should be tested by whether it was suitable for the country and the people rather than whether the action suited some other dependent territory. Before other advances could be made, the two great practical tasks of establishing law and order and improving health had to be accomplished. These led to the third great practical task of education, using the term in its most comprehensive sense. The further social, economic and political advancement of the people began with these initial tasks.

Then I dealt with the policies of protecting the land rights of the native people and controlling land use and distribution, including my decision not to have separate closed communities of European farmers. I described labour policy and indicated the change in the Territory conditions in respect of employment. Other topics were economic development, agricultural training, financing native enterprises, production of food supplies, political advancement and the strengthening of the Administration. It was a fair recapitulation of what was being done. I think it justified the claim made in the peroration that the Government had a clear purpose and was making a steady effort. An immense work remained.

We Australians have got a great job ahead of us. We are not doing enough but if you could meet, as I have met, the many young Australian men of character who are already on the job in Papua and New Guinea you would not have the least doubt that, as a people, we have got the quality for the task. If you could see, as I have seen, the progress made year by year, you would not have the least doubt that we are making ground. But the greatest challenge to us and the hope of greatest achievement are still ahead. We have done enough to know that we can do even better.

There I stood momentarily towards the end of 1956 on a small hillock of optimism. I had worked hard. I had accomplished a great deal. I had also grown in knowledge of the Territory, its people and its problems. I was getting a better staff. I had grown in confidence. I had become deeply interested as well as involved in this special field of government. Hitherto I had also had the practical advantages of benevolent autocracy, making decisions without contradiction and without encountering any political interest among those whom the decisions primarily affected or among those who gave me the authority and the funds with which to govern. This situation would not last. As the result largely of the initial success, I was about to inherit many complexities in the new situation that had been created, new tasks arising out of the tasks that had been accomplished, and interests and political pressures largely awakened by my own endeavours. My benevolence would be disputed and my decisiveness in government would be fogged at times by political argument. Our own campaigning on behalf of the Territory was bringing to an end the easy days when few people outside the Territory were interested in what we were doing.

Looking back on the first five years of my ministry, I think a strong influence on much of my work was my reaction against the colonialist attitudes I found in the Administration and among the European population of the Territory. I was hesitant at first, for I had no theories of my own and no experience in this field of politics. Consequently, much of what I did first was to check tendencies that I thought were wrong and contrary to the general purpose of Australian rule of a dependent territory. Then I tried to bring a new outlook and, when I did not receive the results of any new thinking by others, to grope myself towards some broad statements of policy and principles to guide our activity.

PART III

THE SECOND FIVE YEARS
1956–1960

[18]

EXASPERATION AT DELAY

In the second five years of my ministry I had a growing sense of urgency. I had clearer ideas about what ought to be done and at the same time a more bitter disappointment when they were not done. My determination was greater, my efforts more strenuous, but the results were less satisfying and my administration became more peremptory.

Some of this may have been due to my own shortcomings. I was not outstandingly successful in finding the right men to get things done and was prone to make demands without making sure that an officer was capable of responding to them. Luckily Lambert could work as hard as I could and was just as tough as I was, but like me he was not very good at leading lame horses to the plough.

There were two exceptional circumstances. Recruitment was still very difficult owing to the high level of employment and the expanding opportunities in Australia itself. Attempts at recruiting from overseas were not notably successful. Other demands on my attention were also increasing. During this period I was taking over both Cocos Islands and Christmas Island and setting up Australian administration there and was making major moves in development and aboriginal welfare in the Northern Territory. In Cabinet, Parliament and the electorate we had unusual pressures, and my rise in ministerial seniority meant that I took a greater share of them. Hence I could not keep my eyes continually on Papua and New Guinea. I would make a decision, think that all was clear for action and turn to other urgent matters, only to check back one or two months later to find that nothing had moved.

In the Department at Canberra, we were gradually building up some strength and competence, but in the Territory the greatly increased administrative demands had not been matched by a sufficient growth in administrative efficiency. Numbers of staff grew and the educational standard of recruits was higher, but because of the limited number of candidates for promotion within a small public service, we had to rely a good deal on new and untried people for newly created jobs. We were seldom able to find men and women already accustomed to this type of public administration or to living in this kind of community. It often took a year or two after they were recruited before we started to get good value out of even the best of the newcomers. We had to wait while they adjusted themselves to a new environment and a new way of working.

Every recruit created the additional problem of providing him with a house and an office. In the main towns and particularly Port Moresby we had to keep building the substructure of administration while we expected quick results from the superstructure. Typists and clerks were just as hard to get as geniuses.

Many of the officers worked under difficult conditions, but some of the newcomers were less accustomed to improvisation than some of the earlier officers had been. Moreover any new man faced a further difficulty of accommodating himself to the ways of a strongly entrenched and closely knit group of old hands of the colonialist days. He either became like them or had the discomfort and the impediments suffered by an outsider. In either case his capacity to work suffered.

I still sought for an impetus that would come from the top in the Territory itself. It was my constant disappointment that it did not come. In July 1956 I suggested again that the Administrator had far too wide a range of duties. While the Government looked to him to be the effective head of local administration, he continued under local custom to carry an increasing burden of duties resembling those of a governor in one of the Australian States. Could we separate these 'honorific duties' from practical administrative tasks? I asked the law advisers to examine again the possibility of the appointment by the Governor-General of a Deputy Governor under Section 126 of the Australian Constitution and the assignment to him of certain vice-regal functions so that the Administrator appointed under the Papua and New Guinea Act could 'come down from the top of the hill' to do the hard work and leave the occupancy of 'Government House' and all that went with it to the Deputy of the Governor-General. Nothing came of the suggestion. I still think it was a good idea and that the strong opposition to it, both in Canberra and in Port Moresby, was ill-considered. Looking forward, such an arrangement would also have smoothed the constitutional path to self-government.

In the meantime we had tried to give Cleland a good Assistant Administrator. We picked the best we could—he was really Lambert's discovery—but he had the handicap of being an 'outsider', had a rather rough time of it in the Territory without ever being able to complete the adjustment, and did not last long. An Acting Assistant Administrator sent up on trial—a man who had proven himself a highly successful officer in other posts—also could not break through the local barriers, had an equally uncomfortable time, and was transferred out of the Territory to a more useful role, where again he gave highly creditable service.

At the beginning of 1957 we tried again, setting our sights on a senior man in the Territory itself. The move was complicated by a certain amount of funny business in Port Moresby where one of the oldest and least suitable of the old colonialist type was the fancied candidate. I would not have him because of my judgement on his administrative capacity. Lambert helped me through the tangle and we overcame some local resistance and I appointed John Gunther in

February 1957, even though I knew it meant the loss of an outstanding Director of Health. This was a success.

In the same month I appointed Neil Thomson[35] as Public Service Commissioner. After Head had returned to the Commonwealth Public Service Board, I had appointed T. A. Huxley as Public Service Commissioner. He worked hard on many of the basic problems of forming a public service and faced many difficulties with little help from others. In December 1955 he chose to return to another position in Australia. We borrowed E. W. Dwyer[36] from the Commonwealth Public Service to act as Commissioner during 1956 —he was unwilling to take a permanent appointment—and then were fortunate to find Thomson. It was my own idea that experience in the public service of a State was nearer to the realities in the Territory than was the Commonwealth Public Service and I had asked Lambert to try to get someone from one of the States. Thomson had been on the staff of the New South Wales Public Service Board for fifteen years, rising to the rank of senior inspector. He was also qualified as a solicitor. He brought good qualifications and experience and best of all an enthusiasm and a dedication that made him of great value to us. The work, which he did tirelessly and at some expense to his own health and perhaps also to his career prospects, command fuller recognition than he has received as one of those who can rightly be regarded as the builders of a self-governing Papua and New Guinea. I valued Thomson's competence, patience and diligence very highly. Somehow he managed to survive and master the local resistance.

The appointments of Gunther and Thomson in February 1957 seem to me to mark the beginning of an improvement but did not immediately end my frustration.

Perhaps I should illustrate first the kind of exasperation I was feeling. I can do so by brief reference to notes I made at the time on a number of different topics. At the end of January 1956 the Administrator came down to Canberra at my request for consultations, to quote my letter to him, 'to see if we can clear our minds and reach firm directives regarding the objectives of policy in Papua and New Guinea during the next three years'. I expressed a hope that 'we would be able to lay down some order of priority in the major tasks to be undertaken and to sketch a timetable for the achievement of the various tasks which I propose to set for the Administration'. In addition I said I wanted to discuss further action to be taken on several outstanding matters. These included native labour, native courts, local government councils, agricultural extension work, the Education Department, Crown Law Department, prison reform, mixed-race people, the situation in the Gazelle Peninsula, housing and accommodation for public servants, and uncontrolled areas. That list summarizes matters on which I was most dissatisfied. In my minute I also spoke of the need for more uniform progress for the advancement of the native peoples over the whole Territory and the need for a further spreading of administrative works and a decentralization of administrative activity. (Minute of 20 January 1956.)

In a further minute, of 26 January, I spelt out the purpose of these talks. First, we should clean up all major matters outstanding. This should result in the early submission of recommendations which, when approved by the Minister, would mean that final action could proceed at once. Second, we should lay down a programme of action. We should define in exact terms the task to be done, reach a clear idea of the way in which it was to be done, and establish a timetable for action. Third, if from these discussions we discovered that further directions on policy were needed, I would give them.

These were high hopes. We had the talks on 1 and 2 February. I was disappointed with the outcome. The discussion dealt more with difficulties and doubts than with how to get things done. Since I am writing now chiefly about broad problems of administration and my own exasperation, I will not digress on the substance of any of the particular subjects raised. The chief outcome of the discussions was a series of recommendations made to me by the Department on 23 March and approved on 3 April, but unfortunately most of the recommendations could not go much further than asking the Administrator for further study and consideration and preparation of further proposals. At the same time, however, we inaugurated procedures of regular programming and reporting so that I could keep track of the results.

Further illustrations of my methods and my disappointments will be found in other minutes. On another subject I wrote in January 1956, 'What I want now is exactly what I wanted last August—the immediate preparation of proposals for legislation to give effect to my direction of 19 July 1955.' In yet another field of interest I had given instructions in February 1954 for the creation of an auxiliary division of the public service so that we could introduce into the public service indigenous employees who were not yet qualified educationally for normal appointment but might be trained on the job. Approvals on various details of the scheme were given in November 1954. In January 1956, the work was still incomplete. In August 1956 I was still demanding action. In reciting this disappointing history, I quoted it as yet another example of long delay and asked Lambert to study it closely to find out what was really causing the lag between the giving of a ministerial direction and the commencement of any effective action. In another minute in August 1956 I drew attention to delays in bringing the Lae Hospital into use and complained that the only result of a recent inquiry had been an 'off-hand note from the Acting-Administrator'. I said that it was the function of the Minister and Department to make these inquiries, not for purposes of censure but in order to help improve the functioning of the territories. I insisted on fuller information without further delay. A little earlier, in a minute about corrective institutions, I had expressed concern at the gap between decision and action. On subject after subject I had occasion to complain of delay. One such minute on 7 November 1956 concluded, 'This is just another instance in which, a decision on policy having been made and a direction given, nothing has happened. At point after point in the Territory we are coming up against this sorry fact that the Government is unable to have its decisions put into effect. Why?' On 25 January 1956 I minuted a submission on the problem of the mixed-race people: 'In my view this shows a deplorable neglect to an extent that almost suggests indifference on the part of the Administration to the problem itself and to the instructions given from time to time over the past five years for handling the subject.' On the provision of housing, the disclosure of 'inexcusable delay' in giving effect to a direction, led me to write on 29 December 1956, 'Five months after approval of the programme, I am informed by the Administrator that there has been considerable delay but up to date there is no information about whether any work has started or when it will start. It is apparent that the delay has arisen over matters that should have been attended to before the original submission was made.' On another question, in a minute of 11 February 1957, I tabulated the history. On 15 August 1956 I had asked the Administrator for his recommendations. On 4 September, 3 October and 26 November 1956 and 14 January 1957 reminders were sent. On 31 January 1957 the information was received. A departmental submission was made on 7 February and the ministerial decision was given three days later. My attempt to find out why the delay occurred brought predictable answers. The Administration claimed shortness of staff. Lambert gave instances in which the Territory officers did not know how to go about the job given to them.

The interlocking of the two answers is illustrated by the experience on housing. I had tried to extract from the Administration a recruitment budget, the rate of recruitment being necessarily related to the provision of places in which officers could live and offices in which they could work. At the beginning of 1957 the Department gave me a progress report on the provision of accommodation in towns, showing that in the first six months of the year we would have a total recruitment of 200 and a total availability of 243 beds. Hopefully, I wrote, 'Keep up the pressure. If at any time it becomes possible to increase the rate of recruitment and suitable candidates are available, we should do so.' We had inaugurated a system of routine monthly reports to keep track of progress. The May report showed that in April we had only got twenty-two extra bed spaces when fifty-three had been promised. A minute of 28 August 1957 summarized my view of the subsequent history:

> After the Administration had failed lamentably to grapple with the demand for housing, a team of officers was sent up from the Department to try to show them how to do their own job. As a result of this visit a programme was prepared and, although it fell short of the Government's hopes, it was accepted. This programme was agreed to by the Administration as a programme which was capable of performance. It certainly was not a programme which set a target. It represented what they could do and was certainly far below what the Government wanted. Now the Administration has shown in three successive months that it cannot even carry out this reduced programme.

I instructed the Department to take further steps to help get houses and asked Lambert, who was in Port Moresby at the time on other business, to discuss the problem with the Administrator at once. We tried again, but at the end of the year, in yet another minute, I was sadly noting, 'The Administration is still not producing the results I want and the housing programme still does not seem to me to have been prepared with practical wisdom or carried out with the constant energy that are necessary to get results.' (Minute of 5 November 1957.) I reflect now that it was a very mild sort of rocket for a minute written on Guy Fawkes Day.

Some of my other minutes in this period concerned neglect to follow instructions. In the 1956–7 Budget, instructions had been laid down that priority in the purchase of vehicles should be given to the four-wheel-drive cars and trucks for outback and developmental work. In Australia itself Cabinet, at a time of import restrictions, had laid down rules for purchase of more modest official cars from Australian manufacturers rather than imported cars. From a newspaper, I learnt that Port Moresby had spent a large sum in sterling on a luxury car for the Administrator. After I had scolded him for this, it was disclosed, when the Australian Department of Supply questioned a requisition, that the Administration was buying more high-priced cars with a low Australian content for town use by senior officials. (Minutes of 28 August and 6 September 1956.) On a visit to the highlands in the middle of 1957 I commented strongly again that motor-cars for higher officials in the towns were being provided before the basic needs for utility vehicles had been met, and gave an instruction that in the 1957–8 Budget not a single motor-car was to be purchased unless the requirements of the more remote districts for four-wheel-drive vehicles and trucks had previously been met. (Minute of 28 June 1957.)

In other cases, in which my instructions affected some of the comforts of the senior public servants themselves, it was only human nature that diligence sometimes flagged or that instructions were overlooked. One instance led me to allege in August 1957 'obstruction of policy'. It concerned fees for liquor licences. Cabinet was demanding that more local revenue should be raised— I shall discuss this demand in chapter 23—and my minute reads in part, 'Although the attention of the Administrator was drawn in May 1955 to the need for raising more money from licence fees there have been two years of temporizing.' (Minute of 29 August 1957.) The inaction looked like unwillingness of public servants to pay more for liquor. Another instance concerned rentals on Administration houses. Understandably the public servants who occupied the houses were not as active in responding to proposals to charge a near-economic rental as they were in matters of a different kind.

During 1957 there were also a number of instances in which something went wrong and special investigations were required. Following a report by the Administrator on one incident concerning the breakdown of an officer, the Public Service Commissioner was instructed by me on 16 December to make an investigation into the adequacy and efficiency of the organization of the Department of the Administrator and the Department of Native Affairs for maintaining oversight of the work and welfare of field officers. (Minute of 16 December 1957.) In the same month I started an investigation into the Animal Industry Division. I wrote, 'I have not been impressed very much by anything said or done on cattle in the Territory . . . That is why I want a fresh, tough and imaginative mind, with technical competence, to look at the question.' (Minute of 11 December 1957.) This was occasioned by disappointment at the results of a cattle introduction scheme.

Earlier a separate Organization and Methods Inquiry had been started into the Department of Native Affairs. (Minute of 27 November 1957.) In October, following complaints about delays in a contract for building schools, I had asked urgently for a report from the Administrator on why such temporizing occurred. (Minute of 30 October 1957.) In the same month Lambert had completed a review, undertaken at my direction, into the operation of

Administration sawmills at Lae and Keravat. I minuted his report: 'My own conclusion is that the lack of oversight and direction at the top levels of the Administration gives cause for very serious concern. The Government is bound to rely on the Administrator and the heads of departments in the Territory to see that the requirements of policy, economy and efficient administration are met . . .' (Minute of 4 October 1957.)

I quote these instances as illustrations of the sort of disappointment I was experiencing at this time. There is no area in which I have a greater sense of failure than in my inability to get the Territory Administration to work harder and do its job better. One reason for the poor performance was simply that we did not have enough really competent and experienced men in the top positions and they lacked the support of good routine office workers—the typists, record keepers and base-grade clerks who do the drudgery of administration. Another reason why results were not as good as I hoped was that the system of decentralization by giving greater responsibility to district commissioners for general direction of administration in their districts was limping badly because some of the district commissioners were just not good enough for the job. My own idea was that a man from any of the senior levels of the Administration could be made a district commissioner. In the Territory, however, the posts were regarded as the close preserve of the Department of Native Affairs. The Administrator, who made the appointments, stuck loyally to this group in spite of my suggestions to him to look elsewhere. In three or four instances when Cleland selected one of the younger and more promising Native Affairs officers to be a district commissioner, a successful appeal against the promotion meant that his chosen man was replaced by an older officer whom Cleland had already judged to be unsuitable. The consequence in some cases was that we had district commissioners who had been capable patrol officers and correct district officers but had little training in what to do at an office desk, and sometimes scant sympathy with the unfamiliar things that agricultural officers, school-teachers, project managers, accountants, and other strange 'blow-ins' were bent on doing and had been instructed to do. The other difficulty was that, as work in the districts became more varied, the various specialist branches tended to look solely to the head office of their respective departments and not to the district commissioner as the deputy of the Administrator in their district. Four or five of the district commissioners did very well and gave energy and direction to all that was undertaken in the district. Others were distinguished chiefly by living in a rather better house than their fellow-officers.

We also bore the unavoidable handicap of absences on leave. I used to be taken by surprise, after a new venture had been approved, to find that key men were on leave and would not be back for some months. In the pre-war days, when transport to and from Papua and New Guinea by steamboat was slow, a system of leave was devised under which officers had three months on full pay after twenty-one months of service and a longer period every six years. Officers probably needed that sort of break in those days. In the post-war years, when conditions were not so trying, some officers, not feeling an acute need for recuperation every two years, preferred to build up their leave credits and perhaps to add on some additional credits for working on public holidays. At the end of something short of six years' service they would go off on a grand tour of the world for nearly a year on full pay. At any given time the absence from the Territory of middle-rank and senior officers on leave was critical. This seemed to be more marked from 1957 onwards as more and more of our new recruits on whom we were depending and who were getting the advantage of local experience were then beginning to take long periods of recreational leave after five or six years' work.

Alongside this was the fact that all our public servants were members of a minority community of Europeans which had been accustomed to dominate everything that was done. Many of our officers, especially field officers, had a great and selfless dedication to their work among the indigenous people and, in the case of patrol officers, medical officers, medical assistants and many others in remote places, lived close to the people. Port Moresby, Rabaul and Lae however were becoming urban communities where many of our Australian officers saw the indigenous people only as people on the fringes of a European community—messengers, houseboys, caddies on the golf links, or in a similar relationship.

While some of the newer and younger men lived active and disciplined lives, playing vigorous games and keeping physically and mentally sharp, some of the more senior people lived very much 'in club', visiting, drinking, eating and gossiping in the same circles as soon as work had finished, and looking for the esteem of the members of the circle. It was a colonial 'Main Street'. This pattern of what was correct and acceptable conduct had a deadening effect. In case of error or shortcoming, there was a great group loyalty and a most efficient way of covering up. Within this group, through those very pleasant traders, planters and distinguished citizens and a few pre-war officers and some of the ranking people of war time, an undisturbed pre-war code still prevailed and the observance of this code was a condition of self-regard. There was a strong sense of community among this section of Europeans and strong loyalty to their own community.

One cannot repeat too often the fact that up to this time the only articulate opinion in the Territory on any matter was that of Europeans. The only media of communication, whether by newspaper or radio, were really by Europeans to one another, for the little radio sessions for the natives and the little village mimeographed sheets were in reality at that stage just giving baby-talk to babies.

Looking back on this period, and thinking only on my problems of administration, I realize now that I was far too correct and considerate and not forceful enough. I waited for the Administrator to study questions and to make his own recommendations. I gave him assistance to that end by sending officers into the territory to assist his officers. I relied on the Territory Administration too much and left the execution of policy to them. Lambert and I took such measures as requiring monthly reports and assisting Territory officers to prepare work programmes and action plans while respecting their responsibility to carry them out. I should have moved in much more heavily and brushed them aside more often. I was restrained from doing so because I felt the objective was not only immediate action to secure an immediate result but the building up in the Territory of a local administrative structure in readiness for self-government. We were not only working for the Territory today but for the nation of tomorrow. The irony of the situation was that, although I exercised this restraint and was not as ruthless and peremptory as I should have been and was perpetually trying to get the Territory Administration to accept heavier responsibility and always holding back Lambert and his departmental officers from trying to run the show, I earned a reputation for being autocratic.

The attempts to force the pace in the Territory and the perpetual but necessary correction and pushing of the Administration led to the charges that I was trying to run Papua and New Guinea from Canberra. The catch-phrase 'remote control' was current. Any journalist or parliamentarian who visited the Territory was likely to meet sooner or later some old hand who had been given a hurry-up or had been shown a better way of doing his job and, over a drink or two in the local club, the visitor would be told about 'interference' from Canberra. I was more sensitive to these stories than I should have been simply because it seemed unfair that I should be blamed for running the Territory from Canberra when I kept on trying to spur it on to running itself, and was rejecting the chance to get a quicker result if I let Lambert do more.

This continued resentment against direction from Canberra was also linked in some quarters with ideas about local autonomy. Much of the talk in the Territory about 'self-government' still really meant government by the local whites and a situation in which senior European officials would be left alone to do what they thought best.

My sensitivity over this misunderstanding of my views led me to give a somewhat laboured address on 'The Legend of Remote Control' to the New Guinea Society at the Australian National University in Canberra on 12 May 1958. The address exposes in some detail the state of my mind and records some of the administrative problems of the day.

At the outset, I illustrated the meaning of 'the legend of remote control' by quoting a recent article written by an Australian journalist after an 'on-the-spot investigation'. One phrase used was, 'dancing like puppets at the end of the 1800 mile strings which stretch from Canberra'. This was one of the many forms in which the legend of remote control appeared. 'The dead hand of Canberra' was another favourite cliché.

I asked the critics to be more precise about the meaning of 'remote control'. In trying to think through this question, we had to pay respect to the existing system of government. Constitutions could not be brushed aside as though they were irrelevant to administration. The laws of the Australian Commonwealth and the agreement between Australia and the General Assembly of the United Nations in respect of the Trust Territory of New Guinea required some intervention in Papua and New Guinea by the Australian Government. Under the Papua and New Guinea Act of the Australian Parliament the whole of the administration of the Territory was subject to the directions of the Australian Government. The Minister for Territories (and not anyone in the Territory) was accountable to the Australian Parliament for whatever happened in the Territory. Some constitutional change might be desirable, but even the most adventurous approach in this decade would not take the Territory wholly out of the sphere of responsibility of the Australian Parliament and of the Australian Government.

I continued that a distinction should be drawn between the development of self-government and the functioning of the administrative services provided by the Australian Government during a period when the Territory in fact had something a good deal less than self-government. Europeans in the Territory were apt to become confused on this point and to suggest in public that the Australian Government was hostile to self-government when it took some action concerned only with the efficient functioning of an administrative service for which the Australian Government was still responsible. Criticism that could fairly be made against a Minister who disregarded representative institutions was different from the criticism that might be made unfairly against him for giving directions to an Administrator who was appointed by and answerable to the Minister. To advocate that local public servants should be able to do as they wished—or not do what they disliked—without reference to the Government was not the same as advocating self-government for the Territory. Campaigners for self-government should see that to give more power to a Territory Administration established the power of a local bureaucracy but did not establish a local democracy. At present administrative practice rather than constitutional change was the question at issue. I continued as follows:

For over thirty years before the war the two Territories of Papua and New Guinea were neglected by successive Australian Governments and one of them was governed for a long period by a strong personality impatient of any rule except his own. The post-war period is different both because of changes among the peoples of the Territory and because the pressures on the Australian Government both from inside and outside the Territory are immeasurably greater. Much more has to be done and we are not allowed as much time in which to do it. In this situation, however, a good deal of pre-war isolationism survives and there are people in the Territory, both among officials and among private settlers, who think longingly of the 'good old days' and can dream of nothing better than to be left alone. In this post-war period every one of us has to freshen his thinking about the tasks of government in the Territory today and about the administrative structure and practices that will best enable us to perform those tasks.

My aim is to encourage building up in the Territory the institutions and the services of government in preparation for the eventual attainment of self-government. Any constitutional advance will be of little good unless it has been preceded by the political advancement of those who will be called upon to take part in government and by the development of the complete machinery of government and of administrative skills among those who will have to run the machinery of government. We develop in this way, if we can, by tutelage and by throwing an increasing measure of responsibility on the services in the Territory. Because I know that when self-government comes it will be self-government of a country in which the indigenous people are in the vast majority, I believe also that the aim I have stated will not be realized solely by developing and strengthening the power of a white colonial administrative upper class or by advancing solely the political power of an immigrant minority.

Parallel with this aim is the aim of securing higher administrative efficiency, particularly promptness in administration, by decentralizing; and the aim of reaching wiser and more soundly based decisions on policy by associating the officers of the Territory Administration more and more closely with the shaping of policy, by requiring the Administration to make more decisions for itself, and by drawing on the experience of Administration officers to a greater extent in making any decisions that necessarily remain the responsibility of the Australian Government.

I then recounted the measures taken to develop the Territory public service. More and better-qualified people had been recruited, the basic reorganization of the service had been nearly completed, in-service training had been introduced, a beginning had been made to bring the indigenous people into the service by creating an auxiliary division of the service for training them, and, by consultation and guidance, attempts had been made to give a better understanding of how things could best be handled. We had embarked on measures designed to encourage local officers to think about what they were doing and to teach them how to do it. We had tried, not always with a great deal of success, to draw out of the Territory the reports and the planning on which policy would be based.

Parallel with this we had seen the development of the Legislative Council and an attempt to create representative institutions. More of this work had been done by direction from Canberra than as the result of any action originated in the Territory. This was an example of remote control in order to help the Territory to escape eventually from such control.

I then enlarged on two other considerations that obliged a Minister to have oversight of the Administration. International responsibility for whatever happened in the Territory rested on the Australian Government and it was obliged to give an annual account of what happened. So long as the Australian Parliament retained legislative superiority and voted a substantial part of the revenues of the Territory, the Minister would be required to answer to the Parliament and meet criticism in Parliament. In face of criticism it was no answer to say that the matter had been left to the Administration and was none of the Minister's business. A Minister did not shelter behind his officers; they sheltered behind him.

I then referred to the continuing need to freshen the minds of Territory officers and avoid the growth of colonialist attitudes. While officers with local experience could often be right, they were sometimes blind. For example, recently in the preparation of new labour legislation, Territory officers proposed to give legislative sanction to a system under which one employer, having made an agreement with native labourers to work for him, could hire out those workers to some other employer at prices arranged between them without any reference to the employee. What is more, they seemed unable to understand that there could be any possible objection to that and, after departmental discussion had failed to shift them, they were overruled by my ministerial direction. My direction was yet another instance of remote control, yet I was sure that in this day and age the hiring of labourers like a team of bullocks was contrary to the interests of the people and contrary to the obligations we had accepted and the policies we were trying to pursue. Such a system would be politically indefensible either domestically or internationally.

In closing, I admitted that my talk had been rather one-sided and it might seem unduly critical of the Territory Administration. I had spoken frankly and drawn on the more striking instances in order to illustrate as sharply as possible why a Minister at Canberra was led to make judgements and give decisions that were castigated as 'remote control'. In fact I had only spoken of part of our work. It had not been immediately relevant to mention the 80 per cent or more of our total transactions in which Minister, Department and Administration worked closely and harmoniously together.

[19]

WIDENING PUBLIC INTEREST

Around 1956 and 1957, public interest in our work in Papua and New Guinea began to widen. Whereas in the previous five years it had been hard to find anyone outside a restricted circle to discuss our problems or to listen to our claims, we now were even asked questions about them.

There had always been a small number of Australians who had a direct concern with the Territory—those who had served or were still serving in an official capacity, those who had business interests, those who were associated with missionary efforts, and a small handful of university people, chiefly anthropologists. One simple and direct reason for the increased interest was that each of these groups was growing in size—more officials and their friends and relatives, more business people looking for new openings or improving on old ones as public expenditures and export production rose, more missionary effort, and a few newcomers in the academic field, although the academic rush did not really start until the 1960s.

There were some external events to stimulate interest, such as the Indonesian claim to Netherlands New Guinea. Furthermore, as our administrative activity grew and new things started to happen in Papua and New Guinea, we made the news more often. Journalists mostly gave attention to the unusual incident and it was very rare to find any concern about the basic situation or the broader problems. Any patrol report that gave a peg on which to hang some imaginative story about a 'Shangri-la' in the mountains inhabited by people who knew nothing of the outside world was sure to get space. Any constructive story in health, education, labour or industry seemed to leave the journalists bored.

In our own efforts to extend Australian knowledge of what was happening, we went straight to the targets that mattered. My principal target was the Parliament and I took special steps to keep members well informed.

I made an all-party approach. Basically I saw no reason why what the Labor Party did in the Territory should be different from what the Liberal Party or the Country Party did. The major issues that divided one party from another in Australian domestic politics did not seem to me to be relevant to the major issues in the administration of the Territory. Nor did I think there was any real conflict between the interest of any political group in Australia and the

213

purpose we were trying to serve in Papua and New Guinea. Some persons in Australia would have qualified my simple view. For example some rural interests thought that copra from the Territory in the hands of margarine manufacturers was a danger to Australian butter; some Australian commercial interests thought that the market in the Territory for imported consumer goods should be kept as a closed field for Australian traders; some Australian manufacturers thought that New Guinea logs should be reserved for Australian mills, while others thought that New Guinea raw materials should have no claim to a share of the Australian market if the same materials were available more cheaply from elsewhere; some Australian trade unionists were still nervous about products of 'cheap black labour'; the Australian seamen and some Australian ship-owners were ready to work together to keep the growing seaborne traffic to and from New Guinea ports a privileged route for ships on the Australian registry; some Australian patriots, whose war-time experience was uppermost in their minds, thought Australia had some kind of proprietary right because a high price had been paid in Australian lives in New Guinea in two world wars and they expected some tangible reward to Australia for its efforts; others thought of New Guinea chiefly as a field of Christian missionary effort, and their attitudes towards Australian administration were influenced by the wish that this missionary effort should not be hampered and, so it seemed to me, that it might continue for ever; some thought of New Guinea as a land of opportunity, meaning opportunity for themselves either to obtain land or congenial employment or a chance to do well in trade or industry.

While this list does not cover the whole range of sectional interest by Australians in the Territory, it is broad enough to suggest that interest in the Territory was influenced by many considerations other than Australian political party alignments.

In the early post-war years, when Ward was Minister for External Territories, he and some of those associated with him had given an impression that what they were planning had something to do with socialism. Occasionally Labor Party spokesmen still contrasted the purity of the motives of socialists with the impurity of the motives of Liberals. Occasionally, too, some members of the Liberal Party gave them ground for this statement by harping on the theme that a non-socialist party should let private enterprise have a go in New Guinea, and it seemed to me that Spender had given some support to this view by the way he expressed his encouragement of development of the Territory's resources. As I saw the situation, however, both Government and Opposition found a common principle when they declared that the interests of the indigenous people were paramount. From the start I wanted to get away from the absurdity of a debate about Papua and New Guinea from prepared positions of socialism and anti-socialism and I tried to establish a common ground on the interests of the native inhabitants. I was willing to see private enterprise as one of the instruments of economic development if it were the instrument best suited to a particular situation, but I opposed any idea that opportunity for European private enterprise was the objective of our administration just as I opposed the idea that State ownership, planning and control was the only way in which the interests of the indigenous people could be advanced. So I sought and worked for an all-party policy on the one ground that all parties shared—the interests of the native peoples.

In trying to commend policy as bipartisan, I tried also to broaden the approach to the claims of Papua and New Guinea on Australia by stressing our national responsibility rather than our national advantage. Earlier claims about the importance of the Territory had leant rather heavily on its strategic importance. Both Labor and non-Labor parties made much of that claim. In some quarters I still relied on the old appeal, usually saying that an undefended New Guinea or a New Guinea in the hands of an enemy would be a danger to Australia. My main arguments however are well illustrated in a speech I made in the Budget debate on 1 September 1954:*

> But after we have referred to the strategic importance of Papua and New Guinea, after we have developed to the full all the arguments that we can propose about the development of its resources, we come back to the main argument which is the argument of national responsibility . . . What we do as a nation in the development of this Territory is something we do in order to live up to our own standards, and in order to live up to our own ideals of national responsibility. I suggest that this is a national reason, far more compelling than any of the other reasons, strategic and economic, which might be argued very persuasively . . . I should like to think that all parties, irrespective of any political chances or changes inside Australia, would consider this national responsibility as being a continuing one. A point we need to remember is that, irrespective of what is happening in Australia, irrespective of changes that may take place in this Parliament, and irrespective of anything that may happen in the political fortunes of either party, the essential nature of that situation in Papua and New Guinea will be unchanged . . . I should like to think . . . there will be consistency and something greater than partisanship in our approach to our national responsibilities in the Territory.

In keeping with this view, I set out deliberately to achieve an all-party policy. I distributed information evenly on both sides of Parliament. Commencing in 1952, I promoted annual visits by all-party teams of parliamentarians, each tour lasting from two to four weeks by a working party of six members, whose reports on what they inspected were always discussed subsequently with them by me and my department in some detail. Gradually we built up in Parliament a group of thirty or more members who knew something about Papua and New Guinea at first hand and were seized of its problems. The effect began to show for the first time in the estimates debate of 1956.

In addition to these organized working parties, when members' travel privileges had been extended, I also encouraged and facilitated visits arranged by members themselves, and such visits became frequent. Arthur Calwell, Deputy Leader of the Opposition, made several such visits and each was followed by long discussions between us. I think I had more helpful and encouraging conversations with Arthur Calwell about Papua and New Guinea than with any other member of Parliament on either side of the House.

* *Commonwealth Parliamentary Debates* (H. of R.), vol. 4, pp. 847-8, 1 Sept. 1954.

On the Government side, Shane Paltridge, Denham Henty and Donald Cameron were Ministers who had some knowledge of the Territory and a keen interest in it. Early in 1957 the Prime Minister made a three-day visit and in October Fadden visited the Territory to perform the opening ceremony of the Bomana Hospital, Port Moresby, and to make a tour of the principal centres.

In the senior levels of the Commonwealth Public Service we were also broadening the knowledge of the Territory. From time to time, as occasion arose, we enlisted the co-operation of various departments in particular studies and this not only gave us the benefit of their services but awakened in some of the secretaries and assistant secretaries of departments an interest in and knowledge of what we were doing.

In Cabinet I still had to battle for funds each year, as did most other spending departments, but on most other matters I had little difficulty. Few of the recommendations on Territory policy touched matters of lively concern in Australian domestic politics. It was a field in which, as the outcome of an all-party approach to our problems, we seldom attracted criticism and sometimes gained support from the Opposition, and in the electorate, although our work in the Territories probably did not gain many votes for the Government, it did not lose them any goodwill among the populace, for we had achieved some sort of reputation of 'doing a good job'. Officers of the Department and of the Territory Administration had close association in the course of their work with many sections of Australian opinion who had a direct concern with one phase or another of life in New Guinea, and I myself spoke often, wrote numerous letters and had discussions with most of those people who were directly concerned in one way or another in developments in the Territory. I think we went successfully behind the backs of the press and got favourably in touch with sections of Australian opinion that mattered.

The most difficult arena—indeed the only difficult one—was the Government party room. A New South Wales member, Roy Wheeler, and a Queensland member, Malcolm McColm, had become the spokesmen for a section of Australian business with interests in the Territory and were perpetual critics. In my memory, they stand as the only two constant and determined political opponents in Parliament of what I was trying to do, but from time to time they found small groups of supporters among Government members. It is part of the nature of Australian politics that the toughest fighting for any Minister is in his own party room. Once he has won the victory there, he knows he will win in the House, but my situation was unusual inasmuch as I had to fight very few battles in the House and could find support on both sides. Most of the opponents of the policies I advanced and most of those who tried to defeat me on particular issues were in the Government party room, but this observation should be balanced by the fact that in the Liberal Party there were also a few who were interested in the broad picture and the ultimate objective as well as in the particular incident and who backed me solidly and helped defeat the critical minority.

In the debate on the Territory estimates on 30 September 1959,* I reviewed

* *Commonwealth Parliamentary Debates* (H. of R.), vol. 24, pp. 1573-5, 30 Sept. 1959.

my experience as Minister in seeking an all-party approach. I said the trust Australia had for Papua and New Guinea was not a trust that had been confided to any single political party, nor to any section of the Australian people, but a trust that belonged to the Australian nation. In this spirit I believed that there could be a common meeting ground between Government and Opposition in trying to work out those policies which would ensure that the trust was faithfully discharged while at the same time the enduring interests of Australia were well served. I continued,

> It would not be exact to say that there is no difference between the present Government and the Opposition in the administration of Papua and New Guinea. There are, indeed, differences in emphasis and differences in method. At the same time, I believe that there can be continuity in administration so long as there is constancy in our purposes and principles, and that these purposes and principles are shared by both sides of politics in Australia.
>
> It has been one of the pleasures of my own term of office that it has been possible at various times to discuss in general and particular many questions relating to New Guinea with members of the Opposition and to benefit from their comments. Similarly, on the Government side of the chamber there are honourable members who, by reason of past association or as a result of their visits to the Territory, have taken a special interest in its problems and from time to time have discussed these problems with me. I would hope that this free interchange of views can continue, no matter which party may be in power, and that we may look at the problems of the Territory in the light of the trust we share and not in the darkness of political dispute.
>
> It is true that a Government cannot escape its responsibilities, nor can an opposition surrender its functions, but this is one of the subjects on which it is possible that both sides of politics would aspire to a national, humane and Christian view and, in doing so, arrive at what is broadly the same answer to the problems of this Territory. May I express the hope that we will continue, as members of different parties, to apply to any question that arises in Papua and New Guinea the test of what will best serve that country and its people, and not the test of what can be turned to advantage in our party struggles on the mainland?

The contrasting of socialism and private enterprise again entered into the argument in the controversy over the introduction of direct taxation in 1958 and 1959. My critics in the Liberal Party said in effect that I was just as bad as the socialists and unsympathetic to private enterprise. I tried again to get away from this false antithesis and also to remove the silly notion of some of my Liberal critics that private enterprise meant looking after the whites, and socialism meant looking after the blacks. I wanted to re-emphasize that the contrast between socialism and liberalism was a contrast in methods of reaching the same objective. Justifying myself in the debate in the House on 30 September 1959, I said,

> Liberalism . . . when it emphasizes the importance of the individual, does not mean unbridled opportunity for the strong to do whatever they wish to do; it means expanding opportunity for every person, weak or strong . . . The liberal respect for property . . . is a respect for a small property no less than a respect for a large property . . . and, applying liberal principles to

Papua and New Guinea, I assert that the private enterprise of every native villager is just as sacred to liberalism as is the private enterprise of any European . . . In my thinking, private enterprise means the enterprise of the indigenous people as well as of the European. Furthermore, because of the conditions in the Territory there are obvious limits to the scope of European enterprise. That limit is set by the interests of the indigenous people. European enterprise cannot go beyond the point at which it would cause the displacement of people or place barriers in the way of their advancement.

By and large I believe I succeeded in parliamentary circles in laying the foundations for a bipartisan policy in Papua and New Guinea and hence of consistency and continuity in the administration of the Territory in spite of any political changes in Australia. We had got away from the direct contrast made by Ward and Spender.

In October 1959 I tried to obtain Cabinet approval for establishing a joint committee of parliament 'to assist Parliament to perform its functions in respect of Papua and New Guinea'. Cabinet did not agree with me. Checked on this, I recommended the setting up of an ad hoc parliamentary committee for the single purpose of examining and reporting on Part V of the Papua and New Guinea Act—the part dealing with Territory legislation—but, although discussion began on 27 October 1959, no decision was taken. Perhaps Cabinet reluctance to take these moves may have been influenced to some extent by the current difficulties in regard to the setting up of a joint committee on foreign affairs in the face of demands by the Leader of the Opposition, H. V. Evatt, which were considered unreasonable.

In our attempts to extend Australian knowledge of and interest in the Territory, our second target was formed by those Australians who already had some link with the Territory—churchmen, businessmen, trade union executives, and professional men (lawyers, doctors, anthropologists, social scientists). I made a special effort myself by correspondence, discussion, distribution of information, supply of material for their periodicals, and addresses to meetings to bring them up to date on what we were doing and planning and to facilitate visits by them to the Territory. Senior departmental officers helped considerably in the same way. We made opportunities for senior officers from the Territory who came to Australia, either on official duty or on leave, to talk with such people. This activity merged with our increased efforts at recruiting, especially in connection with our schemes of cadetships in several departments of the Administration. We prepared special booklets for recruiting and distributed information folders to schools and libraries. We started to make our first films. We arranged frequent visits by parties of the indigenous people to Australia. We organized exhibits at agricultural shows in Australia. We developed extensive mailing lists.

In making our first films, we were lucky to attract the personal interest and sustained enthusiasm of Maslyn Williams, a producer with the Commonwealth Film Unit. In making this first film for us, he showed that he could work to our specifications and respond readily to our prescribed requirements and yet could build imaginatively and creatively to give the set task an extra quality of his own. In the course of making a succession of films, we also accumulated a good store of material for which we found an outlet on television shorts to stimulate popular interest.

In 1960 our departmental information work expanded into the publication of a magazine *Australian Territories* six times a year and its distribution on a large but selective mailing list all over Australia.

By these means we built up, on the fringe of public affairs, a useful body of well-informed opinion in the places where good information mattered. For this work considerable credit belongs to Dudley McCarthy, who was at that time an assistant secretary in the Department. He had been a colleague of mine as one of the historians in the *Official War History* team under Gavin Long and had earlier experience of New Guinea, first as a patrol officer and then as an officer in the war-time campaigns, and his initial training had been as a school-teacher. He was a congenial and like-minded colleague with a warm personal response to all social questions. He was one of the very few officers who spoke the same language as I did and, since he travelled often with me in the Territory, there were probably very few who knew as much of my mind as he did. He had a good, sound, shrewd and manly judgement of other people, combined with a charitable tolerance. I owed a lot both to his companionship and to his counsel. Apart from that, as assistant secretary handling most social questions in all the territories, he made a significant contribution to the advancement of the welfare of people in both the Northern Territory and in the external territories under Australian administration.

The flow of books on Papua New Guinea did not start until about 1960. One exception was Colin Simpson, whose *Adam with Arrows* was published in 1953 and *Adam in Plumes* in 1954. These books had a popular success and stimulated much romantic interest in the country and some pride in the part Australians had played and were playing in its history. The author worked diligently with official assistance in obtaining material. Few of his successors have been as entertaining to read or as reliable in their statements as Simpson was.

In about 1959 there were growing signs that New Guinea might become a more popular subject for publishers and that an occasional journalist might be interested in broader questions of the present administration and future development of the Territory. Then those of us who were engaged officially in the affairs of the Territory passed rapidly from a stage when it was hard to find a journalist to take any interest in what we were doing to a stage when they did not want to listen to anything we said because they all knew so much more about everything than we could possibly tell them. In both stages our assiduous attempts to supply information were mostly disregarded as dull. Nowadays one occasionally hears well-founded criticism of governments for their use of 'public relations' in a way that suggests that clever salesmanship is more important than sound policy. Part of the origin of this deplorable situation can be found in the temptation to the practising politician, when he finds that the journalist takes no notice of his factual statements or the sober information in annual reports, to practice all sorts of publicity gimmicks to attract the attention of the news media.

Personally I had much happier associations with the academic workers, especially the anthropologists, than with the journalists and gained some insight into my own administrative problems from what the academics said and wrote. I would permit myself one observation about academic studies. Some research workers focus so strongly on one spot that they fail in broad illumination. So often someone who does distinguished work in one field fails to understand, indeed sometimes will not even seek to understand, what is happening in other fields. The 'recognized authority' becomes obsessed with his own expertness and forgets he has studied only one small patch in a very big field. This lack of intellectual modesty might have been more amusing than harmful if it had not sometimes spread into an assumption by 'recognized authority' that the answer to the problem on which he had worked was also the answer to every other problem that arose in administration. Too many post-graduate men and women get into a narrow specialization without having a broad enough educational base. Perhaps I exaggerate. If I do, it is the acid fruit of a season in the sixties in which the plants began to be over-fertilized with academic advice. Sometimes too we were in the position of having to listen to a self-recognized authority on the cultivation of henbane telling us humble market gardeners how to grow cabbages.

[20]

A TURNING POINT IN EDUCATION

My sense of urgency and my purpose of drawing more of the indigenous people into the public service of their own country led me to look for some results from the effort made in the first five years to put more of the young people into schools. My impatience at the low yield of youths qualified for higher training influenced my renewed instructions on education policy.

There was no early prospect of having the services of anyone with higher skills. In April 1956 we had fifty-six native scholarship-holders at secondary schools in Australia. Theoretically these students, who were the best indigenous candidates for secondary education we could find in the whole Territory up to that time, might have proceeded to tertiary education. In fact, very few of them were able to get beyond the Junior (or Intermediate) examination because of the inadequacy of their primary schooling. The way to the production of students who could take a full secondary course and proceed further to university lay in the primary schools in the Territory. That is where our main educational failure still was.

I expressed my views in a long minute of 23 April 1956 to Lambert and Cleland. I repeated that the first priority was still to bring primary education within the reach of far larger numbers of people. For practical reasons—and by this I meant both the need that existed and the interest of the native people themselves in getting a good job—the next priority was in training for employment in the Territory. This meant technical schools, training on the job, and attention to the problem of adjustment to a new way of life. 'The Territory', I wrote, 'needs people for a variety of administrative services (including clerks, medical assistants, agricultural and forestry workers, truck drivers, printing office employees, linesmen, messengers, typists, infant welfare and mothercraft workers, nurses, teachers and so on). The territory needs people for local government and co-operatives (such as clerks and storemen, clerks of local government councils, carpenters, mechanics and so on). The Territory needs people for private enterprise (such as tradesmen, mechanics, operators of various machines, clerks, storemen and so on) . . .' I then returned to a favourite theme. All departments of the Administration had to help in the education of the people. Schooling was one task which was the sole responsibility of the Education Department and 'at the present moment' it must try to lay a sound foundation of primary education over the whole of the Territory in close co-operation with the missions. Occupational training and training for citizenship was a job for all departments of the Administration.

Turning to secondary education, I referred to the secondary scholarships in Australia as a response to two factors both of which had a 'temporary application'. The first was the personal claim of the child to consideration when there were no secondary schools in the Territory. The second was the need to 'produce as quickly as possible larger numbers of indigenous people who can be used to assist the further advancement of their countrymen'.

> There is a conscious purpose . . . to produce more rapidly a number of people who will become the instructors and the leaders among their own people to assist us in handling the tasks set by progress in the coming decade. In plain terms the Government is spending money because it hopes to obtain without undue delay a corps of more highly educated men and women who will provide staffs to help the indigenous people in their advancement in health, agriculture and economic activity and who will give leadership in social and political change.

Taking this view, I thought that the vocational guidance and after-care of the secondary students in Australia should be closely linked with the Territory and directed towards employment in the Territory. I warned against the 'temptation to find gratification in the personal success or the transformation of the few. In most cases this personal success means that an individual has become so unlike the mass of his people that the rest of his life is going to be uncomfortable for him and not of great value to them.' I wanted the youths who had been given educational opportunity to start serving their own people.

Looking back on this period, across the gap of the years, I appreciate now that I may have been focusing too sharply on one aspect of education. The strenuous endeavours to get things done in the Territory and the growing recognition of the need for more hands to do the work had joined with the earlier recognition that effective self-government called for native staff for the administrative and technical services of the country and that a move into a higher standard of living should be accompanied by an economic capacity in the individual to support himself in his new way of life. Hence I was tending to think perhaps too narrowly of education as a training of men and women to do a service to the community and to earn a living for themselves. It is also apparent that, at that stage of their advancement, the Australian tutelary power was creating the jobs to be done and deciding what we wanted workers to do. At the outset of my ministry I had said in effect that I had no views on educational theory but wanted the people to have a better chance of schooling. Now I was saying in effect that we should put more children into school in order to turn out more people able to help with all the urgent jobs waiting for them. The higher the level of schooling the better, because the need for the more highly trained was just as urgent as the need for those with a basic training. Thus, under the urgency of getting things done, I had come to express a functional view of education with which in an Australian setting I really had little intellectual sympathy.

At this time we had begun to move into the establishment of secondary schools in the Territory for both general and technical education, and on my instructions Lambert went to Port Moresby early in 1957 to work out a further programme with the Administrator for the 1957–8 estimates. He reported that the position was 'unsatisfactory'. Both the accommodation and the supply of trained teachers were inadequate. He had obtained from the Director of Education an immediate programme calling for the recruitment of thirty-seven European secondary teachers and a works vote for further secondary schools and houses for the new teachers. The limit on any programme was set by the capacity of the Administration to handle it. This modest step was all they were capable of taking at that time. Once again our hopes were disappointed. The Administration did not do all they had undertaken.

In planning this forward move we had also placed some hope on the increase in the number of native teachers trained to a higher standard than village school teachers. The figures on which we had based our hopes were not realistic. Lambert reported that the statistics had been improved by making a compromise and lowering the standards to fit the capacity of the trainees rather than the requirements of the job.

At about this time we had strengthened the division of the Department of Territories which handled educational questions and I began to receive better analyses and assessments of the reports sent down from Port Moresby. We began to realize that the hopes that had been raised by the figures supplied by the Territory Education Department were ill-founded. We had said that our aim to get an effective system of primary education, turning out annual quotas of children well prepared for secondary education, would not be realized until the standard of native teachers had been raised. We had pressed for more attention to teacher training and had received reports that purported to show that what we required was being done. It now appeared that in fact the accomplishment was slender. For example in September 1957 I obtained a detailed memorandum from the Department analysing the most recent report from the Territory on training of native teachers. It evoked a rather doleful minute from me to Lambert:

> The chronicle of my attempts to get more effective work in the Education Department over the past five years is a recital of despair and frustration. The Administration has apparently been unable to ensure that directions given in this field by the Government will be carried into effect and therefore it seems to me to be another instance where it will be necessary to consider a special investigation leading to stronger and, if necessary, drastic steps at my own direction to bring about the change that the Government wants. [Minute of 12 September 1957.]

After discussion with Lambert, I instructed him that, since the territorial Administration was 'not working in a practical and effective way to produce the results which they have been asked to produce', the Department should make a survey and give me early recommendations on what steps could be taken immediately to get better results in the current year and to ensure that in the succeeding year this important task was tackled effectively. (Minute of 16 September 1957.)

The short answer was that the trouble was the administrative incapacity of Groves. We were also continuing to have difficulty with Groves over his attitude to mission schools. During 1957 and 1958 I received friendly representations from church leaders about the difficulty of co-operation in advancing our common aim of improving the schools. I again had occasion to write critically to the Administrator on several occasions for not making the Education Advisory Board function as intended. My concern came to a head early in 1958 when I reminded the Department and the Administration that we had to do everything possible to raise the standard of education in mission schools and ensure that curricula and teaching methods were in conformity with our aims. We could do this through financial aid, inspection and discussion and we should also ensure that teacher training was available for native mission teachers. I also laid down, against some opposition from the Administration and the Department, that the teacher-training institutions in the Territory should be open to native teachers for mission schools as well as for Administration schools. I saw this as parallel to our other attempts to raise the level of education in mission schools and also thought that it would help to bring native mission teachers under Australian influence and broaden their approach to the future development of the Territory and its people. I commented, 'All native mission teachers ought to be able to serve their people's needs here and now as well as in the hereafter'. (Minutes of 11 February and 3 May 1958.) I could not hope for much until Groves went. I wrote in February, 'I have regretfully come to the conclusion that it will be difficult, if not impossible, to bring about any significant improvement under the present Director of Education, whose opinions about mission schools are quite firmly embedded and whose merits lie in other fields than the diplomatic handling of situations like this one.'

In 1958 Groves reached the retiring age. It was decided to advertise widely in the hope of obtaining an outstanding man as his successor. The response was more numerous than exciting. The committee appointed to interview the final panel of applicants found two who were better than the others but was divided in preference between them and enthusiastic about neither. I received no firm recommendation. I decided to appoint the most senior man already in the service, G. T. Roscoe,[37] partly on the ground that none of the others was 'so far superior as to warrant the passing over of a man already in the service', but largely because Roscoe only had two years to run before retirement and this would give us another chance to find an outstanding man, whereas the appointment of the man on the top of the outside list would mean that we would have him for the next ten years. What I had seen personally of Roscoe also impressed me. He was a school-teacher and was aware that the work of an Education Department had something to do with getting more and better schools and teachers.

The appointment, which was my own decision against advice, turned out well. Roscoe got down to the job of putting children into schools and teaching them. His methods were more practical and prompter than those of his predecessor. On 8 January 1959 I accepted in principle a plan prepared by the new Director for extended primary education and asked the Administrator to prepare definite proposals regarding the additional measures to be taken in the financial year 1959–60 in accordance with this plan. I expressed appreciation of 'the vigorous and practical approach of the new director to his tasks'.

By September 1959 Roscoe had prepared a fuller plan for the development of education and cleared it through the Public Service Commissioner. He came to Canberra for discussion with me in early November. The major item was the recruitment of more European teachers and measures to expedite the training of native teachers. A further proposal was for the encouragement of mission schools by raising the rates of subsidy and providing capital grants for buildings. He also expressed the view that the aid of native local government councils should be obtained in providing buildings for schools, with Administration co-operation in the supply of materials. He stressed the urgent need for teachers' colleges in the Territory and faced the problems of building and staffing them. He also tackled several ancillary needs. I approved his proposals in principle and directed Lambert to give prompt attention to them and give me an early submission on the precise measures to be taken to put them into effect. (Minute of 13 November 1959.) This memorandum and discussion were the first substantial, constructive and practical proposal I had received in eight years in response to my repeated requests for giving high priority to education. It marks the beginning of a new era in providing schools in the Territory.

In August 1960 we found a need for further special discussions in Canberra to expedite the programme. We set in train recruitment of more teachers in several different categories. Happily the response to our advertisements was heavier than we had hoped and we looked forward to a really impressive change in the commencement of the 1961 school year. But in September came a report from the Public Service Commissioner in Port Moresby proposing a reduction in numbers because of the incapacity of the Administration to absorb them. I directed that priority for education be maintained and told the Administrator to take immediate action to provide for absorbing the increase. 'The Government looks to the Administrator for a special effort to give effect to the decisions', I wrote. 'If he is unable to promise a successful effort he should have let me know within a week so that we can take the necessary steps.' (Minute of 27 September 1960.) This was intended and was received as a direct warning to Cleland that he had to make the task his personal responsibility or face the consequences.

[21]

GIVING THE WORKERS A FUTURE

Early in 1956, following the first approach described in chapter 14, I drafted a statement on native labour policy. This was originally circulated departmentally and communicated to the Administration and later it was made public. It sets out more clearly than any other document my approach to the protection and regulation of native labour at a time when there was no workers' organization of any kind and when the only representations about employment were those made by employers. The major interest of the Administration up to that time had been to serve the twofold purpose of maintaining a supply of labour and protecting the labourer by prescribing and policing the terms and conditions of his employment. My statement read as follows:

The policy for the control and regulation of native labour is intended to serve the following aims—
(1) To advance the general policy for the political, economic, social and educational advancement of the inhabitants of the Territory; the development of the Territory's resources and the maintenance of good order and government, particularly in the following respects—
(a) controlling the nature and the rate of social change among the native peoples;
(b) the education of the native;
(c) promoting an association with the European community favourable to the native's own advancement and good relations between the races;
(d) the association of both European and native in the development of the resources of the Territory in order to sustain a higher standard of living and improved services.
(2) To protect the native worker against unfair treatment, damage to his health, or deterioration in his habits.
(3) To ensure that the native worker honours his obligations.
The methods by which these aims are served will have to be adjusted from time to time to meet changing circumstances in the Territory. At present, it is considered that policy will be best served by measures that maintain village life and the attachment of the native to his land. The education of the native in ways of living, use of tools and new technical methods, and

personal responsibility is to be regarded as a major consideration; and strict precautions for the physical and moral well-being of the worker are to be maintained.

In serving these aims of labour policy, it will be remembered that the parallel policy of economic development means that industrial enterprise requires the efficient use of labour.

In February 1956, largely as the result of work done in the Department on the Jones-Marsh report, I was able to make some decisions on native labour policy. I minuted the papers: 'Although it has taken some time . . . I should like to thank the officers responsible and congratulate them on the clear and practical way in which the present submission has been prepared. It has brought the outstanding matters to a head and greatly facilitated prompt decisions on my part.' (Minute of 20 February 1956.)

The principal decisions I made at this time were eventually incorporated in Native Labour Ordinances. Among the purposes they served were to limit casual labour to employment near the villages where the worker resided, to give an opportunity of free engagement for employment to those native workers who had acquired skills and who were able to fend for themselves in a 'foreign' community, and to improve the terms and conditions of labour working under agreement and revise the safeguards against various undesirable practices in respect of this labour. We also gave attention to wage fixation methods and, having reached the opinion that the majority of the native workers had not yet reached the stage where they could successfully engage in collective bargaining, and having provided for free employment for those who could make individual agreements with employers, we decided to create an employment advisory board, consisting of two representatives of the Administration, two of employers and two of employees to recommend minimum wages, margins for skill, tests and certificates of competency and provision for maintenance of dependants. I also instructed the Administrator to prepare proposals for a departmental reorganization to help give effect to labour policy and to draft new legislation. For some time I had seen the need for a special Department of Labour instead of leaving native labour to be administered by the Department of Native Affairs.

Time passed. In the Territory discussion was going on mainly with employers, and various points were being raised before the drafting of legislation commenced. Most of this discussion arose from the interests of the employers in obtaining labour. The planters' associations made representations over my head to the Prime Minister. I thought we had done enough already to get the views of all concerned and to prepare sound proposals, so on 12 April 1956 I wrote to Lambert:

> In order to precipitate action on this matter—in the same way as it was necessary for me to precipitate action on lands policy in face of various resistances—I propose to make a public statement early next week setting out (a) the statement of policy I have already formulated; (b) the decision to introduce a new Native Labour Ordinance; (c) the successive inquiries made to obtain information and the opinions and the successive steps taken in the preparation of these proposals; and (d) the main changes envisaged.

The main point at issue between the Administration and me concerned the engagement of what was known as casual labour. The ease and convenience of such casual engagement to the employers, including officers of the Administration, was seen in the Territory as a useful feature at that stage of development. To be able to pick up a boy locally to work without too much formality was a great convenience even for the public servant who wanted help in the house or the garden. Probably too the views in favour of greater use of casual labour were a groping towards a system of freely engaged labour as the next step beyond labour under agreements. In my view, however, any easier attitude towards casual labour was going to give a higher risk of the exploitation of the labourer and the encouragement of poor social conditions for the dispossessed, landless and defenceless native workers who were squatting in shanty settlements on the fringes of the towns. Free engagement of labour required something near equality in the bargaining position of wage-earner and employer and should be sought by a different approach.

My own views on the situation were set out at length in a minute of 23 April and, since I regard it as a basic document in the development of labour policy, I quote it extensively. It is also fair to the Administration to reveal the arguments they advanced and I overruled.

1. I disagree profoundly with the approach to this subject by the Administrator. His inability to understand the directions given on native labour policy is clearly indicated in paragraph 2 of Annexure A of his memorandum of 24 March. In quoting what he described as 'relevant extracts' from my statement on native labour policy, he deliberately omits sub-paragraph (a) which sets out that our first purpose in regulating native labour is 'control of the nature and the rate of social change among the native people'. Presumably, he does so because he thinks this sub-paragraph is not 'relevant', yet it is the historical foundation of the native labour policy in the Territory and was deliberately given first place when I listed the four purposes which native labour policy was to serve. The ignoring of this point reveals not only inability to understand the policy the Government had laid down, but also a most disturbing gap in the Administrator's understanding of the problem he is discussing.

2. The reason why the percentage of recruiting in any area is controlled; the chief reason why the recruiting is closely supervised and one of the major reasons why districts are closed to recruiting from time to time; the reason why the term of engagement is limited and why native labourers have to be returned to their villages after a period of service—indeed, the reasons for most of the restrictive provisions in the native labour legislation —lie, and have lain for the past half century, in the purpose which the Administrator now ignores as not 'relevant'. For half a century, successive Governments have been carefully regulating the employment of natives away from their homes for the express purpose of ensuring that village life is not disrupted, the village food supplies not diminished, and the village cycle of marriages and births not interrupted by reason of the prolonged absence of the young and able-bodied men. Care has been taken, hitherto with a fair measure of success, to see that the native social order is not changed too rapidly by the breaking up of the chief social unit—the village —or by destroying those elements that give coherence to native society. Careful measures have been taken against the displacement and dis-

possession of the native people. During my own term of office, reminders of the fundamental importance of these considerations have been given by me on several occasions whenever the subjects of lands policy and casual labour have been under notice. The special concern of the Government over the risk of building up a 'landless proletariat' and over the congregation of 'foreign' natives on the outskirts of the larger towns, has been made clear on several occasions and action has been taken to try to reduce both risks. Yet now I am faced with the amazing proposition that native employment, which is one of the chief factors in producing these risks, can be regulated without close regard to these social factors and that the social consequences of employment are not 'relevant'.

3. In the simplest and most emphatic terms, I feel obliged to tell the Administrator that his arguments on this point are not only unacceptable but show no understanding of the policy he is expected to carry out. He seems also to have realized imperfectly that the regulation of native labour has to be regarded, as all measures must be regarded, as instruments for advancing the overall objectives of our policy, as well as for handling the particular subject to which they refer.

Here I should interpose that part of the Administrator's argument was that a gradual breaking down of the system of employment under agreement would help towards a higher standard of living for the native worker and for the growth of personal responsibility on his part. My objection was that increasing the sort of employment that was known as casual labour at that time would not help towards these ends but would retard their advancement. On this point, I wrote,

5. Undoubtedly, in the course of the years, there will be pressure towards an industrial system under which native labour is freely offered and freely engaged. As this point is approached, it is probable that the native people themselves will organize industrially to protect their own interests and to sell their labour to the best advantage. In the next few years, with an increase in the number of native workers who have technical skill and an ambition for a standard of living that village life cannot provide, more and more native workers will be employed outside the agreement system. We certainly have to be prepared to deal this situation whenever and wherever it occurs. But casual labour, as the term is understood in the current legislation, is certainly not a method for dealing with that prospective situation. Nor can it be regarded as an alternative to the system of employment under agreement for the large body of native workers who not only do not have technical skill but who are still at so early a stage of their social advancement that we must still rely on the village organization to give meaning and satisfaction to them as individuals and to offer the best prospects of their further advancement as a group.

6. It seems to me that one strong element in shaping the submissions which are now made in regard to casual workers has been local concern in the Territory with the situation that has arisen because of 'desertions' of workers engaged under agreement. I am told that an increase in casual employment would both help to overcome the difficulties which employers face and would also be congenial to native workers themselves. Up to date I have only been offered opinions or statements by interested parties and would require some facts before accepting either these opinions or these state-

ments. Even if they are accepted however, I think the argument would have to be completed first by proving that the agreement system was not working smoothly solely because of those features in which it differs from the casual labour system and second by proving that the fundamental purposes which the agreement system serves can be served equally well by a casual labour system. I do not think that either of those propositions can be proved. We also have to be careful about any argument which says that desertions produce casual labour and therefore if you allow more casual labour you will have fewer desertions for, loosely handled, such a line of thinking may bring us to the point that in permitting or encouraging casual labour we are virtually permitting or encouraging desertions. The Secretary, in his submission of 20 April, has put this phase of the situation squarely when he says: 'The Administrator's case . . . is a very strong one provided that you accept the principle that the casual labour system is to be promoted to such an extent that the agreement system must necessarily disappear within a few years.' It is plain that, for reasons indicated in paragraphs 1, 2 and 3 above, I do not accept that principle.

7. There are two points on which we have to be careful in arguing about the provisions to be made in the legislation under notice. The first concerns the application to be given to the term 'casual worker' in the future. We are proposing that elsewhere in the legislation provision should be made for the issue of 'free employment certificates' to advanced native workers who wish to work anywhere in the Territory and who are considered to have the skill and some capacity to look after themselves. Some of the Administrator's chief arguments about casual labour would apply to these 'free employment workers'. Don't count them twice. Having excluded them from the class of 'casual labour' do not use arguments that apply to them in order to make a case about 'casual labour'. The 'casual worker' who is now under discussion does not include those who are likely to obtain free employment certificates, but only those who have little or no skill, those who are not very far advanced and those who could not manage their own lives outside their own villages and who would not normally take wives and families with them to their employment . . . The second point on which we have to be careful is that we do not try to use a casual worker system to overcome problems that have arisen in the application of the agreement system, for reasons that have nothing to do with the differences between employment under agreement and employment by casual engagement . . .

The conclusion to which I came was that casual labour of the kind covered by the use of this term in the Territory should be discouraged whenever it led to prolonged absence of low-skilled and unsophisticated native workers from their own villages and from their own families and whenever it tended towards the congregation in the urban areas of groups of 'foreign' natives—a term in popular use for any native persons living in a place other than their native place—or the building up of a semi-permanent group of landless shanty-town native people who were still at an early stage of social advancement. In too many cases it seemed to me that casual labour was attractive both to employers and to some Administration officers as a means of readily obtaining labour from a pool of unemployed and needy native workers without accepting all the obligations placed on the employer by the agreement system. Casual labour as proposed by the Administration was not the same as free employment and was not the best path to the desirable objective of free employment. At any rate I took the responsibility of making the decisions on policy. Then came the usual disappointment. The drafting of the ordinances to give effect to my decisions was certainly complicated work. The next submission, raising some further difficulties, was not made to me until October. It was incomplete.

'To minimize further delay', I gave approval first to a separate ordinance to create the proposed employment advisory board. I rejected a proposal by the Administrator that the representatives of the native employees on the board should not be native employees but 'persons who have their interests at heart'. While recognizing the difficulties, I said that the effort to find two native representatives had to be made. 'As in other phases of our work', I wrote, 'the principle of representation has to be fostered in the beginning in the hope that an artificially created form of representation may gradually develop into a more truly representative form of institution.' (Minute of 7 November 1956.) I agreed to increase the membership of the board to seven by adding a chairman, and I myself suggested that this chairman be 'a full-time salaried appointment at not less than the level of salary of the magistracy and with a similar measure of independence from departmental instruction'. A wise and understanding officer in this post 'might become one of the chief agents for beneficial and gradual change during the difficult transitional period we are going to face in native industrial matters in the next ten or fifteen years'.

With prospective developments in mind, I also proposed that the word 'advisory' be dropped from the title of the board and that it be known simply as the Employment Board. In the short term, a limit on the board's powers could be set by the description of its functions. In the longer term, with increased responsibility, expanded functions and stronger native membership, it could exercise powers unlimited by the word 'advisory'.

On 16 June 1957 in Port Moresby I announced publicly that, 'following detailed investigations over the last three years', the native labour policy had been reformulated and a new native labour ordinance would be brought down in the September meeting of the Legislative Council. I said that new legislation would provide for agreement labour in two classes—first, married men accompanied by their wives and families to their place of employment, and second, single men, widowers and married men not accompanied by their wives and families. The legislation would also provide for 'free employment' for advanced native workers who had the skill and capacity to work outside the usual native labour agreements and who could command higher remuneration than the mass of native labour. They would be permitted to work anywhere in the Territory. Similarly provision would be made for workers to take job contracts. All native workers would be issued with 'work cards', which would give the worker a record of his engagement and his entitlements and would allow a prospective employer to satisfy himself that an applicant for work was not already under an agreement to work elsewhere. The new legislation would also propose a wage-fixing machinery in the form of an employment board, on which employers, native employees and the Administration would all be represented. I then quoted in full the three aims I had laid down for the control and regulation of native labour, and continued that the methods by which these aims were served would have to be adjusted from time to time to meet changing circumstances in the Territory. (Press statement of 16 June 1957.)

The passage of native labour legislation through the Legislative Council was attended by keen debate and, to help the Administrator handle the situation in the Council, a conference between Administration and employers' representatives was arranged in Port Moresby in January 1958. McCarthy attended from Canberra.

There was a great deal of discussion in the Territory both before and after the legislation was introduced into the Legislative Council, and the major measure was not completed and assent given until December 1958. It was to come into operation on a date to be fixed by the Administrator. Drafting of regulations and other preparatory work in the Territory delayed its commencement until October 1960, over three years after my final policy decision.

The Native Employment Board Ordinance was assented to in April 1958. Regrettably, in the passage of the Bill through the Legislative Council, the Administrator apparently overlooked the directions given and accepted an amendment widening the board's powers. At that stage, when the direct representation of native workers on the board was certain to be weak and possibly inarticulate, I was unwilling to see it exercising the power of examining 'all matters relating to the employment of natives', for I knew that its majority, including Administration officials, were in one way or another all employers of native workers. (Minute of 2 December 1957.) I advised the Governor General to withhold assent to that paragraph of the Bill that would have given it this unlimited function in respect of employment. An amending bill to repair the oversight was assented to in August 1958. The amended ordinance was not commenced by notice by the Administrator until July 1959.

Separately, during 1957, the Administration prepared a draft bill for the Transactions with Natives Ordinance in order to introduce a system under which native workers could enter into contracts to do specified work. In recommending assent to this ordinance in December 1958, I added a direction to the Administrator to watch the system closely and make a special report on its operation in twelve months' time so as to make sure that it was not used as a cheap form of employment for wages.

Towards the end of 1958, at the departmental level, the Secretary of the Commonwealth Department of Labour and National Service, H. Bland, began to express an interest in labour conditions in Papua and New Guinea. Both Lambert and I, from our knowledge of him, thought Bland must be 'up to something', but we could not quite make out what the 'something' was. At times it looked as though he might be laying the groundwork for an extension of his own departmental functions into the field of industrial relations in the Territory. Whatever it was, Bland's show of interest troubled rather than enlightened us and came to nothing.

There was a clearer and happier relationship with the Secretary of the Australian Council of Trade Unions, Albert Monk, with whom I had some previous friendly associations. Monk, in conversation, told me in effect that the Australian trade union interest, which some years earlier had been almost solely concerned about the competition of 'cheap black labour', was changing at least in some quarters to an idea of helping to organize their comrades, the indigenous workers, into trade unions. Monk himself accepted my view that industrial relations in the Territory had their own distinctive problems and that the interest of the indigenous employees at this stage might be better served by methods directly related to Territory conditions than if the Australian trade unions were to handle their affairs. We agreed on an exercise which led to a visit to the Territory by a group representative of Australian employers, employees and the public service. It was a highly educational tour, not least in revealing to its members that labour policy and industrial relations in the Territory were not the same as in Australia. It helped me to ensure that industrial organization would proceed in the Territory in response to Territory conditions and not as a subsidiary of Australian mainland trade unions.

During 1958 I felt growing concern at reports about what was described locally by both officials and the newspapers as 'native unemployment'. In reality the situation was the outcome not of a fall in employment opportunities but the congregation in the urban areas, especially Port Moresby, of native workers, some of whom may have 'deserted' from employment under agreement, some of whom had failed to return home to their villages when their engagements under agreement ended and some of whom had drifted in to the town for any one of a dozen personal reasons which all might be broadly summarized as the attraction of city lights. Some of them joined their 'one-talks' (people from the same part of the Territory) who were in employment in the town and camped in the boy houses in the back yards of the town, but most of them were in crude shanties and shelters in the gullies and patches of scrub on the outskirts of the town. They lived a sort of hand-to-mouth existence with an occasional job. The situation had grown up gradually and almost un-noticed until it forced itself to the attention of officialdom as a nuisance. To describe it as 'unemployment' seemed to me to mask the basic social problem of which it was evidence. To use its existence as an argument in favour of casual labour seemed to me to ignore broader questions of the standard of living, housing and social services for rootless people living on the fringe of urban life.

During 1958 my attention was distracted by other worries and I see signs in my own notes that I slackened my grip on the subject of native labour in the second half of the year and then grabbed at it again in a rather irritable mood. In a note to Lambert in January 1959 I wrote, 'I find my mind is rather in a jumble about various matters that have been discussed with me or submitted to me in reference to native employment'. I complained that several different matters had been 'thrown at me from various directions and without much reference from one to the other' and I had difficulty in sorting them out. 'For all I know', I said in confession of my own shortcomings, 'it may be that departmental officers have been working in orchestral harmony on native employment. So far however the results have not come my way, and since the new year I have been hesitating to make any decisions on native employment until I can see the whole pattern clearly and comprehensively.' I asked

Lambert to get one of his officers to draw together all outstanding matters in one paper so that I could have a talk with him and the various officers who seemed to be handling different aspects of the question. (Minute of 28 January 1959.) I started pressing the Administrator to bring the new Native Employment Ordinance and the Native Employment Board Ordinance into operation.

In April 1959 F. D. C. Caterson[38] was appointed chairman of the Native Employment Board, but my plan to create a separate Department of Labour had not made the progress for which I had hoped. There still seemed to be divided opinion and hesitation, if not opposition, about policy in the Territory. I should have intervened in a much more peremptory fashion but failed to do so.

Towards the end of 1960, on a submission made by the Department of Territories, it appeared to me that the Native Employment Board was assuming a role in negotiating wage agreements which had not been envisaged for it. In a minute of 13 October, while approving an agreement between a group of employers and a group of employees which the board presented, I wrote that it was never intended that the board should act in the way of an arbitration court, a conciliation commissioner or a tribunal, and if we decided to have that kind of machinery in the Territory, we would create it for that purpose. I used the occasion to ask the Department to prepare a broader submission about future industrial relations, linking it with a proposal that had already been made to me for the creation of a Department of Trade and Industry, in which there would be a Labour Division.

In early November, in creating the new Department of Trade and Industry, I had some hesitation about the Labour Division and arranged for further discussion with Caterson and Lalor and the Public Service Commissioner. As a result, I decided, against advice from some other quarters, to create immediately a separate Department of Labour in the Administration and gave directions to the Public Service Commissioner to prepare his proposals for its establishment and functions and instructed the Administrator to prepare legislation. I also asked the Department to draft for my early consideration a new statement on labour policy. (Minute of 23 December 1960.)

The formative influence in this instance was exercised by Caterson and Lalor. Unless I misjudge the situation, some of their earlier endeavours had been blocked in the Territory until, as Minister, somewhat tardily, I broke down the barrier.

At the same time, from my own thinking, I set down certain points to be included in the new statement of policy. These were:

(a) My previous statements on the broad aims of labour policy should be reaffirmed.

(b) In these statements . . . we should place the emphasis on the social, economic, and educational advancement of the people.

(c) In these statements we should also respect the principle of no racial discrimination. Although in fact the largest body of labour in the Territory is provided by the indigenous people and most of the native labour works at levels of skill and remuneration below that of the European employee, we treat that as a circumstance and not as a principle in any industrial organization.

(d) We add to the previous statements a principle regarding fair and equitable terms and conditions of employment. It is a matter for judgement whether we should add anything about the adequacy of wages to maintain the customary standard of living and the capacity of industry (or the economy) to pay, or whether we leave that for a future pronouncement by a court or other tribunal.

(e) We add the principle of free association of persons engaged in a trade or industry and the legal recognition of such associations.

(f) We add a principle regarding the right of negotiation, the legal recognition of agreements reached by negotiation and the provision of machinery to facilitate negotiation.

(g) We add the principle of conciliation and the provision of facilities for conciliation.

In giving this guidance to the Department, I added a few comments of my own. In explaining why, in paragraph (b), I referred only to 'social, economic and educational advancement'. I wrote,

It is neither necessary nor desirable to link industrial organization and political organization. Basically this is not the job of a public service but one for the community to do just as it chooses when it is able to choose. Our task of tutelage and guidance does not extend to making industrial organizations, either of employers or employees, into political organizations . . . My own view is that the political advancement of the people will be better served if their political organization is based on broader questions than employment. We have to think of the self-governing state of the future, in which the membership of any political party will be composed largely of native people and I would doubt whether there would be much profit to them in dividing themselves into a party of native wage-earners opposed to a party of native self-employed persons or native employers. I would foresee great damage to the country if self-government were to start with a division between an urban proletariat and country-dwelling occupiers of land. Furthermore, in the period before self-government comes, any political organization based on employment would necessarily put most of the Europeans on one side and most of the indigenes on the other and that racial division in politics is one of the dangers we have to work to avoid. In any case, the base and the form of political organization are matters for the people themselves to determine in due course and we should carefully and scrupulously avoid making any analogies with Australian history or present Australian political practice and let political development take place in response to the circumstances and needs of the Territory and its people.

The other comment was that we should be cautious at this stage about the creation of tribunals. If in the light of experience it was found necessary to create industrial tribunals, we could create them and clothe them with the necessary powers.

Another decision, in keeping with a submission by Caterson and Lalor, was to create a position of industrial adviser in the Public Solicitor's office. Caterson became Secretary for the Department of Labour.

At this time I also had to take the personal initiative and press hard to get action on workers' compensation and industrial safety in the Territory.

By an earlier direction, requiring strict attention to the holding of coroners' inquests on native fatalities, as recounted in chapter 16, I had arranged to receive regular returns on all inquests. In August 1956 I noted that the return for the first six months of the year included a number of industrial fatalities. Three native workers had died in road accidents, one on a launch, five at work, and four others in situations that were not clear. In a minute of 27 August I asked questions about industrial safety precautions, compensation for death or injury, and what had been done in the thirteen cases under notice. I called for a submission before the end of September. An interim report by Lambert on existing provisions for compensation led me to observe that they were quite inadequate. 'On what principles', I asked, 'does one assess the value of the life of a native and arrive at the conclusion that the maximum is £100?' I pressed for an early submission. (Minute of 19 September 1956.) On 17 October 1956—the day I received the submission—I approved a recommendation made in general terms for the preparation of legislation on both industrial safety and workers' compensation and directed that the subject be 'kept under close notice'.

There were differences of viewpoint in the Territory. The Administrator appointed a committee. Its report, when placed before me on the last day of February 1957, impressed me as 'sound and businesslike'. I approved their recommendations on 4 March and minuted the papers. 'Please ensure that there is no delay in drafting and introducing the necessary legislation. Our timetable is already five months slow.' (Minute of 4 March 1957.)

In the meantime, having received another return of coroners' inquests, for the second six months of 1956, I asked the Administrator to send fuller information in seven cases in which the question of compensation could have been raised.

In August 1957 I received a disappointing report. The drafting of a workers' compensation ordinance was considered to be so closely tied up with the drafting of native employment legislation that it could not be completed independently and, as for the native employment legislation—a total of nine ordinances—'it is not clear when finality will be reached'. It was hoped to have industrial safety legislation ready in 1958. I accepted the reality that the Administration had been unable to complete the drafting in time for the Legislative Council session in September 1957, and wrote, 'This legislation has to be ready for the first meeting of the Legislative Council in 1958.' (Minute of 28 August 1957.)

When the draft of a compensation bill was placed before me in May, I objected to the figures of compensation set for the death of a native worker. The 'best rate', which applied to the lowest-paid workers, was much lower than the original proposals. The Department's submission argued in support of the Administrator's proposals and recommended approval of them. The case rested partly on the needs of the worker, paying regard to the fact that, unlike a white worker, he had 'the village economic and social framework behind him'—which seemed to me to mean that the village could look after the widow and children of the dead man and hence they were not really his dependants. The case also rested on the capacity of industry to pay. I refused to approve. I wrote, rather angrily,

I cannot accept the so-called 'revised approach'. It results in a compensation for death of a worker that is contemptuously low, and it bears the marks of having been devised to produce such a result rather than as a correction of faulty logic in the initial approach. There would also be political difficulty in justifying in Australia and overseas our amendment of our original proposals. [Minute of 26 May 1958.]

The Administration officers were rather miffed because their own views had not prevailed and they continued to dawdle. An acceptable bill for the ordinance was not ready until November 1959.

The industrial safety legislation had a similar history of delay. I find from my notes that in October 1958 I was repeating that it had a high priority. On 24 January 1959 I wrote again, 'Please expedite work on industrial safety.' In March 1959 I was listing a succession of further delays and requiring action. On 7 July the subject was 'still dragging badly' and I set 6 August as a deadline for the final submission. The department beat the deadline by two days and gave me a twelve-page submission on 4 August. I approved their recommendations for a comprehensive system of industrial safety on the same day. 'It has taken us two years to get this far', I wrote. 'See if we can put in a fast finishing run. This has a high priority.' (Minute of 4 August 1959.)

One field in which we made encouraging progress was in a native apprenticeship scheme. An Apprenticeship Ordinance was made in 1952 and under it the Native Apprenticeship Board was created. The first two years were spent in careful preparatory work, the opportunity for arranging apprenticeships at that time being limited both by the lack of openings and the lack of youths with the basic education required for further training. From 1955 onwards however under the chairmanship of John Hohnen,[39] managing director of New Guinea Goldfields, the training of native youths to a level of skill that would lead to steady employment in the Territory commenced in earnest, with a good measure of community support, co-operation of employers and tradesmen, and eventually close liaison with the technical schools set up in the Education Department as well as with such departments of the Administration as the Post Office and the Printing Office. The work of the Native Apprenticeship Board produced for me as Minister one of those happy situations in which my steady encouragement was welcome and I had little more to do than appreciate the good results achieved by the efforts of a dedicated group under Hohnen's leadership. Although in 1958 the total of apprentices in training, about two hundred, may have seemed small, they proved to be powerful leaven in the large lump.

As I have indicated above, I now feel that I might have done better in matters of native employment between 1958 and 1960 and should have taken control more positively of this subject instead of leaving so much to officials. If I had been constantly attentive to this subject, I could have cut though the passive resistance and the apparent conflict of views in the Territory and given a better chance at an earlier stage to the small constructive element in the Administration. Nevertheless by the end of 1960 we had made a good foundation and I believe we had removed some of the dangers to the development of a sound employment policy and opened up some new opportunities to the native worker to share in the material progress of his country.

At that time the only strength the people of Papua and New Guinea had in taking part in the economic life of their country was their possession of land and the demand for their labour. I like to think that I preserved both of these advantages for them.

Employment of native labour was a major educational and social factor in the reshaping of Papua and New Guinea. For many people their first continuous association with any people outside their own clan was when they went to another part of the Territory to work. Their first knowledge of new goods, new tools, new techniques and a cash economy was often brought about by employment. Their first exposure to new risks either in health or habit came with this entrance into the outside world. At any given time, 70 000 of the young able-bodied men would be away from home working under agreement and, since most of them returned to their villages at the end of their period of work, they brought back to thousands more a story of the outside world. What happened to them in the course of their employment helped to shape the outlook of hundreds of thousands of people. On the whole, I think that the report carried home by most of them was a good one. They had also learnt a few skills and some new ways which helped in the advancement of their own folk at home. Nevertheless I always felt that one of the opportunities we missed was in using even the low-skilled employment as a form of training.

[22]

POLITICAL PROGRESS

At this point in my narrative I should assemble the evidence about my attitude to constitutional change during this period in the Territory's progress. That evidence is voluminous in the shape of contemporary statements, instructions and notes for my own use, so I will be narrowly selective.

A few points have to be made in answer to some stock criticisms. I had always seen quite clearly that the end of all we were doing was self-government and eventual independence for Papua and New Guinea. Where I would not commit myself, for I had no firm views on it, was on the form that self-government would take or the terms of the future relationship between Australia and an independent Papua and New Guinea. On these I expressed hopes, in general terms, for a system that would be democratic and in which justice and respect for the rights of the individual would prevail, and for a relationship with Australia that would be close and harmonious. I hoped for a peaceful transition following negotiation of the constitutional change, and worked to avoid either revolution or a seizure of power by a minority or by a determined and ambitious leader.

I had used the phrase 'free, close and permanent' in referring to the future association with Australia. The word 'permanent' was misinterpreted, first at home and then internationally, as though I had advocated a continuing control by Australia. In its context the word clearly meant that we were to work out a relationship that would be a lasting one, in contrast to a brief one, as a result of having been freely agreed to by both parties. We would not cut the ties or cease to take an interest in the independent country, for, as I had also said, I foresaw that after independence Australian assistance would still be needed. It is gross distortion to suggest, as some persons have, that I advocated some form of continued authority by Australia over Papua and New Guinea.

Another misrepresentation of my views came from bad newspaper reporting. After the Cohen lecture in Sydney (see p. 192), a member of the audience spoke at some length at question time about creating Papua and New Guinea as a seventh State of the Australian Commonwealth and sought my views. Not wishing to engage in an argument with that particular person about a proposal I thought personally to be quite unrealistic but I knew had an appeal to some of the European members of the Territory Legislative Council, I simply replied

239

that this was one of the possibilities for the future. I was reported as having said some of the things my questioner, and not I, had said and of being in favour of this solution. I never entertained any such policy myself and never worked towards that end. Every now and again a newspaper would revive the incorrect story, and the suggestion for 'a seventh State' was to be revived from time to time by other persons.

A small number of critics sometimes spoke of our attempts at political advancement as 'forcing them to accept the Westminster style of government'. This is partly true. I tried to ensure that the transition to self-government and to independence would come by constitutional means and not by insurrection or seizure of power, and it is true that, in doing so, I envisaged a peaceful process by which the Australian Parliament would pass a measure transferring powers and functions to Papua and New Guinea, and I hoped that the transfer would be to a parliamentary democracy and not to an oligarchy or a dictatorship. I therefore worked to accustom the people to the ideas of representation, the responsibility of government to the people and a public service that carried on the tasks of administration for the benefit of the whole country and not for the benefit of officials or for the perpetuation of the power of one faction. I tried to accustom them to the idea that the law was interpreted and justice was done through courts that were independent and trustworthy. Following these efforts I tried to ensure that as many of the population as possible be fitted to take part in choosing their representatives and in understanding what was being done by their government. I also believed that the success of a parliamentary democracy would be impeded if there were a big gap between a sophisticated few and the great mass of the people and, although I could not hope for complete homogeneity in the community, I believed that the diverse peoples of the country, divided by language, habit and ancient enmities, had to find some common ground before they could govern themselves as a nation. My concept of a nation was perhaps rather narrowly based on British and Australian history. Although nations might be brought into existence by the powerful conqueror or overlord, they only prospered when they found their own identity and purpose.

To this extent—the broad picture of eventual nationhood and the broad concept of the methods by which it might be reached—I was influenced by my own traditional link with the Westminster style of government and I was also doubtful whether the model of the Soviet Union or the recent experience of some newly emerging countries in other continents offered much prospect of future happiness to the people of dependent territories. As for the rest, my view was that this was a matter for the people of Papua and New Guinea to work out. While trying to establish ideas of representation, responsibility and justice, I tried to leave the structure of the future government as open as possible.

Another point on which I had no firm views was the date for self-government. I thought that both the form of government and the time for a change should be chosen by the people themselves and not imposed on them. I can fairly be criticized for not forming firm views of my own and for not imposing my will on the people. I can also be fairly criticized for not choosing to fix a target date for independence and for not imperiously driving the people towards that historic moment. In my view, freedom of choice included freedom to decide when to make the choice. I thought it was inconsistent to argue that it was wrong for the trustee to say what type of government the people should have in the future, but right to lay down a date when they had to have self-government.

Some statements I made about the prospective period of preparation for self-government expose me to the charge that I did not assess accurately the rate of change in the Territory. I used terms like 'ten, twenty or thirty years' when, as events turned out, the period between the time I was speaking in 1957 and 1958 and the date of independence in 1975 was eighteen or nineteen years. At worst I was ten years out in my guess. Some critics have unfairly quoted what I said in 1957 as though I had said it in 1973.

I put my point of view in a public statement of 10 July 1960:

> I have expressed readiness to give immediate target dates for educational, social and economic advancement because I believe that it is now possible in the light of great progress in the post-war years to do so. We would only be making guesses or expressing hopes if we attempted to give target dates for self-government for we cannot predict with certainty what the effect of social and economic change will be on the people, what the speed of change will be or what the people of the Territory will themselves want in the future.

This interpretation of a policy of self-determination had been given the label of 'gradualism' by some academic writers. If the term means taking one step after another—the normal means of human progress—it may be defensible as a label. If it means going slowly or cautiously, it is untrue. A fairer label for my policy on political advancement would be 'growth'. I was doing my best all the time to force the growth and watched eagerly for signs of it. Because I believed that political change was the outcome of growth and not the cause of it, I also believed that the growth had to be in the roots, the trunk, the branches and the leaves of the tree and not only in the fruit. A fully representative legislature, responsible government and a constitution for an independent country were the product of the growth of a community and not something that could appear, like miraculous apples produced without a tree, before growth had taken place.

Public discussion of political advancement in Australia in the 1950s seemed to me to concentrate too narrowly on the legislature as though the number of native members in a legislative council was the only index of any political advancement. Up to 1958 we had concentrated on training in the handling of affairs by democratically elected local government councils, training in economic affairs through co-operative societies and the enterprise of groups and individuals, and training in public administration through membership of the public service and native participation with Europeans in membership of councils and boards of various kinds. These efforts had brought us to a stage where in 1958 an increase in the native membership of the Legislative Council could take place effectively.

Before I deal with the changes in the Legislative Council I must say something of our work in local government and in bringing the indigenous people into administration. From an early stage there had been local councils of a sort in places like Hanuabada, on the outskirts of Port Moresby, and at villages around Rabaul. The Papua and New Guinea Act 1949 provided for the establishment by ordinance of native village councils with such functions as the ordinance provided. An ordinance was made in 1949 and the creation of councils by the Administrator commenced. The early councils, closely super-vised by district officers, mainly served the purposes of the Administration but introduced the idea of having elected representatives from each one of a group of villages. In 1954 an amending ordinance changed the name to Native Local Government Councils and from about 1956 a more purposeful move was made to promote the formation of councils throughout the Territory and to introduce the idea that local people could handle their local affairs. Several of the younger officers in the Department of Native Affairs took up the task with enthusiasm. It became a matter of pride and clear evidence of successful administration when a district commissioner could report progress in the work of local government councils.

In 1956 there were 10 councils covering 227 villages and 45 000 people. In five years the totals rose to 43 councils covering 1011 villages and 305 395 people. In the same period their total revenues rose from £44 000 to £312 000.

The approach was simple. The initiative came from the Australian officer. With variations suited to circumstances he said in effect to the people, 'Don't you think it would be a good idea if you had a council just like the people over at ———?' (He named some neighbouring group whom they envied.) When curiosity had been stimulated, he told them in effect, with local variations, that when they got a council, they would be able to do such things as build a council house, get a lighting plant, start a rice-mill, have a saw-bench, buy a vehicle or do something else which they coveted but which was beyond their means as individuals in a village. My impression, gained from conversation and observa-tion, was that this picture of material benefits was much more attractive in the early stages than any idea of 'governing themselves' or 'running their own affairs'. They were told of the advantages of accepting a tax—the levies varied but were usually about £4 a year for an adult male and £1 for women and younger men—in order to get funds for common purposes, and this was usually readily acceptable to them.

When interest had been aroused, they were told something of how to form a council and given the idea of choosing people to represent them. They were taught about elections. On a few occasions, in remote villages, I witnessed a first election. Everyone was gathered. There was a state of hushed expectancy. The patrol officer, who had told them all about it, stood in the centre. He asked those who wanted to be candidates to come forward. The first came forward rather shyly and self-consciously. After the second and third, and with some giggling and nudging and rising chatter, others joined them in a rush. The patrol officer put the candidates in a line with a gap of several yards between each and then called on the villagers, men and women, to stand behind the candidate they supported. It was something like children picking up sides for some impromptu game. When all were in their chosen places, the patrol officer and his cadet counted heads. The candidates with most supporters behind them were declared elected up to the required number. There was a babble of talking but still a mixture of puzzlement and solemnity while the patrol officer told them about arrangements for the first meeting.

I also saw an election, at a later stage of progress, by the 'whispered ballot'. This one was held under a tree. Two 'returning officers', both Native Affairs officers, sat at a table with prepared rolls and charts spread in front of them. The people stood apart. A name was called. The voter came forward. He or she whispered to the returning officer the name of a candidate. A vote was recorded, and the voter moved into the group of those who had already voted. Another name was called. When no one was left in the first group, the roll was checked. There was some conferring. Where were So-and-so and So-and-so? An explanation was given. One was in hospital and one had gone to the coast. The poll was complete. While the people waited, the progressive count was checked and rechecked. In a solemn and important way the returning officers stood up and in a loud, clear voice the senior one declared the results of the poll. There was some cheering, but not much, and a minor argument, rather short-lived, started somewhere in the rear of the crowd. The children, who had been subdued, squatting nearer to the village, started scampering about. Diligent women resumed their work. The elected councillors were called forward by the officials for congratulations and advice.

One of the earliest duties of a newly formed council was to appoint its own clerk, usually a younger man who had learnt to write and who had been instructed in how to keep minutes and an account book. In some of the very early councils the work of running the council, keeping its records, prompting its decisions and looking after its funds often fell on a patrol officer, but very quickly we moved into the training of native officials, just as we had trained clerks and assistants for co-operative societies, and soon created a local government branch of the Administration with officers concentrating on this work. The level of work being done by councils and the competence of people serving their villages either as elected councillors or as appointed officials rose.

Some of the small early councils were formed into larger groupings of villages for reasons of efficiency and promoting community interest over a wider area, and so statistics for the number of councils were not always as good an index of the progress being made as were the numbers of the population served.

There was much patient and dedicated work and this was one activity in the late fifties with which I found good reason to be pleased despite an occasional disappointment. On my own frequent visits to the Territory, I had always made a point of including visits to council meetings in the programme and of recognizing a village council as the appropriate body to extend a welcome to a visiting Minister rather than any other institution. On the itineraries of other VIP visitors, a council meeting was often a showpiece. This attention encouraged the councils and the village people to feel that this new side of life was important. Gradually a change came from a time when we had to persuade the people to form a council to a time when some at least were asking whether they could have a council.

Essentially, however, this was an activity promoted by the Government before it was sought by the people. It was promoted as a first step towards self-government and as a measure in political education. Through it we introduced the people to the practice of choosing their own representatives to handle their own affairs, to the mechanics of conducting an election, holding a meeting in an orderly fashion, keeping a record of what was done, deciding on a tax for themselves and deciding how the revenue should be used, by employing their own staff to work for the whole community and paying their wages out of money provided by the community. We also taught them to expect their representatives to account for what they did on behalf of the community. All these ideas were new to them.

We then used the movement as a means of broadening the concept of a village to the concept of a region, with a grouping of village councils to consider questions of common interest and to engage in joint undertakings, and then to broaden this concept still further into a concept of common interests throughout the country. The first Papua and New Guinea Local Government Conference was held rather tentatively in 1959, but at the second, in November 1960 at Vunadadir (near Rabaul), there was an attendance of thirty-nine delegates and twenty-eight alternates from the thirty-nine local government councils in existence throughout the Territory—the number had been reduced by the earlier grouping of small councils into larger council areas—and a number of observers from districts where councils had not yet been formed.

In promoting these local government conferences I found the need for some caution. In a note to the Administrator in October 1960 I wrote,

> The agenda of any conference of local government councils should be intensely practical and a direct extension of the work the councillors are already doing in their respective councils rather than an encouragement to them to have a feast of talking on matters for which they will not themselves have to carry any responsibility. This lesson of responsibility is one of the fundamental lessons we have to teach in political advancement and our officers should perpetually try to get the native people to face up to the things they can and should do themselves rather than encourage them to drift into the popular Australian habit of carrying resolutions, expressing vague wishes or making demands on someone else to do everything for them.

I also directed that prompt and practical attention be given to the resolutions agreed to by the conferences and the conference informed of the action taken. At the same time we had to be careful not to let the local government conferences become a substitute for increased native participation in the work of the Legislative Council or assume a higher importance in the minds of the native people than the Legislative Council.

In the work of the councils, our experience was that the success of a local council depended a good deal on the emergence of a few strong characters to give leadership and to take over from the patrol officer or local government officer the guidance he had given in the formative stages. It was remarkable how common it was for the community to produce these natural leaders. In those few cases where they were lacking it was hard work to keep the councils going.

Another characteristic I noticed in the early stages of many councils was the

After the opening of the Legislative Council

Front row: Sir John Northcott, Colonel J. K. Murray, D. M. Cleland, C. R. Lambert

The author, hands clasped, at left

A councillor from Wabag in the highlands, with the council insignia attached to the traditional headgear

A local government council in session

cautiousness, if not suspicion, with which the councils watched the clerks or other officers. The clerks might be bright young men who could read and write but they were not to be allowed to start telling older and more seasoned people in the village what they should do. There was strong conservatism in most communities and the johnny-come-lately and the juniors were kept in their place. The people were not handing over too much too soon to their 'bright boys'.

Without this foundational work in the local government councils it would have been impossible to take subsequent steps towards self-government. What our officials did in this regard in the period from about 1956 to 1960 was one of the soundest and most valuable achievements in my term of office.*

Another major step in political progress between 1958 and 1960 was to promote the participation of native people in the administrative services. The principal measures initially were the creation of an auxiliary division of the Territory Public Service as a training ground and changes in the widespread employment of a class of workers hitherto called Administration native servants.

The Territory Public Service, narrowly defined, was almost wholly a European service. By December 1956, however, the native people were already involved to a considerable extent in the work of government. There were over 1000 native medical assistants, over 5000 native teachers in Administration and mission schools, over 2000 members of the Royal Papua and New Guinea Constabulary, and 48 native agricultural assistants and over 200 others in training. At a lower level, there were thousands of helpers classed as Administration native servants. I was not satisfied with the terms of their participation in government.

First, in order to give some of them a career service and the opportunity of graduating into the ranks of the public service alongside the Europeans, I created an auxiliary division of the Territory Public Service. The creation of the auxiliary division met with some scepticism in the Department of Territories and suffered from lack of enthusiasm in the Territory Administration. My attempt to overcome both was hampered by the fact that an organizational change of this kind required the working out of a good deal of detail. For example, after we had worked out scales of salary relative to other scales in the public service, new difficulties were raised about entitlement to compensation and retirement benefits relative to those scales of pay, and the argument about this point went to and fro between Canberra and Port Moresby for more than a year.

As early as July 1953 I had directed attention to the need for finding an appropriate way of bringing the native people into the public service of their country. The situation at that time, as I saw it, was that, although the Administration employed a great number of workers described as 'native servants' and although some of them had been in such employment for a long time, they had no chance of advancement or of training and no recognized

* To avoid any confusion I should add that during the same period we were engaged in a separate activity in local government affecting the principal towns and the replacement of town advisory councils by a municipal authority. This work stemmed from a report made in 1956 by J. R. Winders following an investigation concerned mainly with the non-indigenous people, who then comprised the principal population in these towns.

place but were only temporary and casual employees. Most of them did little more than fetch and carry for the Australian officers. Furthermore there was little possibility at that time of finding any native candidates for entry into the Territory Public Service at the same educational standard or level of duties as other public servants. As an interim measure, another division, with its own prescribed standard of entry, prescribed standards of pay, job descriptions and conditions of service, seemed to me to be essential if we were to start to build the foundations for an indigenous public service and replace casual employment as a 'native servant' by a career service. In a further minute of 3 September 1953 I asked for studies to be made, and this resulted in a submission to me on 3 February 1954. On 10 February I directed the Public Service Commissioner to 'proceed as expeditiously as possible with the preparation of proposals for an auxiliary division'. My idea of an auxiliary division was that it should be a division of the public service in which young native officers could be trained in the job, while becoming increasingly useful to the Administration, and then qualify for promotion into classified positions in a Territory Public Service, which would have steadily increasing numbers of Papuans and New Guineans. In November 1954 I received the first proposals and gave immediate approval to them.

Then the lag began. One minor difficulty after another was raised. I kept on scolding the Administrator, but to little effect. After eighteen months I wrote a long memorandum on 17 May 1956, which I quote below (p. 247) since it deals comprehensively with several administrative questions. This restated the policy and demanded early submissions of proposals. Nothing emerged in the next three months. In a minute of 13 September 1956 I expressed my disappointment at the gap of three years 'between the giving of a policy direction and the creation of the division'. The same minute spelt out my purpose because I realized that, in spite of my earlier directions, both the Department and the Administration were still habituated to a wholly expatriate service:

> The building up of competent staff in Papua and New Guinea and the improvement of the organization of the public service are the foundation on which the success of our administration in the Territory rests. Realizing the way in which pressure on administration, as the result of the progress of the native people, is certain to build up year by year, we cannot afford to lose any opportunity to strengthen and train the service. In less than five years' time the demand for competent and experienced officers is going to be perhaps double what it is now and the only way to be sure of having them in five years' time is to recruit them now.
>
> In the building of this foundation, a very high value has to be given to the recruitment and training of the indigenous people. For a commencement this will have an immediate practical effect in obtaining more hands to help do the many tasks that have to be done . . . In addition, we will never be able to cope with the growing demands in health, education and so on unless we recruit native officers and train them to work among their own people. In the longer term, the introduction of the native people to the public service becomes even more important. As the years go by . . . they will have to take an increasing part in the business of government and will expect to have the right to do so. We have to build soundly now to ensure that this future service inherits sound practices and sound traditions.

I directed that no effort should be spared to have the division in existence before the end of the year. Once the division was established, we should apply ourselves energetically to building it up and training it. (Minute of 13 September 1956.)

On 19 December 1956 I approved the establishment of the division and on 3 January 1957 approved of plans for training its members. After commending the Public Service Commissioner for his work, I emphasized the importance we placed on the success of this innovation. Later in the month I received his recommendations for the first twenty-eight appointments to the division.

A pernickety assistant secretary of the Department of Territories gave me eight typed foolscap pages of reasons why I should refer the recommendations back to the Public Service Commissioner for further consideration. I noted that the Department seemed 'to err on the side of formalism' and approved the admission of the first twenty-eight candidates on 29 January. Then there was a lot more fiddling around but, after a further jolt from me, the next batch of 161 candidates were admitted to the service on 27 June. Their appointments included clerical assistant, medical assistant, technical assistant, health assistant and teacher, and among them was the first woman member of the division, Miss Hilda Naime.

Alongside our efforts to provide career opportunities for the people, a very helpful move was made at this time first by the Commonwealth Bank and later by the trading banks in providing opportunities for the training of native bank clerks. This, together with what Carter was doing in the Post Office, and what the Departments of Health and Education were doing in training medical assistants and teachers, helped a great deal in changing the old pattern in which native youths were valued as house boys, labourers, messengers and plantation workers but had few openings elsewhere.

At this time, as will have appeared from other actions I have recounted, I was trying hard to get a sounder administrative base from which to work for constitutional change. A view I held clearly was that, at that particular stage in the development of Papua and New Guinea, when the opportunities and interests of the indigenous people in self-government were slight, the most urgent and most importantly practical tasks were to familiarize them with the ideas of representation and responsibility and the procedures of government by promoting the institutions for local government, and to give them fuller participation and a rising capacity for carrying on the tasks of public administration by employing them in the public service. Otherwise constitutional change would only mean giving more power to an articulate European minority and a public service manned by Europeans. My views were spelled out in the memorandum of 17 May 1956 to which I made reference above. I wrote,

We still have not made enough progress with the general question of the employment of non-European residents of the Territory (Asians, mixed blood and indigenes) in the public service . . . One of the long-term objectives of policy is to build up in the Territory a competent and efficient public service in which there will be an ever-increasing proportion of officers who have the Territory as their home. There are two reasons for this. First, we will never be able to provide enough staff from Australia to handle the expanding tasks of government and provide the services needed in the

Territory. Second, the advancement of the indigenous people towards a larger share in government will be unbalanced and its seeming advantages to them will be unreal if it is only a political advancement. Participation in administration will probably do more than anything else to ensure that their participation in politics is sensible and responsible. Any political change that gives more power and responsibility to the indigenous people will only lead to confusion and failure if they have not previously become accustomed to the handling of affairs. This is just as true of the building up of an administrative service as it is of the fostering of representative local government councils.

It is therefore a definite objective of policy to promote the training and recruitment of the indigenous people for appointment to the public service of the Territory, and to make suitable provision for their entry into the public service as a career.

Because of local circumstances, there will have to be some flexibility in the measures taken to achieve this objective. The final purpose is to create a public service in which all Territory-born persons can have a career, with recruitment and appointment according to their qualifications, with prospects of advancement to any position for which an officer is qualified, with the regulations regarding salary, conditions, leave and other entitlements drawn up according to the principles customarily followed in an Australian or British public service, and with superannuation. Before that purpose can be reached however it is recognized that it may be necessary to advance stage by stage from one make-shift arrangement to another. There is no objection whatever to improvisation of various kinds, so long as the final purpose is seen clearly and so long as none of these interim measures conflicts with or impedes the steady progress towards the final objective. It is imperative that we make a start without further delay and do not wait until the circumstances allow us to introduce the perfect scheme in one day. [Minute of 17 May 1956.]

At the same time as I was trying to create the auxiliary division of the public service, I was trying to make reforms in the class of employee known as 'native servants'. There was a great deal of looseness in the engagement and employment of these temporary and casual workers. I gave instructions that proper rates of pay, classifications, increments and conditions of employment be laid down by the Public Service Commissioner and that the number of employees be limited to an establishment fixed for each department and made subject to regular review. I required economies in the use of native labour in this form and special provision for training and other measures to raise their efficiency. Those who qualified should be transferred to the auxiliary division to give them a permanent career, and the approved establishment of 'native servants' automatically reduced.

This insistence on change was not popular in some quarters where officers preferred the old ways and liked to have a lot of helpers on call. My own approach is well illustrated by a minute of 23 April 1957 telling the Administrator that his latest report on the 'native servants' was 'quite unsatisfactory':

I asked for factual reports. How many are employed? What are their duties? How long have they been engaged in these duties? How many are being given training, by whom, where and for what object? . . . Let the Administrator start by assuming that I have an impression that native labour is being wasted by the Administration—that too many are employed for the work to be done—that those employed are not being trained to increase their capacity—and let him further assume that the only way in which that impression will be changed will be by producing figures to the contrary.

Bit by bit I got my way. The auxiliary division grew. The terms of employment of Administration 'native servants' were regulated and the numbers reduced. Quite a number of the significant men in the political life of Papua and New Guinea, fifteen years later, when the country moved towards independence, were men to whom I had given their first chance to learn about government by my decisions in 1956.

In 1957 and 1958, alongside my efforts to introduce native public servants into the Administration and to promote local government, I was watching very closely for signs of political interest in the Territory. I can find no record nor can I recall any instance when any of our officers in the Territory at that time drew attention to any such political interest. On my own visits to the Territory I started a practice of encouraging the people to talk to me. I asked that, as a standard part of my programme, district officers arrange for the people in any place I visited to come together to say whatever they felt like saying to me. There were scores of such gatherings. In some centres, such as Lae or Rabaul, I might hold a meeting attended by representatives of all native groups. In remote villages I would sit down informally in the shade with every inhabitant of the village present. The procedure was always roughly the same, varied a little according to the sophistication of the audience. I would say, in effect, that I had come to their place to see how they were getting on. I wanted them to say whatever was on their mind so that I could tell the Government in Australia and make sure the Government did what was right. Then I waited. The length of time I waited never worried me but it sometimes obviously tried the patience of some Australian officer who was wanting to show me his pet project. Sometimes a spokesman would commence by reciting three or four matters on which he had obviously been primed by a district commissioner—such as that it was time we built a better office for the district headquarters—but then someone would speak up about what was nearer to his own heart, and one thing would lead to another. Gradually, after the news had spread that this was what the Minister always did on his visits, it was taken for granted that I really wanted to hear what they had to say. People started to talk readily. Most of the things they talked about were local questions about fixing up this or that local disability. The broader questions usually concerned such questions as getting a school for their children or giving the village a better chance to get some money by growing this or that crop or a complaint about a delay in fulfilling a promise made by this or that department.

This was politics of its own kind. It was the politics that one might meet in any rural branch meeting of a political party in Australia. When are we going to get a better road? Why did you only put that 'big-head' in gaol instead of really making him suffer? When are you going to send us a teacher? Always listening to the people in this way and being careful not to prompt them or to do much talking myself, I think I came close to them. One of the most encouraging things ever said to me in New Guinea was when I made an overnight stop at Kerowagi after I became Governor-General. I recognized one of the men with whom I had talked about ten years earlier and, addressing him by name, asked him how his people were. He gave me some account of them and added, 'It's not like when you were here, Mr Hasluck. Then we had someone we could talk with. Now we have no one to talk to, not even our own people.'*

Another practice I adopted in the larger towns, such as Port Moresby, Rabaul, Lae, Wewak and Madang, was to receive deputations. It had been customary for the Planters' Associations, the Public Service Association, the town advisory councils, Chambers of Commerce and other European bodies to seek interviews. After one busy day of receiving deputations in Port Moresby I made a remark to John Guise, whom I met by chance in the street as I was walking out of the offices, that none of the native people had sent a deputation. The next time I visited Port Moresby I had requests for interviews from six of them and the practice started. In keeping with this view I also encouraged the formation of various organizations of the native people and this encouraged them to be the spokesmen of their members.

This idea of the accessibility of the Minister was cultivated by me as part of the political growth of the community. It was a means, too, by which I came to know personally more of the native people who were starting to take part in the affairs of the community.

The deputations talked mostly of housing, opportunities in the public service, wages, price of food, marketing of produce. I listened and helped where I could. When anything was done to correct a disability or extend a benefit, the native deputations showed far more appreciation of my interest than European deputations ever did. Perhaps the difference was that the native deputation said, 'The Minister fixed it for us', and the Europeans said, 'We made the bastard put it right.'

I also made a practice, where opportunity offered, of asking some of the more articulate younger native men to meet me on my own socially, say for a late afternoon drink—it was all lemon squash and lolly water for them in those days—and encourage them to tell me what they thought of the future. They were mostly working for the Administration and usually rather shy, but it is plain that what they thought about most was better chances for education, job opportunities in the public service, and houses at rents they could afford. One fruitful meeting of this kind that I remember very clearly was a small evening gathering when a few of them talked of the employment conditions of native workers and ways of improving them. They had heard about trade unions but were rather suspicious of them and wondered whether there was

---

* My method of sitting down and letting the people talk was really the method that had customarily been followed in the early days by patrol officers and district officers. It fell into disuse in later days for various reasons. Officials became busier and their work more highly specialized and so they were concerned only with their own duties and not with having a general talk. Mechanical transport changed the habits of travel. Persons occupying public office, both expatriate and indigenous, tended to become more self-important, as they came closer in imitation to the ways of 'advanced' countries, where the gap between those in office and those who are being 'governed' seems to be a worsening phenomenon.

some other way, say the appointment of an Australian officer who would argue with the white employers on their behalf whenever there was a dispute.

Now, all this was the stuff of politics but it was not pointing towards constitutional change. At all levels of sophistication there was still an idea that government should be left in the hands of Australians and there was still much reliance on the decisions of an Australian official. At the local government level the people could grasp the idea of representation, of raising revenues by taxing themselves and of making decisions and carrying out services. When I threw out a few feelers, I could sense very little interest and in many places no interest at all in doing the same thing over the whole country. Among some of the better-educated there was a response to the idea of having more representatives in the Legislative Council and of some of the native officers eventually rising to more senior positions in the public service. John Guise, who was far and away the most articulate at that time, spoke eloquently to me on one occasion in 1957 of the hope that one day there might be an indigenous officer as a district commissioner. That seemed to be the scope of political ambition at that time. On self-government they seemed to balk at the lack of any Territory-wide community of interest among the people. They did not yet feel as one people and one country.

In the statements I made, it will be noticed by any careful reader how often I kept on saying that self-government would come and reminding my hearers or readers that in self-government the majority would be formed by the indigenous people. There was of course still talk of self-government in the sense that the Europeans would be predominant. The only pressure for constitutional change up to this time had come from a committee of the Legislative Council in 1954. It had reported in favour of changing the membership of the Legislative Council to increase the number of elected members in proportion to the official members. 'Elected members' meant members elected by a roll of non-indigenous voters. On this I wrote in a minute of 4 April 1957.

In the view of the Government the two requirements for any change in the structure of the Council designed to give the membership a more widely representative character are, firstly, progress in the political advancement of the indigenous people so that they may participate effectively in the work of the Legislative Council to a larger extent (I underlined 'effectively') and, secondly, progress in the electoral strength and political interest of the non-indigenous population.

For the immediate present, the Government believes that the most fruitful efforts for the political advancement of the indigenous people can be made in the field of local government and it is an instruction on policy that increasing efforts shall be devoted to this work . . . The Government is watching closely the growth of local government in the villages and groups of villages in various parts of the Territory in order that an extension of the representation of the native people in the Legislative Council, either by appointment or election, may be made as soon as it can be justified.

Regarding the electoral strength and political interest of the non-indigenous people, the only guide the Government has is the result of the elections held in October 1954. The total enrolment was only 2771 and, in the two electorates in which elections were held, only 750 votes were cast.

The Administrator was asked to incorporate my instructions on this and other points in a statement to the Legislative Council. The occasion for doing so was the announcement of a decision by the Government that no change in the structure of the Council would be made at present. At the same time the Government had approved the drafting of a bill to deal with the qualifications of members of the Legislative Council in order to place beyond question a legal doubt on the validity of their acts. When this Bill was before the House of Representatives in May 1957, I found occasion to say that we could not change the structure of the Council until we could do so in a manner that would give greater representation to the large indigenous population. Papua and New Guinea must grow towards self-government, but Parliament had a solemn responsibility to see that the management of the Territory's affairs did not fall into the hands of only one section of the Territory community.

After this Bill had been passed, I set the Department working on the possible reform of the Legislative Council. In a minute of 11 November 1957 I asked them to prepare a paper reviewing all proposals for change in the membership and powers of the Legislative Council and the 'general nature of the problems and the possibilities of reform'. I also expressed some 'tentative ideas' of my own. These included the following suggestions:

(1) The presiding officer should not be the Administrator but an officer elected by the Council and responsible to it. The presiding officer should be the custodian of the rights of the legislature and not, in effect, a representative of the Executive. The Administrator would have a better opportunity for being an effective 'leader of the Government' if he were not in the chair.
(2) A better balance between official and non-official members would be to have the numbers the same or to give the official members a majority of not more than one so that they would have to justify their proposals by gathering the support of at least some of the non-official members.
(3) The power of appointing non-official members should be broadly based rather than in specified categories. I was inclined to add to the number of nominated non-official members without prescribing what interests they should represent.
(4) The number of members elected on the present roll of non-indigenous voters or the number of European nominated members could not be increased without at the same time increasing the strength of the representation of the native community.

On native membership of the Council I wrote,

In the present conditions it is clearly far too early to provide for any election of native members and it will be difficult enough to find really effective native members by the system of nomination. Our past experience has been that, at any one time, only one out of three of the native members has proved really effective. This may be due in part to mistakes in choosing native members but I think it is largely due to the fact that there are not yet enough native leaders who are both articulate and able to think on a Territory-wide scale.

I speculated whether it would be possible to provide for the local government councils to combine to nominate representatives to the Legislative Councils and to make this the beginning of direct representation for the native population. In subsequent discussions and visits to the Territory in the next eighteen months I modified these doubts and moved to the idea of direct elections by the native people. The success of local governments, especially in the highlands, persuaded me that even communities still wholly illiterate could learn how to vote and produce representatives who could act for them.

I asked the Department to produce a preliminary statement by 15 January 1958 and to aim at the draft of a submission to Cabinet 'not later than 31 March'. In January 1958 further discussions were arranged in the Territory, Lambert and McCarthy attending from the Department. Consideration of the results of these discussions was delayed. An interim submission was drafted, but Cleland, who had been absent from the Territory on leave, asked that no action be taken on it and started fresh discussions. By March I became very annoyed and a terse minute of 10 March concluded, 'I should like a clear statement of Administration views by someone qualified and authorized to make it. The legislation was prepared in consultation with the Administration. They cannot talk with two voices.' I was aware that the Administrator wished to hold on to as large an official majority as he could in any legislature in much the same way as any elected leader likes a large majority in the House of Representatives, but I had already made plain my view that the official majority should be reduced and that it would be better if the passage of legislation always required the support of at least a few of the non-official members, including non-official native members.

I was ready in 1958 for the next constitutional change but, as will be recounted in the next chapter, my timetable was upset. My planning was for fiscal reforms in 1957 followed by constitutional reform in 1958. But, firstly by reason of delay at the official level in preparing proposals and secondly by reason of a major public controversy on our fiscal proposals, the timetable was upset.

We ran into bitter controversy over the introduction of income tax in the Territory. Early in 1959 I rearranged the timetable with a view to having legislation ready for the Australian Parliament by February 1960. (Minute of 25 February 1959.) This was upset when there were resignations from the Legislative Council over the taxation issue and eventually a case before the High Court challenging the validity of the Council's creation and its competence. Until these matters were out of the way, we could not make progress with constitutional reform. In a public statement of 20 April 1960 I explained that this was the sole reason why I could not seek final decisions about the future of the Legislative Council.

In the same statement I referred again to the work done in local government and quoted the commendation given by the last visiting mission of the United Nations on 'the rapid expansion of local government councils, which signifies a forward step in the political advancement of the people'. My own comment:

> Democracy has already put down its roots and at the end of ten years we have a quarter of a million people who are going to the polls. They have become accustomed to the democratic process of electing their own representatives to manage their own affairs. You would search far and wide through all the dependent territories of the world to find any comparable political advancement among a people who started at so primitive a level.

At the end of April 1960 I obtained authority from Cabinet to prepare detailed proposals for a change in the structure and membership of the Legislative Council, the objective being to submit draft legislation to Cabinet in time for the Budget session towards the end of the year. Cabinet said no public inquiry was to be held, but I was asked to take suitable opportunities to discuss the proposals in the Territory in order to prepare the ground for the introduction of reforms. Cabinet's final approval on the amendments to be made was withheld until they saw my further submission.*

In a visit to the Territory in early July 1960 I discussed the proposals for the reform of the Legislative Council with representatives of all sections of the community and was able to inform Cabinet of my first-hand impressions of the situation in the Territory. In a statement at Port Moresby on 19 July I summarized a number of factors affecting constitutional change and presented our proposals as one further stage in a planned progress towards self-government and a result of success in the measures we had taken for political advancement of the people. I stressed too that the prospective reforms were not the only step towards self-government. There also had to be great social advances—that is, changes in the way people lived and in their relationships to one another and to the community at large—great economic changes, and growth of local administrative and political capacity. These changes would come by hard work year by year.

In making these statements in Port Moresby, foreshadowing the change without giving details, I was aware that they would be read by Europeans and by very few of the indigenous people. Hence I was consciously addressing myself mainly to a European audience in the Territory.

At that stage we were facing the problem of nervousness and, as a consequence of the controversy over taxation, some resistance to Government policy from the expatriate community. Journalists, following their customary practice of having an 'angle', were looking for stories of 'insecurity' and 'winds of change'. They made dishonest distortion in picking one phrase out of context in a press conference given by Menzies on 20 June 1960 on his return from a Prime Ministers' Conference in London. I had accompanied him on his overseas tour but had returned earlier. At the press conference Menzies discussed the future of the Commonwealth of Nations and then passed to review developments in Africa and said that if in doubt about the granting of independence to a dependent territory it was better to go sooner than later, echoing a phrase used by Harold Macmillan regarding Africa. Asked if he would apply that view to New Guinea, Menzies replied that he would apply it to any country, but continued that Australia would go on doing a faithful job in New Guinea. Either he or his successor might reach a point when, although self-determination might seem premature, it would be better to take a risk rather than delay so long that the demand for self-determination became explosive and produced hostility.

Some journalists reported and some commentators repeated their reports as though Menzies had said explicitly that Australia should get out of New Guinea sooner rather than later. In the ears of many of the Europeans in the

* I was overseas with Menzies at the time and the submission I had prepared was piloted through Cabinet by the Acting Minister for Territories, F. M. Osborne.

Territory this was understood to mean that the Government would soon be 'handing over New Guinea to the natives'.

The journalists also tried to build a story that there was some difference of view between Menzies and myself. There was no such difference. Both the Prime Minister and I tried in successive statements to correct the distortion. The matter of immediate relevance is that the episode, together with the circulation of other rumours and gossip, gave rise to more uncertainty in the minds of Europeans in the Territory and to much more talk about 'insecurity'. Although some of this talk was politically motivated and was akin to the small boy's threat to take his bat and ball home if he were not allowed to play the game according to his own rules, there was also much genuine concern about what was going to happen.

The position as the Government saw it—and there are several statements by both Menzies and myself to show this fact—was that the Territory and the Australian Government in its trust for the Territory needed the expatriates. We were trying to recruit teachers, medical men, technicians, scientists, engineers and others for the sake of the advancement of the country and its people. White investment and management were needed for economic development. At that stage new industries would not be established if the expatriates did not establish them. As Menzies said in a speech at Brighton, Victoria, on 13 July, if the view gained currency that we ought to be out of New Guinea in a few years, the development of New Guinea towards self-government would be greatly postponed.

I said in the statement of 10 July in Port Moresby,

Social, economic and political change will only come with the help of Australians—not only public servants but others. Good economic foundations for the self-governing Papua and New Guinea of the future demand Australian investment, management and technological skill. The Government wants all three. The people of the Territory cannot progress without them.

The need we saw to maintain confidence in the future was having a strong influence in shaping the public statements made about constitutional change. When the press was repeating stories about 'a feeling of insecurity' and 'people leaving the country', we had to reassure the European population, while knowing that journalists were on the watch for words or signs that would give another peg for another story about Australia's early withdrawal and the exodus of whites in fear of a black takeover.

In my own statements I always made it plain that the eventual outcome of all we were doing was to be self-government and that this would be attained by a process of self-determination. Some months earlier, in a statement in Port Moresby on 4 December 1959, I said,

We know that the end of the job comes when the Territory in its own time and in the way of its own choice attains self-government. We know that self-government means government by the predominant majority, who are the indigenous people. In all we do we respect their rights and try to protect their future. In advancing towards the final goal the Australian has his rightful place in this country. When the goal is reached we trust that we will both deserve and receive the respect of the indigenous people for our rights. Both now and then the two peoples need each other and can serve each other. Any other footing except a recognition of that mutual need and a willingness to give that mutual service will certainly be insecure.

There was a corresponding concern among the indigenous people lest Australia should abandon them. The common talk among the Europeans that Australia was 'pulling out' became known to native leaders. On my visits to the Territory I had frequent pleas from them that we should stay. In July 1960, at gatherings of these leaders at Rabaul, Lae and Port Moresby, I gave them the assurance:

So long as you need our help you can depend on us to give it. So long as you want us to stay you can depend upon us not to desert you. We believe that New Guinea and Australia need each other. Our wish is to work in partnership with you, going hand in hand, doing things together for the benefit of this country and all its people.

It was heartening to hear the deep murmurs of approval and to feel the fervour of the handshake of each native leader at those meetings. They had wanted to have some such assurance.

During my visit to the Territory in July 1960 I met about thirty different deputations, both from Europeans and indigenous groups and had three large meetings with the leaders of the native people at Port Moresby, Rabaul and Lae. As the result of these inquiries and advice given to me, I gave to Cabinet my considered view that, in the political field, we were at the moment ahead of the awakening interest of the people themselves. Any pressure from inside the Territory in the next five years was more likely to come in demands for education, in eagerness for cash incomes, in feeling among the comparatively small group against any racial discrimination of a social kind, and some possible discontent among the growing section of native people who had left their villages to congregate on the outskirts of towns and who, denied the support of their villages, now found it hard to live at the standard to which they aspired.

On 10 August the High Court delivered its judgment that the Papua and New Guinea Act, under which the Legislative Council was created, was valid. After consultation with Menzies I had already placed my submission in the hands of the Cabinet Secretariat and it was circulated at once. (Submission No. 800 of 11 August 1960.) The decisions made by Cabinet on 17 August were put into effect by the Papua New Guinea Bill (No. 2) 1960 and supplementary legislation by the Legislative Council for Papua and New Guinea, and elections for the new Council were held early in 1961.

Although Cabinet did not go quite as far as I wished in some respects, the effect of the changes was to raise the total number of elected members from three to twelve and the number of indigenous members from three to a minimum of eleven (six elected and five appointed) with a possibility of further appointments.

The changes accorded with majority opinion in the Territory at that time both among the indigenous people and the expatriates. Some elements in the Administration were hesitant about going so far in reducing the official members, although there were a few officers who would have been bolder in extending native membership. The idea of representing the native people by electing some and appointing others was favoured by the leaders of the native people, chiefly as a means by which people in districts of recent contact who had not yet learnt anything about voting might be represented.

A full report of the matter is given in my speech to the House of Representatives in introducing the Bill on 22 September.* The Opposition, led by Arthur Calwell, supported the Bill. The new Council was opened on 10 April 1961.

As well as the increase in membership and particularly of the elected elements, three other decisions I obtained from Cabinet seemed to me at the time to be highly important. One was the acceptance of the principle of the common roll of native and non-native voters, backed by my knowledge that both indigenous and European residents of the Territory, while hesitating for the present, agreed that this should be the objective. The second was the replacement of the Territory Executive Council by a new Administrator's Council, including non-official and native members, which I saw as the embryonic Cabinet of the Territory, associating the representatives of the people with the executive and adding to the various measures for preparing the people for self-government. The third was the fact that we had prepared the way for a more rapid and direct evolution towards self-government with the prospect that the Territory legislature, after a brief period of gaining experience, would choose what the next step would be and when to take it.

As I have indicated, the decisions of August 1960 were taken against a background of apprehension both among the indigenous and among European residents of the Territory. They were also taken at a time when the political climate in Australia was not favourable to change because of the reaction against the exaggerated stories in the press about 'fear', 'uncertainty', 'the winds of change', 'pressure of international opinion' and close analogies between Africa and New Guinea. One of the political problems of which I was necessarily aware was that many Ministers and members were more keenly conscious of the need to reassure the people in the Territory of all races than they were of the wisdom of early constitutional change. By causing this general effect, the newspaper stories had not advanced the cause of constitutional change but made it more difficult.

---

* *Commonwealth Parliamentary Debates* (H. of R.), vol. 28, pp. 1285-91, 22 Sept. 1960.

[23]

THE ROW OVER INCOME TAX

In 1958 I ran into great controversy with the introduction of direct taxation. The history of the episode goes back to July 1955 when in a pre-budget series of Cabinet meetings I sought a forward commitment for a development plan. Cabinet directed that efforts be made to increase substantially the revenues obtained in the Territory, including taxation of the European community. Although increases were made in import duties, export duties and fees and charges for services, it was obvious that further substantial increase in revenue could only be obtained by the introduction of income tax. So in 1956 the Australian Treasury was asked to assist the Department of Territories in drawing up suitable income tax legislation.

In a minute of 3 January 1957 I asked Lambert to give me a progress report, saying, 'it will be useless going to Cabinet with proposals for the Budget unless we are able to report that we have carried out Cabinet's request'. I stirred him up again in March, but the Department had not made much progress before the pre-budget meetings of Cabinet in July–August 1957 and, informing Lambert of the outcome of these discussions, I wrote that I was greatly embarrassed by the fact that effect had not been given to the Government's direction. I had a tough time in the Cabinet discussions for the 1957–8 Budget. There was some ground for Treasury criticism of the Administration's control of expenditure and they also pointed out that the percentage of the Territory Budget to be met from local revenues had fallen instead of risen. Consequently I gave instructions in a minute of 3 September that local revenues in the coming year were to be raised above the £4·5 million which the Administrator had proposed. This increase would help to avoid severe pruning of the Territory estimates and would also meet Cabinet's requirement that the local revenues be 30 per cent or more of the total of the Territory Budget.

As an aside, I should mention that I was also critical of the approach by the Administration to budget problems, and in the same minute I gave directions about priorities. It seemed to me that Port Moresby was favouring itself in disregard of places where the need was greater. I ruled that before any cuts fell on the works programme, the most rigorous economy was to be enforced elsewhere.

The priorities in works were to be set by the demands of policy. Accommodation to enable recruitment to proceed was a high priority. The highest priority in recruitment was for field staff in health, education, native affairs and agriculture and, as far as practicable, accommodation should be provided in the field. Native hospitals and schools were also a high priority. Another established aim of policy was decentralization and deliberate efforts to bring about a higher measure of uniformity in the advancement of people. That meant that we put more into districts like the Sepik, the Western and Southern Highlands and the Gulf than into the older districts. The money available for vehicles was to be spent solely on four-wheel drive vehicles and trucks for use at out-stations and in the field. In the older towns the cars should be pooled for general use instead of allocated for exclusive use. Some privileges enjoyed at Port Moresby were to be ended. These directions, coupled with the demand for raising more local revenue, left some of our senior people at Port Moresby rather unhappy.

Then I had another problem. The Australian Treasury interpreted the Cabinet decision to mean that a ceiling had been set on the Territory Budget, by the figures of £11 million for the Commonwealth grant and £4·5 million of local revenue, giving a total expenditure of £15·5 million. My department started to work to this ceiling. I then reopened the matter with the Prime Minister and Treasurer and obtained the clear understanding that the Territory Budget could exceed the total of £15·5 million by the amount by which local revenue could be made to exceed £4·5 million. I then pressed the Administrator to raise more.

We received proposals that would raise local revenue to £4·9 million, with the Administrator fearing 'adverse reaction' from 'the severity of the measures'. I accepted his figure and in subsequent weeks held him to his responsibility of choosing the way of raising revenue while I stood up to criticism for having demanded more local revenue. In the event, however, the Territory only raised £4·7 million. So this first attempt to place greater financial responsibility on the Territory ended in more grizzle than gain.

In this setting, having already lost one year, I renewed the direction for a review of the methods of taxation. (Minute of 9 October 1957.)

In the debate on the estimates in the House of Representatives in October 1957, I publicly suggested that the method of raising revenue in the Territory was not as scientific as it might be. Over recent years, I said, our budget-making had been shaped largely by a search for sources of revenue without sufficient regard to equity between various sections of the community or to the economic effects. In the course of the coming year I proposed to carry out a financial review of Territory revenues.* Later I repeated this announcement in Port Moresby.

The direction given in 1956 had resulted in the preparation of a simple and brief income tax measure. It contained however a number of proposals novel to current Australian practice, and the Australian Taxation Commissioner, who was the only authority available to Cabinet with any experience of taxation law and administration, advised against adoption of the proposals. As the result of a renewed direction in 1957, further proposals were prepared based on

* *Commonwealth Parliamentary Debates* (H. of R.), vol. 17, p. 1678, 23 Oct. 1957.

Australian Commonwealth practice with some modifications to meet Territory conditions. I placed these before Cabinet in March 1958.

Consideration of this submission by Cabinet was deferred. My planning had been to introduce the necessary measures in the Legislative Council for the Territory in May 1958, so that collections of income tax would commence as from 1 July 1958. It was found however that difficulty in drafting legislation would make the introduction of income tax impossible before 1 July 1959 and so my submission to Cabinet was regarded at that stage as having been circulated for information only and it was not formally considered by Cabinet. I was disappointed that, after two years, my department and the Treasury had made so little progress in producing a practical scheme and had done very little to prepare the administrative arrangements for collection of income tax. At the second occasion for decision we were held up by this unpreparedness.

Facing the unwelcome delay, I chose to give Territory residents and other interested parties a chance to express their view before the final decision was made. I wonder whether this was wise. In doing so, I really encouraged them to organize campaigns and to mobilize opinion into a substantial opposition. It may be good democracy but bad politics to start a dialogue with a tiger while it is still enjoying its meal.

On my instruction, a fifty-page abridgement of the departmental review of revenue-raising methods was tabled in the Legislative Council in Port Moresby in October 1958 in order to give all sections of the public a chance to study it and present facts or opinions about it before the final policy decision was made. After four months of public argument, I presented to Cabinet in a submission of 11 February 1959 the case for and against change with a recommendation that various forms of indirect taxation be abolished and replaced by direct taxation on income. These recommendations were approved by Cabinet on 23 February.

The opponents of income tax swung immediately into attack both in the Territory and in Australia. One move was to seek a public inquiry by an 'independent' commission into the whole question of levying income tax. Various arguments against the change in methods of raising local revenue were raised in debate in the Legislative Council of the Territory. In the Government party room at Canberra some Liberal members opposed the proposal. A few Ministers started to have second thoughts. The newly formed Taxpayers' Association of Papua and New Guinea sent a deputation to Canberra asking for the postponement of the measures pending a full inquiry into the impact of the legislation on the economy of the Territory. It seemed to me that they identified the economy of the Territory with their own personal fortunes.

During March, April and May I had a busy time in Cabinet and in the party room in answering objections, some pertinent and some captious, and in taking advantage of the pertinent criticisms to ensure the practicability of the new system. In early June Cabinet confirmed their decision and in July approved some amendments to improve the draft legislation. The measures were passed by the Legislative Council on 14 July 1959.

In brief, the decision was to abolish export duties, which fell mainly on copra, rubber and cocoa, to adjust import duties in a manner designed to lessen costs of living and costs of production, and to introduce income tax both on

Snigging logs of hoop and Klinkii pine for the plywood mill at Bulolo

The author with guard of honour at Hollandia, July 1957

The Prime Minister, Sir Robert Menzies, with local people in the Wahgi Valley

Attractive low-cost housing, Hohola, near Port Moresby

personal incomes and on companies. The avowed purpose was to distribute the burden of taxation in a way that would be more nearly equitable among tax-payers and less restrictive on economic development. The revenue to be raised from direct taxation gave only a slight balance over the loss of revenue from abolishing export duties and adjusting import duties, but the prospective effect was that, as the prosperity of the Territory population grew, so would the local revenues be able to grow without additional impost.

I take full responsibility for forcing the issue. I believe Cabinet made a sound decision and it was right to make it at that time. My views were shaped by three different considerations. One might be described as fiscal. In seeking larger grants for the Territory each year, I was under strong pressure from Treasury and Cabinet to increase the local revenues of the Territory. There was an expectation that local revenues would be about 30 per cent of the total annual expenditures in the Territory. In ten years the Territory Budget had grown from a total of £4·5 million to a total of £17·5 million and I wanted it to rise more rapidly in the future, now that our administrative capacity had improved and some of the substructure of government had been laid down. During the ten years, local revenues had grown from £1·5 million to £5·5 million, but we had done this partly by raising fees and charges on services and largely by seeking an increased yield from the export duties and import duties which fell unevenly on the community. For example a producer who was making a bare living paid the same rate of export duty as a producer who was making a very good living. The trader, who passed on the import duty to his customer, continued to make a profit and paid no tax of any kind, but his customer, whether as producer or consumer, met higher costs. These methods of raising more local revenues gave poor prospects of any further growth in revenue without creating greater inequity in the community and placing further handicaps on the Territory economy.

The social and economic transformation, both among the Europeans and the indigenous people, had produced a more complex society in which wage- and salary-earners, traders, service industries, contractors and tertiary enterprises took a much more significant place than they used to have in the old plantation and trade-store economy.

In these fiscal arguments I had strong support from my departmental officers and the Australian Commonwealth Treasury. Perhaps some of them reduced the question to the simple one, 'Why shouldn't the Territory people pay income tax?' The main question for us however was, 'What is the most efficient and equitable way of raising local revenues?' The answer was direct taxation and we applied ourselves to creating the system of direct taxation best suited to Territory conditions and most conducive to further development in the Territory. One other element in the situation was seen in the number of persons making a good deal of money in the Territory, free of tax either in the Territory or in Australia, and spending or investing it in Australia and leaving little of it in the Territory.

The second set of considerations that influenced me were less widely shared and, although strongly persuasive in my own mind, I tended to keep them to myself so as not to complicate the controversy. This reticence was also linked with the need I felt not to scare either the native people or the Europeans, whose services and investment we needed, with fears that Australia was in a hurry to get out of New Guinea. I was moving towards the next stage in constitutional reform. The Legislative Council would become more widely representative and the change would also be a step towards self-government, not by the European minority but by the indigenous majority. I judged it to be wise to put all fiscal matters on a sounder base before attempting the next constitutional change.

Allied with a change to direct taxation was another change which attracted less notice. After some difficulty and much urging on my part, I had gained Treasury acquiescence in proposals for raising local loans with an Australian guarantee. I wanted local loan raising to attract the savings of the Territory community itself in order to help meet Territory needs, as well as to provide a clear pattern of finance for a self-governing country.

One reason for shaping a new system before we reformed the Legislative Council was coldly practical. Until reform came we had firmer control over the Council than we might have after reform, and I guessed that in an enlarged and more widely representative Council, anything to do with taxing themselves might have a hard passage. I did not want a new Council to start with contentious bitterness or to hold up my plans.

More importantly I saw that many of the native people were moving rapidly away from a subsistence economy to a cash economy and were starting to have money incomes either as producers or as wage-earners. I did not want to have the introduction of direct taxation mixed up with any arguments about 'taxing the natives'. I wanted direct taxation to be the established system well before we were dealing with any significant body of native income-earners or native politicians.

Thirdly there was the persuasion of what might be called tidiness, doing first things first. I wanted to complete the next stage in administrative change and then go to constitutional change. Both direct taxation and local loan raising, supported by a local administrative structure and staff, would give a better base on which to build for self-government. Another associated auxiliary for which I was also working was a statistical service.

The unfortunate outcome was that when taxation reform aroused intense opposition I lost two years instead of the expected six months in moving to the next stage in applying policy. My hope had been for political and constitutional change in 1957 or 1958. It could not come until 1960.

The intensity and bitterness of the opposition to direct taxation were most unpleasant. Quite properly the blame was attached mostly to me, although some 'bureaucrats', vaguely so described as living in Canberra, also suffered vituperation. A section of business people, who, by local domicile or local registration of companies, had been enjoying nice tax-free incomes in the post-war years, saw the threat to their privileged position and they defended it by every means at their command. Because they included the owners of the local newspapers, they became the source of most of the information that other Australian residents of the Territory received about the proposals. The misrepresentation was colossal and unscrupulous. Salaried men, including our own senior officers, were led to believe that they were going to suffer heavily, although in fact the rate of taxation was low and the concessions extensive.

Among our officials, the Treasurer, Harold Reeve, staunchly, loyally, and consistently stood by the policy and paid for it heavily in local unpopularity. I could not have asked more of any officer than what he gave as his duty. But we had very few fighting on our side in the Territory and many were stirred up against us. We could not get our version of the story published or any of the news about the proposal fairly reported.

On one visit to Port Moresby I had the idea of making a ten-minute broadcast from the ABC radio station to explain the proposals but was refused time. The argument of the manager was that in matters of political controversy the rule was that equal time had to be given to Government and Opposition and, since there was no Leader of the Opposition in the Territory, no time could be given to the Minister for Territories as spokesman for the Government. I was told that the Administrator could go on the air because he was 'impartial' but, in this particular controversy, the Administrator was rather too impartial for my needs. On a later visit, a ministerial direction from the Postmaster-General said that the 'equal time' rule should not be used to bar me from explaining the proposals over the air.

Both in the Territory and in Australia I spent a good deal of time meeting deputations and individuals, receiving their representations and trying to answer their objections. Some of the meetings with accredited bodies were a reasoned presentation of argument or fact. Others were quite otherwise. When I recall one of these meetings in Port Moresby, where distinguished local citizens harangued the attendance while I sat patiently waiting for a chance to say something, I also remember a passage in the report of Chief Justice Mann on the Navuneram Incident, which likewise arose from a tax dispute.* The Chief Justice wrote,

> One of the great difficulties encountered by the officers of the Administration . . . was that on some occasions when the officers had spent a great deal of time carefully answering questions and explaining the matters in issue the natives seemed to close their minds to any argument based on reason and simply refused to take notice. The natives themselves illustrated this by explaining that, according to their practice, they have two different ways of speaking. One is the normal serious way of discussing any topic of importance and the other is termed in pidgin 'tok bilas' which may be translated as 'showing off' or 'acting the goat'. This latter mode of address is a silly, cranky, irresponsible way of talking accompanied by extravagant gestures and erratic movements suggesting some form of mental affliction . . . It is a characteristic of the natives which appears to be very real and which seems to be related to a state of mind in which the natives simply will not pay attention to a statement that they do not want to hear.

I heard a lot of 'tok bilas' from whites.

Patience and waiting like a shag on a spit post for your wings to dry before taking the next plunge was the best tactic at the time. Gradually we began to still the unreasonable fears and meet the criticism. The planters long resident in the Territory were perhaps the first organized body to accept the good sense of what we were doing. Then some of the salaried people, including some of

---

* Report of Commission of Inquiry into the Navuneram Incident, New Britain. Parliament of the Commonwealth of Australia 1959, Command Paper No. 41 (Group G), p. 9.

our own senior officers, began to realize that the scheme was not as vexatious as they had been led to believe. Business and professional men in Port Moresby and Rabaul, and those who were making a lot of money in the Territory but planning their own future in Australia, maintained the fight.

Luckily the indigenous people were scarcely involved in any of the argument, and very few of them were directly affected at that time by our decisions.

The legislation passed, Reeve arguing manfully amid the unhelpful silence of many of his official colleagues. Then the determined few, in a final effort to defer if not defeat the measure, challenged the validity of the acts of the Legislative Council by taking a case to the High Court of Australia. The Court's judgment, given on 10 August 1960, not only virtually ended the controversy over direct taxation but freed us at last to get on with proposals for the reform of the Legislative Council. It was considered that while the question of whether the Council was validly created was *sub judice*, we could not proceed with proposals to change its structure.

One sorry fact which was new in my political experience was the unscrupulous way in which a smallish group of self-interested Australian businessmen, who were getting large financial gains out of the progress of the Territory, tried to preserve their privilege by destroying me politically, working through the Liberal Party organization, of which some of them were members, and Liberal Party members of Parliament. They wanted me removed from office and were not nice in their methods. In Australia, the experience also brought me some disillusionment with the Liberal Party.

For the historian, I would commend for careful reading the parliamentary debate of 12 May 1959. My chief supporters in that debate were Calwell and Beazley from the Opposition. I would also commend the debate on the Territory estimates on 30 September 1959. Again Calwell was among my supporters, and my critics were Liberals, although also one of the staunch defenders of my policy was the Liberal Harry Turner. By then I had easily survived the deliberate and planned attempts to have me removed from office because of my alleged hostility to what my critics called 'private enterprise' and what I myself regarded as ugly greed. Yet out of this period of attack inside the Liberal Party, some ill-repute remained and some unfavourable popular notions about me had their origin.

One of the happier memories of this period was a tour of the Territory I made in company with Hubert Opperman and Fred Chaney, two parliamentary colleagues, one the Government Whip and the other the Assistant Whip from the Liberal Party. Their company was by no means unrelated to my need to influence the Liberal party room, but they were also very congenial travelling companions and shrewdly helpful in assessment of the local political scene.

Opperman, in spite of his prominence in Australian political life, was even more widely and honourably known in the Territory as a world champion cyclist, and his fame went before him. At Kavieng, in our search for opinion and our hope to win friends, we went at midday to the local pub in company with the district commissioner, Michael Healy.[40] Seven or eight Europeans were leaning on the bar. Healy took me along the line to introduce me. One by one they grunted and turned their backs on me. But, last in the line, was a cheerful little man with a big grin. He was ready to talk. I thought he must be one of those chaps who became amiable when they have much drink taken. 'Glad to see yer', he said in a friendly way. 'Good of yer to come up here. S'a wun-wun-wunfull country.' I said I thought so too. Here at last was someone who seemed really pleased to meet me. He spoke again. 'Where's yer bike?' I said 'Eh?' 'D'ja bring yer bike with yer?' he asked. The district commissioner intervened. 'This isn't Mr Opperman', he said. 'This is the Minister.' The little man grunted and turned his back on me too.

[24]

MASS COMMUNICATION AND COMMUNITY
DEVELOPMENT

About 1958 I felt a growing need for closer and surer means of communication between the government and the people in the Territory. Both groups were changing and consequently their relationship had to be re-examined.

The old days, when the link between the government and the governed was a face-to-face talk between a patrol officer and the villagers, and when the daily relationship between the expatriate and the indigenous people was between a plantation manager and the labour line or between 'master' and 'boy', had long since passed. Wholly different situations and relationships now existed, but the means of communication had scarcely changed. We needed to exchange views and information on more subjects and on more complex situations but had not yet developed adequate ways of doing so. In the work of government we had taken measures in health, education, agriculture, employment, trading and management of economic activity that also had undisclosed effects on the lives of people. These measures necessarily were changing some of the old habits, the old ties and compulsions of community life, and the obligations of one person to other persons in his daily life, but we had done little or nothing to help the social adjustments a new way of life might require.

Some of my concern was also related to the earlier concern I had with what I called adult education. The active generation which had missed the chance of any schooling should also be helped to learn, both because at present they were the most active and influential group and because, in the future, there could be danger of tension between an uneducated older group and an educated younger group in the same community. Learning for the adult should come in various ways directly related to his own daily life and interests. We could not give him schooling but we could teach him a lot in other ways in our daily association with him. One special need in this process of learning by the adult was to improve the means of communication between the indigenous man and woman and the expatriate official and other expatriate residents.

I talked and wrote a lot about these matters. Most officials at Port Moresby seemed to think of mass communication as a government information service run by journalists. I was thinking of a relationship with people to be developed by everyone in touch with them—an activity inseparable from the whole

266

process of social change and hence a process of sharing ideas and developing discussion with a view to the people's participation both in doing and in deciding what to do. I believed that one of our fundamental necessities for sound administration in a dependent territory was to keep close to the people and to accustom the people to the idea that they had a part to play in conducting the affairs of their own country. One of the great assets in the period of early contact had been the closeness between officers in the field and the people whom they were serving. Trust grew out of that closeness. Moving into another phase of contact and facing new administrative tasks and new problems of government policy, we should work for a similar closeness but we could not expect to achieve it by the old methods. Administration was now more complex, covering more subjects and affecting more people in a greater diversity of situation. There had been a move away from a period when almost everything was done locally to a new period when some actions had to be co-ordinated over the whole Territory and decisions were being made centrally. We had to find new methods or we would lose the trust of the governed. I could see signs of widening separation. The gap was of a different kind to the old gap between them and us. It was like the difference between a situation in which a patrol officer, sitting on the steps of a rest house in a village, was able to say all that needed to be said in the hearing of all who needed to hear it, and a situation in which a departmental head at a desk in Port Moresby or Canberra gave directions that would affect two million people. How could he say what was needed to be said and make sure that it would be heard and understood by all who needed to hear it in the Sepik, in the highlands, the Gazelle Peninsula, the Gulf, the urban districts of Port Moresby or in the far islands? How could we find means by which all those who heard and understood the direction could make known what they themselves thought of it? I was hoping to maintain the closeness of communication, not trying to set up a publicity office to sell the decisions of the Administration or to cover up its mistakes. Some officers in the Administration did not seem to understand that there was any difference. They kept on thinking that I wanted proposals for an expanded information department, with more information officers available to produce official bulletins and films and shiny pamphlets to publicize the Territory. I wanted to find methods that would bring the governors and the governed closer together.

The Administration also seemed to me to be handicapped by its own conception of its duty to run the country and help the people. They were too narrowly concerned with their job of handling situations and making sure that nothing went wrong. I was looking for ways in which more people would become involved in shaping the changes that were taking place.

One tentative approach to the problem is illustrated in a minute I addressed to the Secretary of the Department of Territories on 9 February 1959. I had made earlier requests for a submission on mass communication and I now asked whether, while fully recognizing the position of established native leaders, we could make fuller use of the younger men and women who had received a better education in the post-war years. I asked specifically for a survey of those who were available in this group to help in 'a more positive approach to this double task of promoting understanding and increasing the participation of the native people themselves in the advancement of the Territory'. In May, having received no response, I stirred up the Secretary and Administrator again. Somewhat wryly I recognize now that there may have been a failure in communication between Minister and officials because I never got a full understanding by the Secretary and Administrator of what I had in mind. They did not build on my suggestions and I think one of the short-comings of the Administration from 1959 onwards was in failing to work closely with and encourage the bright young men and women who were now beginning to emerge after ten years of painfully slow work in education.

A fuller exposition of my ideas was included in a memorandum I wrote in March 1959 in preparation for talks to be held in Canberra with Lambert, Cleland and Thomson about the future of the Department of Native Affairs, following the report of the Commission of Inquiry on the Navuneram Incident. I asked the three of them to 'examine critically' a further suggestion:

Thinking over the progress of our work in the Territory and trying to look at the nature of some of the emerging problems in the Territory, I feel that we have before us an immense task of what might broadly be described as social and community development. To illustrate the meaning which I attach to this phrase I ought to give a few examples. There is a problem of finding means of communication between us and the masses, of understanding better what the mass of people are thinking and of helping them to understand what we are thinking. There is the problem of literacy and of devising imaginative forms of education in order to promote literacy among those masses who will never go to the conventional schools because they have passed the school age. There is the task of promoting community projects, not solely for what the projects themselves will bring in the way of advantage to the community, but also for the sake of the effect they will have in the development of new attitudes and habits and a civilized outlook in the community. These community projects will be of various kinds and will differ greatly from place to place according to the opportunities that are offered and according to the interest which the people reveal. There are also the economic activities, both those represented by the co-operative movement and those which are fostered by agricultural extension work. In many cases I think that what is being done in the co-operatives may be having an economic effect but may be failing to have its full social effect because of the narrowness of the co-operative attack, or may even at times be producing undesirable social effects. Similarly projects like the Tolai cocoa project may have economic value but possibly exacerbate or complicate some of our other problems simply because they do not take sufficient account of the effect of the economic undertaking on the community and on the direction of social change. Do we continue to foster these economic movements in isolated compartments or do we attempt to tie them with a general purpose of social and community development? I have a similar feeling regarding the growth of local government councils. We have thought of these mainly as a means of political advancement because there is some pressure from the world outside and a growing interest within the Territory itself for some form of political advancement. But again we have to try to integrate any political advancement with social and community change. Another phase of our work among the native people which comes within the broad field of social and community development is the work that we are doing in order to encourage the progress of the womenfolk. Then there are such general problems as housing, better home management, village clubs, community centres and undertakings of that kind. I have mentioned all these just by way of illustration of the sort of activity of which I think when I use the phrase 'social and community development'.

. . . We are fostering a great number of changes. What can we do to root all these changes deeply in the soil of the community in which the change is being made? How can we make sure that we are not only changing a number of individuals but are also helping them to develop the society in which they have to live? . . .

. . . Considerations such as those which I have outlined, combined with many other considerations arising out of my observation of change in the Territory have led me to speculate whether or not there is a need to create within the Administration a Department of Social and Community Development [which] . . . would use the arts of persuasion to lead the people towards self-help and participation in community efforts for their own advancement . . . If such a change were to be made, my general conception of what would happen in the future would be that, from time to time, at the appropriate moment, the Administrator, having observed the conditions which exist, would designate areas as being ready for the special work of the Department of Social and Community Development. Once such an area had been so designated, the other Departments would be expected to refer to the Department of Social and Community Development the particular projects in which they would like to have expert help or co-operation and the Department of Social and Community Development would be expected to examine local conditions and prepare a programme of measures suited to the local conditions and devise the methods by which the programme could best be achieved. The Department of Social and Community Development would also provide the specialist officers and the experts needed in addition to those available in existing departments and would devise the special techniques for putting its proposals into effect and for securing the co-operation of all the other Departments concerned. One major measure that would certainly be needed would be to create a number of positions for a campaign of mass communication, the positions including technicians to operate the various media as well as the officers to prepare the material . . . The idea behind the work is to promote better living for the whole community and at the same time to bring about the active participation and if possible the initiative of the community. For a beginning, when that initiative is not coming as the result of some native energy, it is necessary to use techniques for arousing and stimulating it in order to secure an active and enthusiastic response to what the Administration is trying to do. I am sure that we are now entering a phase in Papua and New Guinea where we have to be far more imaginative than the Administration has been in the past regarding the methods and techniques which we use. We have to be cautious about adopting fancy ideas for the sake of their novelty or their popular appeal. We have to make sure that the methods and techniques which we devise are effective and will produce, economically, the results which we are seeking. But we cannot be content to go along in the way in which we have been going. For example, in the past we have really been waiting until the people were taught to read before we attempted to communicate to them by printed matter. The spoken word was limited to a certain amount of wireless broadcasting and to the word of mouth of the visiting patrol officer. In a country where the people cannot yet read we have to use the gramophone record, or the film strip or the tape recorder, in the same way as the leaflet, or the poster or the placard might be used on the Australian mainland. If we want to make an announcement widespread over the country the only way to make it may be to send out gramophone records, or tape recordings, or film strips which will be shown to the people and this requires that in a very large proportion of the villages there should be both the instruments for dissemination of this information and persons capable of operating them. We need more active and imaginative minds at work on this phase of our problem. We even have to be prepared to do a few silly things and make a few errors for the sake of the greater achievement which we hope will follow.

I have previously expressed the view that we cannot do better than the human resources available to us in the Territory. We have to make what use we can of the instruments which lie ready to our hand. Yet I am convinced that it will be profitless for us to think of the future of the Department of Native Affairs or to attempt to re-write its functions and revise its structure along the old-fashioned ways. I hope that from the discussions on 6 April we can begin a different sort of approach more fitted to the different sort of world into which we are moving in that part of the Territory where we have been in contact with the people over many years . . .

Lambert, Cleland and Thomson all had a copy of this memorandum. I asked them to get their officers to work on my ideas, not hesitating to 'criticize or pull to pieces the suggestions', and to try to work out a new approach. Later we had the discussions. I doubt whether I really got through to the minds of the three key men. I waited for a submission.

In April 1959, when directing Lambert, Cleland and Thomson to report on the structure and functions of the Department of Native Affairs, I also asked them to examine the following matters and report on the best administrative arrangements to be made in respect of them, whether in the Department of Native Affairs or in some other department: (a) methods of mass communication to the native people, (b) the advancement of native women, (c) social and community development generally. (Minute of 7 April 1959.) Early in July 1959 I reminded them that I was still waiting for a submission on mass communication. 'It is the sort of thing on which we should not be nervous about a proposal for a quarter of a million expenditure straight away and half a million when it fully develops', I wrote. 'Please give this a higher priority.' (Minute of 13 July 1959.) In a further minute in early August I directed that a higher priority was to be given to both mass communication and primary education. The suggested item of £40 000 which they had put in the draft estimates for mass communication was 'quite unacceptable' and I continued,

I want some energy and imagination shown. For months I have been asking the Administration to develop its proposals and up to date I have received nothing. The programme of action under this heading must be submitted at once so that the adequacy or inadequacy of the items on the Estimates can be tested realistically.

Are they making any provision for such items as the following:
(a) Language instruction for European officers.
(b) A school for native interpreters.

(c) The purchase of mechanical aids such as gramophones, recording appliances, regional radio transmitters, projectors, and the means of preparing material for communication through these aids.

(d) Publication of a regular newsletter or 'school paper' to give information about current events and Government policy and action to educated native people.

(e) Preparation of charts of indestructible or durable materials for distribution to villages.

(f) The making of five and ten-minute films for designated instructional purposes.

(g) Measures likely to set free more experienced Native Affairs officers to keep more closely in touch with groups of native people.

(h) Measures of adult education in the villages.

(i) The appointment of new specialist staff to carry out duties in connection with the above suggestions.

(j) Arrangements for the appointment of a permanent film, photographic and sound recording unit in the Territory for producing material to aid us in communicating with the native people.

I do not know whether these suggestions are good or bad or whether there are better suggestions to be made but they will indicate the sort of proposals which I expected I might receive in response to my repeated requests.

A definite and purposeful start has to be made in the 1959–60 Estimates.

Please take up with the Administrator again these policy directions and ensure that effect is given to them in the drafting of the Estimates. [Minute of 13 August 1959.]

When this minute reached the Department, it apparently woke up a sleeping clerk, for a few days later, without further word, a report dated 9 July by a Committee of Inquiry on the subject reached my desk. Why, I asked, had it taken over a month to be presented in spite of my repeated and urgent requests for recommendations on this subject? The report itself left me dissatisfied. I said it was 'thought-provoking and extremely useful in describing the problem', but I did not think much of the suggestions for action. The report seemed to envisage some sort of journalistic enterprise, running a Government newspaper under an editor-in-chief. I said again that the means to be used 'to improve communication between us and the native people' should not be confused with the function of an information service. The sort of function I wanted performed would more properly reside in an Education Branch or Native Affairs Branch than in the Information Bureau. I directed that the officers from the Territory should come to Canberra as quickly as possible to straighten out the matter by discussion. (Minute of 17 August 1959.)

I am unaware of the pushing and pulling that may have gone on in Port Moresby in preparing the proposals, but the discussions in Canberra left me with an impression that at a senior level there was still little comprehension and some resistance. Maybe part of the trouble was that the ambition of some officers to organize a Department of Information of their own on the conventional model of an organization to give wide and favourable publicity to Papua and New Guinea obscured the view of the totally different activity for which I wanted priority.

The proposals for creating a new division were received early in 1960 from the Public Service Commissioner, Thomson. The Department of Territories made a number of critical comments and I raised a number of objections of my own. Mostly the grounds for objection were the vagueness of the statement of aims and functions, and doubts about the way in which the submission set out the qualifications and duties of the various positions it was proposed to create. I wrote, 'I want this to go ahead as quickly as possible but there are so many doubtful points in the attached papers that I cannot give broad covering approval.' The departmental comments and my own minute were sent to Thomson and he was asked to come to Canberra to settle the matter by discussion. (Minute of 29 February 1960.)

In the same month, I had my regular annual talks with Cleland in Canberra on a variety of topics. One item was listed by me as follows:

Contacts with the indigenous people and the present state of our relationships with them. My main concern will be with statements that have been made to me by recent observers that we are not as closely in touch with the native people as we used to be; that the gap between Administration and the indigenous population is widening; and that we have imperfect knowledge of various changes that are taking place among the indigenous people. This topic will also involve consideration of the role to be played by all departments of the Administration, as well as the Department of Native Affairs.

At my request, Lambert had a follow-up discussion with Cleland in Port Moresby in April. This revealed a continuing tendency to look at the problem as one concerning the efficiency of the Department of Native Affairs. Lambert reported to me that the Administrator admitted that contact with the indigenous people was not as good as it used to be. He saw this deterioration mainly in the Native Affairs Department and ascribed it partly to the expansion of activities and the lack of staff to keep pace with the growth, partly to the large proportion of new and young officers who were not well versed in the 'techniques of contact' and the effect of the introduction of motor vehicles which gave field officers both the means and the wish to get back to headquarters quickly instead of following the old patient methods of the patrols on foot.

Proposals to improve the Native Affairs Department were linked with proposals on a general reorganization of the structure of the Administration. I was not willing to accept these proposals in toto for reasons unrelated to the question of communication with the indigenous people and asked for a new submission on that particular question. (Minute of 20 April 1960.) The first response came at the end of June. 'This is lamentable', I wrote. 'The Administrator's message means that for the past three months (i.e. since my talks with Cleland in early April) this urgent matter has not received the attention I required.' (Minute of 28 June 1960.)

As an aside I may mention that when, in August, we received proposals on the improvement of the Public Relations Office which had been created in the Territory early in my term as Minister, I gave the warning, 'Do not mix up this question with the entirely separate questions of mass communication, adult education and extension services . . . or the questions of international affairs, United Nations reports and statistical services . . . Each of those fields has to be filled separately by persons with a wholly different set of qualifications.' (Minute of 2 September 1960.) The warning was necessary because there was some body of opinion in the Territory Administration and in the Department of Territories in favour of a comprehensive Department of Information to handle all these subjects and more.

A Division of Extension Services was created in the Department of Education, and in 1960 a senior officer of the Department of Education, L. R. Newby,[41] was put in charge of it. Some of my ideas were put into effect by the new division. In the creation of this new division, I expressed a preference that it should 'act as an initiator and as an expert service department'. Other departments should also be used in mass communication.

In mass communication and adult education I did not succeed in doing all that I knew should be done. I doubt whether I even succeeded in making plain to the Administrator and Secretary what I wanted to do. I could only have done better if I had taken the subject out of their hands and, instead of expecting them to make a submission, had given them a detailed direction on what had to be done. Even if I had done so, however, I doubt whether I could have got the results that were required.

This gap between those who govern and those who are governed exists in every political society. The autocracies, the monolithic states, bridge it most quickly by making decisions absolutely and enforcing them. In the democracies various means are readily available for making bridges—the printed word, the spoken word, the picture, the demonstration, the political campaign, the parliamentary election. There are newspapers, books, public meetings, radio and television as part of the daily life of most of the people and, in those democracies where one language is common and most of the population is literate, there are many opportunities for the governed to be informed about what the governors are doing, and for the governors to be influenced by the hopes and the opinions of the governed. Even in the democracies, however, the gap remains.

In the conditions in Papua and New Guinea in 1960 the vast majority of the people were not literate and had no common language and there were great disparities between the way of life of one group and another. Most of them were undergoing changes that were weakening the influences giving cohesion to the community without shaping influences giving life to a new community. For the most part, government was in the control of a small foreign minority and acted according to standards set and policies declared in another country. On a purely practical level it was necessary to find suitable appliances and equipment to facilitate communication. Outside the small European minority there were few people who could read English and among these few only a limited number who were familiar with the concepts and the vocabulary of politics. Instead of trusting to chance that meaning might filter through the barriers of language, we needed skilled communicators using novel methods of communication.

In such a situation we had little to copy in method from democratic Australia. In reality, when one looked critically at Australia, one saw increasing signs of failure and a widening of the gap. That failure was revealed by the way in which Australian government and Australian politicians and institutions resorted to various devices of publicity and 'public relations' in the hope of recovering from the failure. When one looked at Australian experience, one saw the way in which those in government were taking the gap for granted and moving more and more into the use of public relations officers, publicity campaigns and information services, not to close the gap but to sell themselves and commend their achievements to those on the other side of the gap. Yet, although the situations were quite different, those through whom I had to work seemed to be able to give me nothing but methods derived from the Australian failure to be applied to a situation wholly different from the Australian one. They thought in terms of measures for publicity and public relations exercises, which have more to do with the arts of persuasion than the arts of communication, more to do with journalism than with education, more to do with salesmanship than with promoting better understanding.

Some of the most effective work was done here and there by an exceptional young officer relying more on his own good sense than on any direction from his seniors. On visits, I was encouraged now and again by seeing the way in which an agricultural officer or a health officer or a school-teacher, engaged in his daily work, was not only teaching people how to grow a new crop or to practise hygiene or to read and write but also helping them to build a new community. There were not enough of these isolated efforts and they were not brought together in one concerted effort. Indeed there was a tendency for some senior officers to regard young enthusiasts as 'freaks' or to remark sagely but uselessly that they 'still had a lot to learn'.

The Division of Extension Services did some useful work as a sort of handyman who could be called in to do a job of making or mending. For example when we made the next political advance, the division worked very effectively in teaching people how to enrol and vote and take part in election campaigns. Newby won deserved credit for his success in several of these practical tasks. Overall however I was disappointed in my hopes for wider constructive measures for community development and mass communication.

[25]

THE IMPEDIMENTS TO EFFICIENCY

In the immediately preceding chapters it may seem that I have placed too much blame on the officers and made too many excuses for myself over the delays in action. I have tried not to be unfair and my purpose has been not to pass judgement on others but to complete the description of the situation we faced. This difficulty in getting prompt and efficient action was a significant part of the situation.

Starting with a small and poorly qualified public service, we had expanded so rapidly and had assumed so many additional administrative tasks that we had outstripped the attempt to build an efficient organization. In seven years public expenditure had more than trebled and the total of European staff had risen from a round figure of 1100 to a round figure of 2800. To gain this figure we had recruited over 2500 new European officers in the three years from 1954 to 1957, for the wastage from retirement for age or medical reasons, resignations and dismissals was running at the rate of about 500 a year.

Thus, although we had a larger service and had tried to recruit at a higher level of qualification, we still had many inexperienced officers working in situations unfamiliar to them on tasks for which they had not been adequately trained, while the older hands were moving into a situation much different from the period of early contact and some of them had not adjusted to the change or even fully recognized that change was taking place.

In September 1957, at my request, Lambert had a discussion in Port Moresby with Cleland and Thomson about the state of the public service. He reported that they agreed that there were three faults: (a) lack of adequate direction, supervision and discipline, (b) over-centralization of departmental business, (c) lack of administrative experience and know-how. This had resulted from the growth of the service at a rate beyond its capacity to train and recruit leaders adequately qualified by experience. The Public Service Commissioner and his staff, in their preoccupation with routine public service matters and the re-organization of various departments, had not been able to take stock of the whole organization to ensure efficiency and economy, and the organization and methods team the Commissioner had at his disposal was 'somewhat raw'. Lambert's view, which I accepted, was to place this highly specialized organization and methods work under a Deputy Public Service Commissioner specially selected from Australia as being highly qualified in this specialized field. The job would require 'two or three years of concentrated effort' and once it was done the work could fall back in to the routine organization of the Public Service Commissioner's office. (Minute of 12 September 1957.)

Before I discuss some of the measures we took to try to improve the service, I should like to make some general observations of my own. My difficulty from about 1956 was not so much in deciding what to do as in getting things done promptly and effectively. Some of this may have been my personal failure. Some of it was a consequence of the system of government and my own scrupulous respect for that system.

The powers of a minister in the Australian system of government are limited. We have inherited a system that surrounds authority with safeguards. An Australian minister who knows the system and who behaves correctly need never worry about his power to stop public servants from doing anything he does not want them to do. His worry is how to get them to do something he wants and they do not. In many governmental situations this is all to the good. Wise and diligent ministers are the best safeguards against bureaucratic despotism, and a minister's authority as part of the executive and his responsibility to Parliament put him in a place where he can make sure that the official does not step out of his appointed role in a parliamentary democracy. During my parliamentary career I have seen some new ministers do foolish things and try to act independently of the system simply because they were frightened of the superior knowledge and skill of senior public servants. They need not have been frightened, for if they learnt their own job and were diligent in it, they would have no difficulty in keeping the public servant in his place. On the other hand, however, ministers in a parliamentary democracy face considerable difficulty when they try to make officials move more quickly or do something they have not been accustomed to do.

The officials are necessary and mostly they are better trained than any other helpers a minister could recruit. The senior men in the public service have a greater store of experience and a more detailed knowledge of the structure and procedures of the system of government than a minister is likely to have and any minister handicaps himself and may wander into a bog if he disregards this store of experience and knowledge and tries to take short cuts. He is wise to use the public service. Furthermore a minister faces the physical fact that he does not have the time or the means to do everything himself. He gives directions but has to rely on officials to put them into effect. Yet, at the same time, officials have their own independence, their own routine of working and their own responsibilities. They are also subject to the rules and regulations of their own service and are obliged to use established procedures. Consequently a minister who tries to be a general, planning a victorious campaign, will find that he is not fully in command of his troops. He can say to one, 'come', and to another one, 'go', but the coming and the going are subject to many rules and conventions, established procedures and fixed habits which the minister cannot alter. They may also be subject to ideas which any experienced public servant may have himself about what is the best thing to do and what is the best way to do it, as well as being necessarily subject to such questions as

Coffee growing was a most successful introduction: a grower inspecting his crop

Subsistence activities produce the overwhelming proportion of food-stuffs: fisherman returning to his village with the day's catch

Traditional skills turned to economic account: a village carver of the Chambri Lakes preparing curios for sale

The spectacular achievements of aviation should not obscure widely continuing reliance on sea and river transport: loading an Administration trawler at Milne Bay

whether the Administrative Arrangements Order places the function in this or that department and whether statutory authority exists for the proposed action.

From my own experience as a public servant I am well aware of the justifiable delays that occur when a need is seen by the public servant for inter-departmental consultation or, even inside one department, for discussion and consultation between the various branches and divisions of a department. I am aware too that when a public servant may have some reluctance or hesitation or professional cautiousness about giving immediate effect to a ministerial direction, these justifiable discussions or consultations may be extended to bring about a delay that is scarcely justifiable. In a hard-pressed department the priorities a minister may declare become subject to the priorities applied at the desk of every senior officer and the delays that may come after the papers have been passed to a more junior officer. An unfilled vacancy in one section of a department or the absence on leave of the 'officer who handles that file' or, lower down the scale, the dilatoriness of a clerk or messenger, may all impede the ministerial will, and it is physically and constitutionally impossible for the minister to remove the impediments to prompt action. Ministers may wave their fountain pens like swords and shout commands, but they wait in an heroic attitude for the cavalry to follow them in a dashing charge in a new direction.

Personally I respected the public service and our system of government so conscientiously and with such theoretical purity that I tended to perpetuate the conflict between my own peremptory demands for immediate action on a question and my insistence that everything went through correct departmental channels and that action was taken on submissions prepared by the department and placed in sequence on the proper files. I made demand after demand for action but always required that the proper procedures be observed and that the department have its due opportunity and carry out to the full its responsibility for advice up to the point of ministerial decision. My own decisions were prompt. The preparation of advice was often protracted. The taking of action was often delayed. I fully respected the position of the public service and at the same time got angry with it.

This difficulty in getting things done was complicated by reason of the fact that, as well as a Department of Territories, there was a Territory Administration. The way to get quicker action might have been to let the Department of Territories dominate the Administration. I chose to continue to run them side by side and continued trying to build up local administration in the Territory with that degree of separateness which would prepare the Territory for the almost total administrative separateness required when self-government was achieved. My piety in serving the theory was splotched by much ill-temper in suffering the consequential delays.

I should not have done otherwise. In other settings I have seen impatient ministers, with more ambition than experience, try to act independently of the public service through their own staff or by dealing directly with some non-governmental agency or group. Even if they escape a most awful flop, I doubt whether they achieve better results than could have been achieved through the system. The tendency in recent years to create a personal secretariat for a minister seems to me to be contradictory of the basic principles of our form of parliamentary democracy. There is danger in inexperienced enthusiasts who believe they are not answerable to anyone except their own minister. I prefer a system that has safeguards and would stop any minister from having his own private army of secretaries lurking in the background with lots of bright, explosive ideas hanging from their belts and no one but the minister to say when they can pull out the pins and throw them into the unsuspecting crowd.

Yet with a system of safeguards, we have this constant problem of getting prompt action on new ventures. One method that has been used successfully is to create a special authority to do a designated task. The Menzies Government had two outstanding examples of such success—the Snowy Mountains Hydro-Electricity Authority and the National Capital Development Commission. This device only succeeds when a precisely defined task can be given to an authority technically equipped to do that particular task. I toyed with the possibility of finding some field of activity in Papua and New Guinea which might have been confided to a special authority. Public construction, especially roads, bridges, schools, hospitals and housing, might have been such a field. In theory, we would have done well to have created a Papua New Guinea Development Commission, under the Minister for Territories, with responsibility for the planning and execution of designated projects. For a variety of reasons this was not within the reach of practical politics. My judgement was that I could not have got Cabinet approval for it. I would not have been able to ensure that it had the required funds. It was highly doubtful that I could find the right men for it.

Thus we worked throughout a period of more intensive effort, still handicapped by lack of capacity and still working in the old framework of a Territory Administration centred on Port Moresby, and a Department of Territories in Canberra.

As seen from the preceding chapters, I was perpetually dissatisfied with the poor response to my demands for action on various fronts. I have to take the final responsibility for this failure. I failed to find and to appoint and to use enough first-class officers in senior posts to carry out the work. I failed to give the leadership that would have led everyone to work twice as hard as in fact they did. I failed to shift people around ruthlessly and to throw some of them out of their jobs or move them to places where they could not obstruct. My fault was in behaving too correctly. I might have done better too if, using ministerial powers under the Papua and New Guinea Act, I had personally intervened more often and more directly in the work of the Territory Administration instead of respecting the established procedures and the established positions in the local hierarchy. Another possible fault was in demanding too much and giving nearly all my demands the label of 'urgent'. I tried to make some slow coaches run like express trains and they wobbled more than ever.

One of our continuing administrative problems was finance. We still had to fight hard for funds, and both in Cabinet and in discussions with Treasury, our effective control of expenditure was a condition of an increased annual grant. We had to get value for money by reducing wasteful or misplaced expenditure and we had to demonstrate that we had the administrative capacity to use the money granted. Because Territories were making new demands for funds for activities unfamiliar in Commonwealth administration, I think we were under stricter Treasury scrutiny than some of those working at home on familiar tasks. Some of my officers were inclined to look on Treasury as a nark. My own view was that such strict scrutiny of expenditure was an essential condition of good government and, while I fought to get more money, I accepted the condition of tight control.

Sound estimating was also an essential element of sound planning, and a bid for more money would lead to no improvement unless matched with a growth in capacity to use the money. From about 1957 onwards we were able to strengthen the section in the Department of Territories concerned with finance and I was well served by a succession of officers trained in Commonwealth Treasury procedures and well able to analyse any problem of financial administration. Among my notes I find a most unusual relic—a faded bouquet. On 28 May 1958 I expressed my appreciation to Lambert of the way in which the Department was now presenting its financial submissions. I wrote, 'The clarity and orderliness of the presentation and the thoroughness of the preparatory work have been of great assistance.' As I remember it, the man chiefly to be praised was Claude Reseigh.[42]

The continuing problem was in the Territory, and although the Treasury Department in the Territory was much improved under Harold Reeve and then under A. P. J. Newman, the habits of the Administration generally were otherwise and the Territory Treasury was less influential and not so strongly backed as it should have been in trying to teach good habits to other departments of the Administration. I believe in a powerful Treasury, not to determine policy but to help ensure that policy is soundly based financially and is applied with financial responsibility. In later years, in Australia, seeing from the sidelines the ill-consequences of the lavish provision of money for half-developed projects or for financing the pet idea of some ephemeral holder of political office, in disregard of Treasury advice, I have been more strongly confirmed in this belief.

Early in 1958 I received the report of a departmental officer, W. T. Gleeson,[43] after an investigation into the control of expenditure by the Administration. We hoped that this would show the way to an improvement and started to apply the Gleeson report. It seems to me now however, across the space of years, that most of the people in the Territory Administration never fully understood nor accepted the idea of financial responsibility. Many of them were accustomed to the easy way of saying that if only Australia would provide the money, they could do all sorts of wonderful things, but they did not take the next step by helping to get the money or relating their claim for money to a capacity to use it and a programme for action. Part of our annual problem of under-spending the grant was due to the inclusion of items in the estimates without sufficient inquiry on supply and capacity.

On 27 May 1958 I wrote a personal letter to the Administrator saying, among other things,

> In the Cabinet at the time of the preparation of the 1957–58 Budget in particular, I was considerably handicapped in trying to raise the level of the financial grant for the Territory because I could not contradict in truth statements made regarding the capacity of the Territory Administration to

make proper use of the funds which I was seeking . . . The situation revealed by this year's accounts . . . will make it extremely difficult, if not impossible, for me to maintain in the forthcoming Budget discussions my claims for better consideration to the Territory . . . What causes me far greater concern is that the incapacity of the Territory Administration, as revealed in the present financial review, is defeating the aims of Government policy. The building up of adequate staffs, particularly on the professional and technical side, is being impeded by the lack of accommodation. The extension of our health and educational services is likewise being impeded by the lack of the basic facilities. Unsatisfactory conditions in the housing of our own native Administration servants, including the Royal Papua and New Guinea Constabulary, persist because of incapacity to carry out the necessary works. Unfortunately, I fear that the position disclosed by the present financial review will not only mean that we have delayed the achievement of policy to the extent of half a million pounds' worth of works which we have not done in the current year but that we will find that inescapably the rate of progress will be slowed down in future years by the revelation of our shortcomings.

Year by year I become impressed more and more by the dire urgency of the tasks to which we have set our hand in Papua and New Guinea. We must bring greater drive and greater urgency into every aspect of that task . . . I feel that the main source of the trouble is located in the Territory itself and will have to be found and removed. May I count on your utmost co-operation in this regard.

In the Department, Lambert had introduced procedures which, with the co-operation of the Administration Treasury, helped us to watch the progress of expenditure throughout the year. By February 1959 he reported to me again under-spending on capital works and recommended adjustments. Earlier in the financial year Lambert had reported to me on the Territory works procedures. On 16 March 1959 I wrote again to the Administrator:

I am most disturbed by the shortcomings revealed in the report which indicate, firstly, a complete absence of proper procedures to ensure efficiency and economy in all stages of planning, execution and financial control of governmental works in the Territory and, secondly, a widespread absence of a proper sense of responsibility in these matters on the part of senior officers of the Administration.

I informed him of the steps being taken to improve the procedures and to ensure that they were observed. My letter concluded, 'I look to you to take all necessary measures to ensure adequate, efficient and economical planning, execution and control of capital works in the Territory in the future.' I continued to watch this subject closely, with the aid of Reseigh, during the financial year 1959–60. In January 1960 the lag in expenditures on capital works still seemed serious.

Unfortunately I found that our concentration on the control of expenditure so as to lessen the under-spending of our votes had tended to encourage the argument that capacity to spend should govern our bid for funds. Defensively some officers were taking refuge in the plea, 'This is all I am able to do.'

Preparing for the budget series of Cabinet meetings for the 1960–1 estimates I reminded the Secretary and the Administrator that the pressure should be for increasing capacity and using it to the utmost. Our case to Cabinet should rest on the urgency of the work. Instead of using limits of capacity as an argument for limiting the finance available, we should use it as an argument for exceptional efforts to build up capacity to meet needs. The pressure of events demanding that we do more should be the keynote of our case to Cabinet. We should ask for more and ensure that we had the capacity to use it. In a separate minute to Lambert on the works programme, I said that my response to his very real doubts about the capacity of the Administration was 'to bend all our efforts to make sure that the Administrator can do the job set him'. The pressure must be for greater performance. The targets for houses, schools and roads should be raised. In a discussion of tactics with Lambert, I said,

> The point I want to put into the Government's mind is that any lack of capacity in Papua and New Guinea cannot be regarded as the incapacity of the Administration. It is the incapacity of Australia and that is the way the world sees it. Hammer this into the Treasury and your own officers so that they stop thinking: 'This is all the Administration can do' and start thinking: 'Is this all Australia can do?'

I added that our outlook should be that the Government wants results. 'If the present tools, equipment and men cannot do the job we have to get tools, equipment and men that can do it.' (Three minutes of 1 July 1960.)

These were bold and optimistic words. In Canberra and particularly in Cabinet I still had to face the reality that I was a competitor with every other Minister for additional funds and there was not as much political advantage in spending money in New Guinea as in spending it on something nearer to the Australian electors. After the retirement in 1958 of Fadden, who had often been helpful to me in Cabinet and who was ready to reopen an argument with his own Treasury officers, I had to deal with a less intelligent and imaginative Treasurer in Harold Holt. I had to work hard to get money from Fadden, but he was always able to understand what I was talking about and, though a very shrewd politician, had a sense of Australian patriotism that was higher than politics. Like others who came from the northern parts of Queensland, he could respond to the idea that what happened in New Guinea was important to Australia as well as to New Guinea. Fadden was the only competent Treasurer in my eighteen years in Cabinet and I missed his hard-headed financial sense as well as his friendship when he retired. I preferred convincing Fadden by making a case than getting an extra half million from Holt by reason of affability and a gimmick about good public relations.

As already indicated, one basic problem was the state of the Territory public service. We had been recruiting purposefully but had to compete with a strong Australian demand for qualified people. We had inaugurated cadetships for university students in agriculture, education, forestry, medicine and veterinary science, as well as another scheme for cadetships for patrol officers. We planned regular intake in general administrative categories and, as the need arose, created new positions at more senior levels to obtain qualified men for new tasks. We could not get enough suitable applicants for all the positions we advertised.

The Administration staff of expatriate officers rose to 2986 in 1958 (of whom more than 2500 had less than seven years' service in the Territory) to 3236 in 1959 and 3632 in 1960. The 4000 mark was passed in 1961, but the majority of them were still comparatively new to the Territory. While a doctor, a scientist or a technician may readily adjust himself to performing the duties of his profession or trade in a new environment, the officer engaged in general administration has to acquire a good deal of local experience before he is fully useful. Sometimes a person recruited at a senior level to take charge of a new activity would find difficulty in adjusting himself to conditions different from those in which he had worked successfully in Australia. The younger administrative recruit did not always find the opportunity in the Territory service for getting a sound training in public administration. Although we were gradually building a better-qualified public service, we suffered a serious lack of officers capable of filling positions at or near the top.

In an attempt to improve the prospects, I inaugurated two moves. One was the holding of courses for senior officers at the Australian School of Pacific Administration. A group of senior officers nominated by the Public Service Commissioner were given a six months' course at the school and were allotted a subject on which they were to engage in discussion and research and produce a report. The subject I chose for the first course in July 1956 was 'Native Economic Development'. The first course included some heads of department as well as some considered to have the potential for promotion to higher offices. The idea was to accustom them to thinking about the problems of the Territory and to applying the results of their thinking to the practical tasks of administration. Then, in the following year, I inaugurated a scheme for having 'policy workshops' in the Territory. Selected officers were brought together at some convenient centre in the Territory for a long weekend, together with officers from the Department of Territories and the headquarters of the Territory Administration. These policy workshops were held regularly and I think had a good freshening effect on officers as well as a training value. The idea was to familiarize officers in the district with the broader problems of the Administration and to educate them in administrative measures to handle such problems.

This approach was in keeping with the views I held about planning. I never saw much value in setting up separate planning staffs. I believed that planning and the shaping of policy should be interlocked with the administration of the plans and the application of policy. Those who were doing should be encouraged to think, and anyone who was thinking should also be directly engaging in doing.

At the same time, we were forming a Public Service Institute to help public servants to improve their education and particularly to encourage and assist some of them to proceed to degrees of Australian universities through external courses. We saw the Institute as the possible forerunner of a university.

In June 1959 I again expressed my concern at the failure of the Territory Public Service to produce better officers for higher executive positions. The occasion was given by a memorandum from the Public Service Commissioner on the subject. Perhaps drawing on a better knowledge than I had of the material available, he suggested that it was premature to make detailed proposals for 'an executive development programme' at this stage. I said that the position was too urgent to let this pass. Why did we not recruit officers at a higher educational standard? Why did a high number of them not add to their educational qualifications after recruitment? Should we raise the inducements for graduate recruitment and give extra rewards for officers who completed approved courses? Were we doing enough to find officers who had the potential for promotion? Were we doing enough for the special in-service training for officers over thirty-five years of age? Were our incentives good enough? Could we stop the wastage of promising men?

This wastage of some of the best of our younger men was becoming more serious. A young and active professional man recruited in his late twenties might give good service for seven or eight years, but then at about the age of thirty-five, with wife and young family to consider, he started to look to a future with more stability and better prospects and we lost him.

I continued to press for better men in senior positions. It fitted my views on how decisions were made and work done. In a minute of 17 June 1959 I said, 'We are having too many working committees. I would rather see someone at the top level making practical proposals from time to time for immediate adoption.' Nevertheless the problem of filling senior executive positions remained. Lambert and the Public Service Commissioner gave to me towards the end of 1959 some proposals for recruiting and training officers for higher positions. They were interested in finding, by new recruitment or by selection within the service, the men who after training could be promoted above the dull strata of 'old hands' who were near the top of the service. They also sought inducements to bright boys to stay in the service instead of seeking better rewards outside it. While approving their suggestions, I stressed the need for a few 'big men for big jobs'. I asked, 'Where am I going to get first-class men with a comprehensive view, analytical power and administrative capacity to handle land tenure problems, economic development, communication with the native people, labour problems, et cetera?' (Minute of 3 November 1959.)

As will be related below, we were also giving attention to a revision of the structure and functions of the Administration and, discussing this revision in April 1960, I returned to the theme that 'the main and urgent problem' of the service was 'improvement in the top-level efficiency'. No shuffling of functions would be of any use unless we could obtain better top-level appointments. (Minute of 25 April 1960.) This minute followed an earlier discussion with Lambert in which, as I recorded it at the time, 'we became aware that there was no one in the Territory service capable of filling certain specialized senior positions at present, but that there were some younger officers coming on who might be trained for such positions.' (Minute of 31 March 1960.)

In this context too I found that my views on planning as an integral part of the processes of administration may not have been fully accepted or understood either in the Department or the Administration. A submission placed before me by Lambert in January 1960, revealing lack of foresight in the Territory, led me to write at some length on the theme:

I was under the impression—and I think Cabinet has been under the same impression—that since the Government's acceptance of the principle of expanding expenditures in Papua and New Guinea and the first submission to Cabinet of a three-year programme, forward planning has proceeded by the regular projection of that programme another year ahead of each successive Budget. If any of my colleagues had asked me I would have replied with complete confidence that we worked to a three-year programme with annual adjustment in the preparation of each Budget and that this three-year programme was based on comprehensive and coordinated planning in the Territory Administration. Perhaps I have not watched this as closely as I should, and I should like to know whether my confidence has been misplaced . . . It is the responsibility of the head of each department in the Territory to plan the work of his department at least three years ahead and, if he finds his planning impeded by lack of certainty in his mind about policy it is his responsibility to obtain a decision on policy. It is the responsibility of each district commissioner to foresee the needs of his district and to plan at least three years ahead for meeting them. It is the responsibility of the Administrator to see that all this is done, and when it is done, to exercise his own superior knowledge and judgement in co-ordinating these plans and of working to get them accepted. Within the Administration itself planning of this kind finds its expression in the draft estimates, the works programme and the public service recruitment programme . . . If the administration and the Department could not immediately, on a chance request by Cabinet, place on my table an exact statement of what we are going to try to do in the next three years in any major field of activity in Papua and New Guinea then I think they have fallen down on the job . . . Ministerially this three-year planning is influenced (a) by directions given ad hoc about policy or shifts in emphasis or changes in priorities, (b) by approval or modification of submissions made from time to time and (c) by approvals of expenditure and appointments. If you can see any place where there is lack of clarity in ministerial direction or uncertainty or delay about ministerial approvals please draw attention to it at once. [Minute of 28 January 1960.]

Possibly some of my disappointment with Administration performance and some of the inability of the Administration to do all I wanted it to do were due to our differences in outlook on this question of planning. They, or some of them, may have been waiting for me to present them with the grand plan. Occasionally there was criticism in the press, possibly derived from careless talk by officials, that we needed a plan and did not have one. On my side I was assuming that they accepted their responsibility for forward planning as part of administration when in fact they had not all done so.

Another criticism came from the expectation of the United Nations visiting missions that they would be handed a plan. In that milieu, plans are an acceptable substitute for action. We were perhaps rather too honest with the visiting missions and told them what we were doing and trying to do and the reasons for it. They were accustomed to a world in which everyone had published a plan and moved on stepping-stones of expired plans to an ever-receding millennium described in a new plan. Lambert was tempted towards trying a bit of glossiness on our own, and the Australian Department of External Affairs at that period also thought well-produced plans with more diagrams than sense would look nice. I said to Lambert, 'The objectives of planning are not to supply answers to External Affairs to pass on to the United Nations. That is a by-product.' I listed my views of the objectives of planning. They were to ensure (a) clear and wise decisions and a comprehensive view of the Territory's problems, (b) a proper balance between various forms of effort, (c) the effort of each branch fitting in with and assisting the total effort, (d) capacity being used efficiently and being continually improved in keeping with the Territory's requirements, and (e) problems and the means of solving them being foreseen.

I will probably incur criticism for not publishing grand plans. The criticism, if it is to be made, should really lie against my belief that sound forward planning is inseparable from administration, and my expectation that those engaged in administration were projecting their work on a rolling programme of three years in the way in which they had been instructed to do. Apart from the reasons I have already given, this approach seems to me to have been both sound and necessary because so little was known about many aspects of life in the Territory, so much was being newly discovered as we extended our work, and reactions to change were not readily foreseeable. Fundamentally however I always had much scepticism about the power of any government to shape history by writing blueprints of social change.

The enthusiasm for producing plans and the consequent waste of time and talent in seeking 'development by drawing board' seems to have been an infection caught from the early days of the Soviet Union by persons who did not study the historical necessities in the Soviet Union and the theoretical impulse that shaped the 'five-year plan' approach to the tasks of government of a new nation and who never took fully into account the frequency of the failure to achieve such plans. I believe an administrator needs vision to get his direction right, principles to guide him in the choice of method, and a clear purpose to give him constant determination, that he has to proceed step by step with his feet on the ground, and that nothing is changed without a lot of hard work. Planning becomes foolish if it sets up an illusion that a plan replaces these necessities, and unfortunately my experience has been that so many earnest, dedicated and skilled back-room planners in and around Australian governments in the last quarter of a century have fostered that illusion.

Meanwhile we were also trying to improve the structure of the service. On 6 April 1959, in conference with Lambert, Cleland and Thomson, we discussed the need to re-examine the structure of the Administration and, as one outcome, I asked the three of them to form themselves into a committee to examine and report on the structure and functions of the Administration with particular reference to the following matters: (a) whether any change is needed in the structure of the Administration, (b) whether the present boundaries between departments of the public service require any adjustments, (c) the definition and allocation of functions to departments, (d) the internal organization of each department, (e) the co-operation of departments and officers in common tasks, and (f) the composition of the public service and the role the indigenous and the expatriate officer will play in the public service of the Territory in future years, with the consequential effects on policy for recruitment, terms and conditions of service and planning of the future development of the public service. I authorized them to appoint a working committee of appropriate officers of the Territory Public Service and the Department of Territories to prepare material for their consideration. (Minute of 7 April 1959.) In the following October, expressing the opinion that the work was lagging, I minuted, 'It is a big job I know but it requires to be pushed ahead rather quickly.'

I received a report in April 1960. I agreed with the creation of a new Department of Trade and Industry and the consequential disappearance of the Department of Customs and Marine; the redistribution of the functions of the Civil Affairs Department and its eventual disappearance; and the creation of a central planning committee, not as a body with the sole function of planning but as a committee to co-ordinate the planning done in all departments and to help ensure that each department was making its three-year forward programme. I refused to accept a proposal to abolish the Department of Native Affairs at that stage, saying that 'it would be bad for the morale of some of the best men in the whole service if we were to remove by one stroke their proud identity'. I said the change could be brought gradually by transferring the best of them, at the age of thirty-five to forty, to senior posts elsewhere in the service. My own opinion was that some of the best men we had in the service, and certainly some with the broadest knowledge of conditions in the Territory, were to be found among the younger men who had come into Native Affairs as post-war patrol officers if only we could add to their field experience some training in administration. I rejected a proposal which would have given numerous new functions to the Department of the Administrator:

In practice your proposals would make it one of the most cumbrous branches in the whole Administration. I want the Administrator and the Assistant Administrators two or three of them if necessary to take effective action to see that the whole machine works efficiently, and to make sure that policy and planning come to a focus. Your proposals would turn the Administrator into another departmental head or, if he did not become that, into someone sitting out on a limb—even if it is the topmost limb. (Minute of 25 April 1960.)

In the same minute I returned to the need for improvement in the top-level appointments. One of the reasons for not accepting the subcommittee's report in full was that I could not see that it would help us in this 'main and urgent problem'. No shuffling of functions would do any good unless we got better men at the top.

As 1960 progressed, it seemed to me that Cleland, who had served a hard term and who was still giving honourable and distinguished service in other aspects of his Administratorship, was not keeping pace with the intensified demands for functional administration. Relationships between Cleland and me were close and friendly and I valued very much his opinions and admired the way in which he carried out the public duties of Administrator. The only worry in my mind was how to get prompt and effective action in our urgent administrative tasks. The fundamental difficulty was in the very nature of the established office of Administrator and the basic problem of requiring one man to be the representative of the Australian Government, a political leader, and the working head of an administrative machine. No man could do all three and, in Cleland's case, I think that the third function was not as well performed as the others. As the result of my earlier prompting, the upper structure was revised by giving the Administrator two Assistant Administrators instead of one to share his burdens, and reallocating responsibilities between the three of them.

Two of the departments which came most closely under notice in the review of the structure were the Territory Department of Works and Department of Native Affairs. As indicated above, much of our problem of financial control was in the works programme. This department, in progressively taking over more works from the Commonwealth Department of Works, had not developed proper procedures of its own and also had probably started to do more than its staff could handle. In 1959 it was in difficulty. Gradually, thanks mainly to Lambert and Thomson and officers from Canberra, we introduced new procedures, created new positions, and improved the management of the department. We then extended beyond improvement in administrative structure to a re-examination of some of the more basic concepts of the works programme—the standard of building, use of local materials, training of village labour for works to serve the villages, low-cost building, the encouragement of private contractors and many other matters in the consideration of which we had been inhibited by the outlook of the Commonwealth Department of Works. In this regard Reseigh did a notable work in his clear analysis of problems and practical approach to the ways and means of achieving policy. Among other things, he was mainly responsible in 1960–1 for the details of a village schools programme of £400 000, providing schools and teachers' quarters for our 'emergency education plan', using as well as the Territory Public Works Department the technical instructors and technical trainees of the Education Department and the labour of village communities. This was perhaps the first large-scale development of low-cost building with the maximum use of indigenous labour. In a limited way, there had been some earlier projects by an energetic district commissioner for the housing of native employees of the Administration, but our previous experience with Commonwealth Department of Works to get low-cost buildings for simple needs had been very frustrating.

The problem set by the Department of Native Affairs seemed to me to be basically due to the fact that its officers were now dealing with a diverse range of situations. They were still patrolling and doing first-contact work in newly opened areas and, at the other end of the scale, had such urban situations as that of 'foreign' natives in Port Moresby and the tangled discontents of the Gazelle Peninsula. By reason of seniority the department was still being run mainly by pre-war officers whose own habits of life had not changed as rapidly as those of some of the people to whom they ministered.

In 1957 I had given instructions for an inquiry into this department but, after the Commission of Inquiry on the Navuneram Incident had reported, I revoked this direction and, following discussions with Lambert, Cleland and Thomson, asked the three of them to examine and report on the structure and functions of Native Affairs. The terms of reference I gave to them were comprehensive and included such other matters as the training of officers to ensure that they were equipped to deal with the various phases of native administration from the early contact period to the sophisticated stage; better liaison in the field with other departments; the handing over of magisterial duties to stipendiary magistrates; methods to ensure closer personal contact of field officers with the native people; and a system of intelligence to ensure that the Administrator was fully apprised of the thoughts and aspirations of the native people. (Minute of 7 April 1959.)

This investigation merged into the wider investigation into the structure of the whole Administration, and their recommendation was to abolish the Department of Native Affairs and distribute its functions among other departments. As I have already written, I was not prepared to accept this, believing that abolition of the department at that stage would have had a bad effect on the service and would have been misunderstood by the public.

Although the membership of the Territory Public Service was still overwhelmingly European, the path of change was becoming clearer. By 1961 the auxiliary division had grown to 582 and there were 28 indigenous officers who had qualified for entry to the main body of the public service. Expatriate officials totalled more than 4000. We could see the prospect of an early increase in indigenous candidates for appointment on the same standards of entry as the Europeans. This would raise more urgently the question of rates of pay. The emoluments of expatriate officers included an element of compensation for working away from home, and their entitlements to leave and other benefits derived from the assumption that their home was Australia. Should an indigenous officer receive the same rewards as an expatriate officer? I rejected the idea of having one rate of pay for whites and another for coloured if they were doing the same work and had the same qualifications, and this view inclined me towards seeking a solution by having the same standard salary for both and calculating expatriate allowances separately.

Another consideration was that the prevailing income level for the indigenous people was very much below the standard rates of salary in the public service. Was it right to load the independent country of the future with the burden of an enormous payroll by introducing European-scale salaries—derived from the standard of living in Australia and from a comparison with salaries paid to other white-collar workers in Australia—instead of giving the indigenous official a salary derived from the standard of living in New Guinea and a comparison with the salaries of other workers with similar qualifications in Papua New Guinea?

At the same time we had claims from the expatriate officers for increases in their salaries and allowances and some expression of concern among them about what was going to happen to them when self-government came. Some of them saw the simple solution as generous provision by the Australian Government for their early retirement. In 1956, to overcome some difficulties not solely related to Papua and New Guinea, we had revived in Canberra the possibility of a colonial service covering all Territories. It was thought that we might create a Territories division of the Commonwealth Public Service composed of all officers of the Department of Territories, the Northern Territory, and the external territories of Australia. I directed that for the present the proposal not include Papua New Guinea, partly because of some temporary advantages in having a separate service and largely through fear of the effect on the morale of the service in Papua and New Guinea. Eventually however the expatriate public servants in Papua and New Guinea might become part of the proposed new division. (Minute of 28 March 1956.)

The proposal came to nothing, but some news of it leaked out and it became plain that the public servants in Papua and New Guinea did not want to merge into the Commonwealth Public Service. Three years later I was still countering rumours. In a public statement in Port Moresby on 15 May 1959, I said categorically, 'There is no proposal to absorb the Territory Public Service into the Commonwealth Service and the Government's policy is for a separate service.' At a later stage, when anxiety among some public servants about what would happen at independence became sharper, I put forward in discussion with the Public Service Association the possibility of transfer of officers to the Commonwealth Public Service. They would have none of it. Part of the reason was an unexpressed fear. Those territory officers who were poorly qualified would be the first to be replaced and many of them would never have a chance of qualifying in the Commonwealth Service for a position as comfortable and rewarding as the one they had in the Territory. There was growing uncertainty about the future in the Territory and this undoubtedly had its effect both on efficiency and on recruiting of new staff. We not only had to avoid scaring investors and industrialists for the sake of economic advancement; we had to avoid scaring possible recruits and serving officers for the sake of better administration. Our difficulties in this regard grew because for a period the favourite angle of journalists was stories about people 'getting out while there is time' and of Government plans to withdraw. The independence of Malaya had given currency to many stories about the 'Malayanization' of its public service.

We kept on recruiting steadily but our gains in strength were reduced by resignations. From 1959 this caused some concern. An analysis of the situation gave me only the consolation that I was at least making a few persons romantically happy. In the financial year 1959–60 we lost fifty-eight recently recruited nurses from the Department of Health. Most of them resigned to get married in the Territory. I was running a thriving Lonely Hearts Club. Some cruder spirits used to refer to the recruiting of young nurses as 'building up the stockpile'.

With the expanding economic activity, there were increased opportunities for employment of young men in other avenues in the Territory. Wives who missed the picture-shows and the shopping centre persuaded husbands to go south. The glamour of New Guinea attracted applications from a number of candidates who never really intended to stay there longer than two or three years. There were the individual cases of family complications or personal difficulties. Some unfortunately resulted from such avoidable disappointments as poor accommodation or lack of stimulus in the job.

[26]

THE ECONOMY TAKES SHAPE

Around 1957 and 1958 the increasing interest in Papua and New Guinea was sometimes expressed in proposals for more rapid development of its resources. Now that I had established more firmly the policies on land and labour, I saw a clearer path towards economic activity although, in my judgement, our social measures were still so incomplete especially in newly opened districts that it would not be wise to concentrate on economic advancement to the neglect of social advancement or to create imbalance between economic change and social change. I also felt strongly that all economic advancement should be of such a kind that the participation of the indigenous people was not excluded and especially that action was not taken which would pre-empt the resources of the self-governing country.

Some of the advocacy of economic development seemed to me at times to mean only that Australians should be given a chance to make money in the territory in order to spend it in Australia. It was as simple and straightforward as the impulse of energetic and hard-working young Australians to go outback and take up land. Out of such hard work and enterprise the Australian pastoral industry had been built. Some energetic and enterprising people saw New Guinea as a similar field for pioneering enterprise. The difference was that Papua and New Guinea was another country and when their hard work and enterprise brought similar success they would have built an industry for an independent country and not an industry for Australia and their position as pioneers in it would still be under question.

Some of the Australians who were pressing for opportunity in the Territory saw this fact realistically and consequently looked for big returns quickly before they got out. Others who saw it nourished a hope that there would still be a place for them and their families in the self-governing nation of the future. I was sure the first lot were wrong and I could only hope that perhaps the second lot might be right. Quite a number of those Australians who pressed for development however seemed to give little thought to the fact. They just took present conditions for granted and assumed that development was good in itself and that everyone would think so for ever, irrespective of what sort of development took place and of the terms on which it was made.

290

Another kind of advocacy of economic development, coming mainly from governmental circles in Canberra, stressed the need for Papua and New Guinea to start paying its own way and developing its own resources to produce exports to match the rising figures for imports financed by Australian expenditure in the Territory. Some of the chief critics of my policies belonged to this school and were apt to misrepresent my views by saying that I did not recognize the need for making Papua and New Guinea economically viable, whereas my view was that exploitation of natural resources should take place in conditions that safeguarded the future of the people and should not have priority over but go hand in hand with their social advancement. In the light of the knowledge of resources at that time, I assumed that self-government would come before Papua and New Guinea was fully able to finance its own services and that continuing grants from Australia would be needed.

Those who simply advocated economic development as a good in itself seemed to me to have an incomplete view of the situation. Although I accepted their ultimate objective of making the country self-supporting or as near to it as possible, I did not believe in giving measures for economic advancement priority over measures for other forms of advancement, or leaving the field of economic opportunity wide open to all comers.

Yet we did need initiative and investment from outside the country. Without expatriate enterprise there would be little economic development of any kind, for at that stage there was no early prospect of finding the capital and the managerial and technical capacity inside the Territory. Strenuous governmental efforts might ensure some indigenous participation in capital-raising and in production but any major project would have to be organized, financed and managed from non-indigenous resources.

My objective was to try to get the development without impairing the chance of future indigenous participation. This was a much more finely balanced task than the one that faces the Premier of an Australian State in trying to encourage development in his own patch of Australia. Yet some critics imagined that it was all much the same sort of thing and that a more capable minister would have promoted economic development more dramatically.

Another relevant fact was that most of the opportunities for development at that time were seen in agriculture and this was an area in which, as shown in chapters 12, 13 and 14, the policies on land and labour were involved most closely and one in which the opportunities for native participation could be more readily foreseen. Both for subsistence and for cash cropping, either for the local market or for export, the indigenous people were already active. Hence any project for major agricultural development could not be looked at simply as a project for expatriate investment and management with occupation of unlimited land and employment of unlimited indigenous labour. Furthermore agricultural production for export had to be related to persistent problems of marketing.

Discussion of economic development kept coming back to agriculture. All of the official advice placed before me by the Department and the Administration was to the general effect that the natural resources of the Territory were limited. The extent of the cultivable land was said to be only a small part of the total area because the terrain was too swampy, too high, too rugged or too steep. The prospects of development were governed by the weakness of world markets for tropical agricultural products.

We searched for other opportunities. The advice on mineral resources was not encouraging. Gold production had been declining year by year. Surveys made by the Australian Bureau of Mineral Resources had not pointed to any other commercial opportunities in minerals.

Oil search had been carried on for many years both before and after the war by private enterprise in the Gulf district of Papua. For a time, prospects seemed hopeful and, following a visit I made to the drilling sites, we set in train studies of the action that would be required in the event of the discovery of oil in commercial quantities. Hopes were not realized. The major commercial prospect was in natural gas. We combined with the Burmah Oil Company in feasibility studies for its use, but no viable project emerged.

Another prospect that caught my own imagination was the use of the water resources of the Territory, especially those of the Purari river system, for the production of great blocks of hydro-electric power. A prospective use of this power emerged with the discovery of bauxite on the Australian mainland at Weipa (Queensland) and Gove (Northern Territory). With my Cabinet colleague, Senator Spooner (Minister for National Development) I was closely concerned with a long series of hard-headed discussions with British Aluminium, Consolidated Zinc, Comalco, Pechiney and others, and the two of us made a number of consequential submissions to Cabinet from 1957 to 1960. These complicated affairs and my part in this phase of Australian development are wider than the story of economic progress in Papua and New Guinea. In one phase of the talks, however, we had the exciting prospect of development in Papua based on power generated on the Purari river system. A great deal of detailed work was done before the prospect faded. The reality was that the exploitation of those water resources was subsidiary to the discovery of a prospective use of the power generated. We did preparatory work and drafted water resources legislation, and some of this work may well be useful in future years.

During this work on bauxite development, I first began to value the talents of R. S. Swift,[44] one of Lambert's assistant secretaries. His clearness, keenness and analytical power and the toughness behind a mild manner and a helpful approach made him one of the most competent public servants with whom I ever worked on a long-drawn-out and involved task.

The third possibility other than agriculture was timber. The plymill established by Commonwealth New Guinea Timbers at Bulolo was still the biggest industrial enterprise in the Territory. Some smaller mills were also operating, partly for supply to the local market and partly for export. By 1960 the timber industry—sawmills, plymill and joinery—were employing over 2000 workers, mostly indigenes, this being about half the total employment in factory operations in the Territory. The export of forest products had passed £1 million a year and was the most significant export item other than agricultural products. The Administration had made detailed studies of forest resources but there was still some uncertainty in the advice given to me about the potential for development. There were still many problems of accessibility of stands of timber, the

Few places were inaccessible to Papua New Guinea's pilots: perched on a narrow ridge is Omkalai airstrip in the highlands

An informal conference: principal chief Ninji (left) and another high-lander discussing the future with the author

mixed growth and varying quality of timber in the virgin forests, and methods of regeneration to give perpetuity to the forests and continuity to the industry. In general, except where the ultimate intention was to clear land for agriculture, there was much caution about commercial exploitation of the forests. On the whole I thought cautiousness at a time of limited knowledge was commendable and I let the Forests Department of the Administration set the pace for the good of posterity rather than putting pressure on them for a more rapid development of the timber industry for the sake of immediate results. The main outside interest in timber was for the export of logs. I saw limited advantages to the Territory in that. The work of the Forests Department eventually led to my approval in May 1962 of a five-year programme to increase timber production, but for the time being I let the foresters set the pace.

Thus, in spite of our hopes in oil, water resources and timber, and lacking any indication of the possibility of mineral development other than the production of gold, the prospect for economic development in the second half of the 1950s was still centred on agricultural production. The only significant contribution to mineral production, at a time when European sluicing and mining of gold were dwindling, came from an active encouragement of gold winning by indigenous people trained and guided by Administration officers.

Our main export crops were coconut products (copra and coconut oil), coffee, cocoa and rubber. All three increased production during my term. In ten years exports of coconut products rose in quantity, in round figures, from 77 000 to 107 000 tons, rubber from 2000 to 4300, cocoa beans from 300 to 7300, coffee from 30 to 2300. The total value of exports of all kinds doubled. This in itself was a considerable achievement.

Although no exact figures are available for the agricultural production for local consumption, the increase in food crops was also considerable. Most of this development was by native farmers. By 1960–1 more than 3000 native farmers had been given agricultural training. The extension staff numbered 137 European officers and about 300 native agricultural assistants. New crops had been introduced, better methods taught and yields increased. Agriculture Department staff had also helped to ensure native participation in the growing of the export crops, especially coffee and cocoa.

In all this work I claim no credit for initiation but only for giving encouragement and taking a close interest in what the officers were doing. The Territory was well served by some capable officers of the Agriculture Department who also enjoyed a high professional reputation in their field. Frank Henderson,[45] who had done notable work in establishing cocoa growing in the Territory, succeeded Larry Dwyer as Director of Agriculture in 1959. Hard-headed, practical, uncompromising and professionally competent, he was the sort of man I liked and could understand. He knew how to work and there was no kidstakes about what he did and said. With him were officers like Conroy,[46] Bridgland,[47] Hughes[48] and Newton[49] who had clear ideas about what they were doing and, better still, what they wanted to do. At the Canberra end, the Department of Territories also had a few officers—E. J. Wood,[50] D. Lattin,[51] Ian Cartledge[52] and Swift—who were essentially practical and had good administrative training and, in this area perhaps more than any other, the officers in the Administration and those in the Department seemed to be able to work together to good effect, supplementing each other. Agricultural development was an area in which Lambert probably was strongest. It was also an area in which we were able to draw on Australian resources of professional and technical advice more successfully than any other. The Council for Scientific and Industrial Research, the Bureau of Agricultural Economics, State Departments of Agriculture and other mainland instrumentalities worked helpfully with the Territory Administration. The Planters' Associations in the Territory and the Highland Farmers and Settlers' Association, under the leadership of Ian Downs, who had left the Administration for private enterprise, worked constructively. As Minister I found myself for once in the congenial position of helping the work of an eager team.

It brought me some unusual and fascinating experiences. Visiting most of the agricultural stations in the Territory, I was introduced into the mysteries of growing and processing such unfamiliar crops as coffee, cocoa and rubber. Co-operation with Australian industry revealed new facts about what happens to copra and the taste of chocolate. As cocoa growing expanded, we ran into some problems on marketing. I approached Australian chocolate makers to persuade them to buy New Guinea beans. They said in effect that our beans had the wrong taste. To learn what they meant, for hitherto I had thought all chocolate was the same, I toured all the large factories to see chocolate being made. At the end of one tour the manager took me to the laboratory where their chemists kept track of quality. A dozen or so separate handfuls of New Guinea beans were set out on a bench and from each sample a small block of raw chocolate had been made. We sniffed and nibbled, detecting the foreign odours. It was as elaborate as wine-tasting. Get rid of those foreign odours, they said, and the beans would be bought. I arranged at once for a party of planters and agricultural officers to come down to go through the same demonstration. The manufacturer co-operated fully, the desired quality was produced and the Territory growers had a better market.

I learnt that copra and coconut oil had many uses besides the production of butter substitutes. Indeed, facing an attempt by Australian primary producers to exclude or limit the importation of copra from the Territory so as to protect the Australian dairying industry, I was able to present figures showing that, in making margarine in Australia, less copra was used than peanut oil produced by other Australian primary producers in competition with Australian dairymen. The processed copra served many industrial and cosmetic demands and a wide range of culinary uses as well as being used for butter substitutes.

On particular products sections of Australian farmers were just as narrow as sections of Australian trade unions in their opposition to the importation of the products of 'cheap black labour'. Our attempts to promote the growing of peanuts in the Markham Valley were resisted as a threat to Australian peanut growers. I found more response to an appeal for special consideration when I went to manufacturers than in other quarters. Cadbury and MacRobertson, the chocolate manufacturers, who drew their main supplies of beans from West Africa, co-operated in ensuring a market for Territory beans and in developing the industry. Several coffee merchants, though not all, did the same. Nestlé continued to buy our beans for the manufacture of instant coffee when they could have imported the whole of their requirements of 'coffee flour' already ground from Brazil more advantageously. The Olympic Rubber Company took Papuan smoke-dried rubber for tyre manufacture while we were still trying to work out the terms of a rubber agreement with Malaya and an acceptable policy on rubber importation.

As indicated, my own principal role in agricultural development was on the marketing side. In this I was able to work closely with John McEwen, with whom I had always had a pleasant relationship as a ministerial colleague. An understanding of each other had begun when McEwen was chairman of the Australian Agricultural Council and I became a member of the council on the claim that, in agricultural matters, the Northern Territory and Papua and New Guinea stood in a position comparable to that of one of the Australian States and that I was in effect the Minister for Agriculture for both Territories. Additionally my responsibility for the two Phosphate Commissions meant that my presence on the council gave state Ministers for Agriculture a link with the source of the major raw materials for farm fertilizers. In turn my membership gave the Territory a useful link with Departments of Agriculture throughout Australia and we benefited a good deal from the interest and advice of departmental officers, and on particular problems were able to work closely with them. Eventually we had the pleasure and benefit of a full meeting of the Agricultural Council in the Territory.

The Department of Territories and the Department of Trade worked closely together. It was necessary for them to do so, for internationally the Territory had no identity of its own apart from Australia, and access to world markets for Territory exports was subject to Australian commitments, both multilateral as in the General Agreement on Tariffs and Trade (GATT) and bilateral as in trade agreements with particular countries. These agreements had been negotiated primarily to serve the interests of Australian industries and so, in discussions related to the marketing of Territory products, either for preferential treatment in Australia or for quotas and prices overseas, it was necessary for us to make a case for special treatment for Papua and New Guinea and in some instances to justify an Australian application for a waiver from GATT. My own memory of relations with the Minister and Department of Trade, the permanent head of which at that time was J. G. (later Sir John) Crawford, is of understanding and co-operation. This close association was also of value in adding to the number of people in Canberra who had some interest in and knowledge of New Guinea.

My general purpose in marketing was to assure the Australian market for Territory products. There were some strong arguments for this. To purchase these products and give the Territory an export income helped a dependent country to become more nearly viable and was the most useful supplement Australia could make to grants-in-aid. Much of the Territory production was complementary to Australian production. One could also argue that there were advantages to Australia in having guaranteed supplies of key commodities from a local source in the event of any crisis cutting off supplies from elsewhere. At the same time I could not press too far with any thesis that the Australian and Papua and New Guinea economies should be wholly complementary, for we also wanted to grow some crops that Australia grew and for our own economic advantage we hoped to replace or reduce imports from Australia of rice, meat and other foodstuffs.

We had already set the pattern in rubber. The Government accepted a scheme under which Australian manufacturers were granted a rebate on rubber imported from Malaya if they took up the whole of the Papuan rubber offered, quality for quality and price for price. In earlier discussions I had tried to obtain a margin on price as a form of encouragement to the Papuan industry, having regard to the strategic importance to Australia of assured rubber supplies, but this was not acceptable.

Without going into details, I can record that the discussions on rubber left me tied to the formula of 'quality for quality and price for price' in the entry of Papua and New Guinea exports into Australia. They also left me cautious about letting inquiries into Territory industries go before the Australian Tariff Board and about trying to base any arguments on costs of production. I found there was too much of a tendency to equate the conditions of Territory industries with conditions of mainland industries and our hope was to prove that Papua and New Guinea was a special case.

I find historic interest, recapturing the mood of the day, in my minute of 15 April 1958 taking issue on remarks in a memorandum from the Administrator:

> I gained Cabinet acquiescence in the view that it was the function of the Administration and not the function of the Tariff Board to decide what measures (other than Australian protective duties) should and could be taken to help the rubber industry. That fact is a challenge to us to do the job. The only way to keep other people from butting into your affairs is to handle the affairs properly yourself.
>
> We should also recognize as a matter of cold fact that, to an increasing extent, our attempts at economic development in Papua and New Guinea will be related to our success in ensuring full and free access to the Australian mainland market for Territory products. In that struggle we will encounter more and more questions related to the efficiency of Territory industries. Our own people in the Territory should be made aware of the sort of hard-headed questions that will come at any time and under any Government from an Australian Department of Trade or from an Australian Treasury and the sort of questions that will be forced under the notice of Australian parliamentarians by producing or manufacturing interests in Australia. We will not win these fights by playing back tape recordings of the anguished squeals of Territory planters.

As a gloss on this minute, I should add that my view about Tariff Board inquiries was that, while the Tariff Board might properly inquire into the efficiency, the costs of production and the economic justification for protection for an Australian industry, it should not start examining Papua and New Guinea claims as though they were an application from a home-based industry for protection, nor should any Papua and New Guinea claim be based on arguments that invited such an inquiry. We were likely to do better for ourselves by other methods and I did not want to renew arguments for tying the Territory into the Australian tariff system.

What we gained for rubber was also applied to coffee. I stated the objective in a minute of 3 March 1959:

... to ensure that, quality for quality, PNG coffee should have first claim on the Australian home market and the certainty that the whole production can be absorbed there (if necessary under Government compulsion) at prices which bear a reasonable relationship to world prices. We should be extremely cautious about giving any encouragement to the notion that coffee growing in PNG by Europeans is ever likely to be subsidized or given substantial preferences in order to give set margins over a calculated cost of production by Europeans.

Early in 1958 it had become apparent that a major rise in world production of coffee over the past seven years without an equivalent rise in world demand was pointing towards a crisis in coffee marketing. Prices were declining. I asked for a departmental note on the outlook for Papua and New Guinea. At that time, departmental officers found some reassurance in the fact that our Territory production was a tiny fraction of world production and that its prospective increase would still give it only a quarter of the Australian consumption. Australia was the natural market for Papua and New Guinea coffee. The current policy of import licensing would control entries from elsewhere, and the Territory product had duty-free entry compared with a duty of 3d or more per pound on imports from other countries, as well as the advantage of a shorter transport haul. Australian consumption was expected to increase.

I thought this somewhat optimistic. The officers admitted that world prices were likely to fall and that the Territory price would have to keep in line. They also conceded that the import licensing policy, adopted to meet problems in the Australian economy, was only an expedient and could not be relied upon as a permanent means for giving Territory coffee an advantage in the Australian market.

The fall in prices was of course the point of most immediate interest to the European growers in the Territory. Their investment in establishing themselves had been based on one price and now that their plantings were coming into bearing, they saw the prospect of a much lower price. Some of them saw a simple solution in an Australian guaranteed price.

In July 1958 I asked the Department to take the initiative in arranging a conference between merchants, agents, growers and the Administration. The difficulties in persuading people to serve their own self-interest by getting together are sometimes ludicrous. Some merchants did not want to meet in Papua and New Guinea, some growers did not want to meet in Australia, the Administration had doubts about this and that, and both the Administration and the growers hesitated over the agenda. Eventually a meeting with incomplete representation was held at Goroka in January 1959. There was a wide disparity between the views of the growers and the merchants on a fair price. Further conferences followed and gradually arrangements for marketing were worked out acceptably. All this was done at the departmental level on my instruction that the Department was to help bring growers and merchants together. The view I took was that European growers, as owners of the coffee, could not avoid their responsibility for making decisions about marketing their product and I resisted suggestions for a Government-controlled marketing with subsidized prices. I also resisted suggestions for a cost-of-production survey to establish a basis for a guaranteed price in Australia. At the outset I said that the departmental interest was to see that the Territory produced the variety and quality of coffee that the market wanted and to persuade the merchants to take it and the growers to market it under mutually acceptable terms. Our broad objective should be to ensure that, 'quality for quality, at world prices, the Territory coffee grower can be sure of selling his crop up to the full capacity of the Australian market to use it, regardless of whether there is a world surplus'. (Minute of 1 October 1959.)

Regarding a cost-of-production survey in particular and marketing in general, I also said that the eventual pattern of agriculture in Papua and New Guinea would have a large component of native growers and that figures based on the expectations of a European grower for a return on his investment and his labour would be partly fictitious. I had also seen too many instances in Australian primary production where cost-of-production surveys had set in train a process that brought artificial prices, the subsidizing of non-economic industries and the inflation of the price of land. I wanted to keep the young Territory free from these complications and not hand over, at the time of self-government, a structure of primary production based on expatriate values, high prices for land, and cheap labour, which an independent and indigenous government would find unreal and intolerable. Some of the settlers in the Territory and some of my own advisers were inclined to find examples in Australian primary production. I was inclined to see the Australian experience of subsidized prices as inapplicable and even as a horrible warning.

By 1958 the indigenous growers were becoming more significant in the production of coffee. The figures in 1959–60 were 580 tons produced by indigenous growers and 957 tons by non-indigenous growers. By the following year the indigenous crop had grown to 1200 tons. The Highland Farmers and Settlers' Association had admitted indigenous growers to its membership and claimed to speak on behalf of such growers, but most of the native growers did not have direct representation and it was the responsibility of the Administration to protect their interests and give attention to the conditions likely to suit them best in the future.

Separately and at a slightly later stage we faced the problem of possible restriction of coffee production under a world marketing agreement. When that issue arose, we successfully made a case to the international conference for special consideration for Papua and New Guinea as a developing country and obtained a quota of production which enabled coffee growing to continue at the planned level at that time.

The pursuit of this aim to gain an assured market in Australia for Territory products was complicated by the growth of secondary industry in the Territory mainly in replacement of imports from Australia. We were trying to get advantage both ways, making sure that we could enter the market in Australia and trying to keep the Territory market for ourselves as far as possible.

Stimulated by the higher governmental expenditure and the general development, the Territory moved into secondary industry for local consumption. Breweries and 'lolly water' factories were among the earliest. Twist tobacco for issue to native workers was another. Furniture and joinery, concrete building materials made from imported cement, paint, metal fixtures, general engineering workshops and a number of other private industries followed. By the financial year 1959–60 there were over 140 factories employing over 4000 workers, of whom three-quarters were native workers, with a pay packet totalling £1·4 million, for a capital investment of £5 million, and an output valued at £9 million a year. Encouragement was given by the tariff policy of free entry to industrial machinery and in some cases to raw materials, and protection during an initial period, as well as by taxation concessions.

This development meshed with our technical training and apprenticeship schemes and by June 1960 the enrolment at technical training schools had risen to 576 and the number of youths serving indentures to 270. Private enterprise co-operated well in helping to train the local people and in their economic advancement.

This diversification of the Territory's economic life also required a reconsideration of trade policy. At an earlier stage I had intervened in the matter of public tendering for supplies and works to the Administration to ensure that local suppliers were given a fair chance of obtaining contracts in competition with tenders from the Australian mainland. It seemed to me that the previous system of equating quotations to a figure f.o.b. Sydney had not given a fair chance to those tenderers who were able to supply at a designated port in the Territory and I tried to make sure that they had the natural advantage of being based locally.

During 1959 the Department handled a succession of inquiries about the establishment of industries in the Territory. It seemed to me that the submissions for decision ad hoc did not show enough thought about the years ahead. In a minute of 12 October 1959, after approving recommendations regarding the setting up of a factory to make twist tobacco, I asked the officers to look more closely at three broad questions. One was the way the Contracts Board operated in the Territory and I thought that was mainly a matter for the Administrator to examine so as to make sure the methods of calling and examining tenders and letting contracts were sound. The second concerned the operations of a tariff committee in the Territory—an inter-departmental body which hitherto had performed a fairly straightforward administrative task. If it were to be called on to make investigations as a consequence of applications by Territory industries for protection from imports, we would have to consider whether it would be better to replace it with an independent board and, if so, what powers, methods of investigation and staff would be needed by such a board and what procedures should be followed in handling the board's reports. The third question concerned a trade policy for Papua and New Guinea. I said that the decisions already made for fostering local industry would, if generally applied, have far-reaching results in trade relations between the Territory and Australia, in the trade relations of Australia and overseas countries, and in respect of Australia's obligations under GATT. I asked the Department 'to do some thinking around this subject, having in mind both the long-term interests of the Territory in respect of the marketing of exports and in providing much-needed local employment at high standards'. (Minute of 12 October 1959.)

It will be recalled that a decision had already been made, soon after my term commenced, to keep the Territory Customs separate from the Australian Customs. In seeking a preferred position in the Australian market for such Territory products as rubber, coffee and cocoa and in making arrangements to assure Australian supplies of copra, however, we had set up a special relationship between the two systems and there was also an expectation among some Australian manufacturers and traders that the Territory market belonged to them because Australia was spending lots of public money in the Territory.

About this time a committee on trade which had been formed by the Government members in the Australian Parliament, under the chairmanship of Peter Howson, started to take an interest in the trade of Papua and New Guinea and was encouraged to do so by McEwen and me. We both thought there would be value in having a group of Government members well informed on some of the trade problems of the Territory.

A long minute I wrote to Lambert about the committee's work summarizes better than any other contemporary document my own approach to the question. I asked Lambert to arrange for Wood to attend a meeting of the committee and give information about Territory trade. My minute continued,

As Mr Wood will be aware from a recent conversation I had with him, the main points we will wish to establish ourselves are:
(a) That the development of Territory production and trade is of the utmost importance to Australia because, unless we provide a solid economic foundation for the Territory, Australia will have to face the provision of increasing grants from Commonwealth revenue in order to maintain the services of the Territory.
(b) That many Territory products supplement Australian production and should find their natural market in Australia in preference to similar products from foreign countries, and this will not only be of advantage to the Territory in the planning of its economic development but will also be of advantage to Australia in the saving of overseas exchange.
(c) At the same time there are some Territory products which have to be sold on the world market and Australian negotiation in trade matters should take account of the claims of the Territory.
(d) With the expansion of Territory production and trade the Territory is itself beginning to encounter some of the typical problems of both policy and administration which arise in any trading economy and the Territory will need to benefit from Australian experience and have the support of the Australian Department of Trade in handling these problems.
(e) It is clear that one of the major practical tasks ahead of the Territory Administration is ensuring opportunities for an increasing population to find either wage-earning employment inside the Territory, or to find opportunities for earning a cash income from production so that the population can sustain the higher standard of living to which it is advancing. This necessarily involves both the promotion of new industries in the Territory in order to provide employment, the extension of agriculture, and the mastering of attendant problems of marketing the products at an economic price.

I arranged a further discussion with Wood before he saw the committee and added the somewhat cynical comment, 'From our point of view the value of the committee is in educating them in our problems but at the same time it is advisable to make them feel that we hope to benefit from any conclusions they may reach.' (Minute of 11 November 1959.)

On one of my visits to the Territory in December 1959 I received representations from some of the local contractors and made an opportunity of discussing the situation with several businessmen and Territory officers. After I returned to Canberra I asked Lambert to draw up proposals for 'more positive measures of promoting local trade and industry'. Discussing the situation with him, I spoke of the growing need for employment for the indigenous people at higher levels of skill and remuneration. This need was linked with the need for European investment, management and technical direction. Our aim should be to limit and eventually reduce the number of Europeans in low-skilled occupations. When our technical education plans showed results, we would also replace the white worker in supervisory jobs and the running of machines. Indigenous labour and not expatriate labour was basic to the economic development of the Territory. 'Except in a few specialized roles,' I wrote,

trade and industry in Papua and New Guinea cannot find a sound foundation if it has to depend on attracting and rewarding expatriate labour. Furthermore many social and political difficulties would needlessly be caused by such a policy. In short, while European management and technical and professional skill will clearly be needed for many years to come, the other European labour has to be regarded as transitory. [Minute of 7 March 1960.]

I had already decided that a new department was to be created in the Territory Administration to promote economic development and I suggested to Lambert that its main concern would be to encourage local industry and trade. As well as taking measures to assist local industry, the Administration should reconsider its own policies as the biggest customer in the Territory. Each year it was spending millions of pounds on works and the purchase of supplies. Was it directing as much of this as possible to maintain employment in the Territory? Statements had been made to me in the Territory to the effect that the local works contractor and supplier did not have equal opportunity with Australians in public tendering. On this point I entered on a detailed discussion of this aspect of the problem, specified a number of complaints made to me about Administration procedures to be investigated and gave directions intended to ensure that the Territory contractor or supplier had equal opportunity with all other contractors and suppliers to obtain Administration contracts.

The other side of the picture was that some Australian firms which had been traditional suppliers of the Territory's requirements thought they had a right to the market because the 'Australian taxpayer' was supplying so much of the money. My policy was one of 'equal opportunity' for the local tenders but that the system of open tendering should not be used to give preference. There were other and more appropriate means of encouraging local industry. (Minute of 7 March 1960.)

During the course of 1959 and 1960 I tried to direct the mind of Cabinet towards questions of a trade policy for Papua and New Guinea. The Territory needed an economic foundation, I said. How far would Australia go in modifying her own domestic policies in order to help build that foundation? How far would Australia go in modifying the trade arrangements made with other countries in the interest of the Australian economy and thus avoid any adverse impact on the opportunities for Papua and New Guinea exports on the Australian market? I am not at liberty to discuss Cabinet business in detail but will recount enough to show what I was trying to do. In November 1960 Lambert's work on trade policy and economic development resulted in the drafting of a Cabinet submission. I asked Cabinet to approve that Papua and New Guinea exports complementary to the Australian economy be given an assured market in Australia, price for price and quality for quality; that, in respect of these industries, the Australian Tariff Board be asked to advise on the level of tariff protection in Australia needed to give this assured market and that the Department of Trade be asked to take certain steps in regard to trade agreements with other countries; that Papua and New Guinea exports such as plywood, passion-fruit juice and peanuts be regarded in the same way as the same commodities produced in Australia for marketing purposes in Australia; and that Cabinet approve the policy of encouraging the development of local consumption industries in Papua and New Guinea even where this might mean protection under the Territory tariff system against some Australian products.

At least I was frank about what the Australian Government would need to do if it wanted to encourage the economic development of the Territory. The most I got at the time was a decision that further work was to be done on the subject by an inter-departmental committee and subsequently a Cabinet committee. The Ministers and Departments designated for the work were Territories, Trade, Treasury, National Development and Primary Industry. We did not get very far very fast. The inter-departmental committee held several meetings in 1961 and produced several papers on a number of current problems and had a useful effect both in identifying some of the problems and improving the education of officers. I cannot recall that the Cabinet committee produced anything of value to us in my time.

During this period I had been trying to get a more comprehensive survey of the whole question of development. In January 1959 Lambert and I had long discussions. He was probably the strongest single influence on me in these matters. He was a practical operator and very tenacious, knowledgeable and competent in dealing with one tough problem after another but he tended to see a succession of administrative tasks rather than an overall picture of the Territory. I wanted an overall strategy and a comprehensive view of the economy. Looking outside the official circle, I could find some academic work on particular topics but no soundly based description or discussion of the Territory economy as it was now and as it could be.

Towards the end of 1960 Lambert and I discussed again the need for a comprehensive survey of the whole question of development. Lambert brought under my notice the reports published by the International Bank for Reconstruction and Development on Nigeria and Thailand. That was the sort of thing we needed. My memory is that at first Lambert had in mind organizing a group from Australian resources to do a similar job for us. The people we thought about, both academic and administrative, were already very busy and there was faint hope of getting full-time work from them. After studying the reports on Nigeria and Thailand I had doubts whether we could obtain the services of qualified persons from any other quarter than the World Bank, and in a minute of 13 December 1960 asked Lambert to examine further the prospect of obtaining the help of a mission from the bank. I suggested consultation with the Treasury, which had administrative responsibility for Australian interests in the bank and with the Department of External Affairs and said this should be followed by a submission to Cabinet recommending that the Government request the bank to appoint a mission and setting out the proposed terms of reference. I asked for a draft of the submission 'as early as possible in the New Year'. This was the beginning of something which two years later a United Nations visiting mission took the credit for suggesting.

Late in 1961 I made an attempt myself to survey the whole subject when I accepted an invitation from the New South Wales branch of the Economic Society of Australia and New Zealand to speak on the economic development of Papua and New Guinea. I worked hard at this paper, calling on the Department for facts and figures. The address is my own composition and I think it was the first broad survey of its kind presented to the Australian public or to Australian economists. In writing it I was mindful of the fact that Cabinet had not fully endorsed my own views and that as a Minister I could go no further than the Government would be prepared to go in stating policy. Hence I sometimes described the issues to be decided, without venturing on a decision or even a personal opinion. The paper, 'The economic development of Papua and New Guinea', has been published in full, first in the *Australian Outlook*, vol. 16, no. 1, and second as a separate publication by the Commonwealth Government Printer, and, since it is readily available, I commend it to the reader's notice as a more complete statement on economic development, as seen in the middle of 1961, than anything I can write here. It is an essential supplement to the present chapter.

There was a good audience when I delivered the paper. They listened attentively. I had hoped for much from the discussion. Some of the economists might give me a lead. All I remember is that one member of the audience delivered himself of what sounded like an undergraduate's tutorial essay on the economies of primitive societies in Africa, and another person, not an economist, expounded at length on my alleged failure to develop an 'elite' in Papua and New Guinea. I was disappointed at the time. Perhaps the silence of the economists, either at the meeting or at the subsequent reading of the paper, which was widely distributed, meant that they acquiesced in my conclusion:

Because of lack of suitable raw materials and lack of human skills, the economy of Papua and New Guinea must depend chiefly on agriculture for development for some years to come. This will require continual expansion of markets for a comparatively narrow range of tropical products, already in some cases in adequate or over-supply.

The present budget is financed two-thirds by Commonwealth grant and much of the social service coverage (e.g. education and health) is inadequate. Similarly the economic capital structure (e.g. public works and training for employment) is incomplete.

Population increases resulting from present policies will add to the budgetary and practical difficulties unless economic development keeps ahead of population increases.

Pressures for early self-government will result in self-government before the country can be properly prepared economically (apart from institutionally, administratively, socially and politically) to sustain itself. It will be necessary therefore to rely on external aid—chiefly from Australia, but possibly also from international agencies—for at least several decades . . . The economic reality is that Papua and New Guinea is a dependent territory and will continue in fact to be dependent on someone for very many years to come.

That was the way we saw the situation in 1961. Having this view, we had devoted a large part of our activities in the previous five years to the promotion of new crops that might be marketable either as exports or locally in replacement of imports. Among the best commercial hopes for new exports were fibres, tea and pyrethrum.

In the Territory some research work was being done on the growing and processing of hard fibres. As customary we tried to interest possible users of the product. In a minute of 27 November 1957, on a departmental submission proposing certain discussions, I wrote,

I regard this field of possible development as of the highest importance for the Territory because of the size of the potential Australian market if Papua and New Guinea can produce suitable fibres, the strategic and economic importance to Australia of supply, and the probable suitability of fibre production for PNG social, agricultural and economic conditions.

What I meant in the third point was that the fibre crops could be readily grown by the native people on their own land and the produce delivered to processing factories in their own districts without the need for change in landholding or transfers of labour. There could also be immediate or early payment for the product after delivery. Local processing works would provide some opportunity for local wage labour. I saw the development of tea growing in much the same way.

My minute about fibres instructed the Department to follow up the opportunity 'far more enthusiastically and energetically' than they had proposed, to broaden the discussions and to try to arrange a visit to the Territory by the potential users and to bring the officers engaged in the fibre experiments into the discussions. I asked the officers to have in mind that 'the promotion of fibre production in the Territory, if investigations prove that it is warranted, would be given a high priority in our agricultural programme'. My imagination was stimulated by the enormous demand in Australia for hard fibres for cordage, containers (including wool bales), carpets and upholstery backing. Our experiments at that stage concerned sisal, agave, manila hemp and New Zealand flax, with a continuing interest in kenaf. Wood gave me a report on progress in March 1958. 'This is a hopeful beginning', I minuted on 25 March. 'Please press ahead vigorously with this project.'

Representatives of various Australian interests were taken on a visit to the Territory and were reported to be impressed by the possibilities. In August 1958, after reviewing progress, I directed that a commercial pilot project be undertaken as early as possible and all reasonable steps taken to maintain the interest of the Australian commercial users of fibres. 'Beyond the economic activities already established', I wrote, 'I can see no agricultural development that offers better opportunities than fibres for giving a stronger economic foundation for Territory progress.' (Minute of 4 August 1958.) We also tried to rouse the interest of overseas concerns. In this connection we arranged a visit by an East African expert on sisal, G. W. Lock, who investigated the potential on behalf of a large London company. He said in effect that no part of New Guinea was as good as East Africa. My Canberra officers were much discouraged and thought we should discontinue our experiments. I supported the more hopeful Territory workers and in a minute of 27 January 1960 summed up my views about 'our enduring problem of broadening the economic foundations of the Territory':

> In coarse fibres we have in Australia one of the largest potential markets so far untouched by Papua and New Guinea. Potentially it is probably a larger market than that available to any of the established products of the Territory. The need for income-producing crops for native land-owners and the need for job-creating industries are both so important that, unless the discouragements are overwhelming, we have to increase and diversify our efforts to find opportunities for developing towards both aims. We can use the Lock report to help in the sound and practical planning of our experimental work on fibres but at this stage I regard it as an argument for doing more work on all fibres and certainly not as an argument for doing less.

Towards the end of the year I reaffirmed this view and gave a further policy direction that the Administration was to give a high priority to investigational and developmental work on hard fibres of all kinds covering the growing, processing and industrial use of them. (Minute of 21 November 1960.)

My approach to tea was similar. Since our early experiments at Garaina, some Europeans had made plantings, notably Bobby Gibbes, at his plantation, Tremearne, in the Sepik district. That redoubtable war-time aviator and airline pioneer in the Sepik had some hundreds of acres. I called on him at Tremearne more than once and was infected by his enthusiasm, even if a little doubtful about a leaf-plucking contraption he had built and demonstrated on one occasion in a way that suggested it might have more interest for the Defence Department as an agent of devastation than for planters. The tea I drank at his place was agreeable. I took some packets of it to Australia and the Cabinet attendant, Alf Stafford, co-operated in putting it into the Cabinet teapot for afternoon tea during one series of Cabinet meetings. My colleagues conceded that it was very much better than Bishop Scharmach's black cigars, which had been placed in the Cabinet box on a previous occasion. Other Australian friends said it was 'quite good'. We could grow palatable tea.

My own conception of the future of the industry was that the tea would be grown by indigenous farmers on their own land and delivered promptly to a factory established at a focal point. As an attraction to the European investment needed to establish the factory, I was prepared to grant a limited percentage of the land for European planting with stipulations that the factory handle native leaf. The problem was to find a large enough area of suitable land for such a group scheme and then to find the European investor and skilled tea manufacturer to join the scheme.

The planting of pyrethrum was commenced in the highlands under plans developed by Henderson, and steps were taken to interest overseas users of the product. There was a steady though limited market for the product in Australia for the manufacture of insecticides and I suggested that as a first stage we go ahead purposefully to get the whole of the Australian market. (Minute of 3 July 1961.)

For the replacement of imports we concentrated on food crops and meat production. In June 1956 I had again given the direction, 'The encouragement of the local production of foodstuffs is to be kept in the forefront of agricultural policy.' (Minute of 5 June 1956.) This emphasis on food production was renewed in January 1958. Discussing the action plan for rice growing, I wrote of the need to reduce expenditure on imports as well as to increase export income. Necessarily during the period of expansion and capital development the value of imports would exceed the value of exports, but we should try to bring them more nearly into balance. My minute continued,

> Another growing problem is the provision of occupation and a cash income for the indigenous people as they advance towards civilization. Not all of them will be able to grow cocoa, coffee and the like which produce big money but some will grow food crops for sale to others. The growing of food crops is also a useful beginning in cash cropping in the transitional period before the people are very far advanced, because the link between production and sale is much closer than in the case of export crops . . . Food production will also be of importance with the introduction of industries requiring labour. In food production, rice has the advantage over many other commodities inasmuch as it can be stored and used under a variety of conditions. Whereas at the present time we have a local market worth one million pounds a year, I am convinced that, with the growth of local industry and with the raising of nutritional standards, the local market could very soon be ten times as much. Rice may come to represent one of the main economic opportunities for the indigenous people who stay on the land and, even if that opportunity lies in the future, we have to lay the foundations now so that it may be grasped in due time . . . The objective is to grow in the Territory at least all the rice which the Territory consumes. This is not just a matter of agricultural practice (as the Territory Administration so often regards it) but a matter related to the economy of the Territory and the founding of industries for the Territory. [Minute of 24 January 1958.]

This minute arose from a report which Wood had submitted on the annual report by the Administrator on the rice action plan. Wood's analysis of the reasons for lack of progress impressed me as cogent. He said that most of the local pressure on the Territory Department of Agriculture came from the Europeans, who wanted to know about cocoa, coffee, rubber and copra but not about rice growing, and the Territory Department of Agriculture responded to the pressure. Another reason was that, largely as the result of the Poggendorff report, a wrong emphasis was being given to the idea of producing rice on a large scale commercially with irrigation and the maximum use of mechanization. While this might be the best method in the long term, the best prospect in the short term was upland rice on village holdings and from mechanized European farms without irrigation. A third reason was that an artificially low price was being paid for Australian-grown rice, and the incentive to local growers was less than it might be. In some places there was 'insufficient enthusiasm' by some Administration officers and it seemed that there was even active discouragement to the native people against growing rice because a local officer had his own opinion that it was better for them to plant something else. (Submission of 19 December 1957 and minute of 23 December 1957.)

Efforts I had inaugurated soon after taking office to promote the cattle industry had not yielded the results for which I had hoped. There were several reasons for this, not the least being that suitable cattle from Australian areas free of disease and tick were not easy to obtain and transport was difficult to arrange. No cattle boats were available to carry beasts in large numbers. Another reason was the simple fact that cattle do not reproduce their kind quickly. Another was the limited availability of readily accessible pasture and, linked with that, the difficulty of internal movement of stock to the pasture from the port of entry. Some of the slowness in overcoming such problems may have been the fault of the Animal Industry Division, which was made the subject of an organization and methods investigation at the instance of the Public Service Commissioner and Lambert in 1957 and 1958. Quite separately and without touching on the functioning of the Territory Public Service, I initiated in December 1957 an investigation by A. L. Rose into the possibilities of cattle raising with a view primarily to the production of meat for local consumption. Rose, who was Director of Animal Industry in the Northern Territory, was well known to me and I had a very high admiration for the work he had done officially in the post-war re-establishment of the cattle industry in the Northern Territory. I drafted the terms of reference for his inquiry after consultation with him. It might be worth explaining that one of my original terms, 'Training and providing of employment for native people in the livestock industry', was deleted only because Rose, in characteristic fashion, said that although he knew a lot about cattle, he did not pretend to know anything about people.

Rose made an interim report in November 1958 and the Administrator was asked to submit his comments and proposals as early as possible. The immediate objective I then had in view was to build up the existing strength of 17 000 head of cattle in the Territory to a mixed herd of about 70 000 head to provide 15 000 carcasses a year, that being the equivalent of the current rate of meat imports into the Territory. In the development of the industry, the native people were to be trained both to be stockmen and to manage small herds of their own on their own land. In cattle raising, except when grazing on the cover crops on coconut plantations, the size of a herd would be limited by the area of land available in one block under native custom.

From this point we began to see some progress towards our objectives and also started to interest the native people themselves in cattle raising. Having regard both to the availability of land and the capacity of the native husbandman, this meant a scheme for small-holders in the highlands. There were many strange problems of animal husbandry to be mastered, for the native people's experience with stock hitherto had not gone beyond pigs and poultry which rooted, pecked and rambled at will.

At an early stage in our work on the development of resources, we had become aware of the difficulty of raising capital for developmental projects. With agriculture as the main prospect, this largely meant capital for the individual farmer to establish his farm or plantation. The problem was seen in part as the provision of credit facilities, and some constructive work was done in the Department. We had established a native loans fund in 1955 for furthering native economic projects in primary and secondary industries and in commerce with a limit of £5000 for any one borrower. A long minute I wrote in September 1956, reviewing and commending the work the Department had been doing in this field, also sets out very fully the views I held then about the pace of economic development and the balance that should be kept 'between the rate of development in European settlement, with its demand for land and labour, and the development of agricultural production by the native people'. All the pressure and the strong interest of officials both in the Department and in the Administration was in respect of European economic ventures, and some officers were eager to promote settlement in a bigger way. I found a need for repeated emphasis of other aims. In this particular minute I asked whether, in addition to our control over the granting of land, we should influence the rate of development of land by the use of the machinery through which credit was made available. One reason for using credit facilities as well as the granting of land as a means of keeping a balance arose from the varying conditions in the Territory and the need to observe the local situations accurately and make a number of 'successive and separate decisions to meet the variations that are observed between one place and another and from one time to another'. Some land held by Europeans had never been in our control and some passed out of our control by being granted to applicants. My minute continued,

> The encouragement of European settlement, intermingled with native settlement, is one of the aims of policy. Normally the Government would prefer the financing of European settlers to be left to the banks and it is only to the extent that the banks are unable or unwilling to finance the individual European settler that Government intervention would be favoured. At this stage of the Territory's history it would be desirable that any machinery set up for providing credit for agricultural settlement by Europeans should be under the control of the Minister to a sufficient extent to ensure that its activities did not run counter to any directions given on overall policy. For example, we would not wish to see a credit institution promoting a demand for new agricultural land by Europeans at a time when land was not being made available or creating a demand for native labour at a time when recruitment of labour was being restricted.

I suggested that there be separate machinery to provide credit facilities for native farmers and for Europeans. An important part of the machinery for native credit facilities would be the education of the native client both in farming and in financial responsibility. For the sake of this tutelage and to avoid the ill-consequences of native land-owners becoming subject to moneylenders, it was desirable that only a government institution provide credit facilities for the native farmers 'at least during the early years of their enterprise'. I stressed the urgency and wrote,

> This urgency extends to credit facilities for natives as well as Europeans. We could certainly make a start with credit in respect of land already held by Europeans or at present open to application by them, but we could not go far with a credit scheme for Europeans which encouraged further settlement unless at the same time we had in operation a scheme which would promote further activity by native farmers, either as individuals or in groups. In this connexion I think that we have to look beyond the co-operative movement, which has served and will continue to serve a useful purpose in stimulating some native enterprise and participation by them in the development of resources, to the requirements of individual native enterprise. The suggestion in the departmental memorandum that there is at present little demand by natives for credit and that advantage has not been taken of the money available under the Native Loan Funds Ordinance seems to me to tell only half the story. We cannot wait passively. It is part of our problem and part of our task to promote agricultural development among the native people. Our agricultural extension work, which had as one of its primary aims the production of more and better food for local consumption is already moving into the teaching of farming for cash and must move further in the same direction. Policy requires that native agriculture advances before European settlement advances. We want both. You must get one before you get the other. In all our economic developmental planning for the Territory, native agriculture is an essential element because the extent of European development of resources has to be related at all times to the possible degree of native participation in that development. I regard proposals for credit facilities for natives as being a natural outcome of a policy which educates natives, which retains land in their ownership and which teaches them better agriculture. We need these facilities if our policy is to flower and bear fruit.

I asked the Department to 'move as quickly as possible and . . . take it up with the Administrator at once'. (Minute of 6 September 1956.)

In this connection I was cautious about proposals for war service land settlement in the Territory. There was a good deal of pressure on me from a group of members in the Government party room, from returned servicemen's organizations and from individual ex-soldiers in the Territory to extend the Australian scheme of war service land settlement to the Territory. At the departmental level such ideas were resisted both by Treasury and by the Department of Primary Industry, largely on the grounds that a scheme devised for Australian land settlement was inapplicable to European settlement for tropical agriculture in Papua and New Guinea. My own view was that, as a matter of equity, we should not deny to returned soldiers in the Territory benefits already available to returned soldiers on the mainland, but that we should not use war service land settlement as 'a means of attracting new settlers or of sponsoring any large-scale scheme of assisted land settlement. We should not seek to take up a large area of land for soldier settlement but rather help to finance returned soldiers on properties interspersed among other properties held under normal conditions'. (Minute of 19 April 1956.) After protracted discussions to overcome the objections of other Australian departments, a Cabinet submission was made in October 1957 and approval obtained for working out a limited scheme. It finally took shape, not as a settlement scheme, but as a scheme for providing credit for ex-service settlers in Papua and New Guinea who were already occupying agricultural land holdings in the Territory or who had lived in the Territory for at least five years and obtained holdings through the normal method of application for land advertised as available for leasing. I announced it on 23 May 1958. This scheme was also extended to native ex-servicemen, although at a different scale of advances, having regard to different requirements in respect of acquisition of land, costs of establishment and differences in production capacity, and their other financial resources.

After a lapse of years, a younger generation may be unaware of the comradeship of war between Papuans and Australians in the New Guinea campaigns. The Papuan Infantry Battalion, raised from volunteers, was among the first Allied troops to engage the enemy when their country was invaded in July 1942, and this and other native units continued to fight alongside Australian troops until 1945, developing great skill in jungle warfare. At the end of 1944, as well as over 35 000 native labourers working in the forces, there were approximately 6500 men in uniform and thousands more employed as guerillas and locally recruited carriers. After the war, they continued their association with Australian soldiers as members of the Returned Soldiers League in Papua and New Guinea. The league, under the leadership for most of the time of R. Bunting,[53] played a highly useful role in the community both in the public-spirited way it took part in the life of the community and in the way it helped to promote the advancement of the indigenous people and better relations between them and the Australians. The European members of the league who had served in Papua and New Guinea had good reason to respect their war-time colleagues and they honoured in peace time the claim of comradeship.

The credit assistance given to native ex-servicemen was accompanied by special help from agricultural extension officers and, to make sure that they understood the scheme, a special advisory committee toured the Territory to discuss it with them. As an illustration of the scope of the scheme, in the second year of its operation, certificates of eligibility were issued to 46 Australian and 252 native applicants.

Under the Native Loans Fund Ordinance of 1955, loans could be made to co-operative societies, local government councils, other groups of indigenes and to individuals. Its purpose was to provide credit for indigenous persons who lacked tangible security. At first, very little advantage was taken of the opportunity but in about 1959–60 the interest began to quicken and thereafter some hundreds of organizations and individuals received loans for plant and equipment and for land development. The scheme was enlarged and amended to meet the new conditions.

While still keeping the objective of a balance between European enterprise in agriculture and the progress of native agriculture, about 1961 I began to see an emerging need to do something about credit facilities in the Territory for development generally instead of relying on the commercial banking system to provide what was required under the standard banker-customer relationship. The role in the Australian Territories of the recently established Commonwealth Development Bank was also under discussion among departments in Canberra. Lambert put the problem to the inter-departmental committee on trade policies, saying that most of the bank lending in the Territory was for short-term and intermediate credit, such as temporary advances to cover requirements until crops were marketed. Would the banks undertake the long-term lending that had been a feature of rural development in Australia? They might feel uncertainty about the long-term prospects for tropical products and about the political future. The committee had before it figures showing that the ratio of advances to deposits in the banks in Papua and New Guinea was about 34 per cent whereas in Australia it was about 60 per cent. As one outcome of this discussion, I wrote to the Treasurer on 14 April 1961 asking if he would take steps to ensure that the banks gave closer and more sympathetic attention to the needs of the Territory for credit.

The examination of this question and the related question of capital formation continued and in September I asked Lambert to extend the discussion to the Australian National University, where Crawford had become Vice-Chancellor, and to the Development Bank. (Minute of 11 September 1961.) We did not get very far during my term as Minister. The question was a complex one and some relevant information was not available readily or exactly. The more people we consulted, the stronger the argument became for a comprehensive investigation by several different kinds of experts. There was a real shortage of qualified persons, free from other commitments, to devote much time to the task. Perhaps the chief reason that little progress was made was that the prospects of obtaining a broad examination of the economy of the Territory by a mission from the World Bank, as a result of the move made by me in December 1960, led to a tendency to defer this single problem until the fuller report had been made. Unfortunately, for a variety of causes beyond our control the World Bank mission was not able to commence its work until 1962.

My own inclination would have been towards greater use of public funds through a public authority established in the Territory and operating mainly to finance development by native people. I reached this state of mind mainly because I thought that in all steps for economic development there should be opportunity for indigenous participation or arrangements under which in the future the ownership and exploitation of the country's resources would be accessible to the indigenous people by peaceful and legal transfer and not by expropriation. I also had a view that the opportunities visible in the 1950s were not such as to attract foreign investment except on terms that in the long run would be against the interests of the country and the people. Economically there were few chances of marriage and many risks of seduction. But the opportunity to test my doctrine did not arise and, if it had, I know I would have had lots of trouble with that section of my party room which had made a sacred text of private enterprise.

Continually, in all phases of our work for economic development, I felt the need to keep on preaching about the predominant interest of the native people.

In some cases I may have been preaching to the converted, but in economic projects I found there was still a good deal of heathen blindness and some sophisticated scepticism both among our own officers and among members of the public concerned with Territory affairs. Three phases of my preaching concerned land tenure, the need for resettlement as a means of improving the access to land by those who would use it to economic advantage, and the training of the native farmers. The questions of land tenure and resettlement will be dealt with in the next chapter.

The training of native farmers was a more straightforward task. I thought of training at two levels: the first, helping the native people who were already gardeners or farmers to be better farmers and gardeners and to learn about new crops, new implements and new methods; the second, giving higher training in agriculture to persons who already had the required basic education. In a minute of 1 August 1956 I stated the aim of creating in the Territory an agricultural college with a standing in tropical agriculture comparable with that of the agricultural colleges on the Australian mainland in temperate-zone agriculture. A departmental officer, J. O. Smith,[54] made an investigation and report and, following further work on it by Swift and discussions with Territory officers, I approved of the recommendations and asked the Administration to prepare plans to implement them. (Minute of 10 October 1957.) Progress was slow. In a press statement of 6 November 1959 I announced a plan for teaching agricultural subjects in primary and secondary schools, forming agricultural project clubs, establishing local agriculture schools in co-operation with local government councils, and establishing district boarding schools of agriculture. These were still only plans.

Progress in agricultural extension work among native people was more readily attainable. There had been some extension work for some time and, at a conference with Cleland and Lambert in my office in Canberra in February 1956, I tried to clarify policy and directed that the effort be increased. A little over a year later in April 1957 I marked a departmental paper on the situation for the Administrator's attention and directed that further work be done in collaboration between the Department and the Administration. After several reminders, we received a document from the Administrator in October 1957. I approved parts of it but asked that other parts be reconsidered.

About the same time, in response to a request for an assessment of what was already done, I received a report from the Administrator on work in advancing native agriculture during the financial year 1956–7. The analysis of this report by Wood showed some encouraging results in various districts. In one district, village agricultural committees were operating. In others, native income from copra had improved as a result of the introduction of inspection of the product for quality and supervised marketing. In one district, producers' co-operative societies had been accepted and, in other districts, a rural progress society was the instrument for introducing new crops and marketing the produce. Agriculture officers had supervised the operation of central fermentaries for native cocoa growers in the Gazelle Peninsula. Throughout the Territory, better use was being made of native agricultural assistants and trainees in extension work. But the effort was still somewhat sporadic and there seemed to be no clear view of the overall purpose. I pressed for the views of the Administration and the Department on a more comprehensive and more intensive effort and for a clearer directive on policy.

No submission was received by me until 5 November 1958 when a Federal election campaign was in full swing and the papers were laid aside until it was known that the Government had been returned and that I was still Minister for Territories. One of my first actions in my new term was to redraft the paper the Department had prepared setting out the objectives of agricultural extension work, and on 8 January 1959 I returned the papers with my own draft of the 'Aims' and, in a covering minute, wrote,

> I regard the work of agricultural extension among the native people of Papua and New Guinea as having one of the highest priorities in our work in the Territory. In the next three years increasing effort is to be put into this phase of our work. On the one hand the purpose is to improve the food supply of those people who are still living in the villages and on the other hand it is the intention to use this native agricultural extension work as part of the much more intensive work which we have to do from now onwards in providing a better economic foundation for the life of the Territory. As you are aware, I have always held the view that the native people already have the land and the manpower. They also have in most districts a tradition of gardening and an interest in agricultural enterprise. The surest and most permanent way towards getting certain forms of economic development in the Territory is through the improvement of native agriculture. We should realize that the economic strength of the Territory is increased when local production can supplement imported foodstuffs to a greater extent as well as when local production becomes available for export. We should have both aspects of economic development in mind when we give our attention to extension work among the native people. Moreover the high educational value of this work cannot be overstressed. It is a point, like health measures, at which our efforts for the native people touch something which is directly understandable by them and is seen as directly affecting their welfare. [Minute of 8 January 1959.]

My revision of the draft statement submitted by the Department set down the aims of agricultural extension work as follows:

1. The aims of agricultural extension among the peoples of Papua and New Guinea are:
   (a) to raise the level of subsistence in the villages by
      (i) improving the nutritional value of the foods eaten;
      (ii) introducing new foods;
      (iii) ensuring a year-round supply of food.
   (b) to introduce the economic means of supporting a higher standard of living by
      (i) introducing crops and stock suitable for production for sale having regard to the situation and circumstances of each village;
      (ii) assisting in the disposal of the produce;
      (iii) introducing, where necessary, the plant and equipment for the processing, storing and marketing of such produce;
      (iv) educating the village people in technical and commercial procedures.

(c) to assist to bring about the optimum use of the agricultural (including pastoral) resources of the Territory and to contribute to an increase in agricultural production in the Territory;

(d) to contribute to the educational advancement of the people both by technical training and by a change in their interests and outlook;

(e) in serving the above aims to improve the methods of native agriculture including methods of selecting, clearing, enclosing and cultivating land, the rotation of crops, the use of better implements, animal husbandry, fish farming, poultry raising, and all farm and garden practice.

2. These aims, while primarily the concern of the Agricultural Extension Service, can only be fully achieved by co-operation among officers of many branches of the Territorial Public Service, in particular Native Affairs, Education, Health and Lands. District Commissioners have the responsibility of ensuring that co-operation takes place according to the needs and opportunities in each district.

The remainder of the statement set out some of the practical measures to be taken to give effect to this new directive and listed in some detail the duties of agricultural extension officers. I elaborated some of the problems. There were hundreds of thousands of native farmers to be reached. With the present levels of social and educational advancement it was impossible for most of the native farming community to understand land-use procedures in the way that Europeans did. Hence consultation with the native population was a necessity, but close attention had to be paid to the correct timing of approaches to the native communities. For the present it could be expected that change would come in local, not Territory-wide, changes and hence the extension service would have to carry the responsibility of moulding local trends to an overall national policy. Native farmers and gardeners often might have motives and incentives different from those of the Australians, and the extension officer should appreciate that there were psychological and social problems as well as agricultural problems in introducing changes. Change could only be effective if made voluntarily by the native people, and hence change would have to be gradual to be permanent. I also pointed out that the full attainment of the objectives would depend on the completion of the investigations being made by the Department of Agriculture to find what were the most appropriate systems of agriculture for each environment of the Territory.

The instructions left considerable flexibility about the methods to be used in arousing the interest and organizing the effort of the native farmers in making changes. Rural progress societies, co-operative societies, private enterprise, and other methods could be used as required by local circumstances. I had observed in the Territory a tendency by some of our best European officers to become the dedicated apostles for one preferred method and to regard the only sign of success to be the creation of the sort of organization they favoured. I thought we should be less rigid.

One of the consequences of this directive was the preparation of a report entitled 'Forward Planning for Agricultural Extension Work' by the Administration and Department working in collaboration. Main credit for this very useful report belongs to Wood and J. O. Smith, of the Department. It set out a three-year plan, starting in the current financial year (1959–60), and its proposals were approved by me on the day they were received, for I had been kept in touch with what was being examined by the officers. Agricultural extension was to be intensified in the next three years by increasing the number of native agricultural assistants by 180 to a total of 300, completing the agricultural training programme to a stage when over 1000 native farmers would be trained each year, increasing the number of extension stations and adding to them extension centres to a combined total of 52, recruiting officers to the professional staff and 10 project managers, increasing patrolling, and forming three regional extension teams to provide services for native demands for development arising unexpectedly in various parts of the Territory. These and accompanying measures, including new methods and aids for demonstrations and training, were expected to bring widespread improvement in native agricultural practice. The effect on increased production of food crops either for subsistence or sale could not be estimated, but in copra, cocoa and coffee it was estimated that the potential production of the plantings at the end of the three-year period would mean a doubling of income from copra, a tenfold increase in coffee and a fivefold increase in cocoa.

In approving the plan, I said that the programme was to be reviewed at the end of twelve months to see whether it could be further expanded or whether any adjustment was needed. I expressed appreciation to the officers concerned for 'their useful report and recommendations'. (Submission and minute of 25 November 1959.) For once I was pleased and hopeful. Already our earlier efforts were showing results. In a press statement on 30 October I had reported that the estimated value of cash crops produced by native growers had risen from £1·7 million in 1957–8 to £2·4 million in 1958–9. I now confidently believed that in a few years their income might well be ten times as much.

At the end of the first twelve months, in approving of some adjustments, mainly as additions to the programme, I said that the plan was the minimum requirement and every encouragement should be given to the Agriculture Department to improve on it. (Minute of 24 January 1961.) A year later another satisfactory report was made. At the end of the third year, the plan was lagging only in the construction of some of the necessary buildings. I made encouraging noises and repeated, 'This is a key activity in our economic planning.' (Minute of 22 March 1962.)

The plan approved in November 1959 was extended in October 1962 when I approved a five-year plan of extension work under which professional extension staff would be raised to 240 and the number of indigenous agricultural assistants to 900; further training colleges and extension centres were to be established and patrolling increased.

The Agriculture Department did the work well. Henderson was a forceful and practical director. In spite of some difficulties in recruiting, he brought together a keen and active team of young officers and the response from the native people was good, for this was a field in which we were trying to fill a need that many of them had already realized for themselves. The work had its own complications and for a fuller understanding of the underlying problems I commend to notice an article by W. L. Conroy, 'Traditions and Trends in agriculture'.*

During this period we also gave further attention to some of the tasks ancillary to economic development.

On one of my visits to the Territory towards the end of 1959 I formed the impression that the allocation of money for roads had been rather haphazard, responding to pressing needs rather than making forward programmes, and that some of the road expenditure had been wasteful. Contrary to my expectation, no comprehensive plan of road building had been drawn up by the Administration. It was apparent too that we were now about to enter on a difficult period in the maintenance of those roads which had been pushed out into various districts with a great deal of vigour and enthusiasm by Native Affairs officers with the aid of village labour. Improvised bridges were becoming unsafe after a few years' use. Villagers were losing their enthusiasm in some districts for road building. Increased traffic, resulting from increased registration of vehicles and increased tonnages of crops to be marketed, was greater than the roads could bear. I asked the Department to obtain information for the shaping of an overall roads policy and a road works programme for the whole Territory. (Minute of 22 December 1959.)

Further discussions with the Administrator followed. We made some improvement but not as much as I would have hoped. At the same period the increased volume of cargo for transport to inland centres, following our rapid development, set us new problems of converting temporary airstrips built by patrol officers into landing grounds suitable for heavier aircraft. Moreover the growing interest in Papua and New Guinea had brought closer and more exacting supervision of aerodromes and aircraft by the Australian Department of Civil Aviation. The adventurous pioneering days of flying, of which so many thrilling stories can be told, were virtually over by 1959. A more sedate and safer period of flying was beginning, and one that made more exacting and more costly demands on the Administration. On my instructions, following one of my visits to the highlands, we worked out a plan for co-ordinated road and air transport, selecting certain routes for construction of major roads and, on other routes, selecting certain airfields for development as major centres for air transport with feeder roads radiating from them. Although this plan did not come into full effect in my time, a beginning was made. Our real shortcoming was in the planning and building capacity in the Territory either from public authority or private contractors. We had ideas but lacked strength.

Another good beginning was in the creation of the Electricity Commission. Steadily over the years the electricity supply in all the main centres had been greatly improved and a commencement had been made with a major hydroelectric generating system for Port Moresby. At the beginning of 1959 I approved the establishment of an Electricity Commission to control the generation and distribution of electricity throughout the Territory. It eventually came into operation in 1961.

Early in 1956, good progress having been made in re-establishing the ports of the Territory and improving the facilities, Lambert and I discussed the ques-

* *Australian Territories*, vol. 2, no. 4 (July 1962), pp. 21-7.

tion of better control of ports and harbours. Lattin made a preliminary survey of the problems. He continued his work and early in 1957 presented a fuller report and used it as the basis for a conference with Administration officers in Port Moresby in March. It was a good piece of work. In expressing my appreciation of Lattin's report, I used the phrase 'careful, thorough and perceptive'. (Minute of 2 April 1957.)

Subsequent work in the Territory was slower. There was some resistance in the Administration, which still wanted to have the direct handling of almost everything in the Territory and did not care for the idea of independent authorities. There was also a lot of argument during the preparation of legislation to create a Harbours Board. I lost patience in January 1960 and entered again into a matter I had hoped would have been concluded in the Territory once the direction to create a port authority had been given. The Administration doubted whether the time had yet arrived for having a Harbours Board. If there were a board, they doubted whether it should handle its own finances or employ or control staff of its own. They thought the Administration should still handle all waterside labour. They wanted to create port advisory committees, very narrowly representative, to be a check on the activities of any board. They were unsure whether the board should control all ports. I wrote, 'I favour a single port authority for the Territory and think it should be a real authority.' (Minute of 20 January 1960.) I gave them a hurry-up in March and received a submission in July. The Administration was still hesitant. I referred to their proposals for a board with limited functions as a 'half-emerged chicken'. I was unconvinced by their views about the port advisory committees. They wanted them to be composed of 'level-headed businessmen' while I insisted that they should be fully representative of all interests and should include a native member as representative of waterside labour. (Minute of 5 July 1960.) Although the decision was made by me in 1960, the ordinance creating the Harbours Board did not get through the Legislative Council until 1963.

The decision on the creation of a port authority was clear and was conveyed to the Administrator in November 1960 and was publicly announced. Two-and-a-half years later it had not been applied. A note I wrote in June 1963 exposes a situation that in this and other matters caused me great concern. We were being defeated by the bureaucracy that was growing up in the Territory. I pointed out that before the decision was made all aspects of the matter had been considered and considerations of policy and practical advantage weighed. It was always open to the Administrator himself to ask the Government to reconsider a decision, but he should submit his view promptly to the Minister and state his grounds clearly and cogently so that an immediate decision could be made as to whether the matter should be re-examined. It was a matter of considerable concern to the Government that a decision of the Government was not immediately questioned (and indeed all the indications on files in Canberra were that steps were being taken to implement the decision), that at no stage did the Administrator personally make any recommendation that required the Minister to reconsider the decision but that, as the result largely of work being done at less senior levels of the Administration, no effect had yet been given to the decision. The plain fact was that a decision of major importance conveyed to the Administrator on 11 November 1960 had not yet been carried out two-and-a-half years later. 'I am almost in despair', I wrote, 'over getting anything done in Papua and New Guinea when I find that decisions lead to no action unless I personally follow up every step of the consequential proceedings.' (Minute of 21 June 1963.)

In addition to the statutory authorities to handle utilities, we also sought to strengthen the Administration on the economic side. As previously recounted a Department of Labour and a Department of Trade and Industry were created early in 1961. Later in the year, when we revised the upper structure of the Administration and created a second position of Assistant Administrator, the reallocation of duties made one of the two Assistant Administrators responsible for Economic Affairs. Reeve was promoted to the post.

[27]

ACCESS TO LAND

In the attempt to improve and extend farming by the indigenous people, we came up against the problem of the availability of land. I had checked the alienating of land for use by the white settler. We now had to face the fact that land retained in native ownership was not always available for the native farmers who were ready to work it for a cash income. Systems of tenure which had been developed in a subsistence economy among clans sufficient to themselves were not suited to a cash economy, in which crops were grown for export, a long-term yield was sought from tree crops, and capital investment was made for implements, plant and machinery.

The use of land under the old system was not exclusive or comprehensive for one farmer but might be subject to the rights held by others in respect of hunting, gathering of jungle fruits, or materials for building. The old system did not always provide for one man a large enough area to sustain an economic operation linked with export marketing or with sale of the product in other parts of the Territory.

The socialization of farming or collective farms or the co-operative society did not seem to offer the answer. Emerging from a subsistence economy to a cash economy, the indigenous community produced individual enterprise. The exceptional, go-ahead, industrious man, who saw a chance to get money for his family group by organizing the labour of his family group, was a common phenomenon in agricultural development. The response to opportunity and eventually the drive to fuller use of the land came from an incipient capitalism rather than from communal effort. There may have been an element of imitation of the European way in this tendency, but it came in spite of the fact that most of the official promotion of farm development pointed towards co-operative group activities. My interpretation of the fact—I had no doctrinal leaning—is that the New Guinean is strongly individualistic.

Another aspect of the problem was the uneven distribution of fertile land. Some districts which had sustained large populations at a low level of subsistence offered few opportunities for growing cash crops for income. Yet their people, having heard or seen the success of other groups in becoming comparatively prosperous on cocoa, coffee, garden produce or some other marketable crop, were eager to do the same sort of thing for themselves. So the problem of access to land presented itself in different forms in the well-favoured districts and the less fertile districts.

In 1956 I had given direction for urgent attention to future land policy. In doing so, I expressed a doubt whether what we were doing for the registration of native land was based on a true and exact knowledge of native land rights. The work of the Native Lands Commission had revealed firstly that the system of native land-holding was much more complicated than had been thought and that it varied considerably from place to place, and secondly that the registration of native lands would probably not be completed in the lifetime of anyone now at work on it. I also expressed a doubt whether the policy we were applying would ensure that at any given time a native farmer who wanted to use land would in fact be able to obtain it. We had to make up our minds whether customary native land ownership should be altered. If there were to be a change of policy, should we make a clean break or introduce a new system gradually in successive stages in selected areas of the Territory?

In starting work on this problem, Lambert tended to concentrate, as I saw the situation at a later stage, somewhat narrowly on the problem of re-distributing land to ensure that it would be available to the native farmer who would make economic use of it. In October 1956 I authorized him to open discussions on his proposals with officers of the Administration in Port Moresby, although warning him that 'no such scheme of redistribution of land should be applied in any case without the free understanding and voluntary co-operation of the native community immediately concerned.' (Minute of 8 October 1956.)

A year later I called for the files in order to review personally the work that had been done. I found that a good deal of useful material had been gathered and the Administration had prepared some recommendations, mainly for doing further work in order to gather clear information about the existing position and the changes that would have to be made. While approving the recommendations, I spoke of the risk of placing emphasis on the production of reports without moving into action. I thought the officers needed to look at practical measures needed for redistribution of land and resettlement of people as well as at questions of land tenure, although I confessed my own uncertainty about the next practical steps to be taken. 'The immensity of the practical task', I wrote, 'is almost as staggering as the complexity of the theoretical problem.' But, I said, the problem was already acute in some districts—'for example, in the Gazelle Peninsula where the economic activity of the people is creating a demand for agricultural land that cannot be met from their own traditional system, and in the Sepik district where people who are on poor land will have no chance of sustaining a higher standard of living unless they can obtain land which will yield to them a cash income; and throughout the Wahgi Valley where the dense population which was previously located in the mountains will have to move on to the valley floor if it is to provide food for increasing numbers.' I said that, in addition to thinking about the problems of land tenure, we also had to think about the practical methods of re-settlement and the engineering works, such as drainage, that might have to be carried out before resettlement could take place. I asked for the immediate

submission of a more definite programme of the work to be done in the next
twelve months. (Minute of 22 October 1957.)

No submission was made to me, but it would seem—although on this point
I am not sure—that the views I had expressed had led officers of the Administration to go ahead with a number of detached schemes to make land available for economic ventures in various districts. In June 1959, after a period of
inattention in 1958, I asked what had been done. (Minute of 17 June 1959.)
A submission by Lambert in October 1959 led me to review again all the files
on the subject and I formed the opinion that we had not yet found a clear
answer to the preliminary questions I had posed in 1956 and, until we made
fundamental decisions for a change in lands policy, we could not make a
decision regarding the nature of a new system and the method by which a new
system should be introduced. My minute continued,

> It appears to me, both from the present papers and from many other
> indications I have seen on scattered departmental files that, in lack of a
> clear decision on the foregoing matters and in lack of any oversight by the
> Administrator, in various parts of the Territory individual officers or groups
> of officers have themselves been making a tentative approach to the settle-
> ment of these problems. We appear to have had various schemes introduced
> by local decision and without apparently complete cognisance of them by the
> Administrator. In my opinion some of these small local schemes of land
> settlement contain principles which would be unacceptable to the Govern-
> ment. It is therefore imperatively necessary for us to make at once a firm
> decision about the basic principles which have to apply in any new system of
> native land ownership. [Minute of 26 October 1959.]

To illustrate the point, I suggested some of the principles to be observed
in any new system of land tenure. I said that tenure could only be from 'the
Crown'. (That phrase, suitable for 1959, might now be better expressed as
tenure from the single sovereign authority of the State.) We could not allow
a system in which land was held under grant from any other authority and
I expressed doubt about some of the local group schemes in which a farmer's
title to the land and his tenure of it purported to be issued by a group which
itself had uncertain title and tenure. Any transfers of land should be registered
by 'the Crown' and, in all the shifts and changes of land ownership and
occupation of land, the only recognizable title should be a document issued
by 'the Crown'. Consequently all land tenure matters had to be handled
administratively through the Territory Lands Department and not concluded
by any other administrative authority. I further suggested that, unless and until
native ownership of a plot of land was converted into a title issued by 'the
Crown', the customary native land ownership was to be respected and only the
issuing of a title by 'the Crown' could affect that customary ownership or use.
The customary native land ownership could not be converted into a title except
by processes that respected the wishes of the native person who at present
claimed ownership or use of the land. I assumed that we would maintain the
principle that only the Administration could acquire land from native owners.
Would there be any distinction between (a) acquisition in order to grant
subsequently a formal and transferable title to the same owners, (b) acquisition
for subsequent allotment to native farmers other than the present owners, or

(c) acquisition for general allotment to applicants under the Lands Board system? If there were to be tenure from 'the Crown', 'the Crown' would first have to acquire the land. Hitherto, in acquisition of land, we had consistently maintained the principles that the native owner must be willing to sell and that the Administration should decide that the land was not needed for the present or future needs of those natives who had rights in it. Should we convert this to a principle that, in defined circumstances, the Administration should decide what was the best use to be made of the land and, in determining the needs for the land both present and future, think of the native people in general and not only of the occupants of the land?

We should reach a clear understanding on these and related questions before we made decisions on the method of redistributing land. I asked for 'basic principles for lands policy' so that a clear direction could be given to the Administrator that these principles should be observed in any of the local schemes already commenced and that any scheme contrary to these principles should be adjusted or cancelled. Then we would work out detailed proposals regarding the nature of a new system of tenure and the method of introducing it and prepare the administrative structure. 'I have it in mind', I wrote, 'that this third step should mean not simply laying down the appropriate administrative structure but embarking on positive and vigorous measures of economic development. That is the real goal to which we are moving.' (Minute of 26 October 1959.)

I asked for an early submission containing recommendations for 'the redefining of lands policy and the principles to be observed in carrying out that policy'.

Already a number of native farmers were the holders of leases granted by the Administration and the practice had started of advertising small farm blocks for application for leasing by native applicants. These steps were taken in respect of land already at the disposal of the Administration, such as land that had been forfeited by European lease-holders.

Our task would become easier if we had more land readily available. Early in 1959 I gave a direction that when the Administration had completed the subdivision of the land it already had, it should approach the owners of freehold land with a view to voluntary sale. It should also build up information about the location of unused freehold land and the demand for land in various localities so that, in due time, consideration could be given to compulsory acquisition of unused land to meet the demand by landless people.

The Administration made some minor purchases from Europeans but reported early in 1962 to the effect that generally the reason why freehold land was not being used was that it was unsuitable for agriculture. I was dissatisfied and called for an exact report on how much idle freehold land there was, where it was, and what examination of its suitability for agriculture had been made. 'Please keep in mind', I wrote, 'that the fact that land already alienated is idle affects the handling of the broader question of inducing native landowners to make their land available for general settlement. Also keep in mind that our major problem in the coming years is not going to be in finding land for new European settlers but in finding land for native settlers who have no land of their own.' (Minute of 30 March 1962.)

The first report showed over a quarter of a million acres of alienated land which, in my own interpretation of the figures, was 'not being properly used by those who hold title to it'. Some of it might not be suitable for cultivation but most of it was close to established centres and lines of communication and would be more readily available for settlement than land not yet alienated. The Administrator was instructed to report precisely the measures he was taking to investigate this land and to ensure either its early use by the present owners or its acquisition for settlement, if necessary by compulsory process. 'It is difficult to force the major conversion of land tenure, which we now have to contemplate', I wrote, 'if there are considerable areas of alienated land lying unused.' (Minute of 17 July 1962.) I complained that the Administration had been 'meandering' since early 1959.

I still had not gone as far as I wanted when I left the portfolio in 1963. I foresaw the problems and tried to have them examined in a practical way so that change could be initiated intelligently but I do not think enough was done under Australian administration in this important field.

Another necessary preliminary to any large-scale resettlement of the native people was obtaining more exact information both about population and land. In a broader context, following requests from Port Moresby, Lambert had arranged for a visit to the Territory of a team from the Commonwealth Bureau of Census and Statistics to make a number of specific studies. In approving his proposals in April 1961, I pointed to one item—a study of pressure on land in the Chimbu, Wabag and Maprik areas—as 'far and away the most urgent' and added, 'I will be making specific demands on the Administrator shortly to prepare long-term proposals for resettlement of population in these and other areas and it is essential that we know the basic facts.' (Minute of 27 April 1961.) The bureau found difficulties through staff shortages and lack of facilities. I again urged the importance of the work. 'Until it is done,' I wrote, 'we will be handicapped in our attempts to obtain a comprehensive view of the economic situation in the Territory.' (Minute of 18 May 1961.)

In my view the subsequent progress was 'far too leisurely'. In October and November 1961 two officers of the bureau visited the area to investigate the possibility of doing the work. In March 1962, discussions were held in Canberra and the conclusion reached that further discussions were needed. In July and August 1962 a further visit to the Territory led the way to preliminary action and in September I was informed that the full plan for the survey was being prepared. (Minute of 14 September 1962.)

Lacking the necessary information, a comprehensive decision on resettlement of the native people had not been initiated during my time as Minister, but a start had been made with smaller projects in separate localities.

One other direction I gave at this time was that we should try to encourage and make use of any contributions the indigenous people themselves could offer on resettlement: 'The more we can make them feel that the schemes which we put into effect are their schemes the better will be the prospect of success.' (Minute of 30 October 1961 apropos of some correspondence with John Guise.) In some of the local schemes, I believe that field officers in the Department of Agriculture and Department of Native Affairs did work in this way with the local communities. Local co-operation was essential to success.

I am not so sure that at headquarters similar regard was always paid to indigenous opinion.

During 1961 we were engaged on drafting a Uniform Lands Ordinance. Three observations I made on the draft received from Port Moresby reflect some of the differences of outlook between the Administration and me. I took the view that appeals against conclusions reached by the Lands Board and approved by the Administrator's Council should not go to the Administrator but to some authority apart from and, in this context, superior to the Administrator. Secondly, on the compulsory acquisition of land I took the view that if in the future it was thought necessary to acquire a large area of land for a particular purpose—for example for a native resettlement scheme or to obtain rights over water for a power scheme—it would be better to do it by obtaining approval from the legislature by means of a bill dealing with that particular project rather than to give the Administrator a general power in the present Bill to declare any project he favoured to be 'a public purpose' and to take the land. I also insisted that no distinction be drawn between native land and non-native land in the provisions regarding resumption. The fact that the vast preponderance of land was native land was an argument for a conservative approach to land resumption. Thirdly, I suggested that there should be a legal obligation on the appropriate officer of the Administration to promulgate notices on land matters among the people in the area concerned and to take other necessary action to ensure that no native interest in land was overlooked. The mere gazetting of notices or the tacking of them on a notice board was not enough in Territory circumstances. Finally I emphasized that the 'basic purpose of land laws is to recognize or confer rights in land and to protect and maintain these rights. Land laws are not passed simply to facilitate the activities of government. In this Territory especially the importance of establishing rights in land and inculcating and maintaining a respect for those rights is fundamental to a great deal of our other work.' (Minute of 15 June 1961.)

After the drafting had been completed, I gave a direction that exceptional measures were to be taken by the Administrator himself to ensure that the native members of the Council, both elected and nominated, understood the purpose of these measures and knew the effect on them of the passage of the Bill: 'Land is one of the most sensitive political points in the Territory,' I wrote, 'and whatever is done must be done with the support of the native members.' (Minute of 1 March 1962.)

A more marked difference of view arose between the Administration and myself over the drafting of a Bill concerning the Land Titles Commission. In my view the functions and powers of the Commission should be narrowly limited to those necessary to carry out the conversion from customary tenure to an individual title granted by the Administration. Their function should end when the title had been granted. They should not make adjudications on disputes that arose from their own decisions. They should not become a court for dealing with land matters generally nor take over any of the functions of the Supreme Court or Lands Department. (Minute of 2 August 1962.)

The submission of the Bill to the Legislative Council was approved, but the way it was handled in the Council, in seeming disregard of the views of native members, caused me extreme annoyance. The position as I saw it was set out in a minute at the end of May 1963, when events in the Council were brought under my notice by a recommendation from the Department to approve certain amendments proposed by the Administrator. Apparently in February some objections to the Bill were raised in the Council by native elected members, but no notice was taken of these objections until the native elected members followed the unusual course of invoking the aid of the public solicitor to prepare a case for the amendment of the Bill. This seemed a strange employment of his office, but what I wanted to know was why no one in the Administration paid any attention to the objections made in the Council and why native members of the legislature had to go to the public solicitor for help. Was no other assistance available to them? Did they hesitate about seeking the aid of the Administrator or the officers of the Legislative Council? Since John Guise, a principal objector in the Legislative Council, was also a member of the Administrator's Council why was not the Administrator's Council used? This seemed to me a matter to which Cleland might well have devoted a few hours of the time of the Administrator's Council, a major function of which was to associate the legislature with the executive in policy matters. I also commented that when eventually the public solicitor made his submission on behalf of the native elected members, there seemed to be a lack of appreciation by the Administrator of the urgency and importance of the matter. The first communication made on the subject was an undated memorandum signed on behalf of the Administrator and apparently received in the Department of Territories on 21 May. I could not even be sure from the documents that the Administrator had personally taken part in the examination of the matter. I said that, while I felt bound to accept the amendments that had already been accepted by the Administrator, I would not endorse without fuller consideration the proposal to reject other requests for amendments. The minute concluded,

> The Administrator should be informed that it is paramount in a measure of this kind that the confidence of the native landowners in the system of conversion should be established at the start and that the measures and procedures should be such as to reduce to the absolute minimum any resentment or disputes after conversion has taken place. It is also essential to have public support of the measure in the Legislative Council by the elected native members in circumstances of prior consultation and explanation which leave no grounds for any subsequent complaint that they did not understand what they were doing. In particular, in the Administrator's Council, Mr Guise must be given proper opportunity of presenting his views on this legislation. [Minute of 30 May 1963.]

Economic policy also necessarily had an impact on labour policy. Both the demands of industry for workers and the redistribution of land would accelerate the growth of a landless class of employees. There would be a transformation of the structure of the community, and part of our administrative task and a strong influence in the shaping of policy would be to ensure that the indigenous wage-earner shared in the benefits of economic development. In thinking of the exploitation of the resources of the Territory, we had to include among those resources the labour of its people. Just as the land and the products of the soil, the timber, the fisheries and—if present prospects were falsified by new discoveries—the minerals should not be pre-empted by reason of action taken for their development, so the labour of the indigenous people should not be disposed of in any way that would put the landless labour force in a position in which it would not share in the benefits of change or would only be able to gain a share in those benefits by violent action regardless of all other claims.

Furthermore the inequalities of opportunity for the Territory population both by reason of the uneven distribution of the natural resources of the country and the wide disparities in the advancement of the people, presented the prospect that economic progress would be uneven, the material benefits of economic change would not be distributed equitably among the population, and the shifts in occupation and place of residence brought by the economic development of a wider ranger of national resources would affect social relationships and even the structure of society with consequent effects on the individual person. Consideration of such prospects as this made me cautious about the easy enthusiasm for any sort of development, but especially those projects that called for permanent transference of labour. Musing on economic history, one reflects that the trans-Atlantic slave trade was in large part the consequence of quick response to economic opportunity in North American plantations, and that the most deplorable consequences in the nineteenth century of the industrial revolution, such as depressed labour, slum dwellings and class enmities, followed actions that were regarded as worthy steps of economic progress. The idea of economic change in response to economic opportunity could be 'a good thing', but the means chosen and the neglect to look ahead for the possible consequences might make it 'a bad thing'. I wanted to look at the future of the Territory comprehensively. I could not separate economic change from social and political change and, since we still had a tutelary responsibility and a trust for the people, I could not make economic policy solely on economic arguments. Consequently it may have seemed to some that I was cautious and conservative. Certainly some decisions made after I ceased to be Minister would not have been made in the same way if I had still been there.

[28]

A MIXED BAG OF SOCIAL QUESTIONS

Apart from the major problems with which I have dealt, there were a number of social questions, not directly related to each other, which called for decision. Among these were the advancement of women, racial minorities, 'foreign natives' in towns, the right of the indigenous people to drink alcoholic liquors, racial discrimination, and various aspects of the health services. In most of them my own role was the accustomed one of calling for action and keeping the policy objective clearly in view.

From an early period in my term, I had become aware, from conversations with various persons in the Territory and from my own observations, that the work we were doing for the advancement of the people was creating a special problem in the relationships between men and women in native society. The simplest way to state the problem is to say that men were advancing faster than women. Men had much more contact with Europeans. Men went away from newly opened districts to work and to see the outside world while women stayed at home. A large number of men and very few women were permanently engaged in Administration service. Most of the school-children were boys, except in some of the mission schools.

Then I also became aware that the problem was much more complicated than would appear from this simplified explanation of how the problem arose. In native society itself there were many situations in which women were subordinate to men and in which women were subject to compulsions or restrained by customs that did not apply to men. One familiar and oft-quoted example of the way in which the schooling or higher training of girls might be resisted was the interest parents had in keeping a marriageable daughter un-spoilt for the sake of a better bride-price. While aware that native custom set limits on the advancement of women, one could not generalize about it because custom was not the same in every language group. My own disposition was to accept the prospect that eventually native societies would work out the relationships of men and women in these changing conditions but that we would give them a better chance of doing so successfully if the subordination of women was not further increased as a result of our efforts. The women as well as the men should take part in the changes brought by schooling and our other work.

327

The Administration, Churches and some voluntary organizations had been doing something to help women, mostly in the older regions of contact but, although I encouraged these limited efforts, I do not think that I judge them unfairly if I compare them to the work of a mothers' union in a village. There were sewing circles, afternoons for craft work and much friendliness and a little bit of something to eat. I also valued very much the work of the Girl Guides in giving identity and importance to women as well as training them in some novel skills, and I increased official financial aid to the movement. Throughout the term of Cleland as Administrator, his wife gave notable leadership and much enthusiasm to all these communal efforts and saw that women had due recognition in them. Several of the wives of district commissioners applied themselves ardently under the leadership of Lady Cleland in helping the womenfolk to keep pace with the men.

I reached the opinion however that the advancement of women had to be stated more clearly as an aim of policy and that stronger official activity was needed as well as the voluntary and feminist work. In this regard I should acknowledge the influence on me of conversations I had on several occasions with two exceptional women anthropologists, Margaret Mead and Camilla Wedgwood, who had made earlier attempts to direct attention to the problem. During 1954 I had also met, at an airfield in the Wahgi Valley another woman anthropologist, Marie Reay, then working among the Kuma people, and checked my own impressions against her deeper research. These distinguished women should not be held responsible for any inadequacy in the action I took but they did influence me towards action.

On 18 March 1955 I wrote a minute directing the Administrator to start a three-year drive to overcome the lag in the advancement of women and to take measures in education, health and other phases of administration to ensure that men and women advanced side by side. In this minute I said that the basic principle was equal opportunity for men and women. We had to pay regard to existing social organization and native custom and remember that we were advancing the welfare of the native people as a community and not expounding the cause of feminism. Another minute, of February 1956, reaffirmed this direction on policy.

Towards the end of 1956 I received from the Department a memorandum summarizing what had been done and what was planned. I wrote:

What has been done is admirable but quite inadequate and simply carries on a course of action which has been followed for some years past . . . No proposals have yet been received on the three-year drive and the report now furnished gives no indication that anything serious or effective has been attempted. On education measures, I want to know whether all primary schools, Administration and mission, are receiving girls on exactly the same terms and in equal numbers to boys and, if not, why not. [Minute of 7 November 1956.]

The Administration was stirred up and a committee for women's advancement was formed to prepare a plan. In March 1957 I approved this committee's recommendations, expressed appreciation of its work and asked for a further report in six months' time on what had actually been done. (Minute of

15 March 1957.) In October I asked if the report had been received. (Minute of 22 October 1957.)

Behind the dusty curtain of silence I detected a rustle and a scurrying. The Administrator had delegated the problem to some busy little men at Port Moresby in the Departments of the Administrator and of Native Affairs and their sex prejudice and smallness of mind, as well as the old belief that only experienced male officers knew what was good for the native people, led them to concoct proposals for an organization under their own direction carrying out their own ideas. The chairman of the committee for women's advancement had been a senior woman officer of the Administration, Barbara McLachlan,[55] a graduate of the University of Sydney and a trained teacher, who had been engaged in this branch of work for some time. After her work on the committee, she had gone abroad for postgraduate training at the University of California under a World Health Organization fellowship. Yet, after her return to the Territory, she was not consulted any further or brought into discussion of the reorganization of the work. The busy little officers who had devised the new organization had discussions with others and correspondence with Canberra without any reference to her and without giving any indication to Canberra that her views had been disregarded.

I had formed a good opinion of McLachlan's intelligence, vision and capacity and wanted her views. I also had doubts about the value of the proposals put before me. These doubts were linked with hesitation in the Department of Territories about plans for creating the proposed 'social development branch' in the Territory and about the personal capacity of those Administration officers who were obviously designing positions they intended to occupy themselves in the new branch. In their structure, only one woman officer would be recruited and that at a subordinate level.

I found too that McLachlan's report and recommendations, addressed to the Administrator after her return from her period of overseas study, had not been acknowledged but had been shelved in the Department of the Administrator.

This was a classic case of successful obstruction and male conceit inside the public service. It took some time for me to learn the state of play but eventually, on a visit to Port Moresby in June 1958, I went over the events in company with the Administrator and the Public Service Commissioner and, on return to Canberra, reopened the question and renewed the direction on policy.

At the same time, in the Department, McCarthy was analysing a report which had been received from the Administrator on the 'progress' of the advancement of native women in the first six months of 1958. In the three years of 1956, 1957 and 1958, when my earlier instruction to 'overcome the lag' should have shown an effect, the percentage of girls in total enrolments in Administration schools had moved only from 21·2 per cent to 23·8 per cent. This, as McCarthy drily remarked, was 'less than would be expected from a vigorous campaign to educate native girls'. There were no figures for mission schools and apparently the 'vigorous' campaign had ignored them. Other papers for the end of 1958 and early 1959 suggest that correspondence from Canberra was being bogged down among the clerks and in May 1959 I asked Cleland to give the subject his personal attention. We then had a period of greater activity, with McLachlan taking a notable part in the achievement. I kept closely in touch with this work, for I felt it needed continuous encouragement in the face of signs that not only native society but also the Territory public service was male-dominated.

I disclaim any high motives or theories about women's rights or women's liberation. My interest was practical. A social transformation was taking place and, unless women shared in the transformation, there would be social imbalance and unnecessary stresses, strains and impediments. I had no ambition to establish the pattern of man-and-woman relationships in the New Guinea community of the future but thought it common sense to enable the people to work it out for themselves without the women being at a disadvantage. I wanted to avoid a social situation in which most men had changed to a new way of life while most women were still living in the old way.

Another practical consideration was that women were needed to help the advancement to which we were committed and the work would be retarded and possibly fail if they did not take part in it. The best way of improving the nutrition of children is to teach their mothers. The best way to improve a family is to change the outlook of the housewife. One could multiply such examples. In the schools, the health services and the administrative offices we needed women workers as well as men. In public life and in the shaping of the transformed society, women would have to take a part, or all the answers to all the difficult questions would be given by men and, although women as well as men are sometimes selfish and stupid, it is lucky that the areas of stupidity and selfishness do not coincide. I knew that many complications were likely to arise from existing native social organization and native custom and codes of conduct. Let the anthropologists enlighten us on them while the clerks continued to trot out these complications as a reason for doing less. Let the ardent feminists become emotional about the mission of women's liberation. My practical concern and my guide on policy was simply that a social transformation was taking place and the whole society needed to take part in the transformation.

There is a fuller story yet to be told by some better-qualified person about the place of women in New Guinea society. Not as much was done in the advancement of women in my time as I would have liked. I found my early encouragement in the fact that we did gain an increasing number of girls for training as teachers, nurses, preschool instructors and similar vocations, that some women took public office, that with the growth of local government councils some women took an active part in them, that when further economic and political change came, women had a share in handling the affairs of their district or country, and that when promotion or higher office came to a native man, he frequently was accompanied by a wife who had shared in and assisted his success and could go further with him. I like to think I can claim some of the credit for results of this kind.

During this period I also moved to bring to finality the question of Asian and mixed-race minorities. As previously recounted, I had already made decisions against old practices which excluded Chinese from the main business areas in towns and restricted the granting of land in town and perpetuated the idea of a separate Chinatown in centres such as Rabaul and Lae. I had also ruled against their exclusion from electoral rolls for the Legislative Council and laid down that the ultimate objective was a common roll for all residents of the Territory. In the commercial and social life of the community I had tried to set a clear pattern of non-discrimination. Looking to the future, I had stated that the objective was to avoid a multi-racial society and to have only one immigrant racial group alongside the indigenous racial majority. In keeping with this objective, I had set rigid limits on new immigration into the Territory so that at the time of self-government the problems facing the indigenous majority might be simplified.

Nevertheless the separateness of the Asian resident in the Territory and the exclusion of an underprivileged mixed-race minority of almost equal size continued and both Asian and mixed-race people had either a subordinate or an undetermined legal status and uncertain citizenship.

Mixed-race people and Asians were almost equal in number, but whereas the Asians were clearly identifiable and closely knit, the mixed-race people were of all kinds and had no single community but only local groupings.

Most of the Asians were Chinese and most of them had been born in the Mandated Territory of New Guinea and had the status of Australian-protected persons. The remainder comprised older people who were resident in New Guinea before Australia accepted the League of Nations Mandate, and some who had been admitted under exemption for temporary residence in the late thirties and were still there at the time of the Japanese invasion. All had established their homes in the Territory. The total number was less than 3000 and they were located mostly in the vicinity of Rabaul, Lae, Madang and Kavieng.

All sorts of opinions were presented to me about the Chinese community, some good, some bad. Some persons, both official and private, represented to me that the Chinese were a security risk, exploiters of the native people, unscrupulous business rivals or undesirable neighbours. They warned me that the Chinese were getting too much land. Others told me that they were useful and industrious members of the community. Some spoke of unfair discrimination against them. This last-mentioned group could quote in truth a number of practices by officers of the Administration, especially in regard to land acquisition and business opportunities, that continued the pre-war outlook on Chinese. In August 1956, after having received yet another memorandum rather unfavourable to the Chinese, I wrote to Lambert, 'I think it is about time we faced the issue squarely and I should like you to have a Cabinet submission prepared on the subject. My own view is that it should end with a recommendation for the granting of citizenship.' (Minute of 15 August 1956.) I had some discussions with my colleague Harold Holt, then Minister for Immigration, and he and I agreed that we should make a joint submission. So the Australian Department of Immigration was brought into the close examination of the subject.

The Cabinet submission was approved for circulation on 21 May. In the preparation of it, officials both in the Department of Territories and Department of Immigration foresaw many difficulties and raised some doubts about policy. In this instance both Ministers had more advanced views than their officers. Someone other than myself and with knowledge of what happened after my time will have to write a fully rounded history of the Chinese in

Papua and New Guinea. For a judgement to be made on my own decisions, however, I quote at some length from a minute I addressed to the Secretary during the preparation of the submission to Cabinet:

There are several reasons why I find the Department's analysis and conclusions unacceptable.

First, I do not think that the Department has attempted at any point to examine closely the facts of the situation in the Territory. The Department has taken as an axiom certain opinions held on the conduct of Chinese as a result of conditions observed elsewhere in the world . . . I do not accept the axiom you accept and so I cannot follow your argument.

While we may draw on what accurate information we can obtain of experience elsewhere, the starting point has to be a close knowledge of the origin, organization, nature and conduct of the Chinese community actually existing in the Territory. It is a very small community. A growing proportion of it is native-born and Australian-educated. Most of them have had their only protection and status in the world during the past twenty years either as British subjects or Australian protected persons. The policy which I have directed shall be rigidly applied is designed to restrict their associations with any countries except Australia and the Territory; to prevent any new immigration and to turn them away from dependence on China either for brides, business assistants, teachers, or preachers; and to persuade them that their only hope for the future lies in an association with Australia. A large proportion of them are Christians, either Roman Catholics or Methodists. The business, financial and productive opportunities for the more successful members of their community depend more upon their relationships with Europeans than with the natives. I think the departmental memorandum may have been based solely on a picture of the Chinese as a fellow running a trade store, buying copra from natives and finding his opportunity solely at the expense of the natives. There are such Chinese. There are also today Chinese whose trading, contracting and financing are of a different kind in the heart of the European community. In brief, I doubt whether the Department has a complete, up-to-date and accurate picture of the Chinese community in the Territory and, having those doubts, I treat the Department's opinions with considerable reserve.

The ends of policy . . . have been directed towards avoiding if we can the ill results that have followed elsewhere. If I accepted the departmental view that ill results are inevitable in all circumstances, then I would feel obliged in the interests of Australia and the people of the Territory to take a wholly different line, deporting every Chinese who was not entitled to be in the Territory and placing more rigid limits on the activities of those who remain. Instead, we have sought the method of trying to give them opportunity, to try to identify their interests more closely with the interests of the European community, to bring about their dispersal rather than their concentration, to persuade them where possible to get out of Chinatown, to encourage the younger generation to go to school in Australia, and so on. The Department apparently believes that this is all hopeless and wrong. If that is the departmental view, I can see that it would also feel obliged to resist the proposals in the draft Cabinet submission on citizenship. That proposal is, of course, the natural culmination of the policy that I have directed should be followed in the past six years . . . If the Department does, in fact, hold the view that the whole course of policy towards the Chinese in the past six years is wrong —i.e. wrong because it is doomed to fail by reason of your belief that 'once a Chinese always a Chinese' (and hence an exploiter of natives and potential traitor)—then the Department has an obligation to make a clearly reasoned submission to me to that effect within this week and to do its utmost to make the Government change its policy. But if that submission should be rejected, then the Department has an obligation in future to accept and work for the accomplishment of the policy laid down by the Government. [Minute of 14 May 1957.]

The Cabinet decision, which was announced by me on 18 June 1957, gave the opportunity to Asians resident in the Territory to become Australian citizens by applying for naturalization, in much the same way as non-British migrants to Australia could gain citizenship. One consequence was that as Australian citizens they could be admitted to Australia for permanent residence as well as having a status identical with other Australians in the Territory. This decision was of some significance in a history of Australian immigration policy as well as in a history of Papua and New Guinea.

Later, with a broadening of Australian policy to extend the opportunity of Australian citizenship to Asians who had been resident in Australia under exemption for more than fifteen years and had satisfied other requirements, the number of Chinese in the Territory eligible for naturalization was further widened and my officers calculated that the decision to extend Australian citizenship could apply to all except about 200 of the Chinese in Papua and New Guinea.

In recalling these matters, I have a memory of two subsidiary incidents. One was when the Chinese Consul-General from Melbourne started to make representations to the Government on various matters on behalf of the Chinese resident in Rabaul. As politely as possible I told him that the affairs of these Australian-protected persons or Australian subjects were none of his business. I won a minor skirmish both with my colleague the Minister for External Affairs and with the Consul-General in making it plain that he had no entitlement of any kind to speak for them and that his representations should not be made.

The other incident centred on a very pleasant social occasion one afternoon in Rabaul during one of the visits of the Prime Minister and Dame Pattie Menzies to the Territory. One of their official functions was a reception by the Chinese community in their own hall. In courtesy and social grace this function far outshone any other arranged in the Prime Minister's honour, and moreover at that time the Chinese hall, built by themselves, was the most pleasantly modern building in the town. In collusion with a Chinese friend, I had contrived a small diversion. A succession of well-spoken, well-dressed, well-mannered young Chinese men were brought up to the Prime Minister. In the course of conversation Menzies would usually ask where they had gone to school. It was a good opening gambit. In succession each one replied, 'The same school as you, sir. I was at Wesley College, Melbourne.' The Prime Minister was delighted and made a great point of talking in later years about the Wesley College old boys' reunion in Rabaul. The then permanent head of his department, Sir Allen Brown, was also a Wesley boy. Similarly, at the same time, Dame Pattie was meeting a succession of charming young ladies who had been to the same private girls' school in Melbourne as her own daughter.

Encouraged by the success with the Asians, I turned attention to the mixed-race people and asked the Department to give me more detailed information about their numbers in various categories, occupations and mode of living. There were wide variations both in racial origin and in present conditions. My view was that persons of mixed race, numbering approximately 2000, should have an opportunity of deciding whether they should seek to align themselves with the immigrant racial group or with the indigenous racial group. There remained the question of their acceptance by the group they chose. I made an early submission to Cabinet to give an opportunity to certain mixed-race persons who chose to align themselves with the European minority to become Australian citizens, as Asians could do, but my recommendation was rejected. This was a setback and a personal disappointment to me, for I thought it unfair and I also thought that the fear that we might open Australia's doors to all the progeny of mixed mating was unreal.

In spite of Cabinet's decision, I still held before my department the ultimate objective of helping the mixed-race people to make a choice to align themselves either with the immigrant racial group or with the indigenous racial group. In the meantime I set out to mitigate their disabilities in the Territory. We were able to take some measures for better housing, education and employment and preparing them for entry into the Territory Public Service. The difficult question of their legal status remained without an answer. I set the Department to work to find a way in which they might be given a Territory citizenship without the right of permanent residence in Australia which Cabinet had denied to them. (Minute of 29 August 1960.)

I also asked the Department at this time to widen their work on Territory citizenship so that, in advance of self-government, there might be an opportunity for a person of any race who was a British subject or a protected person to be covered by the same citizenship as an indigenous inhabitant of Papua and New Guinea. Looking towards self-government and eventual independence, we also should look at the difference in status between the Papuan, who lived under full Australian sovereignty and a New Guinean living under Australian protection in a trust territory.

Discussing the outlook in May 1961 and using as an illustration the policy of having a common roll for future elections, I said that the Territory should start soon to move from the present condition, in which residents of the Territory were classified in various ways, to a condition in which all persons permanently resident in the Territory and having the same rights would have a common description of themselves. 'Keeping this prospect in mind,' I said, in a minute to Lambert, 'you should stop your officers from burrowing in search of difficulties and turn to thinking how all the people resident in the Territory can find and accept a single common status and have an identical standing under the laws of the Territory.' I added that this work on citizenship was closely allied to the work on the removal of racial discrimination from the laws of the Territory, 'on which the Administrator has been lagging so badly'. (Minute of 31 May 1961.)

We did not get far with this work on citizenship, mainly for lack of anyone with both the qualifications and the time to devote himself to these problems.

On visits to the Territory I saw repeated instances of the disadvantages of the mixed-race people and in September 1961 I said that we had to make 'another desperate attempt to straighten out this situation. In human terms a gross injustice is being done to many of these people.' (Minutes of 7 September 1961 and 9 February 1962.) I was particularly concerned with the plight of those families of part-European parentage who had been brought up in the European manner, had English as their only language and were never likely to find acceptance among the indigenous group. Knowing Cabinet's earlier attitude, I judged that the only chance for them would be to have their individual applications dealt with under the discretion given to the Minister for Immigration. Some of these cases were put to the Department of Immigration for examination and eventually I got a Cabinet decision to the effect that a mixed-race person could apply for Australian citizenship with right of entry into Australia, and each case would be considered 'on its merits'. This decision relieved some of the individuals from unfair treatment but I myself would have liked to go further in giving effect to the hope that, before self-government came, all separate mixed-race groupings could be dissolved by the choice of the people themselves to be identified either with the indigenous people or with the expatriate people.

I directed that work towards the establishment of a Papua and New Guinea citizenship should continue, but no significant progress had been made when I surrendered the portfolio. (Minute of 29 November 1962.)

Another social problem was presented under the heading of 'foreign' natives in towns. The early pattern of life had been simple. The towns established by Europeans were small. Most of the indigenous people continued to live in their own villages adjacent to towns. Those native people who had come from other parts of the country to work lived either in barracks (the constabulary), in a compound (for example waterside labour or constructional workers) or, in the case of domestic servants and the staff of small establishments, in 'boy houses' in the back yard of their employer. Those engaged as plantation labour lived in quarters on the plantation. When the towns became larger and urban industry and Administration employment increased, the number of native workers living away from their own villages also grew. Freely engaged and casual labour and footloose native people who wanted to see the world added to the numbers of 'foreign natives' in towns, and little colonies of squatters appeared on the outskirts, living in ramshackle huts made out of whatever materials could be picked up, having little or no provision for sanitation or services. The constraints and disciplines of village life were also absent.

We were facing a social problem requiring urgent remedy. Perhaps I was to blame to some extent because, although I foresaw that one of the accompaniments of change would be the growth of an urban proletariat, I had also expressed the view that we should not promote or expedite the transfer of people from village to town unless we could be sure of a broader base for their social, economic and political advancement. This view may have led some officers in the Territory to think that, for the time being, people would stay in their villages, that there was no problem of urbanization and that there was no specific direction from the Minister to do something about town natives. Then, in the late fifties, we were hit between the eyes by the facts.

The situation was first brought to my own notice not by any formal report or submission made to me by anyone in authority but as a result of a conversation on one of my own visits to the Territory with an earnest officer of the Native Affairs Department whom I met at an evening reception at Government House, Port Moresby. I had met him elsewhere in the Territory and so I asked him conversationally what work he was now doing. He told me about his work in Port Moresby and then, after having apologized for mentioning it, spoke to me a lot about the town natives who were 'causing trouble'. When I asked him why he had not reported on the situation through his own department, he said that he had written two reports but that no one seemed to be taking any notice of them. He had been told simply that the natives should be sent back to their villages.

The next morning I found a pretext to look at things for myself and question a few other people. I asked for a submission on what should be done. The recommendation made to me after my return to Canberra was that a 'survey' of the position be made. I wrote,

> It is obvious that one of the most urgent social problems that is emerging in the Territory of Papua and New Guinea is the presence in nearly every town of groups of 'foreign' natives. I am sure that in the Administration there are already a number of officers who have observed the problem closely and are ready to present both the facts on it and the proposals for handling it. Because it is urgent I have little patience with proposals for making yet another 'survey' and doing nothing until the 'survey' has been completed.
>
> My own impression is that the nature of the situation varies a good deal from town to town and that the kind of action needed also varies. One can distinguish however at least three different groups of people.
> (a) There are the transients, strictly defined, who are passing through towns and for whom temporary accommodation is needed together with enough care and recreation to keep them out of mischief.
> (b) There are the groups of people who are staying in town for a period (e.g. in employment, on a visit, or to look for employment) but who retain close links with their own home villages and either intend to return there or could easily be told to return if the need arose. They need housing either in the place of employment or in some convenient place and they need the facilities to assist in promoting their welfare and providing for their recreation. In some places they retain strong communal interests (e.g. the Keremas in Port Moresby).
> (c) There are the groups who are living away from home almost permanently and have little intention of returning home and, in some cases, would be hard to send home. In this group there are some who could be regarded as a fully urban people with steady jobs, permanent homes and families. It has to be considered whether they should continue to live in 'compounds' or whether they can be established in new suburbs or villages.
> Each group raises special problems of employment, housing, food, health, schooling and recreation. Each creates special difficulties in relation to petty crime, race relations (including relations with other indigenes) and political

change. The Administration has to accept responsibility in all these matters.

In general, it is better at this stage to maintain the old-established policy of preserving, as far as possible, and for as long as possible, the association of the people with their own villages, for social change will come better in the village, the path of their advancement will be so much clearer there, and any evils, such as hunger, can be dealt with more effectively there. This means in practical terms that any people who have no good reason to be in towns should be induced to return home. It also means that in providing for the town dwellers we have to avoid adding unduly to the attractions of the town. Subject to these considerations however it is the task of the Administration to ensure proper attention to all the matters mentioned in this minute.

I propose to discuss this matter with the Administrator in Canberra in March. I want to know (a) What is being done? (b) What it is proposed to do? (c) What are the best staff arrangements to be made to ensure consistent and increasing attention to this problem? (d) What role can the churches and missions play? [Minute of 22 February 1960.]

Arising from the discussions, various actions were started. A housing authority was established. A two-year programme to house Administration servants was started. Increased attention was given to schemes in the towns for low-cost housing at a better standard. Measures were taken to ensure better care and supervision. As a result a major improvement was made, especially in Port Moresby largely due to the dedicated efforts of a district commissioner, David Marsh.[56] The social situation was improved.

Looking back, however, I wonder now whether I should have had a more constructive approach to the growth of the urban proletariat. I think I did right to slow down that growth at that stage. It is also true that at that time the existing disadvantages and distresses of 'foreign' natives in town were more obvious than the requirements for a fuller life for the larger numbers of town-dwelling indigenous employees who would be produced by our own policies on education, opportunities in jobs other than labouring jobs, fuller participation in the conduct of the social, political and economic affairs of the country and the growth of secondary and tertiary industries. There would also be an increase in the number of marriage partnerships outside the traditional village groupings, and the appearance of second-generation families which had a looser native association or no association at all with a village. In many other ways we were preparing for a different sort of society in the future, but I doubt whether we started to prepare early enough for the urban and suburban wage-earning class of the future or to shape the situation in which the urban proletariat would emerge. We had to make an initial effort of repairing a social problem before the Administration could do much in a constructive way.

The 'right to drink' was a highly emotional issue. One of the oddities of the rule over dependent territories is that at one time it was the mark of enlightenment to prohibit the supply of alcohol to the native people and at another time it became the mark of enlightenment to remove the ban. The first ordinance enacted when William MacGregor became Administrator of British New Guinea in 1888 was one prohibiting the supplying of natives with arms, ammunition and liquor. The mandate given to Australia by the League of Nations over the former German possessions in 1920 required that 'the supply of intoxicating spirits and beverages to the natives shall be prohibited'. Both territories had liquor ordinances in keeping with this obligation before they were joined in an administrative union, and a liquor ordinance made for the Territory of Papua and New Guinea in 1946 made it clear that these earlier ordinances and the regulations under them were to continue in effect.

The Papua and New Guinea Act 1949, of the Australian Parliament, Section 72, read as follows:

> Subject to such exceptions and exemptions as are provided by Ordinance, the supply of intoxicating liquor to natives is prohibited in the Territory.

The effect of this section was to allow the possibility of a relaxation of the prohibition if the law-making authority for the Territory was in favour of it. I myself tended to read the Act as permitting something in the nature of local option for the Territory community. I also understood the intention to be that, as the indigenous people changed in habit and outlook, exceptions and exemptions might be necessary to give the privilege of drinking alcohol to some categories of persons while maintaining a general prohibition against drinking for those who were not exempted. There had been a similar approach to the problem among the Australian aborigines, although the lessons of that system were that the 'dog-collar acts' caused as strong a grievance about racial inequality as did total prohibition and that the exempted aborigine was always under strong pressure to be an illegal supplier of drink to his unexempted kinsmen.

When I became Minister for Territories, the only opinion being expressed in the Territory of Papua and New Guinea was in favour of maintaining total prohibition. Native people, as I have remarked elsewhere, were not then expressing opinions but, so far as I was aware, in 1951 there was little or no demand by any of them to have the 'right to drink'. Nor, with the possible exception of the Gazelle Peninsula, was there any drinking among the native people. The prevailing opinions (that is, the opinions of Administration officers, missionaries, planters and businessmen) were that drinking would do harm to the native people or lead to trouble (that is, trouble for the white community in the form of disturbance of the peace, nuisances, unruly conduct and misbehaviour of all kinds, both real and imagined, by native men under the influence of drink). The lesson still drawn from the early history of the Pacific Islands and of New Guinea was that strong drink was the principal agent in the corruption of native peoples. At that time I never heard anyone express a view other than that strong drink was a corrupting influence on primitive societies.

I used to wonder whether some native moralist ever drew conclusions about the effect of alcohol on the behaviour of Europeans and in the corruption of an expatriate society isolated in a strange environment. Drinking, both socially for daily cheer and alone and morosely, either for escape or to fortify the spirits, was a significant part of the pattern of life among the white population. I also noticed how many of the legends of the Europeans in the country had to do with redoubtable drinkers. In some circles, as in Australia, drinking every evening after work, was a social ritual. There were of course among the Europeans many temperate persons and many total abstainers, but the social pattern of drinking was certainly clear enough for any native man or woman who felt that it was a mark of sophistication to covet alcohol in imitation of the whites. 'Good for me, but not good for you' was a poor text for a speech against liquor for native people. The houseboys and servants in clubs and hotels were expected to serve it freely but never to take a surreptitious sip. The contradiction became more marked when, with advancement, native people themselves became fellow-guests with Europeans. The native member of parliament was expected to take his glass of 'lolly water' from the tray while the European clerks picked up their whisky or beer.

From about 1956 some pressure for change became apparent. From 1958, in any discussion with native leaders or in meetings with local government councillors, the question was occasionally raised in the coastal towns in the form of a polite enquiry whether policy was likely to be changed. Just as frequently, whenever the winds of change carried the faintest whiff of alcohol, deputations from other native groups would urge just as earnestly that the prohibition not be lifted.

At the end of 1957, so far as my memory and my notes serve me, the Administrator first raised the question formally with me. It was suggested that a senior officer go off on a sort of world tour to find out what was being done about strong drink in other countries. That particular proposal, which bore the marks of having been drafted by the intending traveller himself, seemed to me too much like a proposal to give an officer a trip abroad at public expense and I rejected it but used the occasion to say that I thought the problem should be looked at as a local problem to be solved in the local setting. Let them observe and report on what was happening in Papua and New Guinea. I did not want to decide what was best for the New Guinea people by finding out what someone else had decided was best for the North American Indians or the Eskimos or the Bantu.

In conversations with the Administrator I said that the responsibility lay on him to watch the local situation and to make whatever recommendations he thought the situation required. In a matter depending so much on a judgement on local conditions, I would not move without his recommendation and would hold off pressures for change as long as he thought I should do so. I also said that there was a local political situation to be faced. A considerable body of opinion, mainly among the Christian missions, might wish to maintain prohibition and, if he thought there should be a change, he should do his best to carry missionary opinion with him. In due course if a change were proposed, I would face my own political problem in Australia but he need not worry about that and could make his judgement on what was best on local evidence.

I had several subsequent conversations with Cleland. By 1961 the demand for the 'right to drink' was becoming stronger in coastal urban areas and it was reported that illegal drinking in the urban areas was growing. Then the case presented by those who sought the 'right to drink' hardened into a claim for 'equality' and an allegation of 'discrimination', and they were encouraged by some European apostles of freedom for dependent peoples. There was little interest in the topic in the outer areas and continued opposition to change by those, both native and European, who thought drinking would harm the native people.

Cleland seemed to me to handle the local situation very coolly and capably. One of his basic problems however was that the state of the law was making some of his best native leaders appear as 'law-breakers' whom it would be folly to prosecute. Yet, by turning a blind eye to breaches of the law, respect for the law was being weakened. In general, if I read Cleland's mind aright, his view was that some change was inevitable but it should be held off as long as practicable. Throughout I maintained the view that the initiative rested with him. In 1959 he sounded out those attending the annual missions conference. The majority favoured a continuance of total prohibition. In 1961 he presented the issue more starkly to the missions conference. They agreed unanimously:

> With the development of the people towards self-determination this conference is of the opinion that, in principle, such determination should also be extended to measures introduced for their protection and which now are deemed to be discrimination. Therefore it recommends that any change in the present laws covering the use of liquor by the indigenous people should only be decided by the will of the people expressed through some form of local option and be covered by adequate safeguards.

The conference also recommended that the Administration embark on an educational campaign on the use of alcohol.

The same question was put by the Administrator to the council of social services, which had been formed among the various missions and other organizations doing social work in the Port Moresby area. This council was in favour of some relaxation of prohibition.

On 12 February 1962 Cleland made a formal report to me surveying the whole problem and recommending a relaxation of the law, the setting up of an independent commission to advise on the means and methods of doing this and, subject to the report of this commission, the repeal or amendment of Section 72 of the Papua and New Guinea Act. I took the matter to Cabinet because of the possible political implications in Australia. The setting up of the commission was approved.

The commission of inquiry was headed by Judge Nelson from the bench of the County Court of Victoria and included two indigenous representatives, two missionaries, a Territory magistrate and a woman welfare officer. Its unanimous report was received in October 1962.

The acceptance of this report led to the passage of the new liquor ordinances by the Legislative Council for the Territory. The first steps were intended to accord with the views expressed by numerous indigenous witnesses before the commission that the removal of prohibition should be a gradual process. In an interim period, restriction was placed on advertising and other ways of encouraging the consumption of liquor, and the Administration gave financial aid and other assistance to a campaign of temperance education.

Any judgement on the action taken in 1962 has to be based on experience during a period after I ceased to be Minister. My own observation of the immediate effects of the relaxation was that it eased some social situations when native and expatriate leaders mingled as guests but that in hotel bars one immediate result was to promote rather than lessen racial strain. Some native drinkers made themselves objectionable and the conduct of these few brought a reaction from the white drinkers who then tended to isolate themselves or to go elsewhere to do their drinking. Antipathy grew. Separateness continued. It was a poor path to equality.

In health administration I had no major problems requiring any change in policy. On Gunther's appointment as Assistant Administrator, I appointed one of his senior officers, R. F. R. Scragg, as Director of Health. He had good experience in the Territory, a sense of dedication to its people and a scientific approach to medical problems. While perhaps not as strong a driving force as Gunther had been, he gave good direction to the work of the department, and the difference in their talents was well suited to the changing situation.

During this period we commenced a special effort to organize Australian thoracic surgery teams to handle the large number of the patients who had been identified in our anti-tuberculosis campaign as requiring surgery. Following a direction given in April 1956, I minuted the scheme, on 15 May 1956, for 'immediate' action. We had ready co-operation from Australian surgeons and hospitals, and a succession of fully equipped teams (surgeons, anaesthetists, radiologists, nurses, therapists) of the highest professional standing went to the Territory where the local director of the tuberculosis work had assembled literally hundreds of patients in readiness for them. It was an unprecedented and dramatic way of tackling an urgent task and deserved wider public recognition than we were ever able to obtain for it. The co-operation of the eminent Australian surgeons gave us a level of service and an inspiration to our own medical men which otherwise we could not have commanded.

We began to see the results of our hospital building programme. Unfortunately the completed jobs were not always as good as they might have been. Design and construction for major projects seemed to be governed more by the ideas of the architect and engineer than by the requirements of those who were going to use the hospitals, and the complaints of the users seemed to come after the work had been done instead of while it was being done and was still remediable.

Another aspect of hospital building was the continuing tendency in some districts to persist with the old distinctions between hospitals for Europeans and hospitals for the native peoples. At the end of 1956 I called for an analysis for all capital expenditure on medical services, after noting that at Wewak it was proposed to spend £120 000 to provide nine beds for Europeans and at Wau £120 000 had been spent on a European hospital where the average bed occupancy was four, including 'the regulars who have to be put into hospital now and again to get over their breakdowns'—a euphemism for 'drying out'. In both places the facilities for treatment of native patients in hospital were substandard and completely inadequate. Yet on population figures and the incidence of disease there was no doubt that the major task was with the native people. (Minute of 29 November 1956.)

In October 1959 I received the first results of a direction I had given twelve months earlier for the preparation of a plan for medical training in Papua and New Guinea and asked that it be converted at once into a programme of action so that items of expenditure could be included in the 1957–8 Budget. I said it was 'one of our highest priorities'. (Minute of 9 October 1956.) In the following February I insisted again that 'a substantial commencement has to be made in the financial year 1957–58' and wrote to Lambert as follows:

As in the case of the breakdown in housing, it will be necessary for an appropriate senior officer or officers of the Department to go to Port Moresby and force these matters to a practical outcome without any further delay. Please make arrangements to that end . . . Before the end of April I want to see definite proposals, in the form of a claim on next year's Budget, including definite proposals for works, recruitment etc. . . . While the plans for the coming year will necessarily have to take into consideration the availability of candidates of training, the works capacity, the staffing position etc., our attitude must be that this work has a high priority, that we do not accept limits but try to overcome them, and that we keep on raising our demands and putting more and more pressure on the Administration. It is apparent, too, that something similar has to be done in education, with which my dissatisfaction is growing. In developing the medical training plan, the Education Department has to be given its clear target for the production of qualified candidates for training. Further than this . . . the Education Department has to make its own teacher training programme more forceful and determined. The officer or officers who go to Port Moresby on the medical training plan might also engage on the production of an expanded practical effort for education in 1957–58. [Minute of 4 February 1957.]

In the event, we did not get further in 1957–8 than an increased effort in training recruits to the Department of Health with the existing facilities and some fuller plans for 1958–9. The local medical school did not come into operation until 1960–1. An intention I formed in 1955 and a high priority I fixed in 1956 produced results in 1960.

About this time my personal attention was drawn by two Australian psychologists, Dr A. J. M. Sinclair and Professor D. W. McElwain, to the problems of mental health among the indigenous people and I arranged for Sinclair to make an inquiry. His report was received at the end of 1957 and referred by me to the Administrator for urgent attention. Eventually, in 1959, we established a mental health service and Dr B. G. Burton-Bradley was appointed.

About the same period we intensified our efforts in the malaria eradication campaign and extended health services to the people by establishing rural health centres in co-operation with local government councils.

Credit for work done on all these social questions rightly belongs to those engaged on it in the Territory, but I would be justified in making the passing observation that they would have had far less chance to do what they did if it had not been for the close ministerial interest I took in it and the backing I gave to them. In these matters, as exemplified in the advancement of women, I became aware of the way in which the improvement and enlargement of the administrative staff of the Territory public service was tending to produce the type of public servant at head office in Port Moresby, similar to his counterpart in Canberra, who had zeal and diligence, an itch to run everything and a religious devotion to the jargon of planning and co-ordination but who had little interest in anything he did not understand or had not himself originated.

[29]

A NEW ERA FOR THE COURTS

Probably there was no subject in which the gap between the Administration and myself was wider than the administration of justice. Here more than anywhere else I found a difference of outlook and slowness or misunderstanding in giving effect to my instructions. There is of course wide room for argument about the best policy for establishing and conducting a system of courts and applying the law in a country such as Papua and New Guinea during a period when it is being administered as a dependent territory in a state of tutelage by a trustee power. What also had to be appreciated is that the situation was not static and the question was not only one of doing what was best in the present but what would be best for the remote future. It seemed to me that some of those persons in the Administration who had a different outlook from me were thinking about a situation that had passed, others were thinking only of the immediate tasks of the present and few were thinking of the future.

The first group was influenced very much by the old tradition. The legend of Hubert Murray, pre-war Lieutenant Governor of Papua, who is described by his latest biographer as 'The Australian Pro-Consul', still cast a romantic spell over the higher offices in the Territory and helped to perpetuate an idea of the supremacy of the Administrator over all that was done. Whereas I interpreted the post-war constitution and conceived the structure of government as giving Administrator and Chief Justice separate eminence in two different fields, neither superior to the other, the habit of the past led some of the officers of the Administration to put the Chief Justice below the Administrator and not alongside him. I made repeated but not wholly successful attempts to make my views clear. In 1953, being presented with an arrangement already made, at a time when the office of Assistant Administrator was vacant, I had reluctantly allowed the Chief Justice to be Acting Administrator during Cleland's absence on leave but expressed the view that it was a wrong procedure. In 1955, when Cleland was again going on leave, he proposed that the Chief Justice should again be acting Administrator during his absence. I said this was quite improper and the Assistant Administrator had to be given the acting post. I think Cleland made a false analogy with the Australian States where, in the absence of a Governor, a Chief Justice, as Lieutenant-Governor, acts for him. When the Chief Justice was about to retire in 1956, Cleland wrote nominating various persons in the territorial service to be considered for appointment in his place. I thanked him for his interest but made it clear that the selection and appointment of the judge was not the concern of the Administrator, and judges were not in any way responsible to him. All appointments to the Supreme Court bench in my time were made by me after consultation with the Prime Minister, Attorney-General and the Chief Justice of the Territory and with no one else.

A little later I used a sharper tone in telling another section of the Administration that, in matters of pay and conditions, they were to stop treating the judges as though they were clerks in the public service, and on another occasion when the salaries of judges were being reviewed, I directed that these were to be equated to other judicial salaries in Australia and its Territories and not fitted into the pattern of senior officers of the Administration. I still remember the incredulous and gasping concern of one of the old hands when I said it did not matter if this meant that the Chief Justice got as much as the Administrator. As late as June 1962, in order to end an argument about travel expenses by judges, telephones, use of official cars and similar claims, I had to write once again saying that judges were not to be regarded as members of the public service or to have their conditions laid down by comparison with any officer of the Administration. (Minute of 7 June 1962.)

These are small things but I cite them only as indications of the way in which a pre-war tradition of the subordination of justice to administration persisted in some quarters and made difficult the closing of the gap between my outlook on the administration of justice and Territory practice.

A more closely reasoned view contrary to my own was advanced with some cogency by the second group of opinion, based on experience of the tasks faced in the Territory and an analysis of the current situation with which officers had to deal. The most intelligent and consistent exponent of the view of this group was Fenbury, who had returned from the United Nations to a senior post in the Administration in 1959. One of his arguments was that native scepticism about the efficacy of a court system would grow when legal procedures outstripped the evolution of indigenous society. A concept of justice could be introduced without introducing legalism. We might think we had succeeded in establishing a Westernized system for the administration of justice, uniform over the whole population and consistent in application as a result of the 'centralism' implicit in the position of the Supreme Court at the apex of the structure, but, when tutelage had ended, the Western Administration might be succeeded by a community that did not have a Western outlook and preferred to seek the satisfaction of claims, protection of rights and redress of wrongs in a different way from the Western way. Hence the courts before which native persons appeared should have local jurisdiction and apply local custom, and could only be understood by the people if they were linked with the local situation and the authority of government as represented by the district officers.

In this brief summary I may not be doing full justice to Fenbury's views but I have sought to indicate that, based on long experience in handling actual situations, there was a respectable body of well-reasoned opinion in the Territory contrary to policy. I respected these views to the extent that, in keeping with my devotion to a policy of growth and my method of working through the proper procedures, I gave the Administration every possible opportunity of offering advice on each step recommended by others and I was willing to make adjustments to counsels of perfection so long as we kept clearly in view the ultimate objective of establishing the concept of justice, building up a 'common law' of the Territory, and devising a system of courts accessible, independent, honest and consistent.

Unfortunately the Administration did not always respond. My earlier memorandum asking questions about native courts evoked no reply. As will be seen later in this chapter, my submission of the recommendations of the Derham report to the Administration produced very little comment or advice and on some matters left me with an impression of resistance and obstruction rather than of reasoned analysis.

I wish I were more certain than I am that I made the right decisions on policy in regard to the administration of justice and I wish that I had been given wider discussion and more time for studying the whole question. I was thinking mainly of the future and I doubt whether what I was trying to say was clearly understood in the Administration. Hence the advice that reinforced me came mostly from lawyers bred in the British and Australian traditions of the rule of law and not from field officers of the Administration.

As already indicated, I had gone along fairly easily with the existing system for the first five years, partly because of the limited results yielded by the Bailey inquiry and largely because of respect for the two senior members of the Territory Supreme Court Bench, Mr Justice Phillips and Mr Justice Gore. They certainly brought out all that was best in the old system so admirably that it is understandable that when the time came for their retirement in 1957, the Administrator looked in the future for 'more of the same', whereas I thought 1956 was about the time to make a change.

Towards the end of that year the Chief Justice, Sir Beaumont Phillips, with whom I had formed a close and friendly relationship, discussed with me at his home in Port Moresby his wish to retire and the state of his health. In January 1957 he publicly announced his intention to retire and very shortly afterwards went on sick leave. During the ensuing months, while he was under medical sentence in Melbourne, I came closer to him even than before. His calmness and even cheerfulness, the reminiscences he continued to share with me and the helpful comments he made about future arrangements in Papua and New Guinea made those meetings memorable. Phillips was one of the notable characters in the early days of Papua and New Guinea, where his experience went back to 1926, and he had cheerfulness, tolerance and common sense. Before he died in May 1957 I was able to introduce to him his successor as Chief Justice and he was able to give the new man the benefits of his own experience on the Bench.

The new Chief Justice was A. H. Mann,[57] a leading member of the Melbourne Bar and a Queen's Counsel. I found him with the aid of my parliamentary colleague, Percy Joske, also a Melbourne silk, and gained the support of Prime Minister Menzies in the approach to him. Mann not only responded to the invitation to take the appointment, which was in professional terms not as tempting as other prospects he might have had, but did so with a strong sense of duty and a dedication to the task. He fully shared my own ideas of the importance of doing all we could to build up a system of justice before independence came to Papua and New Guinea and establishing a tradition of the total independence, probity and accessibility of the courts. He also appreciated the need for building in the Territory a code which, while based on English common law, would in time, through judgments of the courts, interpretation and the recognition of local customary practices, create a recorded system of what I chose to refer to as 'Territory common law'. Mann was undoubtedly the best-qualified lawyer the Territory had ever had up to that time, either on the Bench or in Government service and, as and when opportunity arose after his appointment, his presence as Chief Justice led other men of good legal standing to accept appointments to the Bench.

Mann was one of the best appointments I made. He had his difficulties and his disappointments and was subjected to some vexation and suffered some frustration in not being given all the facilities the Administration had been directed by me to give to him. I was annoyed too that some pettiness was shown to him and his wife on social matters. I went out of my way on visits to the Territory to emphasize the superiority and the separateness of the Supreme Court and its justices from the Territory public service and to recognize Mann's rank on all public occasions. I also made it clear at all times that the Supreme Court and the Chief Justice were established under the Papua and New Guinea Act of the Australian Parliament and were not the creation of the Administration.

The appointment of Mann as Chief Justice coincided with other moves to improve the administration of justice.

Towards the end of 1957 my attention was drawn to the fact that a large body of laws providing for segregation or discrimination on social grounds were still in force. I had been under the impression that this situation was being corrected, for in dealing with the ordinances placed before me in draft form I had repeatedly stressed the policy that there was to be only one law for both white and black. Finding that this work was not being done, I gave a firm instruction to the Administrator to make a review of all existing laws, including regulations made under the statutes, and to prepare proposals for removing any discriminatory provisions. In January 1959, after looking at the matter again, I asked Lambert to ensure that a high priority was given to the work and expressed doubt whether we would see any effective work from the Administration. In theory the work ought to have been done in the Territory but in fact, twelve months after the original instruction, all that had happened was that a committee had been appointed, and, as I said at the time, the information given about the number of meetings held and the amount of work done was so extremely vague as to leave some doubt whether any significant progress had been made. The assurances by the Administrator about work in the future were equally vague. I directed Lambert to find out whether any review of laws involving segregation and discrimination had in fact been made by a competent person and to prepare proposals for a complete survey of existing legislation, referring instances of segregation and discrimination to a suitable authority for advice, and drafting legislation 'to repeal or amend the laws which cannot be justified as inescapably necessary for good order and government and (not or) for the advancement of the welfare of the indigenous people'. (Minute of 5 January 1959.)

Lambert responded promptly and I instructed him to take further action saying, 'It is repugnant to the principles and objectives of the Australian Government that any such discrimination and segregation should continue'. I said that no such laws were to be continued without the approval of the Minister given in each case on a firm recommendation that they were required for the advancement of the welfare of the native people or their protection from harm. This work should have a high priority. (Minute of 24 January 1959.)

Lambert submitted his report and two memoranda from the Administrator dated 2 and 10 February. In Lambert's judgement not much progress had been made and the committee in the Territory was 'tackling the problem at the outside fringe instead of the core'. He found that 'the more blatant discriminatory provisions' were contained in the native regulations of Papua and the native administration regulations of New Guinea, made in the Territory. A 'direct attack' on these regulations was likely to produce the best results. I instructed him to expedite the work. (Minute of 18 February 1959.)

It was apparent to me that the ministerial direction on policy was not fully accepted by some sections of the Administration. Some senior officers still held the old view that those closest to the native people knew best how to 'handle' them and they still saw their responsibility in simple colonial terms of looking after the interests of the natives in the way they thought best. When they discriminated against the native people, they were not conscious of any prejudice against them but rather had an intention of protecting them or making special allowances for them or teaching them how to behave. In this and in related matters I saw signs of some puzzlement among some senior officers why the Minister who gave pre-eminence to the interests of the indigenous people did not also accept the need for special laws for natives only. Their puzzlement was also related to the view that there should be special courts, special laws and generally a separate system of justice for natives.

Even after the work of removing discrimination from existing laws had started, the Territory officers were still drafting new legislation which contained discrimination. For example in July 1960 I asked the Administrator to re-examine the Roads Maintenance Ordinance and eventually I moved for its disallowance. I wrote that this ordinance 'perpetuates a dual system of the administration of justice—one for natives only—whereas the tendency of policy is to have a single system'. (Minutes of 7 July and 17 August 1960.) In rejecting Administration advice, I felt a need to present the issue more starkly to officers, for I thought they had a continuing tendency to go along in the old ways and not to face such basic issues as whether or not there should be a dual system of law and of administration of justice. The two propositions seemed to me to be corollaries of each other. One system of courts meant one body of law. One body of law meant one system of courts.

Uppermost in my own mind was a question of what foundation of law and justice we would lay for the self-governing country of the future. Probably some of those who did not share my views saw what I was doing as an attempt to impose the Australian system of justice on Papua and New Guinea. As I saw it, a system of laws made by white men for natives only, and courts conducted by white men to try natives only were open to much stronger objection as an imposition of white man's rule on subordinate peoples than one set of laws administered in one set of courts for all residents of the Territory. What I was mainly concerned about in the short term however was to familiarize the people with the idea of justice as a principle to be applied without discrimination in all situations, the idea of law as a code that applied evenly and justly to all citizens, and the idea of courts of justice as institutions that were independent, not subject to, the direction of those in authority, not to be used as one of the agencies of governmental administration, and equally accessible on the same terms to all persons. In too many newly emerged countries there were the signs of the colonial system of domination by white over black offering an easy transition to the substitution of a dominant black for the former dominant white group, leaving no greater liberty or freedom and possibly less just treatment for the subordinate indigenous populace than they had under colonial rule. Those were the main reasons why I wanted one body of law and one system of justice.

These problems continued to give me great concern, for it was a field in which both old-style colonialists and a number of new-style young men in the Administration obviously were loath to accept policy direction. Some political scientists as well as officers in the field flourished the derisive word 'legalism' as a broom to sweep my ideas away.

I insisted on receiving progress reports and I set target dates for completing successive stages of the work of removing discriminatory laws. In May and October 1961 and February 1962 the progress reports were marked 'Please expedite'. On the report in May 1962 I lost patience, noting that up to date the only measures prepared for repealing discriminatory legislation were on minor and, in some cases, trivial matters. Five years after my firm instruction, the progress was still disappointing, but the assurance given to me and the prospect I announced publicly was that all discriminatory clauses could be removed by the end of 1963 except for legislation in which a deliberate decision had been taken that special provisions were needed. I had also given a direction that, where it was proposed to retain special provisions, the native people should be consulted to ascertain their wishes whether the differential treatment should be retained or repealed.

With the appointment of Mann I set out to review the whole system of courts in the Territory. One of the early remarks the new Chief Justice made to me in conversation after he had taken a first look at his new duties was that, quite apart from legislation, the most direct form of legal discrimination was to conduct two sets of courts with one for natives only. He also made the observation that a 'Territory common law' could only be built up by recorded judicial decision. It could not be built up by the decisions applied by non-judicial officers of the Department of Native Affairs giving decisions ad hoc in local tribunals with the main objective of fixing up a local situation.

Soon after the appointment of Mann I asked him to come to Canberra for a discussion on the future and asked him to let me have a memorandum, together with his own recommendations, on the system of courts in the Territory. In the course of our discussion we also spoke of law reform and the revision and consolidation of Territory laws. We touched on some practical problems such as buildings for the courts, the training of interpreters and the recording of Supreme Court decisions.

Under Lambert's direction the Department in Canberra had been trying to find a way of carrying on the work of law revision which had lapsed with the death of Fry and the closing down of the law revision section. They had also tried to tie this in with my directions against discriminatory legislation. They had not been able to get very far, mainly for lack of an officer with suitable legal qualifications and the limited response to their attempts to gain specialist assistance from the Australian Solicitor-General's office and the Law School at the University of Sydney. Lambert summed up sadly, 'I am afraid that there is not sufficient competence within the Department to contribute much to this subject and I suggest that we await the submission of the new Chief Justice.' My own view was that the questions of law revision and the administration of justice were separate though parallel questions and would have to be considered on their own. (Minute of 20 July 1959.)

A week later the Chief Justice sent to me a paper 'Outline of Points Calling for Investigation and Revision in the Legal System'. I referred it to Lambert. I then had discussions on my own with the Attorney-General, Sir Garfield Barwick, and with Menzies. The outcome was an approach by me to Professor David Derham, of the University of Melbourne, to conduct an investigation with the following terms of reference:

> To enquire into the existing system of the administration of justice in the Territory of Papua and New Guinea and make suggestions for its improvement having regard to both the present and future requirements of the Territory. [Minutes of 29 July, 13 August and 1 September 1959.]

Professor Derham presented his report in December 1960.

The Derham report is now available to the public,* so I shall not attempt to repeat all its recommendations or to summarize the arguments in support of them. I believe it to be the fundamental document for the study of the administration of justice in Papua and New Guinea. I accepted the advice of this eminent authority, subject to further comment and advice from the Administrator on the ways of putting policy into effect. My views and my intentions, confirmed by the Government and especially by Menzies himself who had a special interest in this phase of our work, are expounded at length in a statement I made to the House of Representatives on 24 October 1961.* I believe this was the beginning of a new era in the administration of justice. In this speech I said, 'The measures I am outlining . . . are intended to lead towards the development of a Papuan and New Guinean institution with

---

* Report on the System for the Administration of Justice in the Territory of Papua and New Guinea, by David P. Derham, Professor of Jurisprudence, University of Melbourne, 21 Dec. 1960. (Typescript prepared in 1973 by the Department of External Territories for distribution to libraries and for circulation by the author.) Appendix C and parts of appendix H were omitted from this copy of the report.
* Commonwealth Parliamentary Debates (H. of R.), vol. 33, pp. 2347-50, 24 Oct. 1961.

steadily increasing participation by the indigenous peoples.' My concluding words were, 'Our present task is to build an implicit acceptance of the rule of law in Papua and New Guinea on foundations that will outlast political change. To do that we not only have to create institutions, we have to educate a whole community.'

I studied the Derham report with care before referring it to the Department and to the Administration and in early February 1961 directed that 'immediate action should be taken to put the recommendations into effect'. I asked Lambert to put a single officer in charge of the subject to ensure that my directions were followed up without any delay. The Administrator was to give an 'immediate report' on when and where the recommendations on courts of summary jurisdiction could be adopted and the successive stages in which the use of such courts could be extended. The Public Service Commissioner was to examine the creating of the necessary positions for both European and native officers and the arrangements to be made for their special training. The Administrator was asked for recommendations on the future organization, recruitment and training of the police force. Recommendations should be submitted on the Derham proposals regarding native local government councils. The views of the Australian Attorney-General's Department and the Territory Chief Justice were to be sought on the Supreme Court Ordinance which was already in draft form. A report should be obtained from the Administrator and the Comptroller of Corrective Institutions as a first step in a review of the whole prison system. Professor Derham's recommendations on the Territory Department of Law should be examined in the first instance by the Department of Territories and the Australian Attorney-General's Department and, as soon as possible, the Administrator and Public Service Commissioner should come to Canberra to give precise form to the proposals for reorganization. The section of the Derham report on land disputes and land ownership should be linked with the work already being done on land tenure and that work should be thoroughly tested against Derham's observations. I stressed the urgency of these matters and set target dates, mostly in April and May, and also directed that provision for reform both in buildings and in staff, should be included in the 1961–2 estimates. (Minute of 8 February 1961.)

The only result I had received at the end of four months was a recommendation for the introduction of an ordinance for the abolition of the jury system until such time as it could be extended to all inhabitants of the Territory. The Administration had wanted this before the Derham report recommended it. As I had no response on the other matters, I tried to coax them into action by deferring this recommendation until it was included in a comprehensive submission on all the Derham recommendations. (Minute of 15 May 1961.) In the same month, arising out of talks in Canberra with the Public Service Commissioner about the Crown Law Department, I wrote that on a major subject of this kind I would not make decisions piecemeal. We had to deal with the subject comprehensively. Specifically I said that the Administrator must complete his recommendations on courts of summary jurisdiction at once. (Minute of 23 May 1961.) A week later the Department of Territories made a submission for further work on the question of land tenure, and its terms led me to ask, 'What is the impediment to approving and putting into effect

Professor Derham's recommendations without any further delay?' I asked them to show me precisely the cause of their hesitation. (Minute of 31 May 1961.) Strangely enough on the following day the left hand of the Department, apparently not knowing in what dark corner the right hand was groping, made another submission supporting the Administrator's recommendation for extending certain work he was already doing on conversion of land tenure and not betraying that it had ever heard of the Derham report.

In mid-June I received a submission on courts of summary jurisdiction. This revealed differences of opinion between the Department of Territories and the Administrator. I sent it back for reconsideration, saying that I inclined towards the Administrator's proposals. They seemed to give practical effect to the intentions of the Derham report and, where they differed in detail from it, they could be regarded as a first stage in giving full effect to the Derham recommendations. Nevertheless the Administrator should be asked to show precisely where he wanted to depart from the Derham report. (Minute of 19 June 1961.) The further submission was made at the end of September and I approved its recommendations, including the acceptance of some variations the Administration wished to make in the Derham report. (Minute of 27 September 1961.)

It then became the job of the Administrator to prepare the necessary legislation, and the prospect was that it would be brought in at the sitting of the Legislative Council in June 1962. In my preoccupation with other matters, I assumed that all was running smoothly and apparently the Administrator was in a similar state. At any rate the officers of the Administration and some inexperienced and inattentive officers in the Department of Territories, working without any further submission to obtain further approvals, brought about such a tangle that I was led on 11 June 1962 to send a telegram to the Administrator to cut through a situation I described as 'confused'. I wrote, 'Please use your personal judgement whether the Bill should be introduced, remembering firstly we want early reform, secondly the Bill must ensure the new system is soundly constructed. I am personally unwilling to clear an unseen Bill unless reassured it has your personal approval and its provisions are regarded as workable by the Chief Justice.' I had no reply and later I discovered that the telegram was never delivered to Cleland, although marked 'Personal to Cleland'.

The Bill was introduced without any attention having been given to my telegram and, when a copy of it was eventually seen by me and examined at a more senior level in the Department, it was found to contain some provisions not covered by the approvals already given. As the Bill was now before the Council, this presented me with the problem of how far I should go in directing that changes be made in a Government measure. In the discussion that followed, I restated policy:

(1) There is to be a single system of courts administering a single body of law.
(2) By a single system of courts I mean
    (a) There shall be equal access by all races to all courts.
    (b) There shall be no court constituted to deal only with native offenders or litigants and there shall be no court in which in practice only native

offenders or litigants appear or in which the law applied or the procedures followed is different from those applied or followed in other courts.

(c) All courts are to be equally independent of the legislative and the executive.

(d) All courts shall be part of a single pyramidal structure having its apex in the Supreme Court.

(3) Courts of Native Affairs are to be abolished and nothing similar to them is to be substituted for them.

(4) Appointments to the Bench of the lower court (or courts) should be, so far as possible, 'professional' appointments in the sense that the person appointed is free of all other duties and is appointed because of his quali-fications to occupy the Bench. There is no objection to associating honorary justices or assessors with the professional magistrates particularly during a period when the indigenous people are being trained to discharge magisterial functions.

(5) Whether there is a structure composed of Supreme Court, or alterna-tively a structure composed only of Supreme Court and District Court is not a matter on which I have formed any opinion. If there is to be a Local Court below the District Court it must strictly conform to the policy direc-tions given above.

(6) If the Local Courts Bill applies the policy set out above it can proceed. If it does not it has to be amended.

(7) If there still remains any differences of opinion, I give the decision in favour of the Administrator's proposal for local courts as well as district courts, it being understood of course that the local courts conform strictly to the policy set out above. [Minute of 3 September 1962.]

Many aspects of the 'confused' tangle are not within my personal knowledge, but I was left with an impression that the Derham recommendations were not being analysed but resisted.

A related question was the appointment of magistrates and the training of staff for the courts. The Public Service Commissioner made prompt recom-mendations in May 1961 on the training of native staff. The Department of Territories messed around with it and it was not put to me until May 1962, when I approved of the scheme. A little later, as part of a general review of progress made, I asked for a fuller report and directed that the utmost possible should be done to associate the native people more closely with the administra-tion of justice and in particular to expedite the selection and training of candidates for positions as magistrates, clerks of courts and interpreters. Pend-ing the availability of trained magistrates, the Administrator should consider the possibility of appointing native persons, literate in English and of standing in their communities, to be assistant magistrates. (Minute of 1 August 1962.)

Regarding the magistracy, it was well into 1963 before much progress had been made with the approved changes.

In mid-1962, approaching the second anniversary of the Derham inquiry, I sought a report from the Department on the progress made. After dealing with each item in turn, the report summarized the 'overall position' by saying that legislative action was incomplete and administrative action lagging. Action had not been concluded on any one of the Derham recommendations. I sent a copy to the Administrator with a direction that all outstanding matters be expedited. (Minute of 2 August 1962.)

Regarding law revision, after reading a separate submission about difficulties of having the work done in the Territory Department of Law, I instructed that action be taken to provide staff in the Department of Territories to undertake the work. 'The work has to be done', I wrote, 'and it is plain that the Territory Administration is both incapable of and uninterested in doing it.' (Minute of 2 August 1962.)

The proposals for the reorganization and better training of the police force and the reorganization of the Crown Law Department also dragged badly. Some of the neglect was in the Department and some in the Administration. I gave repeated reminders. (Minutes of 28 November 1961 and 4 February 1962.) Eventually in February 1963 I had a personal discussion with Cleland about the delay in separating the police force from general administrative activities of the public service and insisted on the early implementation of the decisions made in 1961, including those for improved training. (Minute of 21 February 1963.)

One subject in the reorganization of the Department of Law on which there were differences of view was the creation of an office of public solicitor. Some of my advisers seemed to think that the office was needed only to help 'impecunious persons' and gave it a low classification. I said part of the role of public solicitor in Papua and New Guinea was to guide an ignorant people into the proper use of the processes of the law, and for a time, at least, his work would have far-reaching social and political implications. If he gave good advice, he would prevent disputes and discontent from simmering. He could become 'a friend of the people' and had to be a man of judicial restraint and self-discipline. (Minute of 28 November 1961.) Finally I had to cut through resistance and direct that the office be created. (Minute of 4 February 1962.) Then there was a move to limit his functions to criminal cases against native offenders and I had to direct that he could also give assistance in civil cases. (Minute of 19 February 1962.)

The details I have given regarding the implementation of Derham's recommendations do not make a full account of the subject but have been quoted partly because they became the occasion for renewed directions on policy and partly as illustrations of the difficulty in the way of action.

My failure to do all I wanted to do may have been due to several causes. The basic decisions may have been inapplicable or unsuited to the conditions in Papua and New Guinea at that time. That proposition can be judged in the light of what happened in the subsequent decades and, without making that judgement, I seek only to make clear what I was trying to do. As I saw it at the time, however, two of the causes of failure to achieve all I wanted was that in both the Department of Territories and the Administration of the Territory my views and Derham's recommendations were not fully accepted. I doubt whether the Department thought the subject was as important as I did and, at times when other matters were pressing, the handling of the subject fell below the senior level. In the Administration, I believe that the Administrator personally accepted the policy and also agreed with it but, beyond his direct oversight, other officers in the Administration never fully accepted the policy and some of those departments and officers whose functions and status were in question worked against it. The fact, as I see it across the distance of years, was that the Administration did not use its opportunities to change the mind of the Minister and to modify policy, but resisted the application of policy.

On this subject I was doctrinaire and hence, as well as reasons of practical convenience, any argument would also have had to cover some points of doctrine and I doubt whether there were more than a few persons in the Administration interested in doctrinal dispute. My belief was that the ends of justice are not fully served either by adjusting a situation in order to meet the convenience of society or by delivering a decision in order to uphold the authority of the State and make it easier for authority to function. Justice also requires the protection of the individual against the State, and respect for and fair treatment of the individual as a member of society. The bent of my mind towards democracy leads me to place emphasis in all things on personal rights and personal responsibility. My conception of the law and of a system of courts is that they protect these rights and identify that responsibility and convert it into a legal obligation or a legal liability. Any form of rule, any formulation of laws, any system for the administration of justice and any social order that does not recognize personal rights and personal responsibility seems to me to be imperfect. Without such recognition, such catch-cries as freedom and independence seem to me to be meaningless. 'Arbitration and conciliation', 'fixing things up', 'serving the common interest', 'doing what is best in all the circumstances' and 'the greatest good for the greatest number' are phrases that may express some practical sense about ways of avoiding trouble but they have nothing to do with justice and leave truth in the discard.

One statement in the Derham report that left me flabbergasted was that the reforms I had required on the prisons system in March 1955 were 'very far from complete as yet'. Derham praised the corrective institution at Bomana (near Port Moresby) where 'excellent practical training courses' were being given, but found that at other places visited 'the change has so far been in name rather than in substance'.

I had been misled. I immediately called for a fuller report. I received a lengthy screed of self-justification and, after studying it, wrote, 'I can only regard the results of five years as a failure on the part of the Administrator to do promptly and effectively what the Government required to be done. The Administrator is to present at once a precise statement on what he proposes to do to get better results with an explanation of where and why the breakdown has occurred.' (Minute of 16 June 1961.) The response came in February 1962. I was not satisfied with it and said I wanted 'a factual report on what buildings are in existence, what staff is in fact on the job, what training is in fact being given and what facilities for training do exist'. (Minute of 7 March 1962.) After discussion with Lambert, I agreed that the first step should be a stock-taking to get a clearer picture than the Administration reports presented, and find out what provision had actually been made for corrective institutions in the five-year plan. The invaluable Lattin was given the job. (Minute of 21 March 1962.) As usual, he did his work well, but his report led me to the sad conclusion that, except at Bomana and Boram (near Wewak), 'very little is being done to give effect to policy and few facilities for doing so have been provided'. (Minute of 31 August 1962.) Policy was confirmed and better action required. The sorry history affected me more than usual because I had allowed myself a little vanity as a prison reformer.

There were a few other consequential developments from the decisions in the Derham report. One which I welcomed as a desirable outcome but which caused dismay in some other quarters was that, with the aid of the public solicitor, indigenous people began to take cases to the Supreme Court from the lower courts. Some of these cases concerned land matters and, although it is beyond my competence to comment on the interpretation of the law, I suggest that the fact that redress of grievance on land matters was sought through the courts was a significant historical event, and the substance of these early judgements is important in any study of lands administration and the growth of a corpus of Territory law.

There were also appeals against convictions. One such case in May 1962 arose out of certain disturbances on Buka generally referred to as the Hahalis trouble. Some of the native people were prosecuted and one of them, Hagai Sale, who was convicted of obstructing a police officer, appealed to the Supreme Court. The Chief Justice upheld the appeal on three grounds. Two of the grounds concerned the way in which the charge was laid and the question whether the policeman who was obstructed was an officer within the meaning of the regulations. In these matters the defendant obtained the advantage of arguments on fine points of law with which hitherto native defendants had been quite unfamiliar. The third ground revealed a matter of more serious concern. The case had been commenced in a Court of Native Affairs, and the Chief Justice held that this was not the appropriate tribunal to decide disputes between the Administration itself and the native people. The action should have been commenced in a district court. Moreover, in choosing to take proceedings in a Court of Native Affairs, the officials concerned, knowing that the regulations for a Court of Native Affairs did not allow a non-native to be the complainant, had put up as a dummy complainant a native who had no interest in the matter. The Chief Justice held therefore that the proceedings had not been properly instituted.

It annoyed me very much that, after all we had been doing to reform the administration of justice, as late as 1962 officers of the Administration apparently decided that the interests of the Administration could be served if they brought offenders before a Court of Native Affairs, dealt with them speedily without special provision for the representation of the accused and got a quick conviction and arranged a bogus complainant so that this could be done. As I wrote in a personal letter to Cleland, 'You may think this is a good native administration, but it is hard to convince a sceptic that it is the same sort of justice that we would expect to receive ourselves . . . It was probably a good thing that some of the appeals to the Supreme Court succeeded, as it helps to complete a story of just measures and proper respect for the rights of the native people.' (Personal letter of 5 June 1962.)

During 1962 and 1963 consideration was also given to the amendment of those sections of the Papua and New Guinea Act dealing with the judiciary and the Supreme Court. A submission I made to Cabinet in March 1963 was deferred. The Attorney-General, Barwick, had expressed doubts and, since he was absent overseas in his capacity as Minister for External Affairs, it was impossible to reach a conclusion. It seemed to me that Barwick's doubts were linked with some ideas he was developing at that time about the relationship between all Federal courts, and he had brought the Supreme Courts of the Territories within his conspectus. My own concern was to amend the Papua and New Guinea Act so as to ensure that the jurisdiction of the courts of that Territory could not be affected either fortuitously or by intention by local ordinances or regulations or by the creation by local action of new tribunals outside the system of which the Supreme Court was the apex and on terms that excluded appeals to the Supreme Court. Although in the final issue a Minister could protect the established courts system by moving for the disallowance of an ordinance or giving a direction to the Administration, I would have liked to put my conception of the courts into the Constitution of the Territory.

PART IV

THE END OF TERM
1961–1963

[30]

WEST NEW GUINEA

I will not enter here on any discussion of the issues between Indonesia and The Netherlands or the shaping of Australian foreign policy. My starting point is the fact that West New Guinea remained under the administration of The Netherlands Government after sovereignty over the Netherlands East Indies was transferred to Indonesia at the end of December 1949. The stipulated negotiations twelve months later on its future political status left that position unchanged.

In 1954 Indonesia made its claim to West New Guinea a subject of international debate. The Australian Government's view, expressed on several occasions by the Minister for External Affairs, R. G. Casey (later Lord Casey), and other representatives at the United Nations General Assembly, was that sovereignty in West New Guinea rested with The Netherlands and that, in conformity with the United Nations Charter, The Netherlands was carrying out its obligation to administer the country in accordance with the Declaration Regarding Non-Self-Governing Territories in Article 73 of the Charter.

This meant, so far as my own functions as Minister for Territories were concerned, that we saw West New Guinea, like our own Territory, as a place where the interests of the inhabitants were paramount, that their political, economic and social advancement was to be ensured, and that the goal was self-government. We were also encouraged to believe that there was a close similarity between the peoples of the two territories and that they shared common problems and had common opportunities, different from the problems and the opportunities facing the peoples of Indonesia. In External Affairs statements much was made of the 'social affinity' of the people in West and East New Guinea.

In June 1950 the newly-appointed Governor of West New Guinea inquired of the Administrator whether Qantas Empire Airways, which was at that time operating airline services in the Australian Territory as well as the service to and from Australia, could run a service from Wewak to Hollandia so as to provide West New Guinea with an outlet other than through Djakarta. Qantas arranged a survey flight in May 1951, but the original ground for interest was modified when the Dutch inaugurated their own service from

Biak to Europe and an internal link between Biak and Hollandia. Nevertheless the survey flight provided the first opportunity for administrative contact.

Under approval given by Spender, the Acting Government Secretary (S. A. Lonergan), the Director of Public Health (John Gunther), the Acting Director of District Services and Native Affairs (Ivan Champion) and three other officers paid a two-day visit to Hollandia, were shown all they could see in the time and talked with their 'opposite numbers'. They furnished reports to the Administrator on what they learnt and in due course I studied these papers myself.

One point that I learnt from these papers and from a subsequent and more extensive tour which my Parliamentary Under-Secretary, John Howse, made on my behalf was that the population of West New Guinea was more mixed than the population of our Territory. At the eastern end of the Dutch territory and in the inland regions the indigenous people were much the same as those across the border under Australian administration, but the people in the coastal areas and at the western end of the Dutch territory showed some contrasts. Proportionate to total population there were more Asian (including Moluccan and other Indonesian) immigrant peoples and more Eurasians than in our Territory. The indigenous population was not as large in West New Guinea as in the Australian Territory. There were some Malay-speaking communities. By reason of their pre-war and war-time communication with the outside world and other historical causes, some of the coastal people, speaking Malay or Dutch, were more advanced educationally and economically than any of the indigenous people in our Territory and, even although they formed a small minority, these coastal sophisticates had no counterpart in our Territory, where in 1951 it was rare to find indigenous persons who were engaged in any economic activity other than as labourers. In administrative resources, institutions, equipment and European staff, however, the Dutch lagged behind the Australians.

A second fact that worked on my mind when the international controversy sharpened was that the Dutch administrative influence did not extend very far into the interior. At that early stage the principle of self-determination, which was often invoked and usually connoted a plebiscite, had a limited practical meaning in West New Guinea, for the inland people had scant knowledge even of Dutch rule let alone any ideas about an alternative to it.

At the beginning, links between Dutch and Australian officers were friendly but not close. They were all busy about their own affairs. We had an early interest in improving communication with Hollandia and towards the end of 1952 also made a start to establish uniform quarantine regulations and procedures to protect both territories from introduced pests and diseases.

Early in 1953, following a Cabinet discussion, I informed the Administrator, in a personal and confidential letter of 24 February, of the Government's wish to promote closer liaison to strengthen the Netherlands Government in its present resolve to stay in West New Guinea but I warned him that the subject should be handled 'unobtrusively and with discretion' and that officers of the Administration 'should on no occasion press beyond their own immediate field of work into the fields of higher policy'. He should make it his personal responsibility to keep closely in touch with Canberra to ensure that liaison was established in 'a routine and rather commonplace way'.

The effective beginning of other forms of co-operation was made in July 1953. Joseph Luns, the Netherlands Foreign Minister, and W. V. A. Kernkamp, Minister for Overseas Parts of the Realm, visited Australia for discussions. Casey and I exchanged information with them about plans for development of our respective territories, and their officers discussed with the Department of Territories practical measures of co-operation at the administrative level. The Australian Government undertook to establish a regular air service between Lae and Hollandia. Both Governments agreed to exchange information on mutual problems in agriculture, health and quarantine, education and social development. The basis of these arrangements was stated to be the similarity between the peoples of Australian and Netherlands territories and the mutual problems faced by the two administrations.*

From 1954, when Indonesia sought support in the United Nations for its claim to West New Guinea, the shaping of administrative co-operation became more closely linked with the shaping of Australian foreign policy. This presented me with two minor difficulties which can be roughly summarized by saying that our Territory Administration did not know much about foreign policy and the Department of External Affairs did not know much about the Territory.

There were some signs of an ambition in Port Moresby to promote discussions between Administrator and Governor on the future. I took care to keep administrative co-operation to the working level in such fields as health, agriculture and native labour conditions and checked the Administration from concerning itself with inter-governmental matters. Purposefully I also encouraged more attention by the Administration to the Sepik and Gulf districts, alongside the Dutch border, for both had been much neglected. In March 1956 Cleland was given permission to accept an invitation to visit the Governor of West New Guinea and in July 1957 I made a brief visit to Hollandia myself accompanied by Howse and Cleland.

From that brief visit, relying more on discussions than on what I saw, I formed an impression that the Dutch administrative effort up to that time had still only touched the fringe and that there was some uncertainty among senior officers about what was likely to happen and how long they would be there. Career opportunity in their colonial service had shrunk and New Guinea was a place of exile much further from the main stream of their national life than our Territory was from home and opportunity in Australia. I held the view that, to serve Australia's interest and to help our own work in New Guinea to succeed, we should encourage the Dutch to stay in West New Guinea and to do more than they were doing. The Dutch would be like-minded and predictable neighbours, while we did not know what an Indonesian rule led by President Sukarno would mean in West New Guinea. I also thought that the long-term interests of the people of the whole of New Guinea were more likely to be served if two governments, both committed to the goal of self-government for the people, were to work towards that end. The Dutch and

---

* Statement by Minister for External Affairs, 7 July 1953, *Current Notes*, vol. 24, no. 7, p. 396.

Australians would help both communities to advance side by side to a new status beyond that of a dependent territory and then let them decide their own future, whereas the success of the Indonesian claim was likely to mean the permanent attachment of West New Guinea to Indonesia and make the future of the hundreds of thousands of people in West New Guinea subject to the interest of the tens of millions elsewhere in the Republic. Personally I never dwelt long, as did our spokesmen in the United Nations, on questions of legality of the Dutch title. Although at that stage of the advancement of the people I thought that an act of self-determination would have little meaning, I believed that continued Dutch administration would give some chance in the future to the people to make a peaceful choice of their path, while the transfer of sovereignty to Indonesia would remove that chance for ever.

In this state of mind, I took part later in 1957 in ministerial discussions with Luns and the new Minister for Overseas Territories, G. P. Helders, and personally prompted the terms of the agreement on administration co-operation which was finally endorsed by both Governments in February 1958. The principles we declared were that policies were to be based on 'the interests and inalienable rights of the inhabitants in conformity with the provisions and the spirit of the United Nations Charter' and directed towards 'the political, economic, social and educational advancement of the peoples' in a manner which recognized their 'ethnological and geographical affinity'. We expressed our determination to promote 'an uninterrupted development in this process until such time as the inhabitants of the territories concerned will be in a position to determine their own future'. The two Governments undertook to appoint liaison officers in Port Moresby and Hollandia respectively, to have an attaché on New Guinea affairs at The Netherlands Embassy in Canberra, and to hold periodical conferences between representatives of the two Governments and between officials of the two Administrations.*

The straightforward argument in support of administrative co-operation was that The Netherlands and Australia, having the same goal of self-government by the free choice of the peoples of the respective territories, should work on parallel lines, keeping in pace with each other, so that the peoples would advance together with common practices and mutual understanding, so that, when each was independent, they could continue to work together as neighbours, and so that, if they chose, they could eventually join as one people in one nation. In the shorter term there were also common practical problems (for example in health measures, extension of law and order, introduction of new crops, technical training, public utilities and communications) on which the two Administrations would find mutual advantage in exchanging information and ensuring effective liaison between officials.

The possible doubt that lingered in my mind is expressed in my use of the phrase 'work on parallel lines'. I knew Euclid's definition of parallel. Officially however we allowed at that time no public qualification of the faith that the peoples of the island of New Guinea were one people (distinctive from other neighbouring peoples) or of the hope that they would find one destiny.

I still found a tendency in Port Moresby to build up their part in admini-

* Statement by Acting Minister for External Affairs, 6 Nov. 1957, *Current Notes*, vol. 28, no. 11, p. 882.

strative co-operation beyond the level intended. I had to correct them over the appointment of the liaison officer in Hollandia. 'There is not the slightest resemblance between the proposed appointment and a consular post', I wrote on 5 March 1958. 'The proposed liaison officer has no representational functions; he will not be accredited to anyone; he is not to engage in public relations work or anything of that kind; he is not expected to make any reports or submissions on the political relationships between the two territories.' I described his work as 'to facilitate co-operation at the administrative level between the two Administrations . . . He sees the opportunities for co-operation, draws attention to them and, under direction from the Administrator, makes the arrangements for exchanges of visits, meetings, inspections and so on . . . If and when either Government wants to have a representative at Hollandia or Port Moresby it will make other arrangements'. When the first of the periodical conferences was held at the official level, I also found a need to limit the agenda to matters that could be discussed by officers without involving ministers in any policy commitment. In later administrative conferences I found a need to make the same restriction.

While a measure of friendly co-operation between the two Administrations was encouraged, we had to ensure that government-to-government communications only went through diplomatic channels. The Dutch seemed at times to be seeking to use the Hollandia-Port Moresby link for matters on which our Administrator had no authority. I felt a need to be cautious about acting as though there already was or would be a political connection between the peoples of the two territories. If the Indonesian claim succeeded, I did not want them to have a ready-made case for having East New Guinea too because of its 'affinity' with West New Guinea. In a minute of 23 November 1959 I said explicitly,

> If The Netherlands wishes at any time to raise any matters relating to the political future of either the Territory of Papua and New Guinea or of Netherlands New Guinea they should be raised by The Netherlands Government with the Australian Government through the Minister for External Affairs and it is not within the province of either the Administrator or officers of the Department of Territories to discuss with the representative of another government these matters of high policy.

It seems to me to be a fair summary of the Dutch hope to say that they wanted administrative co-operation, firstly to help the advancement of their territory, secondly to get Australia more deeply involved in West New Guinea and drawn towards fuller support of the Dutch in resistance to the Indonesians, thirdly to promote internationally the idea of the unity of the whole of New Guinea so as to make the Indonesian claim look like an attempt to divide a country and people who should be one, and fourthly, as a result of all this, to strengthen support of their policy by the people of Holland. To succeed in all these objectives, they also had to make their own people who were working in West New Guinea feel confident that their work was worth doing and that they would have time to complete it.

While Australia wanted to keep the Dutch in West New Guinea until that country attained self-government, the means by which we did this and the extent to which we supported Dutch policy in changing circumstances were matters of Australian foreign policy for determination by Cabinet and there was much information and many considerations to which the Administrator was not privy.

Necessarily there was repeated reference of the West New Guinea question to Cabinet. The Cabinet records for this period are still closed and I respect the confidentiality of discussions in which I took part. It is public knowledge however that from about 1959 onwards the shaping of Australian policy on West New Guinea was further complicated by signs of possible military action by Indonesia and growing uncertainty about British and American attitudes. The Australian Government, while continuing to support the Dutch, had to consider possibilities other than continued Dutch administration of West New Guinea and a continued gradual progress towards self-government, and also how far Australia could stick her neck out if the British and the Americans were not of the same mind. They also had to take notice of an opinion held strongly in some Australian political quarters that the success of the Indonesian claim to West New Guinea might be followed by a claim to East New Guinea.

In these circumstances, the Department of Territories revived an argument that Australian interests might be well served by widening the concept of New Guinea unity into a concept of a united Pacific area into which there would be no ground for an Asian intrusion. The development of a wider Pacific sphere, with the aim of self-determination by the Melanesian peoples, it was hoped, might mean that in the short term Australia would not offend Indonesia, that we could create a situation that would put Indonesia at a disadvantage if she ever did claim East New Guinea, and at the same time still leave it arguable that West New Guinea belonged more properly in this developing Melanesian sphere than to the Indonesian archipelago. By this means too the principle of self-determination could be maintained. The practical conclusion of this line of argument in January 1960 was that, while Australia continued the policy of administrative co-operation between our Territory and West New Guinea, we might also take positive steps to promote a close association between our Territory and the British Solomon Islands Protectorate. I brought this argument clearly before Cabinet and advised them on the practicability of the idea. I also wrote personally to the Prime Minister on the subject.

As background to this action on my part, I also record that four years earlier than this, on 23 January 1956, I had written to Casey on the same subject and as a consequence we had made a joint submission to Cabinet. In March 1956 Lambert had made a visit to the British Solomon Islands in order to add to our first-hand knowledge of its problems and in May 1956 Cabinet had allowed me to develop proposals for administrative co-operation with the Solomons although unwilling to consider any move towards a transfer of administration. As a result of the work since 1956, I was in a position in January 1960 to inform Cabinet that, if they wished it to be done, we had the knowledge and capacity to undertake greater responsibilities in the Solomons.

At the end of May and in early June 1959 Lambert made a visit of three weeks to West New Guinea. His report, wholly factual, was the clearest and most comprehensive account we had of what was being done by The Netherlands. It showed that since 1951 there had been a steady rise in expenditure and a big improvement in both the numbers and the quality of staff. Early in 1959, with the appointment of P. J. Mollison[58] as liaison officer at Hollandia—an earlier brief appointment of another officer had not worked out well—we began to receive regular monthly reports, which kept us informed of developments and plans. From time to time I brought the reports under the personal notice of both Menzies and Casey.

Early in 1960 Theo Bot, the Netherlands Under-Secretary for New Guinea Affairs, made a visit of inspection to New Guinea and afterwards we had useful talks in Canberra solely on administrative co-operation. An incident connected with his visit will serve to illustrate another problem in the handling of West New Guinea questions. On his way home Bot was questioned by newspapermen in Washington, where he had been for talks at the State Department. He was reported as saying that his Government was prepared to 'pull out' of New Guinea whenever the United Nations ended Australian trusteeship over the eastern part of the island and also that Netherlands New Guinea would have its first local parliament in 1960. He was also reported as having touched on the future possibility of some form of union between Netherlands New Guinea, the Australian territory and adjacent islands.

On his return to The Hague, Bot issued the 'correct version' of what he was reported to have said. This was that if the United Nations Trusteeship Council deemed that Australian New Guinea, after a certain period, was ripe for self-government, he was of the opinion that the Netherlands part of New Guinea would be just as far with the development of its people. He did not specify any period and no exact answer could be given yet to the question when the population of Netherlands New Guinea would be ripe for self-determination. He had been told by some Papuans that the Dutch pace of development was too fast. The idea of a Melanesian union was nothing new. The Papuans (the phrase the Dutch always used for the indigenous people) themselves ought to make the choice. Neither Australia nor The Netherlands would take such initiative on their own.

What Bot said was unexceptionable for us, but the way it was reported led to all sorts of rumours and misunderstandings, some of them to the general effect that we were going to get out of New Guinea as fast as possible and some to the effect that the Netherlands and Australia were cooking up a scheme for uniting the two territories.

In May 1960 I had ministerial talks at The Hague. I had accompanied Menzies to the Prime Ministers' Conference in London and, during an interval in the programme of the visit, he asked me to go to Paris, where the summit conference between Eisenhower and Khrushchev was to be held, and then to The Hague to discuss matters affecting the territories.

The Paris visit was unexpectedly dramatic. Following the incident in which an American airman was arrested by the Russians on an alleged espionage flight in a U2 aircraft over Soviet territory, the summit talks were called off. By sheer coincidence I flew into Paris on the day of the crisis. The air service from London was delayed and, instead of arriving calmly with hours to spare before a luncheon appointment with the French Minister for Overseas Territories, I landed at Orly within a few minutes of the time I was due in the heart of Paris. But the French had everything arranged. I was hauled out from the long line of descending passengers, taken straight to a car and, with sirens screaming, we raced to the exit. The streets had been cleared—presumably not for me, but for the comings and goings of Eisenhower and Khrushchev—and so, with an escort of eight motor-cyclists (three ahead, three behind and two outriders beside the car), sirens screaming, we tore into and through the city at high speed, gendarmes holding up all other traffic. Here and there a waiting crowd waved, either mistaking me for someone else or merely wondering who the hell I was, and occasionally some deluded group raised a cheer. In a state of bewilderment I was escorted out of the noisy convoy into a grand building, hurried upstairs, offered a chance to wash my hands and was then presented by my ministerial host to fellow-ministers and officials who had been doing pre-lunch exercises for nearly an hour. We had a delightful lunch once I recovered from the disadvantage of having been credited with such fluency in French that there was no need for anyone to try to speak in English or even to pronounce their words deliberately.

Later I had official discussions with the French mainly about the work of the South Pacific Commission and the Trusteeship Council. Then I went to Brussels for similar talks with the Belgians, who at that time also had their own political worries about the Congo, and finally to The Hague.

My reports to Menzies on this series of talks, dated 27 May 1960 are still closed documents but, in my own judgement, there will be no breach of official secrecy if I disclose part of the discussions at The Hague on West New Guinea. My talks were with the Prime Minister (Professor de Quay), Luns, the Minister for Home Affairs (E. H. Toxopeus), and Bot, who had become State Secretary for Home Affairs. In an audience with Her Majesty Queen Wilhelmina I found that she too had a keen interest and what might be regarded as progressive views about the future of New Guinea as well as a deep feeling for the welfare of the people. Her Majesty discussed various aspects of the question for close on an hour, while herself pouring our cups of tea and passing the buttered scones.

The Dutch ministers told me of their plans and their timetable for setting up a Legislative Council in Hollandia. My interpretation of the situation revealed in our very frank talks was that The Netherlands and Australia had similar views about the objective of self-government, parallel development and the tempo of advancement, but both of us recognized that we might have to choose different methods to suit the situation in which each country found itself. The Dutch recognized that Australia had to consider not only West New Guinea but her future relationship with Indonesia. We recognized that The Netherlands had the intention to stay in West New Guinea until the people had self-government but that her capacity to do so depended on the support of the United States and Great Britain in restraint of Indonesia.

My impression was that in 1960 The Netherlands Government was feeling the pressure of events in the Belgian Congo and the indications of possible military action by Indonesia and also felt that they were being 'deserted' by their allies. They did not want to fight Indonesia and saw that the best hope of deterring Indonesia from fighting them was the political influence of Britain and the United States. In their disappointment with Britain and the United States they were inclined, against their better judgement, to introduce self-government before the proper time had arrived in the hope that world opinion would be against any attack by Indonesia on a newly independent, self-governing West New Guinea. Another domestic problem for The Netherlands was the advocacy by the Dutch Socialists of a United Nations trusteeship over West New Guinea, although for the present the government had majority support in their own parliament for a policy of steady and more gradual advancement towards self-government.

In further discussions of the future of New Guinea I made it plain to the Dutch ministers that Australia was unable to commit itself to a union of the two territories so long as we had responsibility for the administration of our own Territory of Papua and New Guinea because, I said, this was a matter that the inhabitants should determine for themselves after they had both attained self-government. The Dutch ministers accepted this point and I imagine that they were also intelligent enough to guess that we were unwilling to have the handing over of West New Guinea, under trusteeship, to Australian administration presented to the world as one of the alternatives to Indonesian rule. We agreed on the value of administrative co-operation although we saw this could only carry us a certain distance and there was a need for more frequent meetings of ministers.

I returned to Australia knowing the prospective date of the next constitutional change to be made in West New Guinea and the prospective structure of their proposed Legislative Council. As shown in chapters 22 and 33, we were already working on the next constitutional step to be taken in Papua and New Guinea, and both the Dutch ministers and I, appreciating that neither should embarrass the other, saw the need for keeping in close touch over the progress of our respective measures.

Following my visit to The Hague, there was a reciprocal visit to Canberra by Toxopeus in October 1960 for further ministerial talks. In April 1961 we arranged for an exchange of visits between delegations from Australia and The Netherlands and representatives of the two territories for the opening of a session of the Legislative Council in Port Moresby and the inauguration of the New Guinea Council in Hollandia. As a result of legislation passed by the Australian Parliament in 1960 and elections held in March 1961, our new Legislative Council had more indigenous members, both elected and appointed, and more elected members than the old Council.

Representatives of other governments also attended. There was great rejoicing. Journalists swarmed. Once again the unfortunate Bot was the centre of misrepresentation by the press. My comment to the Prime Minister at the time was,

It was apparent before I left Sydney on the evening of Monday 3 April that the press was searching for a story that Australia was accepting commitments towards the Dutch. I personally refused to comment. Before leaving The Hague Bot gave a background interview to an Associated Press correspondent, who lodged the story as coming from Hollandia. As published, this report contained a statement about expected Australian aid. The correspondent has personally admitted to Bot in Hollandia that this was misleading. Meanwhile other correspondents, hearing of the original story and feeling that they had been scooped, approached Bot at a social reception. They received nothing but a flat denial. Bot gave no interview to any correspondent in Hollandia . . . Bot definitely assures me no statement was made or interview given to Australian journalists at any time.

After Toxopeus and Bot had been made aware that Australian journalists had sent reports suggesting a military commitment by Australia, and basing their stories on false claims to have had interviews with Bot in Hollandia, they issued a statement including the following passage:

> Mr Bot, when questioned about the Dutch attitude in case of an armed attack, said Holland would resist with all resources at her disposal but said the limited forces in New Guinea are not meant to cope with any large-scale attack. Mr Bot said the present Dutch forces could handle infiltration. In case of a major attack, which he did not consider a real possibility, he said it would become a matter for the United Nations. Nobody could expect Holland to meet such an event single-handed. In that case he expected Pacific powers like the United States and Australia could not remain indifferent.

Unfortunately the original reports based on guesswork received more prominence than the only authentic statement Bot made in Hollandia.

There certainly was no military commitment by Australia in respect of West New Guinea, and we understood Bot's allusion to the United States and Australia to mean that after any major Indonesian attack had been referred to the United Nations, we would support United Nations action.

Another story by Australian journalists in their search for a new 'angle' in the reports on the celebrations in Hollandia and Port Moresby was that the Dutch were going ahead, being more progressive than we were, and that Australia was deliberately holding back. Again there was the suggestion of some sort of misunderstanding or strain between the two Governments. The stories gave scant attention either to the necessity facing the Dutch or to the differences in powers, functions and structure between the Council in Hollandia and the Council in Port Moresby.

International developments during 1960 and 1961 were influencing the Dutch towards more dramatic proof of their policy of promoting self-government. Indonesian military strength and the possibility of its use were becoming plainer; international support for the Dutch in their Charter policy of political, economic and social advancement of the people was less firm. At the General Assembly of the United Nations in September and October 1961 Luns sponsored a plan for self-determination, transfer of sovereignty to the Papuan people, and interim administration by an international development authority, with a continued Dutch financial contribution.

The administrative co-operation continued but there were two occasions when I felt the need to warn our Administration against being drawn into wrong situations. 'No matter how keen may be our friendship or sympathy for the Dutch,' I wrote to Cleland in a letter of 3 July 1961, 'we have to keep these matters under our own control. As well as making sure we do retain control over our own relationships in point of fact, it is equally important in these times that we should be careful about appearances.'

One occasion that prompted this caution was a move that looked like arranging a conference between the peoples of the two territories. I told Cleland that the only conferences we had approved were between the two Administrations. The other occasion was an almost unbelievable suggestion from Port Moresby that a detachment of the Pacific Islands Regiment might be sent to West New Guinea to join in the celebration at Manokwari of the first anniversary of the formation by the Dutch of the Papuan Volunteer Corps. I told Cleland that there was the greatest possible objection to moving any part of the Australian armed services into West New Guinea even for a celebration.

I shall not recount the Australian diplomatic activities during 1961 and 1962 nor the events that culminated on 15 August 1962 at the United Nations headquarters in New York when the representatives of The Netherlands and Indonesia signed an agreement under which The Netherlands transferred the administration of West New Guinea to a United Nations Temporary Executive Authority, which had discretion to transfer full administrative control to Indonesia at some future time. An 'act of self-determination' was to be carried out during this second phase. The transfer to Indonesia took place on 1 May 1963. From the time of the meeting of the General Assembly in 1961, however, it was clear to me that we were facing a situation different from that in which the agreement for administrative co-operation had been made. I never had any illusions about what self-determination meant and agreed with those who described it as an 'act of ascertainment'—something short of a plebiscite.

In these circumstances I saw increased urgency for mapping the border. Except in one section, at a bend in the Fly River, the line of the frontier did not follow any natural features but was described on paper as following a meridian. Except at the two ends it was not marked on the ground and there was some doubt whether the posts at the ends were accurately sited.

The matter had been under notice since 1955 but nothing much had been done. The country was difficult. Australia had limited capacity for such work. There seemed to be some reluctance in the Department of External Affairs to approach The Netherlands on laying down a frontier at a time when we were giving them full support in the United Nations. Our own national mapping authority in Canberra had other preoccupations. In November 1958 I had approved the setting up of a Technical Border Commission and in November 1961, after much importunity, I received its recommendations for the creation of a Dutch-Australian Border Commission and for taking related steps. After a number of minor border incidents had reinforced my case, I managed at length to obtain approval and funds from Cabinet in July 1962 to start aerial mapping and establish a priority for this work. Nevertheless progress was still unsatisfactory and, after transfer of West New Guinea to Indonesia had taken place, we still had some uncertainty about the exact line of the frontier. As a temporary expedient for administrative purposes I approved of the erection of sign-posts on the main tracks crossing the border, with notices on them to the effect that somewhere within the next few hundred yards the track crossed from Australian into Indonesian territory.

This expedient was necessary because Cabinet had required control over quarantine and immigration and because our own patrol officers and other persons needed to know which villages were under their care and to make sure that during a period of possible tension there were no accidental infringements of the frontier and no unjustified claim of Australian responsibility over any villages or people on the Indonesian side.

Looking back over the distance of years, it seems now that some of the Australian fears of what might happen after Indonesia gained West New Guinea may have been exaggerated. At the time, there was considerable concern about the possible danger from animal and plant diseases. In contrast with the period of Dutch rule there would now be free traffic throughout the Indonesian archipelago. Whereas Dutch quarantine had been reliable, we had doubts whether Indonesian quarantine would be effective. There was also some concern about possible attempts at the subversion of village people against Australian administration.

When change had seemed certain, I had directed that a chain of new patrol posts be established in the border region, so that, in conjunction with the existing posts at Kiunga (on the Fly River), Telefomin (in the mountains), Green River (near the Sepik River) and Vanimo (on the north coast), we could be in touch with all the people on the Australian side of the border region and, either by direct observation or by reports from the village people, be sure of knowing what was happening at any time and have landing strips and administrative centres from which we could work in any emergency, such as a cholera epidemic, unusual movements of population or the unwelcome activities of strangers.

I had known the long-established posts for some time and during 1962 and 1963 I personally visited these and all the new posts up and down the border on two occasions, both to give our young officers some idea of the combined requirement of alertness and calmness in order to be aware of anything unusual but not to become involved in any incidents, and to encourage them in the difficult conditions in which they had to work.

These visits were among the most interesting I had during twelve years as Minister. I flew mostly in a two-seater single-engine charter aircraft down the magnificent gorges of the central mountain spine or over the vast waterlogged plains of the Fly and Strickland Rivers, sometimes amid great cloud turrets whose grandeur and majesty, touched with evening light, had an unearthly beauty. In a mosquito-sized aircraft among great mountains of cloud one gains a sense of immensity and self becomes insignificant. This brings its own calm, for one is only a small speck in great space. I came under the spell that so many lonely travellers from the first explorers onwards have felt in the New Guinea wastelands.

Our precautions were creditable, I believe, and the Administration officers who were engaged in the work at those patrol posts did a first-class job. In the event, the transition from Dutch to Indonesian rule brought few border problems. The definition and the mapping of the frontier was still a live question after I left the portfolio, and it became my duty as Minister for External Affairs to continue discussion of the matter in Djakarta, first with Subandrio and later with Adam Malik. I found ready co-operation from the

Indonesians both when Sukarno was in power and after he was deposed. We had one or two quarantine scares, not serious, and some problems of helping village people to find out whether they were on one side of the border or the other.

For a period after the ending of Dutch rule we also had some problems in respect of what were called 'refugees'. Some of the stories current at the time did not always distinguish clearly between the various classes of persons so described. Since the policy and responsibility for admission or rejection did not rest solely on me, I will not presume to enlarge on the situation. In general the Australian Government tried to act in accordance with established international usage. Our main concern in the Department of Territories was with those who had crossed the border, mostly at the northern end and, having been rejected by the Australian Government, had to be sent back home. My instruction to the Administrator was that he should pay careful regard to considerations of humanity and do what he could to avoid unnecessary distress to the travellers. Any recent arrivals who had no claim to admission should not be put on the road again if they were exhausted after their journey or in need of food, rest or medical attention, but should be given a chance to recuperate. A holding camp was set up at Vanimo for these purposes. The Administration Departments of Health and Native Affairs handled this well.

One last act of tidying up was the withdrawal of our liaison officer from Hollandia. To avoid any precipitate break, he was kept there for a few months after the transfer of sovereignty, but I made it plain that as soon as possible we should 'ease ourselves out of administrative co-operation arrangements'. Unless it could be established that East New Guinea and West New Guinea were moving towards a single objective, there was no case for administrative co-operation as we had known it up to date but only a case for 'trying to maintain friendly relations as best we can with the people next door'. This could be better handled as part of our international relations and by appointing an External Affairs officer at Hollandia. My view was accepted. Mollison was recalled to Port Moresby in October 1962, concluding a most valuable period of service, and the Minister for External Affairs appointed one of his career officers, R. N. Birch, to Hollandia. This marked the formal ending of the administrative co-operation arrangements while we were working towards self-government for both territories. Other forms of co-operation with Indonesia could be developed later to suit the new circumstances.

Another consequential move was the improvement of our own work in the districts adjoining the border. I wrote a long minute on the subject on 5 February 1963 following a visit I had made to the Sepik. Our district commissioner at Wewak at that time was R. Cole.[59] I had seen a lot of him during successive visits and had enjoyed and profited from the talks we had when travelling together or sometimes sitting on his lawn overlooking the sea on the lovely tropic evenings. Cole had depth of experience of this region, having been in operations based on Maprik during the war, and was also a capable administrator of his district and a good leader of the officers under him. We discussed many possibilities together, and the directions I gave and the problems I defined in my minute owed much to him.

In closing this chapter, memory prompts me to recall the happy personal associations I had and the friendships I formed with my Dutch colleagues. Joseph Luns, Foreign Minister of The Netherlands for fifteen years, became known to me even more closely after I had taken the portfolio of External Affairs, but it was over West New Guinea that I first came to know his realism, his sense of fun and his racy and sometimes vehement way of demolishing other people's arguments. It was always stimulating to be in his company. Toxopeus, Kernkamp, Helders and Bot did not stay so long on the political scene. They all had the sort of education that would have given them the label of 'academic' in Australian public life. I found it very refreshing to be working with men who, when business was over, could talk of something else and, who when business was on, could examine a question against a wide background of knowledge and pick up an allusion or understand a phrase with some exactness. I had a snobbishly intellectual delight in their company that I did not find often in my usual round of duty. At Canberra the Netherlands Ambassador, Tony Lovink, had become a personal friend mainly because, early in our acquaintance, we started horse-riding together on Sunday mornings. At that time we each had a retired racehorse as a hack and memory still recaptures in vivid detail that long grassy upward slope on the outskirts of Canberra where, on stinging cold mornings, with the wind in their nostrils, we let the horses have their head and galloped laughing side by side for a mad and glorious mile.

One memory I have of one of my visits to Hollandia is of fire-walkers. Somewhere in the Dutch territory there were people who had this tradition. I observed the display closely and with growing incredulity. There was no doubt that the stones were so hot that a green banana leaf thrown on them shrivelled to ash in an instant. It was equally plain that men in bare feet, without any preparation of their soles, walked deliberately across those stones for up to ten paces without suffering harm. It was a mystery beyond my comprehension. Perhaps it would be beyond the comprehension of fire-walkers if they could see the strange ways in which politicians tread and survive.

The attention given to West New Guinea over a period of seven or eight years had some effect on opinion and outlook among both the indigenous and expatriate population in Papua and New Guinea. The 'feeling of un-certainty' of which the whites complained was further promoted by various press stories and rumours about what was likely to happen and what the intentions of the Australian Government were supposed to be. There were signs too of some fear among the indigenes as well as the Europeans about Indonesian ambitions in the future. Although the security people claimed to have evidence of local 'subversion' along the lines that the Indonesians might help to drive the Australian 'exploiters' out of East New Guinea as well as driving the Dutch 'exploiters' out of West New Guinea, I gave little credence to the report. My impression was that most of the indigenous people in our Territory who were at all aware of the events were anti-Indonesian in senti-ment and accepted the view that the Indonesian claim meant that West New Guinea would be denied self-government. At the end, after transfer to Indo-nesia, there was much evidence of ill-feeling against the United Nations, which already was badly regarded by most of the native people. In the Sepik district the native people, particularly their leaders, asked me repeatedly, in effect, 'If the United Nations can give away the people across the border, will they also be able to give us away to someone else?' The short-term effect of the events in West New Guinea was for the majority of both whites and indigenes that they sought further assurances that Australia was going to stay in East New Guinea. It strengthened the feelings among the people of the Territory against early self-government.

[31]

TURNING POINT

The year 1962 seemed to me at the time to be a turning point in the history of Papua and New Guinea. Hard work below ground had been done and progress seemed to quicken.

In this period I had many occasions of encouragement in the opening of hospitals, schools, roads, bridges and other buildings and in little ceremonies arranged to welcome the first fruits of one activity or another. From many memories I draw only two widely different stories.

The first memory is of a visit to the newly opened patrol post at Nomad, high in the mountains of the Southern Highlands in the head waters of the Strickland River. Its opening was almost the last action in the amazing story of bringing all the Territory under control. The Nomad people were of pygmy size but hard with muscle—little savage men who looked at the stranger with a dark penetrating gaze. It seemed as though some wild creature inside were peering out from behind the mask of the face.

The patrol post consisted of an airstrip, which was a bit hard to find among the clouds, and two or three native-material huts perched at the edge of a great declivity. Down below, a river ran invisibly but audibly beneath intertwined jungle growth. A score or so of the pygmies were watching from a distance when we climbed out of the two-seater. One, a sort of spokesman, came close to us, gave a subdued greeting and fingered my clothing in curiosity. Only men were to be seen. They had not yet allowed their women and children to come into the patrol post.

As the two young patrol officers and I made our inspection, the men slipped quietly from one obscure place to another and looked at us around the corners of the huts. They were still unsure what the patrol post really meant. They were naked, except for a tough, hard belt of bark around the soft part of the body, protecting liver and spleen from the arrows of enemies. Each man carried a bow as tall as himself and a clutch of arrows. They had not yet consented to lay their weapons down when they came into the patrol post.

The pilot and I had some food and a yarn with the two boys. They were still at the stage of trying to win the confidence of the people and had a lonely and watchful life on their own. They had only been there for a few weeks. There

374

had been no incidents. These boys were completing the policy of bringing the whole of the Territory under administrative control. As keenly as ever, I felt the immensity of the task that had been done over the past ten years and was thrilled with the young Australians who had done it. Less than three years later the Nomad people were voting for the House of Assembly.

My pilot on this occasion, in a single-engine Cessna chartered from the Missionary Aviation Fellowship, was Max Myers. We had a somewhat hazardous flight from Nomad to Mount Hagen when the weather closed in and the pilot had to find his way on a roundabout route by flying blind for a while, for the cloud was dense up to 10 000 feet, and then descending cautiously a couple of times in search of a place he knew. On the second attempt we saw the ground and crept along the valleys, close to the tree tops, underneath the heavy and unbroken canopy, watching for familiar landmarks. The pilot thought he recognized a stream and followed it to find another stream which he identified by some magic of his own. We crept along to Mount Hagen in the fading light and landed to the surprise of the locals, for the airfield there had been officially closed for hours and anyone who knew we were in the area had assumed we must have stopped for the night somewhere else. The truth was that, in the conditions, there was no other place the pilot had a chance of finding. If we had been about twenty minutes later, we would not have found Mount Hagen.

I flew several times with Myers. He was a noble character, gentle in manner and of great courage. A few years later, flying for the Missionary Aviation Fellowship in Africa, he crashed and was killed.

The second memory is of a different kind: the presentation of certificates to the first nurses (six men and eight women) to graduate from the Papuan Medical College in April 1961. By that time there were over two hundred students in training on a three-year course, leading to a fourth year for specialists. They were the first of the bright new generation trained at a higher standard to serve their people and their country. Students, staff and distinguished visitors had morning tea together. I felt a fatherly pride in all the students. When we had started in our health services, we had done the best we could with illiterate people from the villages who had been given training in first aid and taught when to refer the sick to the nearest hospital. Now, ten years later, these eager and well-qualified graduates were starting a new order. They had come from all over the Territory and had met for the first time at the college. In their happy comradeship and common bond of service I glimpsed the unity of the nation of the future. I felt as hopeful and enthusiastic on that morning as any of the young people. Something was shifting at last.

While memories such as these brought strong encouragement, and while the statistics showed an upward turn towards a new future, there were also some occasions of doubt because I felt I had not succeeded in carrying the Government with me as far as I had hoped.

On several occasions from 1959 onwards I tried to get a broad discussion in Cabinet on our policy in Papua and New Guinea and twice submitted formal papers for that purpose. There was little result. Each year during the Cabinet meetings on the budget, I submitted a paper setting out the facts and arguments in support of my claim for an increased grant, but the Cabinet discussion, such as it was, always centred on the single practical question of whether the claim should be reduced, and, although the Ministers heard my story, there was never any real discussion on whether our policy was sound or our aims well directed. My 'background paper' was only 'noted'. The most I got were directions about such practical steps as increasing local revenue or applying stricter economy standards and stopping extravagance.

In these circumstances I sought mental reinforcement by an occasional discussion with the Prime Minister outside Cabinet. From about 1958 or 1959, I think, Menzies, following his visit to the Territory in 1957, began to respect more than he had done originally, whatever qualities I had and to appreciate more fully both the intricacies and the value of doing the right thing in Papua and New Guinea. I myself, as I came closer to Menzies, was learning to value his great qualities more highly.

A lot of silly comments and many untrue statements have been made about Menzies by persons who never had the advantage of working close to him. He had a far better mind than anyone else in and around government in Australia during the quarter of a century in which I was close to affairs. He knew more, he could see a point more quickly and more exactly, he could think clearly and reach a conclusion reasonably and accurately after hearing the facts and arguments. Some foolish persons have referred to Menzies as a great speaker, as though that summed up his talents. They should recognize that Menzies expressed himself well because he knew what he wanted to say. When, at length, aided by the pressure of changing political events, I found the opportunity to engage his interest, I found that Menzies could understand what I was trying to do and why I was trying to do it far better than anyone else and he gave me the only real intellectual stimulus and encouragement on the rightness of our policy that I had from the Government during my most difficult years with the portfolio of Territories.

Following my policy statement to Parliament in October 1960 and the statements in the same month made by the Governor-General (Lord Dunrossil) and me at the opening of the new session of the Legislative Council in a new building at Port Moresby, I had a talk with the Prime Minister about the future and was encouraged to hope that the Budget for 1961–2 might give a chance for a major step forward. Early in January 1961 I started the Department on the work of preparing the submission. It was to be based on the Cabinet decision and the public announcement we had made of our readiness to fix target dates on educational, economic and social advancement. The submission was to set out our programmes in each of these fields and the dates on which we hoped to complete successive stages of the work.

This work eventually led to the preparation of a five-year plan. When it was ready, I said to Lambert in a minute of 3 May 1961 that, before I put the plan to Cabinet, I ought to try again to get a major decision on policy, especially the scale of effort in the Territory and any changes in the direction of the effort, and I would like to have some preliminary discussion with the Prime Minister (who at that time was also Minister for External Affairs following Casey's retirement in February 1960), the Treasurer and the Minister for Trade. What was Australia trying to do? What were the present and prospective changes in conditions in the Territory? What were the pressures from outside the Territory, both international and Australian? 'This is one of the points of time', I wrote, 'at which we must try to engage the attention of Cabinet in our problems in a realistic but far-sighted way and obtain either endorsement or correction of what we are doing.' I wanted 'to gain an entrance at a high policy level' to a decision on our draft five-year programme.

Some notes of my own, dated 5 May 1961, of a discussion I had with the Prime Minister disclose my outlook at that time on the scale and direction of our effort in the Territory. I reminded the Prime Minister of our undertaking on target dates and suggested that, in fixing targets, we had to make an adjustment between various factors: our judgement on what would be best for the people of Papua and New Guinea; the international political pressures on us; our capacity to provide money and men; a calculation of what Australia could afford and how much the Australian taxpayer would approve; and our judgement, in the light of a guess about the final outcome, on what it was worthwhile for Australia to do. Analysing the last-mentioned point, I suggested that our strongest motive derived from a sense of trust towards the people and from our national self-respect and pride. Defence considerations were still strong in some quarters, even if the purpose were mainly to deny the use of the area to any other power. There was some economic interest, for the production and trade of the country were growing and most of it was complementary to Australian production, while products such as rubber and tea could be of importance to our balance of payments. We also had an interest in ensuring that our nearest neighbouring country had stable government and did not become a political vacuum into which some other power could move. Could we therefore assume that there could be no withdrawal from Papua and New Guinea until we had completed the task we had set ourselves? What would we regard as the end of our effort? We might say that the end would come with the choice of self-government by the people but, in my judgement, one certainty was that self-government would come before the country had ceased to need outside help. Because of pressure from outside and the rapidity of changes inside the Territory, the prospect was that self-government would come before the Territory could support itself financially, provide food and work for its people from its own resources at the higher standards they were now seeking, staff a competent and honest public service, have a system of justice that would protect the individual, and assume full responsibility for foreign affairs and defence.

I continued that there were degrees in self-government, as the Australian evolution from responsible government through Dominion status to full nationhood illustrated. In the changed world conditions and the different circumstances, I doubted whether, after Papua and New Guinea had achieved self-government, Australia would be able to maintain a kind of 'Mother Country' relationship with Papua and New Guinea as Britain had done with Australia until after World War I. Nevertheless my judgement was that for another thirty years Papua and New Guinea would require our help. I expected that for about ten years from 1961 the need for outside support would continue to rise steeply. After that the slope would be more gentle and in about fifteen years from 1961 the need might start to level off and decline rather slowly towards the thirty-year mark. Then there might still be major needs, particularly for financing the development of resources.

My view was that we should work to produce a sound result rather than any kind of quick result so that we could get out from under. We had publicly expressed the view that the rate of advancement was set by the response of the people. It would need courage, skill and patience under insult to maintain that view.

I expressed my own historical philosophy by saying that rulers had limited power to control the course of change and to regulate the pace of change. (Perhaps Menzies was the only politician of the day who had the intellectual temper to evaluate such a remark, for he was a statesman singularly free from the over-confidence, petty vanity and vexation of spirit that mark most of those smaller men who think they are making history and shaping the course of events.) I then said that, in practice, a great part of the wisdom of administration was in making sure that we anticipated the changes taking place and were ready to meet new needs before they emerged. Having jobs for people who had been educated, having enough food for a growing population and having an opportunity for people to share in government when they were ready to do so were not simply matters of regulating the pace of change but rather of observing closely and understanding clearly what changes were about to take place. Colonial troubles often seemed to arise from tendencies in colonial administration to decide what should happen and when it should happen rather than to observe and understand what was already happening. We had to try to ensure that there was intelligent anticipation both at the Cabinet level and perhaps even more importantly at the level of Territory Administration.

I further argued that the projected expenditures in the Territory, linked with a claim for a larger Commonwealth grant, were based on such intelligent anticipation as we could make on the facts as we saw them. At a number of points, however, the answer given by intelligent anticipation had to be modified by the limits on capacity. For example intelligent anticipation would require us to do far more on land matters, agricultural extension and native land settlement than the Government proposed to do at present and the needs in health and education were greater than those the Government proposed to meet. Limits were set by the availability of trained staff, the capacity of the Administration to use them and the views of Government on increased effort. Consequently, in proposing a five-year plan, we should recognize that, from year to year, adjustments would have to be made. Within the period of five years, rapid change might produce unexpected new needs. We should think along the lines of a continual projection of the plan five years ahead.

I advised caution about accepting direct international aid to raise our capacity and preferred to rely on indirect aid from organizations such as the South Pacific Commission, World Health Organization and the Food and Agriculture Organization. I then passed to the argument that the effort Australia was making by increased annual grants to Papua and New Guinea should relieve her of part of the obligation to contribute to other forms of international aid. There had been pressure from the Minister and Department of External Affairs for increased Australian contributions to international aid and they were strong rivals for my claims on the Budget and contested my views that we should count what we spent in Papua and New Guinea as part of our contribution to help other countries. As an aside, I may mention that when I became Minister for External Affairs and reorganized the whole external aid administration, my view prevailed.

The conclusion of my discussion with the Prime Minister was that my claim on the Budget for Papua and New Guinea could not be cut down unless Cabinet made a decision that Australia should do less than was necessary and possible.

At a later stage of the discussion we looked at the questions of whether there were sources of revenue other than the Australian taxpayer and whether we could use our money more economically. We went into some details of local revenues in the Territory from income tax, customs duties and fees and charges and the possibility of increased local borrowing. On this point I revived a suggestion I had made earlier in my term that there should be a loan works programme, serviced from Territory revenues. Although in present circumstances this would not relieve the Commonwealth from the necessity of providing most of the money, as it did for State loan works programmes, it might be useful to establish the practice. At the inauguration of self-government, the existence of loan obligations that could be transferred to the new government would reduce the area of argument. Incidentally this tied in with the attempt I was making to separate such public utilities as electricity supply and harbours from the normal tasks of administration. I suggested that Treasury should also study the possibility of obtaining financial assistance from the International Bank for Reconstruction and Development.

Looking for possible economies, I referred to the high cost of expatriate staff —costly to recruit, costly in wastage, in rates of pay, in long absence through liberal leave provisions, and in demand for houses. Yet we needed them, and favourable conditions were a necessary inducement. The only possibility of change was through the recruitment of indigenous officers, and a limit was set by the availability of candidates with the required education.

I tried to have a similar discussion with the Treasurer, Harold Holt, who had succeeded Fadden in December 1958, but did not get far beyond the figures of my prospective claim for a five-year programme. Holt had many good qualities but a limited capacity for consecutive thought.

An ad hoc committee of officers from the interested departments was set up by the Prime Minister to look at the figures. I still hoped that this committee, while concentrating on what scale of effort was required and what Australian expenditure was justified, might help to bring about the general discussion of policy before the Budget was shaped. (Minute of 9 June 1961.) The committee made a report entitled 'Programme for Accelerated Development in Papua and New Guinea'. Cabinet had a week-long series of meetings on the Budget. Sadly and tersely I minuted the papers to Lambert on 18 July: 'This report has not been considered by Cabinet. The grant for 1961–62 was fixed without admitting the report to discussion. At a suitable opportunity we will have to discuss what we do about target dates.'

The Estimates of Expenditure for 1961–2 totalling £25 650 000 were the normal progression in the pattern of expanding expenditures set in 1953. That was an election year in Australia. Money for Papua and New Guinea was still not a vote-winner, and one by-product of my work for an all-party approach was that the Government did not have to justify itself to the electors.

Towards the close of the parliamentary session, I had another long talk with Menzies about the undertaking to declare target dates, and subsequently prepared a draft of a statement on a five-year programme to commence in the financial year 1962–3 with expenditures rising progressively to £50 million in 1966–7. This draft was described in my covering letter, dated 23 October, as 'modest in its aims' and striking 'a realistic balance between the capacity of the Administration and the expected response by the native people'. The accompanying paper gave details of projects and proposed that the programme should be reviewed at the end of each financial year and extended so that the five-year plan was perpetually renewing itself. With the approval of Menzies I made the statement about target dates and the five-year programme in the House of Representatives on the last day of sitting and outlined what we proposed doing.* Among other reasons why I wanted to make this statement and have the Prime Minister's explicit approval of it was to give the Administration a challenge and to set it a precise task.

Early in 1962, the election having been won and my portfolio being unchanged, I started to prepare a claim on the Budget for the first year of the programme. But with half the financial year gone, the disheartening news came from Port Moresby that the Administration would not be able to do what was expected of it in 1961–2. 'We cannot accept the shortfall predicted by the Administration', I wrote on 31 January 1962. 'The Administration's job is to get the results wanted . . . We have to put the pressure on the Territory to work as it has never worked before.' I added specific directions that the education programme had to be improved, that there had to be some hard work and more drive on roads, airfields, wharves and bridges, that the lands target should be reduced only if settlers (which mainly meant indigenous settlers) were not available, that the local government target should only be lowered if there was lack of response by the people. (Minute of 31 January 1962.) We tried to thrash out some of these matters on a visit I made to Port Moresby in February. The forecasts on which the programme had been prepared had been supplied by the Administration. I felt I had been let down badly. When the talks were reviewed by Lambert, I said the outlook was 'wholly unsatisfactory and quite unacceptable'. We must get the results that the Government wanted and the Administration had promised.

But in May, facing our critical period again, the news from Port Moresby was little better. 'This is very disheartening', I wrote. 'At a time when we are trying to move into greater efforts the Administration has given us a setback (a) by revealing to Treasury a general weakness in financial control that is likely to affect our claims for higher grants and (b) by falling short on performance on the works programme.' Before I faced another financial year, the fault must be overcome and I must have an assurance that the Administration could do what it planned to do. (Minute of 28 May 1962.)

By the end of the financial year I had received a report from the Administra-

* *Commonwealth Parliamentary Debates* (H. of R.), vol. 33, pp. 2529-32, 26 Oct. 1961.

tor on which I commented somewhat bitterly that the claim that the financial position was 'under constant and close scrutiny' only pointed to the conclusion that the scrutiny was inefficient. For 1962–3 the Department had to act as a watchman so that inefficiency would be detected earlier and repaired. The permanent cure was to strengthen the Administration and I asked for proposals to do that. At a time of increased activity, we could not afford to be let down by incapacity in the Administration. (Minute of 4 July 1962.) In a later minute I said, 'We have to find a few persons of greater capacity to take a job in the Territory.' (Minute of 20 July 1962.)

In these circumstances, the preliminary estimates prepared in consultation with the Administration, asked for less money for 1962–3 than had been envisaged for the first year of the five-year plan. I kept pressing for improving the capacity and I set the Department to work on preparing the case for the Cabinet meetings on the Budget. Apart from directions on specific points, I made one or two observations that reveal my interpretation of the political mood. I said that, although United Nations resolutions might be the peg on which to hang a submission, the substantial matters to be covered in a submission to Cabinet had to be practical. I wrote,

> You can take it for granted that Cabinet knows about international pressure, anti-colonialism, 'winds of change', the sort of editorials the Australian newspapers print, the sort of despatches the External Affairs people overseas write and all that field of discussion. What they do not know are the facts about the Territory itself and its people. Ministers can speculate for themselves about what will follow if this or that occurs overseas or in Indonesia. What they are unable to speculate about with equal confidence is what sort of administrative actions in Papua and New Guinea will be practicable, how much they will cost, what results they are likely to have and are they preferable to some other course of action . . .

I had been too optimistic about my reduced bid for funds. We did not do as well out of the 1962–3 Budget as we had hoped. I wrote to the Prime Minister saying that our claim had been closely related to the five-year programme and the announcement of targets. Because this claim had been cut by £1·4 million, I felt I should let him know that it would become apparent that we were not proceeding as vigorously as we had declared we would and that I would have considerable difficulty in meeting the targets of social, educational and economic advancement. (Letter of 2 August 1962 to the Prime Minister.)

Once again in this series of Cabinet discussions there was no comprehensive discussion of policy, but the Ministry invited me to bring forward a paper later in the year 'as a basis in a full discussion on the Government's policy in relation to the Territory'. This was ready in November 1962. We did not have much of a discussion.

From February to May 1963 we again went through a period of strenuous preparation and met a similar result. Our claims on the 1963–4 Budget were again reduced in spite of all the preparatory work we did, and again we had little or no discussion about policy.

Without infringing the confidences of Cabinet, I feel free to discuss some aspects of the situation. One disillusionment is that in my twelve years as

Minister for Territories Cabinet never had a thorough and well-informed discussion of our policy and objectives in Papua and New Guinea, although I was always trying to get one. The nearest I ever got to the re-examination of policy was the occasional discussion with Menzies, who encouraged me to feel that I was on the right lines, and the occasional approval by Cabinet of particular submissions on single topics. For example Cabinet approved that target dates should be announced but neither originally nor later faced the associated question of how to give effect to the announcement. Cabinet approved each step of constitutional change that I recommended but, having decided on one step, gave no special consideration to what the succeeding step might be or what associated measures might also be necessary. In some ways this could be read as a mark of confidence in the Minister for Territories. Let policy be what he said it was. In another way it was a mark of the relative unimportance politically of whether we did this or that. Some of my former colleagues would probably say that they were a team of hard-headed politicians and not a bunch of academics. At Budget time Ministers treated the claim for a larger Commonwealth grant for Papua and New Guinea in much the same way as they treated any other claim from a department for more money and, while granting increases because more work was obviously being done and because a special case had been made for this or that activity, they made the increases still subject to the same arguments about expenditure as departmental votes without arguing about the aim of policy and the best way of achieving it. The most devastating objection to an increase concerned the capacity of the Administration to use the money granted and the weakness of its financial control, but Cabinet never concerned itself with the attendant problem of Australian responsibility to make the Administration efficient. At times it almost seemed as though the view held was that, since Australia had met imperfectly its responsibility to govern the Territory efficiently and provide adequate staff, it had lessened its obligation to provide funds for the Territory.

When our expenditures in the Territory rose and we began to develop the substructure of self-government with a Territory legislature voting on its own Budget, a Territory public service, local government, semi-governmental instrumentalities, and a Territory sense of community, my senior departmental officers and I both tried hard but vainly at our respective levels to establish the point that the annual Commonwealth grant to Papua and New Guinea was not just another item in a number of departmental claims but one contribution to the construction of a separate budget. Hence we argued that Cabinet should look in the first instance at the Territory Budget and then decide to what extent it should support it from Australian revenues, instead of making a comparison between the Papua and New Guinea claim for a grant and other departmental claims and saying that Papua and New Guinea was trying to get a higher percentage increase than other claimants. If they had examined the Territory Budget intelligently as a budget to which the Commonwealth was contributing, they would have had to take some interest in the policies that the Territory Budget was intended to serve. They never really did so.

I wrote on this topic after the reduction of our claim for the financial year 1963–4:

The justification for the amount claimed as a grant lies in the [Territory] Budget. If the amount of a claim is reduced because of economic reasons applying to the whole Commonwealth Budget that is another matter, but if the claim is reduced largely because the percentage rise is considered to be too great, and without closer examination of the Budget which the grant will support, then I suggest with all respect that it is an unintelligent judgement. It is certainly a judgement that the whole basis of policy on which the draft Territory Budget has been constructed has been altered. In other words, the Government changes policy without re-examining it and perhaps even without being fully aware of the effect of the changes in policy which it is making. For example this year, without knowing fully what it was doing, Cabinet in reducing the grant decided that a halt should be called to the policy of an increased effort in education and the speedier conversion of the public service from an expatriate service to an indigenous service. These are the new and adjustable elements in the Budget.

What soured me at times was that if I showed disappointment or kept on pressing a case, the new Treasurer and some colleagues appeared to think I was just a greedy person who was after a bigger slice of the cake, whereas my true disappointment was that I had not been able to get Cabinet to face the question of what the Government wanted to do in Papua and New Guinea and what Australian interests were and how much we should do to serve them. I had tried to get Cabinet to make a decision on the total amount of the Territory Budget before making a decision on the size of the Commonwealth grant to the Territory. Cabinet however simply made a comparison between the percentage increase in Australian departmental votes and made their decision on the claim for a grant without hearing any explanation of the problems of the Territory Budget.

At this stage in the Territory's history, I felt the point I was trying to make was so important that I would not let the Cabinet decision rest. After the reverse in Cabinet, I called in W. H. Scott[60] and Lattin from the Department to help me prepare a special case for the Prime Minister and Treasurer. I had first met Scott when he was Chief Auditor in Papua and New Guinea and had valued his help in trying to bring some order into the Administration's financial control. He transferred from the Auditor-General's Department to become a special projects officer in the Department of Territories in 1960, and in 1962, with the movement of Reseigh to another division, became assistant secretary for the finance and economics division. In 1964 he was promoted back to the Auditor-General's Department but for four years in Territories we had the advantages of the service of a man who knew all about the public accounts and a lot about our work in Papua and New Guinea. He helped greatly in my attempts to get a new approach to our relations with the Commonwealth Treasury.

The point I made in the talks with the Prime Minister and Treasurer—and for this account I draw on the notes I prepared myself on 24 July—were that, in respect of Papua and New Guinea the Minister for Territories faced on a smaller scale exactly the same problems as the Commonwealth Treasurer had to face in the construction of a budget. The major difference was that the Territory Budget always had to be a balanced budget and we could not use the device of budgeting for a surplus or budgeting for a deficit when we met any unusual problem in budget-making. Before approaching Cabinet for the Commonwealth grant, the Minister had already prepared draft estimates and had already been through the whole of the process of examining various pro-posals submitted by the Territory Administration and, in consultation with officers of the Commonwealth Treasury, had already ensured that the need for economy and conformity with policy were met. In the last two years my own concern had also been to ensure that the draft estimates would meet the targets approved by Cabinet in the five-year programme. This approval of the draft estimates was the basis of the claim for a Commonwealth grant. When Cabinet reduced the amount of the claim for a grant, we were immediately set a new problem of reconstructing the Territory Budget. The room for adjustment was restricted.

I dramatized the actual situation in which Cabinet had placed me when it decided that, in a draft budget of £36·6 million, revenue should be cut by £1·9 million. It would be the same, I said, if, after Cabinet decisions on the Australian Budget had been made, the Treasurer set down his final figures for a budget of, say, £1500 million and was then informed 'by some superior authority' that his revenue estimates had been cut by £85 million and that this change had to be absorbed by the Budget without affecting the amount of any surplus or deficit. In the Territory we were proposing to meet our problem by raising another £700 000 locally and cutting expenditure by £1·2 million. This was analogous to a last-minute requirement of the Commonwealth Treasurer that he cut expenditure by about £45 million and find an extra £40 million by more taxes and borrowing. I then dealt with the detailed items necessarily affected by Cabinet's decision. I demonstrated that year by year we incurred an inescapable increment from earlier decisions and, in an area of expanding effort at a time of rising costs, the total of each successive Budget was higher than the previous one before we even made any proposal for new activities. A table of figures showed that in 1963–4, on the basis of the 1962–3 Budget, the total expenditure would be £32·8 million, an increase of £3·2 million over the previous year. To finance a budget held back to the 1962–3 level and allowing for a natural progression of revenue, a Commonwealth grant of £23·3 million would be required. In fact, Cabinet had decided to make it £24·8 million, cutting down our claim for £26·6 million, and so the only increase made by Cabinet to finance new undertakings, and to bear a residue of the cost in a full year of decisions in 1962–3 that had financial effect for only part of that year, was £1·4 million. 'In terms of advancement towards declared targets for development' the increase to be made was 4·3 per cent. Yet Cabinet, comparing one year's grant with the previous year's grant, as though it were an item of departmental estimates, had justified its reduction as holding the Territory back to a 20 per cent increase on the previous year and argued that Territories was still 'doing better' than others.

After the discussions with the Prime Minister and Treasurer, £500 000 was restored to the Commonwealth grant making it £25·5 million, and I undertook to raise local borrowings from £900 000 to £1·7 million and local revenue from £8·6 million to £8·8 million, giving a budget total of £35·8 million compared with the original total of £36·4 million and the forecast made two years earlier of a total of £40 million for the second year of the five-year plan.

This slight improvement was obtained on an argument for a forward drive in education and the need to avoid any reduction in our proposal to recruit 250 expatriate teachers at the beginning of the 1964 school year. While glad to get the money, I regretted that I still had not gained full acceptance of my thesis about the Budget. In a minute to the Secretary of 26 July, forwarding the file of papers I had used in my ministerial discussions, I suggested that we seek a procedure in future years by which we could get our Territory Budget cleared by the Treasurer or by a small subcommittee of Ministers before the Cabinet series of meetings on the Commonwealth Budget. 'The conditions under which the Cabinet discussions are held make it quite impossible for attention to be given to the separate budgetary problems of the Territory,' I wrote, 'and yet any decision on the size of the Commonwealth grant is clearly unintelligent if it is made apart from consideration of the size of the Territory Budget.'

[32]

HIGHER EDUCATION

The five-year plan announced by me in Parliament on 26 October 1961 provided for the development of more secondary, technical and teacher training schools and estimated that by 1966 there would be 10 000 students enrolled in post-primary and secondary schools, 2000 in technical schools and 2000 in teacher training schools. In addition, a central administrative training school would be established and training of nurses and assistant medical practitioners in the Territory Medical School increased.

On recent visits to the Territory I had made a point of checking personally the progress of schools, and my notes for this period show a frequent request for further statistics on the number of children at school, teacher training and progress of building.

In June 1961 I also intervened in the early stages of the recruitment of a Deputy Director of Education saying, 'We have to pick an applicant who shows a really good prospect of being the best Director of Education we have yet had. In effect it is the appointment of a Director of Education on probation. Consequently I said that the Minister was directly interested, as in the case of the selection of the head of a department. (Minute of 29 June 1961.) My intervention resulted in the appointment of L. W. Johnson[61] and, a year later, his appointment as director in succession to Roscoe. (Minute of 25 June 1962.)

Under both Roscoe and Johnson I had greater confidence that the educational programme was being carried out effectively and that its yield was predictable. Since 1958 the enrolments in secondary schools had been growing and by 1961 the schools system was beginning to produce candidates for higher education in sufficient numbers for us to be able to turn more purposefully towards tertiary education in the Territory. Up to that time the very small number of indigenous people who reached tertiary level had been given their opportunity in Australia.

About the same time, we were engrossed with questions about the higher training of officers for our own administrative purposes. We had pressed ahead with plans for training both our Australian officers and indigenous candidates for performing various governmental functions and of course every

386

training scheme or institution became a claimant on those indigenous pupils who had reached the secondary school stage.

Parallel to this, attention was being given to the future of the Australian School of Pacific Administration (ASOPA), located at Mosman in Sydney. There was much departmental concern, stemming from Lambert, about its syllabus and its general efficiency. There was a tendency among some officers to make decisions about what we did in the Territory on tertiary education contingent on what we did about ASOPA. I saw the situation the other way round and thought any decision on the future of ASOPA was contingent on what we did about higher education in the Territory. Much earlier I had rejected suggestions that ASOPA might be made the forerunner of a Territory university and had given it a role closer to that of an administrative training college. I did not want to make further decisions about its future until it became clear what institutions we could create in the Territory.

In a minute of 14 April 1961 I suggested that we should separate the question of the development of training institutions and higher education in the Territory from the future of ASOPA and give 'urgent and comprehensive attention to the question of administrative training and higher education in the Territory'. We should try to advance rapidly to the point of decision on the location of various centres of training, their need for land and buildings and the inclusion of appropriate items in the 1961–2 Estimates. In these institutions we should integrate both indigenous and non-indigenous students. Up to that time there had been distinct differences in the needs of our non-indigenous and indigenous trainees, because of differences in basic education. For example in the work we had done in the Public Service Institute to tutor public servants for Australian university degrees or for institute examinations to improve their qualifications, we had helped only Europeans, while in the work to prepare members of the auxiliary division to qualify for admission to the third division of the public service, we had helped only indigenes. In the future there would be more candidates for common training.

In May I tried to draw together the various approaches to the question by directing that a committee composed of representatives of the Department of Territories, the Prime Minister's Department (which had responsibility at that time for the Commonwealth Office of Education), the Administration and ASOPA should investigate the whole problem of tertiary education and higher training. The chairman was J. E. Willoughby, the departmental representative.

The Willoughby committee reported in August and recommended that a central residential administrative college be established in Port Moresby as soon as possible, a university college, linked with an Australian university, be established in Port Moresby not later than 1966, a multi-racial full standard teachers' college (that is, one producing teachers at something nearly equivalent to the standard of an Australian teachers' college) be set up in the Territory as soon as possible, plans be made for the provision of a higher technical training institution, and secondary education throughout the Territory be expanded to bring more native people to university entrance standard.

I welcomed and appreciated this report, which was essentially a departmental paper, although I found it inconclusive on some points and not wholly clear on others. I referred some questions to the Department for further examination or clarification. After receiving the Department's further sub-mission, I approved of the recommendations in the Willoughby report as a basis for detailed planning, and directed that priority be given to the establish-ment of the Administrative Staff College. (Minute of 11 October 1961.)

I kept up the pressure. A principal for the college was selected, an interim council appointed, a site allocated and talks started on the design of a per-manent building. In a press statement of 8 April 1962 I was able to announce that the college would come into operation in 1963. In the same statement I announced the commencement of planning for a university college and the allocation of an area adjacent to Ward's Strip, Port Moresby, for development as a higher education centre.

Shortly after this we suffered a setback through the death, in turn, of E. J. B. Foxcroft,[62] who had represented the Prime Minister's Department in all this work, and of Willoughby.

Since our thoughts at that time were to establish a university college along the lines recommended in the Willoughby report, departmental officers had concerned themselves with finding an Australian university that would be associated with this venture in the same way as, in the beginning, the Univer-sity of Melbourne had been associated with a university college in Canberra and the University of Queensland with a university college at Townsville. I had written to the Australian National University (ANU) in April 1962 to open discussion with them. After Willoughby's death, however, matters were not handled well. Too many cooks were eagerly stirring too little broth.

I was also becoming unsure whether we were on the right lines. On 22 October 1962 a discussion took place between the Prime Minister, Sir John Crawford, then Director of the School of Pacific Studies at the ANU, and myself. Sir John made it plain that the ANU did not want to take over the planning of university education in the Territory, although some of his col-leagues had previously shown a strong disposition to do so, but would prefer to concern itself solely with deciding what the ANU itself should do. I gave the Prime Minister my view that we should set up a commission with a person of some eminence as chairman to report to the Government on all matters of higher education in Papua and New Guinea with particular reference to the proposed university. As the result of this discussion, departmental work on a university college was suspended. (Minute to Lambert of 25 October 1962.)

I was about to leave for Nigeria as leader of the Australian delegation to a Commonwealth Parliamentary Conference—a visit which incidentally gave me a chance to look at the university at Ibadan—and on my return to Australia started at once to set up the commission under the chairmanship of Sir George Currie, who had recently retired as Vice-Chancellor of the University of New Zealand and had returned to live in Canberra. He and I had been closely associated when he was Professor of Agriculture and later Vice-Chancellor of the University of Western Australia between 1939 and 1952. It was very lucky for the Territory that Sir George was available and willing to set aside some other requests for his services in order to help us. I selected as his fellow-members of the commission Professor Spate of the ANU and John Gunther, after rejecting the names recommended to me from other quarters. It was a very good commission.

On 19 December 1962 I had a discussion with Sir George about the proposed inquiry. I wrote for the occasion a paper headed 'Notes for Discussion' and, after using it for our talk, I left a copy with Sir George. This paper, which gives my views before the inquiry began, is useful historical background to the study of the work of the Currie commission and its influence on the shaping of higher education. The paper also gives a factual summary of the point we had reached by the end of 1962. Consequently I reproduce it in full.

The present plan of the Government is to establish not later than 1966 a university college in the Territory.

In the meantime we will continue with the development of a central residential administrative college, a full standard teachers' college, a medical college and a higher technical training institution. We will also continue the training given to prepare indigenous candidates for service in such instrumentalities as the Department of Agriculture, Stock and Fisheries; the Post Office; the Police Force; and the Department of Native Affairs. Opportunity will be afforded to matriculants to attend Australian universities until such time as courses are available to them in the Territory. The Australian School of Pacific Administration in Sydney will continue for the time being to conduct courses for cadet patrol officers, education officers and others, but it is expected that it will eventually disappear and that the functions it performs will be carried out by the institutions in the Territory such as the Administrative College and the Teachers' College as well as by the Territory University.

The relationship of these existing institutions to the future university may be considered as open to examination and consequently any modifications of their structure that may be found necessary because of that relationship will also have to be considered.

The prospective enrolment of the university college at the time of its inauguration will be a number of expatriate officers of the Territory public service who are studying for a degree part-time, perhaps some children of Australian residents of the Territory and a number of indigenous students who have matriculated by sitting for the Leaving Examination on Australian standards. This initial group of students may be small for a start and they will look to the university college as an alternative to an Australian university. If it is not an alternative to an Australian university giving recognized degrees, many of them may not be interested in attending.

Each year the proportion of indigenous students will increase. Because of the total interruption of schooling by the war and the slowness after the war in building an efficient education system, we are only just beginning to receive an annual quota of youths who, having started school at six years of age or thereabouts, have had continuous and efficient schooling in English through the primary and secondary stages (say, twelve years). There has been a considerable wastage of students throughout the secondary school period in the past, but special steps are being taken now to encourage the bright children to continue at school throughout the secondary course.

It is highly probable however that there will still be a number of candidates for higher education who may have difficulty in matriculating at Australian university standards, or—to put it in another way—there may be a number of students who could benefit from higher education of one kind or another but might have difficulty in completing the usual academic requirements for a degree under normal Australian university conditions.

Another facet of the same problem is that there is an urgent need in the Territory for the service of persons with higher qualifications as school teachers, agricultural officers, laboratory technicians, medical officers, administrative officers, works supervisors, magistrates and so on. Do we demand the full professional qualifications in Arts, Agriculture, Science, Medicine, Law and Engineering or do we accept a lower professional qualification and, if so, do we give them their higher education in a university college with modified standards or in separate institutions?

There is also a very big need in the Territory for technicians of all kinds at levels from the carpenter up to the telecommunications officer and the mechanical engineer. Some can be produced by the technical schools already in existence; others need higher technical schools. All of them, to an extent far greater than in the training of technicians in Australia, also need to broaden their general education in order to enable them to discharge fully their varying responsibilities.

For the sake of the higher technical training and for the sake of the lower professional training some persons have advocated the creation of a 'Polytechnic' either as part of or alongside a university. If it is part of the university do we have, in effect, a university conducting courses at two different levels and issuing two different sorts of 'tickets' to those who pass—degrees and diplomas? Is this practicable? Is this wise?

The same problem will emerge in considering the relationship between the university college and the medical school. The medical school at present trains both nurses (men and women) and 'doctors' (to the Suva standard) and for some time at least I imagine that the Territory will have a great need for these officers. Similarly the training of native teachers will continue for some time to turn out teachers at two or even three different educational levels and the need for village teachers is so great and so urgent that we could not sacrifice the annual quota of teachers to an ideal academic standard.

A number of the candidates for higher education will come from mission schools and some will be destined for mission work or the priesthood. There is a strong interest by the churches in religious studies at the university college.

For the sake of economy of effort it is possible that the university college might assist other institutions by admitting their students to special courses. For example, if the administrative college were to require students to do a course in Public Administration could this be given better at the university? If the medical school required biology could this be better done at the university? The traffic might also be in the other direction.

As students will be drawn from all parts of the Territory it would seem to be essential to plan for halls of residence. Are these to be exclusive to the university or are they to be shared by other institutions? Who runs them?

Questions of location, the area required, ancillary services and facilities, and amenities obviously need consideration.

Out of the total picture will emerge more clearly the exact requirements of staff and accommodation and of finance both for capital expenditure and for maintenance.

It would seem to me that the Government will need advice and recommendations regarding the planning stage up to, say, 1966, and for the first triennium in some detail and a forecast of possible lines of development.

Presumably, soon after the foundation of the university, a commission will be needed to give attention to the second triennium.

Up to date, when considering the linking of the university college to an Australian university we have thought chiefly of the Australian National University. Nevertheless that question and indeed the question of whether or not the venture begins as a university college linked to an Australian university may be considered an open one.

Recommendations will also be helpful on the method of inaugurating the university, the structure of its governing body, its power to make statutes and so on, and, arising out of all this, the draft of the legislation required to establish it.

Subsequently I drafted terms of reference for the inquiry, having rejected a draft submitted by the Department, and early in the new year took my proposals to the Prime Minister. Menzies himself had given post-war leadership to Australian universities and was interested in the situation in Papua and New Guinea. He had shown close interest in what I was doing and readily approved of the inquiry, made his own constructive suggestions on the terms of reference and accepted the members I nominated. On the same day the Department of Territories set to work on the routine of arranging for the commission and drawing up terms and conditions of appointment.

I already had my eye on an executive officer in Fred Kaad,[63] one of the district commissioners in the Territory. I had seen a lot of him on various visits to the Territory. He had completed a degree as an external student of the University of Queensland besides having wide experience as one of our best field officers among the people of the Territory. He had a great faith in the people's capacity. He was personally equipped with good humour and enthusiasm and had been among those enthusiasts who promoted the sending of a Territory team to the Commonwealth Games.

One wholly irrelevant incident that first earned Kaad my friendship and regard was his faithful custody of a duck named Angoram. We were travelling together in the Sepik and landed at Angoram. A very nervous patrol officer had gathered all the local dignitaries to welcome the Minister and had formed them in a hollow square in descending order of rank and local status. Unfortunately when we got to the handshaking, the nervous young man started me off in the wrong direction so that I was meeting the most junior before I met the most senior and a small ceremony which the local people had prepared in my honour was not observed. As I neared the top-ranking 'cap men', I became aware of some chagrin. What should have been the top of the ranking was now the tail and at the bottom instead of the head stood a dignified grey-headed notability of pre-war celebrity. He held his head high and stared straight in front. One hand held a silver-topped staff which was the rod of office he had carried in pre-war days and which he had carefully preserved throughout the Japanese occupation. His other hand was behind his back. As cordially as possible I held out my hand in greeting. He hesitated and seemed to refuse the handshake but then relented and brought his hand from behind his back clutching by the neck a live duck, which he thrust into my outstretched paw. This was the ceremony that had gone wrong. I accepted the gift with manifest delight and, after switching the duck to Kaad, completed the handshake while smiles and grunts of approval broke out all around. The duck had to be carried away with us in the aircraft as a special treasure and, because experienced people said that the donors would keep careful tabs on me to make sure that I did really appreciate it, the bird was installed in honour in Kaad's poultry yard at Wewak, where, on each successive visit, I inquired about the health and welfare of Angoram and exchanged winks with its beady, malicious, yellow eyes.

What better man than Kaad, the proved custodian of a distinguished duck, to look after three distinguished commissioners on higher education—especially because he had other merits. As his assistant we appointed Oala Oala-Rarua,[64] who was at that time in the Public Service Commissioner's office at Port Moresby.

The work of the commission was launched in Canberra on 18 March 1963. Speaking at the opening session, I said that the terms of reference of the commission had been made as wide as possible because, while directing the attention of the commission specifically to the question of university education, we did not wish to limit them to a consideration solely of educational institutions of the same character as a British or Australian university. They should look over the whole field of higher education and have wide liberty in making proposals within that field.

At a later stage of my remarks I emphasized the hope that the proposals made by the commission would be related in a close and practical way to the present and prospective needs of the people of Papua and New Guinea. All education had to be part of the life of the individual and of the life of his community and not just a 'status symbol' or a new set of decorations alongside the road to self-government. Speaking particularly of a university, I said in part,

> When we talk of giving equal opportunity to the coloured inhabitants of a dependent territory, we are sometimes prone to place the argument at too low a level and say that the indigenous person is just as capable of flying an aeroplane or becoming a chemist or a lawyer as the Australian or European. I think that the fuller and richer meaning is to believe as I believe that a dark-skinned man no less than a pink-and-white man is capable of taking part in the search for truth, of making his own contribution towards it and of achieving the highest goals of human understanding. I fervently hope that this will be the achievement of any university established in Papua and New Guinea so that in future years mankind will be able to recognize that Papua and New Guinea has not only received training in various skills but has made its contribution to knowledge and has added to the store of wisdom. These people, too, can help to open the windows of understanding.

The Currie commission's report was presented to my successor in March 1964 and is available to the public.* It led the way to the creation of the University of Papua and New Guinea. While the commission were thus the

* Report by the Commission on Higher Education in Papua and New Guinea. 2 vols (duplicated, Department of Territories, Canberra, March 1964).

principal actors in the founding of the University of Papua and New Guinea, I may also claim to have had some part in the show as their entrepreneur.

In the meantime, while the commission was at work, we had continued with the development of the central administrative college, teachers' college, medical college and the higher technical training institution as well as extending the other forms of training. My view, expressed in successive minutes, was that they should be brought into operation or continue to operate and that, in the light of the Currie commission's report, their relationship to the remainder of higher education could be subsequently adjusted.

[33]

THE HOUSE OF ASSEMBLY

The decisions on constitutional change made by Cabinet in August 1960 were intended to start further progressive changes, some of which could be made administratively. It was planned that the reformed Legislative Council should complete a three-year term and that immediately after its second election—that is, in 1964—it should itself consider the next step towards self-government.

After the experience of the first election and the opening session of the Council in early 1961, however, and following a further visit to the Territory, I revised my outlook and started to plan for further change to take place before the 1964 election rather than after it. In doing so, I was influenced considerably by several discussions on the future with Gunther. In the new Council he became virtually the 'leader of the house' and was my close confidant on what both Europeans and indigenous people might be prepared to do.

Two other highly encouraging elements in the situation were the way in which some of the representatives from what had been regarded as backward areas began to show a talent for politics more realistically than had been thought possible, and the way in which some sections of the white population outside official circles showed a more liberal outlook than I had been led to expect during the controversies over taxation. We may have been benefitting from a backlash after the excesses of that controversy, and some of the solid elements with a long-standing interest in the Territory may have had time to exert influence over get-rich-quick newcomers.

The Government's basic idea in 1960 was that the people of the Territory should help shape the course of constitutional change and make their own decisions on when successive changes should take place. In the speech for the opening of the new Council on 10 April 1961, by the Administrator of the Government of the Commonwealth of Australia, Sir Dallas Brooks, who was in office pending the appointment of a new Governor-General after the death of Lord Dunrossil, that hope was declared as follows:

> At this meeting of the Council the people of the Territory cross the threshold of a new political life. The Australian Parliament, in enacting the constitutional reform which led to the changes in this Council, had it clearly in mind that there should be continuous political growth and progressive

constitutional change. It is their belief that political growth and constitutional change should go hand in hand so that the political advancement of the people is never hampered by having to work through institutions which have become out-of-date and unsuitable; and so that the institutions themselves will never fail to serve their purpose through any lack of political capacity among those who use them . . . We trust that in this Council the leaders of the people will never fail to find their opportunity and that, as the political aspirations of the people expand, this Council will give them the means of shaping their own future until eventually they reach the goal of self-government.

This was one of the passages in my draft I had shown to Menzies for his approval before submitting the speech to Sir Dallas. I was perhaps rather fond of drafting these statements of constitutional orthodoxy. Although, as a politician, I believe I was not in the least doctrinaire on questions of political theory, I confess to being somewhat doctrinaire on questions of political institutions.

The new timetable was given a start when, in its second period of meeting, the Legislative Council turned its attention to the task of choosing the next step. On 21 September 1961 a private member, A. L. Hurrell,[65] discreetly encouraged by Gunther, gave notice of his intention to move for the appointment of a select committee on political development. At its next meeting, on 9 March 1962, the Council set up the committee with two elected native members and two elected non-native members. Later it appointed an additional native member. Gunther was elected chairman and in the succeeding months guided the work of the committee.

The committee, at its first meeting, set itself the target of presenting its first interim report to the Council in October and for that purpose set out to ascertain by public inquiry the need for change in the composition of the Council, and, if there was a need for change, what changes should be made and when they should take place.

Its first interim report, approved by resolution of the Council on 16 October 1962, recommended that there should be a change in the composition of the Council in 1964, that there should be a president and ten official members together with forty-four members elected from a common roll, that in addition there should be ten non-indigenous persons elected from the common roll, as members from reserved electorates, but that this provision should be reviewed before any election in 1967, and that voting should be voluntary, preferential and on an individual basis from a common roll comprising all adult inhabitants of the controlled areas within the Territory, without regard to any educational or property qualification but including a residential requirement of twelve months. In making its recommendations, the committee said that, though they were largely based on the freely expressed wishes of the people, they did in fact go well beyond the conservative proposals the people themselves had put forward. The committee however was confident that the people would respond to this stimulus and challenge.

In a statement welcoming the report, I said the Government had maintained consistently the view that the wishes of the people of the Territory should be sought before any changes were made and that the appropriate channel for the communication of these views was the Legislative Council. For this reason it had encouraged the setting up of the select committee last March. I was also sure that the recommendations of the Legislative Council would be received by the Government as authoritative. It had been planned for some time that whatever changes were adopted would be put into legislation of the Australian Parliament in 1963 so that the making of the reforms could be followed by a period of intensive education on the new procedures among the native people before the next elections were held in about March or April 1964. (Press statement on 10 October 1962.) The interim report was tabled by me in the Australian Parliament on 23 October when I announced that the Government had approved the select committee's recommendations, subject only to any adjustments that might be required as the result of a further report from the committee or to overcome drafting difficulties. We planned to introduce the necessary amending bill in the autumn sittings of Parliament. I added that the Government also believed that, as well as sharing in the legislative process, the people should share in the executive process. Consequently in the new Legislative Council, assuming Parliament approved of the measure to be introduced, some of the elected members would be asked to accept office as under-secretaries to be attached to each of the main departments of government and to understudy the official members. We would also consider strengthening the Administrator's Council in which some of the elected members were already associated with the Executive.*

The second interim report of the select committee was presented on 26 February 1963 and made recommendations regarding electoral boundaries, remuneration and allowances of members, method of voting and similar questions. The committee also recommended that the new legislature be called the House of Assembly. These recommendations were also accepted by the Government.

Separate from the work of the select committee, I had directed the Administrator on 5 September 1961, to set up an internal committee to prepare proposals for efficient electoral machinery, the political and electoral education of the native people and the introduction of a secret ballot and direct voting on the basis of a common roll. They were asked to report by June 1962. This committee did helpful work under the chairmanship of G. W. Toogood[66] on the practical task I had set them, and many of their recommendations were put into practice. They also furnished a further statement based on their view that 'the concept of an electoral roll based on a universal franchise raises a large number of constitutional and allied issues of far-reaching significance', and seemed to envisage a prolonged further period of discussion. Because this departmental paper is still subject to general rules on the archives, I do not feel free to quote it but comment firstly that it will have some historical interest as a reflection of the doubts and hesitations of some senior officers of the Administration at that time and secondly that it had no influence whatever on policy. In a letter to the Administrator I said that this departmental committee should concentrate on the practical matters it had been appointed to

---

* *Commonwealth Parliamentary Debates* (H. of R.), vol. 37, p. 1782, 23 Oct. 1962.

examine. In doing this I was reaffirming my intention to look to the Legislative Council and not to official committees for advice on constitutional change.

Meanwhile during April and early May 1962 the regular tour of the Territory had been made by a visiting mission of the United Nations Trusteeship Council. Its report was presented to the Acting Secretary-General of the United Nations on 21 June and made public on 5 July. The Trusteeship Council considered the report later in the month and approved of resolutions stating that the time had come to create 'a truly representative Parliament in Papua and New Guinea', that it was possible to proceed more rapidly in the political field than was contemplated when the new Legislative Council was inaugurated in the previous year and that preparations for the elections on a common roll, by adult suffrage and direct vote in single-member constituencies should be completed not later than the end of 1963.

The main question this immediately set to the Government was not what it should do in Papua and New Guinea but how it should prepare instructions for the Australian delegation to the General Assembly, whose fourth committee would be taking up the subject in September. The Department of External Affairs became agitated every year about this annual ordeal. I had a preliminary discussion with the Prime Minister and he accepted my aim of distinguishing between our own decision on what was the right thing to do in Papua and New Guinea and a decision on how to prepare an adequate brief for our delegates to the General Assembly. This piece of seeming hypocrisy on our part arose from a considered opinion that the General Assembly of the United Nations was not a deliberative body but a political forum and from our conviction that the people of the Territory should choose their future.

As an outcome of our talk, I prepared a submission for Cabinet. (No. 360 of 17 August 1962.) Its title, 'Papua and New Guinea. Resolutions of the Trusteeship Council', and its opening paragraph make it plain that the main purpose was to prepare a brief for the General Assembly meeting and, to that end, to obtain 'an expression of opinion from Cabinet' on the matters raised. I said in effect that we felt no difficulty regarding the majority of the resolutions of the Trusteeship Council, since action was already being taken by the Government to give effect to what they proposed. The only difficulty was over the proposal for political advancement and the proposals on target dates. The outcome of our discussion can be seen firstly in the statements made on behalf of Australia in the General Assembly and ultimately in the actions taken in respect of political development in Papua and New Guinea. I used the occasion to introduce to Cabinet the ideas I had already formed about what might be done and obtained Cabinet support for them in general terms. This Cabinet discussion in August 1962 cleared the way for the firm decisions made at a later meeting and incorporated in the Papua and New Guinea Act 1963 and contingent Territory legislation.

The relevance of the visiting mission's report and the influence it had was not in shaping Australian policy or changing our judgement on what was best to do but in providing a peg on which I could hang a case in August 1962 for earlier action than the Government had been ready to contemplate in August 1960. The consideration of the report established more firmly than ever the Australian Government's view that we should avoid any sham display but make sure that the successive constitutional changes were effective in practice and that we were laying firm foundations for eventual self-government by building up wider representation and greater responsibility side by side. The decisions also reaffirmed that we should rely upon a representative Legislative Council to take a leading role in deciding when and in what form change should come rather than, as the visiting mission's report suggested, imposing our own decisions on the Territory. I believe the Australian Government was wiser than the visiting mission by seeking to associate the people of the Territory, both indigenous and white, with each step in constitutional progress.

My opinion is that the visiting mission's recommendation for a House of Representatives of 'about a hundred' elected members plus five official members was not soundly based on existing conditions in the Territory. It was also not as significant a step forward as was sometimes popularly represented, for the mission's report seemed to see the value of this augmented chamber as a place for the expression of opinion and said nothing more about responsibility than that a much modified ministerial system of government should be introduced 'as soon as possible'. As an effective step towards responsible government, what the Australian Government actually did in 1963 was more significant than what the visiting mission proposed we should do in the same year.

As an addendum, I should add frankly that I had a poor opinion of the chairman of the visiting mission (Sir Hugh Foot). Both in this mission and subsequently when, as Lord Caradon, he was Permanent Representative of Great Britain at the United Nations, he seemed to me to be primarily an actor —the sort of actor who always tried to upstage other members of the cast. It was no accident that the visiting mission's report was much publicized as the 'Foot Report', while equally distinguished chairmen of earlier visiting missions, in presenting more significant reports, had remained part of a United Nations team.

The Papua and New Guinea Bill 1963 (Act No. 27 of 1963) was introduced by me in the House of Representatives on 7 May 1963. The second reading was carried on the voices and, although there were some divisions in committee on amendments proposed by the Opposition, it can fairly be said that the main provisions of the Bill were accepted by both sides of Parliament. I found some satisfaction in the indications at this stage of the success of my attempts to achieve an all-party approach to policy on Papua and New Guinea. Summing up the debate, I said that all parties found common ground on the right of the people to choose their own future and on the goal of self-government and independence. Where differences appeared, they did not give a contrast between wanting to go 'very fast' or 'not so fast' but a contrast in judgement on certain factors. Among these factors I put the need for national unity, the practical problems of making the system work and the avoidance of a racial clash. My own judgement was in favour of taking two steps in quick succession rather than making one big jump. At the present stage the election of the people from various parts of the Territory would not be an expression of national unity but one of the means by which national unity would be created. To ensure that the new system would work, it was necessary that the people should feel that it was what they wanted themselves and something that they themselves were prepared to make work. To avoid the racial clash, we sought political advancement in which persons of all races were participating and a system in which they could work together.

My speech introducing the Bill and the debate on the measure are fully recorded in Hansard so will not be repeated here. I would however commend these debates to the historian who is seeking an understanding of Australian policy and attitudes or trying to evaluate my own administration.*

During the period of preparation for change in 1963, new measures were taken for the political education of the native people, and our work on local government was intensified.

In this connection in the middle of 1961, arising partly from the Derham report and partly from a review of the Native Local Government Councils Ordinance initiated by the Administrator, I had reconsidered some aspects of policy. There was a difference of outlook on the role of the councils. The Administrator expressed a view that the councils act 'more or less as agents for the Administration' and said that this 'tends to make them more administrative than governmental bodies'. I had a contrary view and directed that councils were to be developed to become bodies exercising powers in relation to matters of local concern without detailed supervision from the Administration, that they should only make rules and carry out executive functions on local matters, that they were not to exercise judicial powers or become land authorities or conduct schools, and that the old-time function of maintaining order and preventing offences on behalf of the central Administration should be repealed. I instructed the Administrator to find the appropriate means of 'making a smooth but early transition from using the councils as agents of the Administration to the functioning of the councils as local governing bodies; and the more rapid development of local government councils as the foundation for further political advancement of the people of the Territory'. In pursuit of this aim and in spite of my wish for more rapid development of councils, I rejected a suggestion by the Administration that we should modify the principle of 'voluntary participation' and impose local government on communities that the Administration thought were ready for it.

The Administration point of view was understandable if one thought only of the value of having a uniform pattern of 'agencies' of the Administration all over the Territory. I was also aware of the difficulties that had arisen in some districts when one group of villages went to the trouble and expense of having a council and another nearby group of villages looked to the Administration to provide all local services without effort on their part. Having basically a different view of what the local government councils should be, however, I thought that most of the value in them would be lost if there were not general community participation and I also doubted whether they would succeed in serving the ends of the Administration if the community did not want to have a council but only worked under the direction of Administration officers. Consequently, in approving that a complete review be made of the councils and the legislation on which they were based, I came down clearly on the side

* *Commonwealth Parliamentary Debates* (H. of R.), vol. 38 passim.

of making the councils local governing bodies and a means of political advancement of the people through the voluntary acceptance of the task of handling their own affairs, with reduced supervision from the central authority, and that they should not be considered as agents of the Administration. (Minute of 11 July 1961.) In some quarters my directions were misunderstood or misrepresented as a move hostile to local government councils. Some keen and good officers who had helped promote the work of councils were perhaps becoming habituated to the idea that councils were their own instruments for better running of their districts.

In a later minute, while the review was in progress, I sought to clarify my views on local government. I wrote that, while a council had to be given powers and functions as a subordinate law-making body, an administrative body, and a policy-making and planning authority, those powers and functions had to be limited by the definition of the field of activity and geographical area to which they applied. I again stressed that in Territory conditions each council had to be 'a school of political advancement'. (Minute of 17 August 1962.)

The review of the legislation on local government and the drafting of a bill for a new ordinance continued in the Territory throughout 1961 and 1962 and, except to give them reminders of urgency, I left the development of these ideas to the Administration. In May 1963 I directed that the Bill, as 'an essential element in the general constitutional reforms' must be presented to the Legislative Council in September and added,

> Exceptional measures should be taken by the Administration to ensure that indigenous members of the Legislative Council and, if thought necessary, indigenous members of Local Government Councils, fully understand the provisions of the Bill and agree that it is workable. If it has not been done already, the Administrator should engage the attention of Mr John Guise, MLC, as a member of the Administrator's Council in this measure and give him the opportunity of doing some work on it before it is introduced. [Minute of 28 May 1963.]

I added the last bit because of other signs that the Administrator's Council was not being used, as it was intended to be used, as an embryonic Cabinet.

Another effort we made at this time was to increase the association of the indigenous people and Europeans on district advisory councils both to accustom them to the idea of working together and to widen the participation of the indigenous people in the political life of the Territory. (Minute of 1 August 1962.)

In February 1962 during one of my visits to the Territory to have discussions with the people on political advancement, some of the native leaders, including elected members of the Legislative Council, asked me how they could learn about 'politics'. I wrote a note at the time:

> My impression is that they are hearing a lot nowadays about advancing towards self-government and about holding elections and having councils but they are puzzled to know what it all means. They want visible and tangible evidence of what government is. In economic affairs they can see something concrete in new crops, money and the goods that money will buy. In government they know about what the Administration officers do day

by day and they know that they have the local government councils and that there is a bigger council in Port Moresby and a much bigger one in Australia. But when people talk to them about self-government or about government in general what do they mean? How does the whole thing work? In what way is it different from what they know already?

To meet this problem, I inaugurated a succession of visits by political leaders to Australia. (Minute of 12 March 1962.) Part of the difficulty we had was that very few even of the more advanced people at that time could learn readily from written material and so the courses were arranged with a mixture of seeing things being done, discussing them and subsequently studying notes on what they had seen or discussed. We mixed up those who understood English readily with those who had no English or limited English so that they could explain matters to each other. Each party, consisting of a dozen or more persons, came to Canberra for a period of two or three weeks, saw Parliament and its committees in action, discussed the role of Prime Minister, Leader of the Opposition, and a Minister with those persons themselves, learnt from members and the officers of Parliament how legislation was made, and saw departments, semi-governmental bodies and municipal authorities in action. At each stage of the visit the members had group discussions with the leader of the party—a senior officer from the Administration. The courses were doubly successful. They taught a lot to the native leaders. The visits were also highly educational for the politicians and officials in Canberra. I recall with pleasure the ready co-operation from Menzies, Calwell, the President of the Senate, the Speaker and the officers of Parliament in helping this success in the series of visits we arranged.

In addition arrangements were made for other native leaders to be brought in groups to Port Moresby during each sitting of the Legislative Council in order to see a legislature in action and to be given courses of instruction of the working of a legislature.

Another big practical task we had to take in hand was the preparation for the elections, including the compiling of the common roll, and the organization for conducting an election, including the physical equipment and the staff and the education of many of the people on how to vote. Out of a million names on the common roll, about 400 000 already had some experience of voting and some idea of the principle of choosing a representative because they had taken part in local government. The others knew little about it and lived in thousands of villages and hamlets in remote parts of the mountainous regions. A mammoth educational effort was made with some novel methods.* The exercise was highly creditable to those who planned it and those who carried it out. The success of the election for the first House of Assembly and of subsequent steps towards self-government owed much to the imaginative way in which this activity was carried on throughout 1963.

---

*Some indication of the size of the job and the work done by the officers of the Administration is given in an article published in *Australian Territories*, vol. 3, no. 6 (Nov. 1963), pp. 19-23.

[34]

GOOD ORDER AND SECURITY

During my term as Minister there were occasional incidents of violence or disorder. In all cases I made sure that I was fully informed of the background and the way in which matters had been handled and in some cases I discussed subsequently with the Administrator additional measures that might be taken to improve the situation or asked for a critical assessment of the lessons to be learnt from the events. I did not choose however to hamper officers in the performance of their duties so long as the approved procedures were followed.

These incidents, which happily were few and far between, required quick action and were matters primarily for the men on the spot to handle. I relied on Cleland to ensure that they handled them properly. It was an area of responsibility in which I believe Cleland did very well as Administrator. He was cool-headed, firm and decisive, but careful about consequences as well as the immediate necessity in any troubled situation. I had confidence in his judgement and in his restraint and supported him at the time of action and analysed the event with him at the time of review.

My judgement is that it is impossible to generalize about the various incidents that arose in the course of twelve years. The nature and causes of each were peculiar and mostly local. There certainly did not appear to me to be any single pattern. One should be careful not to make generalizations about causes, which may have been resistance to authority, or the animosity of one indigenous group to another, messianic movements and group hysteria, disputes over land, revenge, or some other dominant element. Underlying some of them was undoubtedly the fact that a major social transformation was taking place throughout the country and creating unusual situations. The most amazing feature of the twelve years is that violent disturbance or anti-social conduct by individuals in such conditions of stress were rare.

The tribute I would wish to pay to the coolness and good sense of Cleland and several of his senior officers and to many of the wiser Christian missionaries is enhanced when I recall that not only were the indigenous people undergoing this great transformation but the situation was aggravated by the fact that quite a number of inexperienced, itchy and foolish Europeans in various walks of life were also closely in touch with the indigenous people. It is a double tribute to the quality of the indigenous people themselves and to the quality of the leaders of the European community, both lay and clerical, that the transformation took place so peaceably. Any criticism I may have made of Cleland on the side of routine administration is more than balanced by my admiration of his handling of situations to ensure good order in the community throughout a period of rapid change.

In one aspect of this phase of his work there was perhaps a difference in emphasis between us. Cleland and some others in the Territory who had an Army background may have had an occupational weakness for what they called 'intelligence'—the latest confidential report about the worst that might happen if one's gravest fears proved true.

Around 1959 and 1960 some elements in the Territory Administration began to show concern about 'a risk to security'. They produced evidence of new kinds of activity which might promote dissatisfaction and resistance to authority. As a simple example, known Australian communists who visited the Territory ports as members of ship crews sometimes sought out native leaders and tried to influence them in their discontent, and sometimes leaflets with a subversive intention were found. Officers reported sometimes that a zealous missionary was telling the people to obey God's commands rather than those of the district commissioner. As another example, gossip about West New Guinea and Indonesian ambition led to stories about 'secret contacts' across the border. Some officials began to talk of the need for a security service. A few of them developed the odd habit of speaking out of the corner of their mouths when they hinted at all the secrets they knew or suspected.

I would have preferred to rely still on the watchfulness and good sense of our own Native Affairs officers, going about their normal duties and working openly, but perhaps there was a case for special precautions so that any hidden subversion might become known and so that rumour and suspicion among the many could be replaced by exact reports from a few officers who specialized in security.

I certainly did not want any of our own Administration officials to become undercover men. The relationship between the Administration and the native people was, at that stage at least, quite different from the relationship between authority and the community in countries reputed to be more advanced. I thought we should be careful not to impair the trust and confidence between them. If there were any need for undercover work, let it be done by a hired outsider. I rejected suggestions by Cleland that he should have his own 'intelligence' service and I tried to encourage him to keep relationships between our officers and the people in the open.

Early in 1962 the Australian Security Intelligence Organization (ASIO), which had already shown an interest in the local scene, looking at it from an Australian viewpoint, offered some suggestions for an expanded organization and proposed that I set up a committee in the Territory to study the problem. I again resisted the idea of creating a Territory Security Intelligence Organization, saying that if any work of this kind were needed, it should be done by ASIO after receiving our permission and that ASIO should have no function in the Territory other than reporting factually to the Administrator and Minister. I rejected a suggestion that a security organization in the Territory should be an agent 'to advance the Government's policy' and that it should advise on 'counter-measures to be taken by the Administration' to meet 'subversion'. For matters plainly criminal I was willing to have a special Branch in the Royal Papua and New Guinea Constabulary to do the work narrowly appropriate to a police force, but I would not allow our police force to go looking for 'communists', 'enemy agents' or 'subversive elements'.

My views were elaborated in a personal letter to Cleland later in the year. I had seen a report by an ASIO man that some discontent voiced by a well-known native man over a long-standing grievance was due to the subversive activity of an anthropologist working in the area. I said this report was quite unconvincing because I had personally heard the same native man airing the same grievance before the anthropologist ever went there. I expressed the view that ASIO reports over-simplified situations. I wrote to Cleland,

To my mind, the fatal flaw in the approach of the security people is that they tend to relate everything to the subversive influence of this or that person and consequently they fall into the error of thinking that if you remove or silence the subversive influence all will be well. You and I know that any sense of grievance, discontent or resistance may be due to very complex and deep-seated causes, and that our constant job is to try to understand these causes and to take the appropriate action to remove or modify them. While it may be true that persons with a subversive intention may work upon existing grievances or discontent, that fact should not blind us to the necessity of understanding the nature of the discontent better than the subversive agent understands it, and of ourselves working upon the discontented in an imaginative and constructive way . . . You and I . . . have to ensure by all the means we can that increased measures for security do not in any way replace the deep-seated and wide-ranging search for an understanding of all matters affecting the relationships between the native people and ourselves . . . The final outcome in the Territory rests more on what your officers do in all their work in close association with the native people than upon any precautions security may take. [Letter of 1 August 1962.]

In another minute on another occasion, directing that Administration officers were not to become engaged in security intelligence work, I wrote,

I am unshakeably convinced that the administration of the Territory will lose wisdom and calmness and that it will imperil the trust between government and the indigenous people if its officers themselves become engaged in security intelligence work or if senior officers start to live in the atmosphere of security intelligence . . . An efficient security intelligence service is certainly needed but we want to ensure that its work is done by the specialists in this field and that the Administration is not engaged in the work but that, as the occasion arises, the Administration receives promptly the information that the security intelligence service thinks it ought to have. The truth, which unfortunately we do not express plainly, is that once people start on security intelligence work they suffer from the occupational disease of 'twisted neck', always looking over their shoulders. I do not want any of our Administration people to get 'twisted neck'. [Minute of 18 April 1963.]

Cabinet made a decision that 'an adequate intelligence organization to provide warning of infiltration or subversion' should be established. I continued to refuse to allow the Administration to be part of it, insisting that it be a separate and distinct Australian organization. Having read the plans prepared by the security people to put the Cabinet decision into effect, I contemptuously described the paper as 'the most appalling hotch-potch of loose thoughts. It wanders all over the floor like spilt fluid.' I think that was a fair description of most of the stuff I saw both then and later from intelligence committees. I directed that the Administrator co-operate in the creation of an 'adequate organization' to do a narrow and specialized task separate from the Territory Administration and that we receive and consider any reports or assessments, but that these be made directly either to the Administrator or to the Minister. (Minute of 21 May 1963.) In later years, in the portfolios of Defence and External Affairs, when more directly concerned with security, my attitude was much the same.

Because I held these views so firmly, it may seem strange that I should have become involved in the 'affaire Gluckman' in the middle of 1960. Professor Max Gluckman, a distinguished anthropologist on a visit to the Australian National University, was refused a permit to enter the Territory and as Minister I took responsibility. In fact I was overseas when Gluckman's application was made and I was unaware of it until after the permit had been refused. My position, after consultation with the Prime Minister was, as I phrased it during the parliamentary debate, that 'I was not prepared . . . to take any steps to ask the Administrator to reconsider his decision.'

We were caught in a trap which seemed to me to have been contrived astutely by a journalist and some members of the academic staff of the Australian National University. I plead guilty to having been outwitted but not to having been intentionally repressive.

After an examination of departmental files subsequent to the event, I made some notes which show that the whole business was handled departmentally in an unusual way. There were inexplicable delays at every stage between the first application by Gluckman on 1 March and the decision on 21 July to refuse a permit. One consequence of the delays was that both the Vice-Chancellor of the university (Sir Leslie Melville) and I were absent from Canberra at the critical time and neither of us knew anything about the case. The matter apparently was never brought to the notice of Lambert, as head of the Department of Territories, but was kept at a lower level. Some of the official conversations of which I was subsequently informed were not recorded in the files. The attempts made by senior staff at the university to submit additional information and furnish references to establish the good faith of Gluckman were likewise not recorded and never reached the Secretary, the Administrator or the Minister. The Administrator originally granted a permit. Later he was informed orally that ASIO had advised against admission and, after waiting for six weeks to receive written confirmation of this oral advice, he refused the permit. On the very day he did so in Port Moresby the public 'scandal' broke in the Australian press. The journalist's story was obviously ready and waiting for the signal to be given. Then, as Minister, I received a departmental submission 'for information'. As I wrote to Lambert at the time,

The information was rather bare and no attempt was made by the department to direct attention to any unusual aspects of the case. As Minister I accept responsibility for supporting the Administrator and the Prime Minister accepts responsibility for his concurrence but I feel that the departmental submission 'for information' was not perhaps as full as it might have been. In any case, it apparently did not come under your own notice before it was placed before me and I suggest it should have done so. [Minute of 1 September 1960.]

My view of the Gluckman case is that it showed that any report from a security organization should be received only as information and not as 'advice' and should be weighed by a responsible authority against all other available information, and no security question should be handled at a junior level. In my own view, there were insufficient grounds for refusing the permit, and the incident would never have occurred if the application had been handled in a straightforward way at the appropriate level. The Left Wing whooped with joy at the story that the permit had been refused.

Another point on which I differed from the Administration concerned any possible use of military forces in civil disturbance. In January 1962 a move originated in the Territory for making military forces available to aid the civil power if required. This had progressed some distance in discussions in Port Moresby between the Administration and the local Army establishment, and in Canberra between the Departments of the Army, Attorney-General and Territories before being submitted to me. I wrote at once, 'I don't like it', and said that a reference to Cabinet or a discussion by Ministers was necessary before the discussion went any further. In spite of this, the Army, apparently still without reference to their own Minister, kept on working out procedures and sent what was called an 'interim instruction' to the commanders in the Territory, saying in effect that the Army would be ready to comply at once with any request from the civil authorities for assistance in maintaining peace or in restoring law and order and, during a state of emergency, would be ready to assist in maintaining public or other services essential to the life of the community. The submission to me by my own Department reflected a view that this was all very good and necessary as forward planning.

I told my Department to stop. Unless and until it was cleared by Cabinet, what had been done was not approved and nothing further was to be done. The Administrator was told that in no circumstances was he to make a request for military aid without reference to Canberra. (Minute of 22 February 1962.)

[35]

THE INSPECTOR-GENERAL

Looking back on the closing years of my term as Minister for Territories, I realize that, in respect of Papua and New Guinea, I behaved at times like an inspector-general of the service. Various influences made me an inspector-general. Since some of them lie in my own nature, perhaps I may be excused if I use up a few pages in looking at myself.

It is a rare blessing to see ourselves as others see us. A moment of illumination came to me one day in Paris after I had left the Territories portfolio. As Australian Minister for External Affairs I was given a pleasant luncheon at the Quai D'Orsay by the French Foreign Minister, M. Couve de Murville. We chimed together from the moment we met and conversation flowed easily on all sorts of topics—before lunch, at the table, over coffee, and finally in slow progression through the elegant salons to the front door and in a pause on the front steps. We had prolonged deeply into the afternoon what was intended to be a formal hour. As I was departing, I thanked Couve de Murville for being so generous with his time and said how much I had enjoyed our talk. He said, 'I enjoyed it too. It is a rare pleasure to meet a like-minded person.' His last words were, 'From our conversation I would guess that, like myself, you were brought up in a nonconformist household and have been in the public service as an Inspector-General.' This description of me was due to his own percipience and not to any account I had given to him. On the same evening at dinner I said to my old friend Alexandre Parodi, with whom I had sat on the Security Council in New York in 1946, that I had found Couve de Murville congenial company. Parodi said, 'I can understand that. In New York, when we have been arguing, you sometimes reminded me of Couve, but as you and I were warm friends I forbade myself to say so.'

I had a similar glimpse of myself through the eyes of another person a few years later. In a place far from New Guinea, towards the end of a congenial evening in company with a lawyer, we got onto the subject of New Guinea. He had been appointed a magistrate in the Territory near the end of my term but had never met me there. He said that he now found me totally different from what he had been told about me. He had expected to find me grim, narrow-minded and opinionated, but I was quite otherwise and the evening had solved

407

a puzzle that had worried him for years. 'Never having met you,' he said, 'I knew only the reputation you had among some of the officials and all of the journalists and I could never understand why a person so liberal in outlook could apply his ideas in such an illiberal way.' He had formed a picture of me as a person who had admirable objectives but enforced his views like a dictator and never allowed any opinion but his own. He was surprised to find me so tolerant of other opinions, hesitant about enforcing my views and even kindly towards other people.

We soon got off the subject of 'me' to the subject of Australian administration in Papua and New Guinea, of which he himself was rather critical. I found as our discussions proceeded that as a magistrate he had little experience of public administration. When he had thought a little more about the subject, however, he readily conceded that at some point of time in the conduct of affairs someone had to make a firm decision and someone had to take the responsibility of ensuring that a decision was put into effect. He still appeared to think however that a minister should keep on the heights and he had difficulty in understanding the political and constitutional reality that a minister has to answer to Parliament for what is done under his administration and bears the responsibility for all that is done, shielding the officers from Parliament. What changed his mind and helped to end his puzzlement about me was a practical discussion of some of the actual situations in the Territory of which he was aware and on which Territory officers had given him an unfavourable story about me. I reminded him that there was an Administration in the Territory and a Department in Canberra. Often they differed in their views about what should be done and how it should be done. Sometimes they fought each other. Consequently, assuming that neither of them was the boss of the other, no decision would be reached unless the Minister made it. The Minister could end argument by accepting the recommendations from his Department or by accepting those of the Administration, or he could make up his own mind after considering both sides of the argument. I made up my own mind. This meant that in some cases I favoured what the Administration wanted, sometimes what the Department wanted, and sometimes ended the argument by a direction that took something from each. In the course of any year this meant that there were many instances in which the Department did not get its own way and many in which the Administration did not get its own way. Hence, in most critical cases, I was bound to appear to one or the other as a dictator who told them what to do instead of being a good minister who did what he was told. He also appreciated that another practical necessity arose out of the urgency of the task and, in some cases, from the incompetence or lack of energy in some of the soft spots in the staff. If a minister did not drive hard, there would be little decision-making and even less action.

The lawyer accepted both these practical illustrations and magisterially concluded that I was a strong minister and not an authoritarian dictator, while still reserving a doubt whether there was much difference in the effect on the minds of the officers concerned.

This need to make a decision and to insist on action provide the reason for being a 'strong minister' but do not fully explain why I also became the inspector-general. The main reason is that no one else was doing the job. A deeper reason probably is to be found in my own nature and my own approach to administration.

Couve de Murville saw me truly. One of the results of a nonconformist up-bringing is the nonconformist conscience. Another is the belief that faith has to be justified by works. A third is scant regard to a hierarchy so that one does not reverence a bishop or a high official simply for what he is but only for what he does. All three tend towards some harshness in judgement and some impatience over the shortcomings of others, while at the same time they demand facts instead of explanations and excuses. I wanted results. I saw failure where I did not get results, and failure rested heavily on my own conscience. The nonconformist conscience also tends to make a person more keenly aware of what is going wrong than of what is going right.

Furthermore my approach to administration—perhaps somewhat rigid—was shaped both by happy study and sad experience. I was the academic product of the pre-war classical approach to the study of political institutions and I had a good textbook knowledge of the theory and practice of modern government before I had any close experience of it. In my academic reading and writing I was much more interested in political institutions than in political doctrines. As for sad experience, the untidiness and the ineffectiveness of public administration when I was a public servant in the Department of External Affairs under H. V. Evatt drove me into the bosom of orthodoxy and confirmed my respect for the traditions, rules and conventions of public administration on the British model. Good rules are the intelligent formulation of the lessons of experience. I respect them in the same way as I respect sound practice in a workshop. If a piece of carpentry is done in the correct way, it is more likely to be well done than if it is attempted in the incorrect way. If it is done according to the rules, there will be no accidents in the workshop. In public administration, as in any skilled trade or profession, a workman without crafts-manship only makes a mess, and one without diligence only spoils good ideas. Those critics who thought I wanted to do everything myself were astray. My whole endeavour was to make other people do the job but to do it in the proper way, and my impatience was with bad method, disregard of the rules or lack of diligence. One journalist who described me as the 'district officer of New Guinea' was very imperceptive. If he wanted to say something unkind, he would have been nearer the mark to call me an inspector-general or a public service technician, certainly not a district officer. I did not pretend to know more about the situations in Papua and New Guinea than an officer on the spot and I wished to receive information and advice from them and relied on them for action. On the other hand I did know a good deal more than most officers about the working of political institutions and the organization and methods of public administration and tried to keep them up to the mark in these matters.

So much for the peculiarities of my own nature. They alone, however, would not have shaped my behaviour as Minister. That behaviour was my response to a situation, and a different situation could have produced a different outcome.

The situation in the 1960s was that the range of our work in Papua and New Guinea had widened and our staff had increased rapidly. A straightforward task of ruling a dependent people was changing into a more complex operation of running an administrative machine efficiently while dealing constructively at the same time with many new needs for social, economic and political development. There was a need to co-ordinate effort, ensure cohesion in the effort and keep the end in sight. A tremendous effort was also needed to bring more drive into the machine. The outstanding lesson for me from ten years as Minister was that laying down policy and giving directions were not enough. Neither the Administration nor the Department of Territories provided me with an inspector-general, so I became one myself. The Department of Territories was restricted in any inspectorial role because I had consistently checked any attempts it made to run the Territory or to dominate the Administration. Its officers could help the officers of the Administration but could not give them orders. Nevertheless the Department might have done more than it did in keeping track of what happened after decisions had been communicated to Port Moresby and in ensuring promptness. I wondered at times whether the structure of the Department—a matter not under my control—was the best for the circumstances. The Department was organized functionally, not geographically. For example the division responsible for social questions looked after such matters in the Northern Territory and the small island territories as well as in Papua and New Guinea, and the divisions responsible for finance, economic affairs and personnel and administration did the same. A regional subdivision of function might have been better. Within this functional structure, my impression was that departmental officers found, as I myself found, that it was much more difficult to get things done in Papua and New Guinea than in our other large field of responsibility, the Northern Territory.

Furthermore Lambert, who was a prodigiously hard worker and a good public servant, worked with concentration on one subject at a time and had a succession of other big questions to engage him, such as the resettlement of the Nauruans, native welfare conferences, north Australian development, the Australian pastoral industry, the mining of bauxite and uranium, constitutional development for the Northern Territory, and the minor crises that arose sporadically in one part or another of our wide domain. Consequently he was unable, by reason of the multiplicity of his cares and the almost ferocious way he took a grip of each subject as it arose, to keep a broad oversight of all that was happening or failing to happen in Papua and New Guinea. As an aside, it may be mentioned that at this time Lambert had the misfortune to be in a car accident and, although he was only briefly off duty, had a long period of physical pain and the awkwardness of having his right arm in a sling while carrying on his work.

In the Territory public service there was no hope of an inspector-general. We had the constant problem of weakness at the upper levels. Two of the measures we took were not immediately successful. My main disappointment was with a central policy and planning committee and with the Department of the Administrator. Both the committee and the officers of this department had a weakness for discussion and for referring matters to ad hoc committees for the preparation of reports. My judgement is that they hampered rather than helped the two Assistant Administrators. Another weakness derived from the fact that necessarily we had made a number of appointments to senior positions of new-comers without any depth of local experience, and some of these new officers were unaware of the good old public service practice of looking at the files. They hovered around questions on which policy decisions had already been made or clear directions given, simply because they did not use the files. I do not know much about the internal methods of work in the Administration, but the impression I received was that the way in which work was channelled meant that the Administrator was not, at any given time, fully aware of every-thing that was going on but would have to enquire when the occasion arose about what was being done on this or that. His necessary delegation of functional responsibility had tended to limit his personal oversight both of what was coming into Port Moresby and what was going out. Moreover, as I have made plain elsewhere, I think the whole office of Administrator was badly conceived and its functions beyond the compass of any one man. In any case Cleland was unable or did not see it as his function to be my inspector-general.

So I had to plug away myself at this vexatious and wearing task, repeatedly finding out for myself the delay or the digression and always trying to get action and to keep attention directed to the main objectives. Consequently from 1961 to 1963 I used a lot of my energy finding out faults and making correc-tions, repeating demands, being perpetually dissatisfied and getting the reputation of trying to run the whole show.

There may have been some element of self-protection in my increased personal attention to problems on the spot. At the time I only shrugged my shoulders and took it as an occupational hazard that the stock reply to many complaints would be 'blame the Minister'. Even so, I may have been impelled subconsciously to find out more about the mistakes or neglect for which I was being held responsible.

From about 1958 onwards I had developed a new pattern for ministerial visits to the Territory. Instead of making a grand tour and being shown the sights, I stated a definite purpose for each visit and planned my programme to serve that purpose. I worked out a very congenial routine. A Royal Australian Air Force Dakota would be positioned at either Cairns or Townsville and, after doing my day's work in Canberra, I would fly up by commercial aircraft, have a restful night and take off at dawn for direct flight to whichever part of the Territory had been picked for the visit. A two-seater aircraft might be chartered for local travel into airstrips too short or too rough for larger craft but the Dakota was used for the main stages in the Territory and, at the end of four or five days, I could fly directly from the last Territory stop to Cairns or Towns-ville and pick up the commercial flight back to Canberra.

The Air Force crews looked forward to these trips as much as I did, for we visited unusual places. I have very pleasant memories of the time we had together and the service they gave to my staff and me. Another advantage was that the Dakota was a flying office and, when we were above the clouds or over the sea with nothing to look at, we could plug away at the endless desk work that besets a minister. Somehow or other my secretary organized matters so that whenever we came to a place serviced by an airline, there was another locked mail bag from Canberra full of more work for me and, working away at the papers when travelling, I would not have a pile on my desk when I returned home. In this way I came to see the whole of the Territory and its problems more closely perhaps than all except a handful of the most senior public servants. A map on which I marked my visits to the Territory has no blank spaces.

Sometimes there was business to transact at headquarters. We relied a good deal on exchanges of visits by senior officials between Canberra and Port Moresby, but about once a year or a little more frequently I would include Port Moresby in my itinerary. I went there to do business and found scant pleasure in the place. A letter to Cleland regarding a visit in February 1962 exposes my temper. The Administration had sent down to me a nice, leisurely programme for a ministerial visit to the capital with a bit of sight-seeing, a few harmless gatherings and such entertainments as a buffet dinner, a form of punishment I suffer less willingly than any other social activity because it is unseemly to be spilling words of politeness and gobbets from an overloaded plate at the same time as one is trying to shake hands with one person and dodge someone else who is speaking with a mouthful of food and waving an unsteady glass of wine. I had sent a curt telegram cancelling the programme and then wrote more precisely about what I wanted:

My needs will include, in addition to the meeting with the native leaders, the following appointments on Administration matters: at least two hours with the Central Policy and Planning Committee; a good hour with Cannon and an additional hour at least with all those departmental heads who are most immediately concerned with economic development in all its phases; an hour with Caterson and any senior officer or officers he wishes to include plus some additional time with Parrish who, if it is thought wise, can also be accompanied by the leaders of various native organizations for industrial or semi-industrial purposes; an hour with the Extension Services people; an hour or more with the Director and Deputy Director of Education; an hour with Watkins and senior Crown Law people; a private conference of at least two hours with the heads of all departments present; more than an hour with the Public Service Commissioner and the heads of Departments (such as Health, Police, Post Office) which are engaged in training, in order to discuss further proposals for administrative staff training and an administrative staff college; an hour with the Public Service Commissioner, and any others directly concerned with the reorganization of the structure of the public service. At all these appointments it is open to you and either one or both of the Assistant Administrators to be present. I am asking Mr Lambert to be present. As already provided I wish to have a private talk with the Chief Justice, who presumably will also arrange an opportunity for me to meet Ollerenshaw. There will also probably be need for a final session with yourself, Gunther and Reeve to tidy up matters arising from these talks or any matters not covered by them.

Rather than have any social engagements I would prefer to leave the period from six to eight blank on both Thursday and Friday evenings so that I can make ad hoc arrangements for meeting persons informally.

This adds up to a minimum of 16 hours so we have to think of something like 9 a.m. to noon, 2 p.m. to 6 p.m. and 8 p.m. to 11 p.m. on Thursday and Friday.

Occasionally I made the more conventional ministerial visit to the main centres and on such occasions was pressed to receive deputations. I had always taken the view that a minister should be accessible to the citizen and that anyone with a reasonable claim to present a case should be given an appointment. I had also purposely encouraged the indigenous people to tell me about what they themselves called 'trouble'—a term that might mean something big or something very small—and I found I could not be less receptive to the Europeans. Thus I was becoming, without wishing to do the job, something like an Ombudsman for the whole Territory. My notes of deputations cover an enormous range of grievances and requests from the personal problems of individuals to the representations of strongly established groups.

In the course of this closer attention, I became aware of the fact that the Australian Government's decisions and my own directions on policy were not getting through to the officers of the Territory Administration. On many occasions I found relatively senior field officers in all departments who were unaware of directions given and sometimes a keen young officer would expound on what he thought might be a good thing to do, not knowing that he had been expected by me to be doing just that for the past two or three years. I was never sure that I knew the cause of this gap between decision and action. One possible reason was that the Department in Canberra communicated my decisions to Port Moresby incompletely or in paraphrase. It seemed to me however that most of the trouble was in the Territory itself and that the necessary delegation of responsibility both from the Administrator to the departments and from departmental heads to sections had been done in a way that gave dispersal at the expense of firm direction and control. It also seemed to me that as a decision dropped slowly down through the ranks it was paraphrased and interpreted at each stage and what the operative officer finally received was not my direction but someone else's version of it.

Furthermore, in the mental and physical climate of the Territory, the habit of reading was rare. More than once I came across an officer in an outlying centre who claimed ignorance of an instruction but, under my own pressure, turned up his files and found the instruction in a circular which he had not read or had only looked at casually.

In reverse order the same fate seemed to await any screed sent upwards. I recall one instance when an active-minded officer talked critically to me of the rejection of a submission he had made. He thought I had done the rejecting. I followed up the lead by asking if I could see the document and found it lying still unread in the Department of the Administrator at Port Moresby.

Another element in the situation was the continued feeling of separateness from Australia in some sections of the Administration, leading to a tendency to regard directions of the Australian Government as comments made by an outsider rather than as decisions that had to be put into effect. To some extent the existence of this state of affairs may be evidence of my own failure as Minister. If so, the root cause of that failure was that I was consistently unwilling to run the Territory from Canberra and was always insisting that the Administration in the Territory should carry out to the full its function of administration. Even when, as inspector-general, I discovered a weakness, I drew the matter to the attention of the Administrator for him to remedy instead of changing the inspector-general's hat for my ministerial hat and exerting my own powers to discharge the Administrator's functions. If I had been less correct on procedure, I might have forced quicker results and gained easier praise.

Incidentally this care over procedure tends to distort the documentary record in a way that may be less than fair to Cleland personally. The documents show again and again my dissatisfaction with 'the Administrator'. I visited on the official head the shortcomings of almost everyone else in the Territory, but his difficulties in getting action were probably no less than my difficulties. When my minutes contain repeated directions to the Administrator to attend to this or that or complaints of inattention or delay by the Administrator, I was not attaching personal blame to Cleland but observing the procedure I believed to be correct in the relations between the Minister and the Territory Administration. I valued the support of Cleland and the frank and friendly discussions I was able to have with him at all times. I appreciated his difficulties.

There were several reasons for the unsatisfactory situation other than the wrong design in the Territory Administration. The lingering influence of 'the old days' made adaptation to change very slow; the hope of building an efficient public service was hampered by the lack of depth in public service experience and tradition in the Territory and the difficulty in recruiting new officers of high enough quality and training in public administration; local influences in the community still favoured separateness and colonialist attitudes; the administrative task had become more diverse; and the rapid growth in numbers of the public service presented problems of internal departmental management that were not fully mastered. We were also building up the numbers of head-office people who had limited contact with the outlying places or with the indigenous majority and had scant understanding of the practical problems of turning policy into action. I had much impatience at the time but refrain from harsh judgement on individual officers. We had a handful of exceptionally good officers. Most of the others were doing their best, but their best was not always good enough for a very difficult job.

Fundamentally too there was a difference in outlook between a minister who saw the Territory public service as one part of the government of Papua and New Guinea and those officers who were accustomed to thinking of the public service as the whole of the government. I had done a great deal to give the Territory a larger and better public service and now found that I had also strengthened a bureaucracy. On the Australian mainland we are familiar with the presumption of public servants that they really run the country but, because of the strength of the electorate, the news media, Parliament, the Ministry and the supremacy of the law, that presumption can be kept in check. In Papua and New Guinea we had the same presumption but virtually no check on it except the Minister for Territories. In a letter of October 1959 I observed,

> The public servant in the Territory is not very different from the public servant in Australia in wanting to run the country in his own way and in believing that he knows better than any minister. But whereas the public servant in Australia does concede some authority to the Parliament and the executive and lives under the perpetual scrutiny and correction of the

community and the press, as well as the parliamentarian, the public servant in the Territory is not so well instructed in the theory of parliamentary democracy and is encouraged by the local community and the local press to resent any ministerial direction as an interference in Territory affairs.

An amusing experience was frequently to be asked by a citizen to stop the Administrator from doing something that touched that person's material benefit, while in the next half hour I would be roundly criticized by the same citizen for giving the Administrator a direction on general policy. The person who approached me in my unsought role as Ombudsman to ask that I make a public servant do something about a personal grievance might well turn out to be the principal speaker at a public gathering on the same day complaining that I interfered too much.

The public service in Papua and New Guinea stood between the government and the people in a way unknown in the Australian community. In Australia the Ministry is responsible to Parliament, and any elector or body of electors has a chance to make his views known by direct approach to a member of parliament or a minister or through the various media of communication. In Papua and New Guinea the Government's decisions and instructions on policy had to filter through the Department of Territories to the Administrator and from the Administrator down to an officer in the field, who then told a group of people in words of his own and in a manner of his own what the Government wanted done or had already done itself. In the reverse direction, any complaint, request or proposal by a person or local group was made first to an officer, who made his own decision as to whether it was important enough to send higher up and so it crept upwards along the same channels. The form in which it eventually reached the Minister might be considerably different from the form in which it began. The more articulate spokesmen for the people sometimes complained of the difficulty of communication and of the lack of understanding in Canberra, while on my part I was feeling a similar difficulty in making contact with them.

This basic difficulty was made worse by a frequent habit in the public service —a habit common in all public services—of shifting the blame for any shortcoming to a remote place. The easiest way of meeting reproach or disappointment was to say that 'Canberra' was delaying the matter or that 'Canberra' had refused the request. I encountered many cases of this kind. The decisions about land tenure, which had as their objective making more land available for native agriculture, reached one district at least in a way that created the opinion that we were trying to get land from the native people to give it to the whites.

As well as these mechanical impediments to smooth government, there was a more fundamental strain caused by a difference of ideas. The unintended colonialism of the Territory Administration tended to favour an authoritarian and presidential form of government, with the Administrator at the head supported by his own junta of top public servants. This may be the most efficient form of colonial rule. My own purpose, having clearly in mind the certainty of self-government for the indigenous people in the future, was to establish political institutions that could be adapted to that future situation. I wanted an efficient public service but not a bureaucracy. I wanted representative assemblies that, whether in national or local affairs, would be legislative bodies and not the instruments of an authoritarian executive. I wanted a system of the administration of justice that would be independent and not one of the tools of administration. I wanted an Administrator, not a President. There were elements in the Territory, seeing chiefly their own immediate task of ruling dependent peoples, who could not understand or in some cases were wholly out of sympathy with such ministerial views and were slow to carry out directions about local government councils, the courts of justice (both Supreme Court and lower courts), and similar developments. Even at the top level there was incomplete appreciation of the ultimate purpose. Various boards, which I had created to develop as representative institutions, were regarded as an adjunct to departmental functions. The central policy and planning committee, which had been intended as a means of promoting efficient and expeditious work by the public service and co-ordinating its activities, tended to develop as a Cabinet, while the Administrator's Council, which had been intended as an embryonic Cabinet, was neglected in that role and used to help sell Administration views to the legislature instead of being a place where elected representatives of the people brought their influence to bear on the Administration. My suggestion that the Administrator should not be the President of the Legislative Council was suspected as an attack on his status instead of being seen as a necessary enhancement of the status of the legislature and a recognition that it was not to be another tool of the Administration.

Another minor reason why some public servants chafed was that my orthodoxy—or, as one might now say, my old-fashioned ideas—about the public service led me to correct rather sharply some loose practices. I reminded the service of the conventional rules about the making of public statements by officials. I insisted that official business could not be conducted by personal exchanges between 'Bill' and 'Tom' and that every step had to be recorded on the file. I stopped a growing practice under which officers were arranging their own tours abroad and their own invitations to international conferences and I insisted that no officer could travel abroad at public expense unless his travel had been authorized after reference to a Territory overseas travel committee. Similarly I insisted that any proposals for publishing official reports or brochures had to be screened by a Territory publications committee. I said that departmental seniors could not pick their own staff but should follow established public service procedures for recruitment. I stopped a few self-indulgent practices. I insisted that all official matters be channelled through the approved system. Naturally a number of relatively important people three or four rows down from the top thought of such good public service practices as a derogation of that high station in life to which they had been called by providence. The wicked inspector-general was interfering again but, with the aid of the Public Service Commissioner, we got some sort of regularity and responsibility into the service and saved some money for our principal purposes and lifted the service clear of reproach.

Another element in the situation was that after nearly ten years I had developed a deep affection for the land and its people and had begun to develop some of the characteristics of the 'old hands'. We had worked for this country when few others showed much interest. We had stored up pleasant memories. I had yarned on clear tropical evenings in remote places with those who had taken an earlier part in the exploration of Papua and New Guinea and made first contact with its people. I had talked with the people in their villages. I had responded to the grandeur of its mountains and the whispering warmth of the sea on its coast. My sympathy for the indigenous people and hopes for their future had been kindled. In its own subtle way Papua and New Guinea had taken possession of me. Perhaps this showed. Perhaps some of the newcomers and one-week journalists thought I had been deluded into thinking I owned the place, when in fact I was the one who was possessed. In some ways I was finding a closer rapport with the old hands than with some of the more up-to-date fellows I had recruited. Perhaps I had been too long in office and had become one of the 'befores'.

My orthodoxy about the public service also meant that I accepted responsibility. A minister does not shelter behind public servants. Hence the departmental files, when they are opened, will show as well as this book may show a different picture from what was published at the time. My public statements never expressed any of my dissatisfaction or my correction of officers who failed to do what I expected them to do. I took the responsibility for any shortcoming, but my private papers show my constant worry over the great gap between what I wanted and what I got.

This same orthodoxy also requires me to accept full ministerial responsibility for the outcome. My failure as Minister was that performance did not match intention and I did not get the Administration of the Territory to do all that I wanted it to do. In exposing the situation as I have done, I am not seeking to make excuses for that failure but explaining some of the reasons for it and the conditions in which my failure should be judged.

[36]

EXODUS

In December 1963 the Prime Minister asked me to take the portfolio of Defence left vacant by the retirement of A. G. Townley. With the swearing-in of a new Ministry on 18 December, I ceased to be Minister for Territories after having held the post for twelve years and seven months.

I changed posts with a mixture of relief and regret. I had formed many close and happy associations with people in the Northern Territory, Norfolk Island, Papua and New Guinea, Nauru, Cocos and Christmas Island and had become deeply engaged in the welfare and development of all these territories. There was a lot of work I had not yet finished.

On the other hand there had also been some vexations, and a change might be good for all who had felt the strain of my continuous hard driving. A single-topic portfolio would be less onerous for me than the wide range of activity in Territories. Defence policy was a field in which I originally had a much livelier interest and a wider knowledge than I had in Territories. If I had been able to choose my ministerial path in 1951, I would have chosen one that led to Defence. So I looked forward to my new job. Unfortunately further unexpected changes meant that I did not stay as long in Defence as I would have wished but after four months had to transfer to the less preferred post of External Affairs.

My departure from Territories came shortly after Lambert reached retiring age, leaving a vacancy as Secretary of the Department of Territories. I knew that Cleland's retirement as Administrator of Papua and New Guinea would be due in June 1966. Dunk, as chairman of the Public Service Board, produced his list of aspirants for Lambert's place. I would not have a bar of any of them. Privately I worked out my own design to have Gunther appointed Secretary of the Department of Territories, and, in two to three years' time, after he had gained the advantage of the additional experience at Canberra, to appoint him to succeed Cleland. The senior assistant secretary, R. S. Swift, with the advantage of two extra years' seniority, would then be qualified to make a good secretary of the Department. I talked this over with Menzies. He saw merit in it and I would have got my way in spite of Dunk, but the election of November 1963 intervened. With the customary strict observance of the constitutional

418

conventions under Menzies, no major appointments could be made until after the election. After the election I ceased to be Minister for Territories. I handed on the papers and my advice to my successor, but Dunk reappeared with the list he favoured and different arrangements were made.

Menzies was good enough to discuss with me who might take my place as Minister for Territories. The names of two ministers were mentioned. From what I was told later, Menzies put the proposal to each in turn and each recoiled in horror from the prospect. The new Country Party member, C. E. Barnes, who had come in to take the vacancy in Country Party representation left by the retirement of Senator Cooper, was given the job. It was reminiscent of what had happened in 1951 when I had come to Territories as the tail-ender, the only difference being that Barnes was not in the Cabinet.

I handed on to my successor an active and expanding Territory and a five-year forward programme planned to the financial year 1966–7. The estimates for 1963–4, passed by the Australian Parliament in September, provided for an expenditure (in round figures) of £37·5 million, made up of £25·3 million Commonwealth Grant, £10·5 million local revenue and £1·7 million loan fund. When I had started in the job in 1951, the annual expenditure was £6·4 million.

The plans we had made foreshadowed a rise in public service to 10 000, including the recruitment of 2500 additional indigenous officers. In the same period we would enrol 3500 indigenous recruits for training. In addition, 4500 indigenous teachers were to be trained and school enrolment raised to 350 000, including 10 000 in post-primary and secondary schools. The number of people covered by local government councils was to be doubled. Other features of the five-year plan were major increases in agricultural development both by training and by extension work, and 7500 blocks of land were to be made available for native land settlement. Major measures were to be taken in health, including protection from malaria, the tuberculosis survey, and increases in the numbers of hospitals, aid posts and staff. I was satisfied that we now had a strong enough base to make more rapid development possible.

The steeper upward climb to achievement began about 1960–1. Perhaps, in leaving the portfolio, I could feel that I had brought the Territory to a new stage in its advancement towards self-government. The contrast between the situation I found in 1951 and the situation I left in 1963 was so great that I can scarcely credit the rapidity of the change. I had been so closely associated and at times buried so deeply in administrative care that I had to stand off at some distance from the events and be dissociated from them before I appreciated fully the work that had been done. In my time, public expenditure had increased fivefold. The range and volume of administrative activity, as measured by the submissions that passed over my own desk, had increased sevenfold. Exports had doubled in value and had diversified. I had found only a handful of indigenous people engaged in public affairs and left thousands who as councillors, members of the public service, employees in private industry, and members of boards were helping to shape the future of their country.

My mood at the time of departure is revealed in a paper I read to an Adult Education Summer School in Melbourne on 6 January 1964 on the allotted topic 'Present Policies and Objectives' in a course entitled 'The Future in Papua and New Guinea'.* The engagement had been accepted and the address written before I knew that I was to leave Territories but, by kind permission of the new Minister, I fulfilled the engagement and delivered the paper after a little subediting to suit the new circumstances.

The paper also reveals my own approach to the tasks of government. Early in the paper I said that in talking about policies I preferred to deal with practice. For example, if I said 'our policy is educational advancement', I had not said much, but if I talked about the programme for recruiting teachers and for opening more schools, and the relationship between school work and the needs both of the individual and of the community, I would have exposed what policy was—not a high-sounding word to express vague hopes but the sum of a succession of definite decisions each made with a definite purpose in mind. A minister gave no clear lead when he said his policy was educational advancement but only when that aim was translated into decisions. Policy was in part the outcome of a vision of what one wanted to do and in part the outcome of grappling, according to the needs, opportunities and resources, with a succession of problems.

I talked of the overall objective that should be kept clear and constant, and the more limited objectives by which it would be served and which could be varied or discarded to meet changing needs. In making policy decisions a vital question was when to do something. A decision could be foolish either because it was premature or because it was too long delayed. Making the right decision at the right time was one of the most exacting responsibilities laid on a Minister for Territories. I added,

> With all respect to honest opinion, it generally happened in my experience that the best-informed and most expert counsellors usually urged caution and that among those who called for rapid change there have been a large proportion of singularly ill-informed persons. A minister however had to make sure that he is not over-persuaded by those who give expert counsel and that he is not deterred from change because some of those who advocate change are clearly in a state of gross ignorance. He has to make the judgement on what is the right time. In my view, the dominant factors in considering this question of time are whether the measure has a chance of succeeding and whether the step, if successful, will lead clearly towards the attainment of the overall strategic objective. A step that fails is not only useless but may be dangerous. Personally I have always taken a chance in favour of early change and in most cases have taken action ahead of the advice given and demanded exceptional efforts from the service to have things done. Advisers cannot be expected to take risks; a Minister must. The test however is not one of haste or slowness but of moving successfully in the right direction.

Later in the paper, after reciting some of the decisions I had made, I said,

> Looking back, I can claim steadiness in the objective. I could see the objective clearly and had no hesitation by reason of any unsureness of the direction in which I was trying to move. I hope I can also claim consistency

* The full text of the paper appeared in *Adult Education* (Council of Adult Education, Victoria), vol. 8, no. 3 (Mar. 1964), pp. 8-16.

in judgement. So far as it was in my capacity to do so, all decisions were intended to support one another, to serve the same end and to respect the same principles. There is of course room for differences of opinion on whether or not a particular action was well chosen, or whether each move made was in fact the best path towards the objective, or whether each step was taken at the right time.

If any difference of opinion is to be an intelligent one then the starting point has to be a clear understanding of what the objective is. Beyond that lies another basic question whether the objective is in fact attainable. Unless you know the purpose to be served you can very readily complain that a bricklayer's trowel is no use for ladling soup. Unless you know the difference between a trowel and a ladle your opinion on the best way of ladling soup or laying bricks is not worth much. You will however have the customary qualifications for becoming a political correspondent . . .

What is the objective? I suggest that it is self-government for Papua and New Guinea, achieved by a path of peaceful progressive change, and according to the free choice of the people, in circumstances that will give a reasonable prospect that they have both the will and the capacity to make their own choice effective for the benefit of their own people; and that as a self-governing country their social and economic development will continue. We also hope that as a self-governing people they will choose to remain in close and friendly relationships with Australia.

Is this objective attainable?

I can think of some of the pre-requisites of success and in making policy I have tried to help obtain these pre-requisites. One is trust and confidence between the races and between Papua and New Guinea and Australia. This trust requires not only an absence of resentment or the absence of a sense of injury. More positively it has to be a mutual confidence in fair dealing.

Another pre-requisite is a sense of unity among the diverse people of the Territory. They are not yet a people with a common language, a common religion, a common history or a common ambition. Instead there are ancient enmities and many barriers between them. Nevertheless there could still be unity, but the sense of unity will only be strong enough to overcome the barriers of which I have spoken if the people can find some single central point to attract the loyalty of all of them, rising above local loyalties. It is better that they find this central point in a principle of conduct and not in a demand for benefits or an expression of resentment. Some recent independence movements have found no central point except in a slogan to throw out the white man or a movement of 'liberation'. They throw out the white man; they 'liberate' themselves. Then, having no rallying point left and no central idea to which they give their loyalty, they succumb to dictatorial leadership and fall into a subjection from which there is no liberation. We have to help the people of Papua and New Guinea to find the core of their unity, the focus of their loyalty, or the objective towards which we are working will not be realized. But do not let us delude ourselves that we can deliver it to them ready made. Their loyalty has to be satisfying to them. It has to command their respect and support, not ours. It has to attract them—draw them to it—and not merely find favour with us.

A third pre-requisite of success is the establishment of certain traditions and conventions to control their actions in self-government. Let me give some humble examples of such conventions. If a man has a row with his neigh-

bour he settles it by going to court and not by splitting open his neighbour's
head with an axe. If a law is made everyone obeys it and a law means exactly
the same things to everyone. Public servants, members of parliament, and
judges are paid to do their work and they should not be offered nor should
they accept bribes. The Courts are independent of the Government. These
are the sort of things—and I have given only a few random examples—that
have to be bred into the bone (not written in to a bill of rights) if self-
government is to work.

We hope to see a self-governing country. The process by which we hope
to see the change achieved is by constitutional change centred in the legislature of the Territory. Progressively the membership of the legislature grows
and becomes increasingly representative while its powers and functions are
extended. When the point is reached at which the legislature is wholly
elected by the people and when the government of the Territory is made
directly and solely responsible to that legislature, then the fact of self-
government has been achieved. At that point of time it is a matter for the
responsible government of Papua and New Guinea and the fully responsible
parliament to decide what shall be the future status of the country and to
negotiate with the Australian Government either the conditions in which
they achieve complete independence or the terms on which they continue in
the desired relationship with Australia.

For success a self-governing country needs not only a parliament but also
a competent public service; an independent judiciary and magistracy; a
sufficient number of educated and competent men and women to become
candidates for public office; and a sufficient number of knowledgeable and
well-informed persons to give popular leadership in the electorates.

For success a self-governing country also needs sources from which it can
draw its public revenues to support its services and utilities, funds to maintain and extend its capital equipment, and sources of investment for the
development of its resources. Customarily it would also require the institu-
tional structure, both public and private, that facilitates the handling of such
matters.

It also needs economic activity to support the standard of living of its
people and give them gainful occupation; to give the country export income;
and to provide the foundation for further development. With this goes the
need for technical, professional and managerial skills in industry and
commerce and in the ancillary services such as telecommunications, shipping
and civil aviation.

Building a public service, helping a country to become economically
viable and laying a broad base for political activity are all much more
difficult than creating representative institutions or drafting constitutions.
The current fashion in the United Nations and in some sections of Australian journalism is to demand the outward semblance of political change.
Give them a parliament or a president and all will be well.

Yet, in doing so, they talk of the easiest part of the whole task. Anyone
can make something that looks like a machine. But the only value of
machinery is that it runs. If you did not have to worry about whether it
would run or not you could knock together a nice-looking machine with lots
of wheels and pistons and dial faces on a wet afternoon with the same ease
as a modern sculptor turns out metal adornments for Commonwealth Bank
buildings. If you did not worry about whether a new political constitution

would work we could draw up a new constitution for New Guinea before lunch.

We are firmly committed to promoting self-government for Papua and New Guinea and achieving it as soon as possible. Let us also pause to make sure that we have a clear understanding of what self-government is. It is government of the people of Papua and New Guinea by the people of Papua and New Guinea. It means the ending of government by Australia and equally it means the precluding of government by any other 'foreign' power . . . Before we rush out of one door we have a responsibility as trustees to make sure that no other foreigner is rushing in the other door.

Self-government also means, in my book, government according to a form chosen by the people themselves, introduced at a time which they think appropriate and confided to a government which they themselves have entrusted with office. If we renounce our right to impose our will on our wards we do not do so in order that someone else may impose his will on them. They have to shape a government that they can work in the circumstances in which they live.

This gives us a great responsibility. Up to the point of self-government we have to protect the freedom of choice of these people. In blunt terms we have to defend Papua and New Guinea and protect it from invasion, subversion or pressure from any quarter. We also have to have the patience and the courage to stay in the role of trusteeship, however unpopular it may be, until the people themselves are ready to make a choice and, at the moment of choice, we will still have a responsibility to use our own judgement on the prospects of the choice being effective and the best means by which it can be made effective . . .

I am quite certain in my own mind that the form of self-government will come to Papua and New Guinea before the country is economically viable and before it is fully equipped either to finance or to staff the various departments and agencies of government. Someone other than the people of Papua and New Guinea will have to underwrite self-government. I could talk at some length about the efforts that I have made to anticipate this situation—to build up the public service, to try to ensure that the expatriate element of the service will still be available to the self-governing country of the future, to produce a larger body of literate people capable of communicating readily with one another and of making clear and wise decisions as successive issues arise, to give industries to the country, to try to relate standards of expenditure to capacity to meet the expenditure, to promote development of resources. But I know that while our achievement in these directions has been great it is not great enough and the work will not be completed at the time of self-government. Self-government will be an improvisation when it comes but the more we can manage to do now the better the improvisation will be.

For twelve years I have been preaching this sort of thing and stressing urgency. It is part of the irony of political life that, although my own memory of the twelve years is of unremitting efforts, sometimes almost frantic, to convince others of the urgency and to drive them or persuade them to greater administrative measures, I have found myself customarily criticized in certain other quarters for going slowly. On the one hand, with some justice, I have earned a reputation as an immoderate and unrelenting slave-driver always demanding more than can be given and on the other hand I have received the blessing of being called academic, vague and, most damning word of all, sincere—the euphemism for feeble. Yet this question of speed is something that belongs to performance not to policy. The objective even of supersonic flight is a safe arrival . . .

There is a great tendency in some quarters of Australia to talk of our role in New Guinea as that of the last colonial power, as though that were a disgraceful role in which to be cast, and to anticipate all sorts of obloquy for Australia if we do not shed the role more quickly. Against that let me set the reality that the only hope for the future of the people of Papua and New Guinea is if Australia and her allies continue to be ready to defend and support the new nation. Don't be misled by current jargon into the view that we are the imperialist obstacle to their better future. We are the sheet anchor of their hope both now and in the future. We have a respectable role, indeed a proud one, but it will be a hard and ungrateful party of play . . .

At the cost of repetition, may I conclude by repeating that the touchstone for proving the worth of any policy or action in Papua and New Guinea is what happens to the inhabitants—all the inhabitants—of that country. If it destroys them it is bad; if it helps them it is good. And when you are seeking the answer to the question of what is good for the people, do not overlook the fact that they will claim and will have their own identity. They are not going to be imitation Australians but will want to be real Papuans [or New Guineans]. And remember that all continuing political growth, whether it be from the native seed or from a graft, has to draw its nourishment from the soil in which it is rooted.

That was the last time I ever made any remarks about Papua and New Guinea. After I left the portfolio I was careful not to take part in Territory affairs. It is a sound convention of the Cabinet system that a minister leaves a clear field to his successor. So, while I supported Barnes in Cabinet on matters affecting the Territory and tried to keep myself informed, I never went to the Territory or discussed its affairs publicly.

Changes took place. Great progress was made. The pace quickened.

I did not see the Territory for over seven years. After I became Governor-General I made my first vice-regal visit. In Port Moresby the Administrator, David Hay, gave the customary evening reception for hundreds of people in Government House grounds. After all the guests had arrived I excused myself from the presentation line and said that I would drift around in the crowd and find my own way among old friends and new faces without formality.

I talked happily with a succession of people, mostly Papuans and New Guineans with whom I had been associated in one way or another in the old days. I was exchanging some banter with my old friend John Kaputin, who for this occasion had appeared in a very dramatic and brightly coloured African-style garment and I was pretending to mistake him for an ambassador from some distant country and not a local politician.

At this moment I was approached by a tall and consciously handsome Australian whose European-style garments and general deportment gave me the impression firstly that he was not an old hand in the Territory and secondly that he was the most important person present. He introduced himself pleasantly as the Director of Something or Other and said that the Administrator had suggested that he might come over and 'put me in the picture' about the work he was doing. He proceeded to do so. It turned out that he was even more important than his bearing had suggested. But he spoke well about his job and I asked a question or two and made a passing comment.

'Hah,' he said, 'I see you have been reading your brief, sir.'

I probably looked blank, so he explained that when VIP visitors came to Port Moresby they were usually given some of 'the good old paper work' to help them get a bit of background before they were 'put in the picture'. But most of the beggars never bothered to read the stuff. Obviously I had gone to the trouble of 'doing my homework'.

I said that I did have the habit of reading papers.

'Good show, sir,' he said. 'Then let me fill you in with a bit more background.'

A little later I made some remark about the Gazelle Peninsula. He said that I was 'bang on' and that it almost sounded as though I knew the place.

I said I had seen Rabaul—years ago.

He seemed surprised. 'I understood this was your first trip to New Guinea, sir. I didn't know you had been up here before.'

'I did make a previous visit', I said.

'Good for you, sir. But one can't see everything in one visit, can one?'

He continued to 'put me in the picture'.

'Now there arose up a new King over Egypt which knew not Joseph.'

On that thought I come to Exodus.

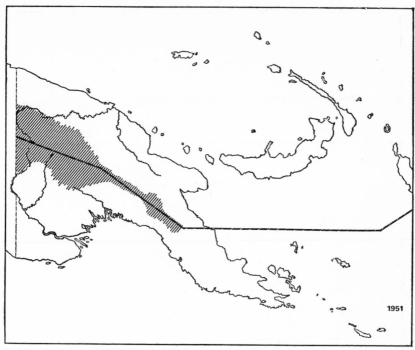

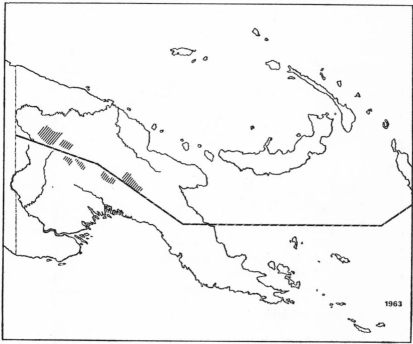

Approximate extent of areas not under full administrative control

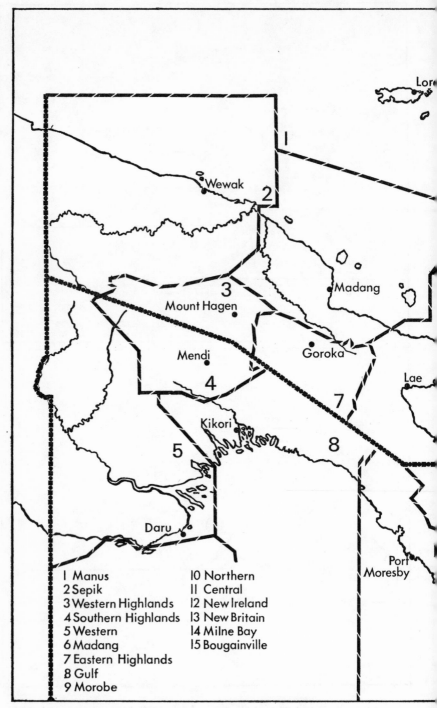

1 Manus
2 Sepik
3 Western Highlands
4 Southern Highlands
5 Western
6 Madang
7 Eastern Highlands
8 Gulf
9 Morobe
10 Northern
11 Central
12 New Ireland
13 New Britain
14 Milne Bay
15 Bougainville

Administrative districts and district headquarters, 1953

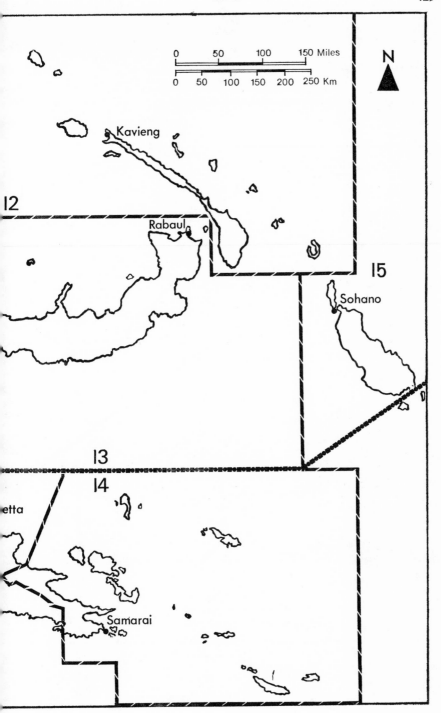

BIOGRAPHICAL NOTES

[1] HALLIGAN, James Reginald (1894–1968), OBE, DipCom (Melb). B. Melbourne. Joined Commonwealth Public Service at age 17. Served as an accountant in the Administration of the Mandated Territory of New Guinea 1922–8. Prime Minister's Dept from 1929, chiefly in External Territories Branch. Appointed Secretary when separate Dept of External Territories was created in 1944. Senior Commissioner for Australia on South Pacific Commission 1948–59; Australian member of British Phosphate Commission and Christmas Island Phosphate Commission 1952–62.

[2] LAMBERT, Cecil Ralph (1899–1968), CBE, FASC. B. Sydney. Entered Commonwealth Public Service at age 15 (Taxation and Attorney-General's Depts). Rural Bank of New South Wales 1933–48. Chairman of Rural Reconstruction Commission 1943–6. Commonwealth Director of Regional Development 1948–51. Secretary, Dept of Territories 1951–64.

[3] MURRAY, Jack Keith, OBE, ED, BA, BScAg. B. Melbourne 1889. Educated Sydney University. Principal of Queensland Agricultural College 1923–45 and Professor of Agriculture in Queensland University 1927–45. Served in World War II as General Staff Officer 2 Training, Northern Command; Colonel Commanding AIF Training Depots in Northern Command and Chief Instructor LHQ School of Civil Affairs, Duntroon. Provisional Administrator of PNG 1945–9; Administrator 1949–52. Member of Senate, Queensland University 1953–69.

[4] HEAD, Ernest Alfred Francis, MBE. Joined Commonwealth Public Service 1913 (Postmaster General's Dept). War service in 1st AIF 1917–19. Public Service Board from 1924 until retirement. Public Service Commissioner in PNG 1949–53. Commonwealth Public Service Inspector in Western Australia 1953–63.

[5] NIALL, Horace Lionel Richard, Kt, CBE, MBE (Mil). B. New South Wales 1904. NSW Public Service 1923–7. Appointed Patrol Officer in Mandated Territory of New Guinea 1927 and rose to District Officer. Served in World War II with AIF in New Guinea mainland campaigns rising to rank of Major and Regional Commander in Angau. Resumed service in PNG Administration. District Commissioner in Morobe 1946–64. MLC 1951–63. Elected member for Morobe in the House of Assembly 1964. Speaker of the House of Assembly. Retired 1972. Knighted 1974.

[6] ELLIOTT-SMITH, Sydney. B. Tasmania 1900. Patrol Officer in Papua and

Resident Magistrate at Samarai before World War II. War-time service in PNG (Commanding Officer 1 Papuan Infantry Battalion 1944–6. Lieutenant-Colonel. Organized Papuan Administrative Unit, the forerunner of Angau in 1941). Rejoined Administration as Assistant District Officer 1946. District Commissioner from 1952. MLC 1952–7. Retired 1958.

7 CLELAND, Donald Mackinnon (1901–1975), Kt, CBE, CStJ. Born Western Australia. Barrister and solicitor of the Supreme Court of Western Australia. Served in World War II with the AIF in Middle East and New Guinea 1939–45. (Mentioned in despatches twice and MBE.) Rose to rank of Brigadier in Angau. Chairman of Production Control Board. Administrator of PNG 1953–67. Pro-Chancellor of University of Papua and New Guinea 1969–75. Chancellor of Anglican Diocese of PNG 1967–75.

8 McADAM, James Bannister (1910–1959), MM, DipFor (Canb). Born England. Educated in Queensland and Australian School of Forestry, Canberra. Queensland Forestry Service until 1937. District Forester, New Guinea 1938. Served in World War II with New Guinea Volunteer Rifles and Angau rising to the rank of Major. Returned to Administration as Acting Director of Forests in 1946. Director from 1951 until death. MLC 1951–6.

9 LEAHY, Michael James, MBE. B. Toowoomba, Qld, 1901. Arrived in New Guinea 1926. Prospector and alluvial miner. Explored Central Highlands 1930–3. Farmer and grazier in Morobe District from 1933. War service with RAAF (Flight Lieutenant). Returned to farming in Morobe District.

10 GUISE, John, KBE. B. Milne Bay District of Papua 1914. War-time service with Angau. Joined Papua and New Guinea Constabulary in 1946. Sergeant-Major. Local government and welfare work for Dept of Native Affairs. Elected to Legislative Council 1961. Elected to House of Assembly 1964. Unofficial Leader of Elected Members. Speaker. Deputy Chief Minister. First Governor-General of Papua New Guinea. Knighted 1975.

11 FRY, Thomas Penberthy (1904–1952), ScJurD, LLM, MA, BCL, Barrister. Born Brisbane. Educated Queensland University, Oxford and Harvard. Served in the AIF in World War II in staff appointments on the legal side. Appointed in charge of Legal Research and Law Revision Section of the Dept of External Territories in 1948.

12 REEVE, Harold Hastings, FASA. B. Sydney 1908. Master builder in Sydney and Canberra 1930–40. Commonwealth Treasury 1941–7. Appointed Treasurer and Director of Finance in Papua and New Guinea 1950–61. Assistant Administrator (Economic Affairs) 1961–6. MLC 1951–61 and MHA 1961–6.

13 NEWMAN, Anthony Philip John, FASA. B. Brisbane 1918. Served with the 2nd AIF in Middle East and New Guinea 1940–5. Queensland State Public Service 1934–40. Joined PNG Public Service 1946. After occupying senior positions in Treasury Dept, succeeded Reeve as Treasurer. Assistant Administrator (Economic Affairs) 1970–3. MLC and MHA of PNG 1963–73. Retired from Public Service 1973.

14 GROVES, William Charles, BA, DipEd. B. Ballarat 1898. Served with 1st AIF in World War I 1915–19. Attended Melbourne University 1920–2. Appointed to Dept of Native Affairs, New Guinea, as Supervisor of Education in 1922. Returned to Melbourne as lecturer in social studies at Teachers' College in 1926. Research Fellow in Anthropology at Sydney University 1930–6. Director of Education in Nauru 1937–8. Adviser on Education to British Solomon Islands Protectorate 1939–40. Served in 2nd AIF with Army Education Service 1941–6 with rank of Major. Inspector of

Schools, Victorian Education Dept 1946. Appointed Director of Education in PNG 1946. MLC 1951–9.

15 MARSH, Reginald, BA (Syd). B. Braidwood, NSW, 1906. Teacher in NSW Education Dept 1926–39. Served with RAAF in World War II (Squadron Leader). Successive senior positions in Commonwealth Employment Service 1945–50. Assistant Secretary Dept of Territories 1953–7. Assistant Administrator Northern Territory 1957–62. Director of Information and International Relations, Dept of Territories 1964–6. Administrator of Norfolk Island 1966–8. Director of Commonwealth Hostels 1968–72.

16 McCARTHY, Dudley, MBE (Mil), BA, DipEd (Syd). B. Sydney 1911. Cadet Patrol Officer New Guinea 1933–5. School-teacher in New South Wales 1935–7. War service with AIF in Middle East and New Guinea (Major). Commonwealth Office of Education 1946–9. Joined Dept of Territories 1952. Assistant Secretary 1958–63. Australian Special Representative at Trusteeship Council 1961–2. Australian Minister to United Nations in New York 1963–6. Ambassador to Mexico 1967–72. Ambassador to Spain since 1972. Australian Senior Commissioner on South Pacific Commission 1959–62.

17 HUXLEY, Thomas Aubrey. B. Queensland 1909. School-teacher in Queensland. Served in World War II with 2nd AIF in Middle East and New Guinea 1940–5. Entered Commonwealth Public Service 1947. Public Service Commissioner PNG 1953–6. Director of Organization and Methods Dept of Army 1956–61. Command Secretary, Northern Command, 1961–6.

18 GUNTHER, John Thomson, Kt, CMG, OBE. B. Sydney 1910. Educated Sydney University (MB, BS, DTM, DTH), also FRACP, FACMA. Medical Officer with Lever's in British Solomon Islands 1935–7. Chairman of medical board investigating plumbism at Mt Isa, Queensland, 1938–41. Medical Officer with RAAF in World War II 1941–6 (Malariologist in 1943; Commanding Officer Tropical Research Field Unit 1944–5). Director of Public Health in PNG 1949–56. Assistant Administrator 1957–72. MLC and MHA 1952–65. Vice-Chancellor of University of Papua and New Guinea 1966–72.

19 WILSON, Rupert Wentworth. B. Sydney 1903. Diplomate of the Hawkesbury Agricultural College. Station manager 1922–32. Tasmanian Dept of Agriculture 1933–46. Commonwealth War Service Land Settlement 1947–52 (Director from 1949). Assistant Secretary in Commonwealth Treasury 1953–4. Assistant Administrator PNG 1954–6. Assistant Secretary Dept of Primary Industry, Canberra, 1956–9. Agricultural Adviser, International Bank for Reconstruction and Development, Washington, 1959.

20 HOLMES, Eric Patrick (1892–1969). B. Charters Towers, Qld. Licensed surveyor. Qld Lands Dept. Served in World War I with 1st AIF 1915–19. In 1923 went to Territory of New Guinea as surveyor and was Secretary of Lands, Surveys and Mines in that Administration 1928–42. During World War II attached to Dept of Interior, Canberra. Secretary for Lands in PNG 1946–52.

21 McCUBBERY, Cyril Patrick, LLB. B. Victoria 1910. Educated Melbourne University. Admitted to Victorian Bar 1934. Served in World War II with 2nd AIF (Captain, twice m.i.d.). Appointed to Crown Law Office PNG 1946. Commissioner of Titles 1951–64. Private legal practice in Port Moresby.

22 MACINNIS, Douglas Evan, OBE, LLB (Syd). B. New South Wales 1903. Served in World War II with 2nd AIF 1940–6, reaching rank of Major.

Commonwealth Public Service as Field Officer, Lands and Survey section of Dept of Interior 1947–50; Legal Officer, Attorney-General's Dept 1950–2. PNG Public Service 1952–64 as Secretary (later Director) of Lands, Surveys and Mines. Member of PNG Legislative Council 1953–63. NSW Public Service from 1964 as Senior Legal Officer, Mines Dept. Retired 1968.

23 GREATHEAD, George. B. Bundaberg, Qld, 1909. Qld Public Service 1927–30. Law studies in solicitor's office Bundaberg 1930–3. Entered New Guinea Public Service 1933. Patrol Officer. War service in New Guinea 1942–5 (Z' and 'M' special units and Angau, rising to rank of Major). PNG Public Service from 1946. District Officer Central Highlands 1946–9. District Commissioner Eastern Highlands 1949–52. Resigned 1952 and engaged in private industry in PNG.

24 PENTLAND, A. A. N. D. ('Jerry'), MC, DFC, AFC. B. 1894 in New South Wales. Served in World War I with 12th Light Horse Regiment and the Royal Air Force. Served in World War II with the RAAF (Instructor 1940–2 and Rescue and Communications Flight from 1942).

25 DOWNS, Ian Fairley Graham, OBE. B. Edinburgh 1915. Entered Royal Australian Naval College. Served in World War II with RAN 1942–5. Pre-war officer in New Guinea Administration from 1935. Officer in PNG Administration 1946–56. Planter. President of Highland Farmers and Settlers' Association 1957–69. Foundation Chairman of Coffee Marketing Board 1964. MLC, PNG, 1957–63 and MHA 1964–8. Member of Administrator's Council 1961–7.

26 WILLOUGHBY, John Edward (1908–1962), BEc (Syd). B. Guildford, NSW. Public servant. Commonwealth Dept of Post-War Reconstruction 1944–7; Public Service Board 1947–50; Assistant Secretary Dept of External Territories 1950–1; Assistant Secretary Dept of Territories 1951–6 and then First Assistant Secretary until his death.

27 DWYER, Richard Edward Paul (1902–1959), B.ScAg (Syd). B. Sydney. Educated at Hawkesbury Agricultural College and Sydney University. Assistant plant breeder NSW Dept of Agriculture 1927–34. Joined New Guinea Administration 1934. Served in World War II with New Guinea Volunteer Rifles at Rabaul and later as Agricultural Officer with Angau. PNG Administration from 1946. Director of Agriculture, Stock and Fisheries 1952–8. MLC 1952–9.

28 CARTER, William Frederick, OBE, AMIEAust. B. Ryde, NSW, 1923. Entered Australian Postmaster-General's Dept 1941; appointed engineer in 1946 and divisional engineer in 1950. War service with AMF (L of C Signals). Appointed Director of Posts and Telegraphs in PNG 1954, MLC 1959–64 and MHA 1964–8. Chief Commissioner, PNG Branch Scouts Association from 1966. Retired in 1975 to rejoin Australian Postal Commission.

29 EVANS, Joseph Horace, OBE, FRGS. B. Portsmouth, England, 1908. Merchant marine with B.I.S.N. Co. and P. & O.S.N. Marine Superintendent Penang Harbour Board 1937–9 and 1946–51. War service with Royal Navy in Malayan waters, South Africa and Europe. Shipping Manager of PNG Shipping Service from January 1953 until winding up in September 1954. Subsequently Harbour Master in PNG ports until retirement in 1964.

30 JONES, John Herbert. B. Liverpool, England, 1897. Served in World War I with AIF at Gallipoli landing. Joined New Guinea Administration in 1921. District Officer in Sepik when Japanese invaded. Coast-watcher. Served with Second AIF rising to rank of Lieutenant-Colonel in Angau and command of

the Northern Region. Joined PNG Administration as Director of District Services and Native Affairs in 1946. In 1953 seconded for duties as Special Representative for Australia at the Trusteeship Council. Member of the Legislative Council 1951–3. Chairman of PNG staff recruitment committees 1955–73.

31 LALOR, William Andrew (usually known as Peter), LLB (Melb). B. Victoria 1920. Patrol Officer in PNG 1946–54. Transferred to Department of Law as Legal Officer 1954. Public Solicitor 1958. Retired 1974.

32 PARRISH, Douglas John. B. 1921. Private employment in Sydney 1936–41. War service with AMF and AIF 1941–5. Patrol Officer in PNG from 1946 rising to District Officer. Industrial Organization Officer with Department of Labour 1961. Chief of Division (Industrial Relations) 1962–5. Acting Secretary and Secretary for Labour 1965–71. Retired to take up employment in Australia.

33 FENBURY, David Maxwell, MC, BA (WA). B. Subiaco, WA, 1916. Entered public service of New Guinea as Cadet Patrol Officer 1937. Wartime service in New Guinea with 2nd AIF (Captain). Attached Government of Tanganyika and British Colonial Office 1946–7. Native Authorities Officer in PNG 1950; District Commissioner from 1955; United Nations Secretariat New York 1956–8; Secretary Dept of Administrator PNG 1962–9; Secretary Dept of Social Development and Home Affairs 1969–73 (retired).

34 LYNCH, Cyril Joseph, LLB (Syd). B. Victoria 1924. Admitted as Barrister, Supreme Court of New South Wales 1949. Legal Officer Dept of Territories 1949–52. Legal Officer Dept of Law PNG from 1952; Deputy Crown Law Officer and Assistant Secretary from 1955; Legislative Draftsman from 1961; Acting Secretary for Law on several occasions.

35 THOMSON, Neil. B. Scotland 1908. Educated Fort St, Sydney, and Maitland High School. Solicitor of Supreme Court of New South Wales. Joined NSW Public Service 1927. Public Service Board Assistant Inspector 1941, Inspector 1947, Senior Inspector 1950. Public Service Commissioner of PNG 1957. Retired 1964.

36 DWYER, Eric William, DipCom (Tas). B. Tasmania 1917. Entered Commonwealth Public Service 1936. Acting Public Service Commissioner PNG (on temporary transfer) from January 1956 to February 1957. Returned to Commonwealth Public Service Board. Later Deputy Secretary Dept of Defence. War service in World War II with 2nd AIF 1940–5 in Middle East and PNG, rising to rank of Captain (m.i.d.).

37 ROSCOE, Geoffrey Thomas, MA, DipEd (Qld). B. Brisbane 1900. Schoolteacher in Queensland 1921. Lecturer at Brisbane Teachers' College 1929. Principal of Charters Towers High School 1945. Chief Inspector of Schools PNG 1947. Chief of the Division of Native Education 1956. Director of Education from 1958. MLC for PNG 1958–62. Retired 1962.

38 CATERSON, Frederick Douglas Claude. B. New South Wales 1919. Chief Industrial Officer for Qantas 1943–59. Appointed Chairman of Native Employment Board of PNG in 1959; Secretary Dept of Labour from 1961. Retired in 1962 to become Industrial Consultant and Adviser to Australian Federation of Air Pilots.

39 HOHNEN, John Harold. B. Sydney 1911. Mining engineer in India, West Africa, England and New Guinea. Managing director of New Guinea Goldfields, Wau. MLC. Chairman of Native Apprenticeship Board. From 1962 mining directorships and consultant in Australia.

40 HEALY, Michael James. B. Brisbane 1910. Patrol Officer in Papua 1927–42. War service with Angau (Major). PNG Administration from 1946 rising to District Commissioner.

41 NEWBY, Lisle Richardson. BA (Syd). B. Taree, NSW, 1918. Teacher NSW Education Dept 1938–41. AIF Army Education Service 1941–6. Teacher Training under Reconstruction Training Scheme 1946–50. Officer-in-Charge aboriginal education, Northern Territory 1951–5. Lecturer at ASOPA 1956–7. Superintendent of Teacher Training in PNG. Appointed Chief of Division of Extension Services 1960. Director of Information and Extension Services 1962–72. Secretary for Health and Education, Nauru.

42 RESEIGH, Claude Edgar. AUA (Adel), DipPubAd, AFIA. B. Adelaide 1910. Joined SA Public Service 1925. Commonwealth Public Service from 1945. Depts of Works and Housing and National Development. Assistant Secretary Dept of Territories from 1953–74. Assistant Secretary Dept of Special Minister of State 1974.

43 GLEESON, W. T. Commonwealth public servant in Postmaster-General's Dept and Auditor-General's office. Transferred to Public Service Board 1946 and was Senior Inspector with the Organization and Methods Division when he made the survey of PNG finances.

44 SWIFT, Robert Stanley, OBE, LLB (Qld), AASA. B. South Australia 1922. Joined Commonwealth Public Service 1937. Chief Accountant with Australian-New Guinea Production Control Board 1948–52. Dept of Territories 1952–68. Deputy Secretary Dept of Interior 1968–70. Deputy Secretary Dept of Primary Industry 1970–4. Deputy Secretary Dept of Agriculture 1975. War service 1941–6 with AMF and AIF, including with Angau.

45 HENDERSON, Frank Cotter (1911–1969), OBE, BScAg (Syd). B. Broken Hill, NSW. Educated Broken Hill and Sydney University. NSW Dept of Education 1933–5. New Guinea Dept of Agriculture 1936–41. War service with RAAF 1942–5 (Flight Lieutenant). PNG Administration from 1946 as agronomist in charge of Lowlands Experimental Station at Keravat 1946–8; Economic botanist 1948–52; Chief of Division of Plant Industry 1952–3; Acting Director of Agriculture 1954–9 and Director from 1959. Assistant Administrator (Economic Affairs) for PNG 1966–9. MLC and MHA in PNG 1961–9.

46 CONROY, William Lawrence, BScAg. B. 1921. War service with AIF 1942–6 (Officer Commanding Malaria Control Unit). Lecturer at ASOPA 1946–9. Joined PNG Dept of Agriculture 1950 and rose to Director in 1964. From 1972 became Special Adviser on Foreign Affairs and Trade to PNG Government in Port Moresby.

47 BRIDGLAND, Leon Ambrose, BScAg (Syd), DipTropAg (Trinidad). B. New South Wales 1924. PNG Public Service from 1947 serving in Dept of Agriculture. Established agriculture training centre at Sogeri in 1952. Superintendent of Lowlands Experimental Station at Keravat. Resigned in 1960 to enter private employment on plantations in PNG.

48 HUGHES, William John (1914–1971), MBE. B. Temora, NSW. Educated at Temora High School. Farming at Temora. War service with AIF 1941–6 in Middle East and New Guinea (2/33rd Battalion, as W.O., later with Angau). Joined Papua New Guinea Constabulary 1946. Transferred to Agriculture Dept. Supervisor of Bubia Agricultural Experimental Station in 1948–69. Retired. Was active in Returned Servicemen's League (State Vice-President from 1963 and President from 1970 until death).

49 NEWTON, Kenneth, BScAg (WA), DipTropAg (Trinidad). B. Perth 1931.

Joined PNG Dept of Agriculture 1954 and became Officer-in-Charge of experimental stations in the highlands and New Britain. Transferred to South Pacific Commission as agriculturalist in 1964.

50 Wood, Ernest John, BEc, DipCom (Syd). B. Sydney 1914. Clerk in company employment. War service with AIF (Lieutenant) 1940–5. Research Officer, Rural Research Division of Dept of Post-War Reconstruction 1945–7. Research Officer Bureau of Agricultural Economics 1947–9. Entered Dept of External Territories as Senior Projects Officer in 1949, transferred to Dept of Territories and became Assistant Secretary (Industries and Commerce) 1956–9 and Assistant Secretary (General Services) 1969–74.

51 Lattin, Daniel Thomas, BA (Melb), BCom (Tas). B. 1914. Agricultural Economist with Tasmanian Dept of Agriculture. Commonwealth Prices Commission rising to Chief Investigation Officer. Joined Dept of External Territories 1948 and continued in Dept of Territories until 1973. Assistant Registrar of Prices Justification Tribunal.

52 Cartledge, Ian Vernon. B. Tasmania 1908. Entered Commonwealth Public Service 1924. Audit Inspector New Guinea 1931–5. Prime Minister's Dept 1935–45. Transferred to External Territories as Accountant and later transferred to Commerce Branch Dept of Territories. Officer-in-Charge Trade Section 1963. Retired 1969.

53 Bunting, Robert Frederick, CBE. B. Samarai, Papua, 1908. After secondary education in Melbourne entered family business of A. H. Bunting, Ltd in Papua, with trading and plantation interests. President of Returned Servicemen's League in PNG from 1954. Lay Canon of Dogura Cathedral. MLC 1958–64.

54 Smith, James Olivant, BScAg (Syd). B. 1916. War service 8th Division AIF (POW, m.i.d.). Lecturer at Hawkesbury Agricultural College 1947. NSW Dept of Agriculture 1949–53. Joined Dept of Territories as Investigation Officer (Agriculture) in 1953. Transferred to Department of Health, Quarantine Branch 1964. Retired 1976.

55 McLachlan, Barbara Anne, BA (Syd). B. New South Wales. Attended Sydney Teachers' College. Joined PNG Dept of Education 1947. Officer-in-Charge Female Education Division 1956–60. Retired 1968. WHO fellowship 1955.

56 Marsh, David Roger Melbourne, OBE. B. Sydney 1921. Field Supervisor Yodda goldfields, New Guinea, 1940–2. War service with Angau 1942–5 (Lieutenant). Patrol Officer in PNG Administration 1946 rising to District Commissioner. Chairman PNG Independence Day Celebrations Committee 1975.

57 Mann, Alan Harbury (1914–1970), Kt, MBE (Mil). Educated Haileybury College, Geelong Grammar, Melbourne University. Admitted Victoria Bar 1938. QC 1955. War service RAAF (No. 10 Squadron in Great Britain). Chief Justice of Supreme Court of PNG from 1957. Knighted 1964.

58 Mollison, Patrick John. B. Melbourne 1913. Joined New Guinea Administration as Cadet Patrol Officer in 1936. War service in New Guinea with RANVR (Lieutenant). Returned to PNG Administration as Assistant District Officer 1946–51, District Officer (1951–7), District Commissioner from 1957.

59 Cole, Robert Rothsay, OBE, MC. B. Dubbo, NSW, 1913. Accountant's office 1933–8. Joined New Guinea Administration 1938. War service with 2nd AIF 1940–5 (Captain). District Commissioner in PNG 1951–64. Commissioner of Police 1964–9.

⁶⁰ Scott, William Herbert. DipCom (Melb), AASA. B. Sydney 1915. Chief Auditor, PNG, 1952–6. Senior Audit Inspector, Canberra, 1956–60, Special Projects Officer Dept of Territories 1960–2, and Assistant Secretary 1962–4. Assistant Auditor-General 1964–6. First Assistant since 1966.

⁶¹ Johnson, Leslie Wilson, MA (WA). B. Tambellup, WA, 1916. School-teacher 1936–41. War service 1942–6. Various appointments in WA Education Dept. Appointed Deputy Director of Education in PNG 1962. Director of Education 1963–6. Assistant Administrator 1966–70. Administrator 1970–4.

⁶² Foxcroft, Edmund John Buchanan (1915–62), MA (Melb). Lecturer in Political Science, Melbourne University 1939–42. Various Commonwealth Depts from 1942. Assistant Secretary in Prime Minister's Dept from 1953. Official Secretary Australian High Commissioner's Office, London, 1955–8. First Assistant Secretary, Prime Minister's Dept from 1958.

⁶³ Kaad, Frederic Pater Christian, BA, DipPubAd (Qld). B. Brisbane 1920. Served in World War II 1940–5 (2/7 Battalion AIF and Angau). Lieutenant. Joined PNG Administration in 1946 rising to District Commissioner. Following severe injuries in aircraft accident he added to his academic qualifications and became Lecturer in Management at the International Training Institute, Mosman, NSW.

⁶⁴ Oala-Rarua, Oala. B. Papua 1934. Secondary education at Sogeri High School. Entered Public Service as a teacher. Transferred to Public Service Commissioner's office. Personal Assistant to Assistant Administrator 1963. Took private employment 1965. Elected to House of Assembly 1968. First Lord Mayor of Port Moresby 1972. Head of PNG Government Office in Canberra 1973. First High Commissioner for PNG in Australia 1975.

⁶⁵ Hurrell, Albert Lloyd, OBE, MC. B. Wingham, NSW, 1916. Educated Hurlstone Agricultural College and Armidale Teachers' College. Agricultural school-teacher in New South Wales, 1937–8. Appointed Cadet Patrol Officer in Territory of New Guinea in 1939. Served in World War II with 2nd AIF in Middle East and New Guinea 1940–5 (Captain, MC). Resumed service in PNG as Patrol Officer. Resigned in 1950 to go farming at Wau. MLC 1958–63. Chairman of Coffee Marketing Board 1965–74.

⁶⁶ Toogood, Gerald William. B. London 1913. Joined Papuan Administration 1937. Served in World War II with 2nd AIF in New Guinea 1942–5. Resumed service with PNG Administration in 1946. District Commissioner 1953. Assistant Director, District Services and Native Affairs, 1954–7. Taxation Commissioner 1958–60. Assistant Secretary District Administration 1962–5.

INDEX

140